THE ALAN FREED STORY

THE ALAN FREED STORY

THE EARLY YEARS OF ROCK & ROLL

JOHN A. JACKSON

Collectables Records Corp.
Narberth, PA

Copyright © 2005 by John A. Jackson

All rights reserved. No part of this book may be reproduced or transmitted in any form or by any means, electronic or mechanical, including photocopying, recording, or by any information storage and retrieval system, without permission in writing from the Publisher.

Collectables® Records Corp.
PO Box 35
Narberth PA
19072

Library of Congress Catalog Card Number: 2005935612

Printed in the United States of America

Library of Congress Cataloging-in-Publication Data

Jackson, John A.
    The Alan Freed Story: The Early Years of Rock & Roll / John A. Jackson.
    p.   cm.
    Includes bibliographical references and index.
    ISBN 0-9773798-0-9 paperback
    1. Freed, Alan. 2. Disc jockeys-United States-Biography.
    3. Rock music-United States-History and criticism. 1. Title.

                                                            2005935612
                                                                                    CIP

Front & back cover photo: courtesy John Cavello, National Television Archives

For my children, Darcie and Tom

CONTENTS

Illustrations viii
Preface ix
Acknowledgments xiii
1. Moondog's Coronation 1
2. Birth of a Disc Jockey 20
3. The Dog Howls 33
4. The Moondog Mesmerizes Manhattan 55
5. Rock & Roll Party 72
6. The Big Beat 88
7. The Boys 109
8. Don't Knock the Rock 138
9. The King Is Crowned 153
10. Banned in Boston 181
11. "We Start 'em; the Others Chart 'em" 207
12. Payola 238
13. As Clean as the Newly Driven Snow 268
14. Payola's First Fatality 307
Postscript 329
Notes 341
Bibliography 373
Discography 387
Filmography 389
Index 390

ILLUSTRATIONS

These photos follow page 112:

1. Freed during his senior year at Salem (Ohio) High School
2. Alan and David Freed
3. Alan and Betty Lou on their wedding day
4. Alan and Alana in Akron, 1946
5. Freed and Jackie, with his parents, backstage at the Brooklyn Paramount
6. Alan and Jackie with their daughter Sieglinde at their Stamford home
7. The Freed family, summer 1957
8. Publicity shot taken c. 1949-1950
9. WXEL-TV publicity still of Freed
10. The Moondog Coronation Ball, Cleveland Arena
11. WJW publicity photo
12. Freed in the WINS studio
13. A 1956 WINS advertisement
14. Brooklyn Paramount billboard advertising Freed's "Easter Jubilee of Stars"
15. Freed with "Big Al" Sears
16. Count Basie, Jackie, and Alan rehearsing for the "Camel Rock 'n' Roll Party
17. Freed with his props
18. The Freed-managed Moonglows
19. Freed's Washington's Birthday show at the New York Paramount in 1957
20. Freed's "Easter Jubilee of Stars" show at the Brooklyn Paramount
21, 22. Freed's 1957 "Summer Festival"

These photos follow page 272:

23. A publicity shot for Freed's third WABC–TV "Big Beat" telecast
24. Freed and Little Richard backstage at the Brooklyn Paramount
25. Freed's "Third Anniversary Rock 'n' Roll Stage Show"
26. Freed on stage in 1957
27. Publicity still from Freed's fourth movie, *Mister Rock and Roll*
28. Monte Bruce, Freed, and Warren Troob in New Haven on May 8, 1958
29. WABC publicity photo, June 1958
30. Publicity still from Freed's fifth movie, *Go, Johnny, Go!*
31, 32. WNEW–TV "The Big Beat" show, August 16, 1959
33, 34. Front-page newspaper headlines, November 1959
35. Freed with WMCA talk show host Barry Gray
36. Freed, surrounded by his fans after the final telecast of "The Big Beat"
37. Freed and his wife Inga arrive at the New York City criminal courthouse
38. Freed's "Christmas Jubilee of Stars" at the Brooklyn Fox
39. The big payola "bust," Elizabeth Street police station
40. Freed at Morris Levy's Camelot Club
41. Freed emceeing "Twist Revue"
42. Freed's simple memorial plaque

viii

PREFACE

WHEN Alan Freed appended the phrase "rock & roll" to black rhythm and blues in the early 1950s, he transformed a music considered alien to other races into a commodity that would be marketed to America's white teenagers. As rhythm and blues caught on with the growing white audience that enjoyed the luxury of money to burn and time to kill, Freed quickly realized he was positioned to become rock & roll's first prominent spokesman-promoter. In New York City, then the media capital of the world, he took up residency on WINS radio and proclaimed himself the "King of Rock & Roll." By 1956, there was no bigger name in rock & roll than Freed, except Elvis Presley. In addition to becoming the New York area's premier rock & roll disc jockey, through his movies, stage shows, national radio (enhanced by WINS's fifty thousand watts of broadcasting power) and television programs, and a European radio program, Freed also became recognized as the leading worldwide figure in rock & roll.

I am of the generation that remembers life before rock & roll. Listening to the radio about the time that Freed moved to New York I became aware of particularly catchy pop tunes including the Crew-Cuts' "Sh-Boom," Bill Haley's "Shake, Rattle, and Roll," and the Fontane Sisters' "Hearts of Stone." But I was as unaware that those songs were white copies (covers) of rhythm & blues songs as I was of the existence of Alan Freed.

As rhythm & blues' popularity increased during 1955, some white copies began to receive competition from the original recordings. Pop radio introduced me to LaVern Baker's "Tweedle Dee," Fats Domino's "Ain't It a Shame," and Chuck Berry's "Maybellene," each of which appeared alongside its white facsimile on the pop music charts (in Berry's case, "Maybellenes' " white copies did not even appear on the charts). It was on a sunny fall day in 1955 that this then-twelve-year-old suburban adolescent came to know the unbounded exhilaration and raw power of rock & roll, courtesy of Little Richard's recording of "Tutti-Frutti." I then realized that nothing in my life would ever again be as it had been.

Not long after that watershed moment I discovered Freed, who, on his nightly "Rock 'n' Roll Party," not only offered the widest variety, and the most exciting of musical sounds I had ever heard but played many of them two and three—sometimes more—times a night.

But there was a darker side to Freed that I and his other listeners had no way of realizing existed. The egotistical and hardheaded deejay, downright obnoxious to those with whom he did not see eye to eye, wielded his considerable power in a whimsical manner. Abetted by a potent self-destructive streak that manifested itself in chain-smoked cigarettes and free-flowing alcohol, Freed became his own worst enemy as he embarked on a career that would include more than its share of opposition. In his book *The Deejays*, Arnold Passman described Freed as a "monumental symbol of the ambivalence of our times, . . . loved and hated . . . powerful and frightened . . . unpredictable and gregarious." There would be no dearth of those eager to see Freed fall from grace, and fall he did.

Along with almost everyone else who discovered rock & roll by way of Alan Freed, I lost track of the deejay after he disappeared from New York radio under a cloud of suspicion created by the growing broadcasting payola scandal late in 1959. Freed had been accused of accepting money to tout many of those marvelous rock & roll records that had become an inseparable part of my life. While those cherished sounds lost none of their luster, I lost some of my innocence when Freed and other deejays admitted they accepted money from record manufacturers and distributors.

It was almost 1961, and I was more concerned with getting out of high school and into college than with keeping tabs on tainted disc jockeys. I knew nothing but that Freed had surfaced "someplace in

California." Three years after his heyday, Freed was all but forgotten by his idolaters and revilers alike, as "Murray the K" Kaufman ruled New York rock & roll radio from Freed's old nighttime slot on WINS.

I have but a vague recollection of reading in the newspapers of Freed's death before the deejay's memory could fade even further, but rock & roll continued to hold my interest, as did the written analysis of the music's history that began to appear in the early 1970s. Sifting through many of those early accounts of rock & roll's history, I found that only myth-laden and often inaccurate fragments of Freed's legacy existed on paper.

Music critic Al Aronowitz wrote in 1972 that "society's greatest fear is not for its heroes, but of them. We put them in jail when they're alive and build monuments to them when they're dead." Freed, said Aronowitz, "lived to be scorned, reviled, and sentenced to prison, his penalty for inventing the term rock and roll [Freed did not in fact invent the term] and then infecting America with it."

History has revealed Freed's prison to be a restraint far more sinister than steel bars and concrete: the expunging of the disc jockey and his accomplishments from their rightful place in the annals of American musical and social history.

In 1973, Terry Cashman and Tom West composed and sang a tune called "(He Was) The King of Rock and Roll," a bittersweet encapsulation of Freed's career that noted the disc jockey's achievements and how he has been forgotten while many whose careers Freed helped get under way went on to "fortune and fame." One of the song's closing lines was "It's a shame the way we decided to say goodbye."

I hoped the song would become a hit and that millions of people would hear it on the radio, but I never again heard it played on the air.

"It's a shame the way we decided to say goodbye." With that impelling thought in mind, I set out to write this book.

JOHN A. JACKSON

ACKNOWLEDGMENTS

THE first essential piece of evidence I obtained in the research for this book was Alan Freed's previously unreleased 1960 testimony before the House Subcommittee on Legislative Oversight. The release of that testimony necessitated a vote by the House Committee on Interstate and Foreign Commerce to do so, and I would like to thank all those responsible, including Rep. Harley O. Staggers of West Virginia, chairman (1973) of the Special Subcommittee on Investigations of the House Committee on Interstate and Foreign Commerce; Daniel J. Manelli, chief counsel (1973) of the subcommittee; Rep. Oren Harris of Arkansas; Rep. Peter F. Mack of Illinois, who succeeded Rep. Harris as subcommittee chairman on April 25, 1960; and W. E. Williamson, clerk (1973) of the House Committee on Interstate and Foreign Commerce.

Another essential aspect of research for this book involved interviewing those who had personal and/or professional contact with Freed. I wish to thank all those who consented to be interviewed for sharing their time and their recollections. I particularly wish to thank members of the Freed family—Alana Freed, David P. Freed, and Betty Lou Greene—who graciously shared with me their memories of Alan.

I wish to thank friends of mine who have assisted with my research in countless ways throughout the years. Among them are Richard Buckland; John Cavello of the National Television Archives; Marv

Goldberg and Mike Redmond, former editors of the 1950s music magazine *Yesterday's Memories* and writers and staff members of *Bim Bam Boom;* William F. Griggs, editor and publisher of *Rockin' 50s* magazine and founder of the worldwide Buddy Holly Memorial Society; Don Mennie, editor and publisher of *Record Collectors' Monthly;* George Nettleton, research authority par excellence; and Helen D. Stevens, Ph.D. in psychology.

Justice Joseph Stone of the New York City Criminal Court (retired) unselfishly spent many hours with me, providing not only his recollections of the 1959 payola investigation and subsequent prosecutions but also valuable legal knowledge and documents of the case. I thank him for doing so.

I also wish to thank Fats Domino enthusiast Rick Coleman of Louisiana; Mrs. Robert W. Lishman, wife of the late chief counsel for the 1960 House Subcommittee on Legislative Oversight; Leonard Newman, former assistant district attorney and former chief of the Frauds Bureau of the New York City Police Department; Fred Weiler; George Moonoogian, and the helpful and congenial staffs of the Salem (Ohio) Public Library, the Cleveland Public Library, and the New York Public Library at Lincoln Center.

Thank you to my editor at Schirmer Books, Robert J. Axelrod, whose professional exhortations enabled me to improve substantially upon my original manuscript.

Finally, I wish to offer a special remembrance of two close friends who are no longer with us, whose boundless enthusiasm for the pioneers of rock & roll and whose vast knowledge of the music provided me with vital support and assistance in undertaking this work. Rick Whitesell was a musician, musicologist, author and editor of *Goldmine*, a record collector's magazine. Marcia Vance was a writer, staff member of *Bim Bam Boom,* editor of Yesterday's Memories, and the most impassioned promoter of surviving 1950s rock & roll artists and their music. I deeply regret that Rick and Marcia did not live to see the publication of this book. To them and to everyone else who helped in any way—rock & roll is here to stay!

JOHN A. JACKSON

THE ALAN FREED STORY

CHAPTER 1

Moondog's Coronation

"If rock had any particular beginning, it was on March 21, 1952."

TEMPERATURES dipped into the low forties that cloudy March evening in Cleveland, Ohio, as show time grew near and the crowd pressed ominously against the four wooden doors that separated the impatient, noisy throng from those already inside the aging ice hockey arena. Another long week had ended. It was Friday evening—party time. Many in the crowd had been drinking, all the better to dance to the rhythm and blues music of the artists—the Dominoes, Paul Williams, and Varetta Dillard—who were to perform.

Some six months earlier, twenty-nine-year-old Alan Freed had appeared late at night on WJW Radio in Cleveland, Ohio. Calling himself "Moondog," Freed began spinning the hottest, nastiest rhythm and blues records in town. Because of the strong response from what was perceived by Moondog as a small yet devoted listening audience, Freed and two others, Lew Platt, a booking agent and promoter since the big-band era, and Leo Mintz, owner of one of Cleveland's largest record stores, who had been instrumental in getting Freed on the air, decided to form a partnership to promote a dance to be billed as the Moondog Coronation Ball.

If Moondog was not surprised by the race—mostly black—of what were then called "hepcats" drawn to the Cleveland Arena (three days earlier Freed had drawn a black crowd to a small dance at Myers Lake Park outside the city) on Euclid Avenue in the heart of the city, he was nonetheless astounded by its size. Although Freed had incessantly plugged the upcoming dance on his "Moondog House" radio program, there appeared no printed mention of the event, save for one brief note in Glenn Pullen's "Swinging Down the Avenue" column in the *Cleveland Plain Dealer*. "I was worried whether there would be enough people to pay expenses for a big place like the arena," Freed had said earlier.

But something was wrong that Friday evening. As the crowd outside the arena swelled to frightful proportions, those nearest the building realized the entrance doors had been closed. Order began to break down, and at 9:30 P.M. "the lid blew off" as the mob of more than six thousand frustrated yet determined youths assaulted the arena in a human wave. They knocked down four panel doors, swept past the astonished, undermanned police, and noisily swarmed inside as ticket takers and ushers scattered for their lives.

"I can still see the crowd below us," recalled Peter Hastings, who was in the arena that night to photograph the dance. "It was getting bigger all the time. I took the picture. Then we got out of there as fast as we could. It was frightening." The arena was soon filled to its ten thousand capacity, but still the crowd grew larger. Bill Lemmon, executive vice-president of WJW Radio, was "flabbergasted" by what he saw. "People without tickets broke down doors. I saw knives flashing. We were up in the press box and we couldn't get out for three hours. It was madness."

By 11:30 the fire department and the police gave up trying to restore order in the overcrowded, supercharged arena. The house lights were turned up. Police Captain William Zimmerman called off the dance, and the police stood by as the now-subdued crowd "slowly and reluctantly filed out."

The next morning, most of the city's residents got word of the events of the previous night at the arena when the *Cleveland Plain Dealer* printed the front-page headline MOONDOG BALL IS HALTED AS 6,000 CRASH ARENA GATE. Glancing at the three-deck headline, most of the *Plain Dealer's* readers must have wondered what a Moondog was. Had they read the five-paragraph story detailing the storming of the arena and the ensuing "confined mass of humanity" inside the structure, they would most likely have had more questions than answers.

The city's afternoon paper, the *Cleveland Press*, described the arena crowd as a "crushing mob of 25,000 . . . hepcats, jamming every inch of the floor." Being an afternoon newspaper, perhaps the *Press* had more time to count heads. More likely, a larger crowd made for a bigger story. The size of the arena crowd was not the sole reason for the commotion generated in the local press either. Although no reference to the fact was made in the early press accounts, "the Moondog Coronation Ball was almost all black," according to Freed's younger brother, David, who was at the arena that fateful night.

Moondog offered his own version of what transpired at his aborted dance when he told his radio listeners, "We were having a real great time until the crushing pressure of some ten thousand people still outside smashed open the doors of the arena and converged on the inside. When that happened and some seven thousand persons without tickets bulged the insides of the arena the whole show went out of control."

"It was strictly a breakdown in the ability of those who worked for the arena and were used to hockey crowds of eight thousand," thought Freed's younger brother. "Nobody'd ever seen anything like that!"

The attention aimed at Freed following the aborted Moondog Coronation Ball came from three sources, each revealing what it thought of the near riot at the Cleveland Arena. The city's white municipal authorities held Freed responsible for amassing the disorderly mob. They threatened to charge Freed and his two white partners with overselling the arena by printing and selling too many tickets. Freed maintained that about nine thousand tickets were sold in advance, arguing that "everybody had such a grand time breaking into the area that they didn't ask for their money back." Bill Lemmon, Freed's boss at WJW, backed him up, insisting the show was not oversold, declaring that "it was those who didn't have tickets that caused the problem." The overselling charges went unsubstantiated, but they were an indication of the trepidation experienced by the city authorities when confronted by Freed's unruly black Cleveland Arena gathering.

Criticism from the city's black community came via Valena Minor Williams, woman's editor for the black newspaper the *Cleveland Call and Post*, who wrote, "The shame of the situation lies not in the frustrated crowd that rushed to the Arena, but in a community which allows a program like this to continue and to exploit the Negro teensters!" *Call and Post* reporter Marty Richardson described Freed's selection of black artists and their music as "low-brow, cheap entertainment . . . frequently obscene."

Derogatory treatment of rhythm and blues music by the black press was not unusual during this period. The *Call and Post,* successor to the black *Cleveland Advocate,* began publication in the late 1920s and was much more insistent than its predecessor in protesting the city's racial segregation in restaurants, theaters, and other public accommodations, yet it, as well as other black publications, "did not make a fetish of integration." By the 1930s the physical consolidation of Cleveland's black ghetto was complete, making the city's average black citizen, as one Cleveland historian has written, "more isolated from the general life of the urban community" than ever before in the city's history. This isolation from the white community heightened the importance of the black press, and between the years 1937 and 1947, national circulation of black newspapers doubled to two million readers.

The underlying cause of the black press's criticism of rhythm and blues music most likely was black upper- and middle-class sensitivity to being subjected to yet another stereotype by whites. Numerous rhythm and blues songs, many written by whites, portrayed blacks as fun-loving, shiftless people who devoted most of their energy to gambling, excessive drinking, and sexual promiscuity. In an attempt to avoid this stereotype, Cleveland's small but vocal black upper and middle classes "sought ways of distinguishing themselves from the rank and file of the black community," but they were caught in a bind. Literally surrounded by white Cleveland, the black upper and middle classes were painfully and constantly reminded of the "cultural short-comings" of the ghetto. Thus, the black press became more vocal in championing cultural, "civilized" functions.

It was no surprise, then, that the *Call and Post*, with a black readership to whom the life-style of the "sidewalk loafer" was incomprehensible, criticized both Alan Freed and "lowbrowed" rhythm and blues music.

But would the *Call and Post* have reacted as it did had Freed's Cleveland Arena mob been predominantly white? Most likely, it would not have, for in the eye of the black middle-class press, Alan Freed's sin was not so much his championing of "gutbucket" rhythm and blues as it was the encouraging of thousands of young blacks to make a public display of themselves to white society that historically attached a negative image to all blacks.

The national media, which had virtually ignored Freed, was also forced to take notice of the deejay, his black legions, and the power of rhythm and blues music after *Billboard, Cashbox,* and the broadcast media reported Moondog's aborted dance. Freed was soon being hailed in the music trade papers as "Cleveland's well-known R&B jock." It was certainly not coincidental, moreover, that on the Monday following Freed's terminated arena dance and front-page headlines WJW Radio increased Moondog's weekly airtime by six hours. After less than a year on late-night radio, Freed and his "blues and rhythm" records could be heard in the Cleveland listening area each night of the week except Sunday.

Caught off guard by the charges of the white municipal authorities and by Cleveland's black press, Freed reacted to the crisis as he would to similar crises in the future. In an act initiated by his distinct and energetic conviction of "right and wrong"—behavior that at its most extreme would exude self-righteous sanctimony—Freed portrayed himself to his listeners as an "underdog," an innocent victim of circumstances beyond his control. What is more, he believed it.

The night following the arena episode, Freed told his WJW listeners, "If anybody, even in their wildest imagination, had told us that some twenty-five thousand people would try to get into a dance, I suppose you would have been just like me. You probably would have laughed and said they were crazy." Not surprisingly, in laying the groundwork of his self-serving theatrics, Freed chose the *Cleveland Press*'s crowd estimate of twenty-five thousand, rather than the *Plain Dealer*'s more modest count, to describe the mob drawn to the arena. If Freed was going to make headlines (and he was), the bigger the better.

"I promise you that everything will be righted, that everybody will be happy!" continued Freed. "I'd like to have you do this for me tonight when you call in your requests to our 'Moondog' show on this Saturday night. I would like you to tell . . . when you call in, that you are with the 'Moondog.'

"And if you're not with the 'Moondog' you can tell them that, too, because if enough of you can show your faith tonight through your telephone calls, through your telegrams, through your cards and letters over the weekend, we will continue with the show. If not, the 'Moondog' program will leave the radio!"

It was the subtlest of setups, but a setup nevertheless. Who was Moondog asking to judge him if not the very multitude of hepcats who stormed the Cleveland Arena the previous evening?

* * *

Cleveland, founded in northeastern Ohio on the shore of Lake Erie at the mouth of the Cuyahoga River by Moses Cleaveland and a company of Connecticut settlers in 1796 was, by 1952, the seventh-largest city in the United States. Until the Great Migration of blacks to northern urban centers began just before World War I, Cleveland's black population comprised less than 2 percent of the city's total population. This relatively insignificant racial minority enjoyed an integrated tradition in Cleveland's schools, public facilities, and day-to-day activities, and the city became known for its "exceptional" race relations.

Accompanying the great influx of blacks between World War I and the early 1920s, the "flowering of racism" began in the city. Because Cleveland's abundance of heavy industry provided for unskilled employment opportunities, the city became a principal destination for blacks leaving the South during the 1940s. But as Cleveland struggled to assimilate large numbers of rural-bred, uneducated blacks, white hostility led to a "crystallization" of discriminatory practices that had begun earlier.

At the time of Freed's Moondog Coronation Ball Cleveland's blacks were outnumbered almost seven to one by whites. The city's black community had previously exhibited what was perceived by local whites and by the black upper and middle classes as acceptable behavior. On the night of March 21, 1952, Alan Freed and the rhythm and blues music he promoted changed that in a matter of hours.

"Race music" (defined by whites in the 1920s as music performed by blacks, specifically to entertain blacks), as it was branded until *Billboard* rechristened it "rhythm and blues" in June 1949, was unheard of by most whites and shunned by upper-class blacks as "garbage trash, a shocking display of gutbucket blues and lowdown rhythms" during the early 1950s. The few white jockeys spinning rhythm and blues on America's airwaves at that time were unwittingly giving black music a new direction—toward the mainstream white radio market. Until then, featuring rhythm and blues on white-dominated radio was thought to be courting financial disaster—who would listen to such a program and who would sponsor it? But certain rhythm and blues songs were starting to appear on the nation's white pop charts, an indication that some whites must have been listening to, and perhaps even buying, this music.

It was no accident that the first true rhythm and blues record to "cross over" from the black charts to the white-dominated national pop charts was the Dominoes' sex-laden novelty "Sixty-Minute Man," in the summer of 1951. The song featured bassman Bill Brown's deep-throated boasting (as opposed to the tenor lead of the more sexually threatening dynamism of Clyde McPhatter) of his sexual prowess, of being able to satisfy his "girls" with fifteen minutes each of "kissin'," "teasin'," and "squeezin'," before his climactic fifteen minutes of "blowin'" his "top."

"Sixty-Minute Man" met with unprecedented white acceptance for two reasons. First, it reinforced the white stereotype of a slow-witted, sexually obsessed black man. Second, and more important, the song, with Brown's sexual braggadocio blatantly overstated, was not taken very seriously by most whites. To them, Brown posed no more of a threat than did "Amos 'n' Andy."

That Moondog Freed was not the first white disc jockey to play rhythm and blues records on the air is inconsequential. What is significant is that he proved to be a deft communicator, one able to move popular audiences. Using only a microphone, a stack of rhythm and blues records, and his charisma, Alan Freed was able to rally some twenty thousand blacks to an innocuous dance staged at a seedy minor-league ice hockey arena.

The Moondog Coronation Ball was meaningful in the development of American popular music, but it was even more significant in the development of Freed's own show business career. Few whites knew of—let alone were avid followers of—rhythm and blues music when Freed became its standard-bearer in the early 1950s. The whites who did know of the music and who did take particular notice of Freed's huge arena gathering were the record manufacturers who owned and operated the scores of tiny record labels that recorded and released rhythm and blues. None of those hustling would-be entrepreneurs were rich from selling rhythm and blues records to blacks, and few, if any, expected they ever would be. But they were industrious, and they were intent on making a living in an industry they knew well. Moondog's Cleveland Arena audience in part showed these men that interest in rhythm and blues was far greater than anyone had imagined it to be. Bill Randle, Cleveland's most popular radio disc jockey in the early 1950s, as well as one of the most influential deejays in the country, said of the Moondog Coronation Ball, "It was the beginning of the acceptance of black popular music as a force in radio. It was the first big show of its kind where the industry saw it as big business."

The huge crowd drawn to the arena by Moondog and his "blues and rhythm" records was also proof of Freed's uncanny ability to use his dynamic showmanship to communicate with his audience. It was said when Freed walked out on a stage, "he generated the same kind of electricity as Mickey Mantle or Judy Garland." A figure possessing Freed's magnitude of charisma needed only a cause to champion before he became a force to be reckoned with. Alan Freed, with a vital push from record-store owner Leo Mintz, chose rhythm and blues music as his cause. Although his timing seemed impeccable, a look at his early radio career suggests that the deejay was a most unlikely choice to have led America's rock and roll bandwagon. And although it seemed to strangers to rhythm and blues as if Moondog burst upon the music scene that March night at the Cleveland Arena, in reality, the "instant" notoriety gained by Freed's aborted rhythm and blues dance was ten years in the making.

Charles Sydney Freed, a Lithuanian-born Jew, came to America as a five-year-old in 1901. As a teenager working as a company store clerk in the western Pennsylvania coal town of Boswell, Freed met sixteen-year-old Maude Palmer, the youngest child of a Baptist coal miner who had emigrated from Wales to the bleak coalfields of Pennsylvania in the early 1900s. The young couple was wed in 1918 and then settled in nearby Windber, a town of 5,000 located just south of Johnstown in the Laurel Mountains.

During their first year of marriage a son, whom they named Charles Sydney, Jr., was born to the Freeds. On December 21, 1921, a second Freed son was born. He was named Aldon James, his first name an amalgamation of Al and Don Palmer, two of Maude Freed's brothers. The following year a third son, David Palmer, was born.

As boys, Aldon and his brothers lived a nomadic existence. In a span of five years beginning in the late 1920s, the Freed family moved three times. After a brief stay in Oklahoma City they returned east, first to Alliance, Ohio, and then on to nearby Salem, Ohio. Founded in 1803 some fifty miles southeast of Cleveland, near the Pennsylvania border, the City of Salem had about 15,000 inhabitants when the Freeds settled there in 1933.

Charles Sr. was hired as a clerk in Sol Greenberger's Golden Eagle Men's Store (for a time in the late 1950s he was a manager there), a position he would not relinquish until his retirement more than thirty years later. He and Maude, who at times worked as a saleswoman in a local dry goods store, would spend the rest of their lives in Salem.

The Freed family grew to six when a daughter was born. But the child, who was named Mitzi, contracted mastoiditis and died when she was three years old.

The Freeds were a family of nicknames. Charles Jr. was known as "Dugie" and David was called "Donnie." Aldon was called "Al J," a name bestowed upon him by his mother. Bob Dixon, a classmate of Al J's, said that Maude was a "very aggressive, very protective mother." In contrast, David Freed described his father Charles as a "quiet and gentle man." Dixon said Charles Sr. was "mild and meek-mannered [and] . . . never raised his voice" to anyone. By all accounts it was the outgoing and talented Maude who dominated the Freed household.

One of Al J's earliest and fondest family memories was of the traditional Sunday evening songfest, at which the Freeds gathered around the family piano ("There was never a time when we didn't have a piano and that we didn't sing," recalled David). Maude played while everyone else sang. Occasionally her beloved minstrel-performing brothers Al and Don enlivened the songfests with bits from their professional stage routine. If nothing else, the intriguing, fun-loving minstrel men ("Some of their style must have rubbed off on me," Freed would say later in life) showed young Al J that there was an alternative to the drab, uneventful existence his father lived. Al J received his fist taste of big city life in 1933 when, as members of the local Episcopal choir, he, brother David, and cousin Bill Sproat traveled by train to Chicago to sing at the "Century of Progress" Exposition.

"Believe it or not," Freed remarked later in life, "when I was twelve years old I wanted to be a symphony trombonist" (Al Palmer, a trombonist himself, had given one of his battered instruments to Al J for the child's seventh birthday). But America soon discovered swing, and Al J became caught up in the exciting, freewheeling music. "I got the dance band bug," he said.

"We always had records," said David Freed, recalling how the entire family eagerly awaited new releases by the big bands of the day. The Freed brothers purchased the records and learned the song's arrangements "before the shellac on the records was dry."

Each week the Freeds tuned their radio to the "Lucky Strike Top 10 Tunes," a program that featured popular songs of the day. A contest in which listeners tried to pick the week's most popular songs was also part of the radio program. Bill Sproat recalled that the Freeds "always picked 'em right."

Although Al J was closer to his younger brother David in both age and in camaraderie, it was Charles Jr. who had a more profound effect on him. Charles was an excellent academic student who also participated in high school science, debate, and acting clubs. He was assistant editor of the school newspaper, as well as editor-in-chief of the high school yearbook. Charles' greatest talents, however, were in the field of music. He was a member of the Salem High Quaker band (and elected band president as a senior), orchestra, and vocal ensemble. He also found the time to lead his own small combo. David Freed said that Charles, an accomplished pianist who wrote his school's fight song while he was still in high school, was "the musician of the family."

Charles Jr. and Al J had what David Freed described as a mutually-antagonistic relationship highlighted by "some heavy differences" (David also said that the studied musician Charles "more or less resented Al's success"). As the swing-smitten Al J entered Salem High in the late summer of 1936 the ubiquitous specter of his multitalented older brother lingered. But Charles Jr.—a tough act for anyone to follow—had graduated with honors the previous spring and was then a freshman majoring in music at Ohio State University, more than one hundred miles away.

Al J, rather than shun his older brother's considerable reputation ("Charlie was brilliant in high school," said Bob Dixon), challenged Charles Jr.'s legacy head-on.

By that time Al J had become a proficient musician in his own right. Chester Brautigam, his high school band instructor who recalled Al J regularly staying after school to practice the trombone, said that he did not have to teach his student how to play the instrument. Salem resident Dan Smith said that on many nights Al J and his trombone could be found at the Salem Country Club, "entertaining all by himself."

As Charles had done, Al J joined the Quaker marching band and the orchestra. Emulating his older brother in another way, Al J helped organize a band they called the Sultans of Swing (named after a famous Harlem dance orchestra). Adopting a jazzed-up arrangement of the popular 1919 "Ja Da (Ja Da, Ja Da, Jing Jing Jing)" as their theme, the Sultans played at local high school dances. "We got fifty cents a man for an evening's work," said Freed. "We couldn't afford orchestrations so we played the blues and Dixieland, which are the easiest to jam."

Freed particularly idolized Benny Goodman (whose brother, Gene Goodman, Freed would one day team up with in a music publishing venture) and the trombone-playing Tommy Dorsey. It was after attending one of Goodman's concerts that Al J vowed, "someday I'll have a dance band of my own."

Al J grew up in Salem with three cousins—Bill Sproat, Billie Hoffman, and Jane Pfund—each of whom has warm, favorable memories of him. But some of those outside the Freed clan who knew Al J had other opinions of Salem's famous son. Classmate Don Rich said that while he considered Freed "a good guy," Al J "wasn't the most popular" boy in high school and appeared as "pretty much a loner."

According to classmate Betty Bischel Lowry, not only was Freed an energetic "go-getter," he was also a "shrewd operator." Mrs Lowry recalled the time when, as eighth graders, she received a "long and mushy" love letter from the apparently amorous Al J. Any romantic notions on Mrs. Lowry's part disappeared before as she finished Freed's love letter, however. He had concluded the letter by asking her if she could get a job for him at her father's dairy.

Bob Dixon, who probably knew Al J better than did anyone else outside the Freed family (they had been classmates from the fifth grade through high school), thought Freed was an "opportunist." Dixon cited a time he and Al J double-dated for a movie. As they and their dates approached the theater box office Freed offhandedly remarked, "Get four, Bob." And Dixon, who said Freed generally acted "as if the world owed him a living," was stuck for Al J's movie tickets.

When Russia invaded Finland in 1940 the Salem movie theater supported the Finnish War Relief Fund by honoring tickets sold through the fund. Dixon said that Freed approached classmate Bob Lyons ("one of those individuals in high school fortunate enough to have a job") and said, "I'm in big trouble. I took out ten tickets to the Finnish War Relief and I lost them. Can you give me ten bucks? I have to make good."

Suspicious of Al J's tale of woe, Lyons and Dixon checked with the local relief fund headquarters and were told, "Freed doesn't have any tickets."

"It was just a scheme, an angle," exclaimed Dixon. "Al was so devious in high school that Lyons and I used to call him 'legal Al' because he could dream up more ways of getting money out of so-called friends than anyone I'd ever seen."

Lou Raymond, who attended Sunday School with Al J, remembered him as fun-loving ("if he couldn't find it, he'd provide it") but, like Dixon, he described Freed as an "opportunist" who was less than perfect. But, added Raymond, "none of us are."

David Freed conceded that there was "factual basis" to some of Dixon's comments about Al J. He admitted that Al J had "a tremendous amount of faults" but, while Al J may have been a hustler, "there are hustlers for good [causes] too."

Never the academic equal of Charles Jr., Al J was content to earn B's and C's in high school ("He wasn't too interested in trying to get straight A's, recalled one of his teachers). Nevertheless, he was the most active member of his senior class. Besides his musical efforts with the Quaker marching band (led by drum major David Freed) and the orchestra, as well as with the Sultans, Al J also landed a leading role in the senior class play. He and 200 classmates received their diplomas on June 6, 1940, at Salem High's 76th Annual Commencement Exercises, where Freed and a classmate performed an instrumental duet of "Carry Me Back to Old Virginny" as part of the program.

David Freed believes that Al J graduated from high school as "somewhat a person of destiny. He had a feeling that he was going to have some impact on the entertainment business."

After graduating from Salem (Ohio) High School in June 1940, Alan Freed followed his older brother, Charles, Jr., to Ohio State University in Columbus. The younger Freed's decision was not a laborious one. As a land-grant institution "State," as native Ohioians refer to the school, was tuition-free to Ohio residents. An education at Ohio State was the most that Charles Freed, Sr., with his meager clothing-store clerk's salary, could hope to provide his sons. At State the younger Freed brother enrolled in a journalism program. It has been written that Alan Freed's course of study was met with disapproval by his father. Alan Freed later said, "He had his heart set on his sons becoming doctors and lawyers. He never thought of a newspaperman being a professional. Just to please my father I switched to mechanical engineering [but] I couldn't make it. I hated every minute of it!"

David Freed disagreed with his brother's recollection. "My father was not ever opposed to journalism. . . . Never would he have been discouraged about journalism. Alan had been editor of the *Quaker* [the Salem High School yearbook] and he was encouraged in that respect."

It is difficult to understand just why Alan Freed insisted on later concocting his tale of opposing his father on his course of study in college. It should be remembered, however, that when Freed was at the height of his popularity in New York, he often "fine-tuned" his background and image. If nothing else, the story stiffens Freed's self-image of an "underdog type" who was forced to overcome adversities before finding success.

Whatever Freed's course of study, it pales in comparison to another event that took place while he was on the Columbus campus. Peering through the window of WOSU Radio, the university station, Freed realized that "that was it. I was gone!" The college freshman was fascinated by the sense of urgency and excitement he perceived behind the glass panes. From that moment on, he was hooked on broadcasting. Young Freed became nearly obsessed with the Ohio State University studio. He mentioned his plight to a speech professor, who then gave the smitten student a few books on broadcasting to read. The professor also suggested Freed hone his diction by reading newspapers aloud. "I hung around, waiting for a chance to announce or do anything," recalled Freed, "but nothing happened."

A disillusioned Alan Freed quickly lost whatever remaining interest he had for his mechanical engineering studies. David Freed said his brother was at Ohio State "for a brief period, maybe a quarter or two," before enlisting in the army. The would-be radio announcer entered the army early in 1941 as a signal corps photographer stationed at Camp McCoy, near the city of Tomah in west-central Wisconsin. "Believe it or not, he ended up stationed in upper Michigan in the ski patrol," said David, the youngest of the three Freed brothers. "He'd never engaged in any winter sports at home [but] in those days you didn't have a hell of a lot of selection."

Alan Freed spent little time on the snow-covered slopes of northern Michigan—about seven or eight months, according to brother David's recollection—before he was issued a medical discharge from the army in the fall of 1941, shortly before the Japanese attack on Pearl Harbor. It has been written that Freed was medically discharged after contracting double mastoiditis, but both David Freed and Alan Freed's first wife, Betty Lou Greene, maintain that Alan Freed was given a medical discharge because of flatfeet. Once again, the mastoiditis story could very well have been Freed "rewriting" his autobiography for the media. Double mastoiditis would have been yet another "adversity" he had overcome. (Interestingly, Freed later did sustain a partial hearing loss from a bout with double mastoiditis.) In any event, it sounded more dramatic than did "flatfeet."

Out of the service, Freed returned to Salem, where he became a government ordnance inspector's assistant on a northeastern Ohio route. Betty Lou Bean (now Betty Lou Greene) lived in Lisbon, Ohio, some ten miles southeast of Salem. She graduated from Lisbon High in 1940, the same year Freed graduated from Salem High. Although Betty Lou, the daughter of a former mayor of Lisbon, had not met Freed during their high schools days, that is not to say she was at the time unaffected by Freed's commanding presence. Because of both students' musical endeavors in their respective school bands and orchestras, Alan and Betty Lou occasionally came into contact. When that happened, Mrs. Greene said she acted "obvious," observing Freed whenever he was close by but never speaking to him. "After graduation I went away to school for a year and he went to Ohio State." Mrs. Greene said she soon left school, returning to Lisbon to work in a government defense plant. The plant happened to be on Alan Freed's inspection route.

"I realized I'd seen him before," she recalled. "We started talking about high school. He would come down and spend the day and most of the time we just talked. I liked him right away."

After becoming acquainted, the couple decided to date, but Freed had no automobile. Betty Lou Bean did. "It was a black Chevrolet and it looked like all cars looked back then—like a hearse!" she said. "I called it 'The Job' because it got the job done." Betty Lou drove to Salem to pick up her date. Freed supplied the gas money.

It has been widely (and erroneously) written that upon leaving the army, Freed returned to Ohio State and earned a degree in mechanical engineering. Once again, this "nonfact" most likely came from Freed himself, later on in his career, embellishing on his achievements. "It's been told over and over that he graduated from Ohio State, but he didn't," attested Mrs. Greene. "He considered Ohio State his alma mater, but he didn't graduate. He never went back."

What Alan Freed wanted most at that time was radio. Despite the ample instances of Freed's career embellishments, it is highly likely that his tale concerning the Ohio State University radio station has some basis in truth. David Freed maintained that his brother had no radio ambitions whatsoever when he went off to State in the fall of 1940. Betty Lou Greene was certain that when she met Freed shortly after he was discharged from the army late in 1941, he wanted to be a radio newscaster. "That was his life," she said.

Freed's dating habits lend credence to his passion for a broadcasting career. Relying on his gas money and Betty Lou's automobile, the couple was soon dating steadily. Hearkening to his college speech professor's advice to practice his diction by reading aloud, Alan would be waiting, newspaper in hand, when Betty Lou drove up from Lisbon. "We spent a great many evenings with him just reading out loud, practicing," she said. Freed was unusually hard on his reading performance, demanding corrections from Betty Lou as he went along.

It was not long before Freed's dating pattern took on a new look. So passionate was his quest for a job in radio that he decided to attend a broadcasting school. The nearest class was held at WKBN Radio in Youngstown, Ohio, fifteen miles from Salem. The class instructor was Gene Trace, then program director at the radio station. When Betty Lou picked up Alan after work, she would drive him to Youngstown and sit in the WKBN lobby while he attended class. After driving Freed home to Salem, she would return to Lisbon.

After absorbing as much of Gene Trace's broadcasting acumen (Freed credited Trace with "doing more to enthuse me and guide me into the radio business than anyone else") as possible, Alan Freed went looking for a job. With America's civilian manpower reserve decimated by the frantic war effort initiated by the Pearl Harbor disaster, the would-be broadcaster was spared the ordeal of endless auditioning at obscure radio stations. In October 1942 he landed a night job at WKST Radio in New Castle, Pennsylvania, a town nestled in the foothills of the Appalachian Mountains near the confluence of the Mahoning, Shenango, and Nashannock rivers. WKST, "the Voice of Lawrence County," was a one-man operation when Freed was hired, and it remains so to this day.

One-man station or not, Freed jumped at the chance to get into broadcasting. His duties at WKST included everything from sweeping up around the studio to announcing on a nightly classical music program. Mrs. Greene said although Freed wanted to be a newscaster and a sports announcer by the time he left Gene Trace's school, at WKST he did "mainly announcing." Freed began work for seventeen dollars a week when, most likely, he would have taken the job for less.

Still carless, Freed made the twenty-five-mile move from Salem to New Castle. When she visited him, Betty Lou stayed at WKST engineer Bob Ash's house, but that arrangement only hastened the young couple's wedding bells. After marrying, Mrs. Greene said she and Freed "moved into a little three-room upstairs apartment" in New Castle.

At the time, Alan Freed showed an active interest in classical music, an interest from his Salem High School days and his exposure to the Cleveland Orchestra. Betty Lou Greene recalled that when she married Freed, he had such a huge classical record library that it was obvious Freed had been collecting records for some time. Among Freed's favorite works were Beethoven's "Pastorale" and Tchaikovsky's "Pathetique" symphonies, as well as pieces by Bach and Brahms, among others. Above all, however, Freed displayed a passion for Richard Wagner's operatic tetralogy *Der Ring des Nibelungen*. Despite a lack of interest in any other operatic work, Freed was nearly obsessed with the *Ring* cycle and would name a daughter Sieglinde, after a central character in Wagner's epic work. "He liked the big bands, too," said Mrs. Greene. "Alan's mother was interested in music. We'd go over there on Sunday for dinner and usually somebody would end up at the piano."

Early in 1943, seeking a full-time radio position, Alan Freed decided to see what his chances of employment were at Youngstown's WKBN, where he had attended Gene Trace's broadcasting school. Trace, by then WKBN station manager, "liked Al and pushed for him," said Betty Lou.

Bob Dixon, the Salem schoolboy acquaintance of both Alan and David Freed, saw things differently. Regarding Freed's job interview at WKBN, Dixon said, "If he'd swept floors in New Castle [which Freed apparently had], he would have told WKBN he'd been assistant manager." He was of the opinion that young Freed "just bluffed his way" through the interview. Dixon was not far from the truth.

Ruth Cruikshank was a secretary at WKBN the winter day that Freed walked up three flights of stairs in the massive wood-frame building on North Champion Street in downtown Youngstown. Mrs. Cruikshank remembered Freed as "good-looking, tall and slender," with a "stage presence, a way about him."

Freed filled out an employment application card on which he

called himself Albert James Freed. It seemed Freed used several names in his younger days. His birth certificate states Freed's given name as Aldon James, but both David Freed and Betty Lou Greene said Freed styled himself Albert J, Albert James ("I think he manufactured that one in high school," said his younger brother, and Al J, as well as Alan.

Freed also added a year to his age on the employment card—for "experience," most likely—giving his year of birth as 1920 instead of 1921. On the application he also said he had acting experience with stock companies in the New England area and had done "summer theatre work and directing," a claim later denied by Betty Lou.

Freed also wrote on the card that he enlisted in the army on September 30, 1940 (at that time he was on the Ohio State University campus), and served eight months. Freed wrote that while in the service he was a trombonist with the Military Concert Band, with the U.S. Army Band, as well as with civic symphonies (there is no hint of musical involvement in Freed's brief military career).

Freed's WKBN employment card was an exercise in "creative writing." Not only had the young radio announcer concocted a new name and birthday, but he fabricated all sorts of experiences he believed would enhance his chances for employment. "It took a lot of guts to bluff his way through, but that's the type of guy he was," said Bob Dixon.

WKBN, founded in 1926 by Warren P. Williamson, proudly displays its original transmitter today in its modern broadcasting complex lobby. The station hired Freed as a staff announcer on February 8, 1943. Besides announcing, he also did some on-the-spot remote broadcasts originating from Camp Reynolds, an army post located near Sharon, Pennsylvania, just across the Ohio state line. Freed and Betty Lou rented a beautiful country home in Salem. It was available to them because the man who owned the house had recently been drafted into the service and his wife was afraid to live outside the city limits by herself. Her fears were not unfounded. After the Freeds were robbed, Betty Lou, too, was afraid to stay there any longer. Freed, who usually did not arrive home from WKBN until one-thirty in the morning, and Betty Lou then rented an apartment in the city of Salem itself, where she worked during the day.

Alan Freed was on the move. Not only was he earning forty-two dollars a week at WKBN, but, more important to Freed, Youngstown's listening market was far greater than New Castle's. However,

WKBN's newest radio announcer was soon experiencing difficulty in keeping his unflagging ambition in check.

Don Gardner, the "Dean of Ohio Sportscasters," began as a sports announcer on WKBN in 1932. By the time Freed signed on in 1943, Gardner was the sports director at the station. Gardner recalled that Freed was soon doing "a little bit of everything" at the station, including some spotting—following the field action with binoculars—for Gardner as the sports director did play-by-play announcing for football games. Gardner said Freed especially enjoyed working football games because he could "rub elbows with the big shots," particularly coaches and officials from Canton and Akron.

Gardner thought Freed was a loner. The sports director believed he was one of a very few able to "get inside" Freed's skin. He said Freed appeared in a big hurry to get to the top. Gardner cautioned the young announcer that very few people ever get to the top, advising him to "take it slow and make a lot of friends along the way."

Gardner said Freed persisted in constantly "looking for the big one," once imploring the sports director to quit his job and move on to Pittsburgh or Cleveland. "He wanted the name more than the money." But a "very comfortable" Gardner turned the ambitious young Freed down. He told Freed to take it easy and he would live longer. "He was a likeable guy," thought Gardner, "but his enthusiasm was always divided between his work and Alan Freed. If he thought he could advance himself he'd step on your face."

Later in his career Freed took on the role of surrogate parent to his young audience. His listeners, in turn, looked upon the elder Freed as a person whom they could trust. Early glimpses of this relationship emerged while Freed worked in Youngstown. It was while Freed and Betty Lou were residing in Salem that Dan Smith became acquainted with the budding young radio announcer who was living in a garage apartment behind a huge house on South Lincoln Avenue. Dan Smith's father owned a grocery store and his son made deliveries, often to the Freeds. Besides delivering groceries and attending high school, young Smith played drums in a local combo. "We went over to WKBN to visit him and to do some recording at the WKBN studio,' said Smith. He remembered Freed as being "very personable and helpful . . . a great guy" who took the time to talk individually with each of the band members. Freed also escorted the youngsters on a tour of the studio. "Being connected to radio, Alan was a person to look up to," said Smith.

As a young radio announcer on the move, Alan Freed experienced his first taste of the awe and reverence that a dynamic radio personality could command. Dan Smith and his youthful buddies may have been the first teenagers to idolize Freed, but they would not be the last to do so.

CHAPTER 2

Birth of a Disc Jockey

> "Alan and I got in some trouble [in Akron] hangin' out too late and having the milkman bring us home."

ALTHOUGH Alan Freed was a radio newscaster and a sports announcer while at WKBN Radio in Youngstown, Ohio, during 1943–1944 he, and many other announcers like him, would someday play a vital role in the development of America's disc jockey phenomenon.

When the first commercial radio stations began broadcasting in the United States in the 1920s, live orchestras provided the bulk of the musical programming. Any talking was done by anonymous staff announcers who were selected for their ability to speak unobtrusively and with dignity. Broadcasters went so far as to prohibit their announcers from using names on the air, lest any sort of listener identity develop. These faceless radio announcers were forerunners of the nation's disc jockeys. They had no idea of the omnipotence their successors would attain once the magical combination of radio and records was established. But in commercial radio's early years that combination was anything but magical.

The first person to play a phonograph record for transmission over the air, the first "disc jockey," was Reginald A. Fessenden, an electrical engineer who at one time worked with inventor Thomas A. Edison. Years later the "Father of Radio," Lee De Forest, laid claim to the title of the "first" disc jockey. Although Fessenden had clearly beaten De Forest to the task by almost a year, De Forest's boast of being the nation's "number-one disc jockey" was only the first in what would someday be an endless stream of such accolades.

Because of the inferior sound quality of phonograph records in the 1920s, there was strong opposition to broadcasting them on the nation's airwaves. The Federal Radio Commission (FRC), formed by the Radio Act of 1927, "attempted everything this side of public hangings to curb the practice," and in 1930 the NBC and CBS networks banned phonograph records from their programming. The use of phonograph records continued, however, even as the FRC decried the practice as "in effect a fraud upon the listening public" and mandated that phonograph records be identified as such before they were played on the air. While the required announcements made it appear as if radio stations were apologizing to their listeners for broadcasting recorded music, the practice continued on independent stations across the country. As the 1930s began, several Los Angeles radio stations already provided their listeners with a nearly around-the-clock sorting of recorded music. As the decade progressed with America struggling through the Great Depression, the disc jockey concept began in earnest as radio announcers ceased being the faceless nonentities they had been during commercial radio's first decade.

The first important record announcer was Al Jarvis, who in 1932 originated the Make-Believe Ballroom concept on KFWB in Los Angeles. Jarvis's "World's Largest Make-Believe Ballroom" utilized phonograph records to create the illusion of a live radio broadcast. In 1935 in New York, WNEW announcer Martin Block introduced the Make-Believe Ballroom concept to the East Coast.

While Al Jarvis and Martin Block were instrumental in introducing the Make-Believe Ballroom concept to radio, "Red Godfrey, the Warbling Banjoist," was busy creating the radio-announcer-as-personality concept. Arthur Godfrey, ex–door-to-door salesman, brought his earthy disposition and free spirit to the public's notice over WFBR in Baltimore in 1929. Smashing records on the air that did not appeal to his liking and poking fun at the commercials of his own sponsors—an unheard of act at the time—Godfrey gingerly toed the line of respectability. Although his early-morning antics attracted more listeners than any other morning program in the area, Godfrey was fired by a shortsighted, uptight NBC executive. Godfrey was snatched up by rival Columbia Broadcasting System (CBS) affiliate

WJSV, where he honed his irreverent style to perfection. "It was this style," wrote music historian Arnold Passman, "popularized by Godfrey when he reached New York during World War II, that was ultimately to become the staple of American radio."

By 1939 network-affiliated radio stations filled 10–15 percent of their programming with prerecorded transcriptions, while some independent stations used them for as much as 80 percent of their programming. While still heavily biased against prerecorded music, broadcasters were beginning to soften their stance against its use.

In 1940 two significant events occurred that not only increased the playing of phonograph records on the air but also paved the way for the radio disc jockey explosion in the late 1940s. First, the FCC requirement for identifying all prerecorded music as such before it was aired was rescinded. Second, the policy of playing phonograph records on the air was legally sanctioned. Since most of the top radio performers of that era had network contracts that called for their stars' exclusive services, such artists did not want to jeopardize their lucrative "exclusives" by having their talents offered free through the playing of phonograph records on other radio stations. Many entertainers, such as Bing Crosby and Paul Whiteman, placed NOT LICENSED FOR RADIO BROADCAST warnings on their record labels, but in a 1940 court case involving Whiteman, the record label warning was held to have no legal basis. It was ruled that a broadcaster, having purchased an artist's record, could broadcast it "without further obligation" to that artist. When the U.S. Supreme Court declined to hear the appeal, the nation's record announcers were on secure legal footing for the first time in radio's brief history.

Because the nation's radio networks still commanded the bulk of the listening audience, as well as a major portion of sponsor advertising dollars, these independent stations created a new set of rules, forgoing the long-accepted fare of live studio music for something more affordable—a disc jockey and a stack of phonograph records.

Despite World War II restrictions on materials, such as shellac, used in the manufacture of phonograph records, and despite the "Petrillo ban"—the response of James C. Petrillo, president of the American Federation of Musicians, to the issue of compensation for playing recordings on the radio—which prohibited music recording in the United States from 1942 until the ban broke down in 1946, live studio music continued to disappear from the radio. By 1942, the year Alan Freed entered radio via WKST, 76 percent of radio broadcast time was taken up with music, with 55 percent of that music being prerecorded. With the ending of wartime restrictions on shellac and the lifting of the Petrillo ban on recording music, the few American record companies doing business had difficulty meeting the post–World War II demand for their product.

Postwar radio also saw the development of the "musical clock" format, which consisted of music, time checks, weather reports, news on the hour, and of course plenty of commercial announcements—all tied together by an ad-libbing disc jockey. Wrote Eric Barnouw, "Such programming seemed to require a minimum of investment. The 'talent' consisted of a disk jockey . . . [who] also helped 'merchandise' his program with appearances in department stores and supermarkets. He might be an 'entertainer' but was also a super-salesman; this became his main economic role."

Radio disc jockeys were now embraced by a booming record industry that had suffered through the Great Depression and the dormant period of World War II. These deejays were becoming essential promotional channels between the record manufacturers and the listening public. They began to be wooed, at almost any cost, to get phonograph records heard on the radio.

Alan Freed left WKBN in Youngstown on November 4, 1944, transferring, according to his later recollections, to WIBE Radio in Philadelphia. These few months present a mysterious gap in Freed's professional career. Betty Lou Greene, Freed's wife at the time, had no recollection of WIBE or of her and/or her husband ever being in Philadelphia. There is no evidence that WIBE existed as a radio station.

Phyllis Simms, who began working at WAKR Radio in Akron, Ohio, in 1949 and was a vice-president at the station in the 1980s, said that S. Bernard Berk, who founded WAKR in 1940, met Freed by chance, "in some sort of retail establishment . . . somewhere in Pennsylvania." Berk was impressed with Freed's voice and thought with "some development" the announcer would be right for WAKR. Any doubts Freed had about making the move most likely disappeared when Berk offered the announcer $62.50 a week.

With its studios located in, and its transmitting tower atop, the lofty downtown First National Tower on Main and Mill streets in the heart of Akron, WAKR was an affiliate of the American Broadcasting Company (ABC) when Freed arrived in 1945. At the time, the Akron listening area was blanketed by Cleveland radio twenty-five miles to the north. The "publicity-conscious" Berk was in the process of trying to convince local listeners that they needed their own radio station.

At first Freed was responsible for a nightly sports wrap-up that followed the 11:00 P.M. news. He also called the play-by-play for the University of Akron athletic teams, an assignment that resulted in Freed's first brush with notoriety. It was hardly the kind of attention the publicity-conscious Bernard Berk sought.

On an evening Freed was preparing to do play-by-play of a basketball game, there was a brief period of silence on the air as WAKR switched its broadcasting lines from the studio to the Akron gymnasium. The broadcasting booth toilets were closed that night, and Freed, under pressure, realized there was no way he could get downstairs and back to the broadcast booth in time for the start of the game. Suddenly people all over Akron tuning in the game heard Freed exclaim, "Jesus, I have to take a piss!" Freed's wife said that unbeknownst to her husband, the WAKR engineers in the control booth had turned on the sound about two minutes too soon.

Freed and Betty Lou were residing in a tiny Akron apartment when Alana Freed was born on August 8, 1945. The couple and their newborn daughter soon moved into a larger apartment, with new furniture compliments of S. Bernard Berk, at Westgate Manor. Not long after Alana's birth, Freed, much to his own surprise, became a full-fledged disc jockey.

Freed was finishing up his sports report one evening at 11:10 when he received a call saying the regular disc jockey for the 11:15 program had not yet showed up. As the only announcer in the studio, Freed was told to fill in for the missing deejay. It happened so quickly that Freed said he did not have time to get excited. He grabbed a nearby pile of records and station engineer Danny Silverman told him which ones to play. The following morning, one of the program's sponsors called Bernard Berk to say they liked the manner in which Freed handled the on-the-spot assignment. Berk evidently agreed. "He fired the other guy and gave me the job," said Freed.

At the age of twenty-four, Freed became a regularly programmed disc jockey in the respectably sized radio market of Akron. The program he took over was a listener call-in show that featured jazz and popular recordings of the day. It was called "Request Revue."

If Freed's WKST position served as the announcer's foot in the broadcasting door and his WKBN position proved to be his initial brush with professionalism, hosting "Request Revue" provided Freed with his first experience as a radio "personality." S Bernard Berk proceeded to give his newest disc jockey "extensive" training, spending "thousands" of dollars in promotional money on Freed. The station owner saw to it that Freed appeared at various school functions and "became a well-known figure in the area." And spinning "the wildest things he could get ahold of"—records by the likes of Ella Fitzgerald, Count Basie, Lionel Hampton, and Woody Herman—Freed gradually built "Request Revue" into the station's top money-maker.

While at WAKR Alan Freed offered the first glimpse of the disdainful behavior he would display toward management and authority throughout his career. WAKR had a "music committee," which sanctioned records for airplay on the station. Not only did the committee decide if a particular record would be heard, but it also determined what time—morning, noon, or night—the record would be heard. If a record was deemed "too wild," the music committee would reject it altogether. Because Freed was on the air until 12:30 A.M., he was permitted to play "more up-tempo" recordings than were allowed to be aired on morning and daytime programs geared mainly to housewives. Despite the fact that Freed enjoyed this leeway in his music programming, "from time to time" he skirted the music committee completely, playing unsanctioned records of his own choice.

On the air Freed played it straight, acceding to WAKR's wishes to keep "Request Revue" on an "adult level." Phyllis Simms said Freed did not use, "and wouldn't have been permitted to use," some of the expressions and style he employed after going to Cleveland. Freed pretty much followed the format he inherited, providing "precious little patter between records."

A frequent visitor to WAKR's studios was Alan Freed's younger brother, David, who, after graduating from Salem High School in 1941, served in the Army Air corps for the duration of World War II. In 1946 the younger Freed enrolled as a radio and speech major at Kent State University, located some twenty miles from Akron. When WKSU, the campus radio station, went on the air, David Freed served as its first program director. "Deejays were just really beginning to get going at the time," said Freed. "I'd say Alan was one of the first to get the feel of the public. He'd go out to schools and meet with the kids. He'd bring kids down to the studio. He turned radio into more of an individual performance rather than just a voice on the airwaves.

Alan Freed was soon working twelve and thirteen hours a day for WAKR, promoting an assortment of recording stars and music that included everything "from pop to the cool jazz bit, to Spike Jones." The "Request Revue" host was then so well known around Akron that whenever he and Betty Lou went out for dinner people approached him for autographs at their table. Although Freed was merely "a big fish in a little pool" at that point in his career, it was the first time that "the public would not leave him alone." Freed could no longer walk the streets on Akron without being recognized.

Freed's arduous broadcasting chores also brought about a lifelong friendship with Hermie Dressel, who was a drummer with the Lyle Davis Orchestra when the two met. One of Freed's broadcasting responsibilities was to emcee WAKR's remote broadcasts of big bands that performed at the ballroom in the Mayflower Hotel in downtown Akron. Bored stiff from the Mayflower's staid "hotel" bands, Freed took an instant interest in Davis's jazz-oriented ensemble. "Jesus Christ," Freed exclaimed to Dressel, "every goddmaned band that comes in here is 'Mickey Mouse'! How come you're here playing some real music?"

It was the beginning of a professional, as well as a personal, relationship for the pair. When Dressel played the Akron area, he would stay with the Freeds. Freed and Dressel nurtured their friendship by "lifting a few glasses" and sharing a few beers at Akron after-hours jazz clubs. Dressel recalled he and the "flamboyant" Freed raising their share of hell, "carrying on" there in the late 1940s. He also said Freed, who became a notorious drinker later on in his life, had his penchant for alcohol under control in Akron. Some of the deejay's biggest kicks came when Dressel brought recording stars such as Woody Herman and Count Basie to the WAKR studios, where the '"wigged out" Freed interviewed them on the air.

By 1947 "Request Revue" was Akron's most popular radio program. As Freed continued to hobnob with show business personalities and as the autograph seekers increased, so did Freed's regard for his own celebrity status swell. The popular disc jockey's career was on the upswing, but there were soon repercussions in his personal life. Devoting himself totally to his professional endeavors, the busy deejay's grueling schedule allowed scant time to devote to his wife and infant daughter. As Freed's popularity continued to grow, so did the strain on his neglected marriage. "At that time my career had to come first, even before my family," he said. "We tried to make a go of it because of the children, but we became complete strangers."

His sponsorship activities at WAKR eventually led Freed to the local Arthur Murray Dance Studio, where, by chance, he met dance instructor Marjorie McCoy Hess, a statuesque, "really attractive" blonde divorcée. "Her name was Marjorie," said David Freed, "but everybody called her Jackie."

Freed's wife was "completely shocked" when she found out her husband was seeing another woman. "We discussed it and Alan denied there was anything to it," she said. Freed maintained Jackie was simply "somebody he'd met." Freed's wife was pregnant again when she discovered Freed was still seeing Jackie. She told her husband she was going to leave him, only to find Freed—who wanted "to have his children with her—would not listen.

Freed insisted that a visit by his troubled wife to her mother and sister, who resided in Coral Gables, Florida, just south of Miami, would do her good. Willing to try almost anything to save her foundering marriage, Betty Lou went south. After a month in Florida, Freed contacted his wife and told her the affair with Jackie was over, that he would never see her again. But when Freed's wife returned to Akron, she discovered the affair was still going strong. Betty Lou, although still "very much in love" with Freed, knew their marriage was over, because "things would have remained that way for the rest of our lives, had I stayed with him."

But Freed, still adamantly opposed to a divorce, told his wife he would fight it. "One night when he came by to see the kids," Betty Lou remembered, "he told me I wouldn't get my divorce, because he knew the judge." When the court divorce hearing date arrived, the judge called Freed and his wife to his chambers and asked Betty Lou if she still loved her husband. She answered that she still loved him. Then the judge asked Freed if he still loved Betty Lou. He replied, "Very definitely!" and added that he did not want the divorce to be granted. Apparently it was no idle boast that Freed made to his wife about "knowing the judge," because the divorce was not granted. "My lawyer was furious," said Betty Lou.

Another court date was set up. This time Mrs. Freed and her attorney came prepared with "a lot of evidence I didn't enjoy gathering." Threatened with having the affair brought out in the open, Freed, most likely after considering the disastrous effect the disclosure of his unfaithfulness would have on his career, agreed to the divorce.

With her divorce granted, Betty Lou took Alana and Lance (who was born in September 1947) to Florida, where they moved in with her mother. Freed never visited his children while they were in Florida, but the deejay's ex-wife never lost contact with his career. Anytime something about Freed appeared in a newspaper, Betty Lou's friends in Akron or her own family in Canton, Ohio, would cut it out and send it to her.

A Coral Gables neighbor of Betty Lou's mother had a cousin named Tom Greene, who was a U.S. Marine. Sometimes when he was on leave, Greene would visit Florida. Before long, he and the divorced Betty Lou were introduced. In time, they began to date and in 1952 they were married.

By 1949 Alan Freed was earning more than $10,000 a year as host of WAKR's top-rated "Request Revue." He may have stumbled upon the position by chance three years earlier, but since then Freed had come on like a house afire. His contract was set to expire at the end of the year, and Freed realized he was largely responsible for his show's popularity, as well as for much of the hefty advertising revenue Bernard Berk collected from satisfied sponsors. Freed wanted some of that revenue, but in attempting to lay claim to it, he clearly underestimated Berk's resolve. It is questionable which incensed Freed more: Berk's rejection of Freed's request for a salary increase or the patronizing manner in which Berk rebuked his star celebrity. The station owner dismissed Freed's request as he would an impudent child's, and the resentful Freed threatened to go elsewhere instead of renewing his WAKR contract. Berk reminded the deejay of the restrictive covenant that was written into his contract. That clause prohibited Freed from broadcasting on any radio station within a seventy-five-mile radius of Akron for a period of one year, should he leave WAKR.

Disdainfully disregarding his WAKR contract, Freed signed with promoter Lew Platt to do a disc jockey program opposite WAKR's "Request Revue." Platt intended to buy airtime from WADC, a rival station located across Main Street from WAKR, and then pay Freed to do a disc jockey program. No doubt WADC was thrilled to be a part of this broadcasting coup. Freed and WADC surely expected the deejay's loyal listeners to follow him over to WADC, enabling Freed to continue to rule nighttime Akron radio.

He had just turned twenty-eight years old. He was a hot item in Akron radio and he knew it, but the brash deejay's aborted stint at WAKR would prove to be the longest period he would ever be employed by another broadcaster. And this would not be the last time that Alan Freed miscalculated his future.

While Freed actually did a couple of radio programs for WADC, Bernard Berk received a temporary court injunction prohibiting the wayward deejay from continuing on the rival station. In a letter dated January 1950, Freed notified Berk of the deejay's intention to form, along with Lew Platt, a company through which Freed would be free to sell his radio program to whichever radio station was interested, Alan Freed and Associates.

The "bitterly fought" dispute escalated when Berk sought to make the court injunction permanent. Freed maintained Berk's restrictive clause was "oppressive" and "against public policy." WAKR attorneys countered, telling Common Pleas Judge Bernard Roetzel that a radio station "depends on its radio audience for its appeal to advertisers" and that Freed was trying to take the "Request Revue" audience to another station. The concept of who a listening audience "belonged to" had never been legally questioned. Obviously, Freed's listeners could not be made to listen to WAKR, but possibly they could be denied the option of listening to Freed broadcast on another radio station. During the hearing, a self-righteous Freed grew outraged, realizing at last that he might be barred from Akron-area radio by a piece of paper held by a station he no longer worked for.

Freed's attorney had summoned executives from other Akron radio stations to the court hearing to testify. The deejay, wishing to establish that he was being singled out for unfair treatment by WAKR, wanted his attorney to ask the witnesses if other local radio employees had restrictive clauses in their contracts. Freed's attorney refused, knowing his client's contract was the only one in question. After asking Judge Roetzel for his "right to be heard," Freed grew so incensed that he attempted to take over the questioning himself. To mollify Freed, his attorney asked the disputed question after assuring the court he was aware it was improper.

As expected, Judge Roetzel disallowed the question, ruling that Freed's WAKR contract "was the only one at issue." He then urged Freed and Berk to "settle amicably" out of court, but after a brief meeting between the two headstrong parties, Freed said WAKR had not "offered me anything it hadn't before."

On February 11, 1950, Judge Roetzel granted WAKR a permanent injunction upholding S. Bernard Berk's controversial restrictive broadcasting clause, in effect barring Freed from broadcasting on WADC or on any other Akron-area station.

What was going on in Freed's mind when he walked out at WAKR? David Freed said his brother was a "bit of a troublemaker . . . stirring things up" at WAKR. He suggested that his brother, "seeing the advantages of publicity," may well have calculated the move. "Alan was not . . . made to be a disc jockey in a small town . . . like Akron all his life."

But if, indeed, Alan Freed had given his walkout from WAKR any thought, he had not counted on the court case going against him. With the decision in WAKR's favor, any publicity the deejay reaped was hardly of any use. Virtually unknown outside the seventy-five-mile radius he was barred from broadcasting in, Freed would have to relocate in an area where he was a complete unknown in order to continue his radio career.

A stunned Freed decided he and his brother David would open up the Alan Freed School of Radio and Television. David Freed, still attending Kent State University as a radio and speech major, became the school's dean. David said he and his brother conducted one class, which lasted "about six months," before the Alan Freed School of Radio and Television "died a natural death."

Whether it was Alan Freed's, promoter Lew Platt's, or someone else's idea, by doing what most longtime radio stars were doing as the 1950s began, the deejay was able to remain in the Akron area and continue his broadcasting career. Freed simply abandoned radio for the limitless potential of America's newest medium, television.

The first postwar television sets appeared in the nation's retail stores in September 1946 at a time when there were only six commercial television stations broadcasting in the entire country. Even Bernard Berk, a foresighted individual with broadcasting acumen, was not savvy enough to envision the newest medium's booming future when he slipped his restrictive broadcasting clause into his star disc jockey's contract. Freed's WAKR contract made no mention whatsoever of television.

In 1950 Cleveland was a city on the move. Already boasting the seventh-largest metropolitan population in the country, that year the city's already extensive heavy industry expanded "at a rate never before equalled in the city's history." Television viewing in 1950 matched radio listening in New York and other major cities across the country for the first time. By the end of the year, there were 107 stations, "practically all . . . operating profitably," on a regular schedule in fifty-eight cities from coast to coast. But broadcasting facilities were primitive. Cleveland's first television station, WEWS-TV, opened in 1947 and the city became linked to Pittsburgh and Philadelphia via television. In 1949, the year WXEL-TV went on the air, Cleveland was connected to the midwestern television market, but by 1950 only one-quarter of the nation's population had access to live network programming. The East Coast and West Coast would not be linked by live television until September 1951.

It may not have been his now-familiar radio, but by switching to television Alan Freed had within his grasp the largest audience of his career, one that dwarfed even Akron's. The ex-radio deejay was totally focused on television when he landed a job hosting WXEL-TV's extremely popular afternoon movie early in 1950. Freed was also responsible for a less-popular show on which he "did some records on late-night TV," when not bantering with his cohost, a locally well-known pianist named Grant Wilson.

Bob Dixon recalled watching Freed late at night during the early era of Cleveland television. He thought Freed's show was "one of the worst things I've ever seen." Utilizing a shoestring-budget "surrealistic" studio set complete with "clouds and stuff . . . he got on there and just played records." When a record ended, Freed and Wilson went at each other in a mock "put-down session . . . doing everything but hitting each other over the head with balloons." Dixon said the show was "really bad," and David Freed agreed that his brother's "television records . . . didn't last long." In short order, Freed was yanked from his late-night television spot.

Alan Freed had tantalizingly tasted stardom in Akron, and it had agreed totally with his very egocentric personality. His relegation to hosting a local afternoon television movie, no matter how popular it was, was the ultimate degradation in Freed's eyes. He could not have felt any better in December 1950 when Ohio's Ninth District Court of Appeals upheld Judge Roetzel's earlier ruling that WAKR could contractually prohibit the deejay from appearing on Akron-area radio.

Convinced more than ever that he had been "wronged" by WAKR, in his frustration, Freed began leaning increasingly on alcohol, not only to pass his idle hours but to dull the pain of his failure. Although he did not realize it at the time, this "failure" would soon lead to a significant breakthrough in Freed's temporarily derailed career. It would be as great, if not greater, than the one he had received five years earlier when an errant Akron disc jockey failed to show for his "Request Revue" program. Not only would Alan Freed's year of banishment from local radio end in February 1951, but he was about to cross paths with Leo Mintz, a man with a vision.

CHAPTER 3

The Dog Howls

"I had a program on WJW, a Cleveland station. The program music, believe it or not, was classical. A friend who owned a record shop suggested that I visit the store. He said I might see something unusual."

BY chance Alan Freed and Leo Mintz, "a very heavy drinker," happened to be drinking in a Euclid Avenue watering hole called Mullins. Mintz owned the Record Rendezvous, a large phonograph record shop at 300 Prospect Avenue, near Cleveland's black inner-city ghetto. A few beers led to idle conversation, and several more drinks led the two to discover a common interest other than alcohol—radio, music, and phonograph records. When Mintz, a longtime sponsor on local radio station WJW (850 on the AM dial), learned of Freed's "exile" to the WXEL-TV afternoon movie, he helped his newfound drinking buddy land a job playing classical music on WJW.

Thanks to Cleveland's almost 130,000 blacks, Mintz's "Record Rendezvous" boasted a steady sale of "race" records, or rhythm and blues records, as they were commonly called by 1951. The myth enshrouding Freed's introduction to rhythm and blues holds that in April 1951 Leo Mintz noticed a growing number of white teenagers frequenting his store, browsing through the rhythm and blues record section, and listening to such black stars as Charles Brown, Fats Domino, Amos Milburn, and Ruth Brown. Taken aback by the "unusual" sight of white youths perusing the heretofore all-black section of his record store, Mintz allegedly summoned his disc jockey friend, Alan Freed, to see the sight himself.

The myth took shape with Freed saying he was "amazed" at the sight before his eyes, a sight the deejay described as "a picture of excitement," with (presumably white) teenagers "enthusiastically listening to a type of music I presumed alien to their culture." As a result of this observation, concludes the myth, Freed went on the air playing rhythm and blues records for white teenagers, and rock & roll was born. This romanticized version of Freed's discovery of young white America's affinity for rhythm and blues music has become gospel over the years, embellished upon by Freed himself, but the facts simply do not support the myth.

In an early account of this historic discovery Freed said he "accepted" Mintz's invitation and saw "dozens of kids . . . listening to the records of some of the people who were destined to become the very top performers in the idiom." There was no mention of race or of the music being "alien" to anyone's culture. Furthermore, existing photographs of Freed's 1952–1953 Ohio dances all depict overwhelmingly black audiences. And despite crossover records such as the Dominoes' "Sixty-Minute Man," the white pop charts remained otherwise untouched by rhythm and blues.

Jack Hooke, co-owner of New York's Royal Roost Records, who originally met Freed on a Midwest record promotion trip in 1952, had been in the music business about four years by then. Hooke said the records in Mintz's store were "played on black radio stations" and were "bought . . . and played by black people only. No white people" knew of them or played them in 1951.

If there was a noticeable number of white teenagers haunting Mintz's Record Rendezvous in 1951, what became of them after that? Freed's aborted Moondog Coronation Ball at the Cleveland Arena eight months later drew a virtually all-black audience. Freed himself, before he consciously set out during his heyday in the late 1950s to "revise" his past, admitted in a more candid moment that during his first years as Moondog his radio program "at first attracted an audience that was nearly all Negro." Only "as time went on" did "more and more whites listen." Freed later said that only after a rock & roll dance in New York City in January 1955 at which it was estimated up to 70 percent of the audience was white did he have the "first inkling . . . that white people enjoyed rhythm and blues." Freed also said his Cleveland dances "appealed most to colored people," so much so that during those years he received "batches of poison-pen letters calling me a 'nigger-lover.'"

The whites in Mintz's Record Rendezvous rhythm and blues section that April day were, most likely, precious few and were not the primary reason Mintz summoned Freed to the store. Mintz noticed his rhythm and blues platters growing more and more popular. If he could persuade Freed to forget about classical music on WJW and replace it with selections of Mintz's rhythm and blues records . . . As Mintz thought about it he could already hear his cash register jingling.

Mintz wasted no time explaining his vision to Freed, telling the deejay, "I'll buy you a radio show if you'll play nothing but rhythm and blues."

"Are you crazy?" replied Freed, who thought that not enough people would listen because "those are race records."

"Not anymore," Mintz allegedly replied.

Freed said he listened to LaVern Baker and Della Reese, "two girls with real contralto voices who know how to tell a story," as well as to the "blues-singing, piano-playing" Ivory Joe Hunter. He also heard the tenor saxophones of Red Prysock and Big Al Sears. More than anything else, Freed was attracted by the honking and wailing horns. "The hoarse, husky tenor sax was . . . a carry-over from swing [Al Sears' career, which began in the 1920s, included stints with Chick Webb, Lionel Hampton, and Duke Ellington, among others]," wrote music historian Arnold Shaw. "In person the tenor man heated up the joint with his eyes shut and the veins bulging in his forehead, he grimaced and bobbed up and down like a rooster, the sweat beading his face in an unabating pour." Freed was instantly hooked by the wild rave-ups of Gil Bernal, Joe Houston, Big Jay McNeely, as well as Prysock and Sears, among others.

Freed agreed the raw, exciting sound of rhythm and blues was appealing to teenagers, apparently even to some white ones, but he was far from convinced to host an entire program of the music. The four heavy beats to the bar, the relatively crude renditions (in comparison to "pop" arrangements), and the blatantly sexual lyrics all seemed to make Mintz's notion seem too crazy—even to the publicity-conscious Freed. He turned Mintz down, telling the record-store owner that "radio is dead." As far as Freed was concerned, Leo Mintz's crazy scheme was also dead.

Mintz, envisioning Freed's entire WJW radio program as one giant commercial for his Record Rendezvous merchandise, remained undaunted. He again approached Freed, reminding the deejay that he did not have to know anything about rhythm and blues. Mintz would tell him what to play. All Freed would have to do would be to introduce the records. Freed told Mintz things were happening too fast and he needed more time to think them through.

Most likely softened by a few beers at Mullins' bar, Freed's resolve began to waver. Still, he wondered how widespread was the appeal of rhythm and blues. "I wondered for about a week," he said, before Mintz once again reassured Freed that sax-dominated black combos would be as popular over the radio as they were at his Record Rendezvous. Hearing Mintz speak of the music's beat, so driving that almost anybody could dance at it, Freed acquiesced, agreeing to go with what the deejay described as a format of Negro blues, gospel-oriented tunes and lots of saxes.

Jack Hooke, who became fast friends, as well as a business associate and right-hand man to Freed, most likely knew more of the deejay's career than anyone else. Hooke explained that Leo Mintz "was interested in selling" his records, bought the time on WJW, and put Freed on the program himself. "He hired Alan, paid him, . . . and gave Alan some idea of what he wanted played." Hooke said although Freed was "pushed" into rock & roll and worked for Mintz, not for WJW, at first, "he got to like the music very much."

Exactly what Alan Freed knew of rhythm and blues music at this point in his career is questionable, although Freed said he was a "confirmed rhythm and blues fan" by the time he got to Cleveland. Freed's indignation toward racial prejudice stems at least from his high school days when he had a black friend named Joe Cooper. David Freed said Cooper was "as close as anybody to Al in high school." A black face in Salem, Ohio, in the 1930s was a rare sight, and a black person socializing with whites, eating meals at a white person's house, was ever rarer. There must have been disapproving comments from neighboring residents when young Freed invited Joe Cooper to dinner. Indeed, there were disapproving voices from Freed's own grandparents. More than likely, the negative comments Freed received regarding his unusual black-white friendship strengthened his conviction of righteousness and solidified his identification with blacks.

Freed also said he gained awareness of black records during his early radio tenures, when race records were sent to the stations where he was working. Freed recalled listening with "fascination," as he remembered songs he had heard during his childhood. He "particularly liked the old Bessie Smith records," which prompted him to do "some jazz research." David Freed said his brother had a "knowledge of spirituals . . . and some interest" in gospel music while Alan was in high school. Alan also retained childhood visions of his minstrel uncles, Al and Don Palmer, in blackface, performing white stereotypes of blacks. What Freed felt about that experience remains unknown.

Whatever Freed's knowledge of rhythm and blues, it is unlikely that he had much, if any, at all before entering radio. David Freed, who was close to Alan during their high school days, said Leo Mintz's Record Rendezvous was "the first place I ever saw a rhythm and blues record." It is unlikely, as close as the brothers were, that David Freed would not have seen a rhythm and blues record until 1951 if his brother had showed an earlier interest in them.

Hermie Dressel, however, lends credence to Alan Freed's claim of being familiar with rhythm and blues by the time Freed got to Cleveland. The musician recalled "prowling" Akron record shops with Freed in the late 1940s and seeing his friend "get really teed off" at the blatant segregation of the "race" records from the "popular" records. It was Dressel's belief that Freed may have "learned a hell of a lot more" about rhythm and blues in Cleveland, but that his disc jockey friend "knew what rhythm and blues was all about" before then.

If indeed Freed "knew what rhythm and blues was all about" before he took to the WJW airwaves with it, he later went into great detail describing the crucial decision to do so. Freed maintained that he had asked some of Mintz's Record Rendezvous patrons what it was that drew them to the "blaring mixture of stepped-up folk songs heard mostly in small Negro night spots." They allegedly told him "it was the beat, the rich excitement the singers and instruments provided." Freed conceded that the "hot, freewheeling platters with plenty of punch complimented, rather than sublimated" youthful teenage energy.

What Freed, as well as rhythm and blues, had in their favor was the state of popular music as the 1950s began. The most popular song of 1950 (with over two million copies sold) was the Weavers' version of "Goodnight, Irene," described as a "naive piece of 'pure corn'" that proved to be "the most embarrassing index to the public taste." Most of the "commercially successful but aesthetically insignificant" pop songs of the year "either echoed some older music or represented a deliberate revival of material already established in the past." Freed said that America's teenagers at the dawn of the 1950s were "starved for entertainment" and had no music to identify with or to dance to. He believed that with the pop charts dominated by "soupy and languid" songs, "ballads and cool, progressive jazz with absolutely no beat," white teenagers were drawn to rhythm and blues by the music's "infectious beat . . . [which was] great for dancing." The deejay said the younger generation's encounter with the "powerful, affirmative jazz beat" of rhythm and blues was "an exciting discovery." As for the few major record companies that dominated the popular music business, the nation's youth could take or leave their product. And by 1951 it looked as if many of them were leaving it.

Exactly how much thought did Alan Freed give to Leo Mintz's suggestion that the disc jockey host a rhythm and blues program in 1951? Several years later, when the rock & roll craze was in full swing with Freed as the new music's greatest promoter, the deejay carefully "filled in the gaps" of that historic encounter in the Record Rendezvous. But everything Freed recalled was filtered through at least five years' hindsight. In the aftermath of Freed's "televised records" debacle on WXEL-TV, most likely any thought given to Mintz's urgings involved the looming possibility of Freed courting yet another disaster. Rather than analyzing why rhythm and blues apparently appealed to Cleveland's teenagers or considering whether indeed it was the music for the coming generation, Freed was most likely wondering if he could survive such a show.

Whatever Freed thought, it was unquestionably Leo Mintz who influenced the deejay to become associated with rhythm and blues. Yet, over the years, most likely with the notion that a businessman out to increase his retail sales was a far less romantic image than someone introducing a "new" music to America's "entertainment-starved" younger generation, Freed gradually shoved Leo Mintz out of the picture.

In perhaps the earliest printed account of Freed's discovery of rhythm and blues, he said, "It found me . . . it was more Leo's idea than mine . . . [he] predicted it would be a national rage in a short time." Not long after that, Freed modified his stance, saying his WJW program "was as much his [Mintz's] idea as mine." By 1957 though, Freed took complete credit for the decision to play rhythm and blues on his program. One account of Freed's beginnings mentioned that while the deejay hosted the WXEL-TV afternoon movie, "this left his evenings open [so] he started a nightly

'Rock 'n' Roll' radio show over WJW, Cleveland." In another story written in 1957, Freed was quoted as saying, "As soon as I got command of those big turntables in Cleveland, I knew I wanted to recapture the lost beat so a new generation could know the fun of dancing. . . . When I couldn't find what I wanted in the studio record library I started exploring the shelves of Cleveland's biggest record store."

It has been said that as Freed reaped the mounting rewards from popularizing rhythm and blues, Leo Mintz grew bitter about his own lack of recognition. Freed himself told of Mintz calling the deejay to complain that although the record-store owner "had the foresight" to program rhythm and blues records on WJW, Freed was "making all the money." David Freed, who knew Mintz personally, saw the record-store owner and Alan Freed as "two of a kind." David Freed said he never heard Mintz complain of his anonymity. He thought "things just jelled with them" on the decision to go with rhythm and blues on the radio.

Of course, playing rhythm and blues records on the air, even by a white man, was not a novel idea. The practice, begun in earnest following World War II, was the result of several postwar developments. Among them were the emergence of a large black consumer market in the northern urban areas of the United States; a relative breakdown of some racial barriers; the expansion of radio broadcasting in general; the growing popularity of rhythm and blues music; and, perhaps most important, yet least considered, the soaring success of the nation's newest mass medium—television.

Before World War II most of America's blacks were concentrated in the rural South, with only isolated pockets of significant numbers of blacks in eastern and midwestern cities. This absence of a sizable consumer market offered radio executives and program sponsors outside the South no reason to offer programs of interest to blacks. It was the South, then, that preceded the North in opening up broadcasting aimed at blacks. In the 1930s and early 1940s black-oriented programming, which included both live and recorded music, was widespread in the South. Numerous small southern radio stations presented black artists who talked, sang, and played blues records on the air. One historian has written that during World War II the role of blacks in American broadcasting underwent "serious appraisal," with the conflict precipitating "a general liberalization within society that would be felt in all forms of the popular arts." Indeed, as the wartime migration of blacks to the northern industrial centers commenced, radio programming was about to be "substantially and irreversibly" altered, especially among local stations, where management recognized a "growing importance of appealing to black listeners." This population shift not only set the stage for the development and popularization of rhythm and blues music but also precipitated the wooing by broadcasters of those relocated blacks as a viable consumer force.

Between 1945 and 1952 there was "intense" pressure within American broadcasting for the development of new radio stations. Early in 1946 this pressure was relieved somewhat when a technical change was made by the FCC, allowing more stations to occupy the same or adjacent frequencies in a given area, which resulted in an outburst of new broadcasting outlets. As a result of new competition, there was generally a greater diversity in programming. Although most of the new stations adopted standard middle-of-the-road programming, a trend of specialization did develop in certain cities. Stations in markets with large black populations soon began to program rhythm and blues to this specialized market. In fact, the popularity of rhythm and blues music and the growing number of black consumers was such that in 1948 full-time radio broadcasting aimed at blacks came into being.

Ultimately, it was the success of two southern radio stations that showed the broadcasting industry the commercial viability of programming rhythm and blues music. "Daddy" Gene Nobles, a white man, played "jump band jazz and well-known black artists such as Count Basie" on Nashville's fifty-thousand-watt station, WLAC, in the early 1940s. Another white deejay, "John R" Richbourg, joined WLAC shortly after World War II. About that time, Nobles and Richbourg noticed that the station began to receive requests for certain blues records made and sold in the South, and they tried to satisfy the requests as best they could. By the late 1940s Nobles and Richbourg played rhythm and blues every weeknight for audiences "from the Eastern Shore of Virginia to the wilds of West Texas and as far north as Canada." Because of the enormous range of its transmitting power, WLAC became a key station for developing rhythm and blues hits in the early 1950s.

While Daddy Gene and John R built up their following of rhythm and blues listeners, two hundred miles to the southwest, in Memphis, radio station WDIA went on the air programming toward whites in 1947. But after one year WDIA lost so much money that its white owners, considering the area's one and a half million blacks, revamped its programming with an all-black format, including its disc jockeys. Almost overnight, WDIA became a commercial success, starting a trend toward all-black programming.

As separate as the white and black radio markets were, almost from the start white men were on the radio entertaining blacks with rhythm and blues music. Bill Gordon, who eventually went on to become a successful morning man in Cleveland, claimed to be the first white to program rhythm and blues records on the air. From 1946 to 1950 Gordon could be heard on WMPS in Memphis, playing rhythm and blues records for the area's large black population. Before long, said Gordon, "many jocks were doing it in the South." When Gordon left Memphis in 1950, Dewey Phillips of WHBQ became the city's principal white rhythm and blues platter spinner.

In 1948 Hunter Hancock began hosting a daily rhythm and blues program over KFVD in Los Angeles. Hancock had been a jazz deejay at the station who, in 1943, began entertaining an audience he described as "average black listeners." Hancock said he was "the first announcer, black or white, to specialize in what later became known as rhythm and blues."

Like Alan Freed, nineteen-year-old Dick ("Huggie Boy") Hugg began playing rhythm and blues music on the air in 1951. Huggie Boy, who called himself "the West Coast Alan Freed," worked out of a storefront window of a record shop in the heart of the Los Angeles black neighborhood. That same year, in the San Francisco–Oakland Bay area, "Jumpin' " George Oxford broadcast forty-nine hours of rhythm and blues a week over KWBR radio.

Other white disc jockeys of the early 1950s who played rhythm and blues music, each with a colorful nickname and personalized style, included Zena ("Daddy") Sears in Atlanta; Clarence ("Poppa Stoppa") Hayman in New Orleans; Danny ("Cat Man") Stiles in Newark, New Jersey; Ken ("Jack the Cat") Elliott in New Orleans; George ("Hound Dog") Lorenz in Buffalo, New York; Phil McKernan in Berkeley, California; and Tom ("Big Daddy") Donahue, who began his career in Washington, D.C., in 1949.

The years between 1948 and 1952 saw a large number of black radio stations program rhythm and blues records to reach what *Sponsor* magazine referred to in 1949 as the "forgotten 15 million black consumers in America." By 1951 most large southern cities had black-oriented radio stations and "the potential rhythm and blues explosion could no longer be halted."

During the first few years of the 1950s the increase in black programming was impressive, "but still represented segregated radio . . . and the exclusion of blacks from the mainstream of popular culture." Because it was regarded by whites as the music of blacks, rhythm and blues ultimately needed a white as its champion in order to gain mass acceptance in American society. Moondog Freed, although not the first white rhythm and blues disc jockey, was nevertheless unique. Historian Arnold Shaw has persuasively argued that "although other white disc jockeys may have devoted full shows to r&b discs, Freed performed the feat of building a large white audience for records that had previously been of interest only to blacks." Freed was to become the leading proponent of the style that came to characterize the northern urbanized disc jockey, and no disc jockey, black or white, would do more than he to promote both rhythm and blues and the music's talented black artists to white people around the world.

Alan Freed apparently had not yet slipped into his Moondog persona on the night of July 11, 1951, when the disc jockey's new rhythm and blues radio program made its debut in the Cleveland area. According to *Cleveland News* TV and radio editor Maurice Van Metre, one night Freed was playing "Moondog Symphony," "a weird number in which a dog sets up a mournful howl," when, on the air, "he attempted to quiet the imaginary cur."

"Come on now, Moondog, please stop howling or you'll wake up the neighbors."

Almost immediately the WJW telephones began to ring as Freed's confused listeners "wanted to know the score." Freed, quick to sense the audience appeal of the freakish "Moondog" recording, adopted the name himself. Once again, Freed had seized the opportunity and was determined to make the most of it. The next evening, with a stack of Leo Mintz's R&B platters and an open microphone, Moondog took to the airwaves, baying like a moonstruck hound. He relentlessly referred to the slow blues instrumental he used for a theme, Todd Rhodes's "Blues for the Red Boy," as "Blues for the Moondog," as if the deejay's incessant repetition alone would change the song title to his liking.

As "Moondog Symphony" played, accompanied by the sound of

bones shaking and rattling in the background, Freed rambled into the open mike, "All right, Moondog, get in there kid! Howl it out buddy!"—as the dog bayed loudly.

"Hello everybody, how y'all tonight? This is Alan Freed, the ol' 'king of the Moondoggers,' and it's time for some blues and rhythm records for all the gang in the Moondog kingdom. We're gonna be saying hello to a lot of folks from all over the Moondog kingdom."

As the music faded, Freed began anew: "Hello everybody and welcome to the 'Moondog House.' And away we go with Wild Bill Moore pickin' up that tenor horn to blow it strong, on the Savoy label, and 'Rock and Roll!'" Freed immediately began to shout into the open mike over the rave-up sax instrumental, "Hey, here we go! Hey, play, hey, all right! Rock it out, Bill. Hey, go, ho, ho!" By then Freed was maniacally screaming over the pounding rhythm of the music. "Hey, hey, hey, hey! Go, go, go, go, go, go! Wow!" As the music faded, Freed continued his frantic pace: "Boy, there's a real rockin' thing to get us off and rollin,' Moondoggers. Wild Bill Moore, the Moondog show, Savoy Records, and Rock and Roll!"

Hermie Dressel recalled that Freed "used to carry on like a madman" in the studio, using "animation, excitement, and forcefulness." Part of Moondog's act included a cowbell and a telephone book. Besides shouting into the open mike as records played, Freed would ring the cowbell or emphasize the heavy beat by slamming his hand on the telephone book. WJW would receive calls from listeners demanding to know what was going on in the studio. After hearing a particular record complete with cowbell and accentuated beat, they went out and purchased the disc, only to discover to their dismay that half the sounds they heard listening to Moondog were not on the record. And Moondog was only warming to the task. His incessant jive patter and sound-augmented recordings compelled attention, and his radio identity began to soar. Hermie Dressel said Freed "tore" the town apart.

"All right, the ol' Moondogger's beatin' it out, folks. One hour fifteen minutes of your favorite blues and rhythm records for all the gang in the Moondog kingdom, from the Midwest to the East Coast."

By January 1952, after a scant five months on the air, Freed was creating waves on nighttime radio in Cleveland. The *Plain Dealer* described February as a "period of adjustment" in local radio. That month Danny Landau, whose nightly "Rhythm Records" had debuted in January on WSRS, abruptly left the station, an apparent casualty of Moondog's popularity. WHK revamped its late-night schedule, putting a new program, "Tom the Piper's Son," up against Freed. WJW countered by again increasing Freed's airtime.

Despite the commotion Freed caused during his first months on WJW as Moondog his relationship to Cleveland's overall radio market should be noted. While Freed may have been making a lot of noise among young rhythm and blues fans, within the total picture of the city's broadcasting activities Moondog was as yet relatively unnoticed.

Traditionally, Cleveland had been central to the pop music business because it served as a "breakout" city, one of several areas of the country in which pop records were "tested" to see if they warranted national distribution. When Moondog began his program in 1951, Cleveland's most popular disc jockeys were Bill Randle and Bill Gordon, both of whom commanded massive white listening audiences. At the start, Freed and his black legions of late-night listeners were unassociated with the white, breakout masses, but as time went on and whites increasingly discovered rhythm and blues, the white audiences of jocks like Randle and Gordon would begin to dwindle. Only then would the pop music industry take notice of rhythm and blues.

At first, even on Freed's own radio station, rhythm and blues music had distinct boundaries. It may have been accepted for late-night programming, traditionally slow in sponsorship revenues anyway, but prime, daytime sponsors were not to be jeopardized by airing those lowdown and nasty black rhythms. WJW's morning deejay, Soupy Heinz (who would later gain fame as comedian Soupy Sales), said if he ever tried to play a record by Dinah Washington or Amos Milburn on his program, he "got called down for that."

Although the boundaries that isolated rhythm and blues to specific radio stations and to certain broadcast times would continue, the boundaries that kept whites from listening to rhythm and blues began to fall. David Freed said that although his brother's "Moondog House" was "never directed . . . to either black or white," in perhaps six months' time Moondog received call-ins and written requests from the white suburbs of Shaker Heights, Cleveland Heights, Brooklyn, and Lakeside.

The nation's record sales charts from early 1952 indicated that the strict racial lines dividing pop and rhythm and blues were about to blur. Johnnie Ray, a twenty-four-year-old white singer discovered by disc jockey Bill Randle, enjoyed unprecedented success on the pop charts and the rhythm and blues charts with an impassioned ballad entitle "Cry." The song reached number one on both charts, reportedly selling more than two million copies as Ray became the first white male vocalist to appear on the rhythm and blues charts. In February, white singer Sunny Gale appeared on the pop and the rhythm and blues charts with her version of "Wheel of Fortune." Ray's and Gale's efforts were significant in that they forewarned of the breaking-down of pop music's racial barriers. Just as important, the sales success of "Cry" and "Wheel of Fortune" in the black community influenced popular-song publishers to be "more willing to submit tunes to independent record companies." Black artists, in particular, would now have a wider variety of songs available to them to record.

Besides making records, the pop music life necessitated touring and performing in public. Every singer coveted a hit record, not only for possible financial reward but, more important, to put them in public demand for personal appearances. The bookings, in turn, could lead to even greater record sales. It was a circular practice that fed off of itself. In the case of blacks, personal appearances were even more vital than they were to whites because the record sales royalties paid to rhythm and blues performers were "virtually nonexistent."

In the late 1940s almost every major northeastern city had at least one theater that catered exclusively to the black audience. Talent packages to appear at these theaters usually consisted of an instrumental combo or orchestra, a comedian, tap dancers, and a couple of singers or vocal groups who would then make the "circuit" of black theaters, usually spending a week in each city. Outside the urbanized Northeast, rhythm and blues entertainment was confined to a "loose-knit trail of night clubs, saloons, and ballrooms" known as the Chitlin' Circuit.

By early 1952 the number of black theaters in the Northeast had dwindled from a high of about forty to about a dozen. Only the Howard Theatre in Washington, D.C., and the famed Apollo Theatre in New York offered entertainment on a regular basis. Cleveland, never a major stop on the rhythm and blues circuit, in early 1952 more resembled the southern Chitlin' Circuit. Occasionally black acts appeared at the Circle Theatre on Euclid Avenue, but it was the city's relatively small night clubs—Cleason's Casino, the Ebony Lounge, the Sky Bar, and the Savoy Club—that kept the local rhythm and blues performance scene in business.

In effect, Cleveland and its large black population was a "wide-open" town in search of an enterprising rhythm and blues promoter when Alan Freed, Leo Mintz, and Lew Platt decided to stage their Moondog Coronation Ball at the Cleveland Arena in March 1952. Following that disaster Freed, as part of his defense, maintained he was not the promoter of the aborted dance, but "only an employee." To prevent a recurrence of the overcrowding that had led to the cancellation of the Moondog Coronation Ball, Freed promised a Moondog Maytime Ball with reserved seats. Nonetheless, there was strong opposition from wary city officials. Deciding instead to begin on a much smaller scale, Freed planned a series of dances for eastern Ohio; in May he flew to New York City to arrange the talent for the dances.

Featuring "thrush" Edna McGriff and her hit song "Heavenly Father," Freed opened at the Crystal Beach Ballroom in Lorraine on June 19. Also appearing at the dance was a rhythm and blues vocal group, the Swallows. Music was provided by Buddy Lucas' band. The following evening, Freed moved from the shores of Lake Erie to the Summitt Beach Ballroom in Akron, the city where he had first experienced celebrity status as host of WAKR's "Request Revue." Freed wrapped up this initial series of rhythm and blues dances the following night at the Avon Oaks Ballroom in Youngstown. As was done with the first two dances, this one was broadcast live over WJW. Freed again drew a predominantly black capacity crowd, and most likely none of those fans realized Moondog had been a sportscaster eight years earlier in that very same city. The three dances were a resounding success, drawing a total of over five thousand patrons. Freed returned to the Summitt Beach Ballroom in August with the Clovers and Charles Brown. This time three thousand teenagers crammed into the ballroom and several thousand more were turned away, but there was no trace of the chaos that had prevailed at the Cleveland Arena the previous March.

Jack Hooke and Teddy Reig were co-owners of Royal Roost Records, a tiny "strictly jazz" label out of New York that recorded the likes of Stan Getz, Erroll Garner, and Kai Winding. Like the other owners of record labels run on a shoestring, Hooke and Reig did it all themselves, including traveling around the country to plug Roost's new releases. Hooke would see the jazz disc jockeys, and Juggy Gayles, a friend who was also a record promotion man, would visit the pop deejays. Hooke and Gayles happened to be heading for Cleveland sometime in 1952 when Gayles said, "Why don't you come with me to see Alan Freed. He's making a lot of noise on the local airwaves."

Hooke had no idea who Freed was, but since he did have a record with him that he thought might suit Freed's program, he went. Hooke recalled walking into the tiny downstairs WJW studio and seeing Freed for the first time, "in a little cubbyhole with just a table, chair, microphone, telephone book, and a bottle of beer!"

Freed was in the midst of a commercial for Erin Brew, a local beer, as well as Moondog's major sponsor at the time. It may have been a commercial, but to Freed this was as much show business as his rhythm and blues records were. "So, folks, you take a tip from the ol' king and give it a try and your very fist sip will tell you that there is a true beer flavor that just can't be beat. Enjoy the finest! Save money! Always ask for Erin Brew, Ten-oh-two.

"How about it, folks? Pop the cap off a bottle and live it up as we enjoy your favorite blues and rhythm records. Wherever you are in the ol' Moondog kingdom, you'll hear 'em all!"

Freed had a knack of creating a popping sound that simulated a bottle top being removed from a beer bottle. He would stick a finger in the bottle, crook it slightly to offer some resistance before jerking it from the bottle, creating a loud "pop." To his listeners, Freed had just opened up another beer. Hooke described the hardworking deejay as a "revelation to watch. I'd been around radio since 1949 and I'd seen radio personalities, disc jockeys, but I'd never seen anything like him! It was wild. It was good show business," said Hooke. "It was one of the first things that impressed me about him."

"Hey, c'mon in!" commanded Freed. Hooke and Gayles cautiously entered the studio, and Freed invited them to sit down. After asking the two record promoters where they were from, he quizzed Hooke about Roost Records. When Hooke showed Freed the record he thought might interest the deejay, Freed took it and played in on a spare turntable. Suddenly, Freed shouted into the microphone, "Here's a new record that just came out!" and he played Hooke's record on the air. When the song ended, Freed played it a second time. Immediately Hooke became concerned that Freed's action was going to cost the record promoter some money.

"We knew guys were taking money [to play certain records]. I had just enough [money] to go on the road!" But Freed never said a word. When he finished his "Moondog House" that night, the deejay asked Hooke and Gayles if they were interested in having a beer.

"He took us to a place on Euclid Avenue called Mullins'," said Hooke. "We had a beer or two or three or four." Hooke remembered Freed as acting "very sociable" that evening. "Four beers and you become friendly." Freed asked where the pair was headed next.

"Pittsburgh," replied Hooke, still warily waiting for Freed to name his price for having aired the record man's disc.

Apparently Freed enjoyed Hooke's company, as he asked him to stay over in Cleveland another day. Hooke, who was still fearful, declined the offer, but Freed persisted. He wanted Hooke and Gayles to meet his wife Jackie, whom he had married three years earlier.

Still looking to escape, Hooke uneasily glanced over at Gayles, but Gayles was thrilled that a hot deejay such as Freed took an interest in the two East Coast record promoters. Gayles suggested to Hooke that they stay over, and arrangements were made for the two to meet Freed and his wife for breakfast. "Alan was there bright and early, accompanied by Jackie," recalled Hooke. After breakfast Freed told Hooke to meet him at the studio that night. Hooke would sit in on Freed's "Moondog House" and then the two would have a few drinks.

Over a few beers at Mullins' that night, Hooke discovered that Freed was an avid Cleveland Indians baseball fan. He told Hooke he had tickets to the next day's game and invited the record promo man to stay yet another day. "I stayed four days," said Hooke. "Alan never asked me for a penny. I think we just struck some kind of spark. If we went to dinner, he'd fight me to get that bill. I could never pick up a tab. I had dinner at his house and he took me to the baseball game. That was the beginning, and Alan became one of my closest friends."

By 1953 Moondog's popularity scaled new heights. Not only did WJW bill itself as "Cleveland's chief station," but it loudly touted Freed's program as the "hottest new show in town . . . the nation's number-one rhythm and blues show." As a white host of the nation's top rhythm and blues program, Freed was in a unique position. Despite the handful of other white disc jockeys programming chiefly to black listeners, rhythm and blues music was still considered in the music business as primarily a black enterprise. In February 1953 the show business tabloid *Variety*, noting the "strong upsurge" in the rhythm and blues market in recent years, maintained that the decision of the 260 radio stations programming rhythm and blues music (and attracting both national and local sponsors) "stems from the music's widespread and almost unique acceptance by Negro audiences."

The growing affinity of whites for rhythm and blues was still insignificant to the music business early in 1953. The thrust of *Variety*'s story was the recent elevation to "key positions" in the music business of the more than five hundred black disc jockeys located "in every city where there is a sizeable colored population."

Apparently *Variety* was not yet ready to abandon the traditional black-white pop music boundaries. Unaware of the growing affinity for rhythm and blues among persons outside the "sizeable colored population" or perhaps unwilling to acknowledge the change, *Variety* instead looked "paradoxically" at the white Gene Nobles, who by then was "one of the most potent" of the rhythm and blues disc jockeys.

Early in 1953 Alan Freed and Jackie resided in a duplex apartment in the exclusive Shaker Heights suburb on the eastern outskirts of Cleveland. Each night the deejay drove five miles to his home. In the early hours of an April morning, Freed fell asleep at the wheel of his automobile and it careened headlong into a tree somewhere along Kinsman Road. Because the accident occurred near a police station, the local police heard the crash. They found Freed unconscious and battered in the twisted wreckage. An adrenaline injection was frantically administered when his heartbeat ceased. Freed was seriously injured, with a punctured lung and damage to both his spleen and liver. The skin on his face had been peeled away. Jack Hooke said the doctors had to replace it and sew it back across the top of Freed's forehead. In all, it took some 260 stitches and extensive plastic surgery to get Freed's face back to a semblance of humanity. "He was not expected to live," said Freed's daughter, Alana. The deejay's doctors told him he was lucky to survive.

As he lay in a hospital bed fighting for his life, Freed said he felt "small and meaningless," like an "infinitesimal speck" on the face of the earth. For weeks he lay critically ill. Once off the critical list, the bettered deejay's doctors gave Freed some grim news: considering the extent and severity of his injuries, they did not expect him to live more than ten years. For the dazed Freed there was news that may have shocked him even more than his doctors' prognosis: "He was told that he could never in his life take another drink," said Alana Freed.

While evidence suggests Freed had no discernible drinking problem until he reached Cleveland, his heightened alcohol consumption was not part of a sudden change in behavior; rather, it was the next stage in an apparently progressive alcohol dependence. Betty Lou Greene said that when she first began dating Freed in 1942, "he didn't drink anything." Don Gardner, sports director at Youngstown's WKBN when Freed worked there in 1943, adamantly maintained the deejay never touched alcohol while working there. Greene said she and Freed occasionally socialized with Gene Trace and his wife and "might have had a glass of wine" while doing so, but that the Freeds kept no alcohol in their house.

Apparently Freed began to use alcohol to an obvious extent in Akron while simultaneously experiencing the growth of his celebrity status and the unraveling of his marriage. David Freed said that his brother was "almost a teetotaler" in high school, but that he began to drink "a little bit more than moderately in Akron." Upon arriving in Akron, Greene said she and Freed began keeping alcohol in their apartment in case guests visited, but that Freed "never came home and fixed a drink." If the couple went out, Freed would have no more than "a social drink now and then." It was also around then that Freed kindled his friendship with musician Hermie Dressel as the pair "lifted a few glasses" in various Akron watering holes. Dressel said Freed "drank pretty heavily . . . [but never] severe enough for him to ever miss a show or to ever goof up on a show." WAKR's Phyllis Simms said while Freed "was not a teetotaler," she was certain his drinking did not affect the deejay's on-the-air performance at the station. "Up to the time he left [WAKR], I never heard that he had a drinking problem."

Jack Hooke said when he met Freed in Cleveland, the deejay was "a ten-cent beer drinker" who eventually "learned differently" and switched to hard liquor before becoming "a very big drinker . . . later on." Hooke "presumed" that Freed's drinking was a contributory factor to the deejay's automobile crash, because "he'd get off his show at two o'clock in the morning and he'd go to that goddamned [Mullins's] saloon." But Freed was alone that night, and in what condition he was, only he knew.

By that time, doctors' warnings notwithstanding, Freed was too dependent on alcohol to do anything but further indulge his habit. As his career progressed, so would his penchant for alcohol.

Despite his automobile accident, Freed's "Moondog House" never missed a beat. David Freed and several WJW disc jockeys saw to it that the show continued, as they took turns sitting in for the injured Moondog. It has been erroneously reported that five weeks after his auto accident Freed resumed broadcasting from his hospital bed, flat on his back, but David Freed maintains his brother did not broadcast from the hospital.

As the days wore on and summer approached, Freed began to regain some of his strength. By then the high-energy disc jockey was stir-crazy, a virtual prisoner to the very hospital care that had saved his life. In June 1953 *Billboard* noted, "Moon Dog, aka Alan Freed, one of Cleveland's top r&b dj's, is back at work and just about recovered from a serious automobile accident nearly two months ago."

After a long hospital convalescence and $11,000 worth of surgery, Freed went home to Shaker Heights, where, seated on a bedside chair with a telephone book and cowbell at hand, Moondog returned to the airwaves with his rhythm and blues platters and jive patter: "Well, here's a letter from Korea: 'Hello, Moondog. My sister lives in Cleveland and listens to your program every night. I'm in Korea now, but I'd like to have you play a song for me and dedicate it to Mrs. Bernice Taylor and all her friends.'

"Be sure to write to the men and women in the armed forces as often as you can, folks. You know there's nothing worse than answering mail call and not having your own name called.

"Now, Faye Adams on Herald and 'I'll Be True.' Yeah, baby! You talk, baby!" shouted Freed into the open mike as the song began, Moondog's cowbell clanging steadily in the background. As the song ended Freed sang the last chorus with Miss Adams.

When Freed returned to WJW he did so looking over his shoulder. On June 5 WERE's Bill Randle, Cleveland's top-rated pop deejay, promoted a local rhythm and blues dance starring Billy Ward and his Dominoes (with new lead singer Jackie Wilson), ex-heavyweight boxing champion Joe Louis and his band, and Bill Haley and His Comets. Further evidence that the racial lines of rhythm and blues were beginning to blur, Haley was white and as yet relatively unknown to blacks. His hit recording of "Crazy, Man, Crazy" (a black expression of the era) had appeared on the national pop charts but did not make the rhythm and blues charts, although the heavy beat of "Crazy, Man Crazy" was more akin to rhythm and blues than pop. Randle's encroachment upon Freed's rhythm and blues territory was a challenge to Freed, but one that Freed believed he would put down quite easily with his own upcoming blockbuster rhythm and blues promotion.

Toward the end of February 1953 an ambitious and aptly named "Biggest Show of '53" began a six-week journey of one-nighters throughout the South and Southwest. The tour package, starring Ruth Brown, Billy Eckstine, and Count Basie, was a resounding success, with disappointed customers turned away from full houses in certain cities.

Because of the popularity of the "Biggest Show of '53," a more-ambitious package tour, one that *Billboard* would, in retrospect, call a "daring project," was organized. "The Biggest Rhythm and Blues Show," starring Ruth Brown, Wynonie Harris, the Clovers, Joe Louis and his band, the Lester Young Combo, and Buddy Johnson's Orchestra, was the largest in rhythm and blues touring history. It would open in Revere, Massachusetts, on July 9, 1953, and conclude a month later in New Orleans. In between, there would be shows almost every night, including a date in Cleveland on July 20. That show would be promoted by Freed, Lew Platt, and Leo Mintz. This time, however, they would not make the disastrous mistake they committed a year earlier at the aborted Moondog Coronation Ball. The Cleveland Arena would again be the sight of the show, but this time seats would be sold on a reserved basis, and no tickets would be sold at the gate.

ALL SEATS RESERVED! stated local newspaper advertisements. M.C.—ALAN FREED, "KING OF THE MOON DOGGERS." Tickets were scaled from $1.50 to $3.00 and clip-out mail-order coupons were included in the ads. GOOD SEATS AVAILABLE! BUT HURRY! warned the final advertisement the day before the show.

"Now it's Joe Louis, the 'dancing comedian,' formerly known as a prizefighting champion, who flings his sombrero into the show business ring," reported the *Plain Dealer* the day before what it termed Freed's "sepia musical show."

The reserved-seat policy solved the crowd problem, even though "almost 20,000" turned out at the Arena. "Joe Louis Packs in 10,000 Trained Squeals for Show," said the *Plain Dealer*'s following-day account. Significantly, the white media, still not fully comprehending the growing popularity of rhythm and blues music, instead heralded Joe Louis' presence as the reason for the capacity crowd at the arena. The *Plain Dealer* failed to understand that Louis and his band were merely incidental to the musical festivities. Still, the *Plain Dealer* described Freed's show as a "phenomenon" because of the impressive turnout by the "race music" and "skat singing" devotees, despite limited publicity. "There was a hot time in the ice house last night when one of the largest crowds ever gathered in the Arena jammed the hall for a Rhythm & Blues Show."

Jack Hooke was astonished. He said the percentage of whites at the "Biggest Rhythm and Blues Show" was "very, very small," leaving a vivid memory of Freed and his wife Jackie walking out onto the stage "amidst a sea of black faces" and raising their hands over their heads in a triumphant gesture to the delight of the uproarious crowd.

The record-breaking "Biggest Rhythm and Blues Show" package tour became the largest-grossing rhythm and blues tour at that time, with turn-away crowds in many cities. The largest crowd was the nearly twenty thousand Moondog drew to the Cleveland Arena. Clearly, there was money to be made in the promotion of a music and its singers, who until recently had been confined to the traditional Chitlin' Circuit.

Moondog followed the "Biggest Rhythm and Blues Show" with two smaller dances, both dubbed the Second Annual Moondog Birthday Parties, in commemoration of Freed's WJW program. At the Akron Armory on August 14 and at Youngstown's Stambaugh Auditorium the following evening, with both dances broadcast over WJW, Freed showcased Billy Ward and His Dominoes, featuring the group's new lead vocalist, Jackie Wilson. Wilson, who had recently taken over for the departed Clyde McPhatter, and Freed would develop a warm friendship as both of their careers soared in the 1950s.

Several newspaper ads and extensive radio publicity on Freed's "Moondog House" program were sufficient to pack the Cleveland Arena, and the deejay's newly instituted reserved-seating policy erased any fear of future crowd control. Yet Freed and WJW had no idea of the extent of Moondog's drawing power. The deejay easily drew almost twenty thousand fans to the arena, but just how big a building he could fill was purely conjecture. Although Cleveland had no indoor facility larger than the arena, a plan was hatched to give Freed and WJW a more accurate indication of the deejay's drawing power. A Cleveland Arena show was booked for Saturday evening,

August 29, but unlike the previous arena show, Feed would rely exclusively on his WJW radio program to publicize the dance. Moondog conducted an on-the-air contest for his listeners, inviting them to submit the names of their favorite rhythm and blues artists. Over 300 winners were drawn at random from the 3,424 responses. Each winner received coupons worth a dollar off the price of the show. There were no newspaper advertisements—no printed publicity whatsoever—for the upcoming bash.

Could Moondog again pack the Cleveland Arena, this time solely by talking about the upcoming dance on his "Moondog House" program? Alan Freed had no doubts. Just give him the microphone and those ten thousand seats would be occupied.

CHAPTER 4

The Moondog Mesmerizes Manhattan

> "[Freed] was a character, a little wacky. I made out his income tax and know that he got . . . big money in the early '50s. But I had to lend him $200 when he left for New York."

ON Saturday evening, August 22, 1953, Moondog Freed emceed his "Big Rhythm and Blues Show," which starred Fats Domino and Joe Turner. With that show, the magnitude of the power Moondog held over his fanatical listening audience was no longer in doubt. Publicity for the show, confined solely to announcements on the deejay's "Moondog House" radio program, resulted in a packed Cleveland Arena. *Billboard* reported that "over 10,000 admissions were racked up."

One of the acts that appeared at Freed's "Big Rhythm and Blues Show" that August was an unheralded vocal quartet called the Moonglows. Sometime in 1952 local singer Al ("Fats") Thomas had noticed a young rhythm and blues group called the Crazy Sounds—Bobby Lester and Harvey Fuqua, who began singing together in Louisville, Kentucky, in 1948, and local singers Prentiss Barnes and Alex Graves—in a Cleveland nightclub. So impressed was Thomas that he told Lester, "I'm gonna take you guys downtown and introduce you to a disc jockey named Alan Freed." Hoping that the influential rhythm and blues deejay would become their manager, the Crazy Sounds accompanied Thomas to the WJW studios, where the group auditioned in front of Freed with a rough version of "I Just Can't Tell No Lie," one of their popular stage numbers.

At the time, Freed and WJW were aggressively promoting the deejay's Moondog music and his Moondogger audience. Although the crude harmonies of the Crazy Sounds failed to distinguish the group from countless others who searched for an opportunity to record, most likely Fred sensed another promotional opportunity at hand and agreed to manage the unknown group, telling them they were now the Moonglows.

Bobby Lester offered a different version of how the Crazy Sounds became the Moonglows. He said that whenever the group rehearsed at the WJW studios, Freed referred to them as his "Moon puppies." After one such rehearsal Lester replied, "No, 'Moonglows' sounds better because we glow in the dark."

However the Moonglows acquired their name, after much rehearsing and "scores of suggestions" from Freed, he and Lew Platt formed Champagne Records and recorded the group in the WJW studios. Freed supplied the music's beat with his telephone book, which, to Lester, "was a pretty funny thing to see."

With heavy airplay from Moondog, the Moonglows' "I Just Can't Tell No Lie," a smoother version of their audition number, sold well locally. Bobby Lester said Freed helped the group considerably. Freed also helped himself. Using the pseudonym "Al Lance," the deejay took songwriting credit for both songs.

The Moonglows subsequently appeared at several of Freed's local dances, but not making much money, they soon lapsed into a part-time act. During the week Lester drove a truck, Fuqua worked at a service station, and Barnes and Graves returned to the band they were in before they joined the Crazy Sounds.

When the Moonglows performed at Freed's "Biggest Rhythm and Blues show," they were spotted by record executive Art Sheridan, who, with Ewart Abner, owned the Chicago-based Chance Records. Chance had had its greatest success with the Flamingos, a rhythm and blues group formed in Chicago in 1952, and Sheridan hoped to do as well with the Moonglows. He signed them to a recording contract in October 1953.

It was also about that time that Alan Freed entered the record distributing business. Distributors acted as wholesalers, as well as promoters (since it was to the distributor's advantage to have a hit record to market), for independent record companies who did not have their own distributing systems. Since the majority of rhythm and blues records were on independent labels, record distributors wielded great power. A distributor could, in effect, hold a small label hostage by reporting lower-than-actual retail sales of a certain record. The label, which had little cash with which to take legal action, also feared its next record might not be shipped at all. As a result, it took what the record distributor gave.

Ohio Record Sales, owned by Record Rendezvous proprietor Leo Mintz and run by his brother-in-law, was one of the leading rhythm and blues distributors in Cleveland. In 1953 Alan Freed's brother David worked for Ohio Record Sales as a record promoter. Now Freed decided to enter the record distributing business himself. He teamed up with Chance Records owner Art Sheridan, who also owned Sheridan Distributors of Chicago. Sheridan saw the venture as a way of gaining a foothold in Cleveland, and who better to have as a partner than the most famous rhythm and blues disc jockey in the area? Sheridan became president of Lance Distribution, Inc. (named after Freed's son). David Freed quit Ohio Sales to become vice-president of Lance. It was he who would do most of the promotional legwork for the new company. Lance, with few record labels signed (Ohio Sales had most of them committed to deals), set up shop in a tiny storefront on Prospect Avenue, not far from Leo Mintz's Record Rendezvous.

Not long after the Moonglows began their association with Freed, another rhythm and blues vocal group came under his managerial tutelage. The Coronets had recently cut a demonstration record, "Nadine," which was written by one of the group's members about his girlfriend. Instead of "sittin' around waitin' on somebody to discover us," recalled another group member, Sam Griggs, who decided to start at the top and sought out Alan Freed at the WJW studios. What happened next illustrates the power that Freed's wife Jackie could wield in dealing with her famous husband.

At WJW, Griggs was met by Lew Platt, who told the singer that Freed would not see him. Suddenly, Jackie appeared and, after listening to Griggs's story, entered the control room to speak with Freed. As a result, Freed gave Griggs "a quick minute" and told him to leave the demo of "Nadine" at the station. Several weeks later the Coronets were contacted by Chess Records of Chicago and signed to a recording contract. Their first release for Chess was a reworked version of their demo, "Nadine." On the label, the writer of "Nadine" was listed as Alan Freed. Released in September 1953, "Nadine" scored heavily with the black listening market in the Midwest, enabling the Coronets to headline shows at Cleveland's Circle Theatre and various local nightclubs. With a hit record and with Alan Freed as their manager, the Coronets thought they were on their way to a successful recording career.

A month after the release of "Nadine" the Moonglows recorded six sides for Art Sheridan. The group's first two Chance releases, on which Freed and Harvey Fuqua were listed as cowriters, sold poorly, however. As the Coronets celebrated what Sam Griggs called "our little hit," the Moonglows were "lying around, starvin' to death." Art Sheridan must have wondered whether he signed the wrong group to his record label.

On Friday, November 13, Alan Freed returned to the Akron Armory to stage a "Harvest Moon Ball." Twenty-five hundred fans paid $2 each and crammed into the building to see and dance to Clyde McPhatter and the Drifters and the Bull Moose Jackson Orchestra. Friday the thirteenth or not, Moondog knew this dance would not prove unlucky. A week earlier, the same package had done well in Steubenville and Youngstown.

The Drifters and Clyde McPhatter could not forsee it, but their careers—and the carers of rhythm and blues veterans Fats Domino, Joe Turner, and Ruth Brown, among others—were about to soar as each crossed over to the white pop charts. In 1953 rhythm and blues recordings became pop hits, notably Ruth Brown's "(Mama) He Treats Your Daughter Mean," Fats Domino's "Goin' to the River," the Orioles' "Crying in the Chapel," Faye Adams' "Shake a Hand," and the Four Tunes' "Marie."

Perhaps the most significant song of the group was "Crying in the Chapel," released in the summer of 1953. The song was originally a country and western ballad, sung by the songwriter's sixteen-year-old son. "Crying in the Chapel" was "covered," or copied, by a least six artists, with June Valli's pop version (fourth on *Billboard*'s best-seller list) the biggest-seller of all. Darrell Glenn (with the original version) and Rex Allen both had big country hits with the song, and the Orioles' rhythm and blues version did well on both the rhythm and blues charts (first place) and the pop charts (eleventh). Of course, Freed played the Orioles' version of "Crying in the Chapel." The song reportedly sold over thirty thousand copies in the Cleveland area the day after Freed first played it. "Crying in the Chapel" provided further evidence of the blurring of pop music's racial, as well as stylistic, barriers. Rhythm and blues, and country and western, versions of the song not only appeared on their own respective sales charts, but on the pop charts as well.

By the end of 1953, Alan Freed had reached another significant level in the development of his career. He was now heard on metropolitan New York area radio. That September WNJR, a tiny, five-thousand watt radio station located in Newark, New Jersey, across the Hudson River from Manhattan, was sold by the *Newark Evening News* to the Rollings Broadcasting Company. Rollings, who paid $140,000 for WNJR, instituted a format of jazz, gospel, and rhythm and blues on the station. WNJR hired rhythm and blues disc jockeys Hal Jackson, Ramon Bruce, Charlie Green, and Hal Jackson and, with an assist from Herman Lubinsky and Fred Mendelsohn of the locally based Savoy Records, station manager Al Lanphear convinced WNJR's new owners to supplement their programming with prerecorded tapes of prominent rhythm and blues jocks from around the country.

On a late-night drive through the Cleveland area the previous summer Lanphear had become intrigued by a rhythm and blues character on the radio who shouted along with the records while a cowbell clanged in the background. Lanphear did not forget Freed, and when the station manager convinced WNJR to add tapes of other rhythm and blues deejays (including Los Angeles's Hunter Hancock and Atlanta's Zena Sears) to their programming, Freed was one of the new out-of-town additions.

By December 1953, WNJR had become the metropolitan area's first full-time black radio station, daily airing eighteen hours of jazz, gospel, and rhythm and blues. Freed's "Moondog House" was taped and mailed to Newark, where WNJR rebroadcast the program from 10:00 P.M. until midnight six nights a week and until 1:00 A.M. on Saturdays. WNJR edited out Freed's Cleveland commercials and replaced them with its own local spots, but the primitive editing techniques provided awful results. "It was the worst thing you ever heard," said Jack Hooke, who also recalled WNJR paid very little for use of Freed's tapes. The fee was of little concern to Freed, however. His attitude, shaped by the deejay's "very aggressive . . . very large ego," was "The hell with the money . . . I'm being heard in the New York area!"

As WNJR provided New York–area listeners with their first taste of "Moondog madness," Freed was busy as ever on the northern Ohio rhythm and blues dance circuit, where his annual Akron Armory Holiday Ball drew more than three thousand fans on Christmas night, 1953. While over twenty-five hundred disappointed fans were turned away, those lucky enough gladly paid $2 each to see and to dance to Billy Ward and His Dominoes, Little Walter and His Jukes, and the Ralph Williams Orchestra at what *Billboard* termed a "dilly" of a ball.

The year 1953 saw the traditional ratio of black-to-white record buyers change. Until then, a rhythm and blues hit meant maximum sales of perhaps 250,000 copies. But that year Fats Domino's "Goin' to the River" and the Orioles' "Crying in the Chapel" both reportedly sold over a million copies each. The rhythm and blues vocal group sound, as shown by the Dominoes and the Drifters, was on the rise as 15 million rhythm and blues singles were sold in 1953. Despite these significant breakthroughs in the pop market, rhythm and blues had not yet gained mass acceptance. Rhythm and blues sales for the year accounted for less than 5 percent of the total record sales, and the biggest-selling rhythm and blues record of 1953, Willie Mae Thornton's "Hound Dog," never came close to appearing on the pop charts.

As 1954 began, Freed's evolution as chief spokesman for rhythm and blues continued. He was unquestionably the most influential rhythm and blues deejay in the Midwest, but try as he might, he was unable to stimulate record sales for the Moonglows. With disappointing sales of the group's first two Chance releases, Art Sheridan held back the two remaining sides recorded the previous October. Sheridan had the Moonglows record six new songs in January 1954, including a cover version of Doris Day's top-selling pop hit "Secret Love." Rush-released to capitalize on the popularity of Day's giant hit, the Moonglows' rhythm and blues version of "Secret Love" caught on and topped the 100,000 mark in sales. Suddenly in demand, the Moonglows played the Circle Theatre in Cleveland and Akron's Esquire Club. They also appeared at another of Freed's Moondog Memory Balls at the Akron Armory. Bobby Lester recalled that Freed had no trouble booking such dances, saying the deejay "got all the acts he wanted, and if he said you were going to sing so-and-so, that's what you sang!"

Meanwhile, Freed's other group, the Coronets, were now not faring as well as the Moonglows. Their second Chess release, issued late in 1953, sold dismally. The Coronets' Sam Griggs said with bitterness that there was some misunderstanding between the group and their manager. Freed expected "great sacrifices" (such as touring with the disc jockey without being paid) from the group. Griggs charged Freed with neglecting the Coronets in favor of his many other professional activities. "We needed management, which we were not getting," he said. The singer described the situation whereby the Coronets were contracturally bound to Freed, despite the deejay's apparent neglect, as "ruthless. No matter how much money he made from us, it could have been more [with conscientious promotion and management of the Coronets]."

Whatever Freed's efforts on behalf of the Coronets, Chess Records declined to issue any further recordings by the group, and despite several subsequent releases on another label, the Coronets never came close to having another hit record.

Some of Sam Griggs's bitterness toward Freed no doubt stemmed from Freed being credited as cowriter of "Nadine." The singer said Freed was listed as such because the deejay "happened to be in a position of . . . power [that] also gave him the necessary influence with any recording company that was hustling records."

Considering Freed's WJW disc jockey duties, his dance promotions, his involvement with the resurgent fortunes of the Moonglows, his interest in Lance Distributing, and his reported interest in becoming a network radio disc jockey, Freed was certainly guilty of not devoting maximum time and effort to the struggling Coronets.

Another milestone in the mass acceptance of rhythm and blues occurred early in 1954 with the unprecedented pop success of a "jump" (up-tempo) tune, "Gee," sung by a New York group called the Crows. The Crows were a black group, but "Gee" was closer in style to pop than to traditional rhythm and blues. Released during the summer of 1953, the song did not become a big rhythm and blues hit, but when sales in Southern California eventually surpassed the 50,000 mark, Los Angeles deejays began to plug the song and "Gee" caught on with white listeners. In February 1954 the music press reported that "Gee" was "making a strong bid for pop market acceptance." The following month, "Gee" appeared on the national best-selling pop charts. Not until April did "Gee" make the rhythm and blues charts, thus becoming the first "reverse crossover" rhythm and blues hit. As a bigger hit among white listeners than among black, "Gee" shattered yet another barrier that had stood between rhythm and blues and the music's acceptance by the general pop audience.

The unprecedented breakthrough of "Gee" made it clear to even the most shortsighted of independent rhythm and blues record-company owners that their product had pop market potential. But for rhythm and blues to transcend the music's traditional pockets or regional strength and develop into a national phenomenon, the music required a strong voice in New York City, the entertainment capital of the world; as one rhythm and blues writer said, "what happened there soon happened elsewhere."

Shortly after the release of "Gee," a seemingly innocuous broadcasting transaction took place in New York. In August 1953 the Crosley Broadcasting Corporation sold WINS (1010 AM), a nondescript money-losing pop radio station purchased in 1946 for $1,700,000 from the William Randolph Hearst radio organization, to a group of Western investors headed by Seattle broadcasting entrepreneur J. Elroy McCaw. Crosley's chairman of the board said the sale of WINS (for the bargain-basement price of $450,000) was "regretfully deemed advisable" in order for the corporation to concentrate on its expanding broadcasting properties in the Midwest and the South.

Pending FCC approval of the sale, J. Elroy McCaw publicly stated that it was his intention to continue with WINS's present personnel and operating policies under the Gotham Broadcasting Corporation. Privately, McCaw had other ideas. WINS may have been a money-loser, but the station commanded fifty-thousand watts of broadcasting power in the largest radio market in the world. McCaw's plan was to build the struggling WINS into a moneymaker and then sell it for a hefty profit. But barely able to scrape together the down payment for WINS, McCaw lacked the cash flow necessary to improve the lot of the money-losing station.

WINS employees soon discovered that their new boss was a penny-pincher. To slash operating costs at the station, McCaw ordered, among other things, WINS's teletype to be operated on a single roll of paper instead of the more expensive double roll; decreed that the station's program logs be typed single-spaced instead of double; and had the electric light bulbs in the WINS offices switched from 150 watts to 60 watts. Staff announcers Lew Fisher and Jack Lacey were given on-the-job crash courses on how to become disc jockeys. The only WINS programs with encouraging ratings were Bob and Ray's highly popular morning comedy show and the Sunday-only "Battle of the Baritones," hosted by staff announcer Brad Phillips.

The station's greatest asset was its New York Yankee baseball broadcasts, but that asset was potentially jeopardized by J. Elroy McCaw's cost-cutting schemes. In the spring of 1954 as the Yankees readied for their try at a sixth straight World Series victory (they currently held the record with five successive world championships), picket lines from Local 802 of the American Federation of Musicians appeared around Yankee Stadium on opening day.

When WINS's contract (stipulating that the station employ a minimum of eight studio musicians) with the AFM expired at the end of March, McCaw had refused to renew it. His attempts to mollify the AFM by offering to hire a single musician fell on deaf ears. The union struck WINS and threw up picket lines not only at the station's Fifty-fourth Street studios, but around Yankee Stadium as well.

New York Mayor Robert Wagner refused to cross the stadium picket line to make the traditional opening-day gesture of throwing out the first ball. Wagner's relief pitcher, the Bronx borough president, proceeded to fire a wild pitch into the stomach of a nearby photographer.

The following day *The New York Times*, noting that "all other union members at WINS and the various unions at the Stadium are apparently passing the picket lines, working as usual," asked why the Mayor ("not an employee of WINS, and not, so far as we know, a musician") had not done likewise. "Some picket lines," opined *The Times*, "deserve to be crossed."

The AFM was soon enjoined from picketing at Yankee Stadium. Although picket lines continued at the WINS station, J. Elroy McCaw refused to hire any studio musicians. The station owner had time, as well as current radio trends, on his side. Despite the efforts of the AFM to preserve it, live studio music as radio entertainment was becoming extinct.

With no live studio music, no recognizable disc jockeys, and no broadcast ratings (save those of Yankee baseball) for his station, McCaw's financial situation grew more tenuous each day. Clearly, a drastic move was necessary for WINS to emerge from the ratings doldrums and become attractive to potential advertisers. McCaw met with WINS station manager Bob Leder and program director Bob Smith to discuss the station's disc jockey situation.

About that time, Alan Freed called Jack Hooke in New York and told his friend he wanted to put on a rhythm and blues dance at the National Guard armory in Newark, New Jersey. Stirred as much by his boundless ambition as by the raw energy of rhythm and blues, Freed set his sights higher than packing the Akron Armory to turn-away crowds. He was "being heard on New York radio," and it was time to show his face there too. Freed intended to make his first Moondog promotion east of Ohio a smashing success and leave no doubt in the minds of his new listeners as to why he was the top-rated rhythm and blues deejay in the Midwest.

Following their established procedure, Freed, Leo Mintz, and Lew Platt promoted the dance, booked by Platt into Newark's Sussex Avenue Armory for the first weekend in May. Freed shrewdly signed the New York–based Harptones, a tremendously popular group in the area, to perform in Newark. Also on the bill were Washington, D.C.'s Clovers, one of the hottest rhythm and blues groups in the country; blues singer Muddy Waters; crooner Charles Brown; Nolan Lewis; Arnet Cobb; Sam Butera; and Buddy Johnson's Orchestra, featuring Johnson's sister-vocalist, Ella.

Most of the advertising for the dance was done by Freed via spots on his WNJR taped program. Jack Hooke, who helped Freed run the show, called it "a sight to see." He remembered standing at one of the armory doors and "grabbing money" from the patrons as they entered. "We had boxes full of money. God knows who stole what!" Freed twice packed the armory with "11,000 screaming teens," and thousands more were turned away. Trade-paper accounts noted that the production produced a box-office gross of $20,000.

Although accustomed to huge crowds on Freed's familiar Ohio turf, both the disc jockey and Jack Hooke were as surprised as everyone else was by the huge metropolitan-area turnout. The East Coast pop music moguls certainly had not expected it either. Not since the days of the swing bands had a single dance generated such an uproar. Tin Pan Alley buzzed with excitement at the midwestern deejay who was then regarded as the reviver of frenzied dance music. *Billboard* reporter Bob Rolontz wrote, "The kids want that music with a beat to dance to . . . Alan Freed has found out what they want." Ironically, the dance was so crowded that dancing proved impossible.

Impressed with Freed's drawing power—"beyond even his own expectations"—*Billboard* examined the demographics of Moondog's audience. The crowd was comprised predominantly of youngsters fifteen to twenty years old. Of greater significance, about 20 percent of the rhythm and blues audience was white.

As Alan Freed returned to Ohio, his status, not only in rhythm and blues circles but in the entire pop music business, was considerably enhanced. Neither Moondog's enthusiastic Newark audience nor his faithful Cleveland radio listeners knew that Freed was about to return to New York on a permanent basis.

When New York record promotion man George Furness (a friend of both WINS program director Bob Smith and Freed) learned of WINS's plight, he told Smith, "Put this guy [Freed] on [WINS], Bob. You guys are crazy if you don't." But after listening to several tapes of Moondog, Bob Leder pronounced the deejay a crazy man. The WINS station manager wanted no part of Freed, but Smith, convinced that Moondog was precisely the deejay WINS needed, eventually persuaded Leder to hire Freed. They had little difficulty convincing the desperate J. Elroy McCaw to sign the midwestern rhythm and blues disc jockey. On May 23, less than a month after his astounding Newark rhythm and blues dance, Freed flew to New York to meet with WINS officials.

To Freed's Cleveland audience, it appeared to be "business as usual" for Moondog as the deejay hosted a Moondog Birthday Ball at the Akron Armory on June 25. On the bill with Joe Turner, Faye Adams, and Five Keys, Al Savage, and Joe Morris's Orchestra was local musician Joe Cooper, a friend of Freed's from the pair's high school days in the late 1930s. The capacity crowd of thirty-one hundred was reported to be more than one-third white, a significantly larger portion than was Freed's Newark audience less than two months earlier. A week later, on July 3, 1954, the broadcasting industry took notice when it was announced that Freed, "one of the country's strongest rhythm and blues disc jockeys," would soon move to New York radio station WINS for a yearly salary of "about $75,000."

The music trade papers jumped on the story. MOONDOG TO WINS; FREED OF WJW TO START IN N.Y. IN FALL, read *Billboard*'s headline. Until then, a disc jockey's move from one city to another had been nothing unusual, but Moondog's reported switch was newsworthy in that it involved the largest sum of money ever paid to a rhythm and blues disc jockey by an independent radio station. Lew Platt attempted to play down Freed's deal. He claimed the WINS proposal was still "in negotiation" when, in fact, only the formal contract signing was yet to take place.

Freed held his final Cleveland production where it had all begun two years earlier—the Cleveland Arena. On August 6, Freed drew ninety-six hundred for what was the kickoff of the month-long "Second Annual Biggest Rhythm and Blues Show," starring the Drifters, the Spaniels, LaVern Baker, Faye Adams, Roy Hamilton, King Pleasure, Rusty Bryant, the Counts, and Erskine Hawkins. The tour drew more than fifty thousand rhythm and blues enthusiasts the first eight days on the road. When it was over, Freed's Cleveland crowd had been topped only by an audience of ten thousand in Chicago.

On August 21, as the "Second Annual Biggest Rhythm and Blues Show" played San Antonio, Texas, it was announced in New York that although Alan Freed was not scheduled to begin his new program until September 7, WINS had syndicated his show to five markets and had hopes of selling it in at least sixty markets. It was also noted that an out-of-town record distributor, Art Freeman, had "kicked up a fuss" among certain New York record manufacturers and distributors after he called a press conference at which he "exposed some of Freed's activities."

Art Freeman was a Cleveland record distributor (Benart Distributing) with an apparent score to settle with Alan Freed. In the presence of local record manufacturers and distributors, as well as reporters from *Billboard, Variety,* and a representative from WINS, Freeman displayed a letter he claimed to have received from Freed, in which the disc jockey allegedly told Freeman the distributor would have to pay to have any of the records Benart handled played on Freed's WJW program. But after making the allegation, Freeman asked the press to sit on the story "until further action, if any," was taken.

David Freed said Freeman and Leo Mintz were in the Cleveland record distributing industry and that Alan periodically befriended Freeman "whenever he [Freed] was fighting with Leo Mintz."

Freeman's unsubstantiated allegations more than likely fell on deaf ears. David Freed believes the rhythm and blues record manufacturers and distributors had a great deal to do with his brother's move to New York and they eagerly awaited his arrival. David said Freed's friends in the business—Leonard and Phil Chess of Chicago and Art Rupe of the California-based Specialty label, among others—watched as he almost single-handedly widened the midwestern rhythm and blues market. They "wanted [the R&B market] . . . expanded everywhere they could get it [expanded]" and subsequently "engineered" Alan Freed's move to New York. Indeed, many in the music business maintained that "New York got up and took notice" when rhythm and blues became a big moneymaker in Cleveland.

As Freed wrapped up his business in Cleveland he continued to manage the Moonglows, but the group's up-and-down career had taken another downward turn. Their summer release of "219 Train" sold poorly. Bobby Lester said the Moonglows were "kind of messin' up" and, as a result, their association with Art Sheridan became strained. Sheridan had recently lost Chance Records' biggest moneymakers, the Flamingos, to Parrot Records. That loss, coupled with the Moonglows' erratic record sales, induced Sheridan to close the doors of Chance at about the time that Alan Freed closed the doors on Cleveland.

With Freed's imminent departure to New York, David Freed had a decision to make. Alan "wanted me to go with him," David recalled, but his own wife was opposed to the move and told her husband that their marriage hung in the balance. In the end, David Freed decided it was time to seek an identity of his own, something he had been unable to accomplish working in close proximity to his famous and egotistical brother: "There was no identity with him. . . . It was Al, and everybody else was just incidental." David remained in Ohio and attended law school. He continued to work part-time for Lance Distributing, which was sold to New York bandleader–turned–record distributor Jerry Blaine.

In New York, WINS was busy preparing a mammoth promotional campaign to capitalize on Freed's arrival. Station manager Bob Leder verified Freed's record-setting rhythm and blues disc jockey salary and cryptically added that a "special incentive plan" might push the $25,000 figure much higher. Although the press, encouraged by WINS for publicity value, bandied about figures ranging from $25,000 to $75,000 when discussing Freed's salary-to-be, the deejay's new contract guaranteed him just $15,000 against 25 percent of the net income, less "applicable discounts and agency commissions," derived by WINS from Freed's radio broadcasts. In addition, WINS agreed to "afford its facilities" to Freed for the promotion of his dances in return for an unspecified percentage (later determined to be 10 percent) of the net income received by Freed from such dances.

Freed's new employer began tossing verbal barbs at its competition. As his September 7 debut approached, the rival WNEW nightly time slot that Freed was slated to fill on WINS became WINS's primary target. Publicly, WNEW ignored Freed's imminent arrival, but Art Ford was inexplicably moved to the daytime (and his show retitled "Milkman's Matinee"), thus precluding a Moondog-Milkman confrontation. But WINS would not let up. For a week the station ran hourly spots that informed its listeners of the "Milkman's" time shift. WINS taunted the displaced WNEW jock with exhortations of "Long live the new king—Alan Freed, King of Moondoggers!"

Freed, true to his flamboyant, live-for-today life-style, arrived in New York on $200 borrowed from WJW station manager Bill Lemmon in Cleveland. By the time he got to New York, he had no money. Besides helping find its new employee a Manhattan apartment, WINS also paid for the deejay's move.

Freed was well aware of the situation he was stepping into. As Arnold Shaw has noted, New York City was "definitely not a R&B town." Radio station ratings belonged mainly to what were described as "good music" stations. Despite an increasing black population and what one local black station in 1952 claimed was a listening market with "billion dollar plus" potential, the New York rhythm and blues market remained as fragmented as ever. In February 1953, *Variety* had reported the New York metropolitan area with having "one of the largest concentrations of Negro jocks [at least twelve] in the country." Despite the fact that a majority of those deejays were heard on low-wattage foreign-language stations, they managed a strong enough hold to get their listeners to tune in during the specific hours they were on the air.

The longest-tenured rhythm and blues deejay in New York and the "accepted white voice" of the city's black listeners was an uptown trumpet player named "Symphony Sid" Torin. Torin, known by rhythm and blues and jazz aficionados as the "hippest guy in the business," began playing jazz-oriented "'sepia" and "race" records in New York in the early 1940s. But Torin, with his "gravelly voice, as deep as a cello tinged with a southern accent," was not a pure rhythm and blues disc jockey in that he favored a laid-back jazz format.

One result of Symphony Sid's sustained local success in what was called the "after-dark Negro market" was the introduction of the "After-Hours Swing Session" on WHOM in 1949. The program was broadcast from the storefront window of the Baby Grand, a Harlem nightspot not far from the legendary Apollo Theatre. It was hosted by black show business veteran Willie ("The Mayor of Harlem") Bryant and Ray Carroll, a white man who had previously worked on the radio with Sid Torin. By 1952 Bryant and Carroll were popular enough to also host an afternoon program of rhythm and blues on station WOV.

The most prominent rhythm and blues disc jockey in New York when Freed hit town was WWRL's Tommy ("Dr. Jive") Smalls. Blues singer Screamin' Jay Hawkins, a Manhattan resident at the time, said Bryant and Carroll "did not command the respect" that Tommy Smalls commanded. Rhythm and blues songwriter-arranger William Miller said that until Freed arrived, "WWRL [with Tommy Smalls] was where you got your plays." But, said Jim McGowan, lead singer with the Four Fellows vocal group and a Brooklyn teenager in 1954, Tommy Smalls was accessible only to those "few whites [who] went all the way up the dial [to 1600 where WWRL was located]." On the eve of Alan Freed's fifty-thousand-watt debut, New York was a wide-open rhythm and blues town lacking a strong, unifying figure.

On September 7, 1954, the day of Freed's New York broadcasting debut, WINS threw a gala cocktail party at the Belmont Plaza Hotel for fellow disc jockeys, record executives, and other music business figures. That evening Freed, with his rhythm and blues records, his telephone book, and his cowbell, was heard live in the city for the first time.

"Hi everybody," began Freed. "This is your ol' Moondog here, with rhythm and blues records with the big beat in popular music in America today, for everyone out there in the Moondog kingdom. Here it is, the number-one rhythm and blues song in New York right now—Ruth Brown, Atlantic Records, 'What a Dream'!"

Ray Reneri, who, as a teenager, first worked for Freed as a "gofer" before becoming one of the deejay's backstage assistants, said that instead of Freed and an engineer isolating themselves in the broadcasting booth, as was the usual procedure, "Freed had ten people in there all the time. They smoked, they drank, and had a party!"

One music business well-wisher who stopped by the WINS studio that first night to offer Freed congratulations was local record producer and manufacturer Bobby Robinson. Lucky Millinder, former swing bandleader and by then a popular Harlem deejay who hosted his own rhythm and blues program on WNEW, also paid Freed a visit. Robinson and Millinder took telephone calls as Freed drank, spun his rhythm and blues records, beat on his telephone book, and, with a breathtaking slur, squeezed in as many on-the-air dedications to his listeners as was humanly possible: "Now we're gonna send El and Jimmy, Peggy and Reno, Judy and Rick, Joyce and Teddy, Marlene and Don, Yvonne and Buddy, Elaine and Vinnie and Bootsie, and Carol and Johnny Accosella; Mary and Jerry and little Junior Lucadamo, Antoinette and Dominic, Carmine Mangarelli and Ralph Reya, and especially to Charlie Accosella, who's been going steady fifteen months, and Lucy, who says, 'I know I getcha mad honey, but I don't mean to. It's just love, that's all!'

"And good luck to the Phi Zeta Sorority on your dance, from Lucy Mangarelli of Mount Vernon, New York, Kenneth Cook of St. Albans, from Joan Harding, who still loves him, and Frankie Johnson of Flushing, from Olga in Springfield Gardens, Long Island. All the kids of Andrew Jackson high—Gail, Jackie, Helena, Dorie, Kenneth, Jerry, Billy, Shadow, Baby, Joan, Olga, Clifford, Connie, Jose, Slim, Mousie, and Tommy—here's Varetta Dillard, Savoy Records, 'Johnny Has Gone'!"

John McCarthy, Freed's WINS engineer, said much of Freed's jive patter was unintelligible. McCarthy also recalled a time he tried to put on Freed's studio headphones but was unable to get them near his head. Freed had the volume up to "double ten," twice the normal volume. Although it has been said that Freed tolerated such high sound levels because he was left hearing-impaired from a bout with mastoiditis, Alana Freed characterized her father's hearing loss as "very slight" and "always very exaggerated." She maintained that Freed always listened to music at high volumes simply because he preferred to.

During Freed's early days in New York, McCarthy said he received calls from confused listeners trying to settle arguments as to whether Freed was black or white. Often a caller, certain that Freed was black, would pause in stunned silence after learning that he was white.

Not everyone accepted Freed immediately. Paul Sherman, a WINS staff announcer the night Freed made his radio debut there, observed Freed's antics and heard the type of music the deejay played. Sherman described Freed's show as "crap . . . loud, phony, unpleasant and artificial." Fellow announcer Lew Fisher happened to be on the night shift with Sherman. They looked at each other and Fisher exclaimed, "Oh my God, I give him three months."

"You're crazy," replied Sherman. "I give him one week."

Jim McGowan said he and his Brooklyn neighborhood friends originally regarded Freed's WINS program as an "intrusion" upon the familiar rhythm and blues scene. Many of McGowan's young black friends were turned off by Freed, not because the new deejay was white, but because of his "ostentatious style." They felt more comfortable with Tommy Smalls (or Hal Jackson or Joe Bostic), who spoke the "jive-language" in a soft-spoken manner. "I think Freed shocked the sensibilities of black teenagers when he came on banging and shouting."

If many black teenagers were initially offended by Freed's showy style, his white audience, most of them unfamiliar with the local black disc jockey style, "automatically assumed that's the way [black radio] was," said McGowan. The singer likened to a tidal wave the surge of white teenagers discovering rhythm and blues in 1954 via Alan Freed. McGowan also conceded that most black teenagers who originally opposed Freed eventually got caught up in his excitement and boundless energy and finally accepted him "because he played the records they wanted to hear." McGowan believes Freed was able to overcome objections to him because the deejay came across with a force that was just too powerful. "He just swept everything else aside."

Jack Hooke said Freed "took this town over before you could turn around," and Ray Reneri recalled walking down any street in New York City at night and hearing "the same station [WINS] everywhere you went." Freed's magnetism was not confined to the New York area. The political activist Abbie Hoffman, who, as a youngster, lived near Boston, "had to rig up a roof antenna to hear ol' Alan Freed bang a telephone book on the table while he spun the Sound."

Freed was initially on the air at WINS six nights a week (except Sundays) from 11 P.M. until 2:00 A.M. In October the deejay was also given the 7:00–8:00 P.M. time slot. He had quickly become the dominant nighttime personality on New York radio. Yet, despite Freed's immediate success, or perhaps because of it, Moondog was about to be embroiled in controversy more serious than he had ever faced in Akron or Cleveland.

CHAPTER 5

Rock and Roll Party

"Teenagers Demand Music with a Beat, Spur Rhythm & Blues."

AS significant a force in rhythm and blues music as Alan Freed was by 1954, there were other forces at work in America that the influential and controversial disc jockey could neither predict nor alter. So long as rhythm and blues music remained within the traditional boundaries defined by the pop music business, the opposition from white America was inconsequential. However, as the popularity of the black music—and the number of whites exposed to it—increased, rhythm and blues began to evoke open derision and outright hatred from certain segments of society.

The first significant opposition to rhythm and blues centered around the music's allegedly "smutty" lyrics—specifically the sexual double entendres that were extremely popular in the genre. Many white listeners familiar with such early 1950s pop hits as "Oh, My Papa," "That Doggie in the Window," and "Come on-a my House" (each of which reached number one on the nation's pop sales charts) were shocked to hear rhythm and blues songs such as "It Ain't the Meat (It's the Motion)," "Sixty-Minute Man," "I Got Loaded," "Rock Me All Night Long," and "Roll with My Baby." Those whites were joined in their criticism of rhythm and blues by upper- and middle-class blacks who were ashamed and embarrassed by the music's vulgarity and primitiveness.

By 1954 the rhythm and blues lyrics controversy was grave. When the Drifters released "Such a Night," a song in which lead singer

ROCK & ROLL PARTY 73

Clyde McPhatter recalled a previous night's lovemaking, a group of East Coast disc jockeys came out against playing records that advocated sex or drinking or that ridiculed blacks. "Such a Night" was quickly banned by various radio stations across the country.

In March 1954, a group known as the Royals (soon to become the Midnighters to avoid confusion with another R&B group) released a song called "Work with Me, Annie." Despite being resoundingly criticized for its overt sexual connotations (specifically, for the use of the word *work,* which critics maintained was a black euphemism for sexual intercourse), "Annie" quickly became an overwhelming R&B hit, which only compounded the problem. Midnighters producer Ralph Bass later claimed that *work* was an old jazz expression that could mean "anything," but later that year, when the Midnighters released a sequel called "Annie Had a Baby (She Can't Work No More)," there was little doubt as to what type of work Annie was fond of.

As Alan Freed made preparations to move to New York City in the summer of 1954, the rhythm and blues lyrics controversy intensified. That July the Robins' "Riot in Cell Block #9" was banned by the CBS Network, and Clyde McPhatter was at it again, this time singing of needing his "honey love" not only in the middle of the night but in the "morning light" as well. The nation's most powerful black radio station, Memphis's WDIA, banned all records with "suggestive" lyrics and double entendres. As Freed took control of nighttime radio in New York City, "Work with Me, Annie" appeared on the best-selling pop charts and the heat on Moondog—who had already been referred to by some Cleveland detractors as a "nigger lover"—intensified.

The *Pittsburgh Courier,* the nation's leading black newspaper, issued a blast against "smutty" R&B records, and Harry Mills of the venerable Mills Brothers singing group charged Freed with playing off-color records on the deejay's WINS program. In defense, Freed cited the fact that two years earlier he had been the recipient of the *Courier'*s Brotherhood Award for his "showcasing Negro talent." The deejay also denied he ever played smutty records on his radio program.

Much of the opposition to the lyrics of many rhythm and blues records originated from within the music industry—members of the American Society of Composers, Artists, and Publishers (ASCAP)— who, until R&B's surging popularity, enjoyed a virtual monopoly on the writing and publishing of America's popular music.

ASCAP was formed in 1914 by a group of composers, lyricists, and attorneys as "a voluntary association to protect their property rights" because their musical compositions were being performed in public without payment of performance fees to the writers and publishers. From the start there were hard feelings between America's broadcasters, who used copyrighted material without permission, and AS-CAP. When commercial radio stations refused to pay performance royalties for the music they played on the air, ASCAP took the broadcasters to court. In 1923 it was decided that the broadcasters were legally bound to pay performance fees to ASCAP for any guild-licensed music played on the air. For the time being, ASCAP's monopoly was preserved.

During the 1930s, ASCAP, with its elite songwriter membership—the Gershwins, Kerns, Porters, and Berlins—controlled nearly all the "good music" publishing rights and the guild collected performance royalties for use of that music by the broadcasters. But in 1937 ASCAP began talk of a proposed 100 percent increase in the royalties paid by the broadcasters.

The radio broadcasters, however, were not about to submit to ASCAP's excessive demands, nor were they about to refrain from broadcasting the guild's music. When their performance-licensing agreement with ASCAP expired on January 1, 1941, the broadcasters had already formed a song-performance licensing society of their own, called Broadcast Music International (BMI).

ASCAP regarded its fledgling rival disdainfully, but BMI, taking advantage of ASCAP's stringent membership requirements—as well as its royalty-payment scale, which favored established songwriters over new ones—managed to lure some ASCAP writers and publishers into the BMI fold. Most important, however, BMI capitalized on ASCAP's relative indifference to the popular music being produced outside of New York and Hollywood. BMI sought out and acquired membership from "have-not" writers and publishers in the country and western and the rhythm and blues fields. Music business insiders, who believed there was no money to be made with black and hillbilly music, had a good laugh at BMI's expense, but eventually they were proved wrong. With the rise in popularity of the grassroots rhythm and blues and country and western music after World War II, BMI controlled the licensing rights to more and more of the popular music heard on the air. Now it was BMI's turn to prosper. By 1950, ASCAP members were "panic-stricken" because BMI-licensed songs comprised up to 80 percent of the music heard on the air in many markets.

David Freed says that because of ASCAP's de facto song-licensing monopoly before BMI's existence, it was nearly impossible for a nonmember of ASCAP to get a song recorded. His brother's impact in popularizing BMI-licensed rhythm and blues "was probably the most vital factor in the bust-up of ASCAP domination. . . . That alone may be the most important thing Alan ever did."

Because many broadcasters also held stock in BMI, and because some disc jockeys also became BMI song publishers, in effect playing their own BMI-licensed music on the air, in November 1953 a group of thirty-three ASCAP members filed a $150 million antitrust suit against BMI, the three major broadcasting networks, and two affiliated record companies (Columbia and RCA Victor). The lawsuit charged that BMI controlled the nation's radio stations and effectively blocked ASCAP from getting its songs aired. The plaintiff in the case was an organization called Songwriters of America, whose seven hundred members all happened to be members of ASCAP.

Ironically, as musicologist Arnold Shaw pointed out, in charging BMI with monopolistic practices, ASCAP members were trying to prevent the "impending breakdown of their own monopolistic hold on pop." Because of his promotion of BMI-licensed music, Freed may have become a target for ASCAP's good-music membership.

Hoping to stem the increased airplay of BMI-licensed songs, ASCAP members spearheaded the attack on questionable rhythm and blues lyrics. (The ASCAP-favoring newspaper *Variety* began referring to them as "leer-ics".) Lyricist and ASCAP board member Billy Rose typified the attack, calling most BMI songs "obscene . . . junk," in many cases "on a level with dirty comic magazines."

"The most astonishing thing about the current craze for rhythm and blues records and their accompanying leer-ics," wrote *Variety's* Jimmy Kennedy, "is that it was ever permitted to happen." Kennedy pointed his journalistic finger at the record companies that allowed their business to be "fouled by marketing filth" and at the disc jockeys—the listening public's link to those record companies. Noted Los Angeles pop deejay and host of TV's musical "Juke Box Jury," Peter Potter, said that "all rhythm and blues records are dirty and as bad for kids as dope." Under the mounting pressure from parents, schools, and religious and civic groups, BMI announced the formation of a screening committee to eliminate "flagrantly pornographic" songs from being licensed for airplay.

ASCAP members' opposition to rhythm and blues—and to BMI—persisted. The guild announced that it would not credit "any performance whatsoever" written by its members in collaboration with BMI writers after January 1, 1955. Although ASCAP's members were not legally enjoined from collaborating with rival BMI members, the guild did bar them from entering into "any sort of deal" with either BMI or The Society of European Stage Authors and Composers (SESAC), a third performance-royalty organization. The antitrust suit brought against BMI by members of ASCAP dragged on, but Alan Freed faced a more pressing problem—opposition to him from portions of the local black community that believed the deejay to be capitalizing on rhythm and blues and jeopardizing the jobs of black rhythm and blues disc jockeys already on the air.

At an uptown rally held in a Harlem YMCA, angry blacks characterized Freed as an outsider who imitated blacks. They wanted Moondog's WINS radio program to be hosted by a black. WINS program director Bob Smith told the hostile gathering that his radio station had not thought black or white, but had aimed at the entire listening market, when it selected Freed. "We just wanted the best talent."

Ex-bandleader Lucky Millinder, then a Harlem-based R&B deejay, defended Freed: " 'Tis said he [Freed] apes Negroes in a jive talk manner that belittles them," said Millinder. "He has the fire and excitement of a Reverend Billy Graham, . . . but in no way does he burlesque Negroes."

Then, Smith said, "things got very heated." The loudest Harlem complainer was Willie Bryant, a local R&B disc jockey who "felt he could do it [Freed's WINS program] better than Alan Freed could." Since Bryant, more than anyone else, directly felt Freed's impact on New York nighttime radio, his criticism of Freed was understandable.

Born black, but with straight hair and a complexion light enough to enable him to pass for white, Bryant was nevertheless denied by those aware of his heritage the opportunity to work the downtown Manhattan nightclubs. He eventually became a radio disc jockey and in 1946 became the first black deejay to host a network radio music program. On local radio, Bryant teamed up with Ray Carroll, a white man, and the pair hosted their "After-Hours Session," broadcast on New York's WHOM from 11:00 P.M. until 2:00 A.M. After featuring

R&B on the air since the 1940s, however, Bryant and Carroll "couldn't get arrested," while the minute Freed hit town his WINS program took off. To Willie Bryant, Freed's eclipse of the black deejay was simply another example of the racial discrimination he had experienced throughout his long career.

"I have nothing against Freed," said Bryant, "and I am not carrying on a campaign against him." But Bryant did express alarm that the anticipated widespread syndication of Freed's WINS program (the station had hopes of syndicating Freed in up to sixty radio markets) would "shove aside" black disc jockeys in favor of whites, like Freed, who specialized in rhythm and blues.

Bryant's protest, however, never amounted to anything. "Alan just got bigger and bigger," said Jack Hooke.

As Alan Freed survived the charge that he was putting black deejays out of work, and as he continued to defuse the controversy over R&B's objectional lyrics, his own popularity continued to soar. In October 1954 Freed engineered the signing of the Moonglows to Chess Records, a significant rhythm and blues label. Bobby Lester said Freed gave the group a letter of introduction to present to the Chess brothers, but when the group arrived at Chess's Chicago office, they did not need the letter after all. "Alan had already touted us to them."

Freed and Harvey Fuqua were listed as cowriters of the Moonglow's initial Chess release, a ballad called "Sincerely." The song's commercial appeal was demonstrated when the McGuire Sisters, a white pop-oriented trio, copied the song note-for-note and enjoyed a million-selling number-one hit with it early in 1955. The Moonglows' original version of "Sincerely" was confined to the rhythm and blues charts, where it showed sales of about 300,000 copies, an impressive figure for a rhythm and blues record, yet disappointing when compared to the McGuire Sisters' pop numbers.

Freed maintained the practice of recording white copies of rhythm and blues songs was "anti-Negro," and in the sense that it was those black singers of the original R&B songs who suffered most from the practice, covering was detrimental to blacks. But the practice of covering, although popularly viewed as an attempt by the major labels to capitalize on the expanding rhythm and blues market, was as old as the record business itself and was not limited to pop covers of R&B material.

During the early 1950s there was no such thing as an artist's exclusive rights to a particular pop song. Columbia Records Artist and Repertoire (A&R) head, Mitch Miller, one of the most influential forces of the era in pop music, said that to reap greater profits from a particular song, a publisher would line up as many artists as it could to record the song. It was the song, not the artist, that was considered the key to financial success in the pop market, and it was not unusual for the major record labels to cover each other with five or more versions of a particular song. As far as songwriters and publishers were concerned, the more versions of their songs that were released, the greater were their financial opportunities.

The vision of tiny, undercapitalized R&B record labels being ripped off by major record companies issuing white pop versions of R&B originals has been greatly exaggerated. During the 1950s, independent R&B record companies often initiated deals between themselves and the major pop labels, ensuring that cover records of their songs were issued.

There were four ways that an individual could gain financial reward from being listed on a pop record label: by being the record label owner, the song's publisher, the song's writer, or the song's performer. The R&B label owner stood to profit from pop cover versions of his song, as it was generally accepted that competition between the original and the cover stimulated sales of the original. Most R&B label owners also had their own publishing companies and generally owned the copyrights to the songs that were covered by the major labels. What the R&B label owners lost in sales of their own records was usually made up (and sometimes exceeded) by royalties received from sales of the cover versions. Many R&B label owners also had their names attached to songs as writers or cowriters, which ensured them songwriting royalties from cover version sales.

As musicologist Arnold Shaw noted, "Only the artists suffered, because the copyright law afforded them little protection." Often the only benefit derived by a black artist from a pop cover of his or her song was wider exposure of the song and increased personal popularity, both of which created a greater demand for personal appearances.

As the popularity of rhythm and blues increased, the most notorious instances of covering a song involved white copies of black originals, but there were instances of black artists covering other black artists, as well as blacks covering whites. By 1954, when the music business saw that a pop cover of an R&B song could develop into a substantial hit, the covering practice was stepped up and black releases believed to have pop potential were considered fair game. Often five or six versions of a particular song were released.

Ironically, Alan Freed, who had overseen the Moonglows' cover of Doris Day's "Secret Love" early in 1954, became personally embroiled in the cover controversy later that year when the Moonglows' "Sincerely" was covered by the McGuire Sisters. Listed as cowriter of the song, Freed had everything to gain by the pop success of the McGuire Sisters' version of "Sincerely," yet he loudly decried the covering practice. In Cleveland, as well as during his early years in New York, Freed played only the original R&B recordings because he believed rhythm and blues music was "honest."

As the Moonglows were covered by the McGuire Sisters, LaVern Baker was victimized by two pop copies of her latest release, "Tweedle Dee." Covered by Vicki Young and Georgia Gibbs, "Tweedle Dee" became a huge hit for Gibbs, who had sung with several big bands, including Artie Shaw's. Overshadowed on the charts and incensed at "note for note" copies of "Tweedle Dee" that cost her an estimated $15,000 in royalties, Baker wrote to her Congressman, Charles Diggs Jr. of Michigan, suggesting he consider a revision of U.S. copyright law so that singers such as she would be protected from "modern-day pirates." Baker told Diggs she was not opposed to other artists recording her songs, but "I bitterly resent their arrogance in thefting my music note for note." Freed, too, was beside himself with anger. "Oh, they can always excuse it [pop cover versions of R&B songs] on the ground that the covers are better-quality recordings," he said, "but I defy anyone to show me that the quality of the original 'Tweedle Dee' . . . or any of those others is poor."

But with the major record companies—as well as many R&B label owners and song publishers—making unprecedented amounts of money from black material, the practice of covering continued to spread. No legislative copyright action was taken, and by the close of 1954 the practice had turned into an industry of its own. Like it or not, there was little that Alan Freed could do about pop covers except to publicize the black originals as best he could.

Freed was vindicated somewhat in August 1955 when WINS announced that in the "interest of fairness to the original artist and label," the station would no longer play "copies" of original recordings. Station manager Bob Smith differentiated between copy records—"note-for-note arrangements and stylistic phrasing of the singer"—and legitimate cover records, which Smith said were an "integral part" of the record industry and "completely ethical." To implement the policy, WINS supplied its disc jockeys with a list of original recordings to be played instead of the copy versions.

Despite the WINS copy-record ban, Dot Records emerged in 1955 to challenge Mercury as the most prolific rhythm and blues cover label. That year Dot, with considerable assistance from a twenty-one-year-old singer from Nashville named Pat Boone, charted no less than eleven of its rhythm and blues covers on the nation's best-selling pop lists. Boone's whitewashed versions of songs by the Charms ("Two Hearts"), the El Dorados ("At My Front Door"), Fats Domino ("Ain't That a Shame," which Boone, a college English and speech major, actually tried to sing as "Isn't That a Shame" before conceding it "didn't work"), Little Richard ("Tutti Frutti"), and the Five Keys ("Gee Whittakers") outsold the originals.

Boone—who now describes his cover records as "antiseptic, sterile-sounding [lacking the] raw, natural quality" of the R&B originals—nevertheless defends them and justifies his own role as a "catalyst, unwittingly and unintentionally," for the acceptance of rock & roll. Had his records not sounded as they did, they would not have been played, said Boone, "and the likelihood of the music being accepted by mainstream America might have been nonexistent." He maintains that Little Richard and other artists were "thrilled" to be covered. "It was their hope that someone would cover their records."

In November 1954, as "Sincerely" moved up the charts, Freed was about to be stripped of his famous Moondog moniker. When the deejay arrived in New York two months earlier he had no idea that he was not the first "Moondog" to curry favor with Manhattan's public. Thirty-eight-year-old street musician, composer, and beggar Thomas Louis Hardin, blind since age sixteen, had arrived in New York City from the Midwest in 1943 and set up shop on the sidewalk outside the stage entrance of Carnegie Hall. Wanting to do his "own thing," the bearded Hardin began wearing Viking garb, complete with a horned helmet. In 1947 he adopted the name Moondog and introduced a set of triangular drums he called trimbas. Hardin also put in a stint as a disc jockey on local WNEW radio "for a fast few days," said Jack Hooke, "before they realized they'd made a terrible mistake and let him go."

When Freed came on New York radio as Moondog, he was soon informed by Hardin's attorney that the deejay had "infringed" on Hardin's name. Now Freed needed an attorney of his own and obtained the services of music business attorney M. Warren Troob.

On November 23, 1954, swathed in a garment resembling a monk's habit ("He looked like Jesus Christ," said Hooke) and seeking $100,000 in damages from Freed, Hardin appeared in the courtroom of Justice Carroll G. Walter. The sightless street musician contended that Freed stole his Moondog nickname after hearing one of Hardin's recordings (a plausible contention, considering that Freed had played one of Hardin's records on the air). Hardin also accused Freed of playing the street musician's other compositions, including one called "Snake-Time Music." The robed Viking poet also asserted that Freed's rise to fame was a direct result of the deejay's exploitation of the blind beggar's pseudonym. Hardin was prepared to offer samples of his musical compositions as evidence. Justice Walter, characterized by Warren Troob as a nearly incapacitated "sick old man," reluctantly agreed to listen.

A portable phonograph was brought into the courtroom and when "Howl of the Timberwolf" and "Moondog Symphony," two Hardin recordings, were played, one reporter described the noise emanating from the phonograph as a mixture of "jungle sounds and Chinese harmonies, complete with clattering chopsticks in the background." As the din echoed through the courtroom, Justice Walter "buried his face in a handkerchief."

On cross-examination, Warren Troob succeeded in getting Hardin (whom the attorney called a "very bright guy, a musicologist") to admit to little more than that he was a street beggar. By that time, Justice Walter had heard enough. "You boys go out and settle it," he told both parties. But when no agreement could be reached, the judge handed down his decision the following morning.

Judge Walter issued Hardin an injunction restraining Freed from using Hardin's recording of "Moondog Symphony" on the deejay's radio program. The judge also said that since Hardin had been calling himself Moondog since 1947, while Freed had not used the name until 1951, Freed's continued use of Moondog might give his listeners the impression that the deejay was actually Hardin or that the two were in some way connected. "Not only did he [Hardin] win about seven or eight thousand bucks [the settlement was actually $5,700]," said Hooke, "but Alan was forbidden to use the name [Moondog]."

Hooke said Freed was both "very angry" and "shocked" that he was legally barred from using the name he used in Cleveland "all those years."

Warren Troob called Judge Walter's decision a "bad one." The "outraged" attorney said he was "more than reasonably sure" it would have been overturned on appeal, but WINS, which had invested a lot in Freed's future, intervened. "They didn't care about the name," explained Troob. "They wanted to get on with the show." Freed agreed with the radio station's position and overruled Troob's recommendation to appeal Judge Walter's decision.

Freed then huddled at WINS with his producer, Johnny Brantley, and Jack Hooke, uncertain of what to call his now-Moondogless radio program. "I think I'm just going to call it the 'Rock 'n' Roll Party,' " said the deejay. Hooke cautioned Freed that the phrase "rock & roll" was widely considered a black euphemism for sexual intercourse. "I don't give a shit," exclaimed the deejay. "That's what I'm going to call the show!"

Alan Freed is generally credited with having coined the phrase "rock & roll" to describe rhythm and blues music. Although the deejay began to refer to his radio program as a "Moondog Rock 'n' Roll Party" while still in Cleveland he referred to the name of his program, not to the type of music he played. As late as March, 1954 Freed described his WJW program as "a rock & roll *session* with *blues and rhythm* records."

Freed maintained that he originally thought of the phrase "rock & roll" after he and Leo Mintz agreed that the racial stigma of rhythm and blues would have to be eliminated "in order to cultivate a broader audience" for the music. As the two listened to rhythm and blues recordings, Mintz predicted that the music would be a "national rage" in short order. "I agreed," said Freed, "'and named the program, *not the music,* 'Rock 'n' Roll Party.' "

What is certain is that sometime before 1954 Freed began referring to his radio program as a "Rock 'n' Roll Party," while describing the music he played as "blues and rhythm." At some later point Freed transposed the phrase "rock & roll" from a description of his radio program to a description of the rhythm and blues music he played. Freed eventually claimed he gave rock & roll its name, and by 1960 the deejay incorrectly maintained he had named the music rock & roll in 1951.

The phrase "rock & roll" appears repeatedly as a euphemism for sexual intercourse in the bluntly sexual lyrics of race, or rhythm and blues, records. If the celebrated phrase is not quite as old as "race" records themselves, the separate use of either *rock* or *roll* to denote sexual intercourse certainly is. Both words, although not paired together, appeared on various race records of the 1920s. The earliest instance of both *rock* and *roll* (although not yet linked) appearing on a phonograph record label occurred in 1922 when blues singer Trixie Smith recorded "My Daddy Rocks Me (With One Steady Roll)." The record inspired other blues songs about "rocking," including "Rock That Thing" and "Rock Me, Mama," but few race records of the 1920s contained both the words *rock* and *roll* in their lyrics.

With the rise of jazz and swing in the 1930s, lyrical references to "rock" and to "roll" strayed from sex and, instead, "connoted a new sensuality of rhythm" and musical beat, as in Duke Ellington's "Rockin' in Rhythm." In the 1934 motion picture *Transatlantic Merry-Go-Round* the Boswell Sisters, a white vocal trio, sang a song called "Rock and Roll," which referred to a type of swing dancing. In 1937 a song titled "Rock It for Me" included the lyric "Won't you satisfy my soul with the rock and roll." Like the Boswell Sisters, the singers of "Rock It for Me" did not sing of sex, but of hot, danceable music.

During the 1940s as race music became more popular the number of songs employing the words *rock* and *roll* in their titles steadily rose. In 1945 Luther Johnson sang of "rocking with Aunt Anna" and "rolling with Aunt Alice." That same year, Wilma Harris promised on record to "rock and roll the house down."

Some record companies began to employ the words *rock* and *roll* in their advertising. By 1944 Capitol Records touted Nat ("King") Cole's West Coast R&B as "Royal Rockin' Rhythm." In 1947 National Records said Joe Turner's rhythm "really rocks," and in 1948 Savoy Records said of a Brownie McGhee record, "It Rocks, It Rolls."

"Rock's" big musical boost occurred late in 1947 when blues shouter Wynonie Harris covered Roy Brown's "Good Rockin' Tonight" and made a number-one R&B hit of it in 1948. After that, as one noted rhythm and blues writer said, "if it rocked, it sold." By 1950 at least a dozen rhythm and blues songs a year mentioned "rock" or "rockin' " in their titles and some, like Little Son Jackson's "Rockin' and Rollin'," came right out and said it all.

At about that time, Alan Freed began frequenting Leo Mintz's

Record Rendezvous. Had Freed no prior exposure to the phrase "rock & roll" he most certainly came across it while listening to Mintz's rhythm and blues platters. Although the deejay maintained that the phrase "rock & roll" came to him in an "inspirational flash" as a "colorful and dynamic" description of the "rolling, surging beat of the music," in all likelihood Freed appropriated the phrase from the rhythm and blues music he listened to.

The night of Justice Walter's decision that barred Alan Freed from continuing as Moondog, the disc jockey and a companion drank at P. J. Moriarty's, a local Manhattan saloon on Fifty-first street. The two spoke of Freed's (and WINS's) intent to emphasize "rock & roll" in the wake of the deejay's lost nickname. Sometime between drinks they decided to copyright the phrase "rock & roll." Such a copyright would protect Freed from further courtroom shenanigans concerning his radio program's new name—"The Rock 'n' Roll Party"—but there was another motive involved in the copyright decision. Rhythm and blues, the music Alan Freed now called "rock & roll," was entering a new era. Whoever held the copyright on the phrase "rock & roll" would stand to collect royalties each time the phrase was used.

If Alan Freed was most interested in spreading the rock & roll sound around the northeast listening area, Morris Levy had other ideas. Levy, born in Manhattan in 1927, grew up near Crotona and Claremont parks in one of the poorest sections of the Bronx. He landed his first job, shining shoes, when he was nine. After assaulting his sixth-grade teacher (Levy said he "took her wig off her head, poured an inkwell on her bald head and put her wig back on"), Levy walked out of school. He was sentenced by children's court to eight years in reform school and, after an early release, found work, first as a dishwasher, then as a short-order cook. In 1941 Levy got his first taste of the entertainment business while working as a hatcheck boy at the Greenwich Village Inn in lower Manhattan. At sixteen he developed photographs taken of patrons at Manhattan's Ubangi Club.

"Morris was a very aggressive young kid," said Jack Hooke. "He had visions of being an entrepreneur, of owning a nightclub." Levy, burly and gruff-voiced, was a man on the move. He and some partners opened a bebop and jazz nightspot called the Royal Roost. In 1949, when his associates jumped ship to form their own club, Bop City, Levy and his brother, Irving, acquired a controlling interest in

Birdland, the legendary jazz and R&B nightspot located on Broadway at Fifty-second Street. By 1952 Levy also controlled the Downbeat, another local jazz club.

One day Levy was informed that he had to pay royalties to the appropriate song publishers for any copyrighted music played at his clubs. Levy, after checking with his attorney, who gave the nightclub owner a lesson in U.S. copyright law, said, "Everybody in the world's gotta pay? I'm gonna open up a publishing company!" In 1953 Levy became the major partner, in association with Phil Kahl, in Patricia Music, a BMI-affiliated song publishing firm.

Levy was introduced to Alan Freed by Jack Hooke, and the nightclub entrepreneur and the disc jockey—whom Levy thought "had a lot of talent, but he was also a little nuts"—discovered they had a common interest in rhythm and blues.

Not long after the Moondog decision a copyright on the phrase "rock & roll" was filed on behalf of Seig Music, a corporation consisting of Freed, Levy, Lew Platt, and WINS. Then the popular disc jockey set out to promote the concept of rock & roll as a specific musical form. *Billboard*'s first mention of rock & roll came as the trade newspaper reported Thomas Hardin's courtroom victory over Freed and said, "Freed is now calling his program the 'Rock and Roll Show.'"

The next logical step was to move Freed's lucrative live rhythm and blues promotions into the rock & roll camp. Morris Levy proposed bringing a show to New York. "I'll take the risk," he told Freed. "You just hit it [publicize the show] on the air and you've got half the action."

Freed's first live New York show was called "The Rock 'n' Roll Jubilee Ball." Because no larger facility was available, Levy booked the St. Nicholas Arena, a renowned boxing establishment. Realizing that the six-thousand-capacity arena was not large enough to accommodate the anticipated crowd, two shows were planned, one on Friday, January 14, 1955, and another the following night.

Although it was reported that Freed's "Rock 'n' Roll Jubilee Ball" would be promoted by "Birdland executive" Morris Levy, there were other parties involved. A key provision of the promotional arrangement was that WINS, for 10 percent of the live show's profit, would allow Freed unlimited radio plugs on the deejay's "Rock 'n' Roll Party" to hype the St. Nicholas Arena show. As part of his on-the-air advertising, Freed encouraged his listeners to submit their choices of favorite artists, from which the deejay would select the most-requested to appear at his "Rock 'n' Roll Ball."

As part of the show's promotion, Freed mailed to members of his rock & roll fan clubs—of which there were hundreds—a printed advertisement and mail-order ticket coupon for the upcoming show. Addressed to "Dear Fellow 'Rock 'n' Roller," the letter referred to the rhythm and blues talent scheduled to perform as "sensational 'Rock 'n' Roll' artists." Altogether, the phrase "rock & roll" was mentioned ten times in the one-page letter. Rhythm and blues was not mentioned at all.

As Freed's St. Nicholas show neared, both the show business weekly *Variety* and the music business weekly *Billboard* touted the deejay's " 'Rock 'n' Roll' Ball" and, although both publications accepted Freed's description of the dance, neither sanctioned rock & roll as a particular musical genre. *Variety* referred to the dance as a "rhythm and blues bash," while *Billboard* continued to describe Freed as a "key r&b deejay."

There was "pandemonium from 8 P.M. to 2 A.M." as seventy-five hundred fans, each of whom paid $2 advance admission (both shows sold out one week in advance), enjoyed the performances of Clyde McPhatter and the Drifters; Fats Domino; Joe Turner; the Clovers; the Harptones; Charles Brown; Ruth Brown; Varetta Dillard; Dakota Staton; Danny Overbea; Red Prysock; Mickey ("Guitar") Baker; the Buddy Johnson Orchestra, featuring Johnson's sister, Ella; and Nolan Lewis. The Freed-managed Moonglows also performed, and Bobby Lester and Harvey Fuqua did a separate set as the Moonlighters.

The size of the crowds and the box-office gross in excess of $24,000 were no surprises to Freed. What made the deejay's St. Nicholas dance a milestone in the acceptance of rock & roll was the racial composition of the audience, which was estimated to have been half white—the first such documented ratio. And although Freed may not have been impressed with the turnout, Morris Levy was shocked, saying "Oh my God, this is crazy."

But despite Freed's predance buildup of his "Jubilee Ball" as a rock & roll affair and despite the fact that following the historic promotion WINS began touting its star property as "America's #1 'Rock 'n' Roll' Disc Jockey," the printed voices of the pop music business held doggedly to their long-standing "rhythm and blues" categorization of the music Freed now called "rock & roll." But a breach of the practice of referring to Freed as a rhythm and blues disc jockey occurred when *Variety*'s Herm Schoenfeld wrote, "The big beat in the pop music business these days is rhythm and blues and the top name in the rhythm and blues field today is Allen [sic] Freed, the rock and roll disc jockey." But when *Billboard* continued to classify Freed as a rhythm and blues deejay who had featured "only rhythm and blues talent" at his St. Nicholas dance, Freed stepped up his on-the-air hype of what he called "rock & roll records with the big beat in popular music today."

"Hello, everybody. Yours truly, Alan Freed, the ol' king of the rock 'n' rollers, all ready for another big night of rockin' 'n' rollin'. Let her go! Welcome to 'Rock 'n' Roll Party Number One'!"

As Freed's theme began, he continued, speaking over the music. "Yeah, top twenty-five rock 'n' roll favorites everybody, according to your mail requests, your telegrams, and your purchases all over the rock 'n' roll kingdom. And we're gonna get off and runnin', warp up with Red Prysock, on Mercury—'Rock 'n' Roll'!" The deejay proceeded to shout incessantly into his open mike during Prysock's breathless sax rocker, "Ho-ho-hey-hey-hey-hey!"

"Oh boy, that's a great one, and a wonderful guy—Red Prysock on Mercury and 'Rock 'n' Roll.' And that's exactly what we're gonna do!"

In a span of less than four minutes—with half that time taken up by Prysock's record—Freed managed to utter his pet phrase, in one form or another, nine times. WINS? Often the rock & roll deejay would not even bother to identify his station for thirty-minute stretches or longer. Freed was now selling rock & roll and WINS simply happened to be the deejay's outlet for doing so at the moment. Perhaps the pop music industry was not yet buying rock & roll but, as 1955 began, unprecedented numbers of American teenagers were.

CHAPTER 6

The Big Beat

"The Big Beat has arrived. . . . Rock 'n' Roll has finally burst loose on the popular music horizon."

BY 1955 there was no stopping the rise of rhythm and blues music. Although industry insiders promulgated the idea that the current popularity of the music was simply a fad, the face of America's heretofore segregated popular music business was rapidly changing. In the first two months of the year the Penguins' "Earth Angel," LaVern Baker's "Tweedle Dee," the Five Keys' and the Charms' "Ling Ting Tong," and Johnny Ace's "Pledging My Love" each became a big hit among white listeners.

WINS owner J. Elroy McCaw could not have been happier. Thanks to Alan Freed and rhythm and blues, his radio station showed a 42 percent rise in advertising sales, compared to the same period the previous year. Overall, WINS showed a substantial profit for the first time in its history.

As Freed's audience—and WINS's ratings—soared, his pet phrase began to take on new meaning. *Billboard* and *Variety* suddenly began to refer to Freed as a "rock and roll" disc jockey, and several record companies—majors and independents alike—began describing rhythm and blues as "rock & roll" in their trade advertising, eager to capitalize on the music's growing popularity. Ironically, one of the first record companies to do so was Chicago's Mercury Records, at the time the most prolific rhythm and blues cover company in business. In March, Mercury advertised that the record company "Rocks 'n' Rolls with 2 Smash Hits." The songs referred to were Red Prysock's saxophone instrumental, "Rock 'n' Roll," and Dinah Washington's "That's All I Want from You." Both were touted in the March 12 edition of *Billboard*, and not coincidentally, both songs were played by Freed on his "Rock 'n' Roll Party."

The major record companies rushed to make the most of the new music, promoting as much of their music as possible as rock & roll. In a matter of months, the pop music business had turned Alan Freed's pet description of rhythm and blues into a generic classification of the music now aimed specifically at America's youth, but the deejay's success in popularizing rock & roll ironically rendered his and Morris Levy's copyright on the phrase unenforceable. "It would have meant filing a thousand lawsuits," said Morris Levy.

Freed demonstrated that rock & roll was too big an enterprise for seedy, smoke-filled buildings such as the St. Nicholas Arena. It was time to bring rock & roll to a more respectable setting. Morris Levy, with strong connections within the American Broadcasting Company's entertainment complex (which included the Paramount Theatre chain), wanted to book Freed's next rock & roll show into Manhattan's famed Paramount Theatre on Broadway near Times Square. But there were problems. Paramount, concerned with the lingering racial stigma of the music, was cool to Levy's proposal. "Who the hell wanted rock & roll on Broadway?" asked Jack Hooke. A "sell job" by Levy produced a compromise with Paramount. Instead of Manhattan, the sight of Freed's first theater engagement would be Brooklyn, at the Paramount Theatre located at the corner of Flatbush and Dekalb Avenues. Not only would this arrangement enable Paramount to keep the integrated crowds away from Times Square, but it would also take some financial pressure off promoter Levy. The Brooklyn Paramount was secured for a much lower fee than would have been required to book Manhattan's Paramount.

For the first time, there would be no dancing at an Alan Freed show—at least no more dancing than could be accommodated by the Paramount's aisles and seat cushions (there were forty-four hundred of them in Brooklyn). The week-long engagement would also include a movie, the purpose of which was twofold: it would give the performers a break between live shows (there were four to seven shows scheduled each day) and it would help clear the theater so that a new audience could be seated (there were no reserved seats, so patrons could stay as long a they wanted to). Ray Reneri said that as a theater-emptier, the movie was a flop. Instead of leaving, many young patrons sat and booed throughout the film.

At 9:30 A.M. on April 12, 1955, the Brooklyn Paramount's doors opened for Freed's "Rock 'n' Roll Easter Jubilee." Following a screening of *The Americano* (the first arrivals saw both the movie and the stage show for 90 cents), the live entertainment got under way at 11:30, heralded by a hard-charging, saxophone-dominated number played by the Alan Freed Band. Fronted by Freed in name only, the deejay's rock & roll band was centered around three veteran big-band swing musicians—Sam Taylor, Al Sears, and Panama Francis. The trio had musical profiles similar to most of the other musicians employed by Freed—artists self-taught and steeped in jazz and big-band swing who by then had turned to rhythm and blues session work in order to make a living.

Samuel L. ("Sam the Man") Taylor, born in Kentucky to a family of musicians, was already thirty-eight years old by the time he joined Freed. Described by one noted critic as "a superior tenor man with a fine grounding in genuine jazz," Taylor also served as Freed's musical director for the deejay's live shows. He joined Sherman ("Scatman") Crothers' Orchestra in 1938, and during the 1940s played in several big bands, including those of Cootie Williams, Lucky Millinder, and Cab Calloway. He was a sought-after New York session musician by 1955.

Albert Omega ("Big Al") Sears, born in Illinois in 1910, began playing the saxophone in 1927. He arrived in New York City three years later and briefly played in a combo that included Fats Waller and Chick Webb. During the 1930s Sears was a member of Zach Whyte's Beau Brummels. In the 1940s he played with the Lionel Hampton and Duke Ellington orchestras, among others. Sears became a rhythm and blues session man in 1952.

David Albert ("Panama") Francis, born in Florida in 1918, began playing drums when he was six. It was while playing gospel music at Miami's Holiness Church that Francis said he learned "much about what later went into rhythm and blues and rock and roll." Francis went to New York in 1938. The following year, he received his nickname from bandleader Roy Eldridge, who, unable to remember the name of his new drummer, got his attention by calling him "Panama," after the type of hat that Francis wore constantly. Francis drummed for Lucky Millinder and Cab Calloway (playing behind Sam Taylor in both bands), as well as Willie Bryant, before turning to session work in 1953.

Others who from time to time played in Freed's band included Haywood Henry, a veteran of the Erskine Hawkins Band; Curtis ("King Curtis") Ousley, originator of the "yakety sax" style popularized on many Coasters recordings; Freddie Mitchell, New York session veteran who briefly led his own combo; Leon Merrian, who played with Lucky Millinder and Gene Krupa, among others; Count Basie Orchestra veteran Ernie Wilkins; and Jimmy Wright, one of the most prolific session men of the early rock & roll era and the man responsible for the spirited saxophone breaks on Frankie Lymon and the Teenagers' first recordings.

Despite a lukewarm reception at the Brooklyn Paramount, the Freed Band—a swing orchestra with a high-energy rhythm section powered by two drummers—became a staple of the disc jockey's stage shows and was responsible for producing Freed's "big beat."

Sometimes the drummer opposite Panama Francis was Freed's longtime friend Hermie Dressel. Dressel said that while other musicians in Freed's band could "lay out" (take a short break) and be covered by the other instruments, the band's drummers enjoyed no such luxury. He recalled developing open blisters on his hands from drumming six or seven shows a day: "It was like digging ditches or pounding nails." There was such excitement inside the theater that the musicians could not hear themselves play, while the sound emanating from the young audience was so intense that the band members could feel the air move. As the band played ("We had eighteen guys on stage, blowin' our butts off"), Freed once came up the steps to the bandstand, walked among the musicians, and shouted at Dressel, "For Christ's sake, what are you doing with the fucking brushes? I can't hear you!" Laying down the big beat was a most serious matter to the disc jockey.

On stage at the Paramount were the Penguins ("one of the best visual acts on the bill"), the Moonglows/Moonlighters, LaVern Baker, the Clovers, B. B. King, Danny Overbea, Red Prysock, Mickey Baker, and Count Basie's Orchestra. For the first time, Freed also included white performers on his show, and given the deejay's stated dislike of rhythm and blues cover records, it at first seems curious that one of the white singers on the bill was Eddie Fontaine. Fontaine, a Queens, New York, lounge singer, had just covered the rhythm and blues song "Rock Love" for X Records, a subsidiary of RCA Victor. Nevertheless, Freed hyped Fontaine's "Rock Love" on the deejay's "Rock 'n' Roll Party." Fontaine, who described his singing manner as "coon-style, really raucous Frankie Laine school," said Freed "took me under his wing" and "Rock Love" "took off like a shot" in the Northeast.

The Chuckles (with Teddy Randazzo), a pop group that, like Fontaine, recorded for X, had a big hit late in 1954 with the ballad "Runaround." Both "Runaround" and "Rock Love" were published by Regent Music, a firm owned by Gene Goodman, with whom Freed was involved in a publishing partnership. In addition, Morris Levy, Freed's manager and promoter, did production work for RCA and was about to enter into a "unique deal" with RCA whereby Levy would "nurture new talent" for the label. It therefore made good sense to all parties involved that Fontaine and the Chuckles (at the time, touring together) not only appeared on stage with Freed but also received heavy airplay on the deejay's radio program.

Billboard unwittingly showed the pop music industry's racial barriers had not yet completely fallen when the trade newspaper noted that Freed's white acts "pleased the kids . . . [but] seemed out of place in the predominantly r&b line-up." The voice of the pop music industry also underestimated rock and roll's appeal, suggesting Freed include some dance or comedy acts in future line-ups in order to "break up the steady stream of record talent."

Despite *Billboard*'s clamor for comic relief, New York–area teenagers could not get enough of Freed's rock & roll. His week-long Brooklyn Paramount run drew ninety-seven thousand people and produced a box-office gross of $107,000 that shattered the theater's all-time house record set in 1932 by crooner Russ Colombo. *Variety* said Freed's opening-night audience was "dancing in the aisles, clapping in time with the music and letting out shrieks at a lively riff or just the announcement of an upcoming performer," although Brooklyn Paramount manager Gene Pleshette, who had also worked at Manhattan's Paramount during the big-band era, said Benny Goodman's and Frank Sinatra's swing audiences were "wilder" than Freed's. Freed described the Brooklyn crowds as "amazing" and said that as they stood on the theater seats Pleshette "was getting nervous." He said Pleshette yelled, "Cut the last number. Finish it up!" "If we hadn't," said Freed, "there'd be no theater left, just a crater!" Pleshette conceded that Freed's audience bounced up and down "pretty hard" on the theater's seats. "Some seats would have to be repaired," he said, but Pleshette considered such damage "only normal wear and tear."

Although Freed's Brooklyn audiences were generally described as "well-behaved and appreciative," and the deejay's show as "clean, and frequently exciting," at one point several teens jumped onto the stage. *Variety* reported that as they were quickly ushered off, one youngster "began shoving a fireman who was aiding in clearing the stage, but he was coaxed into the wings and there was no further trouble." Pleshette estimated that during the week perhaps twenty patrons who made nuisances of themselves were given their money back and told to leave the theater.

Although there had been some reluctance on the theater's part to host Freed's rock & roll show, the attitude changed drastically following the deejay's box-office smash. "Money rules," said Jack Hooke. "That changed their minds about rock & roll." Freed was solicited by other local theaters that wished to host the deejay's next live production, but Freed and Morris Levy chose to remain with the people who had given them a stage when nobody else was interested. The deejay's first Brooklyn Paramount show became a model for the deejay's future productions. Hip New York teenagers would no longer need calendars to keep track of the seasons. Freed's stage shows would appear like clockwork on Easter, Labor Day, and Christmas.

Unfortunately, following one of Freed's Paramount shows that April, a rowdy group of teenagers created a disturbance in a Brooklyn subway car. Despite the fact that it was never proven that the youths involved in the widely publicized incident even attended Freed's show, many outraged New Yorkers pointed to the deejay and to rock & roll as the cause of the disturbance. The accusations that Freed promoted teenage violence would intensify as his own stature as rock & roll's leading proponent steadily increased. Freed would be unsuccessful in overcoming the stigma his critics imposed upon him, and this negative image would facilitate his ruin.

In the 1953 movie *The Wild One*, based on a true story of a motorcycle gang that terrorized a small California town, a leather-clad biker played by Marlon Brando is asked what he is rebelling against. "Whaddaya got?" Brando replies. That scene pretty much summed up the attitude of a small yet highly visible portion of America's teenagers in the mid-1950s. What to rebel against was less important than the act of rebellion itself, and the nation's teenagers, more or less sheltered from the real world of nine-to-five jobs and the pressures of supporting families, were afforded the luxury of rebelliousness at no personal cost. This attitude was seized upon by the pop music business, which realized that rock & roll, which teenagers were adopting as their own music, could be marketed as a form of escapism and rebellion for them. The music business thus sought to exploit teenage tastes in order to broaden its own range of listeners.

Society's reaction to rock & roll was generally one of disapproval, which only served to reinforce the rebellious adolescent attitude and behavior. Even Alan Freed—perhaps the greatest defender of rock & roll—acknowledged that one of the reasons the music was so popular was that it represented "a safe form of rebellion against authority."

Along with the pop music industry, Hollywood played a vital role in linking teenage violence and deviant social behavior to rock & roll. Perhaps the most influential Hollywood production to do so was *The Blackboard Jungle*, which starred Glen Ford and Sidney Poitier and portrayed a New York schoolteacher's harrowing experiences in the city's public school system. *The Blackboard Jungle* offered a terrifying portrait of hoodlumism and violence toward parents and other authority figures. The film also provided most of the adults in the audience with their first taste of the literal power of rock & roll. The only rock & roll song in the film—"Rock Around the Clock," sung by Bill Haley and His Comets—had nothing to do with it, but it did help set the movie's shocking, defiant tone. When *The Blackboard Jungle* was first shown, audiences were jolted by the sound that emanated from the giant speaker systems: "One, two, three o'clock, four o'clock, rock! Five, six, seven o'clock, eight o'clock, rock! . . . We're gonna rock around the clock tonight!" The Comets' powerfully amplified, driving beat produced an energy never before experienced in movie theaters. A hair-raising rush of excitement swept through young audiences as America's teenagers rejoiced, buoyed by the omnipotence felt from embracing as their own something that adults both feared and despised. Although adults may have exited theaters in a state of shock after viewing *The Blackboard Jungle* during the spring of 1955, their teenage offspring left with Haley's music still pounding in their heads and a powerful urge to pursue the exciting new big beat. Rock & roll's already tarnished image was further damaged when instances of teenage street disturbances following showings of the film were widely reported by the media.

"Rock Around the Clock" was not a new song. Haley's cover version of an obscure rhythm and blues song originally recorded by Sammy Doe on the Arcade label had flopped when released a year earlier. With a vital, if somewhat belated push by its inclusion in *The Blackboard Jungle*, however, the song became a number-one hit for Haley and His Comets. In doing so, "Rock Around the Clock" solidified the association between rock & roll and juvenile delinquency. To many adults, *The Blackboard Jungle* was proof enough that rock & roll and teenage violence went hand in hand. Freed saw rock & roll's image being dragged down by the film industry. "Hollywood is to blame [for the violence]," he said. The hoodlum element—in Freed's estimation, perhaps 5 percent of all teenagers—were merely "aping" Brando (and James Dean, who starred in the 1955 movie *Rebel Without a Cause*) in their behavior. "Why malign all teenagers?" asked the deejay.

Freed disliked *The Blackboard Jungle*. "It was unfortunate," he said, that rock & roll had been used in "that hoodlum-infested movie . . . [which] seemed to associate rock 'n' rollers with delinquents." But the music had been exploited, and its connection to violence strengthened, providing "proof" of the evils of rock & roll to another group of critics who feared and loathed it for a deeper and more passionate reason.

The socially oriented attack on rock & roll originated in America's southern regions where, by the time of *The Blackboard Jungle*'s release, teenage-dance promoter Howard Lewis reported that rhythm and blues had become "a potent force in breaking down racial barriers." Most overt in the South, racially oriented protests against rock & roll were equally strong in many northern regions and were felt by Alan Freed and other proponents of the music.

Segregated musical performances had long been the rule in the South, but as the popularity of rhythm and blues increased among whites, semi-integrated shows, in which blacks and whites were permitted into the same building with the two races separated by a rope or other restraint, became commonplace. What followed not only unnerved the local authorities but proved symbolic of what was happening throughout a portion of American society. As the blacks danced on their designated side and many whites, confined to their own side, tried to copy them, the rope would come down and blacks and whites would dance together. Rhythm and blues producer Ralph Bass thought early rock & roll did as much to break down America's racial barriers as the civil rights acts and marches did. But those citizens who viewed such racial developments as dangerous were well aware of the integrated crowds flocking to Alan Freed's dances and stage shows. Freed's image as a lover of things black was strengthened when, in May 1955, the *Pittsburgh Courier* invited him to emcee its "Command Performance" benefit concert for blacks, held at Detroit's Olympia Arena.

Freed had no desire to become embroiled in social conflict and he bristled at any suggestion that he was a racial do-gooder. His only interest in blacks, said Freed, was in rhythm and blues and in heightening the popularity of black artists who had historically been "pushed aside and ignored." But the deejay's distinction between racially motivated actions and his own musically motivated deeds fell on deaf ears. Freed's young audience was unconcerned with the color of rock & roll's performers, while his detractors already had their minds set that the rock & roll disc jockey was partial to blacks.

Many whites who disliked Freed found their negative feelings toward him exacerbated by the deejay's social habits, particularly Freed's propensity for physical contact with blacks. It was not uncommon for Freed to kiss black female singers or embrace black males as they walked off a stage. Nor was it unusual to see the disc jockey in a public place, drinking from the same glass as a black companion or sharing a cigarette. Ray Reneri said when Freed, "this so-called 'madman,' walked onto the stage with 99 percent of his show black . . . a lot of people hated him."

It was purely coincidental that rhythm and blues music began to appear on America's popular music charts at the time the South was stunned by the U.S. Supreme Court's decision outlawing segregation in public schools, but the white backlash to the decision affected the region's attitude to rhythm and blues and to rock & roll. White Citizens Councils (segregationist committees of whites) began to appear throughout the South, railing against the obscenity and vulgarity of rock & roll, calling it "obviously Negro music" and "a means by which the white man and his children can be driven to the level with the Negro." It was not unusual to hear council leaders talk of doing away with the "vulgar, animalistic, Nigger rock and roll bop." This racially motivated attack on rock & roll was echoed in the North, but usually in a more subtle manner than in the South.

When blacks were considered rhythm and blues performers, they were kept at a safe distance from most white audiences. It was not difficult, if one chose, to simply ignore the existence of black artists. But rock & roll permitted—even encouraged—black artists to overstep music's traditional racial barriers. This sudden intrusion of blacks into the white entertainment field, and the integrated audiences that promoters such as Alan Freed now drew to their shows, aroused great passion among many adults.

Of all the cities outside the South, perhaps the metropolis most perilous for a traveling all-black rock & roll show in 1955 was Boston, a bastion of deeply rooted Roman Catholic conservatism. Boston's Roman Catholic hierarchy, typified by the Very Reverend John Carroll, who warned the Teacher's Institute of the Archdiocese of Boston that rock & roll inflamed and excited youth "like jungle tom-toms readying warriors for battle," looked askance at any activity or idea that threatened the status quo. Throughout the city, thousands of Roman Catholics stood in church to pledge to the Legion of Decency not to support purportedly indecent cultural by-products, including motion pictures and rock & roll music.

It was hardly a surprise, then, that when Alan Freed's all-black eleven-act "Diddley Daddy" package show (featuring Bo Diddley) hit downtown Boston on May 20 for a week-long run at the local Loew's State Theatre, the deejay was not given the key to the city by civic fathers. Freed, having astounded onlookers with the magnitude of his success at the Brooklyn Paramount, was determined to take his rock & roll show on the road. After Boston, where Freed was no stranger to those with an AM antenna able to capture WINS's fifty thousand watts of power, the disc jockey had booked three days in nearby Providence for May 27–29. Onstage with Diddley would be the Moonglows/Moonlighters, the Five Keys, Nappy Brown, Dinah Washington, Al Hibbler, Little Walter, Dakota Staton, and the Buddy Johnson Orchestra, with Ella Johnson.

Jack Hooke said Freed met "strong opposition" to the deejay's first Boston visit, led by the Boston Diocese newspaper, which ran a series of articles condemning the "immoral" rock & roll and urged parishioners not to attend rock & roll productions. Hermie Dressel said Freed was told not to put his show on, which only guaranteed that the controversial rock & roll promoter would be there.

One account of Freed's Boston engagement said the "joint was jumping," but that regular patrons stayed away. Although there was an increase in attendance over the disappointing opening-day audience of five hundred patrons, the deejay's week-long production grossed a disappointing $27,000, a far cry from his heady week at the Brooklyn Paramount.

This was Freed's first serious encounter with anti–rock & roll sentiment. Paranoia over the music spread as quickly as the music's popularity as civic authorities from coast to coast, citing press accounts of violence attributed to rock & roll shows, lashed out at rock & roll's proponents. A disturbance at a rock & roll show at the New Haven Arena caused neighboring Bridgeport police to issue a ban on rock & roll dances, wiping out a dance scheduled for May 22 at the Ritz Ballroom, for which Fats Domino had been booked. The Bridgeport cancellation set off a wave of anti–rock & roll reaction. In Boston, having had a taste of Freed's "Diddley Daddy" show, Roman Catholic leaders urged that the offensive music be boycotted. Hartford, Connecticut, authorities threatened to revoke the license of the State Theatre (a site of future Freed productions) after audiences became rowdy during a musical stage show. In Washington, D.C., the police chief urged a ban on rock & roll shows at the National Guard Armory.

Freed, who, said Bo Diddley, "'was gettin' bricks throwed at his house," began to receive hate mail, some of which the deejay took to reading on his WINS "Rock 'n' Roll Party." Freed recalled one of the worst riots he ever witnessed, which occurred in 1944 when a Youngstown audience mobbed the bandstand as Guy Lombardo and His Royal Canadians played. Music does not have to result in violence, said the deejay. "If a stage show is well-policed and well-presented they won't have riots."

The early Boston rumblings against Freed were portentous. As rock & roll's leading proponent, the contentious disc jockey was now on a collision course with America's anti–rock & roll forces. Not that Freed was one to shrink from controversy, but Boston—a city Freed was determined to bring his rock & roll show to again—would ultimately play a vital part in events precipitating his downfall.

Eager to return to the stage ever since his disappointing Boston "Diddley Daddy" show in May, Freed chafed all that summer as he watched his competitors, rhythm and blues disc jockeys Dr. Jive and Hal Jackson, cash in on the newfound rock & roll. Shows by both disc jockeys featured all-black talent (attended nevertheless by integrated audiences) that was now billed as rhythm and blues in Harlem and as rock & roll elsewhere.

The Brooklyn Paramount, scene of Freed's Labor Day "First Anniversary Show," again served as mecca for New York's first generation of rock & rollers. With charges of the evil influences of the music ringing in Freed's ears, it was becoming apparent that most of the rock & roll deejay's support came from his listeners and from WINS radio. Freed's post-Boston anxiety was understandable, for a repeat of his light Boston turnout would only lend credence to the theory being bandied about by rock & roll's assailants—that the music was simply a passing fad.

When Freed booked pop singer Tony Bennett to headline the week-long engagement at the Paramount, the deejay's hard-core fans were shocked. How could the premier rock & roll spokesman give Anthony Dominick Debenedetto, a twenty-nine-year-old singer from Queens, New York, top billing at an Alan Freed rock & roll show? Eddie Fontaine and his Frankie Laine "coon-style" proved adaptable to Freed's setting, but Tony Bennett?

Freed and Bennett were friends, having known each other since 1951 when the singer was unknown and trying "everything from being a race singer to doing Mario Lanza" in a Cleveland nightclub. After several large pop hits, by 1954 his recording career was at an ebb. As the other major record companies did with their pop singers early in 1955 when rock & roll emerged, Columbia (with the blessings of A&R chief and Freed nemesis, Mitch Miller, who also happened to own his own ASCAP publishing firm, Miller Music Corporation) had Bennett record the Orioles' 1948 R&B hit "It's Too Soon to Know" and promoted it as "'an outstanding rhythm and blues rendition." With Columbia trying to pass Bennett off as a rhythm and blues singer, his appearance on Freed's stage makes sense from Columbia Records' standpoint. But what about Freed's motives?

Although Jack Hooke insisted that the deejay had no ulterior motives in booking Bennett and that Freed had done so "on a whim, one night after three or four beers," *Billboard*'s June Bundy, shortly after Bennett's Paramount appearance, wrote that Freed had hired the singer as "box-office insurance" (for a fee of $10,000, plus a percentage of the gate). However Bennett came to be the top-billed star at Freed's rock & roll show, his appearance highlighted Freed's growing propensity to feature white artists on his previously all-black shows, and was consistent with the disk jockey's (and Morris Levy's) desire to popularize rhythm and blues as rock & roll to the widest extent possible. Just how much of an impetus for Freed to move in such a direction was provided by Morris Levy is uncertain, but Lew Platt, still Freed's manager (on paper, anyway), was vehemently opposed to the shift from strict rhythm and blues.

When Freed moved from Cleveland to New York, Platt, in anticipation of expanded activities as the deejay's booker and manager, set up an office there. But the one thing Platt failed to anticipate was the presence of Levy. When the Birdland impresario booked Freed's St. Nicholas Arena dance in January, however, it was obvious to Platt that given Levy's local influence and ambitiousness, he was no longer necessary—indeed, no longer desired—in Freed and Levy's scheme of things. While Platt remained a promotional partner in Freed's first Brooklyn Paramount show in April, shortly thereafer he temporarily withdrew from all his professional activities because of mounting family problems and personal illness. When the promoter returned to New York in October 1955, to his chagrin he found that "other associations [had] convinced Freed to play whites as well as blacks" on the disc jockey's radio program, as well as on the stage. The "other associations" Platt referred to could have been none other than Morris Levy and WINS radio. Platt, described by Jack Hooke as a "very nice man [but] a very square guy, not the New York type," said he "deemed it advisable, . . . because of my need for cash to protect myself," to sell his interest in Freed and "our varied businesses." Noting that "Alan has dropped playing records by people such as Eddie Bo, Muddy Waters, and similar Deep South artists," Platt felt the separation from Freed "advisable, inasmuch as during my absence that several of our associates had started to persuade Alan to gradually drop Rhythm and Blues and to start building pop artists on his show, and a white artists version of 'Rock 'n' Roll.' " With the assistance of WINS, Platt proceeded to make a deal to take over the management of another white rhythm and blues disc jockey, George ("Hound Dog") Lorenz ("he is not as dynamic as Alan," said Platt, "but he is doing a wonderful job. . . he is white, but both the colored folks and white people love him"), then presiding over the Northeast from Buffalo's fifty-thousand-watt radio station, WKBW.

When Freed's stage show opened on Friday, September 2, early arrivals were greeted by life-size cardboard likenesses of Tony Bennett in the Brooklyn Paramount's lobby. Many were destroyed on the spot by angry young fans who had come to see rock & roll's newest attraction, Chuck Berry (in only his third professional booking), white truck driver–turned-singer Lillian Briggs, and rhythm and blues veterans now billed as rock & roll stars, including the Flamingos, the Harptones, the Cardinals, the Nutmegs, Nappy Brown, the Moonglows, and, making his first theater appearance (as well as his New York debut) of his month-old professional career, Chuck Berry. On the Paramount's move screen was *Foxfire*, starring Jane Russell and Jeff Chandler.

After his opening-day performance, Tony Bennett withdrew from Freed's show because of an alleged throat ailment. Leroy Kirkland, Freed's musical director, said the audience screamed, "Who wants him! Get off there!" when Bennett appeared on stage. "I know he's good," said the musician-arranger, "but he just didn't fit the show." Kirkland said Bennett was replaced by Al Hibbler "and the shows picked up because at least he could sing something the people liked."

Berry was Freed's opening act, and the nervous singer broke into a sweat as Jack Hooke shoved him into the wings as Freed made the introduction. As Berry's three-piece combo hit the stage it was welcomed with a cheer that "wiped the doubt clear of any fear of being there." Berry was onstage for all of seven minutes, singing "Maybellene" and then "Wee Wee Hours." He said he received an enthusiastic response from the seemingly "solid white" audience, which applauded "without apparent regard for racial difference" (because of similar enthusiastic responses he drew at subsequent performances, Berry thought the same people returned for each show). Berry's Brooklyn Paramount appearance left the singer thinking, "I might be able . . . to carry on for a while in the big business."

Ray Reneri, a fourteen-year-old rock & roll fan, was in Freed's Brooklyn Paramount audience. Like so many of his peers, young Reneri attempted to get backstage between shows to obtain autographs of the performers. As Reneri slowly followed the flow of the crowd, he was suddenly caught in a surge and pushed through the stage door. In the confusion, he was knocked to the floor and his face was scratched, drawing blood. The injured teenager was quickly spirited into Freed's dressing room and was astounded to be greeted by Freed himself. After being reassured that his young fan's facial cut was not serious ("the cut looked worse than it was," said Reneri), Freed asked Reneri what he had thought of the show. Reneri replied that he thought it was great. Freed invited him to "stick around [backstage] and see the next show" and, by the end of the day, Reneri had become a gofer for the deejay's backstage entourage. For renumeration, Reneri kept whatever spare change was left over. He returned after school the next afternoon and worked until twelve that night. "It was a long day," he recalled, "but they'd drink a lot, . . . so I made about $200 for the week."

With or without Tony Bennett, Freed's week-long Labor Day

stand in Brooklyn shattered his own box-office record set the previous April. Freed split his percentage of the gross with Morris Levy, now his only partner and major influence on the deejay's career. The most significant development to come out of this show was Freed's realization that box-office "insurance" such as Tony Bennett was unnecessary. In the future the deejay would book all his talent at flat fees, "with some artists working the week (and happy to do it) for $200."

Rock & roll's continued growth in popularity was punctuated by Freed's Labor Day success, but no sooner had the deejay silenced those critics who insisted that the music was just a fad than Freed came under attack from opponents who charged him with keeping local high schoolers who listened to his "Rock 'n' Roll Party" up too late on school nights. This latest flak was not only a new avenue of attack against Freed but an attestation to the changing demographics of rock & roll's audience. As the music became more popular (and whiter), the average age of its audience decreased, but any visions of Freed's 1955 rock & roll audiences as pimply-faced adolescents packing tubes of Clearasil in their pockets are not accurate.

In Cleveland, Freed's audience consisted mostly of blacks who were nearly out of their teens or already in their early twenties. As young whites became familiar with rhythm and blues and rock & roll, the average age of Freed's listeners did decrease, but a look at the deejay's early 1955 radio sponsors—a clothing store, an appliance chain, an automobile dealership, an arthritis remedy, and a debt-refinancing company—indicates the targeting of a consumer group older than high school age.

Between rock & roll records Freed hawked a "free ten-day home trial of the thrilling new Kelvinator automatic washer," followed by a pitch to get his listeners into a brand-new Mercury from Lucky Lowell, who, said Freed, would offer each listener a trade-in value for his present car that was "more than you ever dreamed it was worth." If Freed's listeners were threatened with legal action or wage garnishees and repossessions (by Lucky Lowell perhaps?), the deejay told them not to despair, that "no matter how much you owe, how many people you owe, . . . your troubles can soon be over" if listeners would just make a telephone call to the Silver Shield debt-refinancing agency.

Whatever the age of Freed's audience, in deference to the growing number of high schoolers tuning in, WINS bowed to the opposition and scrapped their star deejay's late-weeknight portion of his

"Rock 'n' Roll Party." In its place, Freed took over Jack Lacey's 6:30–7:00 P.M. slot, which increased his "Rock 'n' Roll Party Number One" from 6:30 to 9:00. Freed retained his 11:00 P.M.–1:00 A.M. show on Friday and Saturday nights. He also kept his Saturday morning program from 10:00 to noon, giving WINS's star property a weekly total of twenty-one hours on the air.

In October a flurry of live rock and roll shows in New York, including Freed's one-night "Rock 'n' Roll Halloween Party" at the Brooklyn Paramount; and Carnegie Hall's first all-rhythm-and-blues show, indicated that if indeed rock & roll was a fad, it was a fad still on the rise. Ironically, as more than twenty black artists performed in New York to promote a positive image of rock and roll, their efforts were negated by a white pop trio from Los Angeles and its recording of "Black Denim Trousers." As far removed from rock & roll as could be imagined, "Black Denim Trousers" glorified the stereotype of an irresponsible, antisocial hoodlum biker and so served as much as did *The Blackboard Jungle* to brand rock & roll as an outlaw music to the general public.

As "Black Denim Trousers" reinforced rock & roll's negative image, the music reached yet another milestone in its acceptance. While declaring 1955 the "year R&B took over the pop field," *Billboard* instituted a new record-popularity chart—the "Top 100"—an amalgamation of pop, rock & roll, rhythm and blues, and country and western songs; the best indication to date that America's pop music tastes could no longer adequately be categorized along racial or stylistic lines.

Rock & roll also made a major television breakthrough when Tommy ("Dr. Jive") Smalls hosted a rhythm and blues music segment on Ed Sullivan's "Toast of the Town" variety show on the CBS-TV network on November 20, 1955. While much of Sullivan's large, faithful, and conservative audience no doubt was shocked by the likes of the Five Keys, LaVern Baker, and Bo Diddley rocking and rolling in their Middle American living rooms, some viewers' lives would forever be changed after having heard the exciting new sound. A week later, apparently realizing the folly in promoting pop artists such as Perry Como and Eddie Fisher as rock & roll singers, RCA Victor signed Elvis Presley, a singer with limited record sales and little recognition outside the South, after paying the Memphis-based Sun Records an unprecedented $35,000 for exclusive rights to the "Hillbilly Cat." RCA had no idea of what it had acquired in Presley, but thanks to television, Presley's gyrating antics would soon complicate matters in Freed's quest to make rock & roll respectable.

Freed's local popularity was validated in December when an independent music survey showed the deejay to be "most listened to" by New York–area high school students. The survey also showed rock & roll's rumored decline in popularity to be so small as to be insignificant. WINS was in the midst of a ratings battle to maintain the top spot Freed had helped the station recently obtain. In an attempt to cash in on WINS's success, a rival station, WMGM (at 1050 kilocycles on the dial, a slight twist away from WINS), lured deejay Peter Tripp, who referred to himself as "the curly-headed kid in the third row," away from WHB in Kansas City, Missouri. Tripp's "Your Hits of the Week" program utilized a chart survey countdown (a format Freed already used on his Saturday morning "Top 25") each night from five to eight. Freed and Tripp would go head-to-head for ninety minutes, with an advantage to Tripp for his early-evening start. It was the only advantage Tripp could claim as top-dog WINS gleefully anticipated the confrontation.

Also that December, Freed attended BMI's annual awards dinner, at which "Sincerely" and "Maybellene" were named to the BMI song honor roll for 1955. Thanks largely to those two songs, Freed, a bona fide musician who could read and write music, was "fast gaining stature as one of the most prolific cleffers around." Not coincidentally, "Sincerely" and "Maybellene" were both issued by Chess Records, with which Freed had a close working relationship.

Because of the highly competitive structure of the pop music business, whereby perhaps ten new records out of the several hundred released each week could be added to a station's playlist, the quality of a particular song was not in itself a sufficient guarantee for radio airplay. Not surprisingly, within this cutthroat environment, record manufacturers and distributors resorted to special arrangements and deals ranging from relatively mundane cash payments to more creative devices in order to obtain radio airplay for certain new releases. Although Leonard Chess's son, Marshall, said that in the days before payola was illegal, it "helped us independent record companies get established," Chess, as an alternative to outright cash payments, sometimes invited key disc jockeys and record distributors to select certain songs on which they would be given cowriting credit in return for guaranteed radio airplay for those songs.

Although Freed and Harvey Fuqua were credited as the writers of

"Sincerely" and Freed noted that one of his "proudest memories" was of writing the song, Jack Hooke and Bobby Lester both disagree. Hooke said that "Alan used to sit around and tell people how he wrote ["Sincerely"]," but that the song had actually been written by Harvey Fuqua and Bobby Lester. Leonard Chess, explained Hooke, put Freed's name on "Sincerely" "to help get it played." Lester maintained he and Fuqua wrote "Sincerely" "a long time before we met Alan," but that he and Fuqua had no idea of the song's potential. Lester said the songwriting gift to Freed was done "out of pure courtesy" because the disc jockey was their manager and the Moonglows realized certain opportunities made available to the group never would have occurred if Freed had not been listed as one of the song's writers. Freed said he sat in with the Moonglows and other artists, giving advice during the creation of certain songs.

Although Bobby Lester remembered Freed as "a beautiful man ... we had a lot of fun with," the Coronets' Sam Griggs was not as kind to his onetime manager. Griggs called Freed a "businessman out for a buck," who had "no real creativity." He maintained that "Nadine" was actually written by group member Chuck Carruthers about his girlfriend, but that the Coronets were told that unless Freed was given the writing credit, "nothing else would happen [with the song]."

By far, the most popular song for which Freed received cowriting credit was "Maybellene." In May 1955, part-time cosmetologist and would-be recording artist Chuck Berry was directed by blues singer Muddy Waters (himself a Chess artist) to the Chess offices at 4720 Cottage Grove on Chicago's South Side. Berry carried with him a homemade tape recording containing four songs he had recently recorded. Berry had high hopes for a slow blues he had written called "Wee Wee Hours," but Leonard and Phil Chess had enough traditional blues artists on their roster. They were searching for more "current" material, something that would lend itself to the rock & roll mold and would appeal to young white record buyers. Chess was more interested in a lively number on Berry's tape called "Ida Red," a song Berry called "a joke," put on the tape as "filler." When the singer, recently rejected by Vee Jay and Mercury Records, was told to come up with a new title, Berry obliged. The final version of "Maybellene" was recorded on May 21, 1955, on the thirty-sixth take. What happened after that is uncertain.

One unlikely account of the incident says that Freed was present during the recording of "Maybellene." Almost as unlikely is the notion that after listening to hundreds of Chess releases, Freed selected "Maybellene" on which to have his name attached as cowriter. The most plausible account of how Freed's name came to appear on "Maybellene" was offered by Berry's biographer Howard A. DeWitt. DeWitt maintains that Russ Fratto, a Chicago record distributor and the Chess Brothers' landlord, as well as a friend of Freed's, was present at the "Maybellene" recording session and was so impressed with the song's final version that he called Freed and the two "discussed Chuck's talents," before Leonard Chess flew to New York to talk with Freed. Chess said he gave Freed a dub of "Maybellene" that did not even contain Berry's name, and told the disc jockey, "Play this." By the time the record manufacturer returned to Chicago, Freed had called a dozen times, "saying it was his biggest record ever." In any event, when "Maybellene" was released, Fratto, Freed, and Berry were listed as cowriters of the song.

Berry maintained that because of his "rookiness" in the music business he was "totally ignorant" of the intricacies of songwriting and publishing royalties. It was not until the singer received his first royalty statement for "Maybellene" that Berry discovered Fratto and Freed "had written the song with me." Confronted by Berry, Leonard Chess told the singer that the song "would get more attention" bearing Fratto's and Freed's names.

Indeed, "Maybellene" did receive a great deal of attention during the summer of 1955, including a two-hour airing one night on Freed's "Rock 'n' Roll Party." The song reached fifth place on *Billboard*'s pop best-seller list, selling over a million copies at a time when a good blues record was one that sold in the neighborhood of ten thousand copies and a hit rock & roll record frequently sold hundreds of thousands. "Maybellene" was also the first rock & roll record to totally overshadow the pop cover versions that appeared, another sign of rock & roll's growing popularity.

To say that Freed pushed "Maybellene" simply because he had a piece of it is incorrect. In Berry, Freed saw a talented, dynamic showman, which was exactly what rock & roll needed to once and for all overcome the lingering rhythm and blues stigma that dogged other rock & roll stars such as Joe Turner, Ruth Brown, and Fats Domino. Unlike them, Chuck Berry carried no rhythm and blues baggage with him. Inducements by the Chess brothers aside, although Freed's name never again appeared on another Chuck Berry record, the deejay pushed Berry's subsequent recordings as hard as he did "Maybellene." Furthermore, Freed's exceptional promotion of Berry helped the crafty showman to establish a firm grip on rock & roll's young white audience.

The scene for Freed's twelve-day "Rock 'n' Roll Holiday Jubilee," which began on December 22, was the New York Academy of Music, on East-Fourteenth Street in downtown Manhattan. On stage at the Academy were the Cadillacs, LaVern Baker, Boyd Bennett, Gloria Mann, the Wrens, the Valentines, the Three Chuckles, and Count Basie's Orchestra, with vocalist Joe Williams. Also on the bill, making their stage debut and singing their recording of "Crazy for You," were the Heartbeats, a local group led by James Sheppard. The Heartbeats were managed by William Miller, a songwriter, producer, promo man, and part owner of Hull Records, for which "Crazy for You" was recorded.

Miller had met Freed while visiting WINS on a promotional tour for "Crazy for You." After listening to the record, Freed told Miller the song's beat was not strong enough. "The beat, man," exclaimed Freed, "give me the beat!" But Freed did play "Crazy for You" on his "Rock 'n' Roll Party." "He took that telephone book," said Miller, and by slamming his hand on it into the open microphone, "He emphasized the beat."

Freed had been displaced from the familiar Brooklyn Paramount (Jack Hooke said the theater would not give Freed the deal he wanted) by Dr. Jive, who, featuring white artists for the first time—including Pat Boone—made a bid to chip away at Freed's rock & roll kingdom. Dr. Jive's "Rock 'n' Rhythm and Blues Show" began its week-long run a day after Freed's show opened and, Pat Boone or not, the Doctor's Brooklyn Paramount lineup equaled, if not surpassed, Freed's. On stage with Boone was Bo Diddley, Ruth Brown, Clyde McPhatter, the Flamingos, the Four Fellows, the Five Keys, the Turbans, the Cheers, and Willis ("Gator Tail") Jackson's sixteen-piece band, featuring Mickey Baker.

Freed's "Holiday Jubilee," which began on a Thursday, "opened slowly but picked up tremendously over the weekend." On Monday, December 26, Freed shattered the single-day box-office record. With the doors open each day at nine in the morning, continuous shows all day, and late performances nightly, the "Holiday Jubilee' racked up a gross of $150,000.

At the same time, Dr. Jive took in $85,000 for his week-long run at the Paramount, "a healthy box-office take in view of the fact that Freed was at the Academy," according to theater manger Gene Pleshette.

In its 1955 year-end issue, *Billboard* featured a story about the expanding outside interests in the music business of radio disc jockeys. The industry, said *Billboard*, "has its share of jockeys who indulge in doubtful extracurricular activities—those with secret slices of publishing companies, hush-hush management contracts with recording artists, etc." The story also suggested that some broadcasters were in partnership with disc jockeys in various outside deals, while stating that Freed was "one of the most active and successful deejays in this outside business category." There was also music-trade speculation concerning under-the-table arrangements between certain disc jockeys and various record companies and distributors. Such talk had long bubbled under the surface of the pop music business, but with no end to rock & roll's growing popularity in sight the hushed conversations, particularly among those with a financial interest in the "good" music being displaced on the radio by rock & roll, grew louder. If Alan Freed had not been the chief suspect in those hushed conversations, he certainly was after receiving acclaim from local record manufacturers and distributors at BMI's December awards dinner for the influential deejay's "help" in getting their songs played on the air. True to form, Freed arrogantly stated that—side arrangements or not—he was proud to be thought of as one of radio's most successful disc jockeys.

CHAPTER 7

The Boys

"The first time I handed him [Freed] a record he sat down and talked to me. He listened to the record, but after that, when I'd go up [to WINS] . . . I didn't have to worry. I'd go home and sometimes before I'd get there I'd hear my record being played."

AS 1956 began, America's popular music could no longer be defined by traditional styles and racial barriers. In large part because of Alan Freed and a bevy of independent record companies, rhythm and blues continued to infiltrate previously white best-seller charts and New York City became a cocoon for the final stages of the metamorphosis of rhythm and blues into rock & roll.

Located in storefronts on the west side of Manhattan, from Forty-second to Fifty-sixth streets and from Tenth Avenue to Broadway, were dozens of small independent record labels and distributors eking out an unsteady existence in the burgeoning rhythm and blues field of the early 1950s. Because of the occasional pop hit (such as 1952's "Wheel of Fortune," which appeared on Larry Newton's Derby label) produced by those independent labels, Tenth Avenue—with the highest concentration of independents—came to be called in the business as "the Street of Hope." Each "indie" label owner harbored aspirations that he might become the next to produce the surprise pop hit to intrude on a field dominated by the few major companies. The area's aura of shirtsleeve-style entrepreneurship contrasted starkly to the more formal midtown zone just a few blocks to the east, which housed RCA Victor, Columbia, Mercury, and Decca.

Billboard's Bob Rolontz wrote that there were "no plush restaurants, no uniformed elevator operators, and few Cadillacs" on the Street of Hope. What there was was a group of innovative and energetic hustling optimists who hoped the combination of long work hours, a lot of luck, and whatever else it might take would somehow be enough to overcome the long odds of becoming the "street's" next surprise hit maker.

Among the independent rhythm-and-blues–oriented record companies operating on or near the Street of Hope when Alan Freed hit town in 1954 were Apollo, Atlantic, Baton, Bruce, Derby, Herald/Ember, Jay-Dee, Jubilee/Josie, Old Town/Paradise, Rainbow, and Rama. Rhythm and blues record distributors included Alpha, run by Harry Aposteleris and Johnny Halonka, Jerry Blaine's Cosnat Distributing, and Portem Distributors. Most of the entrepreneurs on the Street of Hope either knew Freed, or knew of him, from the deejay's early days in Cleveland. As Jack Hooke (who regularly made promotional trips for his jazz-oriented Royal Roost label in the early 1950s) explained, other promo men returned from their midwestern swings saying, "There's a guy making noise in Cleveland named 'Moondog,' and what he plays hits the charts." When Moondog arrived in their town, the "boys," as Hooke referred to the New York independent label owners and distributors, could not have been happier.

Far and away the largest and most significant player in the early 1950s rhythm and blues derby was Atlantic Records, founded in 1947 in a tiny office of the Jefferson Hotel on Broadway and Fifty-sixth Street by Ahmet Ertegun, the "playboy" son of a Turkish diplomat, and Herb Abramson, a dentist by profession but also a veteran of the Street of Hope who had worked as a part-time A&R man for National Records in the early 1940s and who in 1956 owned the short-lived Washington, D.C.–based Quality label. Ertegun and Abramson were not only sharp businessmen but also record collectors and true fans of jazz and blues who, according to noted Atlantic Records authority Peter Grendysa, "had an ear for the black sound that others who owned their own labels . . . could not duplicate." When Abramson entered military service in the spring of 1953, ex-*Billboard* staffer Jerry Wexler (the man responsible for *Billboard*'s dropping its "race music" classification in favor of "rhythm and blues") was invited by Ertegun to join Atlantic. With a formidable roster of artists headed by Ruth Brown, the Clovers, and Joe Turner (with the last two featured by Freed at his Cleveland dances as early as 1953), and offering a slicker, cleaner sound than its competitors, Atlantic became the dominant rhythm and blues label, "innovating and forcing" the evolution of rock & roll.

Although geographically separated from Manhattan by the Hudson River, "hard-headed, hard-working, and highly opinionated" Herman Lubinsky was the senior member of the "boys." Lubinsky formed Savoy Records in 1942 in the heart of Newark's already sprawling black area, but unlike Ahmet Ertegun and Herb Abramson, Lubinsky knew nothing about rhythm and blues except that the black customers at his electrical parts retail store bought the music. With his sole objective being to "sell records to colored people," Lubinsky hired knowledgeable producers, including Fred Mendelsohn, Lee Magid, Ralph Bass, and Teddy Reig (who became partners with Jack Hooke in Royal Roost Records), who, when the Petrillo recording ban broke down in 1944, "plunged into recording with a vengeance." As the 1950s began, Savoy was a significant factor, not only in rhythm and blues but in jazz and gospel music. Lubinsky's ties to Freed began in 1952 when the Cleveland deejay lined up two of Savoy's artists, Varetta Dillard and the Paul Williams Orchestra, to appear at the aborted Moondog Coronation Ball.

The next-senior member of the "boys" was ex-bandleader Jerry Blaine, who had worked with Herb Abramson at National Records and who, along with another ex-National employee, Sid DeMay, owned Cosnat Inc., a major rhythm and blues label distributor. In 1947 Blaine bought out Abramson as major partner in the newly formed Jubilee Records. The label name was shelved for a year until Blaine reactivated it in 1948 to replace his "It's a Natural" label moniker (said to be too close in sound to the National label). Like Herman Lubinsky, Jerry Blaine's association with Freed dated back to 1952 when Moondog featured Jubilee artists Edna McGriff, the Swallows, and Buddy Lucas at several of the deejay's Ohio dances. In 1954 Blaine added a subsidiary label called JOZ ("Josie") to his holdings.

In 1947 Al Silver purchased a small record pressing plant and developed an appreciation for rhythm and blues from his work done for several small R&B labels. He entered the recording phase of the industry in 1952 when Fred Mendelsohn asked him to become a partner in Mendelsohn's Herald label, which was started around 1950, but after no commercial success with Herald, Mendelsohn soon sold his interest in the label to Silver. Silver's brother-in-law, Jack

Angel, along with Duke Ellington's son, Mercer, owned Ember Records, but like Herald, Ember was no commercial success and Ellington soon sold his share to Angel. Silver and Angel then joined forces by merging Herald and Ember.

Silver was on his way out of a Joe Morris audition early in 1953 when he was approached by a young woman who began to sing for him. The singer's name was Fay Scruggs (Adams), the song was "Shake a Hand," and Silver's reaction was that "I knew I had to sign her." Freed, who according to Silver broke quite a few of his records in Cleveland, did so with "Shake a Hand" and the record went on to become a number-one R&B seller, while also reaching the pop charts. Silver also said Freed "induced" the label owner to switch the Midwest distribution of Herald Records to Lance Distributing and, later that year, Freed helped make Fay Adams' "I'll Be True" into another number-one R&B hit for Silver.

In 1952 Hy Weiss and his brother, Sam, formed the Old Town label, which they initially operated out of Harlem's Triboro Theatre before moving their operation to a Broadway location in midtown. Hy Weiss, who became a close family friend of the Freeds, credited the deejay with breaking many of Old Town's biggest-selling records.

Apollo Records, overseen by Bess Berman, wife of one of the label owners, was formed in Harlem in the early 1940s before relocating on West Forty-fifth Street, near the Street of Hope. Apollo releases by the Larks and the "5" Royales were among Moondog's most popular hits during his early years on WJW in Cleveland. Also in Harlem, Bobby Robinson, who said he "worked closely" with Freed, formed his Robin label in 1951 (soon changed to Red Robin because of a legal challenge) and became one of the first of the "boys" to capitalize on the New York streetcorner R&B scene by recording local talent.

Joe Davis, former bandleader and a New York indie label veteran dating back to the early 1940s when he formed the Beacon label, started Jay-Dee Records in the early 1950s and enjoyed success with Otis Blackwell, Dean Barlowe and the Crickets, and Lillian Leach and the Mellows. Davis and Freed were particularly tight, and the label owner frequently guested on Freed's radio programs.

In 1953 Sol Rabinowitz scraped together $500 and formed Baton Records, located on West Forty-fourth Street. Freed regularly played Rabinowitz's records, particularly those of the Rivileers, and he helped make the Hearts' recording of "Lonely Nights" on Baton (with the Al Sears Orchestra) a huge hit early in 1955. Also in 1953 Monte

"Al J" Freed during his senior year at Salem (Ohio) High School, 1939–1940. *Courtesy of Alana Freed.*

Alan and David ("Donnie") Freed, Salem, Ohio, 1943. *Courtesy of Alana Freed.*

Alan and Betty Lou on their wedding day, August 1943.
Courtesy of Alana Freed.

Alan and Alana in Akron, 1946, shortly after he had become the regular host of WAKR's "Request Review."
Courtesy of Alana Freed.

Freed and Jackie, with his parents, Charles Freed, Sr., and Maude Palmer Freed, backstage at the Brooklyn Paramount, Labor Day 1956.

Alan and Jackie with their daughter Sieglinde at their Stamford home in October 1956. *Courtesy of John Cavello, National Television Archives.*

The Freed family at the deejay's Stamford home, summer 1957. Left to right, Alana (12 years old); Alan, Jr. (2); Jackie; Lance (10); Alan; and Sieglinde (3). *Courtesy of John Cavello, National Television Archives.*

Publicity shot taken c. 1949–1950, when Freed left WAKR and joined WXEL-TV in Cleveland. *Courtesy of John Cavello, National Television Archives.*

WXEL-TV publicity still of Freed with one of the props he used on his ill-fated television show, c. 1950–1951.
Courtesy of John Cavello, National Television Archives.

"I can still see the crowd below us . . . getting bigger all the time," said photographer Peter Hastings. "It was frightening. I took the picture. Then we got out of there as fast as we could." The Moondog Coronation Ball, Cleveland Arena, March 21, 1952. *Courtesy of John Cavello, National Television Archives.*

WJW publicity photo taken before Freed's automobile accident in April 1953. *Courtesy of John Cavello, National Television Archives.*

Freed in the WINS studio, September 15, 1955. The previous week he had set a box-office record at the Brooklyn Paramount, taking in more than $150,000 from his Labor Day show there. *Courtesy of John Cavello, National Television Archives.*

A 1956 WINS advertisement. Note that while Freed loudly decried cover versions of R&B songs, WINS touted Pat Boone, one of the most successful R&B coverers, as an artist played by Freed. *Courtesy of John Cavello, National Television Archives.*

Brooklyn Paramount billboard advertising Freed's "Easter Jubilee of Stars" in April 1956.
Courtesy of John Cavello, National Television Archives.

Freed with "Big Al" Sears, October 5, 1956, rehearsing for the deejay's CBS radio "Camel Rock 'n' Roll Party" the following evening. *Courtesy of John Cavello, National Television Archives.*

Count Basie, Jackie, and Alan rehearsing on October 5, 1956 for Freed's CBS radio "Camel Rock 'n' Roll Party" the following night. The show was heard on Saturday evenings from 9:00 to 9:30. *Courtesy of John Cavello, National Television Archives.*

Freed with his props—cowbell, telephone book, and a stack of telegrams from his listeners—on the air, October 9, 1956.
Courtesy of John Cavello, National Television Archives.

The career of the Freed-managed Moonglows, frequent performers on the deejay's stage shows, received a big boost when the group appeared in Freed's movie *Rock, Rock, Rock* in 1956. Clockwise from bottom left, Bobby Lester, Harvey Fuqua, guitar accompanist Billy Johnson, Prentiss Barnes, and Alexander ("Pete") Graves. Lester and Fuqua also performed alone as the Moonlighters.

Freed's Washington's Birthday show at the New York Paramount in 1957, at which the deejay's third movie, *Don't Knock the Rock*, premiered. *Courtesy of John Cavello, National Television Archives.*

Freed's "Easter Jubilee of Stars" show at the Brooklyn Paramount. (Note the misspelling of "Bo Diddley" on marquee.) *Courtesy of John Cavello, National Television Archives.*

A New York Paramount billboard advertising Freed's July 1957 "Summer Festival." *Courtesy of John Cavello, National Television Archives.*

"Rock 'n' Rollers Collect Calmly," reported a surprised New York *Times* on July 4, 1957. Teenagers queue for Freed's "Summer Festival" at the New York Paramount. *Courtesy of John Cavello, National Television Archives.*

Bruce, along with arranger Morty Craft and promoter Leo Rogers, started Bruce Records (two years later sold to Rogers, who would go on to form many small labels, including Lido, Tip Top, and Power), on which the Harlem-based Harptones would have great local recording success.

Not long after Freed arrived in New York, Blanche ("Bea") Kaslin, a bookkeeper at Herald Records, decided to try her own hand at the recording business. A good businesswoman but lacking the street savvy and promotional experience necessary to run a successful record company, Kaslin convinced fellow employee William Miller and Billy Dawn Smith (ex-lead singer of the Heralds), who was the manager of several singing groups, to join her. Hull Records, started with $500, became a modest success in 1955, largely because of Miller, who was instrumental in signing a local singing group called the Heartbeats to Hull. Miller and Freed developed a close working relationship, not only because of the writer-arranger's knack of coming up with solid material but also because of Miller's deep ties to the New York–area talent scene ("I was up there on Broadway and Forty-eighth Street for forty years," said Miller). Miller became Freed's "troubleshooter," and if an act scheduled to appear at one of the deejay's stage shows suddenly became unavailable, Freed would get on the telephone and say, "Miller, who can you bring to the Paramount?"

There were many other small independent record labels, including Eddie Heller's Rainbow Records and Larry Newton's Derby label, that never managed to penetrate the periphery of the New York recording scene, but one of the boys who managed to do so in a big way was George Goldner. Of all the boys, it was Goldner who became most closely associated with Alan Freed.

In post–World War II America, Latin music experienced widespread popularity and New York City nightclubs became centers where people of all races came to enjoy the sensuous and exciting rhythms of the samba, the rhumba, and particularly the mambo. George Goldner operated a group of Latin-oriented dance halls in the metropolitan area and after observing the enthusiasm of his patrons (and his Latin wife) he decided to try his luck at recording some popular Latin rhythms. In 1948 Goldner and his cousin, Sam, formed a record company and named it Tico, after a popular Latin song of the day. They set up shop on the Street of Hope, and before long, Tico was the most successful label in the field of Latin music. In 1953 the Goldners moved their operation from Tenth Avenue to a West Forty-first Street location above the local Police Athletic League headquarters. When growing numbers of blacks who patronized his dance halls began requesting rhythm and blues songs, George Goldner, having had great success recording Latin music, decided to try his hand with the popular black dance music.

Rama Records was formed early in 1953, but with no rhythm and blues contacts Goldner could not get his records played in that highly competitive market. To make matters worse, one of Goldner's best-selling Tico artists, Tito Puente, fresh from an extended booking at Birdland, had been persuaded by Morris Levy to sign with RCA Victor Records. The situation looked grim for Goldner, an inveterate horseplayer who was more successful at producing records than he was at picking winners as the racetrack. Running low on cash, Goldner approached Levy and said, "You really hurt my label. . . . You took away my number-one act." When Levy apologized, saying he had meant Goldner no harm, the cash-poor label owner seized what he saw as an opportunity to increase the chance of success for his next Rama release. Aware that Levy's active promotion of jazz tours provided the Birdland owner and music publishing impresario with contacts to black disc jockeys across the country, many of whom could plug Goldner's records, the label owner said, "Well, maybe you can help me . . . get my record on the air." Levy, constantly on the lookout for ways to increase his music business holdings, saw a chance to enter the record manufacturing business and become a partner with George Goldner. At the time, Goldner was delighted. His plan had worked perfectly, albeit belatedly, when Rama's next release, the Crows' "Gee" (which was published by Levy's Patricia Music) began to appear on the pop charts early in 1954. As "Gee" continued to gather momentum and sold in unprecedented numbers, Goldner became the envy of the Street of Hope. By the summer, however, as the Crows celebrated their unexpected good fortune by motoring triumphantly down the streets of their Harlem neighborhood in a spanking new pink Cadillac convertible, try as he might, Goldner could not duplicate the success of "Gee." He had gone so far as to form another label, named Gee, after the Crows's monster hit, but the new label failed to boost record sales and was discontinued after only twelve releases.

It appeared that like many other would-be entrepreneurs on the Street of Hope, Goldner had had his one shot at the big time. Nevertheless, he struggled with Rama for a year, managing to produce a modest hit during the summer of 1955 with the Valentines' "Lilly Maebelle," all the while surviving on the steady sales from Tico. By that time the rhythm and blue/rock & roll scene was in dramatic change, with unknown and relatively inexperienced young vocal groups (such as the teenaged Valentines) beginning to record. To capitalize on this phenomenon, Goldner sought to parlay his recording expertise, Morris Levy's capital, and the defunct Gee logo (but with red and black colors replacing the original green and yellow, and a new numbering system) into a successful rock & roll label.

For the new Gee label's first release, Goldner recorded a local high school group called the Cleftones, whom he had had under contract since that summer. Lead singer Herb Cox described Goldner's oganization as a "one-man operation" in which the record manufacturer "signed the groups, arranged the sessions, promoted the records, and everything else you can think of." Goldner had no recording studio. Most of his sessions were done at Manhattan's Bell Studios. After the Cleftones recorded the up-tempo "You Baby You" and the ballad "I Was Dreaming," Goldner told the surprised group, "Okay, fellas, this is going to be on the Alan Freed show tomorrow night."

The next evening, Cox, sixteen years old at the time, and about forty of his classmates, gathered around a radio and anxiously listened to Freed's "Rock 'n' Roll Party," and "sure enough," said the young singer, "Alan Freed played our record." But after touting the Cleftones as "a group coming out of Jamaica High School" and naming the members individually, Freed played the slow "I Was Dreaming" instead of "You Baby You," which was the side the group expected to be pushed. Cox and the rest of the group did not care. The singer said to hear their record played on Freed's show "was enough; who needed the money!"

Eventually "You Baby You" became the hit side of the Cleftones' first record, but it was not Freed who turned the record over. "You Baby You" was being played heavily in Detroit, and Cox thought Freed "may have taken the lead from what was happening there" in switching to the up-tempo side. The Cleftones had several major rock & roll hits for the Gee label, but it was the group that sang on Gee's third release that thrust George Goldner and Morris Levy into the upper echelons of the rock & roll business.

Calling themselves the Premiers, this group came out of the Harlem neighborhood known as Sugar Hill. After recording session combo leader Jimmy Wright suggested a name change to the Teenagers (although the youngest member of the group, Frankie Lymon, would not turn thirteen until November 1955), the group recorded "Why Do Fools Fall in Love." Goldner released the song the week after Christmas 1955, and the spirited, catchy number outperformed even the label owner's wildest dreams. "Why Do Fools Fall in Love" became a nationwide hit that shot to number six on *Billboard*'s "Top 100" in the spring of 1956. The song was covered by several pop artists, including Gale Storm, but as evidence that rock & roll audiences more and more were demanding "the real thing," none stood a chance against the Teenagers' unique-sounding original. (Many listeners at first could not tell if Lymon's spirited lead-tenor voice emanated from a girl or a boy.) With a national hit record—his biggest recording success up to that time—and Morris Levy's direct link to Alan Freed's "Rock 'n' Roll Party," George Goldner was on his way to becoming the biggest of New York City's "boys."

Of course, the boys had no monopoly on Freed. Hustling indie R&B label owners across the country coveted a New York–area hit or at least some solid Northeast radio airplay, and they possessed the necessary wherewithall to get many of their records onto Freed's "Rock 'n' Roll Party." Marshall Chess, son of label owner Leonard Chess, recalled that at the time "white stations wouldn't play our records." His father had to resort to what Marshall termed "guerrilla tactics" against the major record companies, which included giving "money to the disc jockeys . . . all over the country." Leonard and Phil Chess maintained a virtual pipeline to Freed, whose promotion of Chess/Checker artists began with Little Walter's appearance at the deejay's Moondog Holiday Ball in Akron in December 1953 and continued with the Moonglows, Danny Overbea, Bo Diddley, and Chuck Berry, among others. According to Jack Hooke, when Freed first accepted money from various record manufacturers, he did so in return for having helped create a hit record for them. Hooke said Leonard Chess would tell Freed, "You made me a millionaire. . . . Don't tell me I can't give you something. I have to give you something."

Freed's other major midwestern tie was the "myopic, anemic, . . . high school dropout" Sydney Nathan, who began manufacturing his King records (he later added Federal and DeLuxe) in Cincinnati in 1944. In 1952 Freed began featuring Nathan's R&B artists, including the Dominoes, Wynonie Harris, and Bullmoose Jackson at his dances. It was "wily old Syd" who in 1953 released the first of the tunes ascribed to Freed—"Tongue-Tied Blues," recorded by blues singer Champion Jack Dupree.

Freed was also close to tough-talking Houston nightclub owner Don Robey, who ran the Duke and the Peacock labels. Hooke said that one time Robey came to New York from Texas carrying with him a huge diamond ring. "Hey, man," Robey told Freed, "you just made me 400,000 bucks. Don't tell me you can't take this gift from me!"

Although their companies were located in California, neither Lew Chudd of Imperial nor Art Rupe of Specialty had difficulty getting their records played by Freed. Other California-based label owners, including the Bihari brothers (Jules, Saul, Lester, and Joe) of Crown, Modern, RPM, and Flair; the Messner brothers of Aladdin; and Dootsie Williams, who operated DooTone, saw some of their records make the eastward trek to Freed's "Rock 'n' Roll Party."

While large recording companies such as Atlantic and Savoy were less dependent upon individual disc jockeys like Freed, for some of the boys airplay on Freed's "Rock 'n' Roll Party" was a matter of life and death, not only for a particular record but, in some cases, for the record company itself. Often after Freed played a particular record "it sold ten thousand copies the next day," said Ray Reneri. "It was that fast." He estimated that from 1954 to 1956 the boys sold "a hundred thousand records that weren't even heard outside the tristate area [of New York, New Jersey, and Connecticut]." Perhaps the most striking instance of this provincial success involved a Harlem vocal group called the Harptones. After the group recorded "A Sunday Kind of Love" for Monte Bruce in 1953, the first thing Bruce did was take the Harptones to meet Freed, whom group member Willie Winfield described as a "beautiful person." Raoul Cita, the group's arranger and accompanist, credited the deejay's heavy airplay of "A Sunday Kind of Love" (heard in New York over WNJR before Freed moved to WINS in 1954) with turning the song into an East Coast hit. Freed also gave the group's follow-up record "My Memories of You," the same treatment early in 1954, with similar results. "My Memories of You" was a hit in New York but hardly noticed elsewhere around the country. Freed "also made 'Life Is But a Dream' a hit for us in the metropolitan area," said Winfield. While Monte Bruce sold thousands of Harptones records in New York, "you couldn't find the

[Bruce] label in Chicago or Cincinnati," said Ray Reneri. "It wasn't even being distributed across the country."

The goal of the "boys" was to overcome the self-created and overwhelming odds against having one of their records selected for airplay from the several hundred new releases Freed received each week. Consequently, Freed and the boys worked closely, as exemplified by a sequestered gathering hosted by the deejay in March 1955 that included Saul Bihari, Jack Angel, Bob Rolontz (then with RCA Victor's R&B subsidiary label Groove), and Ahmet Ertegun. What developed from such meetings was an intricate maze of business deals and associations that often took on Machiavellian overtones. About the time Freed began hosting what were to become semiannual "thank you" parties for the boys at Al and Dick's Restaurant on Fifty-fourth Street, the deejay publicly laid to rest the on-again, off-again rumors of his impending association with Coral Records. Freed said his decision not to sign with Coral in an A&R and talent-procurement capacity was made because his relations with other artists and labels "would be restricted if he aligned himself with any one company exclusively."

One of Freed's guests at Al and Dick's in March 1955 was Al Silver, to whom Freed owed a substantial amount of money after Lance Distributing was taken over by Cosnat Distributing. "Alan promised to make it up to me" by playing those Herald records the deejay "felt had a chance to be hits," said Silver. Indeed, Freed made good on his promise, helping Faye Adams' "Hurts Me to My Heart" become a number-one R&B song about the time he arrived in New York. Three weeks after the party at Al and Dick's, Freed broke another Silver record, "Story Untold," sung by a Connecticut group called the Nutmegs. But whether Freed "owed" Silver or not, the record manufacturer soon discovered how whimsical the volatile deejay could be. Not long after a June appearance of the Nutmegs at a Dr. Jive "Rhythm and Blues Show" at the Apollo, Freed received a letter suggesting that because of some allegedly obscene dancing by the Nutmegs on Dr. Jive's stage, the group was unfit to perform in front of young people. Sensitive to the antirock roll criticism swirling around him, Freed verified the incident before pulling "Story Untold" from his "Rock 'n' Roll Party." The Nutmegs, alarmed at being banned by such a potent force as Alan Freed, personally apologized to him for the Dr. Jive incident. Not only did Freed begin to play "Story Untold" again (by July it was the top-selling R&B song in New

York), he also booked the Nutmegs for his upcoming "First anniversary" show at the Brooklyn Paramount.

Phil Rose, who at one time was A&R man for Larry Newton's Derby label before forming his own Glory Records, also discovered how unpredictable Freed could be. Jim McGowan, a member of the Four Fellows, a singing group managed and recorded by Rose, said that because Rose refused to offer Freed any inducements, the label owner initially had difficulty "getting him to play our records." Nevertheless, when the Four Fellows released "Soldier Boy" in the summer of 1955, Freed recognized the song's commercial potential and told Rose he would play it just one time. If "Soldier Boy" drew any requests, said Freed, he would then continue to play it. "He played it," said McGowan (the song became a hit, as well as the Four Fellows' biggest record), "and he began to listen to our music." Consequently, inducements by Rose or not, Freed played the group's records. "I found out that underneath it all he was a hell of a lot more honest in his dealing with people [than were some other disc jockeys]," said McGowan. "He gave you the professional respect and courtesy you deserved."

The boys each discovered that dealing with the egotistical and impulsive Freed was a double-edged sword. While they respected Freed for his ability to generate record sales and help create hits, they resented the disc jockey because of the subservient position they were forced to adopt, to capitalize on his power to give radio airplay to their records. Even those as close to Freed as Jack Hooke, known to industry insiders as the deejay's right-hand man, never knew what to expect. Describing Freed as a "very bad sonofabitch to a lot of people," Hooke said his friend often went against his own word. Freed once promised Hooke the publishing rights to a particular song, but before he made good on the offer, the deejay was reminded by another acquaintance that Freed had promised him the rights to the same song. "Alright," said Freed, "fuck Jack! I'm giving the rights to you."

Of course, the boys could obtain radio airplay from other disc jockeys—most notably, Dr. Jive, called the "black Alan Freed" by some—but by 1956 the fact was that if Freed refused to play one of their records, it was not going anywhere, and the extent to which some of the record manufacturers went to kowtow to Freed bordered on ludicrousness. Sol Rabinowitz named a song recorded by former Count Basie saxophonist Buddy Tate "Jackie," after Freed's wife.

Monte Bruce, after having the Neons record "Angel Face" (and after having the group sign over their songwriting rights to Bruce and agree to pay for their own recording sessions out of future royalties), then added a female vocalist to the group before they recorded "Kiss Me Quickly" for the flip side. The female singer was Mrs. Toni Bruce, the label owner's wife, as well as Jackie Freed's daughter by her first husband. Freed's office and the WINS studios were visited nightly by dozens of music publishers, record distributors, and promotion men, of whom Bob Rolontz wrote, "His [Freed's] thumbs-up or thumbs-down on a record could affect their job or their future. He was wined and dined like an ancient doyen, courted and conned and looked to for a nod, a smile, or a hello."

The Blackboard Jungle's startling success during the spring of 1955 affirmed film's power to create a national hit record (of a song which had already flopped with the public its first time around, no less). In October, on the heels of *The Blackboard Jungle*'s release, a low-budget film with the title *Rock and Roll Revue* appeared in theaters. But while aptly titled to exploit the current rock & roll craze, *Rock and Roll Revue*, a recombined re-release of two films, was nothing more than a series of filmed stage performances by such rhythm and blues stalwarts as Joe Turner, Faye Adams, Ruth Brown, and the Larks. In addition, Count Basie, Lionel Hampton, the Delta Rhythm Boys, Paul Williams, and Sarah Vaughan—hardly rock & rollers by any stretch of the imagination—were also featured in the film. The proceedings were emceed by Harlem disc jockey Willie Bryant. The genesis of *Rock and Roll Revue* aptly condenses the changes that rapidly took place in rhythm and blues circles in 1954–1955.

During the summer of 1954, Studio Films, a small Los Angeles production company, filmed a series of twenty-six musical performances of "top Negro entertainers during their singing and dancing specialties" at Harlem's Apollo Theatre, with the intention of marketing them as a television series to be titled "Apollo Varieties." Studio was unsuccessful in marketing the package to television, a medium that did not regard rhythm and blues as a serious musical form before 1956. Studio then opted to repackage their filmed performances into twelve thirty-six-minute musical shorts and distribute them to movie theaters early in 1955. Ultimately, that package was reedited into two full-length films with the first, *Rock and Roll Revue*, released on a limited basis in April, at the height of *The Blackboard Jungle*'s popularity. The second, *Harlem Variety Revue*, was released nationally in May, and in August *Rock and Roll Revue* was released nationally. Both films were poorly distributed and quickly disappeared from the few theaters in which they appeared, but as rock & roll continued its relentless growth in popularity, Studio combined its two releases into one, retained the now-current *Rock and Roll Revue* title, and rereleased it. Not many more viewers saw the film this time than had seen it months earlier, but *Rock and Roll Revue*'s limited success helped bring the music to levels of popularity never thought possible by its early artists.

The popularity of *The Blackboard Jungle* and the rerelease of *Rock and Roll Revue* did not escape the eyes and ears of Hollywood film producer Sam Katzman, a "B-movie" specialist who during his lengthy career had not turned out anything less than a box-office moneymaker. Katzman decided to go *The Blackboard Jungle* one better and make a film that not only featured rock & roll music but actually showed the performers in action. He would improve on *Rock and Roll Revue*'s format by adding a story line. To begin with, Katzman signed Bill Haley himself to perform "Rock Around the Clock" (which became the film's title), the song that had developed into a youthful anthem of sorts after its inclusion in *The Blackboard Jungle*.

With a wary eye on promotional outlets for his production, Katzman sought Alan Freed to appear in *Rock Around the Clock*. But when booking agent Jolly Joyce approached the deejay and offered him what WINS announcer and disc jockey Paul Sherman called "a small part" in Katzman's film, Freed turned it down. If he was not slated to be one of *Rock Around the Clock*'s stars, Freed would pass on the offer. Katzman did not want to forgo the famous disc jockey's peerless value as rock & roll's publicist and deigned to increase Freed's role in the film. Although the deejay still would not appear on screen until two-thirds of the way into *Rock Around the Clock*, his expanded role was significantly more than a cameo appearance. But Katzman still did not have Freed in the fold. No sooner had the producer accommodated Freed's call for a bigger part than Freed demanded an "up-front" cash guarantee instead of the percentage of the film's gross offered by Columbia Pictures. Freed told Columbia that without the "front money" he would not appear in *Rock Around the Clock*. But the move was simply a bluff on Freed's part. He "would have done the picture for 2 cents," said Jack Hooke. When Jolly Joyce told Freed, "Dummy, take a piece!" a compromise was reached and the deejay "yessed the deal in a second" for $20,000 up front and 10 percent of the movie's profits.

As the Teenagers' "Why Do Fools Fall in Love" shot up the best-selling record charts in January 1956, Freed took a leave of absence from WINS to fly to Hollywood and film *Rock Around the Clock*. Filmed in two weeks, the movie was no Academy Award winner; but then, it was never intended to be. The movie's minimalistic story centered around the question of whether the "new" music—rock & roll as sung by Bill Haley and the Comets, the Platters, and Freddy Bell and the Bellboys—could overcome the traditional sounds represented by the Latin rhythms of Tony Martinez and, in the process, win the minds of adults as well as the hearts of their children. Of course, the answer was an unequivocal yes. With an assist from rock & roll disc jockey Alan Freed (who handily portrayed himself on screen), even bandleader Martinez was eventually won over by the joys of the "big beat." Besides providing teenage entertainment, *Rock Around the Clock* was a pro–rock & roll editorial, aimed at the adult segment of society that opposed both Freed and the music, but Freed was not to achieve in real life the proselytization of his foes. As for the teenage audience, *Rock Around the Clock*'s music was what they craved, and Katzman's production provided plenty of it. The rock & roll stars were on screen for almost half of the film's brief seventy minutes.

Released in April 1956, *Rock Around the Clock* achieved instant notoriety, thanks to incidents of violence such as occurred after a group of youngsters left a theater in Minneapolis and snake-danced about town, smashing windows, causing the theater manager to cancel subsequent screenings of the film. Abroad, the situation was even more volatile. First overseas reports of rioting in the wake of *Rock Around the Clock*'s showing emanated from Dublin, Ireland, which prompted several West German theaters to attempt (unsuccessfully) to obtain antiriot insurance before showing the film in their country. Egyptian authorities thought of *Rock Around the Clock* as an "Eisenhower-led plot" to encourage Middle East turmoil by undermining the country's morale. In Copenhagen a teenage motorcycle gang, the Leather Jackets, viewed *Rock Around the Clock* and then proceeded to terrorize the city's streets. In Iran the Shah banned the film as a threat to Iranian civilization. In Great Britain the movie was shown in more than three hundred theaters without incident until a group of teens exited a South London movie house dancing and chanting Bill Haley's "Mambo Rock" (heard briefly in the film) and stalled traffic on the city's famed Tower Bridge. When the English tabloids blew the incident into a full-scale riot, one theater chain banned Sunday viewings of *Rock Around the Clock*. Somewhere in Liverpool a fifteen-year-old would-be rocker came away from a local theater disappointed. There had been no riot at the screening of *Rock Around the Clock* that John Lennon had attended. The country's music newspaper, *The New Musical Express*, editorialized with a large degree of lucidity that "hooligans were hooligans before *Rock Around the Clock* was ever exhibited" and "they have not suddenly become undisciplined and irresponsible because they have heard Bill Haley and his rocking tempo." Despite, or perhaps because of, the hubbub over the controversial film, Queen Elizabeth scrapped a scheduled Buckingham Palace showing of *The Caine Mutiny* in favor of a showing of *Rock Around the Clock*.

Ironically, although many of rock & roll's stateside critics branded the music as part of a Communist plot, real Russians in Moscow condemned the "fake folk music" of *Rock Around the Clock*. Back in the United States the Communist plot was given some credence by the Party's newspaper, *The Daily Worker*, which, while decrying the film's "relentless commercialism," nevertheless praised *Rock Around the Clock* as a "direct, refreshing film," and rock & roll as "nothing obscene." In pre-Castro Cuba the film was enjoyed by packed houses, and Havana became the scene for live rock & roll revues hosted by Freed's Latin alterego, deejay Rafael Zomavilla.

Given a boost by its unexpected controversiality, *Rock Around the Clock* grossed almost five times the $500,000 it cost to produce. Paul Sherman wryly reflected that Columbia "could have bought Freed for $15,000, and instead he made a fortune [from the percentage of the profits Columbia insisted Freed sign for]." Overall, Freed was "rather pleased" with his film debut, but he reacted to his own on-screen image and manner much the way people react when they first hear their own recorded voices. "He was sure he didn't look [in real life] the way he did on screen," said Warren Troob.

Rock Around the Clock became the prototype for subsequent rock & roll films. Although the performers fortunate enough to be included in them benefited from a rare opportunity to have their music seen and heard by mass audiences otherwise unaccessible to them (television still largely ignored rock & roll as entertainment), they were treated as second-class citizens on the screen. Few rock &

rollers received speaking parts, and their appearances had little, if any, relevance to the films' stories.

Observing the volatile yet mixed reactions generated around the globe by the release of *Rock Around the Clock*, WINS program director Bob Smith and deejay Jack Lacey embarked on a three-week hiatus across the European continent in March. Along the way they sampled the musical climate before returning home to report that Freed was now a worldwide personality and that Europe was "ripe for rock and roll."

Rock Around the Clock, the movie that "riotously introduced rock and roll to England" as well as to the Continent, in a matter of weeks established Freed as a worldwide celebrity. Radio station WINS, seeking to capitalize on the fortuitous situation, arranged for a taped segment of Freed's "Rock 'n' Roll Party" to be aired Saturday evenings on Radio Luxembourg, the most powerful of Radio Free Europe stations. Despite the bad press the music received at home, rock & roll "became a propaganda weapon" overseas, and Freed, with an established European beachhead, made preliminary plans for the "first full-scale invasion of England by rock and roll." With the hope that his Radio Lux "Rock 'n' Roll Party" would create a ready-made audience for him, Freed announced a tentative October concert at London's sedate Albert Hall.

As Freed filmed *Rock Around the Clock*, rock & roll continued to spread from coast to coast. One indication of the music's widening acceptance was an announcement by the CBS Radio Network that Freed was set to host a nationally syndicated weekly rock & roll program for it. A network spokesman acknowledged Freed as the "most popular of the men in rock and roll," and said CBS sought "someone of that caliber" to emcee its new program, which was to be broadcast on Saturday nights from 9:00 to 9:30. The announcement came as somewhat of a surprise because of the fact that both the CBS and NBC networks had made overtures almost a year earlier to several influential disc jockeys, including Freed, to host network music programs. At the time, the networks were rebuked by the local stations that employed the jocks in question because the broadcasting outlets did not wish to compete with their own star personalities. But Freed's CBS program was to be sponsored by Camel Cigarettes, a heavy network advertiser since the 1930s, and by granting permission for Freed to host the CBS program, station owner J. Elroy McCaw had placed WINS "in the advantageous position of doing a favor for a national sponsor."

Although Freed's new radio program was nationally syndicated, it was not broadcast live outside of the New York area because of the financial impracticality in 1956 of establishing a live network hookup for a once-a-week thirty-minute show. Instead, the "Camel Rock and Roll Party" was transcribed onto sixteen-inch discs and the transcriptions shipped to those CBS affiliates across the country (and to U.S. overseas military bases) that agreed to broadcast the program.

Billboard noted that the CBS-Freed arrangement was "of particular interest" to the broadcasting trade in that it was "unusual" for a cigarette company to sponsor a program or a personality so closely associated with teenagers, who were legally nonsmokers. Almost immediately Freed and Camel Cigarettes became embroiled in controversy over whether tobacco companies should be allowed to advertise to such a young audience. Freed (himself an inveterate chain-smoker) was accused of encouraging cigarette sales to teenagers. WINS station manager Bob Smith said a recent PULSE survey showed that "contrary to general belief," more than half of Freed's listening audience was over twenty years of age. Smith and Freed both recalled the deejay's Cleveland beer sponsorship, when Freed enthusiastically drank his sponsor's product in front of an open WJW microphone with no complaints that he promoted underage drinking. Despite the public brouhaha, Freed's new program made its network debut in February 1956, in front of an audience of about one hundred at CBS's Fifty-second Street Studio in Manhattan. To the wonder of many listeners, Freed's house band—which provided musical accompaniment for the Platters, the Four Fellows, and the Cleftones, among others—was that of Count Basie.

William ("Count") Basie, born in Red Bank, New Jersey, in 1904, enjoyed a long and illustrious career during the big-band era. But with the demise of big-band popularity almost complete by the mid-1950s, Basie, like other big-band maestros, had to "acknowledge . . . pop conventions" in order to survive. In 1954 the Count employed blues vocalist Joe Williams and put two hit records onto the pop charts (Basie's first chart success since 1948). By 1955 Basie, a close friend of Birdland owner Morris Levy (whom Basie said was "one of our biggest fans"), could count on being booked into the famed jazz showplace four times a year for three or four week stands at a time.

To commemorate Birdland's fifth anniversary Levy organized his six-week "Birdland Stars of 1955" tour, for which Basie opened for Sarah Vaughan, Stan Getz, George Shearing, Erroll Garner, and Lester Young. Following the tour, Basie made his first appearance with Freed, at the deejay's initial Brooklyn Paramount engagement, promoted by Levy that April. Basie again appeared with Freed at the Academy of Music show, also promoted by Levy, in December. How much, if any, input Freed had regarding the decision to put Basie on the "Camel Rock and Roll Party" is uncertain. The same could be said of Basie, who knew rock & roll "wasn't our thing." The proof of Basie's incompatibility with Freed's audience, as if the noted bandleader needed proof, came at the Count's Academy of Music appearance when he noticed the packed house "would get up and go outside to get their popcorn and ice cream" whenever he came on, not to return until the Count's set concluded. Basie said the deejay's young rock & roll audience "didn't care anything about jazz" and regarded the renowned Basie Orchestra as "just an intermission act." It is an attestation to the behind-the-scenes influence wielded by Levy that Basie, after playing to "an almost empty house" at the Academy two months earlier, ended up as Freed's resident rock & roll band. Nevertheless, Basie said he knew after the first week with Freed's radio program that his band did not "fit in any kind of way." By the summer of 1956 Basie (who, ironically, was to receive *Cashbox*'s "Best Rock 'n' Roll Band" award for that year) was replaced by Sam ("The Man") Taylor and a group of musicians that regularly appeared at Freed's live shows. "Basie is a good friend of mine, and musically he has the greatest band in the country," said Freed, "but it isn't a dance band."

"People were dancing long before there was rock and roll," replied the deposed Count. Basie would never again appear on one of Freed's shows.

About the time that Freed signed to host CBS's "Camel Rock and Roll Party," he entered into an exclusive recording agreement with Coral Records that marked the label's "first full-scale venture into the straight r&b recording field." Freed had been involved in on-again, off-again talks almost a year earlier, to join Coral in some sort of A&R and talent-procurement capacity, but the deejay had nixed the deal out of fear of aligning himself too closely with one label. Freed's contract with Coral was a straight recording deal, however, in which label A&R chief Bob Thiele said Freed would be employed "only as an artist" and would record "dance sets for teenagers to play at parties." Thiele also said the "Alan Freed Band" logo would appear on recordings of other artists whenever "additional r&b flavor" was deemed appropriate.

Finalization of Freed's recording deal came about after Thiele approached the deejay and said, "Why don't we go into the studio and record the Alan Freed Orchestra?" but although Freed subsequently signed with Coral, he never saw the inside of a recording studio. "Leroy Kirkland wrote the arrangements," said Jack Hooke, "and I used to go into the studio and do it all."

Kirkland was born in Jacksonville, Florida, and learned to play the guitar at an early age. He played in several southern bands, including Belton's Society Syncopators, before going in the late 1930s to New York City, where he joined the Sunset Royals, a band that included Sam Taylor. By then, Kirkland was doing as much writing and arranging as guitar playing. After a short stay with the Erskine Hawkins Orchestra, Kirkland began to write, at the request of Sy Oliver, for Tommy and Jimmy Dorsey. During the 1940s, Kirkland recorded with Jimmy Dorsey and received a degree from the Hartnett School of Music. Kirkland was soon hired by Herman Lubinsky to arrange and conduct sessions for Little Sylvia (Sylvia Vanderpool, a future member of the Mickey and Sylvia duo), Big Maybelle, and others. But the polished and professional Kirkland found it "very difficult" to work with rock & roll artists. When he attempted to improve upon the primitive sound of one Savoy artist, Kirkland was stopped by Lubinsky, who said, "I don't want no white music."

Said Kirkland, "That's what the company wanted. They were paying for it, so that's what they got." The arranger said he would often "go to sleep at night and dream of how not to write so good." He also began free-lancing for Columbia's rhythm and blues subsidiary label, Okeh (where he did many of Chuck Willis' sessions), and for the Rainbow label, where he worked with the Bonnie Sisters and Mickey Baker (the other half of the Mickey and Sylvia duo). Kirkland also arranged many of Mercury's Dinah Washington sessions for A&R chief Bob Shad. It was at the request of Shad, who was doing some production work at Royal Roost, that Kirkland arranged and conducted Roost sessions for the Duponts and for Eddie Cooley. "I was doing a lot of work for Roost," said Kirkland, "and Jack Hooke got me to set up the [Freed] band." Thus did Kirkland become Freed's musical director, who "hired all the musicians and everything [else]" for the deejay's stage shows and Coral recording sessions.

Jack Hooke said Freed's Coral recording arrangement was "no big deal" financially. It was also no big deal in a musical sense. The deejay's first album, *Rock 'n' Roll Dance Party—Vol. 1*, released in April 1956 to benefit from the publicity then being reaped from the deejay's appearance in *Rock Around the Clock*, included eight big-band instrumentals featuring Al Sears, Sam Taylor, and Freddy Mitchell, and four pop vocal numbers sung by the Modernaires, a group that achieved great popularity singing with Glenn Miller during the big-band era but by 1956 was struggling to survive the rock & roll onslaught. To create what Coral termed a live "party" effect, Freed narrated the record, introducing each song much as he would do on his radio programs. Although the liner notes touted the Freed band's "hard-driving uninhibited performance," which packed "a stronger kick than six Moscow mules," Coral's collection of big-band instrumentals and pop renditions of "The Great Pretender," "See You Later, Alligator," and "Rock Around the Clock" was of no greater interest to Freed's young rock & roll lovers than were the notorious cover records that Freed himself loudly decried. To make matters worse, sales of rock & roll albums of any sort were almost nonexistent in 1956, the 45-rpm single being the means of conveying rock & roll to its audience. Yet even Coral's release of four Freed singles that year did not stimulate the deejay's dismal record sales. Sadly, Freed's *Rock 'n' Roll Party—Vol. 1* was indicative of the deejay's subsequent recordings, none of which were a factor in Freed's career or in Coral's record sales. Considering the attacks to which Freed and rock & roll were being subjected at the time, the question remains whether the deejay's shilling for the Modernaires and his presentation of instrumental recordings that were more big band than big beat constituted an attempt on Freed's behalf to "legitimize" rock & roll to adults or simply another case of "business as usual," with Freed having lent his tacit approval for Coral to do as it saw fit under his name.

In the spring of 1956 *Billboard* reported that rock & roll had surmounted the "propaganda of pressure groups, the ill-will of Broadway-based music publishers and some pop artist and repertoire directors," yet the nation's media continued to focus on incidences of rock-related violence. In February, riots in Cleveland prompted its city fathers to unearth an ancient city ordinance that barred anyone under eighteen from dancing in a public place. Thereafter, disc jockeys in that city were required to obtain from the police special permission to hold teen dances. In Cambridge, Massachusetts, the city council approved an order that barred disc jockeys from appearing at local record hops, a move that came about after disc jockey Bill Marlowe of WCOP was nearly mobbed at one such function at the Massachusetts Institute of Technology. In nearby Boston, several deejays claimed they had been threatened by gangs at record hops who demanded the jocks play rock & roll. In Birmingham, Alabama, fists and bottles flew and four youths were arrested after a "wild" rock & roll concert in that city's baseball stadium. All across the United States "roughhouse riots" at disc jockey record hops prompted city officials to take action to stop such functions. Meanwhile, the national media did its best to promote rock & roll hysteria. *Look* magazine said attending a rock & roll show was like "attending the rites of some obscure tribe whose means of communication are incomprehensible" and could be frightening to an adult. *Time* said rock & roll does for music "what a motorcycle club at full throttle does for a quiet Sunday afternoon." Disc jockeys themselves were split as to the so-called evils of the music. Fred Robbins blamed some of his colleagues for the wave of violence, saying that by promoting the "musical junk" known as rock & roll, which was "a mere perversion of rhythm and blues, . . . too many [disc jockeys] . . . were failing to live up to the importance of their jobs." The underlying hope of a great many music business insiders was that rock & roll was just a passing fad. *Billboard* reported that a group of rhythm and blues disc jockeys would soon meet "while the r.&b. craze is still at its peak," to discuss ways of combating industry abuses such as payola and offensive lyrics.

With the country warily eyeing rock & roll, Freed booked his traveling stage show into the Hartford (Connecticut) State Theatre for appearances on March 23, 24, and 25, as a warm-up for his Brooklyn Paramount Easter show. Freed was aware of his disappointing venture into Boston a year earlier and of more recent events—most notably, the youthful disturbances that had followed screenings of *Rock Around the Clock*—that had Hartford city officials up in arms over what they termed the "corrupting influences of rock and roll."

The Hartford State Theatre had been a battleground over the future of rock & roll in Connecticut long before Freed arrived. Twenty-six arrests had been made there since the State began staging rock and roll shows in the fall of 1955. As Freed's rock & roll entourage approached, local police claimed that "public safety was endangered" and tried to revoke the theater's license. Although one local psychiatrist characterized rock & roll as "cannibalistic" and "tribalistic . . . [a] communicable disease" that appealed to "adolescent rebellion and insecurity" and drove teenagers to do "outlandish things," the State Theatre succeeded in remaining open. Freed's shows went on, but the Hartford police subsequently cited the arrest of eleven teens who allegedly had attended one of Freed's shows as proof that the controversial deejay's productions were indeed cause for rioting.

Amid such charges of rock & roll "cannibalism" and "tribalism," it was no surprise that rumors began to circulate throughout the New York–area schools that Freed was a mulatto (or, in teenage lexicon, "part nigger"). No doubt the deejay's physical appearance (including his wide nose, a result of his auto accident, and his kinky hair), along with his friendliness to blacks and his avid promotion of black music, lent credence to the rumor.

The racial slurs aimed at Freed were the national culmination of the raw southern racist response by white adults who saw integration (particularly after the 1954 court-ordered public school desegregation) as being fostered by rhythm and blues and rock & roll. As the *Rock Around the Clock* film spread inflammatory images of Freed across the South, Asa Carter, a representative of the Birmingham chapter of the Alabama White Citizens Council (with over sixty-five thousand members statewide), a leader of the anti–rock & roll forces, said the music "appeals to the base in man, brings out animalism and vulgarity" and is nothing more than the "basic, heavy beat . . . of the Negroes, . . . a plot to mongrelize America." Not long after Carter's remarks, members of the Birmingham White Citizens Council, enraged at the sight of their daughters crowding a concert stage in adulation of Nat "King" Cole, jumped onstage and beat the singer. Such violence was an ever-present danger for black performers in the South. Bo Diddley, a Freed favorite, told of South Carolina bomb scares and other forms of intimidation "where the KKK didn't want us performing." Count Basie (at the time, leader of Freed's house band on the deejay's CBS network program) said the attacks on rock & roll reminded him of the racist slurs that were aimed at his music in the 1930s when it was said that "jam sessions, jitterbugs, and cannibalistic rhythm orgies" wooed the nation's youth "along the primrose path to hell." Freed reacted by saying the campaign against rock & roll "smells of discrimination of the worst kind."

Jazz critic and ABC Radio quiz show host Leonard Feather said the music "appeals to morons of all ages, but particularly to young morons," and when the *New York Daily News* ran a fierce anti–rock & roll series that coincided with Freed's Easter stage show, the disc jockey labeled it "completely biased" and said the nationwide anti–rock & roll hysteria was a "conspiracy." While not naming names, Freed hinted that there were certain people out to get him.

While most of the nation's elders "fumed, fretted, legislated, and pontificated" against the monster rock & roll, barely perceptible voices of reason struggled to be heard. The pro–rock & roll argument was not that the music had artistic merit or even that it sounded good, but rather that the controversial big beat had teenagers dancing again. Paul Whiteman, the 1920s "King of Jazz," who was celebrating his fiftieth year in show business, thought the youth of his day were "crazier" than the teenagers of the 1950s. Noting that the "steam" that teens were full of could either "run an engine or bust a boiler," Whiteman said it was "good to see them dancing again." Kathryn Murray, one-half of the noted Arthur Murray dance team, said she and her husband were so enthused about rock & roll that they devoted an entire television program to demonstrating its "playful" dance steps. Willie Bryant, host of ABC radio's "Rhythm on Parade," defended rock & roll by pointing out that "you don't hear music playing on the corners where the fighting starts." Noted songwriter Irving Berlin, after recently celebrating his sixty-eighth birthday, said matter-of-factly, "I wish I had thought of the 'Rock and Roll Waltz' [a number-one pop song recorded by Kay Starr early in 1956]."

Freed's ten-day "Easter Jubilee of Stars" at the Brooklyn Paramount turned out block-long lines of teenagers (who were described by *Billboard* as restless "natives") that at times caused the police to suspend traffic around the theater. The impact of the media's ongoing hysteria over rock-related violence manifested itself locally as a hundred special police, many in plain clothes, patrolled both in and outside the theater. Special flashlight-equipped patrols roved the Paramount's aisles, providing an "intriguing, Alcatraz-like aura" that contrasted starkly to the lighthearted activities on stage.

Freed, infamous for running behind time with his stage shows, did his best to keep this one moving by limiting his own appearances to brief introductions of the acts. The talent—"heavy on groups"—included Frankie Lymon and the Teenagers, the Platters, the Cleftones, the Valentines, the Willows, the Jodimars, the Flamingos, the Royaltones, the Rover Boys, Ruth McFadden, Cindy and Lindy, and Dori Anne Gray. Sam Taylor, Al Sears, and Freed's rock & roll stage band provided the music. On the Paramount's screen was the movie *Battle Stations*, starring John Lund, William Bendix, and Richard Boone.

Hermie Dressel said Freed booked too many acts for the amount of time allotted for his shows, and when the emcee let somebody like Bo Diddley come out for three encores, "the show would just stretch out." Freed was also "getting heat from the record companies to give their acts stage exposure." Indeed, Freed faced the delicate task of presenting a show that was current and would prove popular with his audience while, at the same time, satisfying the boys.

Not surprisingly, George Goldner's and Morris Levy's interests were represented by three acts—the headlining Frankie Lymon and the Teenagers, the Cleftones, and the Valentines (who had been told by Freed that he "couldn't put them on the show unless they had a new record out" and that lead singer Richard Barrett should write one "immediately"). Hy Weiss arranged for two of his Old Town artists, the Royaltones and Ruth McFadden, to appear with Freed, a feat no doubt facilitated by Freed receiving writing credit for McFadden's hit "Darling, Listen to the Words of This Song." The Royaltones, signed to Old Town the previous November, thought they were "on our way" when they were booked to sing "Crazy Love" on Freed's show. Group member James Ifill said the Royaltones were "really on cloud nine" performing there because of the "unbelievable" crowd. But the Royaltones soon discovered the harsh reality of life with the boys. When they inquired about royalties for "Crazy Love" (which reached number four on Freed's own countdown list), Ifill said they were told by Old Town that "we owed them money." Because of the dispute, Old Town refused to issue any further recordings by the group. (Any artist who asked Morris Levy about royalties was told, "You want royalty? Go to England!") Street of Hope arranger Morty Craft's new Melba label was represented by a local group called the Willows, who had a big hit with "Church Bells May Ring." The new ABC-Paramount label, child of the American Broadcasting-Paramount Theatre Corporation, to which Levy had "a strong connection," was represented by the Rover Boys and by Cindy and Lindy.

Freed's overextended shows were not looked upon favorably by the Paramount Theatre because management wanted to turn over as many audiences as possible to increase the box-office take. Freed's attitude was different. If the deejay felt like doing so, said Dressel, Freed would not hesitate to bring an act back for an encore. Herb

Cox, lead singer for the Cleftones, said Freed constantly juggled the show's lineup so the Cleftones would not know from show to show "whether we were on third or eighth, or whether we were doing three or six songs." Although Freed had a great rapport with his young audience, "he had no concept of time," said Ray Reneri.

The Platters, one of the hottest vocal groups in the country, with three successive chart smashes in a matter of months, and the Teenagers, whose first two releases were currently on *Billboard*'s "Top 100" chart, were most popular with Freed's audiences, who did not seem to care what the other acts sang "as long as the rock and roll beat was there." A particularly loud roar went up at each show when Freed's wife Jackie was introduced and took a bow.

Freed's Easter show was the Cleftones' biggest stage appearance of their short career, a career that came perilously close to ending right then and there. George Goldner, taking care of business, had released the group's second record, "Little Girl of Mine," to coincide with the Cleftones' appearance on Freed's show. Herb Cox, the Cleftones' lead singer, said Freed was playing the record "regularly" as it moved up the national charts. The group, which had yet to meet Freed face-to-face, heard he was demanding and that they had better be ready when they were supposed to be. But the Cleftones, high school teenagers with two hits in two attempts, "were getting a little cocky," thinking they "must be pretty good." Carefree, the group appeared late for their scheduled 8:30 A.M. rehearsal time the day before the show opened. An irate Freed gave the Cleftones a thorough dressing-down before turning angrily to the group's manager and demanding, "Who the hell do these guys think they are!" Cox, who surreptitiously listened to Freed's "Rock 'n' Roll Party" each night at low volume so his parents would not find out, was "shattered" by the tongue-lashing received from the person he regarded as a hero. Cox's reaction quickly changed to one of apprehension for having offended the single greatest promoter of the Cleftones' records. "Man, what does this mean?" he wondered.

The Cleftones, outfitted in green tuxedos, wearing red shoes and sporting matching bow-ties, were nervous the day Freed's show opened. Cox said that although Freed "wasn't too friendly at all," he made a point of telling them they "really look sharp." Because of their nervousness, coupled with their lack of stage experience, the Cleftones did not give a good opening-day performance, but they got themselves together on the second day and drew a warm response from the audience. Freed picked up on the audience's enthusiasm and exclaimed, 'C'mon, let's bring 'em back to do one more!" Having already performed the four songs they had recorded for Gee, the Cleftones did not have "one more" rehearsed, so they capped their Paramount performance with a reprise of their set-opening "You Baby You." After the show, Freed visited the group's dressing room to say, "Good show, fellas, good show!" Instead of a disaster, the Cleftones' appearance with Freed proved to be their baptism under fire. Subsequently traveling around the country, the group became "fairly seasoned," said Cox. "But it was always a thrill to do his [Freed's] show."

Freed's ten-day "frantic rock 'n' roll rumpus" at the Paramount grossed $240,000, which broke Freed's own house record there. In his three successive Brooklyn engagements during the past year, Freed first grossed $125,000, then $155,000, and now $240,000, but he did not foresee breaking any more records there because "that's all you can get into the place with a shoe horn."

While Freed was at the Paramount, Dr. Jive Smalls packed the Apollo Theatre for his own Easter "Rhythm and Blues Revue," held from March 30 to April 5. If anything, the ongoing Freed-Smalls rivalry seemed to help both deejays. Obviously there was no shortage of paying customers to go around, and the shows themselves were of a higher caliber as each deejay sought to outdo the other. In this particular case, Dr. Jive, with an assist from Leonard Chess, may have got the best of Freed in the talent department. Chess was represented on the Apollo's stage by the Moonglows, Bo Diddley, and Buddy and Claudia. Several of the local boys were also taken care of with the appearances of Charlie and Ray (Al Silver and Jack Angel), the Solitaires (Hy Weiss), and Dean Barlowe (Joe Davis). Also appearing with Dr. Jive were Brook Benton, a gospel-turned-pop singer, the local Fi-Tones, the West Coast Teen Queens, and Harlem's own Schoolboys, a streetcorner group hoping to emulate the success of the neighboring Teenagers. Clad in sweaters, beanies, and white bucks, the Schoolboys brought down the Apollo house as they sang both sides of their latest record, "Please Say You Want Me To" and "Shirley." Dr. Jive's week at the Apollo was so successful that his show was extended an additional week and the Heartbeats were added to his line-up.

Herb Cox said Dr. Jive, who catered primarily to a black audience, was "pretty much" in direct competition with Freed, "and it wasn't always friendly." When the Four Fellows scored with "Soldier Boy" in 1955 and appeared that June with Dr. Jive to promote the song, Freed, who also drew a significant number of blacks to his shows, refused to play the record until Dr. Jive's show had ended its run. By playing "Soldier Boy," Freed felt he would be promoting his competition, which he refused to do. Since Freed's and Smalls's productions were often staged simultaneously, the rivalry sometimes led to problems for the acts, particularly the black acts, which could only appear on one show or the other. "We [the Cleftones] were personally in a tight spot, an awkward position," explained Cox, who said Freed's shows were always of the "highest standard" and, from the standpoint of money and public recognition, were preferred over Smalls's Apollo productions. "But," said Cox, "we were under a lot of pressure, primarily because we were black," to appear with Smalls. "Some people questioned whether we were betraying the black deejays. They felt we owed them something."

By the spring of 1956, Freed had to his credit not only his local WINS "Rock 'n' Roll Party" and his nationally syndicated "Camel Rock and Roll Party" but also a new international audience via Radio Luxembourg, a staring role in a worldwide-distributed rock & roll movie, and successive record-breaking grosses at his live stage shows. What is more, the deejay presided over more than two thousand fan clubs and he regularly received over fifteen thousand supportive letters, cards, and other messages each week. Still, the personal attacks aimed at the controversial personality grew uglier. Buoyed by a deluge of mail protesting the *Daily News* anti–rock & roll series, as well as by the record-breaking crowds at his Easter show, on April 15 Freed made an appearance on Eric Sevareid's CBS-TV Sunday news program, where, as a "primary target" of rock & roll criticism, he was "allowed" to state his case.

Filmed segments of a Camden, New Jersey, rock & roll show were shown, and several pro–rock & roll teens in Sevareid's live audience were interviewed. Sevareid also had on hand psychiatrists who, when questioned, said the violence attributed to rock & roll was "symptomatic of something wrong with the kids' home environment rather than with the music they listened to." In a special appeal to "Mom and Pop," Freed asked them to remember their own teenage years (and his) when Benny Goodman and Glenn Miller were to them "what the current rock and roll artists are to the youngsters today."

The deejay also claimed that current press accounts of teenage rioting were "grossly exaggerated." Appearing as a "surprise guest" on Sevareid's program was Columbia Records' A&R head and ASCAP-affiliated music publisher Mitch Miller. Miller, who would soon become one of rock & roll's staunchest foes, said that although no music can be called "immoral," the chief fault of rock & roll is that it "makes a virtue out of monotony."

With the opposition ominously circling him, Freed evidently realized he had few allies besides the boys, WINS, and his own legions of fanatically loyal listeners, with the continued support of the first totally subject to the fickle nature of the latter. With his parting words, Freed revealed the assumption—a fatally flawed one—of a bond between himself and his followers that ran deeper than rock & roll: "As long as there are radio stations like WINS in America, and as long as there are people who like [having] me around," said the deejay, "we're going to rock and roll until you don't want to rock and roll anymore, and then when you don't want to rock and roll anymore, I'll give you what you want."

Meanwhile, J. Elroy McCaw continued to transform WINS into a high-income low-budget radio station. Tired of leasing space in Manhattan's high-rent Fifth Avenue area, McCaw initiated a search for a suitable site that he could purchase. The station owner discovered a vacant second-floor in a grimy two-story building at 7 Central Park West that fronted on Columbus Circle and extended north up Broadway and Central Park West to Sixty-first Street. The building's most conspicuous characteristic was a four-story-high Coca-Cola thermometer. There were no broadcasting studios in the building, so McCaw had some walls knocked out and windows installed, and in a flash, he had his new studio. It may not have been soundproof, but it was cheap.

A new address was not the only change for WINS. Bob Leder had had enough of McCaw's cost-cutting schemes and had moved over to rival station WOR. In May, WINS program director Bob Smith left to join his ex-boss. McCaw hired H. G. ("Jock") Fearnhead to run WINS, and one of the new station manager's first acts was to drop the high-salaried "Bob and Ray" show from WINS's schedule and replace it with a new morning talk program called "Contact," which was hosted by resident sports announcer Bill Stern. Stern happened to employ as his "girl Friday" an attractive blonde Scandinavian named Inga Boling, whose life would soon change drastically once she crossed paths with Alan Freed. In the meantime, the WINS budget had once again been trimmed, and J. Elroy McCaw was pleased.

About the time that McCaw found a new home for his radio station, Freed found a new home for himself on the Connecticut shore some thirty miles from Manhattan in the thriving industrial city of Stamford, whose onetime residents included Joshua Logan, Vivian Vance, and Freed's boyhood idol, Benny Goodman. Freed purchased a half-century-old sixteen-room stucco mansion called Grey Cliffe, located on the exclusive Wallach's Point, not far from the residence of William F. Buckley, Jr. Jack Hooke said the place was "falling apart" and that Freed "had to rebuild the house." Also standing on the two grassy acres, bordered by 150 yards of private beach on Long Island Sound was a small guesthouse in which Freed planned to install remote broadcasting facilities from which he could broadcast his "Rock 'n' Roll Party," thereby eliminating the nightly commute to and from Manhattan. It was a prospect that J. Elroy McCaw and Jock Fearnhead were less than thrilled with.

Hermie Dressel, a Freed family friend since the deejay's days in Akron, was a frequent guest at Grey Cliffe. He recalled his first visit there, by which time the renovated house "looked like a stately mansion right out of England." The centerpiece of Grey Cliffe was a balconied, cathedral-ceilinged living room, of which Jackie was most proud. Naturally, she chose to begin Dressel's tour of the house there, but Freed suddenly burst in and exclaimed, "Bullshit! Wait'll you see this," as he collared Dressel and ushered his friend through the mansion, pointing out all eight of its bathrooms, "each a different color and motif."

During his first summer at Grey Cliffe, Freed told one reporter that he had put down $35,000 in cash for the property he purchased for $75,000 and that he carried the balance in mortgages. "That's what we got to show for last year's work—a house with two mortgages," said the deejay. What Freed neglected to add was that one of those mortgages was held by Jerry Blaine and the other by Morris Levy.

CHAPTER 8

Don't Knock the Rock

"I think Elvis Presley is a fine, well-mannered young guy, a wonderful performer with lots of ability. But I wish he'd shave off his sideburns."

IN May 1956, while noting the "striking parallel" between retail best-seller lists in the pop and the rhythm and blues markets, *Billboard* wrote of influential new rock & roll material that was making "tremendous headway" within the pop music business. The new material was supplied by what the trade newspaper called "rock and roll country-style artists"; who sang uptempo songs with a heavy beat. *Billboard* called the music of these artists the "back shack" sound. The particular style of music was not new, as it had long been a common practice for country artists to include dance-oriented up-tempo numbers on the flip sides of their more traditional ballads in order to satisfy the jukebox demand in roadhouses and honky-tonks. This up-tempo country style, called "hillbilly boogie, when it was called anything at all," paralleled the post–World War II development of rhythm and blues and drew heavily from the latter genre. Ironically, before 1956, "hillbilly boogie" singers faced stronger discrimination than did black rhythm and blues singers. While the latter received an increased amount of radio airplay as "rock & roll" artists, the former were avoided by pop and R&B stations as "country" and were shunned by country stations in favor of the more traditional ballad-style singers. These finely defined racial and stylistic music barriers were made obsolete early in 1956 when Elvis Presley's "Heartbreak Hotel" and Carl Perkins's "Blue Suede Shoes" both made unprecedented appearances on *Billboard*'s three best-selling charts—the pop "Top 100," rhythm and blues best-seller, and country and western best-seller lists. With the multicrossover success of Presley and Perkins, up-tempo records by other white country-influenced artists began appearing on some country radio programs, not necessarily out of a personal like of the disc jockeys for such music, but because some of the country jocks "felt it necessary to go with listeners' preferences." To satisfy the new musical demand, record companies began a widespread effort to discover and nurture white rock & roll singers. That May, *Billboard* noted that "everywhere the search is on for another Elvis Presley."

By that time, the twenty-one-year-old Presley was the singing rage of America. Whether people loved him or loathed him, almost everybody had heard of the controversial Presley, thanks to a series of national television appearances by the singer that began in January 1956. Contrary to popular belief, Presley's initial television appearances were not widely viewed. They took place on a second-rate CBS-TV variety show called "Stage Show," which was hosted by aging bandleaders Tommy and Jimmy Dorsey and produced by noted comedian Jackie Gleason. When Gleason signed the relatively unknown Presley (who had been rejected by both Ted Mack and Arthur Godfrey for their amateur-competition television shows) for six appearances at $1,250 each, it was a desperate move to boost the anemic "Stage Show" ratings. Few people watched "Stage Show" on January 28, 1956, as Presley was introduced to America by Cleveland disc jockey Bill Randle as a "young hillbilly singer." The "hillbilly cat" then hurtled headlong into a Joe Turner medley of "Shake, Rattle, and Roll" and "Flip, Flop, and Fly," before concluding, hips swiveling, pelvis gyrating, and arms flailing wildly, with Ray Charles's "I Got a Woman." The studio audience sat stunned, not certain whether to applaud, laugh, or boo. To the staid, sedate middle-aged fans of the Dorsey Brothers, Presley may as well have come from the moon as from Memphis.

On Presley's third "Stage Show" appearance (on February 11) the singer introduced "Heartbreak Hotel," his first release for RCA Victor, featuring a bizarre arrangement of the song in which Presley was accompanied by the Dorsey's screeching orchestra. Following Presley's final "Stage Show" appearance (March 24), on which he reprised—without the Dorsey Brothers—the rapidly rising "Heartbreak Hotel," Gleason declined to exercise the option he held for additional Presley appearances, citing "too much unfavorable mail" received from his viewers as the reason. "People were not only revolted by him," explained Gleason, "but they went out of their way to tell us."

After Presley's "Stage Show" appearances, each more widely viewed than its predecessor, the music industry noted that the radio and television networks were "finally beginning to have programming 'eyes' for rock and roll and rhythm and blues." Taking note of Alan Freed's CBS Radio "Rock and Roll Party," *Billboard* reported that CBS was negotiating for Freed to host a rock & roll show on "Stage Show," and that if Freed's one-shot appearance "clicked," the deejay stood a chance of a permanent rock & roll television show the following year.

While "Stage Show" viewers may have been vociferous, they were relatively few in number and caused no great clamor over Presley. Milton Berle, another famous comedian suffering audience problems, decided he would take a chance with Presley and signed the young singer for two appearances on his comedy-variety show at $5,000 for each show. On April 3, 1956, Presley was introduced as "America's new singing sensation," and (from the flight deck of the USS *Hancock*, docked in San Diego) performed "Heartbreak Hotel" and "Blue Suede Shoes." It was not until this television appearance, seen by an estimated forty million viewers and coinciding with Freed's Brooklyn Paramount Easter show as well as the scathing *Daily News* anti–rock & roll series, that Presley began to generate a nationwide storm of controversy. Such controversy resulted in a polarized response to Presley. While the "phenom from Mississippi" watched "Heartbreak Hotel" reach the top position on six of *Billboard*'s sales charts—retail sales, jukebox play, and disc jockey play in both pop and in country and western—making Presley the first "double Triple Crown" winner in the music newspaper's history, he was canceled after one week of an extended Las Vegas booking because of poor attendance there.

Presley received his two triple crown awards on Berle's June 5 television show. The singer, described as a "rock and roll sensation," introduced "Hound Dog," his upcoming RCA Victor release. Following this television appearance by Presley, the press began bashing the singer in earnest. Jack Gould of the *New York Times* described Presley's act as a "rock and roll variation of one of the most standard acts in show business, [the] hootchy-kootchy." Jack O'Brien of the *New York Journal-American* said that while Presley could not "sing a lick," he made up for his vocal shortcomings with "plainly planned, suggestive animation short of an aborigine's mating dance." Such "abdominal gyrations," O'Brien suggested, deserved equal time from burlesque star Georgia Sothern. WNEW disc jockey Jerry Marshall told his "Make Believe Ballroom" audience that Presley's handlers should be more concerned with seeing that the singer becomes more than merely a "present-day craze," ending up as "Pelvis Presley in circus side shows." New York critic Ben Gross wrote of Presley's "grunt and groin" antics, and syndicated TV critic John Crosby posed the question "Where do you go from Elvis Presley, short of obscenity?" Lost in the hubbub over Presley was the fact that the singer's latest TV appearance enabled Milton Berle to top the rival CBS-TV Phil Silvers show ("You'll Never Get Rich") for the first time in months.

While the critics panned Presley, the controversial singer sold records for RCA Victor at an unprecedented rate. In his first three months with the company, Presley sold 75,000 records a day, over half of RCA's total record sales. By May 4 "Heartbreak Hotel" had reached 1,350,000 in sales. Presley's first album was RCA Victor's first album ever to top sales of 300,000 copies, and the record company had over 300,000 advance orders for Presley's next release ("My Baby Left Me"/"I Want You, I Need You, I Love You") the day before it was shipped. With RCA having gambled with Presley having "emerged a winner," every record company mildly interested in rock & roll (and in increasing sales) began a search for the "next" Presley. Some companies, including Columbia (with Marty Robbins) and Decca (with Roy Hall), sought to make rock & roll stars out of country-oriented singers who had previously recorded hillbilly boogie and up-tempo country and western for them. Others eagerly signed any young white country singers who were willing to perform rock & roll; among them twenty-year-old Roy Orbison ("Ooby Dooby" recorded on Sun Records), seventeen-year-old Mac Curtis ("If I Had Me a Woman" on King), seventeen-year-old Eddie Cochran ("Skinny Jim" on Crest), Johnny and Dorsey Burnette and their Rock 'n' Roll Trio ("Tear It Up" on Coral), and nineteen-year-old Buddy Holly ("Love Me" on Decca). When the winner of Capitol Records' Presley soundalike contest, twenty-one-year-old Gene Vincent, pushed his debut record, "Be-Bop-a-Lula," to number nine on *Billboard*'s "Top 100" during the summer of 1956, record companies intensified their search for white rock & roll singers with country roots. Their musical genre came to be known as "rockabilly" (a combination of the terms "rock & roll" and "hillbilly"), a word that first appeared in *Billboard* in August 1956. Because of the hillbilly connotations that emerged in urban radio markets toward rockabilly, as well as the music's raw, uninhibited sound, rockabilly had a difficult time making inroads into those citified markets.

Elvis Presley next surfaced on Steve Allen's NBC-TV variety show (a consistent also-ran to Ed Sullivan's top-rated CBS-TV "Toast of the Town") on July 1. The "painfully subdued" singer appeared in a tuxedo and tails and sang his latest hit, "Hound Dog," to a sad-faced basset hound. Although it was said that Presley "rolled not—nor did he rock," when the television ratings were in, the singer's appearance enabled Steve Allen to best Sullivan in the ratings for the first time. Sullivan, who previously had vowed never to allow Presley onto his program, was forced to eat crow and signed the singer for three appearances at the then-astronomical figure of $50,000. Presley's first Sullivan appearance took place on September 9 and fifty-four million viewers tuned in, an estimated 84 percent of the total viewing audience. Presley introduced his upcoming RCA release, "Love Me Tender," and RCA promptly received nearly one million advance orders for the record.

In April, Freed had crowed victoriously, as well as prematurely, to his young fans that "the big fight [over rock & roll] is over and you and I have won," but Freed had not taken into consideration the flack that would be caused by Presley. It had been repulsive enough for some whites to observe blacks jump around and wiggle as they sang rhythm and blues and rock & roll while Freed encouraged them to do so. But those artists and their music, however threatening, could still be easily categorized and segregated as black entertainment, even if there were whites in the audience. And although there had long been outcries concerning overtly sexual rhythm and blues lyrics, there existed only a tenuous sexual link between black performers and their newfound white audience. But, as rhythm and blues historian and author Lawrence Redd has written, with Presley's emergence young white Americans had for the first time "a real live sex idol, all to themselves." Presley also led the way in the separation of the musical terms "rhythm and blues" and "rock & roll," which until 1956 had been used interchangeably. By the end of the year, white America would be claiming rock & roll as its own.

Ironically, Freed originally did not even consider Presley to be a rock & roll singer, explaining that he "really sings hill-billy, or country-and-western style."

As Freed prepared for his ten-day "Second Anniversary" Labor Day show, to begin on August 28 at the Brooklyn Paramount, a segment of the music industry "greeted with distaste" the fact that rock & roll was "by no means on the skids as yet." Freed's headline act, making his first New York theater appearance, was Fats Domino, who introduced his latest release, a remake of the standard "Blueberry Hill." As usual, Freed did not overlook the "boys." George Goldner's and Morris Levy's Gee/Rama interests were represented by Frankie Lymon and the Teenagers ("I Promise to Remember"), the Cleftones, and the Harptones. Jack Hooke's Royal Roost artists, Cirino and the Bow Ties, also performed at the Paramount, as did the Shepherd Sisters, whose just-released "Alone" appeared on the Freed-affiliated Lance label (named after the deejay's son). Jimmy Cavello and His House Rockers and the DeMilo Sisters, two acts Freed had been instrumental in signing to Coral Records, also sang on the deejay's Labor Day show. Atlantic Records was represented by Joe Turner, then a rock & roll star at forty-five years of age. Rounding out the bill were the Freed-managed Moonglows, the Penguins (managed by Buck Ram, a good friend of Freed's), blues singer Mabel King, and Jean ("the female Elvis Presley") Chappel.

In the Paramount audience for one of Freed's Labor Day shows were the deejay's parents, Charles and Maude Freed, who, while continuing to spurn their famous son's offer to finance their move to the New York area, had boarded a Greyhound bus and made the four-hundred-mile trip from their beloved Salem to view one of Freed's rock & roll shows. In his son's dressing room between shows, the soft-spoken Charles said that his son had given his young audience "a most important release for the frustrations brought on by my generation." As for his son's attackers, the elder Freed said he wished "those who spend their time attacking our country's teenagers would spend that energy in righting their wrongs" instead of passing them along to the young generation of rock & roll fans. Freed's mother sat with her eyes toward the floor and said nothing.

Meanwhile, a group of teenagers climbed onto a rooftop adjacent to the Paramount, and when their shouts into the dressing room windows went ignored, one of the teens tossed a rubber ball through Freed's window. One account said the teens were apprehended and that the Paramount audience, informed of the incident, "roundly scolded the unruly youngsters."

Freed called such teenagers "bunnies" ("my word for delinquents") and said it was "just outrageous" that all American teenagers should be indicted because of a few like them. For the most part, Freed's record Paramount crowd was well behaved, and the mounted police on hand to keep order were not needed. Freed said his young audiences "know in order to get into the theatre they need only to exercise patience."

The deejay's summer-ending rock & roll show drew over 140,000 patrons to Brooklyn and produced a box-office gross of nearly $221,000. That figure topped the $204,000 mark Freed had foreseen as impossible to break.

Dr. Jive Smalls continued to go head-to-head with Freed, but as rock & roll continued to become whitened, the difference between Freed's Paramount shows and Smalls's Apollo shows became more apparent. While Freed's talent lineups were generally racially balanced, Dr. Jive's remained predominantly (and, in this instance, totally) black.

On July 9, 1956, WINS extended Freed's nightly "Rock 'n' Roll Party" by two hours each evening, putting the deejay on the air from 6:30 to 11:00 each night, except Sunday. The increased airtime meant Freed would be in competition with himself on Saturday evenings when his CBS "Rock and Roll Party" was broadcast opposite his local WINS program.

It was also about that time that a rift began to develop between Freed and WINS management. With the completion of the remote broadcasting facilities at the deejay's Stamford home, which were linked to a master control room in New York, Freed began to do many of his nightly broadcasts there. "The station didn't want it," said Ray Reneri. WINS thought its star personality should be in the studio slamming his telephone book and doing all the things there he had previously done. But, said Reneri, Freed became so popular that "he thought he didn't have to go into the station every day." Freed grudgingly continued to appear at WINS, but there were times when he would show up very late. "He used to come in a half hour, sometimes fifteen minutes, before the show," said Reneri. "He was always going through some sort of crisis, whether it was with the press or with something else." As WINS began to send down memos telling Freed "don't do this, don't do that," the deejay began to feel the pressure. But he would not abandon his remote broadcasts. The deejay's producer, Johnny Brantley, boarded a Stamford-bound train from Grand Central Station each afternoon to bring Freed his commercials, newly released records, and his daily mail—usually more than a thousand letters and telegrams requesting certain records.

Amid the commotion caused by the emergence of Elvis Presley, some music business insiders did not realize that almost three years had passed since the November 1953 filing of the $150 million antitrust lawsuit by the Songwriters of America, charging BMI, the three major broadcasting networks, and RCA Victor and Columbia Records with conspiring "to dominate and control the market for the use and exploitation of musical compositions." As the controversy over Presley raged, the lawsuit remained stalled in the offices of high-powered Washington attorneys. Meanwhile, "Colonel" Tom Parker, Presley's crafty manager, had set up two publishing firms to protect his star—one affiliated with each rival song-licensing agency—no matter what the outcome of the ongoing ASCAP-BMI dispute.

With rock & roll continuing to become even more popular with the emergence of white stars, the Songwriters of America and their supporters mounted a "massive and expensive propaganda campaign" to convince an uninterested public that it had a vital stake in the outcome of the BMI antitrust lawsuit. The media was filled with anti–rock & roll statements and charges of subterfuge against BMI for the methods of promotion of its music on the air. Celebrities including Bing Crosby, Billy Rose, and Oscar Hammerstein sounded off against BMI and rock & roll, but one of the most stalwart of critics proved to be singer Frank Sinatra, who wrote of the "unrelenting insistence" of record companies and movie companies on purveying "the most brutal, ugly, degenerate, vicious form of expression it has been my misfortune to hear." Rock & roll, said Sinatra, was a "rancid aphrodisiac [of] every sideburned delinquent on the face of the earth," sung by "cretinous goons."

Amid this ASCAP-instigated propaganda campaign against BMI and rock & roll (no criticism was ever levied against "Rock Around the Clock," an ASCAP-licensed song), the Antitrust Subcommittee of the House Judiciary Committee, chaired by Emanuel Celler of New

York, which was conducting hearings concerning problems in regulated industries, such as aviation and transportation, on September 27, 1956, turned to a new set of hearings concerning network television. At this point the subcommittee put into evidence an NBC network interoffice memo relating to " 'Payola' and the Product 'Plug' " on television. Noting the growing media attention to instances of alleged payola in television, the memo posed the question of whether there was "a danger that an exposé [in print] of the growing payola enterprise in our industry . . . will spark a government investigation of our industry?" The memo was primarily concerned with "plugs" for merchandise offered on TV giveaway shows, and it did not mention radio or disc jockeys. Still, the memo offered proof that broadcasting executives certainly were aware that payola practices existed within their industry. Not long after the television hearings began, they were suddenly halted so the subcommittee could begin an investigation into the practices of BMI.

Celler, an outspoken critic of BMI and rock & roll, proceeded to speak his mind on the music he despised, conceding it "has its place" and has given "great impetus to talent, particularly among the colored people. It's a natural expression of their emotions and feelings." Celler also expressed his opinion that Elvis Presley ("If I may call him Elvis the Pelvis") and his "animal gyrations . . . are violative of all that I know to be in good taste." The subcommittee chairman also read a list of anti-BMI and anti–rock & roll statements into the record before saying that he was "quite convinced" that should BMI prevail, "we'll never hear serious and good music." Songwriter Billy Rose testified that most BMI-licensed songs were "on a level with dirty comic magazines" and decried the climate on radio and television "which makes Elvis Presley and his animal posturings possible." Rose described rock & roll performers as "untalented twitchers and twisters whose appeal is largely to the zootsuiter and the juvenile delinquent."

After much "name-calling and rock-knocking," the Celler hearings, referring to the alleged BMI "conspiracy," reached the less than earth-shattering conclusion that "the greatest song in the world cannot gain popularity unless the public is given a chance to hear it." More significantly, it was also concluded that the Department of Justice should undertake an investigation into "all phases of the music field," but since BMI had successfully weathered Justice Department scrutiny in 1949 and again in the early 1950s, the House subcommittee's recommendation left the song-licensing agency unfazed. The ASCAP-backed Songwriters of America did not concede defeat, however. They doggedly continued their search for some way to bring BMI to its knees.

As the summer of 1956 drew to a close, Freed's broadcasting horizons continued to expand. Because of what was described as a "strong mail response," especially from England, to the deejay's overseas Radio Luxembourg radio program, Freed began talking about producing a rock & roll stage show in the fall at London's Albert Hall. Warren Troob flew to London to discuss the details. It was also said that Freed had "blue-printed" an extensive European rock & roll tour for the summer of 1957. Ultimately Freed's hectic domestic schedule, combined with WINS's objections to an extended absence by the deejay, precluded any such English hiatus in the immediate future.

Shortly after his Labor Day festivities at the Brooklyn Paramount, Freed took a leave of absence from WINS and returned to Hollywood on September 17 to film his second motion picture. Convinced by the deejay's performance in *Rock Around the Clock* that Freed could carry such a film on his name, Columbia Pictures announced that he would have a leading roll in its rock & roll sequel. The film was originally to be called *Hi-Fi*, but after signing Bill Haley and His Comets to sing six numbers in the production, Katzman wanted to change the movie title to *Rhythm and Blues*, a curious move, considering the widening gap between rock & roll and rhythm and blues. In the end, however, Columbia opted for *Don't Knock the Rock*—what Freed had been saying all along—as the title for its second rock & roll movie. Bill Haley would again receive top billing among artists that included Little Richard, the Treniers, and Dave Appell and His Applejacks.

Picking up where *Rock Around the Clock* left off, *Don't Knock the Rock* centered around a group of hostile adults who banded together to prevent a local rock & roll show from taking place. Freed, again playing himself onscreen, along with singer Arnie Haines (played by actor and Coral recording artist Alan Dale), attempt to convince the adults that rock & roll is no more harmful that the Charleston or the black-bottom dance crazes they had experienced themselves. The height of *Don't Knock the Rock*'s dialogue takes place when the mayor of the town rages at Haines that rock & roll "is for morons, it's depraved!" As the teenagers gathered in the background begin to chant Haines's name, the mayor admonishes them that "children should be seen and not heard," to which Freed replies, "Boy, there's a quote from the Middle Ages!" Ultimately the celluloid anti–rock & roll movement turned out to be simply a "misunderstanding," and as in *Rock Around the Clock* the music was accepted by adults. If only such acceptance could have been gained by Freed in real life.

Musically speaking, *Don't Knock the Rock* was a notch below *Rock Around the Clock*. The film featured Dale's pop-oriented version of the title song (released on Coral) instead of Haley's more popular rendition. By the time of *Don't Knock the Rock*'s release, Haley himself was a has-been in the United States, thanks to Elvis Presley. The performances by the Treniers and the Applejacks were pedestrian at best. Only Little Richard and his driving seven-piece combo saved the film with high-powered performances of "Long Tall Sally" and "Tutti Frutti." Despite the fact that Columbia had expanded Freed's role in *Don't Knock the Rock* over his part in *Rock Around the Clock*, the former failed to equal either the quality or the popularity of the latter.

Meanwhile, the surprising success of *Rock Around the Clock* caused other film studios to jump aboard the rock & roll bandwagon. Freed had no sooner completed filming *Don't Knock the Rock* than he signed a deal with the independent Distributor Corporation of America to star in another rock & roll movie, to be called *Rock, Rock, Rock*. Produced by Milton Subotsky and Max J. Rosenburg for Vanguard Productions, *Rock, Rock, Rock* was intended to hit the nation's theaters before *Don't Knock the Rock*'s scheduled February 1957 premier. Completed in less than two weeks, *Rock, Rock, Rock* had all the markings of the rush job that it was. The movie also starred Teddy Randazzo and the sixteen-year old Tuesday Weld in her screen debut. As nonsensical as *Rock, Rock, Rock*'s plot was (it involved the purchase of a high school prom dress), the acting was worse. Since Weld's singing ability ranked below her acting talent, an unknown singer named Connie Francis sang the soundtrack vocals, which were then ineptly dubbed into the film.

It was *Rock, Rock, Rock*'s musical sequences that made the film a must-see for rock & roll fans everywhere. By granting Freed control over which artists appeared in the film (a power that Freed did not have for his two Columbia films), Distributor Corporation offered the deejay a deal he could not refuse, and as with his stage shows, Freed did his best to accommodate the "boys." Frankie Lymon and the Teenagers, who gave stellar performances of "Baby Baby" and "I'm Not a Juvenile Delinquent," remained George Goldner and Morris Levy's hottest recording act. Cirino and the Bow Ties recorded for Jack Hooke and Teddy Reig's Royal Roost label. LaVern Baker recorded for Ahmet Ertegun's Atlantic Records, and the Johnny Burnette Trio (in their only filmed appearance) and Jimmy Cavello and the House Rockers recorded for Coral, the label that Freed also recorded for. Teddy Randazzo and the Chuckles had song-publishing ties to Freed and to Levy. The Moonglows and the Flamingos recorded for Leonard and Phil Chess, as did the show-stealing Chuck Berry, who duckwalked his way through a spirited version of "You Can't Catch Me," a performance that in itself was worth the price of admission to the movie. The musical sequences were filmed in a huge warehouse-type studio in New York ("Just a couple of cameras and you," recalled the Flamingos' Nate Nelson, who appeared in *Rock, Rock, Rock*), and then they were rushed to California where they were spliced into the film.

Besides the filmed singing performances, the highlight of *Rock, Rock, Rock* was Randazzo's self-buttoning sports jacket. When several takes of one of the singer's livelier numbers—including at least one in which Randazzo performed with his jacket unbuttoned and another in which it was buttoned—were filmed, the best parts of each were then spliced together to form one cohesive sequence. No concern for the state of Randazzo's jacket was given in the editing, and in the resulting scene the singer's sports jacket appeared to continually button and unbutton by itself.

Released on December 5, 1956, as a top-feature attraction in over four hundred theaters across the country, *Rock, Rock, Rock* did manage to beat *Don't Knock the Rock* into distribution. The film played simultaneously in seventy-seven New York–area theaters, "amidst considerable hoopla." *Billboard* predicted that thanks to *Rock, Rock, Rock*, Freed "should be rolling in the long-green." Freed, Chuck Berry, and Connie Francis made an opening-night appearance at Manhattan's Loews' Victoria Theatre uptown, while the Apollo Theatre tried to match the competition by conducting a "Rhythm and Blues Week," beginning on December 7, during which the theater would revive Studio Films' *Rhythm and Blues Review*. In conjunction with the film, Big Maybelle, the Clovers, Etta James, and James Moody performed at the Baby Grand club. At the same time, Clyde

McPhatter, the Heartbeats, Della Reese, and Jimmy Cavello and the House Rockers were at Neopolitan City.

Freed's Brooklyn Paramount "Christmas Jubilee," which ran on December 23–30, simultaneously satisfied both the deejay's rock & roll audience and several of the boys. Featured on Freed's bill were some of the hottest recording acts in America, including the Chicago-based Dells, singing "Oh What a Nite" (Vee Jay Records); the New Orleans duo Shirley and Lee, singing "I Feel Good" (Aladdin); Los Angeles's Jessie Belvin, singing "Goodnight, My Love" (Modern); and Syd Nathan's "next Elvis," the young Texan Mac Curtis, performing "If I Had Me a Woman" (King), a song that received unusually heavy airplay on Freed's radio show, considering that Curtis was a true rockabilly proponent. The country-oriented George Hamilton IV performed "A Rose and a Baby Ruth" (ABC-Paramount), Screamin' Jay Hawkins performed what was to become his most famous number, the alcohol-inspired "I Put a Spell on You" (Okeh), and the Moonglows sang their late-summer hit "See Saw" (Chess). Also appearing on the Brooklyn Paramount's stage were the Freed-discovered truck driver–turned–singer Lillian Briggs and a host of local talent, including Eddie Cooley and the Dimples, singing "Priscilla" (Royal Roost); fourteen-year-old Barbie Gaye, singing "My Boy Lollipop" (Darl); the G-Clefs, singing "Ka Ding Dong" (Pilgrim); the Heartbeats, performing "A Thousand Miles Away" (Rama); and the Three Friends, singing their local hit "Blanche" (Lido).

The Lido label was owned by Leo Rogers, and "Blanche" was published by A.D.T. Enterprises, a firm fronted by Warren Troob for Freed. "Somehow, some way," said group member Joey Villa (né Francavilla), "I knew that he [Freed] was going to push it and he was going to make it a hit." Indeed, Freed did plug "Blanche" heavily, but despite the song becoming a sizable hit in the Northeast, it failed to catch on nationally. Rogers was not equipped to handle a large-scale hit, and complicating matters, the suggestive lyrics of "Blanche" ("I took a walk with Blanche, along the avenue of love and romance") caused numerous radio stations to ban the song.

The Three Friends, not used to performing with a sixteen-piece orchestra, had difficulty during their Paramount appearance. As another group member sang his part off key, Villa anxiously glanced into the wings to his right, where Freed stood, "tapping his feet, smoking about fifteen cigarettes a minute." Not wishing to incur Freed's wrath, Villa headed off to stage left as they finished "Blanche." But the move proved fruitless, said Villa, as Freed sought out the Three Friends and "gave us a balling out."

The success of the Heartbeats' "A Thousand Miles Away" showed that although the practice whereby white pop artists covered songs by black artists continued, because of the increased exposure black artists received on radio, in rock & roll films, in live stage shows, and even on television, much of the record-buying public would no longer settle for such white copies. In the latter half of 1956, no pop cover version was able to dominate the black recording it imitated, while huge rock & roll hits by black artists—including the Heartbeats (their version of "A Thousand Miles Away" reached number fifty-three on *Billboard*'s "Top 100" early in 1957, while the Diamonds' pop cover version failed to chart) and Ivory Joe Hunter ("Since I Met You Baby")—totally overshadowed their pale pop imitations.

Although the $180,000 taken in during Freed's "Christmas Jubilee" ended the deejay's string of record-breaking box-office grosses, it did not put a damper on his 1956 success. Freed's personal gross for the year doubled the $100,000 "neighborhood" figure it was reported the deejay garnered in 1955. The year 1956 was also a good one for the boys. While RCA Victor had Elvis Presley, they had Freed's airplay and his other promotional resources to rely on. Ahmet Ertegun's Atlantic label—which had experienced unparalleled eminence during the rhythm and blues era—produced two of the boys' top ten best-selling records for 1956 (Ivory Joe Hunter's "Since I Met You, Baby" and Clyde McPhatter's "Treasure of Love"), as did George Goldner and Morris Levy's Gee label (Frankie Lymon and the Teenagers' "Why Do Fools Fall in Love" and "I Want You to Be My Girl"). Others in the boys' top ten included Al Silver (the Five Satins' "In the Still of the Night" on Ember), Jerry Blaine (The Cadillacs' "Speedoo" on JOZ), Eddie Heller (the Bonnie Sisters' "Cry Baby" on Rainbow), and Jack Hooke and Teddy Reig (Eddie Cooley and the Dimples' "Priscilla").

Freed and Goldner also had a hand in the second-best-selling record produced by the boys. Local songwriters Bill Buchanan and Dickie Goodman came up with the concept of a disc jockey being interrupted by reports of flying saucer landings, and with Goldner's assistance, the duo put together their "Flying Saucer" novelty "break-in" record. Buchanan and Goodman's next stop was with Alan Freed, whom they convinced to listen to their record. Freed thought the "Flying Saucer" record was funny and that it could not miss becoming a hit. He told them he was going to play in on his show. The next day, WINS was inundated by requests for the "Flying Saucer," which precipitated a quick release of the novelty on the Goldner-owned Luniverse label. Buchanan and Goodman's "Flying Saucer" became a national hit in the summer of 1956.

When Freed entered into the agreement to star in *Rock, Rock, Rock*, he received 10 percent of the film's profits. As part of the deal, Freed formed Snapper Music, a publishing firm that secured the rights to fifteen of *Rock, Rock, Rock*'s twenty-one songs. Morris Levy's associate Phil Kahl held the publishing rights to the remaining songs. Before *Rock, Rock, Rock*'s release however, Freed sold Snapper Music to Kahl and Levy. No reason for the sale was offered, but most likely the transaction was in some way linked to the formation of a new record label by Freed, Levy, Goldner, and Kahl.

The idea behind the formation of Roulette Records was to capitalize on the influx of young white singers having success as rock & roll artists. Levy maintained that Roulette was formed largely because Goldner kept telling him he "didn't know nothing about the record business and it aggravated me." Goldner and Levy had recently received a master recording that had been issued on the tiny Texas-based Triple-D label. The two sides—"Party Doll" and "I'm Stickin' with You"—were performed by a West Texas rockabilly-influenced combo called the Rhythm Orchids. Since both sides showed strong commercial possibilities and each was sung by a different member of the group, it was decided to split the songs and issue two separate records with new flip sides. "I'm Stickin' with You" by Jimmy Bowen and "Party Doll" by Buddy Knox were rerecorded and issued simultaneously in January 1957 as Roulette's first two releases.

When Roulette was still in the formative stages, Goldner, who despite his steady gambling losses remained the senior partner of Tico/Rama/Gee Records, expected to function in the same capacity with the new label. Freed allegedly expected to receive up to a 50 percent share of Roulette. But Morris Levy, whose business practices involved acquiring and consolidating assets and power rather than parting with them, had other plans for Roulette Records.

CHAPTER 9

The King Is Crowned

> "As soon as the name 'rock 'n' roll' begins to sound like an archeological label to the crop of kids just turned thirteen, they'll find something new to call it. But I can't find anything in sight to challenge the big beat itself."

THE formation of Roulette Records temporarily diverted Morris Levy's lingering intention of acquiring Jack Hooke's and Teddy Reig's Royal Roost record label. As early as August 1955, and again in early 1956, Levy had made public his desire to gain control of Roost for use as his own jazz label.

Formed in the early 1950s, Royal Roost had specialized in recording jazz musicians. "That was my thing," said Hooke. "It didn't sell twenty copies, but I loved it." But Hooke's access to Alan Freed inevitably caused the label owner to try his hand at rock & roll. Starting late in 1955, Roost periodically recorded and released songs by local groups, but despite radio airplay from Freed, the records did not sell in any significant quantity. "I went into bankruptcy twice," said Hooke, "and I was struggling." Then, in the summer of 1956, Roost released a song called "Priscilla," sung by Brooklyn-born songwriter Eddie Cooley (who had recently written "Fever" for Little Willie John) and three women who called themselves the Dimples. By the fall "Priscilla" had risen to number twenty-six on *Billboard's* national "Top 100" chart. Jack Hooke finally had his rock & roll hit and "paid off all [of his] bills."

Another vocal group whose Roost recordings had gone unnoticed was Cirino and the Bow Ties. Freed cast the group in *Rock, Rock, Rock*, in which they sang "Ever Since I Can Remember." Ivy Schulman, the six-year-old niece of a Hollywood film executive, also appeared in the film and, backed by the Coney Island Kids, sang "Rock, Pretty Baby." Hooke released both songs on one record, but despite the publicity from *Rock, Rock, Rock*, few copies were sold. An Eddie Cooley and the Dimples' follow-up to "Priscilla," released late in 1956, netted the same dismal results as had the Bow Ties' record, but Jack Hooke was not deterred from his quest for another hit record.

The Duponts were a high school vocal group discovered in 1954 by songwriter-producer Paul Winley at Brooklyn's Boys' High School. Winley was sufficiently impressed by the Duponts to write a song called "You" and have the group record it. Winley then released the song on his own Winley label, but, according to Duponts member Anthony Gourdine (who would eventually become Little Anthony), the record producer lacked the "power" to get his records played on the radio. In those days, power translated to cash in many instances. "It was the days of payola," explained Gourdine. "If you had the money, your record was played." Winley did arrange for his friend, Dr. Jive Smalls to play "You" on the deejay's WWRL program for a couple of weeks and, said Anthony, "it probably sold about twelve copies."

Disillusioned with Winley's meager promotional efforts, late in 1955 the Duponts were introduced to Jack Hooke by another local songwriter-singer named Otis Blackwell. The group auditioned with "Prove It Tonight," a song written by Anthony. Hooke liked the tune and had the Duponts record it. Then he took "Prove It Tonight" to Freed, who thought the song was "great."

"Are you going to play it? asked Hooke.

"Yeah," replied Freed, "and on top of that they're going to open my next show at the Paramount."

The Duponts, accustomed to playing amateur affairs and local $5 competitions, were awestruck by the once-in-a-lifetime opportunity that suddenly lay ahead of them. The unknown group would soon open one of Alan Freed's famed rock & roll shows, not in Brooklyn but in the heart of Manhattan's entertainment district, at the renowned Paramount.

After a year of becoming "whitened" (and after a string of record-breaking box-office grosses by Freed at the Brooklyn Paramount), by

1957 rock & roll was ready for the big time—Manhattan's Broadway, the "Great White Way," which ran through what was then the entertainment capital of the world. Morris Levy had achieved for rock & roll what he originally envisioned after Freed's astounding St. Nicholas Arena success in January 1955.

Freed's first Washington's Birthday stage show was scheduled for the Paramount on Broadway, the scene of a previous generation's displays of pop music mania, exemplified by a 1943 concert at which the audience became so aroused by a skinny crooner named Frank Sinatra that more than four hundred riot police were summoned to the theater.

Although Freed temporarily commandeered the famed showplace, this was but one of three rock & roll stage shows in town that February. Broadway was also the scene of a show hosted by the Philadelphia-based disc jockey Douglas ("Jocko") Henderson, who commuted to Manhattan for his WOV "1280 Rocket" show, which originated from the Palm Cafe in Harlem. Jocko's "Rock 'n' Roll Revue" at the nearby Loews' State boasted a formidable array of talent and, except for the headlining Diamonds (with their hit "Little Darlin' ") and the unheralded Jo Ann Campbell, the show comprised black talent. Enjoying current national hit records were Mickey and Sylvia ("Love Is Strange"), the Jive Bombers ("Bad Boy"), and the Heartbeats ("A Thousand Miles Away"). Lewis Lymon and the Teen Chords ("I'm So Happy") and the Paragons ("Florence") performed their huge New York–area hits, and Jocko's bill was rounded out by the Clovers and the Buddy Johnson Orchestra, with Ella Johnson.

On February 22, the day on which Freed's show opened, Dr. Jive's "Rhythm and Blues Revue" began at the Apollo Theatre. Headliner Chuck Willis ("C. C. Rider"), the Love Notes ("United"), and the Drifters ("Fools Fall in Love") each had a national hit record, while the Channels, the G-Clefs, King Curtis, and Little Joe and the Thrillers were each well known in the New York area. Also appearing at the Apollo—at the time without a record label—were the Flamingos.

As if three rock & roll shows did not offer sufficient entertainment, three rock & roll movies also played in Manhattan. *The Girl Can't Help It*, the first big-budget rock & roll movie (it was filmed in color and featured top Hollywood names), starring Jayne Mansfield, Tom Ewell, and Edmund O'Brien premiered at the Roxy Theatre. Included in the landmark film were performances by Fats Domino, Little Richard, Gene Vincent, and Eddie Cochran, of whom *New*

York Times critic Bosley Crowther said, "The vigor with which they grab the spotlight and beat out their organized tunes reminds one of the way alert bullfighters rush into the ring when a companion is being gored." Freed's second Columbia picture, *Don't Knock the Rock*, accompanied the deejay's Paramount stage show, while *Rock, Rock, Rock* could still be seen at selected theaters in the metropolitan area. Three stage shows and three movies combined for a rock & roll feast of unprecedented proportions. If nothing else, it was a sure sign that rock & roll was now a significant moneymaker.

Freed boasted that although Jocko and Dr. Jive were also in town, his own rock & roll show was still tops. If the scene outside the Paramount was any indication, Freed was on the mark with his assessment. Although the chilly February winds that whipped through Manhattan's shaded man-made canyons made it no night to be outdoors, some of the deejay's fans—equipped with blankets and playing cards—began to queue up on Forty-third and Forty-fourth streets at 1:00 A.M.

As Freed prowled the Paramount lobby before the doors opened, he was told by the police that "he should keep his ass inside the theater" for his own protection. "Bullshit!" replied Freed, who wanted to mingle with the gathering crowd. "I'm going to go out there!" Protected by a cordon of police ("We almost got killed," said Hermie Dressel, who accompanied Freed), Freed proceeded to meander about the Times Square area and purchase all the coffee and donuts he could find. He then took the food back to the Paramount and distributed it to some of the chilled teens waiting outside.

When the theater doors finally opened, the eight-to-ten-deep block-long lines, extending west from Broadway, almost to Eighth Avenue, slowly began to move as thousands of teens (the Paramount contained 3,650 seats, compared to the Brooklyn Paramount's 4,400) jostled their way into the famed showplace. Just as many remained on the sidewalks, resigned to an additional wait for a couple of hours until the next show began. At one point, a segment of the line erupted in commotion. A spirited roar arose as one young male, sporting a prevalent well-oiled, pompadoured "duck's ass" ("DA" to the squares) hairstyle, with sideburns à la Presley, inadvertently crashed through the plate-glass door of a Broadway restaurant. The incident had a sobering effect on the teens, who "fell back from the barriers they had been trying to overturn." By midafternoon 175 police surrounded the theater to maintain order.

Inside, the Freed band appeared on the Paramount's rising platform stage to a tumultuous roar. After the band ran through its rendition of "Night Train," the deejay made his first appearance of what was to be a long day. Freed likened the "scrubbed faces" looking up at him from the orchestra to his own children, saying, "If they want to jump and clap hands, that's all right. If the theater gets a few broken seats, that's their problem." Many of the lively audience wore buttons that proclaimed their love for Elvis Presley as well as for Freed. Some of the teens explained that they "used to belong to Elvis," but they needed a new idol "now that Elvis is about to be drafted." It was difficult to tell who enjoyed the moment more, the emcee or his audience. ("I love being mobbed by kids," Freed once remarked. "I wouldn't want it to stop.") Clad in his garish red-plaid, gold-buttoned "lucky" sport jacket, Freed could not suppress his grin as he introduced himself to his audience as "the ol' king of rock 'n' roll." But Freed's bask in the limelight was brief. With six nonstop stage shows scheduled for the day, he knew he had to get things rolling quickly.

Morris Levy, rebuked in his 1955 rock & roll bid for Broadway enjoyed the last laugh, not once, but twice that February. Not only did he and Freed succeed in booking the Paramount for the deejay's show, but almost half of Freed's lineup—Frankie Lymon and the Teenagers, the Cleftones, Buddy Knox, and Jimmy Bowen—recorded for Levy and George Goldner's Gee and Roulette labels. In fact, except for the headlining Platters, Freed's February show was dominated by artists who recorded for the boys, including the Cadillacs (Jerry Blaine), Nappy Brown (Herman Lubinsky), Bobby Charles (Leonard and Phil Chess), and Ruth Brown (Ahmet Ertegun). And, as promised to Jack Hooke, Anthony Gourdine and the Duponts opened the show, singing their Royal Roost song "Prove It Tonight."

Ruth Brown recalled Freed's "seven-shows-a-day bit" and said that the deejay's heavy airplay of the artists who were scheduled to appear in his stage shows was so intense that "all you had to do was go up on stage and the band hit the introduction and the audience would sing [the song] for you."

Cleftones' lead singer Herb Cox recalled Freed's grueling schedule of six and seven shows a day and said the deejay "quite often worked you to death." But Cox also was quick to cite Freed's unique ability to encourage his audience to make each singing group feel at ease "as soon as they hit the stage." Cox, who maintained that the

Cleftones "gave it all that we could" and performed some of their "most inspired" shows for Freed, credited the deejay for the occurrence. At one particular show that February, the Teenagers' bass singer, Sherman Garnes, overslept and was nowhere to be found when the group was called on to perform. Predictably, Freed was furious, but he solved the problem by convincing the Cleftones to "loan" their own bassman, Warren Corbin, to the Teenagers until the late-sleeping Garnes appeared.

As with many vintage movie theaters, the Paramount (built in 1926) contained a huge balcony. Disc jockey Don K. Reed, then a teenager, was seated in the Paramount's balcony when he suddenly realized that "the ceiling, the walls, the floors [were moving] . . . it was an incredible feeling. You had to be there to really experience that." Hermie Dressel, playing drums, said he and some of the other musicians, as well as Freed, also noticed the balcony began to shake. At 5:00 P.M. the theater management cleared three-quarters of the balcony's sixteen hundred spectators as a "precautionary measure." Three hours later, following an emergency inspection by the city fire marshall, the area was declared safe and was refilled to capacity.

At 10:30 Friday night, almost twenty-four hours after the first rock & roll fans had gathered on Broadway, the last patrons entered the Paramount. By one in the morning the show was over—at least for eight hours, until the next day's performances began. Opening day records were set by the more than fifteen thousand patrons who attended Freed's six shows, as well as by the $29,000 box-office take. Theater manager Robert Shapiro called it "the largest opening show we ever had," adding that he had expected a crowd, "but not such a large one."

The marathon performance took its toll on Freed, who became "hoarser with each appearance" on Saturday. In his dressing room Freed pointed to a large cup of hot tea and honey as he told one reporter, "I'm pinning my hopes on this throat spray and on Grandma's remedy." When asked to explain rock & roll's success, the deejay said the music was simply "swing with a modern name," and he once again emphasized the captivating aspect of rock & roll's rhythm, reviving his theory that the nation's teens were "starving for music they can dance to, after all those years of crooners."

Despite the record-breaking crowds, Freed said he had viewed his Washington's Birthday run as "somewhat of a gamble" because unlike the deejay's previous shows, which were held during holiday weeks when schools were closed, this was his first New York engagement during four school days. When the ten-day run was concluded, however, a total of sixty-five thousand spectators had visited the Paramount.

Freed's Washington's Birthday stage show drew unprecedented press coverage. On his opening day the *New York Times* carried a front-page story with the headline ROCK 'N' ROLL TEEN-AGERS TIE UP THE TIMES SQUARE AREA. Also on the front page was a large photograph of the lines of people on West Forty-third Street waiting to enter the Paramount. The article was continued inside the newspaper, alongside photographs of teenagers standing on the theater's seats ("Blue-Jean and Leather-Jacket Set Find Rock 'n' Roll at Paramount Theatre the Most"), and dancing in the aisles, and of Freed himself. Several rock-related articles about morals and dress codes for teenagers, about proposed studies by psychological "experts" of the rock & roll "craze," and about the lucrative rock & roll merchandising industry that was developing also appeared in the *Times*.

Although Freed's Times Square multitudes forced the press to acknowledge rock & roll's presence, reports showed that the media did not understand the music any better than it previously had. While such newspaper coverage was unprecedented (only rock & roll "riots" made the newspapers in the 1950s), the media's demeaning attitude toward rock & roll mirrored that of society's in general. *New York Times* movie reviewer Howard H. Thompson called *Don't Knock the Rock* a "terrible little film" and said that Freed's stage show "took up exactly where the [movie] . . . left off." Thompson also warned that anybody over thirty who chose to brave Freed's show may have found himself "amid a composite of a teenage revival meeting and the Battle of the Bulge. And O-Daddy-O, with a slight case of St. Vitus Dance, compliments of the house—if it is still standing."

As part of its disparaging attitude toward rock & roll, the media continued to regard interest in the music as a fad, albeit a fad that was now "increasing sales for many segments of American business," including phonograph records, movies, television commercials, clothing, and emblems. And, not surprisingly, there was no shortage of "experts" ready to explain the rock & roll craze to the adult population. Educational psychologists equated rock & roll to a "medieval type of spontaneous lunacy" when one individual's odd behavior was copied by others. One psychiatrist said the rock & roll craze "demonstrated the violent mayhem long repressed everywhere on earth" and concluded that the music "is a sign of depersonalization of the individual, of ecstatic veneration of mental decline and passivity." Teenagers' fanatical reaction to rock & roll ("a contagious epidemic of dance fury") was likened to the Children's Crusade and to the Pied Piper of Hamelin. Freed labeled such talk "nonsense" and said that rather than making them delinquents, rock & roll "keeps them from delinquency."

Meanwhile, reports of the rock & roll frenzy from around the world caused many readers to believe the "experts" were on target in their assessment of the music. Theater seats were torn up in London, and a theater balcony in Jakarta, Indonesia, was caused to "sway precariously." In Vancouver, British Columbia, a rock & roll singer had to be rescued by police after his audience of two thousand teens went wild. Showings of *Rock Around the Clock* continued to touch off riots in Japan, as well as on "just about every continent."

In March 1957 it was suddenly made public that Freed and Morris Levy had terminated their business association. "Freed, Levy Come to Parting of the Ways," reported *Billboard*. The music trade paper wrote that the pair's "multi-faceted business ties" had been "abruptly but not amicably" severed the previous week. Freed's impending Easter show at the Brooklyn Paramount was to be the duo's final joint venture. Freed denied any blowup between him and Levy, and said their split would be a "quiet one" in which the two would "naturally dissolve and silently steal away into the night."

Whether anyone had ever silently stolen away from Morris Levy is doubtful, but in any event, the formation of Roulette Records was apparently at the root of Freed's alleged attempt to do so. It was said that while Freed originally expected to own 50 percent of the new label, "the contract actually called for a much smaller percentage." All Freed would say was that he was "not in accord with some of the policies of the [Roulette] company." According to the *Billboard* story, Freed intended to form his own record company and, having sold his share of Jackie Music publishing to Levy and Phil Kahl as part of the spilt-up, also form a new music publishing company. The deejay also said he would now promote his own stage shows. "I can no longer limit myself to one field," said Freed. "As long as I had so much to do with exposure of this type of music, why shouldn't I get as much as I can out of it."

Whatever the personal dynamics of Freed and Levy's relationship, at least one source has stated that Levy (who "never trusted anyone or anything he couldn't buy") was never certain of the decisions the maverick-minded Freed would arrive at and exploited the deejay's propensity for alcohol to control his unconventional business associate. Chuck Berry, who spent a great deal of time with Freed during the deejay's stage shows and movie productions, said Freed's heavy drinking was "a condition he was increasingly in." It has been alleged that Levy saw to it that Freed was well plied with liquor before the deejay entered into any business negotiations, "presumably to make him easier to manipulate." Whether Levy had a hand in encouraging Freed's drinking or not, Berry said that the deejay's semi-inebriated state sometimes left him with an "inability to carry out his [business] obligations."

George Goldner also was not "in accord" with Morris Levy's business intentions. Singer Lewis Lymon (Frankie Lymon's younger brother, who recorded with the Teen Chords) pointed out Levy's "junior partner" status in Tico, Rama, and Gee records. "You know how junior partners are," he said. "They like to become seniors." Which is just what Levy had in mind for the Roulette label. Not willing to accept those conditions, Goldner sold his share of Tico, Rama, and Gee records, as well as Tico Distributing Company, to Levy and Kahl for a reported $250,000.

One of Freed's new business ventures was the formation, in association with Jack Hooke, of Figure Music Publishing. Hooke, who said he "wasn't doing well" businesswise, was still striving for a follow-up hit to Eddie Cooley's "Priscilla." But early in 1957 Royal Roost Records entered into yet another bankruptcy.

"What the hell are you killing yourself for?" asked Freed. "I'm making all this money, and you're breaking your back with that shit. Give it up and come with me." What Freed had in mind was a publishing company from which Hooke would draw "whatever he needed" as a salary. The deejay told Hooke that whenever there was a profit, "we'll split it, fifty-fifty." Thus was Figure Music created, with Hooke owning a 55 percent controlling interest.

As he had done in the two previous years, prior to his Easter stage show Freed made a short road trip to Boston. Since his first disappointing rock & roll show there in 1955, Freed had faced adversity in that city. His 1957 show provided more of the same. Following Freed's April 13 stage show, blacks and whites reportedly clashed at a local subway station. Two youths were thrown onto the tracks and one of them was stabbed. Only the arrival of a subway train prevented further hostilities, and as a result of the melee, rock & roll shows were banned in Boston until tensions cooled down.

Three days later, Freed's ten-day "Easter Jubilee of Stars" opened at the Brooklyn Paramount. As with the deejay's previous stage show, nearly half of the performing artists recorded for Morris Levy, now in complete control of Tico, Rama, Gee, and Roulette records. Those artists included Buddy Knox, Jimmy Bowen, the Cleftones, the Harptones, Billy Mason and the Rhythm Jesters, and a local female group called the Rosebuds. All but the Cleftones and the Harptones were white, an indication of Levy's intention to blend rock & roll and pop to gain the widest audience possible. Also on Freed's bill were three acts with nationwide hit records: the Dell Vikings ("Come Go with Me"), Charlie Gracie ("Butterfly"), and the Cellos ("Rang Tang Ding Dong [I Am the Japanese Sandman]"). Other performers included Anita Ellis, the Pearls, the G-Clefs, the Solitaires, Bobby Marchan, and the perennial showstopper Bo Diddley. On the Paramount's screen was the theater-clearing movie *The Big Boodle*, a "tame caper of gangsters and counterfeit money, set in Havana," and starring Errol Flynn.

In the works for Freed at the time were two half-hour ABC-TV rock & roll shows to be televised on May 4 and 11. It was Freed's intention to bring rock & roll "into the living room" and thereby "show everyone in the family that this is a healthy, normal music." Reportedly, if the trial telecasts were successful Freed would be given a regular weekly television series that fall.

Freed's first TV "special," televised on March 4 from 7:30 to 8:00 P.M., featured live performances by the Dell Vikings, the Clovers, Screamin' Jay Hawkins, and Sal Mineo. The rest of the show included pop artists Guy Mitchell, Martha Carson, and June Valli. Freed's May 11 show also blended rock & roll and pop. Appearing were rock & rollers Jimmy Bowen, Charlie Gracie, LaVern Baker, and Ivory Joe Hunter, as well as pop singers Andy Williams and Edie Adams. The two shows were a far cry from Freed's notoriously boisterous stage productions, but the toned-down format was the price Freed had to pay to seek a viewing audience wide enough to justify network airtime (as well as sponsorship).

As Freed received network television exposure, the ASCAP-backed songwriting and music publishing forces kept up their attack on rock & roll and on BMI. Although they received little satisfaction from the Celler congressional hearings the previous fall, ASCAP members did manage in 1957 to bring before the U.S. Senate a bill to prevent ownership of BMI stock by individuals engaged in broadcasting or recording. The bill eventually died in committee, but the discussion over its merit once again raised the broadcasting payola issue. As a result, public awareness was heightened somewhat as the nation's newspapers and magazines discussed rumors of disc jockey payoffs to guarantee airplay for certain records. WNEW New York disc jockey Art Ford appeared locally on Mike Wallace's WABD-TV "Night Beat" show and denied rumors that many New York disc jockey's were on the take. Ford reasoned that the city's jocks were "paid so well" that they had no need to succumb to payola's "temptation."

As suddenly as it had been announced that Alan Freed and Morris Levy had severed their business ties, *Billboard* reported in May 1957 that the two had reassociated. According to the story, Freed said that Levy would once again operate as the disc jockey's personal manager for his live performances and television and movie deals. What took place to precipitate the reassociation is uncertain, but Freed, who once remarked that show business careers such as his were "so short you got to get it from all angles," most likely had learned recently a cold, hard fact concerning the New York rock & roll scene: there were more angles at one's disposal working with Morris Levy than without him.

One such angle was television. During the Freed-Levy "split" (Levy maintains he merely "stopped talking to Freed" because the two had an "argument for a few months"), Levy had negotiated with General Artists Corporation for an extended Alan Freed television series to be broadcast over the ABC network. Levy was to be the executive producer and Phil Kahl the associate producer of the series.

Another factor in the Freed-Levy "reassociation" most likely was the $11,000 mortgage held by Jerry Blaine on Freed's Stamford home. It was around that time that Blaine returned to Freed all of the interest money the deejay had paid to Blaine over the past year and "assigned" the original mortgage to Roulette Records, giving Levy control of both mortgages on Freed's Grey Cliffe estate.

Freed stressed the fact that he would not "actively engage" in Levy's other interests (which by then included Tico, Rama, Gee, and Roulette records; Tico Distributors; Kahl, Planetary, and Patricia Music; Variety Artists Management; and Birdland Star Tours, as well as the Birdland and the Embers nightclubs).

It was soon announced by ABC-TV that Freed's April television specials had proved so successful that the deejay would star in a thirteen-week series called "Alan Freed's Big Beat." Freed's series was scheduled to premier on July 12 in the network's 10:30–11:00 P.M. Friday time slot.

George Goldner, who denied any mutual business interests with Freed, maintaining that he and the disc jockey were just "friendly," said he was "surprised" and "shocked" by Freed's reassociation with Morris Levy. Since his sale of Tico, Rama, and Gee records to Levy in April, Goldner had not missed a beat in his recording activities. Almost immediately he formed two new labels, Gone and End, as well as a new music publishing firm called Realgone Music. To kick off his new enterprises, Goldner purchased a master recording of "Don't Ask Me (to Be Lonely)," sung by a vocal quintet called the Dubs and originally released on the tiny Johnson label. Goldner re-released the song on his Gone label in May 1957 and "Don't Ask Me" quickly became a national hit, reaching number seventy-two on *Billboard*'s "Top 100" that summer.

Off to an auspicious start, Goldner went on to record such acts as the Chantels, the Flamingos, and Little Anthony and the Imperials on his new labels, all the while "improving production techniques without destroying the quality of the group sound." Besides employing his noted production techniques (his record labels bore the message "Recorded under the personal supervision of George Goldner"), Goldner also put to use several of what were regarded as standard practices in the rock & roll business. The record manufacturer assigned several of Gone/End's song copyrights to prominent disc jockeys "in hopes" that the songs would receive airplay from those influential jocks. He also reimbursed television and stage-show promoters for payments made by them to Gone/End artists for their appearances on certain shows. Goldner also said he paid disc jockeys and "other station personnel"—including Philadelphia's Joe Niagara ($500 a month for "three or four months"), Detroit's Tom Clay ("approximately" $100 a month for twelve to sixteen months), and New

York's Dr. Jive ("approximately" $1,000 a year)—to play Gone and End records.

Soon after rejoining Morris Levy, Freed sought to bring his scattered family closer together. He now had four children: Alana, twelve, and Lance, ten, from his marriage to Betty Lou Greene, and Sieglinde ("Siggy"), three, and Alan, Jr., two, with Jackie.

In 1956, while Alana and Lance lived in California with their mother and Tom Greene, the two youngest children spent the summer in Connecticut. Alana said she and Lance were treated "beautifully" while they were there. Freed's two older children "just rambled" throughout Grey Cliffe, swam in the pool, and thought, "Gee whiz, this is super!" Then, in 1957, Tom Greene was transferred from the Camp Pendleton marine base to Florida. Freed visited Alana and Lance there several times. He also confided to Jack Hooke that he missed his children more and more. "I want to bring the kids here," he said. "We have to put Tommy Greene on the payroll."

After nine years in the marines, said Betty Lou Greene, her husband "wanted out." She was opposed to the family's move to New York, but ultimately Freed had his way. The disc jockey arranged for Greene to work for Roulette Records and to work backstage during Freed's live rock & roll shows. The Greenes rented a house in the posh Westchester County suburb of Scarsdale, just north of New York City, before eventually moving to New Canaan, Connecticut, a short distance from Freed's Stamford home. Betty Lou said that after moving to New Canaan she was invited to Grey Cliffe at least one Sunday every month and that she and Jackie "became very good friends."

Alana said she began to see a lot more of her famous father (including attendance at his stage shows), but although Freed's four children now spent time together, "there was such an age difference, I didn't really feel that I got to know either [Sieglinde or Alan, Jr.]." She and Lance each had their own bedroom at Grey Cliffe, and Freed's older daughter said she felt "very good about [the visitation arrangements], . . . very lucky we had the time that we had with [her father]."

Freed and Jack Hooke did not feel very good about Tom Greene, who did not share Freed's "true love" for kids. Backstage at Freed's shows, whenever Hooke turned his back, Greene would shout nastily at the teenagers gathered nearby, "Get outta here! Don't let me catch your face here anymore!" "He was the worst," said Hooke, "but we stood for it. As long as Alan was here [New York], Tommy Greene had a job."

One of the first of Freed's shows at which Greene worked backstage was the deejay's seven-day "Summer Festival," which began on July 3 at the Paramount. Freed put together one of his better lineups for this show, including Frankie Lymon and the Teenagers ("Goody Goody"), Chuck Berry ("School Day" and "You Can't Catch Me"), Johnnie and Joe ("Over the Mountain, Across the Sea"), the Everly Brothers ("Bye Bye Love"), the Dubs ("Don't Ask Me"), Jodie Sands ("With All My Heart"), the Moonglows ("Please Send Me Someone to Love"), LaVern Baker ("Jim Dandy Got Married"), Clyde McPhatter ("Just to Hold My Hand"), and fifteen-year-old Canadian-born Paul Anka ("Diana"), the first of rock & roll's teen idols. Lewis Lymon and the Teen Chords, Joe Turner, Teddy Randazzo, and Screamin' Jay Hawkins, local favorites whose records sold well in the New York area, also performed.

Perhaps the most memorable performance at Freed's summer Paramount show was given by Hawkins, whose drunken, diabolical rendition of "I Put a Spell on You" became a big New York hit the previous year, establishing the singer in R&B circles as the "black Vincent Price." Freed thought it would be a great promotional gimmick for Hawkins to emerge onstage from a closed coffin, and the deejay arranged to have one brought backstage. But people who saw the coffin cautioned Freed against following through with his idea. "Don't tell me what to do!" replied the deejay.

Freed confronted Hawkins in a backstage elevator and told the singer, "I have just the thing for you." But when Hawkins saw the coffin and learned of Freed's scheme, he refused to go along with it. "Go on and do it," urged Freed as he reached into his pocket, produced a roll of cash, and peeled off a hundred-dollar bill. Still, Hawkins refused to get into the coffin. "Are you sure?" asked Freed.

"Yes," replied Hawkins.

Freed produced another hundred-dollar bill, but the singer still refused to get into the coffin. But when Freed had $1,000 in his hand, Hawkins "was in the coffin and loving it." His Paramount performance that summer thus solidified Hawkins' ghoulish stage image, an impression that would dog Hawkins throughout his career.

The surging, overflowing teenage crowds drawn to the Paramount the previous February were nowhere to be seen at Freed's opening day in July. To the press, that in itself was newsworthy. Perhaps the rock & roll craze was indeed coming to an end. ROCK 'N' ROLLERS COLLECT CALMLY, trumpeted the headline in the *New York Times*. In the story, much was made of how New York's rock & roll "enthusiasts" had "fooled" the police by "behaving quietly." Photographs bore testimony to the empty sidewalks and needlessly erected police barricades surrounding the Paramount. Although about a thousand teens had gathered on Broadway for Freed's 8:00 A.M. opening, once they were inside the theater, no lines appeared.

Inside the Paramount, Freed's fans "were as enthusiastic as last February." Between shows Freed patiently explained to reporters eager to herald the demise of rock & roll that the music was as popular as ever. He reminded the press that last February the much-heralded opening-day rush occurred on Washington's Birthday, a school holiday. With schools now closed for summer vacation, explained Freed, the crowds would be spread evenly throughout the week. His assessment proved correct. At the conclusion of Freed's summer run, talent booker Tim Gale wryly stated, "Rock and roll may be dead, but Alan Freed just racked up some of the biggest grosses of his career at the Paramount."

Indeed, a Teen Age Survey, Inc. poll showed that rock & roll disc jockeys in New York were "stronger than ever," although there was a trend toward "ballads and sweet music." Freed and WINS radio headed the poll as New York's most popular disc jockey and radio station.

Buoyed by his impressive local ratings, Freed and his prime-time ABC network "Big Beat" television show debuted on Friday, July 12. *TV Guide* noted that Freed would serve as "host and conductor for a new series of half-hour sessions of popular music, featuring recording stars." Freed's debut show—a restrained venture into America's living rooms, where some of the deejay's most caustic critics lurked about—was understandably tame in comparison to his stage shows and leaned heavily on white pop music. The Everly Brothers ("Bye Bye Love"), Ferlin Husky ("Gone"), Don Rondo ("White Silver Sands"), the Billy Williams Quartet ("I'm Gonna Sit Right Down and Write Myself a Letter"), Nancy Whiskey and the Charles McDevitt Skiffle Group ("Freight Train"), and Johnnie and Joe ("Over the Mountain, Across the Sea") each lip-synced their huge chart hits, while a still-unknown local singer named Connie Francis—a half year away from her first hit record—also performed.

The show pulled such impressive ratings that *Billboard* noted some of Freed's "more ambitious plans . . . may have to be delayed" if ABC exercised its option, extending the deejay's television obligations to the end of 1957.

While Freed's "Big Beat" television success was said to be a "healthy sign for the music with a beat," in truth, the "big beat" was being toned down for wider public acceptance. On July 19 true rock & rollers Chuck Berry and Frankie Lymon appeared on Freed's "Big Beat," but so did pop singers Andy Williams, Betty Johnson, Martha Carson, and the Fontane Sisters (who mouthed their cover version of the Jimmy Bowen hit "I'm Stickin' with You"). As with Freed's first "Big Beat" telecast, he again turned the show business spotlight on an unknown singer. This time it was a television-commercial jingle writer who wrote rock & roll records on the side. Twenty-one-year-old Bobby Darin was unhappy that none of his songs had proven successful. Thinking that he could perform his songs better than anyone else, Darin signed a recording contract with Decca Records in 1956, but five single releases of his own flopped and the singer was dropped by Decca. In 1957 Darin was signed to Ahmet Ertegun's Atco label and mouthed his first Atco release, "Talk to Me Something," on Freed's "Big Beat." It would be a full year (and two more unheralded Atco releases), however, before Darin broke big on the rock & roll scene with "Splish Splash."

Amid the accolades for Freed's "Big Beat" television show, the host unwittingly presided over an incident that would allegedly lead to the show's cancellation. "Alan's show closed with the kids in the audience coming out and dancing," explained Jack Hooke. As Freed's second "Big Beat" ended, Frankie Lymon "grabbed a little white girl and started to dance with her." Most likely the event went unnoticed by Freed, but such was not the case with ABC's affiliated stations throughout the South, where, said Hooke, "the flack was unbelievable." Leroy Kirkland, musical director for Freed's "Big Beat," said that after the Lymon incident the show's sponsors said it could continue, "but only if they had all ofay [white] acts. Alan refused, and the show was discontinued."

While Freed's "Big Beat" faced cancellation, there was no public knowledge of the crisis (talent booker Jolly Joyce said the show "continues rating kudos from the rock and roll public"). To his viewers, it seemed like business as usual on July 26 when Freed featured Fats Domino, Clyde McPhatter, and Dale Hawkins on an otherwise country-oriented show with Marvin Rainwater, Jimmy Newman, and Patsy Cline.

Freed's fourth "Big Beat" telecast, on August 2, featured Mickey and Sylvia, the Four Coins, Gogi Grant, and an unknown Mercury Records' recording group called the Tyrones. This would have been Freed's tamest talent lineup ever, but for the appearance of Jerry Lee Lewis, the twenty-one-year-old rockabilly singer from Ferriday, Louisiana, fresh from his national television debut on Steve Allen's Sunday evening NBC variety hour the previous week. The "killer" performed "Whole Lot of Shakin' Going On," a performance that culminated with Lewis perched atop his piano. Unbeknownst to his viewers, this was Freed's final "Big Beat" telecast.

Perhaps the ABC network had bowed to southern pressure when they canceled Freed, but there had been an undercurrent of uneasiness concerning his show since its inception. At the time, the broadcasting networks and their national sponsors were cognizant not only of rock & roll's somewhat limited adult appeal but also of the outright hatred of the music still expressed by society. As Harry Castleman and Walter J. Podrazik noted in their book *Watching TV: Four Decades of American Television,* Freed's "rough, unpolished manner—while perfect for his live stage shows—was unsuited to the demands of network television." Although the deejay did present a toned-down, pop-oriented show, he often seemed "preoccupied in creating the frenzied movement" his live rock & roll shows were noted for. Thus, to those viewers unfamiliar with Freed, the deejay's "Big Beat" telecasts "appeared visually confusing and Freed's own supercharged demeanor somewhat threatening."

Perhaps it was merely coincidence that ABC planned to debut a daily afternoon rock & roll show called "American Bandstand" on August 5, 1957, three days after Freed's final "Big Beat" telecast. "Bandstand" had begun as a local telecast in Philadelphia in 1952, shown on the ABC-affiliated WFIL-TV. It was originally hosted by WFIL radio nighttime deejay Bob Horn and announcer-pitchman Lee Stewart. The show's intent was mostly to fill time in the deadly late-afternoon hours when viewing audiences were at their lowest. Horn and Stewart showed old filmed song clips, made calls to viewers at home, and interviewed guests in the studio at Forty-sixth and Market streets. Horn and Stewart requested a live studio audience, and since a Catholic high school was located nearby, the audience turned out to be predominantly high school girls. Some of the girls began to dance to the musical clips and when a cameraman focused on them, the director put the shot on the television screen. Almost immediately WFIL-TV was inundated by callers who said they enjoyed watching the teens dance and wanted more. Gradually the old film clips were replaced by artists who appeared to lip-sync their records, and "Bandstand" soon drew as much as 60 percent of Philadelphia's viewing audience.

Lee Stewart left "Bandstand," and Bob Horn had the show all to himself. But in 1956, during a time when WFIL's owner, the *Philadelphia Enquirer*, was conducting a campaign against drunken driving, Horn was arrested for driving while intoxicated. Compounding Horn's misfortune, he was accused of statutory rape of a fourteen-year-old girl who allegedly was a member of a local teenage vice ring. Although Horn was eventually acquitted of the rape charge, he was finished in Philadelphia.

To weather the scandal, WFIL needed a personality with a clean-cut image, somebody who appeared beyond reproach. With his freshly scrubbed look and neatly groomed hair, twenty-six-year-old Richard Wagstaff Clark radiated an aura of respectability. As rock critic Richard Goldstein wrote of Clark, "there were no skeletons in his split-level closet, just a lot of two-button jackets and ties." Originally hired by WFIL radio in 1952 as a summer replacement, Clark was kept on. Eventually he and Bob Horn shared an afternoon radio program, but since the hours conflicted with Horn's televised "Bandstand" show, he did only fifteen minutes on radio before Clark took over each afternoon.

Clark replaced Horn as WFIL-TV's "Bandstand" host in July 1956. Neatly dressed, warm, and articulate, Clark proceeded to provide the "necessary stabilizing control and guidance" for a televised rock & roll program. (Capitol Records' Joe Smith said that while Freed came across on television as "gruff, a street man, New York rock and roll, tough," Dick Clark was "Middle America, nice, a white-bread face.")

By 1957 Clark and "Bandstand" were so popular that the ABC network decided to broadcast the show nationally. In the middle of a local television engineering strike that left the show (now called "American Bandstand") a "technical shambles," Dick Clark made his network debut at 3:00 P.M. on August 5. After one week, *Billboard* described the show as a "mild success."

Jack Hooke said Freed at first regarded Clark as nothing more than an "imitator," but the truth was that with the loss of his "Big

Beat" network show, Freed would find it impossible to compete on an equal basis with Clark's impressive national figures.

Following the cancellation of Freed's television series, he renewed talk of a rock & roll tour of England in September or October. The deejay reportedly would receive $25,000 a week for emceeing the tour and bringing with him his own band and "a couple of U.S. acts." There was also talk of Freed hosting an eight-week stage show at the Paramount, during which the deejay would present a new show each week from November until Christmas. Those plans were shelved, however, when it was announced that Freed would return to Hollywood in October to begin filming his fourth rock & roll movie, the semiautobiographical *Mr. Rock and Roll,* which purported to show Freed's involvement with the birth of rock & roll.

No matter how heavy his business schedule, Freed found time to party. He periodically hosted gala music industry bashes at Grey Cliffe that were attended by the boys, as well as other friends, performers, and music-related individuals. "He did entertain a lot," remembered daughter Alana, who recalled a liquor truck from a local store arriving to restock her father's basement bar prior to a scheduled party. It was not necessary that a party be thrown for Freed's friends and acquaintances to appear at Grey Cliffe. Freed's younger brother, David, called Alan's Connecticut estate "sort of a home for the down-and-out" and said that whenever he visited Grey Cliffe, he found several record people or musicians down on their luck there, "drinking Scotch, eating a steak, and listening to music."

Freed's annual summer-ending party came to be a Grey Cliffe tradition. *Billboard* noted that "many top r&b tradesters" attended Freed's party of August 26, 1957. Among the guests were Bob Rolontz (RCA/Vik Records); Bob Thiele (Coral Records); Sam Clark (president of ABC-Paramount Records); Bob Leder and Bob Smith (ex-WINS station executives, then working for WOR radio); Ahmet Ertegun, Jerry Wexler, and Herb Abramson (Atlantic Records); Johnny Halonka and Harry Aposteleris (Alpha Record Distributors); Morris Levy and Joe Kolsky (Roulette Records); and attorney Warren Troob, in addition to other "radio, TV and film personalities." Entertainment was provided by Leroy Kirkland, Al Sears, Panama Francis, Leon Merian, and Teddy Randazzo (who then recorded for Vik Records). Whenever Freed threw a party, he would call Kirkland, his musical director, and ask what the pay scale for musicians was. When

Kirkland told the deejay it was $16 a night, Freed replied, "Well, pay them thirty-two, we're gonna have a party."

This particular party ended with some guests receiving an "involuntary dunking" in Freed's huge, flagstone-surrounded pool, a gift from Ahmet Ertegun that was touted by Freed as being the most expensive feature of Grey Cliffe. On one occasion, Morris Levy allegedly told Freed that Ertegun was upset because the deejay "wasn't playing enough Atlantic records." Freed said that as soon as Atlantic released something the deejay considered "good enough," he would play it. Levy expressed his displeasure with Freed's response and reminded him who had paid for the deejay's swimming pool. Freed responded that if Ertegun "didn't like it, he could fill [the pool] in."

Jack Hooke recalled the time when Freed ("who had never been on a boat in his life") decided that since there was a private dock on his property, he would buy a speedboat. One day Hooke, an avid fisherman, received a call from Freed. "Come on up," said the deejay. "I bought a Chris-Craft." Hooke and the boat, a mahogany-finished nineteen-footer with dual inboard engines, arrived about the same time. As one of the deliverymen handed Freed the keys, the landlubber deejay sheepishly said, "Well, I never ran a boat." The deliveryman told Freed to get on board and he would show the new owner how to operate the craft. Hooke and Freed climbed aboard, and as the deliveryman untied the boat, he instructed Freed to turn the ignition key. Then, pointing to the throttle, he said to Freed, "Alright, push this lever down." Freed gingerly did so, but the boat hardly moved. "Push it down a little more," he was told. Freed jammed the throttle down, and as the boat lurched forward with a powerful jerk, the deejay was thrown back in his seat. Hooke roared with laughter as the deliveryman casually remarked to Freed, "Fast boat, isn't it?

"I don't want to drive it," said the shaken Freed. "Take me back to the dock!" When they returned to shore, Freed grabbed the keys, thrust them at his friend, and said, "Hooke, the boat is yours!"

Despite the partying and carousing at Grey Cliffe's pastoral waterside setting, Alan and Jackie began to experience marital problems and ultimately spent their final years together there living a double life. The harmoniousness of the couple grew to be merely a stage act for the deejay's audience. Betty Lou Greene said that when she and Freed were first married, he told her he thought every man should have three wives—one to be "a wife and a mother, one for a business partner, and one for a social life." Jackie, said Betty Lou, had become Freed's "business partner," and she was not happy with her role.

Alana Freed said although Jackie "did a beautiful job" as Freed's secretary, "it was not what she wanted." The deejay's daughter maintained that Jackie was very much like Alana's mother, in that she "wanted to be a very typical down-to-earth homebody." But her famous husband's life-style and ego did not allow her to live that way. Freed demanded the illusion of a devoted, loving wife and mother who actively supported his career in every way possible. Judging from the mail received by the couple from Freed's listeners, the illusion was successful. Besides dedicating songs to boyfriends, girlfriends, and friends, the deejay's audience would also regularly dedicate songs to "Alan, Jackie, and all the little Freeds." And Freed did his utmost to foster the image (a family portrait of Freed, Jackie, and their four children appeared in his 1957 Labor Day show program book), with on-the-air messages that "Jackie and I" wanted to convey to his listeners and the introduction of his wife to his stage-show audiences. But Jay Hawkins, who likened Freed, Jackie, and Jack Hooke to "the Three Musketeers," also recalled overhearing the deejay and his wife argue backstage about his being away from home so often. "You're married to me and you're married to rock & roll," said Jackie. "One of them has to go!"

Jackie "wanted to be a mother and a wife and to have a home and a husband," said Alana. The life-style she shared with Freed "was not for her."

Shortly after his summer-ending party at Grey Cliffe, Freed returned to the Brooklyn Paramount, where he hosted his eight-day "Third Anniversary Show." The current state of rock & roll was reflected by two acts on Freed's bill who recorded for Morris Levy. The Gee label's Cleftones represented the music's lingering rhythm and blues past, while its future was seen in a twenty-three-year-old white pop singer from Camas, Washington, named Jimmie Rodgers. Rodgers's first Roulette recording, a song called "Honeycomb," which Levy and Phil Kahl's Santly-Joy publishing company owned since 1954, was then on its way to becoming the number-one song in America. "Honeycomb" would also become the first in a string of huge pop hits Rodgers would turn out for Roulette Records and for Levy's publishing firms. Another Roulette artist who appeared at Freed's show was Shaye Cogan, who was married to Phil Kahl at the time.

Jo Ann Campbell, who credits Freed as the "main reason" for her rock & roll career, also represented the new look of the music. Campbell, just turned nineteen, had grown up in Jacksonville, Florida, where she was a high school drum majorette. But before she could graduate, against Campbell's wishes, her parents moved the family to Queens, New York, so Jo Ann could pursue a career in dance. Campbell said she "really hated everything" about the drastic change in her life-style. She dropped out of high school to attend dancing school, and by the time she turned eighteen, Campbell was a professional dancer who, when she was not dancing, was "in my bedroom with the door shut, listening to Alan Freed." She attended Freed's Brooklyn Paramount show in September 1955 and was transfixed by Lillian Briggs, a woman truck driver clad in clinging gold lame who played the trombone and sang. At the time, the good-looking and ambitious Campbell was discouraged by her unsuccessful Broadway dancing career (only four feet, eight inches tall, she was regularly rejected for chorus lines), and upon seeing Briggs she thought, "This is it, I've got to . . . sing rock & roll, and I've got to be on an Alan Freed show."

Ironically, Campbell's first New York rock & roll appearance was not with Freed but with Douglas ("Jocko") Henderson on his otherwise all-black April 1957 stage show at Loews' State. But soon after, recalled Campbell, "Alan Freed beckoned," and the singer, with her sassy stage demeanor and her skintight outfits, became a staple of Freed's stage shows. He dubbed her the "blonde bombshell," a title Campbell says she has "always hated," yet tolerated because it was given to her by Freed, "and I loved him very much." Shortly after her appearance on Freed's 1957 Labor Day show (she subsequently appeared on each of Freed's stage shows until he left New York), George Goldner signed Campbell to a Gone Records' recording contract, and with heavy airplay and other promotion by Freed, she sold a lot of records in the New York area for Goldner over the next two years.

Billboard said that Campbell and Little Richard (featuring his latest smash, "Keep a Knockin' ") were the "hottest acts on the bill," while Freed's other acts, including Buddy Holly and the Crickets, the Moonglows, the Dell Vikings, the Diamonds, Larry Williams, the Five Keys, and Ocie Smith were also "breaking it up" at the Brooklyn Paramount. On the Paramount's screen was *Gunsight Ridge*, a western starring Joel McCrea and Mark Stevens, the ex-WAKR deejay who lost his "Request Review" radio program to Freed ten years earlier in Akron.

* * *

Following his Labor Day stage show, it was announced that Freed was "90 percent sure" of taking the Moonglows, Little Richard, Teddy Randazzo, and Jo Ann Campbell on tour in England from October 20 to November 14. That news caused the music industry to buzz over the "new, important international phase" that rock & roll was about to enter, and *Billboard* noted that Freed's proposed tour "underscores the high interest of American artists in England and also the continuing strength of rock and roll itself."

In September 1957, WINS listeners noticed a radical format change. Previously, except for Freed's "Rock 'n' Roll Party," the station's programming hodgepodge had failed to hold much listener interest. Station owner J. Elroy McCaw had recently noticed a music trade paper story concerning a chain of midwestern radio stations owned by broadcasting czar Todd Storz that were doing well in the ratings war by playing nothing but the currently popular top forty songs over and over. McCaw wasted no time in hiring one of Storz's ex-employees, the "diminutive and wiry" Mel Leeds, to institute a top-forty format at WINS for $175 a week. The impulsive Leeds, who carried with him a "show-biz flair" (as well as a loaded pistol), had been asked to leave Storz's WHB station in Kansas City, Missouri, after an ongoing personality clash with a superior there. Leeds was no stranger to New York, having been an assistant record librarian at WNEW radio before moving west to Kansas City.

Leeds was not dumb either. The new WINS program director returned to New York with tapes of WHB's highly successful radio jingles, and just like that, WINS had new jingles of its own: "For music, news, time, and the weather; Keep your dial where the tens come together [WINS was located at 1010 on the AM dial]! Ten-ten WINS, New York!" Or: "For the news and the music where the records spin, when the tens come together it's W-I-N-S, WINS wins!"

Leeds cleaned out the station's entire library of record albums (rock & roll lived and died with the 45 rpm record in the 1950s) and also restaffed the station. He installed former Storz deejay Irv Smith ("a Smith named Irv") as the WINS morning man. Jack Lacey, one of the few WINS holdovers ("Listen to Lacy"), was assigned a double shift—from 9:00 A.M. to noon and from 4:00 to 7:00 P.M. Staff announcer Stan Z. Burns filled the station's noon-to-four slot. Now it did not matter which WINS deejay was on the air. Adhering strictly to the top-forty format, the station would broadcast the same records, morning to night. Only Freed remained unaffected by Leeds's programming. The program director, wrote Rick Sklar, Leeds's newly appointed assistant, had enough savvy not to tangle with Freed, who "had too big a name and too much power with the record companies."

Leeds and his top forty were an instant success. By October, WINS was the New York radio audience share leader between seven in the morning and eleven at night, and J. Elroy McCaw had not spent a penny on advertising the station. Meanwhile, Freed continued to play whatever he chose, whenever he felt like doing so.

In October 1957, Freed's fourth movie, *Mr. Rock and Roll*, premiered at Manhattan's Loews' State. Made by Paramount Studios and starring, along with Freed, Rocky Graziano, Lois O'Brien, and Teddy Randazzo, *Mr. Rock and Roll* was the loosely autobiographical account of Freed's involvement in rhythm and blues' transformation into rock & roll, complete with a Cleveland record store proprietor calling Freed to his store to witness young white teens grooving to race records. Freed again played himself, this time out to prove to a sniping news editor that rock & roll was not a bad influence on youngsters.

Freed said that teens "will find this a wonderful picture to take Mom and Pop to . . . for they'll find that it explains all about the new and exciting rhythms of Rock 'n' Roll . . . and will enjoy it as much as you do." He then used the eighty-six-minute film to present the talents of Chuck Berry, Little Richard, Frankie Lymon and the Teenagers, LaVern Baker, Clyde McPhatter, the Moonglows, Ferlin Husky, Brook Benton, Teddy Randazzo, Shaye Cogan, and Lionel Hampton.

The *New York Times* called *Mr. Rock and Roll* the "latest quickie film to capitalize on the metronomic musical craze," saying it contained "more songs and less plot" than any of its predecessors. The *Times* concluded by pondering the question "With the rock and roll trend apparently wobbling toward the end of the line, where do we go from here?" Where Hollywood's filmmakers went was back to their studios to produce a glut of low-budget rock & roll films, which attested as much to the movie industry's habit of overexploiting as it did to the continuing popularity of rock & roll.

Freed "had a knack for bringing together a tremendous amount of talent in his movies," wrote music critic John Blair. Giving Freed credit for the deejay's emphasis on black talent in his productions,

Blair added that although Freed appeared only in a "small percentage of the total output of the genre . . . he was, in the minds of the youth, and especially in the profit-oriented eyes of the filmmakers, the spokesman and ombudsman for rock and roll."

Movie success or not, Freed was having difficulty turning his much ballyhooed English rock & roll tour from a press agent's dream to reality. The dynamic deejay thrived on his grueling schedule of radio responsibilities, stage and television shows, and Hollywood films. But WINS, which looked upon Freed's "Rock 'n' Roll Party" as the deejay's primary responsibility, was not happy with their star property's increasing off-station activities. Another Alan Freed rock & roll movie premiering in Hong Kong or another Freed stage show in Boston or Hartford would not help WINS's ratings one bit. Freed, meanwhile, went about his business. He placed a full-page ad in *Billboard*, under the heading "Atomic Alan Freed." A close-up photo of the deejay's head was superimposed over a mushroom cloud. At the bottom were listed Freed's activities: "Radio, TV, Records, Motion Pictures, and Personal Appearances," which were followed by a special "thanks" to WINS "for making it all possible—Alan."

Freed's contract with WINS stated that the deejay was responsible for hiring, and paying for, a substitute whenever other commitments took him away from WINS. As his stand-in, Freed selected Paul Sherman, the staff announcer who had predicted that Freed would not last one week on the station. Born in 1917, Sherman joined WINS as a staff announcer in 1943, after working for a Newark, New Jersey, radio station. Jack Hooke said that because Freed called himself the "King" of rock & roll he dubbed Sherman the "Crown Prince." And when the Prince stood in for the King he was paid twice—once by WINS, for his announcing duties, and again by Freed, for subbing for the deejay. Sherman said Freed paid him "very, very well" and that most weeks he "made more from him in direct fees than I did from WINS."

Sherman described himself as a "square" who "knew from nothing" about popular music (he enjoyed the big bands, particularly Artie Shaw's), but he learned quickly from Freed, who, the announcer said, was "a very bright guy who really knew music." At first, Sherman's program was a "carbon copy" of Freed's. "It was his show," explained the announcer. "I never, either on the air or in my heart, tried to usurp any part of it." Although Sherman said he "liked"

Freed, the two were never particularly close. The Prince said only once had he gone to dinner with the King. Sherman was simply "working for money" and nothing else. While Freed had complete control over the music he played, Sherman had no control. "The music was picked for me by Freed or his producer," said Sherman, who arrived at the studio shortly before airtime "and played what they wanted me to play."

Shortly before Freed rocked Broadway with his Christmas stage show at the Paramount, it was announced that the deejay would head a six-week cross-country rock & roll tour beginning in late March, 1958. Freed's "90 percent sure" English tour was suddenly placed on hold.

Fats Domino, singing his latest hit, "The Big Beat," headlined Freed's Christmas show, which opened on Christmas Day and ran through January 5, but it was the appearance of Jerry Lee Lewis, now twenty-two years old, that caused the greatest stir. There was "tension in the air" as Lewis demanded to close Freed's show. Freed informed Lewis that such a move was not possible because Domino's contract stated that he close the show. Lewis' very presence on the Paramount stage could have meant disaster to Freed if word had slipped out that, unbeknownst to the deejay, as well as to most everyone else, the "killer" had secretly wed his thirteen-year-old cousin Myra Brown three days earlier.

After Lee Andrews and the Hearts ("Tear Drops"), Paul Anka ("I Love You, Baby"), Danny and the Juniors ("At the Hop"), the Rays ("Silhouettes"), the Shepherd Sisters ("Alone"), Little Joe and the Thrillers ("Peanuts"), Thurston Harris ("Little Bitty Pretty One"), the Dubs ("Could This Be Magic"), Jo Ann Campbell, Frankie Lymon and the Teenagers, the Twintones, and Terry Nolan had all performed, Buddy Holly and the Crickets took the stage for a twenty-minute set. Holly, with two records high on the charts ("Peggy Sue" and "Oh Boy!" with the latter credited to the Crickets), thought he deserved to close Freed's show, a contention supported by the encore ovation the group from Lubbock, Texas, received from the Paramount audience. The Everly Brothers followed Holly and the Crickets with a softer set, and then it was on to Lewis and Domino.

The "killer," miffed at Freed, hit the stage with a vengeance. Like a raging madman, Lewis kicked away his piano stool and pounded the keys as if they were afire and he was trying to extinguish the flames.

Lewis' platinum-dyed blond locks dangled halfway to the keyboard as the singer hunched over his piano and careened through twenty minutes of rock & roll, including his recent million-seller, "Whole Lot of Shakin' Goin' On." Just when Freed's audience thought it had witnessed everything that Lewis was capable of doing onstage, he charged into his latest release, "Great Balls of Fire" and, before the song was over, leapt atop his piano to boogie as the house went beserk.

What Fats Domino thought as he watched in the wings, waiting to perform, is unknown. When the Paramount audience finally settled down, Domino closed the show as scheduled, but he told Freed he never again wanted to follow Jerry Lee Lewis onstage.

In a scene reminiscent of Freed's Washington's Birthday show the previous February, by 5:30 A.M. crowds began to gather on Forty-third Street outside the Paramount's main entrance in the bone-chilling fifteen-degree temperature. Several hours later a line at least five deep extended west on Forty-third Street to Eighth Avenue, and then south to Forty-second Street, as police strained to maintain order as the "shrieking, pushing, stamping teens" besieged the Paramount. "20,000 Rock 'n' Rollers Queue for Block in Midtown to Crowd Into Holiday Show," reported the *New York Times*. The crowds proved so large that one-third of the way through the twelve-day run Freed scrapped the traditional grade-B movie (this time it was the British-made *It's Great to Be Young*) and added six additional live performances. Immediately after the final show Freed's cast took part in what Jack Hooke called a "traditional occurrence." As soon as the final curtain closed, "we'd all get buckets of water and have the worst water fight you ever saw in your life. Everybody got drenched!"

With shows running until two in the morning, Freed's rejuvenated big beat grossed more than $300,000. Theater manager Robert Shapiro said the deejay's Christmas crowds exceeded those drawn to Freed's February and July Paramount runs. Freed also set the theater's single-day box-office mark of $32,000, as well as a weekly gross record of $193,000, dating back to the days of Frank Sinatra and Tommy Dorsey.

Freed's spectacular record-breaking Paramount holiday show marked the high point of the vaunted disc jockey's stormy career. He was a world-renowned entertainment personality with four rock & roll movies to his credit. He had established in his name more than four thousand fan clubs, each containing from ten to three hundred members. His 1957 take-home earnings exceeded $123,000.

The year 1957 was also a memorable one for the boys, particularly for Morris Levy. Of the year's top ten best-selling New York–produced popular records, Ahmet Ertegun's mighty Atlantic/Atco complex had three, and Morris Levy had five.

Because of Freed's notable celebrity status, neither he nor anyone else anticipated the disc jockey's stunning fall from this pinnacle of success, an inevitable descent that would begin in just five months—in Boston, Massachusetts.

CHAPTER 10

Banned in Boston

"When kids stand on seats or dance in the aisles, I hold up my hands and ask them nicely to please sit down and we'll continue the show. That's all I have to do."

BY presenting veteran black rhythm and blues performers to a young white audience, Alan Freed pieced together his musical kingdom as he assisted that generation, just beginning to sense its separate identity, discover a type of music it could call its own. With the exception of the music of Bill Haley, urbanized rock & roll radio remained virtually all black until the coming of Elvis Presley early in 1956. In Presley, explained Freed, an idol ("all any musical trend needs") was born, and "the cycle was complete." Now "there was no stopping" rock & roll.

Freed was proved correct in his assessment of the development of the music, and in 1957 a wave of country-influenced white rock & rollers—including Buddy Holly, Jerry Lee Lewis, Buddy Knox, Jimmy Bowen, Jimmie Rodgers, and the Everly Brothers—made their initial appearances on America's national best-selling pop record charts. With Holly and the Everly Brothers in mind, Freed spoke of the "youth revolution" then taking place in popular music in which the new singers (some "no older than their audiences"), most of whom wrote and recorded their own material, helped cause Tin Pan Alley (as well as ASCAP) to "lose its monopoly in the music business." The trend of young white singer-songwriters, thought Freed, "should continue to produce interesting popular music."

White rock & roll vocal groups lagged a step behind their solo counterparts. While no white rock & roll vocal groups appeared on

Billboard's national "Top 100" in 1956, some of them did make local inroads, and by the end of 1957, the appearance on the national charts of the Mello Kings, the Techniques, the Playmates, and Danny and the Juniors signaled a change in the wind for rock & roll.

The year 1958 was the one in which white rock & rollers gained national sales chart parity with their black counterparts. Discussing the music's future that February, Freed said he thought that rock & roll would be around "for a long time to come, although there will be trends set within the field which nobody can predict." One such trend was the practice whereby producers overdubbed a chorus and/or violin strings onto rock & roll recordings in an attempt to make them more acceptable to large urban radio markets.

The rock & roll producer was also to play a far more significant role than mere overdubbing in toning down rock & roll's harsh sound. The next step in the process was the development of white "teen idol" singers, of which Paul Anka (sixteen years old as 1958 began) was the forerunner. A performer since his days in grade school in Ottowa, Canada, Anka had cut one record (financed by his father) in 1956, which had flopped. But Anka scored big in 1957 with the self-penned "Diana" (number two on Billboard's "Top 100"), and he subsequently appeared on two of Freed's stage shows that year. Freed's audience, however, raised on a hefty dose of rhythm and blues, showed little appreciation for the slightly overweight teenager who was younger than many of them. Leroy Kirkland, Freed's musical director, said he "felt sorry" for the young Anka. "The people didn't like him at all." But Anka was a cut above those teen idols who would follow him. Not only was he a decent singer, but he was also a talented songwriter. Of singers such as Frankie Avalon, Bobby Rydell, Freddy Cannon, Jimmy Clanton, Annette Funicello, and the archetypical teen idol, Fabian (Forte), few, if any, wrote their own songs, and discounting Avalon's trumpeting skills, few could play a musical instrument. Some teen idols could not even sing, which had little bearing upon their success. They were all darlings in the eyes of the largely white "American Bandstand" audience, collectively growing younger each day, thanks to Dick Clark's nationally televised daily after-school dose of rock & roll.

The teen idols provided a collection of cute, "safe" faces and wholesome images. The songs they sang were crafted on Tin Pan Alley by a stable of pop songwriters, many of whom worked in teams, who ground out two-and-a-half-minute songs on a nine-to-five basis.

Studio producers, utilizing teen idols and highly polished arrangements, began to dominate the rock & roll music business.

Freed "knew the times were changing," said Ray Reneri, "so he made sure he had a good-looking girl on his show. Jo Ann Campbell didn't sell any records [nationally] to speak of, but we'd take her on the road and . . . she was a fabulous act!" Although Freed made a valiant attempt in adapting to what Reneri referred to as the "teenage thing," it was no coincidence that as the teen idols began to dominate rock & roll, Freed's career began to take a downward turn.

While black rhythm and blues served as a theme for the early 1950s youth culture, that situation existed only until that culture began to develop its own heroes. While the emergence of Elvis Presley meant there was no stopping rock & roll, it also meant trouble down the road for Freed, for the deejay's strong identification with black performers precluded his acceptance by a young white audience that collectively was not capable of relating on more than a limited basis to those black artists.

As 1958 began, Freed did not need to be reminded by Chuck Berry singing about his " 'Sweet Little Sixteen' rocking on 'Bandstand' " that Clark's "American Bandstand," less than a year after going national, not only represented the vanguard of rock & roll but was also the hottest show on daytime television. The underlying factor in the phenomenal success of "Bandstand" was Dick Clark himself, who, it was said, treated rock & roll "first and foremost as a special business enterprise that had to be adjusted to meet the unique demands of television." Clark also recognized the need to showcase rock & roll in "safer, more accessible surroundings" in order to appeal to America's massive afternoon viewing audience, and almost singlehandedly he created the "teen idol" phenomenon. Not only did Clark possess a keener business acumen than Freed but he also had the resources of the ABC network to back it up. In 1958 "American Bandstand" appeared on 105 ABC-affiliated stations across the country and was seen by forty million viewers—half of them adults—each day. With a single spin of a record, Clark was able to give it instantaneous national exposure. No previous disc jockey ever commanded so large an audience. It became an axiom in the pop music business that what did well in Philadelphia would also do well elsewhere, and pop music trendsetting shifted away from New York to that city as the teen idols and their "south Philly" sound came to dominate America's pop music charts. As Jerry Hopkins observed in *The Story of Rock*, "Good singers and good songs may have sold records, but the 'Bandstand' gang sold more."

Freed was well aware of the challenge originating from the "City of Brotherly Love," just ninety miles south of New York, but openly the deejay remained apathetic to the show's meteoric rise. "I don't want to limit myself to only music," said Freed in February 1958, predicting he would do additional movies and eventually take a rock & roll show to England, perhaps in September. "I just haven't had the time to do everything I want to."

Behind the scenes there developed what Jack Hooke described as a "very strong rivalry" between Freed and Clark. At one point Hooke was dispatched to Philadelphia, where he said to "Bandstand" producer Tony Mammarella, "We could have a great thing here if the two of us could get together in some way."

There was at least one occasion when the Freed and Clark forces did "get together" in hopes of a great thing. It involved a New Jersey quartet called the Royal Teens and their recording of "Short Shorts." When Leo Rogers originally released the song late in 1957 on his own Power label, Freed played the song nightly and it began to take off. "Short Shorts" had all the makings of a national hit, but Rogers could not provide the massive distribution required for it to become one. He subsequently sold the record to ABC-Paramount for $15,000, at the time one of the largest cash advances ever paid for a record. Royal Teens member Bob Gaudio, who maintained that the group "saw nothing from Power once they sold the master," earned approximately $1,600 in songwriting and performance royalties from "Short Shorts." Gaudio, who would go on to greater success with the Four Seasons in the 1960s, said he received "a real quick taste of the record business at a very early age" from his "Short Shorts" experience.

Meanwhile, with Power's sale of "Short Shorts" to ABC-Paramount Records, Jack Hooke managed to obtain 50 percent of the song's publishing rights for Figure Music. Hooke's acquisition allegedly left even Freed nonplussed. "Why the people gave him half" of the song's publishing rights, Freed could not understand, "because the record was already a hit." Nevertheless, Freed said Hooke then "took the record to Philadelphia for Mr. Clark to play," in hopes of giving "Short Shorts" national exposure on "American Bandstand." Sure enough, Clark did play the record regularly, and "Short Shorts" reached number three on Billboard's "Top 100" early in 1958.

For the most part, there was little contact between the Freed and Clark camps. Although it was to Freed's advantage to have records in which he held an interest played on "American Bandstand," Freed could do little for Clark, who "represented the future of rock and roll," while Freed "remained tethered to its inglorious past."

As busy as Dick Clark was on the air, he proved even more industrious behind the scenes. He had discovered, even before "Bandstand" acquired a national audience, that certain individuals in the music business insisted on doing favors for him. As 1956 ended, the Philadelphia-based Cameo Records, owned by Bernard Lowe, issued a song written by Lowe and Kal Mann called "Butterfly." Sung by twenty-year-old Philadelphian Charlie Gracie, who had recorded for several years without commercial success, "Butterfly" took off locally. In January 1957, Lowe said he called Clark, with whom the record manufacturer was friends, and offered to give Clark 25 percent of the song's publishing rights if Clark would call deejays around the country and promote the song to them. Lowe said Clark agreed to do so for nothing, because the record manufacturer was a "friend."

Nevertheless, when "Butterfly" became a national hit in the spring of 1957, Lowe insisted on giving Clark a check for $7,000, "because things worked out pretty good." Clark maintained that he and Lowe had no "arrangement" concerning "Butterfly" and that he told the record manufacturer that giving him the $7,000 "was unnecessary." When Lowe "insisted" that Clark take the money, the "Bandstand" host "again said it was unnecessary." Clark did eventually take the money, but Lowe said that when the disc jockey found out Lowe was going to give him a check, Clark asked for the check to be made payable to Margaret Mallory (at the time, Clark's mother-in-law), before changing his mind and asking that Lowe make it payable to the Click Corporation.

Clark had formed the Click Corporation in March to handle song-publishing royalties and artist-appearances reimbursements made to the deejay for performing fees Clark had paid singers who had appeared on "Bandstand." When "American Bandstand" went national in August, Click Corporation became the show's producer.

In May 1957, Clark paid $125 for 25 percent of Jamie Records, a company then $450 in the red. The revitalized label's first release, a guitar instrumental called "Movin' 'n' Groovin'" by nineteen-year-old Duane Eddy, received heavy airplay on "American Bandstand,"

and Eddy made several promotional appearances on the afternoon show. "Movin' 'n' Groovin' " reached the national sales charts in the spring of 1958.

In July 1957, Clark formed Sea-Lark (a wordplay on the spelling of his last name) Enterprises, a BMI-affiliated song-publishing firm. It was to Sea-Lark that George Goldner testified he assigned four song copyrights, in hopes that those assignments would result in Clark's playing of the records on "American Bandstand."

Also in July, Clark and Bernie Binnick formed the Binlark Company for the purpose of investing in the rock & roll movie *Jamboree*, in which Clark and other disc jockeys made cameo appearances.

It was around the time of Binlark's formation that Bernie Lowe bestowed yet another gift on Dick Clark. In August the record manufacturer released a timely, if depressing, song for "Bandstand" viewers called "Back to School Again." Lowe assigned 50 percent of the song's performance rights to Clark. "Bandstand" airplay and guest appearances by the song's singer, forty-two-year-old vaudeville comedian Timmie ("Oh Yeah") Rogers, helped "Back to School Again" rise to number thirty-six on Billboard's "Top 100" by the fall.

With good reason, music writers and publishers appeared eager to bestow gifts upon Clark. Late in 1957 the songwriters of Danny and the Juniors' "At the Hop" assigned to Clark half of the song's copyright. They maintained that the gift stemmed from Clark's writing contribution (when brought to Clark, the song had originally been called "Dance the Bop," but Clark changed some lyrics and suggested the new title), as well as their realization that the song "wouldn't be a hit" without him.

In December 1957, Clark and Harry Chipetz each put up $10,000 and formed a record distributorship called Chips Distribution. Also in December, Clark (50 percent interest), Binnick (25 percent), and "Bandstand" producer Tony Mammarella (25 percent) formed Swan Records. Clark wasted no time in hyping Swan's first two releases, Dicky Doo and the Don'ts' "Click Clack" and Billy and Lillie's "La De Dah" on "American Bandstand," and both songs became national hits early in 1958.

Harry Chipetz said it was the practice of record manufacturers, himself included, "to try to get as many artists as we possibly could on 'American Bandstand.' " To accomplish that feat, Chipetz said he "made out checks to Click Corporation, who in turn paid the artists for their appearance" on Clark's television show.

* * *

As if "American Bandstand" did not present enough of a challenge to Freed, he was also faced with new local competition from the Philadelphia-based "Jocko" Henderson. Jocko had been commuting to Manhattan in order to do his WOV radio "1280 Rocket" program from Harlem when, in January 1958, Henderson left WOV to try his hand at television. Jock's TV "Rocket Ship," a kind of black "Bandstand," made its New York–area debut on a Monday afternoon, broadcast over WATV (channel thirteen) in New York. A crowd of predominantly black teenagers overflowed WATV's tiny, sixty-seat Newark, New Jersey, studio. On Tuesday five hundred youngsters attempted to board Jocko's televised rocket ship, while on Wednesday fifteen hundred disappointed ride-seekers had to be turned away.

Jocko's records always moved "higher and higher" as rocket engines roared in the background and the host deejay served up a constant spate of jive patter: "From way up here in the stratosphere, you got to holler loud and clear! . . . Ee-tiddly-oh and a ho, I'm back on the scene with the record machine, saying Ooh-pop-a-doo and how are you?"

Jocko's jive patter was not original—he appropriated much of it from a veteran of twenty years on Baltimore radio, Maurice ("Hot Rod") Hulbert—but to Henderson's metropolitan-area audience, many of them white, it was new and exciting.

By February 1958, artists who appeared on "American Bandstand" to plug records or songs the publishing rights of which Clark in part owned included Charlie Gracie ("Butterfly"), Dicky Doo and the Don'ts ("Click Clack"), Timmie Rogers ("Back to School Again"), Paul Anka ("Diana"), the Dubs ("Could This Be Magic"), the Chantels ("Every Night"), Danny and the Juniors ("At the Hop"), the Diamonds ("High Sign"), and Huey Smith and the Clowns ("Don't You Just Know It"). By that time Clark had a stake in a song-publishing company (Sea-Lark), two record companies (Jamie and Swan), a talent-free reimbursement company (Click), as well as a record distribution company. It was possible—and perfectly legal—for Clark to acquire the publishing rights to a particular song, to have one of the teen idols record the song for Clark's own record label, to have the record distribution by his own company, to play the record as often as he chose on "American Bandstand," and to have that artist appear on "Bandstand" to plug the record before being reimbursed for the singer's television appearance for which Clark had paid.

That same month, as the "Bandstand" ratings continued to soar, Clark was given a new television program on the ABC network. "Saturday Night," sponsored by Beech-Nut chewing gum, was a half-hour program on which recording artists either sang or lip-synced their latest hits, a program that television historians Castleman and Podzarik said "closely resembled Freed's 'The Big Beat,' only with more polish." The show premiered on February 15, 1958, at about the time that Freed's bid to secure a daily Mutual Radio network program—a deal said to have been "sizzling for months"—was declared dead. Adding insult to Freed's latest injury, Clark's new show originated not from Philadelphia but from the ABC network's Little Theatre on Freed's Manhattan turf.

Freed was not the only disc jockey to face heightened competition, however. *Billboard* ran a cover story that described the all-time-high competition among "key jocks," competition that caused the broadcasting personalities to be "alert for new ideas to offset the ratings threats."

Despite the ascendance of "American Bandstand" and the "south Philly" sound, Freed's prospects were anything but bleak. His WINS "Rock 'n' Roll Party" was still highly rated in the New York area, and Figure Music held the publishing rights to several "hot tunes," among them "Jo Ann" by the Playmates (released on Levy's Roulette label), "Maybe" by the Chantels (on George Goldner's End label), and "Short Shorts" by the Royal Teens. Jack Hooke said he "started taking songs [to record] to George Goldner, among others." Goldner, in turn, said he assigned the publishing rights to "three or four" of his songs to Figure Music in anticipation of radio airplay by Freed.

Freed, almost certainly referring to Dick Clark, said he did not think any disc jockey should be associated with any record company or record distributor "or any phase of the record business," except music publishing, which "was a different story." Freed reasoned that "if top stars like [Perry] Como or [Patti] Page can have their own publishing firms, why shouldn't I?" The deejay pointed out that it was "perfectly legal" for him to pick out certain songs and to publish them, "as long as someone else makes the records." As for Clark, Freed admitted that his daughter Alana "watches him every day." He wished the "Bandstand" host "a lot of luck" and said Clark "has done a great job for the business."

Because of what Morris Levy termed certain "financial difficulties," Freed had encountered a cash-flow problem. On February 28, 1958, the deejay "requested and accepted" from Roulette Records a $10,000 bank check. Levy said the money was given to Freed with "the tacit understanding and agreement" that Freed "would continue to favor and expose records manufactured by Roulette" and that Freed "could forget about repayment" of the $10,000.

Mitch Miller was at it again, firing another broadside of criticism at the music he despised. As rock & roll continued to become more popular, the Columbia Records' A&R chief grew more vociferous in its criticism, and his uneasy truce with Freed fell apart. By then the two no longer even bothered to feign any air of civility between them. In March, Miller addressed a convention of top-forty disc jockeys and lamented the demise of "creative programming," while accusing the jocks of playing to an audience of "eight-to-fourteen-year-olds."

Freed took Miller's attack personally, saying, "It sounded like sour grapes." The deejay also charged Miller with knowing "little about rhythm and blues and native American music. He's always been classical-minded and my feeling is that he's a musical snob." When Mike Wallace invited Freed to discuss the merits of rock & roll on the commentator's television program, weary of hearing the same tired arguments against the music, Freed declined. "Let's face it," he told Wallace, "rock and roll is bigger than all of us."

Again Freed scoffed at those critics who persisted in describing rock & roll as a "craze." The deejay said that teenagers would not outgrow rock & roll "just because they reach eighteen, nineteen, or twenty." He granted that although their musical tastes may change, "that doesn't mean they stop liking rock and roll." Consequently, said Freed, youngsters exposed to rock & roll a few years earlier "are now carrying their tastes right into college, and it looks to me like the colleges will be saturated with rock and roll."

Elvis Presley, the antithesis of rock & roll's emerging teen idols, was inducted into the U.S. Army on March 24, 1958, as Freed and Mitch Miller battled publicly. Presley was not about to drop from sight completely—RCA Victor had enough of the singer's music already recorded for several releases, and Presley's latest film, *King Creole*, had yet to be released—but the singer's accessibility to a fickle public would be considerably constrained. At Colonel Parker's insistence and much to the chagrin of Uncle Sam, Presley shunned a cushy assignment with the army's entertainment division in favor of the regular tour of duty faced by the everyday GI. The move was part of Parker's plan to soften the rebel image that Presley still projected to much of America's adult population, and it was to prove successful. When a humble, "mature" Presley was honorably discharged from the service in 1960, his appearance and his music—as well as rock & roll in general—had been toned down considerably.

As Presley was being inducted, Dick Clark was adding to his already substantial musical empire. In March he formed Globe Record Corporation and a publishing subsidiary, Kincord Music, which would issue records on the Hunt label. In April, Clark began heavy airplay of a record called "Pickin' on the Wrong Chicken" by the Five Stars and released on Hunt. Although Clark's efforts failed to get the record onto the national charts, the undaunted "American Bandstand" host continued his quest to create a hit for his new label. In July another Hunt release, "Down the Aisle of Love" by the Quin-Tones, began to be heard on "American Bandstand," and the group made several promotional appearances on Clark's show to promote the song. By the end of the summer, "Down the Aisle of Love" had become a national hit.

It had been announced in February that Alan Freed was planning a six-week rock & roll tour for the spring. Although the deejay had previously made several brief road trips to various locations along the eastern seaboard from Massachusetts to Washington, D.C., this tour was to be the most extensive of Freed's career. In addition, he would face competition from Irving Feld's "Biggest Show of Stars for 1958." Feld, who had promoted similar extended rock & roll road attractions for several years, had closed out the previous year with his "Biggest Show of Stars for 1957," an eighty-day fall tour of the United States and Canada that starred Fats Domino, Chuck Berry, Buddy Holly and the Crickets, the Everly Brothers, and numerous other top recording artists. Feld's promotion proved to be rock & roll's first successful large touring show. It not only helped popularize the music but also established the rock & roll concert tour business as a significant part of the music industry.

An epic battle between Freed and Feld was in the works, but both promoters faced not only the usual unforeseen pitfalls of touring but also a sagging domestic economy and, in March 1958, the highest U.S. unemployment rate in seventeen years. *Billboard* reported that

Freed and Feld each planned to spend $35,000 a week for talent, and the music trade newspaper estimated that the rivalry would drive usual talent prices up at least 20 percent. Veteran bookers expressed alarm at the inflated fees both promoters would be forced to pay to secure rock & roll's hottest acts.

On that ominous note, Freed kicked off his road show with a two-day warm-up at the Brooklyn Paramount. On March 20 the deejay played the Hartford State Theatre in Connecticut before returning to New York the following day for a getaway date at Loews' Paradise in the Bronx. Then, said Jack Hooke, they "put our acts on the bus," and off they went to do sixty-eight shows in thirty-eight cities, covering a route that would crisscross the northern and midwestern United States and venture into Canada before coming to an end on May 10 in Newark, New Jersey, forty-five days after it began.

Freed boasted a formidable trio of headliners in Jerry Lee Lewis ("Breathless"), Chuck Berry ("Johnny B. Goode"), and Buddy Holly and the Crickets ("Maybe Baby"), while the Chantels, the Diamonds, Danny and the Juniors, Billy and Lillie, the Pastels, Ed Townsend, Larry Williams, Screamin' Jay Hawkins, and Jo Ann Campbell rounded out the disc jockey's impressive lineup.

Feld, whose tour began on April 5, countered with the Everly Brothers ("All I Have to Do Is Dream"), the Silhouettes ("Get a Job"), the Royal Teens ("Short Shorts"), Sam Cooke, Paul Anka, LaVern Baker, Clyde McPhatter, and Jimmy Reed.

During the first week of Freed's tour, Jerry Lee Lewis destroyed several pianos as part of his frenzied performances and, on one occasion, had pushed what remained of the battered eighty-eights off the stage, into the audience. When Freed arrived in Cleveland for two performances at Public Hall on Sunday, April 6, he discovered that the show's local promoter in that city had two pianos waiting for Jerry Lee. But when the unpredictable "killer" turned in what was for him a rather perfunctory performance, the chagrined promoter pleaded with Lewis to destroy one of the pianos during the second show. It was reported that one of Freed's Cleveland shows grossed a "smashing $17,000," while the next day in Canton, Ohio, the show took in $12,000 more. Similarly successful dates followed in the Columbus War Veterans' Memorial, and as Freed's entourage prepared to head north into Canada, *Billboard* reported that the disc jockey's touring "Big Beat" had taken in $150,000 during the first ten days on the road. But after a month on the road, as April drew to a close, gate attendance for both Freed and Feld sagged. To make matters worse, a third traveling show, "The Rhythm and Blues Cavalcade of 1958," was on the road, but it barely managed to stagger through the Midwest before being "pulled from the road" on April 27. Driven by his boundless energy and able to capitalize at the box office with a superior talent lineup and on his own name, Freed's "Big Beat" rolled on across the country. After his inflated talent expenses were met, however, Freed's impressive box-office grosses allowed for little profit. Meanwhile, Irving Feld stated he would be content simply to break even with his own tour.

As May began, the end of Freed's grueling road show was finally in sight. However, if the deejay, described by author Bruce Pollack as an "open and vulnerable target as he roved the countryside," hoped to complete his ambitious tour without incident, he should not have included on his itinerary a Saturday-night (May 3) performance in Boston, a city whose civic authorities did not welcome the deejay and where Freed had repeatedly experienced difficulties with the authorities in the past.

Freed "hated" Boston, said Ray Reneri. It was an attitude the rock & roll deejay harbored since his visit to that city in 1956 when some of Freed's audience left their seats and surged toward the stage. Reneri said many in the audience were hurt when the police "began pushing the kids back." In the ensuing melee, theater seats "were torn up and there was a lot of other damage." When Freed was told to report to the police station house after his show concluded, many in the deejay's entourage expressed concern about the police getting Freed alone and inflicting physical abuse on him. "Make sure somebody stays with me all the time," Freed told Reneri. "If they're going to hit me, I want a witness." Freed was released unharmed about an hour later, and as he emerged from the station house, he told a crowd of reporters gathered there that he thought the Boston police "were a bunch of rednecked old men."

Not long before Freed hit town in 1958, Boston Mayor John B. Hynes lifted a ban on rock & roll shows that had been instituted after Freed's 1957 show which allegedly resulted in some subway station violence. Tensions were heightened, however, when on April 13 a fight broke out in the audience at Irving Feld's show at the New Haven Arena as Paul Anka performed onstage. Although the brawlers were quickly "hustled" out of the arena, it was said that Anka's performance "suffered" from the disturbance. The New England press once again bashed rock & roll, and those Boston citizens previously unaware of Alan Freed's impending visit were warned of what they, too, might expect.

Rhythm and blues musician, historian, and writer George Moonoogian, a seventeen-year-old high school senior in the spring of 1958, had already attended two Boston rhythm and blues stage shows when he and four friends—Bill McGirr, Sal Gucciardi, Mike Chase, and John Coppolla—piled into Coppolla's 1952 red Chevrolet sedan and drove from suburban Haverhill to join thousands of other rock & roll fans inside the seventy-two-hundred-seat Boston Arena on the night of May 3.

Time magazine noted that "5,000 hip kids" were at the Boston Arena, which was located in a downtown section of the city which Jack Hooke described as "the worst section in Boston . . . [where] the dregs of society lived." Since Moonoogian, Coppolla, and Chase had purchased their tickets earlier than McGirr and Gucciardi, the three were seated in the arena's first-level boxes, about twenty yards to the left of the stage and about ten feet from the arena floor, where temporary folding chairs were set up facing the stage. McGirr and Gucciardi were seated one level up, also on the left side of the arena, but further toward the rear.

Moonoogian estimated the Boston audience as "perhaps 60 percent white," although the section he, Coppolla, and Chase occupied was predominantly black. As Freed's show began, Moonoogian said it was "all one could expect it to be." Larry Williams wowed the audience by playing his latest hit, "Dizzy Miss Lizzie," "lying prone on top of a grand piano and playing it that way—backwards." One of the funniest incidents of the show involved Jo Ann Campbell and Screamin' Jay Hawkins, who utilized as a stage prop a human skull attached to the end of a stick. "As Jo Ann rocked off stage, wiggling her rather attractive backside," recalled Moonoogian, Hawkins pursued her wiggle with the skull. "The skull kept nipping away at Jo Ann, she screamed, and the crowd roared approval."

During intermission, McGirr jostled his way to a nearby men's room, where through the smoke-filled air he noticed a group of teens shooting craps with dice as several of the participants swigged wine from a bottle concealed in a paper bag.

Moonoogian and McGirr agreed that as the second half of Freed's show began, "a noticeable feeling of tension began to mount." Jo Ann

Campbell said the show had to be stopped "several times" because of roughhousing in the audience, and each time, "Alan came out and tried to quiet everybody down." Onstage there was electricity in the air. Hooke said the Boston police "were all around us," on the stage and in the wings. "We didn't pay 'em any mind," said Freed's associate. "We were going to do the show like we'd done in every other city."

For a month Freed's entourage bore witness to a smoldering rivalry between Jerry Lee Lewis and Chuck Berry. The "killer" was miffed because even though he received top billing in Freed's printed program booklet, it was Berry who closed each show. Forced to accept performing before Berry, Lewis sought to make Berry's task of following him onstage an unenviable one. After being introduced by Freed, Jerry Lee charged wildly into his set, flailing madly at the keyboard and gyrating suggestively in front—as well as on top—of his piano. As Lewis began a medley of "Whole Lot of Shakin' Goin' On" and "Great Balls of Fire," all hell broke loose. Many in the crowd of five thousand left their arena seats and began to dance in the aisles and converge on the stage area.

Hooke, who had been observing the performance from his usual vantage point off in a far corner of the stage, said such exhibitions by Freed's audiences "happened in every other place" and so were not unusual. But this time a police sergeant appeared onstage and told Hooke that "the kids are out of line" and that he would stop the show if they did not return to their seats.

Hooke pleaded with the officer to "be cool" and promised he and Freed would "take care of it." After locating Freed, Hooke grabbed the deejay and told him, "Alan, you'd better get 'em back in their seats or we're going to have trouble. You know how they [the police] are in this town!"

The way Freed viewed the proceedings from on the stage, his audience's behavior was simply another case of enthusiastic teenagers dancing in the aisles, standing on seats, and crowding the stage for a better view. But George Moonoogian, seated in the audience, was aware of a mounting undercurrent of tension around him. As Freed commandeered the stage microphone, two rival gangs seated near the teenager began to don head bandanas—their identifying battle colors.

"Alright, listen, hold it!" Freed told his young audience. "I have to stop the show for a minute, kids. You have to sit down. I want everybody back in their seats. The show won't go on unless you all get back in your seats!" Meanwhile, Jerry Lee Lewis sat sullenly at his piano.

The audience reluctantly complied with Freed's demand and managed to remain seated as Lewis resumed his goal of upstaging Chuck Berry. But, shortly after Berry took the stage for his show-closing performance, Hooke said the audience came out of their seats again, "strong as ever."

And the police sergeant was yelling in Hooke's face, "I told you I'm going to put on the houselights!"

Hooke knew that such a move "would make Alan crazy," and he pleaded with the police officer not to do so. "I'll tell Alan to get the kids seated again," said Hooke, but it was too late.

The police sergeant snapped his fingers and called for the houselights to be turned up. Onstage, the animated Berry fell silent and motionless as Freed once again stormed to the microphone. "Hold it!' he screamed, throwing an annoyed glance in Hooke's direction.

Freed was interrupted as the sergeant shouted from across the stage, "This show is not going on until everybody's in their seats!" Freed, not accustomed to being upstaged, least of all by a hostile Boston police officer, did his utmost to remain calm. The audience, as if sensing an impending confrontation, grew eerily quiet.

"Alright, kids," implored Freed, "I told you before, this is the way it has to be. You have to go back to your seats for the show to go on. Please go back." Once again the audience returned to their seats, and Freed gave Berry the signal to continue and called for the houselights to be dimmed.

"I'm not putting the houselights out!" snapped the sergeant.

By now, Freed was livid. "You can't do that!" he said. "These kids paid $3 a ticket and they didn't come here to see a show with bright lights on!" But the police sergeant would not yield.

When another officer brushed past the harassed deejay and said to him, "We don't like your kind of music here," Freed could no longer contain himself. Boston Arena manager Paul Brown said the "serious-faced" Freed grabbed a microphone and uttered what Hooke characterized as "the big statement."

There are conflicting accounts of what Freed actually told his audience that night. Hooke recalled the deejay saying, "Kids, the police in Boston won't put out the lights. I guess the police in Boston don't want you to have a good time." It was also Paul Brown's contention that Freed said, "It looks like the Boston police don't want you to have a good time!"

But Freed later maintained that he never specifically mentioned the police, that he had simply said, "We'd like to get the lights out. We're here to enjoy ourselves and they're not letting us." George Moonoogian and Bill McGirr also maintain that Freed never mentioned the police, that he said, "They won't put out the lights, kids. I guess they really don't want you to have any fun."

Whether Freed did or did not specifically mention the Boston police (Freed said his disputed statement was made "off the cuff . . . [an] unfortunate chance remark"), Moonoogian said the statement "certainly wasn't made to incite anyone."

But, as Freed spoke to his audience, a teenager who, along with his friends, had been drinking near Moonoogian during the second half of the show suddenly climbed on top of his seat. Affected by his alcohol consumption, the teen collapsed to the floor. At that point, Moonoogian noticed a colored bandana tied around the drunken youth's head and similar "colors"—identifying members of a local street gang called the Band of Angels—adorning the heads of the drunken teens who surrounded him. He then ominously observed nearby another group of teens who "had on different colored bandanas."

Another gang member picked up a chair and tossed it over the railing onto the arena floor eight or ten feet below, tumbling over the rail with it. Then, said Moonoogian, "various objects started raining down from above."

Paul Brown anxiously paced in his office as the Boston Arena audience buzzed defiantly moments before the rival factions erupted ("There's no other word for it," said Moonoogian). "Nothing really started it, and Freed certainly was not the catalyst," said Moonoogian, who thought the host deejay "probably had no idea" of what was going on in the audience. The violence soon grew fierce enough to be noticed onstage, however, and Chuck Berry ran to the rear of the stage and up the band platform to seek refuge behind his drummer. There were those in the audience who thought Berry's scamper was a part of his stage act, but, explained Moonoogian, they were "too far away to see the look of fear on Berry's face." As objects from above rained down onto the lower level of the arena, Moonoogian turned to Mike Chase and John Coppolla and said, "Let's get the hell out of here!"

The trio headed for a nearby exit ramp and, with "hoards of people screaming and yelling at us," ran through a long underground corridor, kicking open a fire door, and exited the arena. They hurried across the street to the parking garage and jumped into Coppolla's Chevy and locked the doors. "All we could hear were screams and shouts from outside the garage," said Moonoogian, as he, Chase, and Coppolla began a tense wait for Bill McGirr and Sal Gucciardi to appear.

After observing "a great deal of activity near the stage area," McGirr and Gucciardi left their seats and began to walk downstairs, just before the major eruption that sent Berry scampering for cover. They were "just a few yards from the outside doors when a tremendous roar came from behind us and the crowd panicked and started pushing and shoving forward." The two teens were swept out the front doors of the arena in the crowd surge and became separated in the confusion. McGirr, seeing nobody on the other side of the street, entered the parking garage and, "strolling like it was an afternoon at the beach," found Moonoogian, Chase, and Coppolla huddled inside the Chevy.

Gucciardi thought he "was a dead man" as he was grabbed and slammed against a parked car. Suddenly, another teenager approached and said to Gucciardi's attackers, "No, no, he's not one of them!" Momentarily freed, Gucciardi headed for the sanctuary of the parking garage. On the way he noticed a woman knocked to the pavement by a group of youths who dashed past her. Moonoogian thought that five minutes had passed since McGirr reached the garage and "Sal came puffing in." As the five shaken teenagers hastily sped away, they passed a small group of youths on the lower level of the garage who had encircled two other teens who were engaged in a fistfight.

Jack Hooke said they "finished the show in bright lights," but Moonoogian maintained that when the disturbance in the arena audience erupted, Chuck Berry ran for cover and Freed's show never actually "ended."

Hooke said he, Freed, and Jackie, who were supposed to fly ahead to Montreal to make arrangements for the following night's show, "got dressed and . . . left." As they exited the arena, "only a couple of kids were milling around" outside.

Freed said he "stood on a street corner [outside the arena] signing autographs for a half hour or so." Then, said Hooke, "a police officer walked over and hustled us into our car." George Moonoogian found it "hard to believe that Freed was out signing autographs," considering the mayhem he witnessed in and around the arena that night.

(Bruce Pollack wrote of the "unsettled crowd milling by the stage door," which Freed's acts were forced to walk by on the way to the busses after the show.) Moonoogian also disputed press accounts that said Freed's show lasted well past midnight. Boston's blue laws prohibiting entertainment after midnight Saturday was strictly enforced in those days. What is more, Moonoogian said he arrived home in Haverhill at about one in the morning and the trip "took a good hour back in those days."

After they left the Boston Arena, Freed, his wife, and Jack Hooke were driven to the Hotel Statler, where they slept until late Sunday morning. At two o'clock they boarded a plane for Montreal. Freed said that "at no time did we get a phone call from the police or anyone else before we left Boston to tell us anything was wrong." But if the trio thought Boston was safely behind them, they were gravely mistaken.

Freed said that "Sunday night following our show in the Montreal Forum we got a phone call from the *New York Journal-American*, asking us what happened in Boston." The unsuspecting deejay replied that there had been a "minor interruption" at the arena, but that it "really was no problem, I've handled those things before." Freed then stood dumbfounded as the reporter informed him of the sketchy details he had heard. According to the reporter's sources there had been a riot in the Boston streets following Freed's show and, in the melee, someone had been stabbed. Freed dismissed the story as just another overblown press account of rock-related violence and hung up the telephone. "That's the first we knew of any trouble," he said.

On Monday, Freed, Jackie, and Hooke flew back to Boston, en route to that evening's show in Lewiston, Maine. Hooke said that after arriving at Boston's Logan Field, they noticed front-page newspaper headlines telling of a riot that had occurred after Freed's Boston Arena show. They picked up one of the newspapers and proceeded to read "how girls were raped in the bathroom, how kids were cut up inside the arena, and how there was a big riot outside the place," said Freed's associate. "We looked at the newspaper headlines and we wanted to die!" recalled Hooke, who called the press account "the most unbelievable story I ever saw in my life." He and Freed looked at each other, and Freed said to Hooke, "What is this? Where are we? Is this America?"

The wire services jumped on the riot story, and even the staid *New York Times* headlined an account ROCK AND ROLL STABBING, reporting that "teenaged brawlers stabbed a sailor and beat and robbed a dozen other persons early today in the aftermath of a rock 'n' roll show at Boston Arena." According to the story, a nineteen-year-old sailor named Albert Reggiani was stabbed and his two female companions were mauled by teenagers milling around the arena following Freed's show. A twenty-three-year-old woman who had taken two teenaged babysitters to Freed's show reportedly had earrings ripped from her ears by "thugs" outside the arena. In all, nine men and six women were roughed up and required hospital treatment. Boston press accounts told how teens had "beat, robbed, and molested" passersby and said that after police broke up the fights outside the arena, teenage gangs "raced through the streets," in the Roxbury and Back Bay sections of the city, "knifing, beating, and robbing." An all-male gang of about twenty-five, wearing motorcycle jackets and pink bandanas, reportedly "attacked and robbed three men of $50."

George Moonoogian said there indeed was violence after Freed's Boston show—"we were witness to it"—but that the newspaper accounts of it were "certainly exaggerated." He said it was "obvious that the trouble began brewing in the arena audience and was not a direct result of either Freed or the show," and it would have started, "no matter what type of show took place" there. Moonoogian said that as far as he and his friends could determine, what happened that night would have happened "with or without Freed," but that the rock & roll deejay was "good news copy."

As soon as the Boston "riot" story hit the United Press wire service, Jack Hooke received a telephone call from Atlantic Records' Jerry Wexler in England. ("That's how far the story spread," said Hooke.) "You hit the headlines!" exclaimed the record executive, who wanted to know the details.

"There was no riot," moaned Hooke. He explained to Wexler that the press took the entire police blotter for the area near the Boston Arena that night and attributed all the reported crimes to Freed's show. "That's what a 'hot nut' they had for Alan."

* * *

As Freed's stricken rock & roll troupe prepared for its Lewiston performance, local disc jockey Frank Sweeney stood in for Freed. Police Chief Roland C. Arnott doubled the usual guard contingent from four to eight officers, but only one minor scuffle occurred among the four thousand teens at the Lewiston Armory when one youngster momentarily squared off against a policeman who had warned the youth to move away from the stage.

Elsewhere, developments were less encouraging. Freed's Tuesday show in Troy, New York, was wiped out by what were described as the "conflicting reports from Boston," and Wednesday's performance in Providence, Rhode Island, met a similar fate. Of Freed's scheduled Thursday appearance in New Haven, Mayor Richard C. Lee said, "Not only will this show not be permitted, but while I am Mayor there will be no further rock and roll melees in this city."

"The next thing we knew," said Jack Hooke, "they issued an injunction against us appearing in New Haven." Mayor Lee told the press that New Haven "would do everything possible" to keep Freed's show from taking place there.

"We tried to fight it," recalled Hooke. At the hearing to try to have the injunction lifted, Freed's associate was called as a witness. He told the New Haven authorities that when he and Freed walked out the front of the Boston Arena, "there was nothing happening." Hooke said a sergeant from the Boston Police Department then took the stand and said that some of Freed's audience "were raping girls in the bathroom" and that the police "had to pick up girls off the floor of the [arena] lobby."

Mayor Lee concluded from the hearing that Freed had "contributed by a substantial amount to the Boston violence," and he upheld the New Haven ban on Freed's rock & roll show.

Although the initial Boston police reports filed by Back Bay division Lieutenant John T. Corkey dispelled any racial motivation in the alleged violence following Freed's Boston show (George Moonoogian said the confrontation inside the arena "never seemed to be racial, but territorial"), but a later Boston police report by Lieutenant Arthur Quinn stated that at least six white victims claimed that they had been attacked by black men and women, but that the attackers "fled before they could be seized by police."

Mayor John B. Hynes banned all rock & roll shows organized by outside promoters and stated he was "not against rock and roll as such," but that he was opposed to rock & roll dances put on by promoters, because that sort of performance attracted "the troublemakers and the irresponsible. They will not be permitted in Boston and no outside promoter need apply."

Meanwhile, Boston's wheels of justice ground into motion against Freed. District Attorney Garrett H. Byrne, who for the past few years had directed a preventative program to keep the city free of what he termed "juvenile delinquency and unrest," said that "an obvious source of juvenile outbreaks is adult misguidance." When such misguidance "takes the form of rock and roll paganism, my duty is to present the facts to the Grand Jury."

A fresh element was introduced into the Freed controversy when Massachusetts State Senator William D. Fleming introduced a bill to the legislature to ban rock & roll from all state-owned buildings. Saying he did not think rock & roll music was the "primary cause of the trouble" that sent some teenagers along a "path of destruction" following Freed's Boston show, Fleming declared, "I have certain information that certain products—narcotics—were sold."

Freed had returned to New York, where on Thursday, May 8, he received the latest bad news from Boston. A Suffolk County, Massachusetts, grand jury had handed down an indictment against him, charging Freed with "inciting the unlawful destruction of property during a riot touched off at a performance at his rock and roll show." After Byrne announced the indictment, he instructed the Boston police that, should Freed fail to surrender himself for a May 12 hearing in that city, he be "arrested and extradited."

The basis for Freed's indictment was a Massachusetts antianarchy statute issued in 1928 when, after a union representative had encouraged workers to strike, violence erupted on a picket line and the union official was charged with inciting to riot. "He was convicted," said Hooke, "and that set a precedent."

Freed called his attorney and said, "Warren, I've just been indicted in Boston!"

Warren Troob was "enraged" after hearing the charges lodged against Freed. The attorney said he believed the case "had nothing to do with Alan Freed," but was "the work of the [Catholic] church" and its anti–rock & roll crusade. Troob assessed the seriousness of the charges ("Alan stood a chance of going to jail for twenty years," said Hooke) and determined that a Boston-based criminal attorney was essential to Freed's defense. To represent the deejay, Troob retained the services of noted criminal attorney Paul Smith.

Once again, Freed was in the position of having to defend not only himself but rock & roll in general. He termed the notion that rock & roll produced juvenile delinquency "just so much hogwash." Juvenile delinquency, said the deejay, "begins at home, not in a piece of music." If he did not believe that rock & roll was "good, wholesome music," explained Freed, "I wouldn't play it." Citing his own four children, he said, "I'm concerned about what happens to them, and also . . . what happens to other kids."

The rock & roll disc jockey issued a public statement denying any trouble in and around the Boston Arena the night of his show. Freed also criticized the Boston police, who, he said, "threw the book" at the deejay. "I'm the scapegoat for their own juvenile delinquency problem." Freed maintained that his Boston audience was comprised of "the greatest—swell, wonderful kids [a contention George Moonoogian would dispute]. But the police were terrible!" Freed also defiantly said he would not return to Boston to face the charges levied against him, and he also said he doubted that he could be extradited.

Citing the collective opposition of the Catholic church, the Boston civic authorities, the Federal Bureau of Investigation (FBI), and forces within the music industry itself to Freed and to rock & roll, the deejay's son Lance believes "there's no question anymore," but that his father was "set up" in Boston because "he was seen by many at ASCAP as the leader of the movement that made BMI a viable organization." Lance claims that certain documents and memoranda ("pretty disturbing stuff") "suggest" there was communication between the Boston Archdiocese and the FBI concerning his father and how they could "get him there" in Boston.

"If certain forces within pop music were out to nail Freed," wrote Bruce Pollack, "the Boston riot certainly provided the hammer," but although Freed certainly did not lack enemies, both within and outside the music industry, no evidence supporting a conspiracy to set up Freed in Boston has come to light. The Catholic church had been the longest and loudest antagonist of Freed and of rock & roll because, as Arnold Passman wrote in *The Deejays*, "what Alan Freed and, increasingly, others did was to sock it to" the austere New England leadership. Most likely, the church, along with other anti-

Freed forces, leaped into the breach the moment Freed was victimized by the unfortunate violence that apparently did begin at his Boston show. If there was any conspiring to "get" Freed in Boston, it came immediately after the violence and was marshaled by those forces which thought they could at last pin a rap on the rock & roll disc jockey that not only had a chance to stick but could also ruin his career.

As for the FBI, that organization first became interested in the business activities of Morris Levy "at least as early as 1958," after Levy and some partners opened the Round Table Restaurant in Manhattan. New York Police Department sources (the NYPD began putting together a dossier on Levy "some years" after Birdland opened) claimed that those partners included Frankie Carbo, a convicted killer with alleged mob ties, and John ("Johnny Bathbeach") Oddo, an alleged captain in the Joseph Colombo crime family. At the outset of the Levy investigation, neither the New York Police Department nor the FBI had reason to be interested in Freed, but the deejay's business association with Levy eventually caused Freed to fall under the watchful eye of the authorities.

Specific FBI interest in Freed appears to have commenced shortly after the Boston riot incident, when FBI director J. Edgar Hoover was moved to warn the nation of rock & roll's "corrupting influence on America's youth." Hoover also denounced rock & roll riots such as the one at Freed's Boston show as "inexcusable."

Bureau documents released to the public reveal no interest in Freed prior to the Boston incident. An FBI internal memo dated December 2, 1959, however, stated that Freed "undoubtedly . . . has an intense dislike for the Director [Hoover] because of statements which the Director made . . . a few days after the Boston rock and roll riot." Taking stock of the Boston incident, and citing Freed's business involvement with Morris Levy, the FBI began to compile a dossier on Freed.

On Thursday, May 8, the day of his Boston indictment, Freed and Jack Hooke met with the WINS owner, J. Elroy McCaw. "Alan wanted to defend himself" against the Boston charges, said Hooke. He and Freed told McCaw, "We want to go on the air. We want to fight it."

WINS's response was, "If you do anything like that, we don't know if you'll have a job here. In fact, we're thinking about whether you have a job here or not."

Freed's Boston incident was not at the root of WINS's growing disenchantment with its onetime star property. There had been friction between Freed and the station management at least since the deejay began to do remote broadcasts from his Connecticut home, much to WINS's disapproval. Robert Smith, Freed's original program director, described the deejay as "an impossible person to work with on a personal basis." Smith claimed Freed's "ego problem" was the crux of his downfall, noting that it was "huge even before he was anybody in New York."

McCaw had finally turned WINS into a moneymaker, and since Mel Leeds's arrival as program director, the station's ratings had risen to an all-time high. WINS's broadcasting license was worth millions of dollars (as opposed to the $450,000 McCaw had paid for the station). But each new Freed headline caused McCaw, a worrier by nature, to wince. The latest charges, coupled with mounting industrywide payola allegations ("the music industry's worst-kept secret"), might very well ruin the station owner's plan to sell WINS for a substantial profit. If there had been any doubt in McCaw's mind as to Freed's future at WINS, such doubt had been removed by the recent events in Boston. McCaw's star property had turned into his chief liability. Alan Freed had to go. Not only did McCaw decide not to renew Freed's contract (which was due to expire in August), but he invoked the contract's moral clause—under which Freed agreed to "conduct his personal life as not to reflect discredit on or cause embarrassment" to WINS—and fired him on the spot. Freed, who had counted on WINS to pay for his legal defense, was "struck dumb for one of the very few times in his life."

The deejay spent Thursday trying to persuade McCaw to change his mind. When the station owner refused, Freed sought at least a contract extension to enable him to remain on the air until after his sold-out Newark show on Saturday. Many of the acts were to perform there gratis, in exchange for airplay on Freed's "Rock 'n' Roll Party." But if the deejay no longer had a radio program on which he could play those artists' records, they might not perform. Again, McCaw remained unmoved by Freed's predicament, and that night, Paul Sherman replaced the deejay on the air.

While McCaw held fast to his decision to terminate Freed's services, the disc jockey was permitted the face-saving gesture of "resigning." That evening, Hooke announced to the press that Freed had "resigned" in protest over what Freed said was WINS's "wishy-washy" attitude toward him since Boston.

Freed sent a formal letter to WINS station manager Jock Fearnhead, stating that WINS had failed to "stand behind my policies and principles." He also said WINS's attitude toward him was "a hard thing to swallow" and that the station should have given him "a little support after all the unproved publicity from Boston."

Friday, May 9, Fearnhead told the press that Freed's "resignation" had come "as a complete surprise to WINS." Although in cases such as this the public "usually assumes that a person in trouble is fired," said the station manager, that was "definitely not the case" with Freed. "WINS sincerely wishes Mr. Freed the best in his future business activities." With that, the figure most responsible for making WINS one of New York's top radio stations was gone.

Ironically, the only relatively good news for Freed that day came from Boston, where District Attorney Byrne withdrew the scheduled May 12 deadline for Freed to answer the riot charges. Byrne instead ordered Freed to surrender himself in Boston "within a reasonable time."

That evening, Freed was in Hershey, Pennsylvania, to host what turned out to be the final performance of his ill-fated "Big Beat" tour. The chief of the Newark National Guard, Major General James Cantwell, canceled—out of concern for "the public's safety"—Freed's Saturday-night show, which was to have taken place at the National Guard armory there.

With the May 12 deadline for Freed to surrender himself in Boston removed, the unemployed disc jockey remained secluded in New York City, where on that very day Jack Hooke allegedly received a cash payment of $750 from Kenneth Luttman. The payment was allegedly made on behalf of United Artist Records, recently formed as a subsidiary of the United Artist motion picture company. It was the first in a series of alleged monthly cash payments made by that record company to Freed. The arrangement supposedly came about after United Artist national promo man Bernie Friedlander advised his company that "it would be of value to enter into certain arrangements with particular disc jockeys" in order for the fledgling label's records to get played. Friedlander allegedly approached Jack Hooke regarding those "certain arrangements," and Hooke supposedly told him that for $750 a month "arrangements" would be made for United Artist records to be played on Freed's radio program. But when Luttman allegedly delivered the first $750 from United Artist Records to Hooke, Freed's "Rock 'n' Roll Party" was no longer on the air.

The following day, the *New York Herald Tribune* printed an editorial titled "Rock 'n' Riot," which described Freed's music as "not the kind that soothes the savage beast," but, rather, the kind that "makes the savage beast more savage." The newspaper noted that Freed had recently "lured 20,000 shrieking juveniles" to the Paramount and that the disc jockey's Boston show had "touched off a riot."

Speaking of the canceled tour dates of Freed's rock & roll show following the Boston violence, the *Herald Tribune* said, "There was a time when cities boarded their gates against the plague," and, while such action is no longer necessary, "most communities still try to keep known thugs at bay." Noting that but for the Pied Piper of Hamelin, "musicians are not generally thought to be dangerous. . . . Now another pied piper seems to have turned up."

Meanwhile, that new pied piper needed a radio program, and he needed it quickly.

CHAPTER 11

"We Start 'em; the Others Chart 'em"

"There were times that money passed hands and I was in the middle."

ON May 14, 1958, two days after Jack Hooke allegedly received $750 in cash from United Artists Records, Alan Freed was indicted a second time in Boston; this time the charge was "unlawfully, wickedly, and maliciously inciting to riot during a rock and roll show." The next day Freed pleaded not guilty to that charge, as well as to the original charge of "inciting unlawful destruction of real and personal property." Justice Lewis Goldberg set bail at $3,000. After his Boston arraignment, Freed basked in the celebrity treatment afforded him by the very press corps that only two weeks earlier could not wait to print accounts of violence attributed to the deejay's Boston Arena rock & roll show.

In New York, Jack Hooke, "job-hunting" for his recently fired associate, had read in a music trade newspaper that WABC, the flagship station of the ABC radio network, was about to undergo a change in programming format. At a time when the top-forty format was spreading successfully across America's radio dials, WABC remained a programming hodgepodge, with little continuity and no established listener base. The station tried to increase its ratings by wooing Martin Block and his long-running "Make-Believe Ballroom" from rival WNEW, but Block's middle-of-the-road appeal was not the answer to WABC's woes; in 1958 the station was nearly a million dollars in the red.

Hooke got in touch with WABC management and said he would

like to discuss possible employment for Freed. WABC told Hooke that the station planned to program rock & roll "and who better to have than Alan Freed." But although station management was "very interested" in Freed, they told Hooke they could not offer Freed "the kind of money you're used to."

While WABC had "delusions" of what Freed had been paid at WINS, Hooke said that when his associate was fired, he was earning "the same shit at WINS that he got the first day he arrived there!" It was from Freed's stage shows that "the big bucks" came, explained Hooke. In addition, although Freed swore he "never got a dime" from Figure Music, he did have that music publishing company as an additional source of money. Hooke said Freed also received "other money, gratuities, from other people."

Realizing that Freed was in desperate need of any available radio position, Hooke coolly told the WABC brass, "I think we could possibly work that out. What's the most you could give us?" When WABC mentioned the figure of $40,000 a year, Freed's associate said he found it "very hard for me to control myself." He asked them if that was the best they could do, and when it was confirmed that $40,000 was the station's best offer, Hooke, "fighting like hell" to maintain a serious face, said, "Well, let me speak to Mr. Freed and see if he'll accept it."

When Hooke arrived at Freed's Lincoln Towers apartment in Manhattan, where he was secluded, the deejay anxiously asked, "What happened?"

"I think we got a gig with ABC," replied Hooke.

"Wow!" exclaimed Freed, "Are we set? You signed the papers, didn't you?"

Hooke sheepishly replied that he had signed nothing, that he had told WABC "I had to talk to you first."

"You schmuck!" Freed railed at Hooke, ordering him to "get back there as quick as you can!"

The following morning Hooke informed WABC management that the station's $40,000 offer "was acceptable to Mr. Freed."

On May 20, four days after pleading innocent to the Boston indictments against him, Freed and Hooke arrived for the deejay's formal contract signing at the ABC offices in New York. Freed said they were met there by Mortimer Weinbach, vice-president and general counsel for ABC. He also maintained that as he was about to sign his contract—which stipulated a salary of $800 a week for a period of 260 weeks—he was "taken back" by what Weinbach allegedly referred to as an "unwritten obligation" ABC expected Freed to assume. Weinbach allegedly said now that Freed was part of the ABC "family," the network vice-president "trusted" that Freed "would be sure to lay very heavily on ABC-Paramount records." Freed said that Weinbach added that he trusted the deejay "would play nothing but Paramount theaters" with his rock & roll stage shows.

A small announcement stating that Freed would begin broadcasting over WABC from 7:15 to 11:00 P.M. nightly in New York on Monday, June 2, appeared in metropolitan newspapers the following day. Thus began Freed's transition from WINS's "Keep your dial where the tens come together" to WABC's on-the-air claim, "We start 'em, the others chart 'em."

On May 31, Freed and fellow disc jockey Art Ford, in the past an outspoken critic of rock & roll, appeared on CBS-TV's Saturday-afternoon "Right Now" show, moderated by Ron Cochran. Freed had expected the usual adversarial format and was perplexed when he, Ford, and a child psychologist instead formed a panel moderated by Cochran. Ford, who admitted to playing "quieter" rock & roll on his program, agreed with Freed on the groundlessness of the attacks on the music. Ford's only hint of opposition came when he admonished Freed to be "more selective" and to play only "better" rock & roll songs. Freed listened attentively and took exception only after Ford began to espouse the virtues of jazz. Freed called jazz "music for older people" and said that older people "don't make the hits," that it was teenagers, who "want a strong, happy beat to dance to," who bought the majority of the popular records. Freed also landed a blow at ASCAP, blaming much of the anti-rock & roll hysteria on "the whole ASCAP" situation. He again denied any culpability in the recent Boston violence, pointing out that he had previously played forty-two cities "'without incident."

Despite the fact that Freed was back on the air, having hardly missed a beat since his WINS firing, the Boston riot charges against him lurked in the background. On June 4, Paul Smith asked for the dismissal of both indictments, contending that the Boston antianarchy statute cited in the charges against Freed "was unconstitutional as it was applied to Mr. Freed because of failure to cite any intent to overthrow the government." Smith also pointed out that violent outbreaks similar to those Freed was accused of having incited were nightly occurrences around Boston's infamous Scollary Square district, even when there was no rock & roll show there on which to pin the blame. Not surprisingly, the Boston attorney's move for dismissal was denied, and a trial date for Freed was set for January 1959.

By the time Freed signed his contract with WABC radio, the ABC network's rock & roll eggs had all been put in Dick Clark's basket. Since the network had no interest in reviving Freed's rock & roll television show, he was free to arrange any video deal he was able to.

Counting on what they termed Freed's "power to line up top artists," on June 18, 1958, the near-dormant Dumont Broadcasting Company (WABD-TV, channel 5 in New York) signed Freed to do a locally televised rock & roll show each weekday afternoon from five to six, the time previously occupied by Herb Sheldon's "Studio Party." Freed's new show was to be called "Alan Freed's Big Beat."

WABD-TV's plans for Freed's new show included possible national syndication, which would put the deejay's "Big Beat" in competition with Dick Clark (actually coming on the air as "American Bandstand" signed off), but in the process of gaining a television show, Freed was forced to sell a bit of his soul. WABD executives insisted that Freed retain Sheldon's format of employing guests, contests, stunts, and "dancing youngsters" and that there be "no special emphasis on rock and roll." In the words of pop music historian Arnold Shaw, "reacting to Boston, or coaching of WABD, Freed turned to polite rock and roll" on his "Big Beat" television show. Many industry insiders regarded the deejay's newly adapted "subdued announcing style" as his attempt to emulate Dick Clark as the host of a TV record hop that would appeal to adults as well as to teenagers.

Ray Reneri said that Freed "didn't like television" to begin with, because it was "too containing" for the whimsical deejay's impulsive personality. Freed's former assistant explained that if Freed "didn't do a commercial [on the radio] at 8:10, he'd do it at 8:20. He couldn't do that on television."

Reports of Freed's initial "Big Beat" telecast said that the deejay was "positively subdued" in his manner of introducing the curious blend of talent Freed was expected to piece together in order to appeal to the widest audience possible. Chuck Berry, after lip-syncing his current hit, "Johnny B. Goode," was followed by the Four Lads, a pop vocal group who mouthed their current hit, "Enchanted Island." When Freed suggested that the group take "a couple of turns around the room with some of the eager kids," it was reported that the Four Lads instead "made a hasty exit." The juxtaposition of rock & roll and pop music, combined with Freed's commercials for classical music concerts held at New York City's Lewisohn Stadium, pleased few of his rock & roll fans. Although he gradually slipped into a more familiar, harder rock & roll format, Freed carefully refrained from uttering the phrase "rock & roll" on the air (in sharp contrast to his 1955 on-the-air manner when he promoted the phrase as often as possible), instead referring to the songs he played as "the music with the big beat." No national syndication resulted for Freed's "Big Beat," but in April 1959, WNEW-TV (late in 1958 the Dumont station changed hands and was renamed Metromedia [WNEW-TV]) added a Saturday 8:00–9:00 P.M. show to the deejay's schedule.

Not long after Freed's "Big Beat" TV debut, Mitch Miller leaked a story that a "well-known host" of a televised rock & roll show had refused to play a Four Lads record unless he received half of the song's publishing rights. Although Miller was careful not to name the TV host, it was believed by many in the business that the Columbia Records' A&R chief was getting in a dig at his musical adversary, Alan Freed. Miller also insisted that payola was widespread in the pop music business and that one of the reasons Columbia Records was not heavily involved with rock & roll was the label's refusal to partake in the practice.

By the spring of 1958, Dick Clark had become what rock historian Jerry Hopkins termed an "unparalleled success." As Clark became more influential, he continued to expand his music-related business holdings. After Clark and Bernie Lowe formed Mallard Pressing Company in May 1958, to manufacture phonograph records, the "American Bandstand" host had his finger in every aspect of the rock & roll hit-making pie—from song publishing to recording, to manufacturing records, to commanding the ultimate forum in which to publicize the songs to a national audience. That month, Clark filled another gap in the hit-making process when he secured a 25 percent interest in SRO Artists, a talent management company that Clark used to manage Duane Eddy, as well as Clark's own personal appearances. In June, Clark added January Music, another song-publishing company, to his holdings, and in July, he formed Drexel TV Productions to produce his own Saturday-night show.

Rock & roll singers clamored for a guest spot on "American Bandstand," and perhaps none benefited more than Duane Eddy by Clark's publicity, save for Frankie Avalon. Born Francis Avallone in Philadelphia in 1939, as a child performer Avalon appeared on radio and television in the early 1950s with Paul Whiteman. By 1953, Avalon was playing his trumpet in various Atlantic City bands. In 1957 Bob Marcucci signed Avalon to Chancellor Records (and also landed the young singer an appearance in the 1957 rock & roll film *Jamboree*, in which Dick Clark held a partial interest). Avalon said that when he recorded "Venus," "Dick got behind it and it sold over a million copies."

After his first record bombed, eighteen-year-old Jimmy Clanton from Baton Rouge, Louisiana, appeared on "American Bandstand" to introduce his follow-up record, "Just a Dream." The next day, said Clanton, his record company received orders of "over 100,000 from distributors around the country" for "Just a Dream."

Music publisher Marty Mills, of Mills Music Publishing, remarked that "people know that Clark will lay it on [a song] if he's got any stake in it." As far as Clark was concerned, it was "just good business" for him to own a song's publishing rights. He added that any songwriter with a song to publicize would "want me to own it because I could do the best by it."

Despite the additional income generated from his new television program, Alan Freed remained in a financial squeeze. Not only did his Boston legal fees continue to mount, but Freed's family expenses had him near the breaking point. Lozier Caplan, the Salem, Ohio, attorney who handled Betty Lou Greene's divorce from Freed, said that in 1958 the deejay "was supporting two families," which included his own four children and Jackie's two children from her previous marriage.

At a time when he could least afford it, Freed also faced a threat to the most lucrative aspect of his own musical kingdom—his stage shows. Trade paper announcements said that Dick Clark was negotiating for a Labor Day weekend stage show in New York, possibly at the Brooklyn Paramount. Temporarily denied the use of Paramount's theaters because of the Boston incident, Freed contemplated a show of his own, to be held at Loews' State or another Manhattan theater, perhaps before Labor Day so the New York deejay could "get the jump on Clark."

Adding to Freed's financial woes, on July 18, 1958, Alan Freed Enterprises, a corporation formed to back the deejay's stage shows, headed by Jack Hooke, filed for bankruptcy in federal court. Claiming that lost revenue from Freed's canceled spring tour dates following the Boston "riot" had put the corporation under, the suit listed Alan Freed Enterprises assets as "nil," while maintaining the corporation owed Shaw Artists (the 1958 spring tour backers) $24,665, owed Freed $15,000, and had liabilities totaling almost $52,000.

Not long after Freed changed radio stations he also changed wives. Despite her valiant public display of support for her celebrity husband, Jackie Freed had long since soured on his professional grind. Alana Freed said her father believed that "he had a certain image to keep up, and she [Jackie] was a part of that image." Freed insisted that Jackie's place was with him. Despite this philosophy, Betty Lou Greene said there came a time when Jackie refused to go many places with her husband "and stopped doing some of the things she [previously] did with him." And, added Freed's first wife, "that was when he picked up on Inga."

Since Bill Stern's morning "Contact" program had made its WINS debut in September 1957, the commentator and his girl Friday, Inga Boling, had become morning regulars at the radio station's Columbus Circle studios. On certain nights when business kept him in Manhattan until late evening, Freed stayed overnight at his Lincoln Towers apartment instead of returning to Stamford. Often he stopped by WINS the following morning. It was one such morning that Freed arrived at WINS and discovered Inga, a tall, attractive, Nordic blonde. All at once the rock & roll deejay began to spend more nights in New York and fewer in Connecticut. And wherever Freed went, Inga was at his side.

Jack Hooke remembered an incident that took place at Grey Cliffe in the spring of 1958, when Freed, although still married to Jackie, "had already met Inga and was in love with her." Freed's associate said it was "public knowledge" that Freed planned to leave Jackie and marry Inga. Hooke was sitting with his wife at one of Freed's Stamford barbecues when she said to him, "He's a bitch!"

"Who are you talking about?," asked Hooke.

"Alan Freed," replied his wife. "He's unbelievable! How could he have the nerve to have all three of them here?"

As Hooke looked around he saw together in the same room "Betty Lou, Jackie and Inga—past, present, and future."

Freed and Inga were married on August 8, 1958, the day of his older daughter's birthday, but Alana Freed was not happy with her new stepmother. She thought Inga was the "glamour part" of her father's life. The daughter-stepmother rivalry was intensified by the narrow age difference between the two, for Inga was only about twenty-two at the time she married Freed. Inga was "too young," said Alana, and as Freed's daughter matured, she said "it became harder for me to accept her." Alana also claimed not to have sensed "a lot of love and respect" for her father from Inga, "and that turned me off."

During the summer of 1958, George Goldner aggressively promoted his new Gone and End record labels. The Dubs, assisted by heavy airplay by Freed, had kicked the Gone label off to a promising start a year earlier with "Don't Ask Me (to Be Lonely)." And Goldner had paid a tribute of sorts to the deejay in January 1958 when the label owner had his studio combo (Buddy Lucas's band), billed as the Gone All-Stars, record an instrumental Goldner called "7–11," which happened to be Freed's hours on WINS at the time.

Freed was also instrumental in having Goldner record John Ramistella, a young singer from Baton Rouge on Gone Records. Born in New York City in 1942, Ramistella and his family moved to Louisiana in 1945. Ramistella was given an old guitar when he was eight years old, and besides becoming proficient on the instrument, he became a singer aspiring to cut his own record. By the time he was fourteen, Ramistella had saved enough money to pay for what would be the first of several trips he would make to New York and to Nashville in search of a recording contract. It was on one such New York visit that Ramistella claimed to meet Freed out in front of WINS. When the singer explained who he was, Freed told him to come up to the deejay's office the following day. Evidently Freed liked Ramistella's songs more than he did the singer's name. Because Ramistella hailed from the bayou country, Freed suggested that the name Johnny Rivers would sound more authentic than his real one. Besides giving the singer his professional name, Freed put Rivers in contact with George Goldner, for whom the singer made his first recordings. Released early in 1958, "Baby, Come Back"/"Long Walk Home" (Gone 5026) failed to sell, as did the next sixteen sides Rivers recorded for various record labels over the next several years. The rest of the world would not discover Rivers until 1964, when he released his hit recording of Chuck Berry's "Memphis." Morris Levy, who by then owned the Gone/End masters, promptly rereleased "Baby, Come Back" on his Roulette label to capitalize on Rivers' newly found success, but the record sold no better than it had six years earlier.

Freed was also indirectly involved with the success of Goldner's End label, which also started out in the fall of 1957 with a chart hit by the Chantels ("He's Gone"). After the Brooklyn-based Duponts broke up following their aborted performance on Freed's Washington's Birthday show at the Paramount in 1957, lead singer Anthony Gourdine (whose sore throat forced the Duponts to withdraw from Freed's show) joined the Chesters, a Brooklyn group in need of a new lead singer. With Anthony singing lead, the Chesters recorded the soaring ballad "The Fires Burn No More," which was released on the Apollo label. Anthony said that Freed made the song "really big locally," but since Apollo "didn't come out with the bread [payola to have the record played]," the record eventually fizzled.

The Chesters then began to pursue Richard Barrett, a local songwriter who also did production work for Goldner, to give them a listen. Barrett finally relented, and the Chesters, led by Ernest Wright, auditioned for the producer with a song called "Just Two Kinds of People in the World." Barrett said the group's performance stopped him "in his tracks," and he set up a recording session for the Chesters with Goldner. But the label owner was not nearly as impressed as Barrett had been with Wright's rendition of "Just Two Kinds of People in the World." He had the group try a different song and insisted that Anthony sing the lead. Gourdine was reluctant to sing "Tears on My Pillow" (a song he maintains to this day "stinks"), but the group recorded it in July 1958. Goldner, however, was also unsatisfied with the Chesters' name, which he thought "didn't have any 'zing' to it." Anthony claimed the group became "outraged" when promo man Lou Galley suggested they call themselves the Imperials, but when "Tears on My Pillow" was released (with "Just Two Kinds of People in the World" on the flip side), the Chesters had become the Imperials. Shortly after the record was released, Anthony sat on a Brooklyn park bench listening to Freed's radio program when he heard the deejay say, "And now, a new record which is making a lot of noise—'Tears on My Pillow' by little Anthony and the Imperials."

There is disagreement concerning the motive for Freed's "little Anthony" remark, with Gourdine himself contributing to the confusion. In one account, the singer claimed that Freed "did not know it was me" who had appeared with the Duponts on Freed's stage show in 1957 and that the deejay's remark "came off the top of his head." This contention was supported by Freed, who also claimed that his on-the-air reference to "little Anthony" was purely an ad-lib on his part. But Gourdine later changed his story and claimed that Freed "remembered me from the Duponts" and, knowing the singer was small in size ("I was a little bit taller than Frankie Lymon," said Anthony), called him "little Anthony." In still another telling of the story, Gourdine, sensitive about his diminutive stature, attributed Freed's description of him to the fact that Anthony "had a little voice." The singer claimed not only that many people who heard him thought he was a girl (as also happened with Frankie Lymon) but also that "they thought I was a little-bitty boy. For a long time people thought I was twelve, thirteen years old."

Whatever Freed's motives were, after the deejay dubbed Gourdine "little Anthony," the singer said the name "just spread like wildfire," catching on so quickly that George Goldner changed his record labels so that all but the very first pressings of "Tears on My Pillow" credit the group as Little Anthony and the Imperials. Not only did the song become a million-seller, but the other side, said Gourdine, "jumped up and sold about 800,000."

Three days after his marriage to Inga Boling, Freed allegedly received a $400 payment from Superior Record Sales, a New York record distributor. Jack Hooke said there were several instances in which he "was in the middle" when money passed hands to Freed. One such case involved Freed's arrangement with Sam Weiss, of Superior Record Sales, whereby Weiss made out checks payable to Hooke, which Freed's associate "then cashed before giving Alan the money."

Also in August, Hooke and Teddy Reig finally sold their Royal Roost label to Roulette Records, putting it under the control of Morris Levy. As part of the deal, Reig joined Roulette's A&R staff. Hooke was already working as A&R chief for Les Levy's (no relation to Morris Levy) Hanover Records, a position he had been named to the previous May.

The first blockbuster TV quiz show was CBS-TV's "The $64,000 Question," which debuted in June 1955, as a summer replacement for a drama series. Within one month "The $64,000 Question" was the most popular program on television. Tensions mounted each week as ordinary people with extraordinary knowledge in a particular area (a policeman who was an expert on Shakespeare; a taxi driver who knew opera; a young psychologist named Dr. Joyce Brothers, who was an expert on boxing) won unprecedented sums of money. When the top prize of $64,000 was first won in November 1955, the story appeared on the front page of the *New York Times*.

The rival NBC network strove to duplicate the success of "The $64,000 Question" with a quiz show of its own called "The Big Surprise," which was hosted by Mike Wallace. "The Big Surprise" (created by the same person who originated "The $64,000 Question") debuted in October 1955, but while the new quiz show boasted a top prize of $100,000, it failed to live up to network expectations, largely because it lacked the human drama provided by the "$64,000 Question" isolation booth. *Variety* editor George Rosen said that "The $64,000 Question" remained "alone and unique," not because of the large prize money itself, but because of the show's "fine sense of dramatic showmanship values." Despite the show's spectacular success in 1955, Rosen maintained that television "would not be taken over by the 'gimmick boys.'"

But early in 1956, NBC underwent an executive shake-up that resulted in a decision to place more emphasis on flashy but easy-to-produce quiz shows. The network scheduled a new quiz show, "Break the $250,000 Bank," hosted by Bert Parks, immediately following CBS's "The $64,000 Question" on Tuesday evenings. In a related move, the NBC brass dropped a failing quiz show called "Can Do" (which was being drubbed weekly in its Monday-night time slot by the top-rated "I Love Lucy") and replaced it with "Twenty-One," which the network pulled from its Wednesday-evening time slot. Much to everyone's surprise, "Twenty-One" caught on with television viewers, and Jack Barry and Dan Enright, the show's young and aggressive producers, began to create a corporation empire of quiz shows structured in such a way that no network or sponsor could obtain total control of program content.

On November 28, 1956, while "Twenty-One" champion Herbert Stempel was in the midst of his four-week reign, Charles Van Doren, the personable thirty-year-old son of Columbia University professor and poet Mark Van Doren, began his own winning streak on the show. After first dramatically tying Stempel, Van Doren defeated the champion a week later on December 5, 1956, after Stempel had won a total of $49,500.

But not long after Van Doren became the celebrity favorite of quiz show viewers, a contestant from NBC's "The Big Surprise" (also produced by Barry and Enright) complained to the Federal Trade Commission that the show was "other than a true test of skill."

By January 1957, Van Doren's earnings on "Twenty-One" reached $122,000, and the show ran neck-and-neck in the ratings with "I Love Lucy." By February, when Van Doren's picture appeared on the cover of *Time* magazine, the quiz show champion had become a national celebrity. But that same month, the popular champion was tied on "Twenty-One" by Vivienne Nearing, a New York attorney. When the show's ratings were tallied, "Twenty-One" topped "Lucy," the first show in that time slot ever to do so. The following week, Van Doren and Nearing tied again, and "Twenty-One" topped "Lucy" by an even wider margin. But two weeks later ("Twenty-One" was preempted for one week), on March 11, Van Doren lost to Nearing on the very first question, when he could not name the king of Belgium. Van Doren left "Twenty-One" with $129,000 and his own national constituency, and NBC wisely offered the famous English instructor a $50,000-a-year contract to appear each morning with his own five-minute spot on Dave Garroway's "Today" show.

But when Van Doren left "Twenty-One" amid continuing rumors of quiz show rigging, the show's ratings plummeted seventeen points. "Twenty-One" soon dropped out of television's ten top-rated shows and, in the spring of 1957, the integrity of television quiz shows began to be questioned in several leading national magazines. Meanwhile, Louis G. Cowan, who started the quiz show mania when he created "The $64,000 Question," was named president of CBS-TV as the dwindling quiz show audience waited for the next Charles Van Doren to appear.

In May 1958, at a time when a growing ratings lag of network quiz shows precipitated an uneasiness in broadcasting circles, a standby contestant on NBC-TV's "Dotto," while backstage, discovered the notebook of a woman who that same day was a winning contestant on the show. In the notebook were the answers to the questions the woman had answered. On August 7, the standby contestant filed a complaint with Colgate, the show's sponsor. On August 16, a week after Alan Freed allegedly received $400 from Superior Record Sales, "Dotto" was abruptly canceled and replaced by "Top Dollar," another quiz show. Rumors soon began to circulate that a disgruntled "Dotto" contestant had charged that the show was rigged and was talking to New York District Attorney Frank Hogan. On August 28, just hours after the all-time television quiz show prize record of $252,000 was set on "The $64,000 Challenge" (a successful clone of "The $64,000 Question"), Hogan announced that his office, under the auspices of Assistant District Attorney Joseph Stone, would begin an investigation into possible illegal activities by the "Dotto" producers. Although his office said "Dotto" was the only quiz show under scrutiny, there were indications of a wider scandal when, on August 28, Herbert Stempel charged that "Twenty-One" producers Barry and Enright had supplied him with answers before he was told in November 1956 to "take a dive" against Charles Van Doren. Broadcasting historian Eric Barnouw noted that following Stempel's bold allegations, "the smoldering rumors of 'fixed' quiz programs and other broadcasting irregularities blazed into scandal."

Van Doren, then hosting NBC-TV's morning "Today" show for the vacationing Dave Garroway, issued an on-the-air denial, saying he was "saddened and shocked" by Stempel's accusations. A highly respected English instructor who earned $4,400 a year at Columbia before he appeared on "Twenty-One" and subsequently received his own NBC-TV contract, Van Doren said the charges were "enough to shake your faith in human nature" and insisted that he "was never given any answers or told any questions beforehand." Jack Barry and Dan Enright also categorically denied that "Twenty-One" was rigged, but by then, TV quiz shows as a genre were on shaky ground, needing only the slightest push before collapsing.

As rumors of fixed quiz shows flew, Alan Freed was busy promoting his upcoming Labor Day stage show at the Brooklyn Fabian-Fox Theatre, just "down the road" from the rival Brooklyn Paramount. Freed had been denied use of the Paramount theaters for this show because theater executives thought the deejay was still too controversial, after the Boston incident. While Paramount wanted Freed to wait until Christmas to "cool things off," Freed, sorely in need of cash, could not afford to do so. After the deejay finalized a deal with Brooklyn Fox owner Ed Fabian, Paramount executives were reportedly "annoyed" with Freed. It was announced that the Paramount was considering the promoting of a stage show opposite Freed's, which would feature a rotating group of WINS disc jockeys as hosts.

But the Paramount show remained in limbo because of problems in the procurement of talent, for some agents and acts "preferred not to oppose Alan Freed at all."

Aside from the Paramount Theatre squabble, there was trouble brewing for Freed at WABC in the form of Ben Hoberman, who for the past eight years had been a television advertising salesman at XYZ-TV in Detroit. In June 1958, Hoberman became WABC's new station manager. From the start, there was no love lost between Freed and Hoberman, whom Jack Hooke categorized as a "pretty slick dude [as well as] a very tough businessman." Hooke maintained that Hoberman, whose own contract contained an incentive clause awarding the station manager a percentage of the radio station's profits, was aware Freed earned substantial amounts of money from his stage shows and that the new WABC station manager wanted to get as much of that money as possible for the foundering station (and in turn increase his own earnings). Hooke said that Hoberman "came in, and he came in strong!"

There are conflicting accounts of what happened next. Hoberman said that as he monitored Freed's radio program shortly before the deejay's Labor Day stage show, he heard Freed do several unauthorized commercials for the show. Hoberman said the next day he told Freed "under no circumstances would he be allowed to read or do commercials ad lib for his stage shows unless he purchased time to do so like any other advertiser." Hoberman maintained that he also told Freed if the deejay was unwilling to purchase the commercial time, "then there is no need for you to mention anything about this stage show on your radio program."

Jack Hooke said that as Freed's Labor Day show drew near, he and Freed asked Hoberman how much it would cost to purchase advertising spots on the deejay's own radio program to plug the show. Hooke said Hoberman told them that from what the station manager understood, Freed had not paid for individual advertising spots at WINS, that "they got 10 percent of the [stage show] profit" in return for allowing Freed to plug his stage shows on his WINS program. Freed said that when he balked at signing any such percentage agreement with WABC, Hoberman told him he would be "forbidden" to mention his stage shows at all on the air. Hooke said he was with Freed when Hoberman told the deejay, "I'm no Johnny-come-lately. I know all the angles." Hoberman then allegedly mentioned income from Figure Music, as well as "other income," that the station manager knew Freed had, saying he was willing to turn his back on that, "but on the shows I want that 10 percent."

Freed brooded for a week before he yielded to the inevitable and agreed to pay WABC 10 percent of his stage show profits in return for being allowed to advertise the shows on the air at WABC. "Let's have a microphone," Freed told Hooke. "That's all that matters."

Another potential crisis loomed for Freed when his ten-day Labor Day show opened at the Brooklyn Fabian-Fox on August 29. The preshow crowds grew so large that the Fox's doors were opened an hour early to alleviate the crush of teenagers gathered outside. Unbeknownst to the excited young spectators, the Everly Brothers, one of Freed's headline acts, had withdrawn from the show at the last moment. And Freed had not yet arrived at the theater. When the deejay arrived late and was told of the circumstances, he realized that even a minor disturbance coming on the heels of the Boston Arena incident could very likely put an end to his lucrative stage productions. Freed urged his audience to "keep things cool." He reminded them that although critics had predicted four years earlier that rock & roll would not last six months, he and the music were still around, and he had "every intention of returning at least another four years too!" With that, there were rousing cheers as the show began.

Despite the loss of the Everly Brothers, Freed had several other hot acts on hand. Perhaps the hottest one of all was the Elegants, whose Am-Par–distributed recording of "Little Star" was at the top of the charts across the nation. The Elegants' lead singer, Vito Picone, recalled doing several of the Fox shows without Freed because of conflicts with the deejay's WABC radio program. Unlike WINS, Ben Hoberman allowed Freed no Paul Sherman–type stand-in. Freed was required to fulfill his contracted radio obligations before appearing at his stage shows. Besides the Elegants, Freed's Labor Day show featured three other Am-Par–distributed acts—the Poni-Tails ("Born Too Late"), Bobby Hamilton ("Crazy Eyes for You"), and the Royal Teens ("Harvey's Got a Girlfriend").

Am-Par Distributors' growing presence in the pop music structure was indicative of changes taking place behind the scenes. Large record distributors now handled more and more independent record labels as they could provide a small label better distribution, but in doing so, they also wielded life-and-death power over the indies. A distributor could put a record label out of business simply by withholding payment on a hit record or by refusing to push a certain record (or an entire label). By 1958, the indie labels, one of rock & roll's original driving forces, had ceded most of their power and influence to the record distributors.

It was reported that Canadian-born Jack Scott drew "sighs of admiration" from the audience when he sang his first chart hit, "My True Love." But Freed's audience was "sent furthest" by eighteen-year-old teen idol Frankie Avalon, screaming and shouting continuously through the singer's latest hit, "Gingerbread," as well as "De De Dinah." Also on the Brooklyn Fox's stage were the Danleers ("One Summer Night"), Bobby Freeman ("Betty Lou Got a New Pair of Shoes"), Chuck Berry ("Beautiful Delilah"), Bill Haley and the Comets ("Lean Jean"), the Kalin Twins ("When"), Freed favorite Teddy Randazzo ("Little Serenade," the singer's first chart hit), Ed Townsend ("When I Grow Too Old to Dream"), and the Olympics ("Western Movies"), as well as the Cleftones, Larry Williams, and Jo Ann Campbell.

Also on Freed's Labor Day bill were the brother-sister act Gino and Gina. Gino and Gina Giososia lived in the same Queens, New York, neighborhood as Jack Hooke and knew of the producer's ties to Alan Freed. Artie Zwirn, their manager, realized that if anybody could get a record onto Freed's radio program, it was Hooke, and approached him with a song called "Pretty Baby," which had been written by Gino and Gina. Hooke liked the song and so produced a master recording of it. He brought it to Freed, who after listening to it snapped his fingers and proclaimed it "a winner!" The song's publishing rights were assigned to Figure Music, and "Pretty Baby" was released in the spring of 1958. By the time of Freed's Labor Day show, it had become a national hit, rising to number thirty-four on Billboard's "Top 100."

Jo Ann Campbell worked the males in Freed's audience into a frenzy when she suddenly threw off her skirt and revealed skintight shorts (a risqué move for the 1950s). The "blonde bombshell" then picked up her guitar and rocked through renditions of "Jailhouse Rock" and "Hound Dog."

Freed's Brooklyn Fox stand, which produced lines that snaked around the theater, was reminiscent of the deejay's heyday in New York ("Alan Freed Rocks Brooklyn with 'Big Beat' Show," reported *Billboard*), and he wasted no time in flaunting his triumph. Freed placed a full-page advertisement in *Billboard*, thanking Ed Fabian for making it possible for the deejay to break his all-time Brooklyn record with his Labor Day box-office gross of $207,000. Lest anyone have doubts about Freed enjoying his moment of sweet revenge on the rival Paramount theater chain, the $207,000 figure in Freed's ad was set in bold one-and-a-half-inch type and placed alone in the center of the page.

Freed once again rode high, not only because the Brooklyn Fox scene was suggestive of the days when he ruled the rock & roll scene unchallenged but also because of the $84,000 he received as his share of profits from the stage production.

But Freed's relationship with WABC management remained on what Jack Hooke described as a "rocky" basis. Immediately after Freed's Labor Day show, Hoberman summoned the deejay to his office and said the WABC management was unhappy because they felt the station did not make enough money from Freed's show, that "a better deal" would have to be worked out. Freed became so enraged that Hoberman opted to maintain their original 10 percent deal for the deejay's upcoming "Christmas Jubilee of Stars," to be held at Loews' State in Manhattan.

Although no renegotiation of Freed's stage-show advertising agreement took place at that time, another form of renegotiation that involved Freed did occur. Jack Hooke and Bernie Friedlander allegedly agreed to decrease United Artists Records' monthly payments to Freed from $700 to $400. Why the reduction in payment was made is uncertain, but the alleged payments from United Artists Records, as well as from several record distributors, continued to be made on a steady basis to Freed in 1958. On September 29, Freed "did request and accept" from Jerry Blaine's Cosnat Distributing Corporation, a "gift and gratuity" in the amount of $2,000. The next day, he allegedly accepted another $700 check from Superior Record Distributors. On November 21, Freed allegedly received a $500 payment from Sam Weiss on behalf of Superior, while Lester Dees allegedly continued United Artists payments to Freed with $400 amounts being delivered in November and December 1958. On December 18, Sam Weiss allegedly gave Freed another $700 from Superior Record Sales.

In September 1958, Stone's investigation into the alleged television quiz show rigging got under way. The shows' producers—some against their will—began to visit the assistant district attorney's office as many of the quiz shows quietly disappeared from the air. Late in

September, a New York grand jury was empaneled to hear testimony relating to the alleged quiz show rigging.

On October 8, as producer Jack Barry issued an on-the-air defense of his and partner Dan Enright's quiz shows, assuring viewers that "the truth will win out," ex-"Dotto" contestants were telling Stone otherwise. The most damning evidence of fakery surfaced when one "Dotto" contestant handed over to Stone sealed registered letters containing answers he had received and mailed to himself prior to appearing on the show. But the assistant district attorney's investigation was on shaky ground. What, if any, law had the quiz show producers broken with their on-the-air deception? The vast majority of Americans remained unconcerned with, and indifferent to, the growing scandal, while to those who were aware of what was happening, Stone's probe took on "an element of unreality, of a hypothetical crime committed in the imaginary land of television."

On October 16, 1958, CBS network president Frank Stanton, in what was viewed as an attempt to send a message to the Federal Communications Commission that the network could police itself, told the Radio-Television News Directors Association that CBS would cancel all its big-money quiz shows. Stanton said it had been made "crystal clear that the American people hold the networks responsible for what appears on their schedules." Meanwhile, rival NBC canceled "Twenty-One" (whose rating had plummeted from sixth to thirty-sixth in a matter of months) and several of its other quiz shows. But all the while, both CBS and NBC complained loudly that the tainted quiz shows had been produced by outsiders and that the networks had no control over them. The ABC network, which had never relied on big-money quiz shows to the extent that the other two major networks had, gloated on the sidelines as Dick Clark's "American Bandstand" flourished.

In New York, Assistant District Attorney Stone finally uncovered a possible lawbreaker. Albert Freedman, the producer of "Dotto" and "Twenty-One," was indicted for lying to a New York grand jury when he testified that he had not given answers to contestants who appeared on the show.

In November, "The $64,000 Question," the prototype of TV's blockbuster quiz shows, was taken off the air. As other quiz shows continued to disappear from the airwaves (by December 1958, all such shows had virtually disappeared from the home screen), the New York grand jury continued to meet behind closed doors into

1959, and what little public interest had been aroused by the scandal quickly subsided.

As Alan Freed's Boston legal counsel placed advertisements in local newspapers, appealing to people who were present at the Boston Arena on the night of Freed's rock & roll show to come forth as witnesses, the deejay's trial was postponed from November 17, 1958, until January 1959.

Meanwhile, Freed's power struggle with the WABC management escalated when the station attempted to gain control over the records Freed programmed. It was a standard broadcasting practice that all radio stations adhere to a periodically received list of songs approved for lyrical content and cleared for broadcast by BMI, ASCAP, or SESAC, the song-licensing agencies. Jack Hooke said that while disc jockeys on small, independent stations might get away with playing unapproved songs, on the network stations "nothing could be played until it was cleared." Hooke revealed that while "Alan had to have the list," the deejay simply ignored it. The situation was exacerbated whenever various record manufacturers or distributors brought Freed dubs of unreleased records, some which Freed then played on his program, despite the fact they had not yet been cleared for airplay. "Somewhere down the line, ASCAP or BMI would call ABC to complain," said Hooke. Hoberman, in turn, would get on Hooke's back, reminding Freed's associate that the deejay was not permitted to play songs not yet cleared for broadcast. Freed adhered to WABC's playlist for a few days, said Hooke, but "the next thing I knew, there he'd go again [playing uncleared songs]." Each new violation on Freed's part drew Hoberman's ire. "He can't do that, Jack!" complained Hoberman. "I'm going to get fined by the FCC!" WABC then demanded that Freed submit his playlist to the station three days in advance. Hooke said that he and Freed cut the time down to two days, and before long, the deejay's associate was "running to them at the last minute with the list."

Ben Hoberman maintained that the selection of records for airplay on Freed's "Big Beat" remained "Mr. Freed's bailiwick." Although the station manager contended that Freed had the authority to play whatever he chose "within the limits of good taste," it was the opinion of pop music business veteran Bob Rolontz that Freed's WABC radio program "never really equalled the popularity of his WINS program, partly because he was restricted in the records he could play."

Whether Freed was told to play certain records or was given an incentive to do so (or threatened if he did not), the WABC deejay without question played an inordinate amount of "ABC family" records (released on the ABC-Paramount label and/or distributed by Am-Par) on his "Big Beat" program, many of which were heard on no other radio station.

Freed's running battle with the Paramount theater chain continued with his "Christmas Jubilee of Stars," which opened on Christmas Day, 1958, at the Manhattan Loews' State, located at Times Square, just across Broadway from the Paramount. Since the Paramount people had considered Freed too controversial to play their theater in August, they would not have him in December—or ever again, if Freed had his way.

In a curious move, the very un-rock & roll-like Johnny Ray was signed to headline the first half of Freed's Christmas run, with the Everly Brothers ("Problems/"Love of My Life") slated to move in for the show's final five days. It was reported that Ray (who had a moderate pop hit on the charts with "Up Until Now") "tried very hard" to please Freed's audience, but that "the teeners didn't dig him," and Ray "seemed out of his element."

While nobody in the Loews' State audience realized it, six of Freed's stage acts were also set to appear in the deejay's next rock & roll movie, scheduled to begin production immediately following his Christmas show. The six included Chuck Berry, who promoted his two-sided seasonal hit, "Run, Rudolph, Run" and "Merry Christmas, Baby"; Jackie Wilson, who performed his current hit, "Lonely Teardrops" in what was said to be a "highly dramatic style" and whose manager, Nat ("The Rat") Tarnapol, also worked as an A&R man for Morris Levy's Roulette Records; teen idol Jimmy Clanton (who would play a teen idol in Freed's movie), who sang "A Letter to an Angel" and "A Part of Me"; the Cadillacs, who performed their current hit, "Peek-a-Boo," which was only the second chart success for the much-heralded New York group; Eddie Cochran ("C'mon Everybody"); and Harvey Fuqua and the Moonglows ("Ten Commandments of Love"). Also appearing on the Loews' State stage were Frankie Avalon ("I'll Wait for You"/"What Little Girl"); the Crests ("16 Candles"); Dion and the Belmonts ("Don't Pity Me"); the Royal Teens; Baby Washington; the Nu Tornados; and Freed's wife Inga, whom the WABC deejay was trying to make into a rock & roll star. Inga had recently cut her first record, "Silly Willy" (her follow-up, "Get Off the

Phone," would appear shortly), and Freed was giving it steady airplay on his "Big Beat" program. Besides having Inga appear onstage by herself, Freed also came up with a way to work her into another act on the bill.

Joey Villa (who had been the lead singer of the Three Friends on their 1956 recording of "Blanche") was a member of the Royal Teens, who were then at the tail end of their hit "Harvey's Got a Girlfriend," and it was his fate to play "Harvey" in the group's stage act. When Freed introduced the group Villa ran onstage, dressed as Little Lord Fauntleroy in "short shorts" (commemorating the group's biggest hit) and wide-brimmed hat and carrying a giant lollipop.

When Freed first saw the Royal Teens' act during rehearsal, Villa recalled that the deejay approached him and said, "I want to put my wife in there, 'Harvey.' I'd like to have Inga on the show." Villa, wise enough not to question Freed, said he "just kept his mouth closed." Inga's cue to walk onstage came after the Royal Teens sang the line "Harvey's got a girlfriend," to which Villa responded, "So what!" Villa remembered that Inga appeared, "strollin' across the stage . . . in some sexy dress, before suddenly planting a kiss on Villa's face." ("I mean a kiss!" he exclaimed). Then "the audience began whistling and clapping," said the singer, who endured five or six of Inga's kisses for the next ten days. "I had my Christmas gift, believe me!" said Villa.

Despite such stage antics, and the presence of artists with hit records, it was Bo Diddley, without a hit record on the charts, who once again proved to be Freed's showstopper. It was reported that Diddley's electrifying guitar showmanship "broke it up most of all," drawing a couple of encores from Freed's appreciative audience.

Billboard noted that Freed "nearly packed the house" the day after Christmas at Loews' State. What is more, the show's overall box-office gross, somewhere in the neighborhood of $225,000, topped the $207,000 Freed racked up in Brooklyn the previous Labor Day. Under the circumstances, it was the best way Freed could have closed out 1958. Aside from his successful stage productions, the year had been the stormiest year yet in his controversial career. He had walked unexpectedly into the Boston riot incident, only to be further shocked by WINS's nonsupport and subsequent dismissal of him. And although he was quickly hired by WABC, Freed's new job brought new headaches as he became embroiled with management on several issues.

On that unsettled note, Freed left for California in January, 1959, to begin shooting *Go, Johnny, Go*, the fifth of the deejay's rock & roll movies.

Go, Johnny, Go was directed by Paul Landres and produced by Freed. Once again the deejay portrayed himself on the screen. This time he costarred with young singers Jimmy Clanton and Sandy Stewart, as well as with Chuck Berry, a veteran of two of Freed's earlier films. This time, in addition to his musical performances, Berry was afforded a major speaking part. The arrangement proved advantageous to Berry, not only for the prestige but also for the money. Those artists who did not have speaking parts received no monetary compensation. But despite that thrifty production arrangement, Berry said that during his five days spent filming *Go, Johnny, Go* at the Hal Roach Studios in Culver City, he saw "lots of people walking around, doing nothing, it seemed, but surely on the payroll."

The film's minimal plot centered around disc jockey Freed's "creation" of a rock & roll star by incessantly playing the unknown singer's record on the deejay's radio program. The new "idol" happens to be a young orphan boy (played by Clanton), whom Freed subsequently rescues from a potentially life-ruining jewelry store robbery by taking the rap himself. Ironically, so closely were Freed's real-life rock & roll shows identified with the Paramount theaters that a scene in *Go, Johnny, Go* that purportedly showed the disc jockey's 1958 Christmas show was depicted as having taken place at the New York Paramount, despite Freed's actual boycott of that famed theater.

Of course, the ultimate reason for *Go, Johnny, Go*'s existence were the filmed rock & roll performances (some of which, like those in *Rock, Rock, Rock* were filmed in New York and later edited into the film) of Clanton, Berry, Jackie Wilson, Eddie Cochran, Jo Ann Campbell, the Flamingos, the Cadillacs, Harvey Fuqua (as a solo act), and a rare film appearance by Ritchie Valens, who performed "Ooh, My Head" (after reportedly seeing an early screening of the film, Valens said, "I'm not much good, but I hope my mother likes me").

An oddity among the movie's many musical performances was Chuck Berry's rendition of "Little Queenie," in which Freed is shown sitting in on drums. By the closing bars of the song, as Freed loses the song's beat entirely, it becomes obviously that the filmed video and the recorded audio of "Little Queenie" are not one and the same.

In *Go, Johnny, Go* the artists sang their respective numbers, after which everyone lived happily ever after, but Freed was still unable to turn his celluloid fantasies into reality. When late in January 1959 Freed returned to New York from his three-week California hiatus, he said he received a telephone call from Ben Hoberman, who was then vacationing in Florida. The WABC station manager allegedly told Freed that since motion pictures "seemed more important" than the deejay's own radio program, WABC felt Freed's services were no longer needed. Hoberman said the decision to terminate Freed's contract, effective at the end of February, was not the station manager's alone, that other WABC executives had some hand in the move. Hoberman also maintained that WABC's decision had nothing to do with its running battle over payment for Freed's on-the-air stage show plugs, that it came about because of "several incidents [which occurred after Freed's Christmas show], none of them relating to the stage show." ABC network president Leonard Goldenson said that the primary reason for terminating Freed's contract was that the deejay no longer had a highly rated program, that Freed's radio show "wasn't doing any [advertising] business."

Whether he could face the truth or not, by 1959 Freed's popularity in New York was on the wane. Since coming over from WINS, the rock & roll deejay's original hard-core followers had increased in age, but had declined in numbers. And Freed had not won over many new listeners. As early as August 1958, Peter Tripp of rival WMGM topped the Teen Age Survey poll as New York's favorite disc jockey among both high school and college students. To make matters worse for Freed, second place was held down by Paul Sherman, the WABC deejay's original "Crown Prince" stand-in at WINS. Although Freed continued to offer the widest variety of new rock & roll sounds (albeit biased toward ABC-Paramount and Am-Par products) in New York, his "Big Beat" radio program lacked the crisp professionalism that his audience had over the years come to expect. It was as if Freed, surrounded by legal, personal, and outside business distractions, had lost interest in his own program and no longer took rock & roll as seriously as he once had. Freed's listeners had to contend with a steady stream of on-the-air clowning, staff in-jokes, whispered asides and put-downs, and an overabundance of dead air—the bane of any radio station. The deejay's listeners were also subjected to running gags about his engineer, Marty Foglia, and his announcer, Don Lowe.

On the air, Freed referred to Lowe's news broadcasts as "unfortunate thing[s] that I have to do," adding that it was a "good thing" WABC had a very efficient news bureau downstairs, "because we've got a terribly inefficient newscaster upstairs by the name of Don Lowe!" Lowe derisively addressed Freed as "Alvin" (it was a time when David Seville's "Chipmunks"—Alvin, Theodore, and Simon—were the pop radio rage).

One night, as Freed played an ABC-Paramount record by a then-unknown seventeen-year-old Carole King, the record began to skip. "Tell Sam Clark [Am-Par president] to take it easy with those pressings," interrupted Freed on the air. "Clark, you can't do that, man!" Then, after a long pause, Freed quipped, "I didn't say 'Dick' [Clark], I said 'Sam'!"

Constantly dissatisfied with the performance of his board engineer, Foglia, Freed complained how it would be tough to replace him because "they've got a pretty strong union . . . Ben [Hoberman], it's not my fault, if you're listening. It's Marty's fault!"

Freed also conducted a "Ben Hoberman look-alike contest," in which the deejay's listeners were encouraged to draw and submit pictures of what they thought the station manager looked like. "I hope you'll be kind to him when you draw the pictures," Freed told his listeners, " 'cause next week we could all be outta here, you know." Contest winners, explained Freed, would be selected from "the best ten drawings, or worst drawings—whichever our judges [Foglia, Inga, Lowe and John "The Cool Ghoul" Zacherle, then the host of a local TV horror movie show in New York and the narrator of the 1958 novelty hit record "Dinner with Drac"] decide."

Freed refused to acknowledge the changing times and the deterioration in the quality of his radio program, holding steadfast to his belief that WABC was trying to ax him solely because the station felt it was not receiving enough money for the deejay's on-the-air stage show plugs, and for his refusal to use Paramount theaters for his stage shows. The deejay pointed out that his personal efforts had recently landed two major sponsors—Coca-Cola and the Gillette Razor Company—for his "Big Beat" program, and while it was true that Freed's show no longer held down the top spot in the local ratings, it remained a moneymaker, grossing between $85,000 and $90,000 a year for WABC. What Freed thought made no difference, however. Ben Hoberman stuck to the station's decision to fire Freed and gave him four weeks' notice.

Once again, Freed faced the prospect of an upcoming stage show and not having a radio program on which to promote both the show and the latest records of those artists booked to perform onstage. In desperation, Freed asked Hoberman if there was any way his contract could be extended an additional five weeks, enabling the deejay to remain on the air until his stage show took place. WABC agreed to do so, but realizing that they had Freed on the ropes, the station's price was steep. On February 13, less than two weeks after Freed and the rest of the rock & roll world had been shocked by the tragic deaths of Buddy Holly, Ritchie Valens, and the Big Bopper in a plane crash in Iowa, WABC drew up a contract extension for the deejay. The document stipulated that Freed purchase advertising time on WABC to plug the upcoming show and that if there ever came a time that he should "not be one of the sponsors," the station had the right to terminate the agreement "effective as of such time." Not having much choice, Freed signed the temporary pact. Hoberman pointed out that WABC was no longer interested in Freed and had already terminated his services. At the end of his five-week contract extension Freed was to be fired.

But amid rumors of Freed's impending firing and while Ben Hoberman allegedly conducted interviews for the deejay's replacement, Freed suddenly signed a new contract with WABC on March 2, 1959. The stunning turnabout by the American Broadcasting Company did not come about out of the goodness of its heart. Freed, who at the time earned $41,600 a year from ABC, was told that if he agreed to pay WABC the sum of $10,000, three times a year, to plug his stage shows, then a new contract could indeed be worked out. Under the $30,000 kickback agreement, WABC would be getting Freed's disc jockey services for approximately $10,000 a year. While Hoberman admitted that Freed's new contract was not the "usual type of arrangement" for WABC's disc jockeys, the station manager said he thought the large reduction in Freed's salary would be compensated for by his stage show earnings. *Billboard* reported that Freed's new contract signing "silenced rumors of several weeks that he might leave ABC this month."

In one way, Freed felt vindicated by the oppressive financial structure of his new contract. It was proof that he had been correct all along in believing the root of his troubles with WABC was the protracted stage show advertising dispute he was engaged in. Despite the ABC network president's claim that Freed's popularity was declining and the deejay's "Big Beat" program "wasn't doing any business," WABC managed to come up with a new contract for Freed after he agreed to kick back three-fourths of his salary to the station.

As harsh as the $30,000 yearly price tag for remaining on WABC appeared to be for Freed, it was not of major concern to him. The new contract ensured Freed a voice on the airwaves, the deejay's guarantee that his lucrative stage shows would continue, and the continuance of the payments he regularly received from various record companies and distributors.

Shortly before Freed signed his new WABC contract, Roulette Records president Morris Levy announced in the music trade papers that his label "had never been stronger." Most likely, the announcement was a public relations ploy to boost Roulette's reputation. It was said that Levy planned to make Roulette stock available to the public and had already conferred with the Securities and Exchange Commission regarding such a move.

On March 6, 1959, Boston's Assistant District Attorney Edward M. Sullivan announced that one of the charges originally lodged against Freed would be dropped. Since Freed had also been charged with the misdemeanor of inciting to riot, Sullivan said that "no useful purpose" would be served by pursuing the anarchy charge. No new trial date was announced, and Freed's legal fees continued to mount.

Meanwhile, Freed's weekday "Big Beat" television show was doing well enough for WNEW-TV to give the deejay an eight-to-nine Saturday-night edition. Soon after its April 4 debut, Freed's Saturday-night "Big Beat" was reported to be "well ahead of the previous ratings" for that hour.

Freed returned to the Brooklyn Fabian-Fox Theatre for his Easter show, where he hoped to duplicate, if not top, the previous year's record-breaking Labor Day run. His ten-day show, which began on March 27, was loaded with artists eager to promote recently released fast-rising records. Among them were headliners Fats Domino ("I'm Ready"/"Margie") and Jackie Wilson ("That's Why [I Love You So]"), as well as Bobby Darin ("Dream Lover"), Duane Eddy ("Yep!"), Dale Hawkins ("Class Cutter [Yeah Yeah]"), the Impalas ("Sorry [I Ran All the Way Home]"), Fabian ("Turn Me Loose"), and Joe Medlin ("I Kneel at Your Throne"), a vocalist out of Buddy Johnson's band. Two other acts, Thomas Wayne ("Tragedy") and the Skyliners ("Since I Don't Have You"), had enjoyed huge hits that were still selling. Twenty-nine-year-old pop singer Tommy Leonetti, Larry Williams, Bobby Freeman, and the Mello-Kings also performed, as did three stars—Jimmy Clanton, Sandy Stewart, and the Cadillacs—from Freed's about-to-be released film *Go, Johnny, Go*. Rounding out the Fabian-Fox bill was regular crowd-pleaser Jo An Campbell (who was still a year away from her first charted hit record) and Freed's wife Inga, whom the deejay still aspired to make into a recording star. On this show, Inga promoted her latest record, called "Get Off the Phone."

Reflecting the current state of rock & roll, Freed's 1959 Easter show bore scant resemblance to his earlier, legendary group-laden Paramount productions. This time Freed had only four groups—three of them white—in his lineup. And following the show, it was duly reported that one of Freed's "highlight performers" had been none other than sixteen-year-old teen idol Fabian.

Fabian, who, according to Jack Hooke, "couldn't sing a note" but had that "virile image that Dick Clark had built," was slated to perform early in Freed's show. Twenty-two-year-old Bobby Darin, not scheduled to go onstage until later in the show, watched from the wings as, in Hooke's words, Fabian hit the stage "and the joint went wild." Freed's associate said it was "impossible" to hear Fabian, "that's how nutty the kids were!"

Unlike Fabian, Darin had a wealth of talent—"a good writer, a good arranger, and very hip musically, a talented kid in spite of his cocky attitude," recalled Hooke. But Darin also had a deep streak of insecurity and fear of failure which drove him to succeed. Hooke said when Darin saw the audience's reaction to Fabian ("They were out of their heads!"), "he couldn't believe it." Momentarily transfixed on the scene, Darin then returned to his upstairs dressing room. When he came back down, the multitalented Darin, who was on his way to a fourth successive hit record ("Splish Splash," "Queen of the Hop," and "Plain Jane" preceded "Dream Lover"), appeared backstage gesturing with his hands and moving his lips in silence. A doctor was summoned to examine Darin, but no physical ailment could be determined. Hooke said that Darin, worried that he would not be able to match Fabian's fanatical audience response, "mentally lost his voice. When he came back down he could not sing." Darin was scratched from that particular show, while Fabian—originally scheduled to perform on the first four days of Freed's show—was hastily booked for the deejay's final two days.

Despite a March 30 box-office gross of $27,000, the Fabian-Fox's largest one-day take in its history, Freed's Easter show grossed a disappointing $167,000. Once the deejay's expenses were met, the $10,000 Freed was contracturally required to pay WABC for radio advertising exceeded his share of the stage show's profits. That prompted Freed to tell Ben Hoberman that the deejay did not intend to purchase future airtime from WABC on which to plug his stage shows. According to Freed, Hoberman told him that the disc jockey had no choice in the matter but to pay the $30,000, that "Paragraph Twenty" of Freed's new contract (which took effect on April 6, the day after the deejay's Easter show ended) stipulated that Freed "shall purchase airtime from WABC, three times a year." Freed asked how he could be expected to comply with an agreement whereby he would lose money. He demanded that Hoberman lower the $10,000 figure, which precipitated a heated three-hour dispute during which Freed swore that Hoberman told him if he did not like his contract, the station manager would "take his microphone away," leaving Freed with no radio audience and no means to promote either his stage shows or the artists who were slated to appear on them. Hoberman finally agreed to reduce the advertising price Freed was required to pay from $10,000 to $7,000, three times a year, but the deejay's Pyrrhic victory was tempered by the rumor that Hoberman's contract with WABC stipulated that the station manager receive a percentage of the station's profits. Freed protested that he was being "blackjacked" by Hoberman, who sought to increase his own income by squeezing more money out of the deejay.

It was around this time that Freed staged an impromptu on-the-air Jackie Wilson "marathon." Although Wilson's manager also worked for Roulette Records, Ray Reneri said that "no one knew what Alan's association was with Jackie." But Freed and Wilson had a close personal friendship that extended to the singer's early days with Billy Ward's Dominoes. Freed vigorously promoted Wilson's records and personal appearances and at the time had all the more reason to do so. *Go, Johnny, Go* with Wilson one of the film's featured performers, was about to be released in movie theaters across the country. What is more, Wilson's latest record, "I'll Be Satisfied," had just been released. Freed, with the opportunity to simultaneously promote his own movie and Wilson's career, played "I'll Be Satisfied" and then asked his listeners to call and voice their opinions on the song. Freed then told his audience that since they liked Wilson's new record so much, "We're going to play it again." Then, said Reneri, "he played it for forty-five minutes straight and the station manager freaked!"

Freed told Hoberman that it was the deejay's show, and "if I want to play one record for three hours, I'll play it!"

The New York grand jury hearing closed-door testimony concerning the rigging of television quiz shows ended its session on June 10, 1959. Charles Van Doren had testified before the panel in January that "Twenty-One" was not rigged, but by that time "Twenty-One" (and most other big-money quiz shows) had been all but forgotten by an apathetic American viewing public. After hearing testimony from more than 150 witnesses about six quiz shows, the grand jury handed up its twelve-thousand-word report to New York Criminal Court Judge Mitchell D. Schweitzer. The report was not the usual grand jury indictment but rather a "presentment," which called attention to illegal acts without holding specific people responsible for them. Although District Attorney Frank Hogan maintained that more than 100 of the 150 witnesses had lied, most of the quiz show producers in question cooperated with his office and, in return, potential charges against them were dropped (the one exception was the indictment of "Twenty-One" producer Albert Freedman for lying to the grand jury).

Judge Schweitzer sealed and impounded the grand jury report because he believed making the document public would damage those mentioned in it by not giving them the opportunity to publicly defend themselves. But the grand jury members, outraged by the rigging allegations they had been privy to over the past few months, wanted their report made public. The panel claimed it had specifically avoided naming individuals so that no harm would be done by releasing its findings. A compromise was worked out in August 1959 whereby Judge Schweitzer agreed to show the minutes of the grand jury investigation (the actual report was never made public) to Representative Oren Harris of Arkansas, chairman of the House Subcommittee on Legislative Oversight, who had recently announced that his subcommittee would begin public hearings on October 6 regarding the television quiz show rigging.

While the alleged payments to Freed from United Artists Records and Superior Record Sales continued, Charles Van Doren received his Ph.D. in July 1959 and was made an assistant professor at Columbia University. That same month, Alpha Distributors, represented by Johnny Halonka and Harry Apostoleris, allegedly entered into an agreement with Freed "with an understanding that he would expose records distributed by Alpha Distributing Company for payment of $500 per month." It was also alleged that Freed "insisted that the checks from Alpha were to be made to the order of his wife's maiden name, Inga Boling." Halonka supposedly made such payments in the form of $500 checks in July, August, and October 1959 and, while doing so, "brought all his new [record] releases to Freed, who selected those he liked and played them on his program."

In the past year, Dick Clark had added nine additional music-related companies, including Arch Music, an ASCAP-affiliated publishing firm purchased in December 1958, and indirect interests in BAE Music (ASCAP) and Request Music (BMI), wholly owned publishing subsidiaries of Swan Records formed in August 1959. By that time, Clark had begun to branch out of the entertainment field and formed two corporations with which to purchase land in Maryland and in Delaware, while on America's home screens and in record stores Clark's teen idols continued to roll along. Fabian, Frankie Avalon, Freddy Cannon, and Kathy Linden, among others, each had a hit record published by one of Clark's publishing companies.

Jackie Wilson headlined Freed's Brooklyn Fox Labor Day show in 1959, singing his latest release, "You Better Know It," which was taken from the recently released film *Go, Johnny, Go*. Jimmy Clanton, another of the film's stars, performed his latest hit, "My Own True Love." As usual, several acts with up-and-coming hits to promote, among them Dion and the Belmonts, with their two-sided hit "Every Little Thing I Do" and "A Lover's Prayer"; the Skyliners, with "It Happened Today"; the Crests, with "The Angels Listened In"; and the Mystics, with "Don't Take the Stars," appeared with Freed. Trying to join the teen-idol ranks was fifteen-year-old Bronx-born Johnny Restivo, who sang his hit "The Shape I'm In." The Tempos, who, like the Skyliners, hailed from Pittsburgh, performed their big summer hit, "See You in September" and its ill-fated follow-up, "The Crossroads of Love." Freed also showcased Roulette Records' hottest new artists, twenty-four-year-old Ronnie Hawkins and the Hawks, whose first two Roulette releases, "Forty Days" and "Mary Lou," appeared on the national charts. Freed crowd-pleasers Jo Ann Campbell and Bo Diddley were also on hand. After years of trying, Diddley's last two records, "Crackin' Up" and "Say Man," entered the national pop sales charts. Rounding out the bill for

Freed's summer-ending show was Roulette artist Valerie Carr, Johnny October, and the not-yet-famous Bobby Lewis.

Freed managed, albeit barely, to survive his turmoil-filled first year at WABC. He believed he had been badly mistreated and given little respect by his own radio station, yet Freed clung to his all-important microphone. The famous rock & roll disc jockey still had his stage shows and a steady income from at least four local record distributors (Action, Alpha, Cosnat, and Superior), and little else mattered to him at that point.

What Freed did not foresee was that the widening television quiz show scandal, as yet largely unrevealed to the public, would soon be afforded heightened exposure by Oren Harris's Subcommittee on Legislative Oversight. That, in turn, would draw public attention to alleged broadcasting payola practices, of which Freed would be cast as the principal practitioner.

CHAPTER 12

Payola

"What they call payola in the disc jockey business they call lobbying in Washington."

THE House Subcommittee on Legislative Oversight, created in 1952 "to probe the morals of radio and television programs," had since bedeviled the television industry, as well as the FCC itself, with antitrust allegations and inconclusive hearings concerning sex and violence on the home screen. With the New York grand jury's television quiz show rigging revelations, Oren Harris, the bespectacled and subdued congressman from Arkansas, believed he finally had a strong issue to use against the television network broadcasters, whose industrywide power had increased over the past several years by what many thought to be alarming proportions. But during months of research, subcommittee lawyers failed to come up with any federal law that the alleged quiz riggers had broken. Thus, the Harris subcommittee hearings concerning quiz show rigging became a vehicle by which to bring the issue before the American public. It was hoped that a national viewing audience would react as the members of the New York grand jury had reacted—with outrage—and demand federal legislation making such deception illegal and curbing the broadcasting autonomy in the process.

The federal government's broadcasting regulatory agency, the Federal Communications Commission, had its own problems with the House Subcommittee on Legislative Oversight. Because of the growing power of the television networks within the broadcasting industry, the FCC, in the fall of 1955, brought pressure on the subcommittee to look into the networks' operating practices. The subcommittee, then chaired by Morgen Moulder of Missouri, did not issue its first report on the subject until October 1957, by which time Harris had replaced Moulder. Its recommendations, which reportedly "shook the industry," called for sweeping changes in broadcasting, of which the most significant was that the networks be placed under the control of the FCC. Predictably, the networks protested that such changes would destroy the structure of American broadcasting.

During its investigation of the network broadcasters, the subcommittee also began to look into problems involving the federal regulatory agencies (including the FCC), which the subcommittee was to oversee and supervise. At the time, a boom atmosphere permeated America, affecting virtually every facet of business, including the broadcasting industry. Since the FCC had the final say on who would control the limited number of available television stations, private enterprise did not hesitate to use various means to influence commission members in order to gain favorable decisions. Reacting to rumors of FCC corruption, the Harris subcommittee in 1957 hired New York University law professor Bernard Schwartz to serve as its chief counsel. Schwartz was instructed to conduct an investigation of the federal regulatory agencies. Broadcasting historians Christopher H. Sterling and John M. Kittross wrote that "almost from the start, the FCC became a prime target" of Schwartz's probe.

Creating as much embarrassment as surprise for Schwartz, Harris, who presented the image of a crusading legislator to the public, also became a target of the law professor's investigation. Schwartz uncovered the fact that Harris had acquired a 25 percent interest in KRBB-TV, located in the congressman's hometown of El Dorado, Arkansas. Shortly after Harris's broadcasting acquisition, for which he paid $500 and a $4,500 promissory note, KRBB-TV reapplied for a previously denied power increase. Not only was the power increase granted by the FCC, but Harris never made good on the promissory note.

When the chairman of the subcommittee saw no impropriety in the chain of events involving his interest in KRBB-TV, Schwartz was in a quandary as to how he should proceed. Schwartz, who, it has been said, had "little patience for diplomatic conventions," leaked some of his findings concerning Chairman Harris's TV coup to the press. The embarrassed legislator eventually sold his share of KRBB-

TV, but he continued to have jurisdiction over the congressional broadcasting probe. Schwartz, done in by his press leaks, was fired by the House subcommittee in January 1958, but not before he showed that certain investigators could stand a bit of investigating themselves.

The Harris subcommittee probe indicated that FCC members routinely fraternized with broadcasting executives, often collected unethical payments for travel and entertainment, and discussed pending cases with parties that had a vested interest in the outcome. Those findings were stated in a subcommittee report issued in April 1958, which called for a code of ethics for administrative agency personnel and for the right of the president to remove commissioners for "neglect of duty."

The congressional hearings regarding television quiz show rigging, largely a rehashing of the New York grand jury's findings, were as much political theater as they were anything else. After eight years, the laissez-faire Republican administration headed by World War II hero Dwight Eisenhower was drawing to a close. The Democrats, utilizing every opportunity to discredit the Eisenhower administration, whose vice-president, Richard M. Nixon, would serve as the Republican party standard-bearer in the 1960 presidential election, lost no time in attacking their political rivals. The televised Harris subcommittee, chaired by a Democrat, and consisting of a Democratic majority, had a unique opportunity to make political hay by exposing to America the level of corruption tolerated by the Republicans. Not coincidentally, each subcommittee member was up for reelection the following November.

The subcommittee hearings began on October 6, 1959, four days after Alan Freed allegedly received the second of two $500 payments given to Jack Hooke by Lou Klayman of Action Record Distributors. The hearings were conducted in the Caucus Room of the Old House Building, a high-ceilinged chamber where the congressmen sat behind a huge round table fronted by paneling which concealed not only their feet but also the golden spittoons left over from a bygone era. One of the first to testify was Herbert Stempel, who had blown the whistle on the "Twenty-One" producers a year earlier. Soon after came the first public appearance of James Snodgrass and the registered letters that contained answers he was given before his appearance on "Dotto" and that he had then mailed to himself; they ultimately forced quiz show producer Dan Enright to admit what could no longer be denied. On October 9, Enright publicly acknowledged that "controls" had been "a practice for many, many years" on his quiz shows, as well as on others. The following day, FCC chairman John C. Doerfer testified before the subcommittee that he had been "unable to pinpoint any legal violations" in the quiz rigging. Furthermore, said Doerfer, in his opinion the FCC had no authority to act on the matter because of a federal communications law prohibiting censorship by the regulatory agency.

As Dan Enright made his public confession, Charles Van Doren, who had been Enright's star performer and who continued to deny any complicity in the quiz riggings, was nowhere to be found. After being subpoenaed to testify before the Harris subcommittee, Van Doren mysteriously dropped out of sight for several days before suddenly appearing in New York at District Attorney Hogan's office on October 13. Van Doren explained he had been on vacation in New England, but was ready to testify in Washington.

By late October, Jack Barry, Dan Enright, and other quiz show producers openly admitted that most of the big-money TV quiz shows had been rigged. Their excuse for having done so was that "deception is not necessarily bad . . . it's practiced in everyday life." Since the quiz show producers now openly admitted that their shows had indeed been fixed, many of the contestants who had testified before the New York grand jury (some with coaching by the quiz producers) that such rigging had not taken place were now open to perjury charges.

At a news conference held on October 22, President Eisenhower called the quiz show hoax a "terrible thing" to do to the American public. While he saw "no power in the Executive Department" to deal with the problem, Eisenhower also expressed doubt that the FCC had the authority to do anything to remedy the situation. But Eisenhower did order his attorney general, William P. Rogers, to meet with broadcasting, FCC, and Federal Trade Commission officials to look into the situation.

On November 2, 1959, America watched a different kind of television quiz show as the thirty-three-year-old Charles Van Doren, described as a "symbol of ingenuity," awkwardly slid into the witness chair to face the House Subcommittee on Legislative Oversight. Van Doren nervously gulped a glass of water before slowly telling the congressional investigators in a teary-eyed manner that he would "give almost anything to reverse the course of my life in the last three years." He then described the concern of the "Twenty-One" sponsor

(Revlon Cosmetics) in 1956 that Herbert Stempel, viewed as an unpopular figure who was causing "Twenty-One" to lose viewers, was "virtually unbeatable," given his vast array of knowledge. Van Doren, a certified intellectual with "the good looks and engaging manner of a manitee idol," said he was handpicked by the show's producer, Albert Freedman, to defeat Stempel and aid the cause of the "intellectual"—not to mention the show's sagging ratings. Van Doren agreed to do so, but he maintained that although his conscience quickly got the better of him, and he asked Freedman to end the ruse, the producer would not do so. It surely occurred to many television viewers who found Van Doren's admission to being coached particularly galling that he could have ended the hoax at any time simply by giving an incorrect answer on the show. But he did not. Van Doren admitted to the subcommittee that he had been "foolish, naive, prideful, and avaricious" in originally lying to the grand jury. By the time he finished testifying, most of the subcommittee members were visibly moved. But Steven B. Derounian of New York told the contrite witness he did not think an adult of Van Doren's intelligence "ought to be commended for telling the truth." Following his public confession, Van Doren was fired by Columbia University and by NBC-TV. Revlon immediately dropped its sponsorship of all Barry-Enright shows, and within one week all Barry-Enright shows were removed from the air.

While the subcommittee hearings made it clear that both NBC and CBS had duped their audiences with rigged quiz shows, the networks had markedly different reactions. CBS canceled its three remaining big-prize shows—"Top Dollar," "Name That Tune," and "The Big Payoff"—and said it would eliminate other broadcasting "deceits," including recorded laughter on comedy shows. NBC maintained that when "properly conducted," quiz shows were "legitimate entertainment desired by the public" and that network's remaining quiz shows would be "policed, not cancelled." The ABC network, never heavily committed to big-money quiz shows, adopted NBC's position.

Meanwhile, a mood of retribution began to crystallize in the nation's collective consciousness as television viewers realized they had been hoodwinked by the broadcasters and a handful of quiz show producers. The *New York Times* decried the "shocking state of rottenness within the radio-television world" and denounced the " 'get-rich-quick' schemes through which so many people were corrupted and so many millions were deceived." Over a decade after the scandal, one television critic wrote that "nothing television has done in America has had so great an impact—or so evil a consequence—as the revelation that the ordinary people millions had come to admire were in fact common cheats and liars."

As fate would have it, Jack Barry and Dan Enright also owned two top-forty radio stations. After the quiz show team admitted their complicity in the television rigging, ASCAP and other frustrated anti-rock & roll forces had before them a link between the deceptive practices of quiz show rigging and music business payola. Perhaps BMI and rock & roll could be brought down with this issue. The situation called for a dramatic way to introduce the music business payola allegations to a public already outraged by the television quiz rigging revelations. This latest ASCAP-inspired assault on rock & roll would come by way of the Harris subcommittee, setting the stage for Alan Freed to become the Charles Van Doren of rock & roll.

The day that Van Doren confessed his guilt before a national television audience, Superior Records' Sam Weiss met at Freed's Lincoln Towers apartment on Sixty-fourth street with the disc jockey and his radio producer, Johnny Brantley. Weiss had allegedly paid $700 a month on behalf of Superior to Freed since August 1958. It was said that in return Freed would "favor the exposure" of those records distributed by Superior. In Freed's presence, Brantly allegedly informed Weiss that the deejay had decided to institute a "new arrangement for the payment to him for records that he would favor on both his programs on WABC and WNEW-TV." According to this "new arrangement" only four record distributors would be "permitted to make payments to Mr. Freed for the exposure of their records." In turn, each of the four distributors would be permitted to send as many new releases as they desired each week to Freed, who would then select a "Pick of the Week," a "Sleeper of the Week," and a "Spotlight Song of the Week" to be played on his radio or television show. Freed's Pick of the Week would cost a distributor $1,000. His Sleeper and Spotlight discs would each cost $500. Checks, damning evidence of particular transactions, were no longer acceptable to Freed. All future payments were to be made in cash. By that time, however, enough checks had been passed to establish the fact that such transactions had taken place for a substantial period of time. The checks showed that Freed, for whatever reason, was on the payroll of several record manufacturers and distributors.

Brantley also allegedly informed Weiss that Superior was one of Freed's "chosen" four distributors and that the Spaniels' recording of "One Hundred Years from Today" (Vee Jay 328), a record distributed by Superior, would be selected as the Spotlight Song of the Week for November 4 on Freed's WNEW-TV show, while another Superior-distributed record, "Wear This Ring," would be selected as the deejay's Sleeper for the same week. Two days later, on November 4, Weiss allegedly delivered $1,000 to Brantly.

On November 6, 1959, the House subcommittee concluded the television quiz show phase of its sweeping investigation into deceptive broadcasting practices. No sooner had that phase of the hearings been completed than the subcommittee's chief counsel, Robert Lishman, was presented a letter from ASCAP that charged commercial bribery was a prime factor in determining what songs were selected for radio airplay and what records the public was "surreptitiously induced to buy." The letter to Lishman was accompanied by thirteen pages of *Billboard* and *Cashbox* articles dating back to 1948 and alleging a conspiracy of disc jockeys, broadcasters, and BMI existed "to suppress genuine talent and to foist mediocre music upon the public."

Shortly after receiving the ASCAP letter and packet of articles, Harris announced that his subcommittee would next investigate the alleged commercial bribery in the promotion of music, records, and television commercials, as well as advertising plugs inserted by devious means into certain programs.

The practice of payola in the music business can be traced at least as far back as 1863, when the composer of "Tenting Tonight on the Old Camp Ground" gave the leader of the famous Hutchinson Singing Family a share of the song's royalties so that the group would sing the song at their enormously popular concerts. In Victorian England, a young songwriter named Arthur Sullivan succeeded in having one of his compositions, "Thou Art Passing Hence," performed by Sir Charles Santley by giving the singer, a leading baritone of the era, a share of the song's royalties. After Sullivan teamed up with Sir William Schwenck Gilbert, the duo paid substantial sums of money to influential performers as inducements to sing Gilbert and Sullivan compositions. The practice became known as song plugging. By 1905, Tin Pan Alley was paying out a half-million dollars a year to stage stars to plug certain songs. In 1916, the year that the Music Publishers'

Protective Association was formed to curtail payments to song pluggers, the word *payola* first appeared in print, contained in a *Variety* front-page editorial condemning the widespread practice of influence peddling. *Variety* called the practice "direct-payment evil."

The development of the phonograph record put an end to the song pluggers, but with the emergence of commercial radio broadcasting in the 1920s, a new form of payola—given with the intent of getting certain records played on the radio—was born. Although as late as the 1940s there was still dispute as to whether "free" radio airplay helped or hindered a song's sales, by the end of the decade the value of radio airplay in creating a pop hit was no longer in doubt. In 1950 a *Billboard* editorial reported that payola to disc jockeys was at an all-time high. The next year, *Variety* reporter Abel Green began a series of articles about payola with the headline PAYOLA—WORSE THAN EVER.

The small independent record companies that dominated the rhythm and blues market in the late 1940s and early 1950s relied heavily on the payola system to cut through the competition and get their records heard on the radio. With the rise of rock & roll, payola intensified as the myriad of small labels that produced most of that type of music created a record glut that solidified the payoff practices as a necessary evil of the business. By 1959, more than six hundred record labels, many of the fly-by-night variety, released pop and rock & roll records. Survival of the fittest was the modus operandi, and to a large extent, the fittest in the rock & roll business were those who paid the most. Certain cities—Cincinnati and Philadelphia foremost—came to be known in the business as hotbeds of payola, with the payoffs said to be "flagrant and rampant." In Philadelphia some disc jockeys were rumored to have been bought outright with amounts of cash ranging from $50 to $100 a week. One record wholesaler in that city was said to have twenty-five local deejays on a monthly payroll for $25 to $200 each.

Detroit radio stations WKMH and WJBK each featured an "Album of the Week" that could be purchased for $350, for a minimum of six weeks. WKMH deejay Robin Seymour was said to have a 15 percent interest (in his wife's name) in ARC Distributors, which handled fifty labels in Detroit. One Chicago record company executive was said to have a "cash accounting formula" requiring $22,000 to make a particular record popular, while it was widely accepted that the "normal fringe benefits" of certain disc jockeys included gifts of stock in certain record companies.

* * *

On the day that the House Subcommittee on Legislative Oversight received the ASCAP letter and packet, a story about it went out over the nation's newswire services, awakening the slumbering network giant, the American Broadcasting Company, which had only been tangentially affected by the television quiz rigging scandal. ABC president Leonard Goldenson, after learning of the payola investigation from a radio broadcast, said that under the circumstances he thought it "advisable" to draft a company affidavit and questionnaire regarding payola, to be submitted to each of ABC's broadcasting personnel.

The nation's disc jockeys, while residing at the bottom of the broadcasting hierarchy, were "out front" in the public's eyes. Hip to the fact that in the large scheme of things they were quite dispensable, many deejays realized they were being set up to take the fall for indulging in business practices as old as the pop music industry itself. Oren Harris received a telegram from the National Council of Disc Jockeys for Public Service, signed by WINS deejay "Murray the K" Kaufman. Kaufman cited the good work done by the nation's disc jockeys on behalf of charitable organizations such as CARE. He also noted that only 5 percent of all disc jockeys programmed their own music, implying that the majority of radio deejays had no say in what was played on their own programs. Kaufman also protested the payola allegations made against the disc jockeys and demanded a public apology from the Harris subcommittee. Kaufman received no such apology or even so much as an acknowledgment, as rumors of broadcasting payola continued to fly furiously.

On November 6, the day that ASCAP's letter reached the Harris subcommittee and Leonard Goldenson learned of the Washington payola probe, Louis Klayman, representing Action Record Distributors, paid a visit to Freed's Manhattan apartment, where he was allegedly told what Sam Weiss had been told a week earlier about the deejay's "new arrangement" involving four "selected" record distributors. It was alleged that "Humorock," an Action-distributed song, would be Freed's Pick of the Week for November 19.

On November 10, "as a result of widespread public reaction to House subcommittee disclosures of rigging of TV quiz shows," the FCC announced its own hearings on the matter, despite the fact that FCC chairman Doerfer had previously expressed "substantial doubts" as to whether the FCC could act to remedy the broadcasting abuses.

Two days later, Boston Superior Court Judge Lewis Goldberg placed Freed's 1958 riot charge "on file." Judge Goldberg had allowed Freed to change his plea from "not guilty" to "no contest," and the case was subsequently filed at the request of Assistant District Attorney Sullivan. The reason for the action, said Sullivan, was that many of the witnesses scheduled to testify at Freed's trial "were scattered over the country . . . [so] prosecution would be difficult." In addition, the police captain who had been in charge of the investigation had since died. While the no-contest plea removed the legal monkey from Freed's back, the staggering legal fees he incurred in his eighteen-month battle with the Boston authorities still hung over him.

When the broadcasting payola scandal broke, Freed was on what he termed "good relations" with Ben Hoberman, the turmoil of prior months having subsided to a tolerable level. While the deejay was reasonably certain that Hoberman knew he regularly received money from various record companies and distributors, Freed was positive the station manager knew of his stake in Figure Music and in Hanover Signature Records. The deejay recalled receiving an interoffice memo from ABC management on Friday, November 13, which contained an affidavit and three questions relating to payola. The questionnaire, sent to every individual who participated in the selection of music over ABC's facilities, requested "any pertinent information" relating to instances of "acceptance of gratuities in connection with music promotion" and "financial interests directly affected by the broadcast of music." The three questions specifically dealt with payments received for the broadcasting of music, the refusal to play certain music unless a payment was received, and ownership or interest in music copyrights or performance rights "in any music publishing, recording, or merchandising concern." The document stated that if any of the three questions were answered affirmatively, they were to be "explained in detail." The document was to be signed, notarized, and returned to ABC's legal department.

As Freed read the letter, he realized there was no way he could answer no to any of the three questions without perjuring himself. His initial reaction was to do nothing. Three days later, Freed said, he received a telephone call from Hoberman asking, "Where is your affidavit?"

"An affidavit?" queried Freed, stalling for time.

"The affidavit," Hoberman allegedly replied. "Everybody is signing it!"

From the tone of Hoberman's voice, Freed said he surmised that ABC regarded the affidavit signing as merely a formality. Did ABC expect the deejay to simply check no to the three questions, thereby relieving station management from any complicity in the matter? Freed was not about to fall into that trap. He told Hoberman he could not sign ABC's affidavit because he could not answer no to the questions. Freed reminded Hoberman that the station manager knew the deejay was "in the music business" and that he had a music publishing company from which he received payments. He also said he reminded Hoberman that he had received "cases of Scotch, . . . portable radios," and other gifts at Christmas. "I can't sign this because I am going to perjure myself," he told the station manager. Under increasing pressure to sign the document, Freed later told Hoberman he would gladly sign it "when I see Martin Block's signature and Dick Clark's signature."

Hoberman allegedly said that was "impossible" and "out of his department."

"I work for the same company," retorted Freed. "If they sign it, I will sign it." That was the last discussion concerning the payola affidavit that Freed had with Hoberman. The station turned the matter over to its attorneys.

In the meantime, ABC announced a new policy whereby anyone who selected and played records on the air had to divest himself of all financial interests in recording, publishing, and other, related fields. The order placed Dick Clark, who had an interest in more than thirty such companies and who was in the process of forming even more of them, in a quandary. The "American Bandstand" host accused ABC of using a "shotgun to your head" approach when they asked him, "Which would you like to be, in the music business or the television business?"

Clark, admitting he "had made a great deal of money and . . . was proud of it," while having done "nothing illegal or immoral," said he would nevertheless divest himself of his music-related ventures because he "preferred" television and wanted to be a personality. With Clark's business divestiture, ABC proclaimed its "renewed faith and confidence" in his integrity.

On Tuesday, November 17, it was disclosed that the House Subcommittee on Legislative Oversight would dispatch a series of investigating teams, which had already collected substantial evidence of payola plugs, phony commercials, and other broadcasting-related instances of commercial bribery, to major cities across the country. Two federal probers were already in Philadelphia for talks with Dick Clark, and the subcommittee was said to be studying the House Judiciary hearings of 1956, chaired by Emanuel Celler of New York.

Warren Troob had since taken over Freed's payola affidavit negotiations with WABC when he received a call from one of the network's attorneys, who allegedly told Troob that more than 70 percent of the affidavits from ABC's affiliated stations had been signed negatively and returned. Troob said that when he responded that he wanted the same affidavit for Freed that Clark had signed (Clark had been allowed to have his attorneys draw up a personal affidavit to sign), the executive responded, "You must be kidding!" Troob said the ABC executive "was very upset. He thought I was being a wise guy!" But Troob could not have been more serious. The attorney relayed ABC's message to Freed that the deejay must sign the company payola affidavit, but Freed held fast. The deejay said he reminded ABC that when he originally signed his contract in 1958, the network was fully aware that he was in the music publishing business and that he had other outside interests. Freed also allegedly reminded ABC that at that time he was told such things made no difference.

The verbal tug of war continued for a week, with ABC calling to ask, "Are you going to sign? Everybody's signing it," and Freed steadfastly refusing to do so.

Freed's brother David said he thought a lot of disc jockeys "lied under oath" when they signed affidavits for their stations stating they had not taken payola. "Alan wasn't about to do that," he added. "Alan was not going to sign the affidavit just so he could remain on WABC."

In a last-ditch effort to bolster his eroding position, Freed sent a letter to ABC on Saturday, November 21, in which he said the network's request for a payola affidavit "evince[d] a lack of faith and understanding" by ABC and was "improper and uncalled-for." Freed said that ABC's query as to whether the deejay had ever played, or refused to play, a certain record because of a payoff was "ridiculous in the extreme" and that ABC was aware he had always been "extremely zealous in protecting the high quality" of his radio program and would not compromise such quality "for money or any other consideration."

Freed also mentioned that "from time to time" he had an interest in various music publishing and recording firms and was a songwriter, all of which was "a matter of public record and common knowledge."

In closing, Freed accused ABC of "malicious, unfounded accusations" and stated that if signing such a payola affidavit was a "necessary prerequisite" of his employment, ABC should have insisted on him signing it before he was hired. Freed found it "impossible to accede" to the network's payola affidavit request, "for to do so would violate my self-respect."

As Freed was writing the letter to ABC, Warren Troob met with a network attorney. Troob said he remarked in a jocular manner that the ABC attorney probably still expected Freed to sign the affidavit in the manner the network wanted him to sign. "We will expect all three answers to be no," the attorney allegedly replied.

Taken aback by the ABC attorney's candidness, Troob reiterated that his client had no intention of perjuring himself and, as Freed's attorney, Troob would not permit Freed to sign the affidavit. ABC, having gone as far as it was prepared to go with Freed, told his attorney that the deejay had until three that afternoon to return the affidavit signed. Troob headed for Freed's Manhattan apartment to relay the ultimatum.

When Freed heard what Troob had to say, he told the attorney he felt there was "too much American Broadcasting Company news in the newspapers right now, and I think maybe they would like to get somebody else off the front page and me on it. . . . Warren, I think I'm going to get fired anyway, whether I sign [the affidavit] or not," he said to Troob. Freed instructed Troob to call ABC's attorney and tell him the deejay was now willing to sign the payola affidavit, "but ask him if it will make any difference [whether I sign, or which way I answer the questions]."

The call was made, and as Freed had surmised, ABC's attorney said that "it would not make any difference whether he signs it or not, he is fired."

"They paid my four weeks' salary to me," said Freed, "and that was that."

While the Sunday, November 22, newspapers reported that Freed had been "abruptly dismissed" from his WABC radio program, Ben Hoberman insisted that WABC's decision to do so had nothing to do with payola, but was the station's "contractual right." When the WABC station manager declined to offer any other reason for Freed's dismissal, however, it was assumed by most observers that the disc jockey's termination was, in some way, linked to the developing payola scandal.

The unfolding scandal drew immediate responses on several fronts. FCC commissioner Robert E. Lee announced that broadcasting stations that indulged in payola were "jeopardizing" their licenses, "irrespective of the licensee having knowledge of the same." In a hastily conducted survey of New York broadcasters, stations responded "virtually to a man" that their disc jockeys were "clean as a whistle." WMCA and WINS said there was no payola at their stations because their disc jockeys did not select the records they played. ASCAP charged that disc jockey payola was merely a symptom of a more serious malaise—the involvement of the entire broadcasting industry in commercial bribery practices—and, for once, the song-licensing organization was on target with its charges. The growing payola scandal extended far beyond the disc jockey level, and a series of sensational disc jockey firings would not remedy the situation. *Billboard*, citing the abuse of "freebies"—free promotional copies of a record distributed to plug a particular song—claimed that so many free copies of records were given away that it was difficult to tell "what the public really wants." The music trade newspaper also called for a "complete overhaul" of the music industry.

New York's Assistant District Attorney Joseph Stone, who had headed the quiz show–rigging investigation, said that Sam Lacter, head of the Accounting Investigation Unit of District Attorney Frank Hogan's office, noticed a payola-related news account in *Billboard*, describing what Stone called "shenanigans," including alleged payoffs to disc jockeys, in the radio broadcasting business. Stone said that on the basis of the news account, he and Lacter decided "that we ought to take a look at what was going on in the industry."

The district attorney's payola investigation did not begin with Alan Freed as a target. Stone said that at that time he had never even heard of Freed, and Jack Hooke concurred, explaining that the New York Police Department was "after payola itself" and, although Freed "turned out to be the scapegoat," at the outset he was only a "small cog" in the investigation.

While the practice of indulging in any form of payola may have been cause for the FCC to suspend a broadcaster's license and while any individual who received such payola without reporting it as income was subject to federal tax-evasion charges, in 1959 the act of giving or receiving money, gifts, or other considerations to influence disc jockeys and other broadcasting personnel was not a federal crime. Nor was the practice a crime in the overwhelming majority of the states. But New York then happened to be one of a very few states that had such a law on its books.

Section 439 of the New York State Penal Law of 1909 deals with the "corrupt influencing of agents, employees or servants." Under the statute, any individual who "gives, offers, or promises . . . any gift or gratuity whatever," to an employee, "without the knowledge and consent" of his employer, "with intent to influence" the employee's action is guilty of a misdemeanor and subject to a fine not to exceed $500 or to imprisonment of not more than one year, or both. Likewise, an employee who "without the knowledge and consent" of his employer "requests or accepts a gift or gratuity . . . with the understanding that he shall act in any particular manner in relation to his . . . employer's . . . business" is guilty of the same misdemeanor. For the crime of commercial bribery to be committed, it is not necessary that injury be caused to the employer's business.

Alan Freed's firing by WABC precipitated a nationwide disc jockey purge. Just a matter of hours after Freed was dismissed, thirty-year-old Detroit disc jockey Tom Clay, who had commented that payola was like a "little boy who takes an apple to his teacher," was fired from George B. Storer's WJBK after Clay admitted accepting money ("generally $100 or $200") to play records. Clay said it "was not unusual" for disc jockeys to be offered percentages of songs or pieces of record companies in return for playing certain records. The Detroit jock, extremely popular with the city's teenagers, refused to say whether what he had done was right or wrong, but Clay did maintain that payola was a part of the business he was in. Clay said that while he never told anybody that they had to pay to get their records played on his program, record companies and distributors asked him to take money. "Were they wrong," mused Clay, "or were they good businessmen?"

After Storer announced his own payola investigation of Storer-owned stations in nine cities, three of his employees—Dale Young, emcee of WJBK-TV's "Detroit Bandstand," Joe Niagara of Philadelphia's WIBG radio, and Don McLeod—resigned without comment. A few days later, Storer instituted a new program control that barred disc jockeys from playing music of their own choice. Storer officials would henceforth select for airplay what they termed "desirable music."

On Monday morning, November 23, Alan Freed had become a hot news item. FREED FACES TV PAYOLA PROBE; WNEW ASKS DETAILS OF SHOW, proclaimed the *New York Daily News* front-page headline. Inside the paper, it was said that "with Congressional probers hot in pursuit of payola givers and takers," WNEW-TV wanted Freed to "explain how he runs his show," for which he had "full responsibility."

Freed was scheduled to meet with WNEW-TV program director Jack Lynn and general manager Bennett Korn at the station's East Sixty-seventh Street offices that afternoon to discuss the manner in which records were chosen for the deejay's show and how Freed's "Big Beat" guest performers were paid. "We want to know what the situation is," stated Korn. "We don't believe in prejudging a man. On the other hand, we don't intend to be soft or ostrich-like in our decision."

WNEW-TV's decision was anything but "ostrich-like." During what turned out to be a three-hour meeting, Freed was informed by Korn that the station had decided to fire him. "What are you doing," exclaimed Freed, "following ABC, which fired me without any cause?"

"We want to do it nicely," responded Korn, who then suggested they move downstairs, "where the reporters are waiting." Korn told the gathered press corps that Freed's contract would be terminated "by mutual consent" as of December 6, although the deejay's services would "no longer be required" after Monday, November 30. Korn, who was also vice-president of Metromedia (the owners of WNEW-TV), claimed, as had WABC, that the decision to terminate Freed's contract was not influenced by the payola scandal, that "at no time did we suspect he did anything wrong." Korn said the decision to fire Freed had been "long in coming" and stemmed from a long-standing wage dispute between Freed and the American Federation of Television and Radio Artists (AFTRA) over payment of the deejay's "Big Beat" guest performers. While Korn said that WNEW-TV "long ago wanted to control our own show" and no longer felt Freed was "right" for them, the broadcasting executive emphasized that Freed had signed a statement that asserted he had not committed any improper activities while working there, which read as follows: "At no time during my period of association with said program ("Big Beat") and Channel 5 have I at any time committed any improper practice or done or omitted to do any act or thing for which I might properly be criticized."

Why had Freed signed such a statement for WNEW-TV after refusing to sign ABC's payola affidavit? While the deejay could not truthfully deny participating in some of the practices described in ABC's document, he still maintained he had done nothing improper. Since the WNEW statement only vaguely referred to "improper" practices, Freed was able to sign it while acting in a manner consistent with his beliefs.

Freed's only comment to reporters was that he did not feel he had been fired by WNEW-TV. Almost as an afterthought, he added, "We discussed this several weeks ago."

Morris Levy said that after Freed was fired, the disc jockey called him to ask for help. Levy told Freed he would do whatever he could and, in the meantime, to "go home and don't talk to nobody!" But, said Jack Hooke, when the payola scandal broke wide open, "Alan was very publicity-conscious." In sharp contrast to many broadcasting colleagues across the nation who were also under the payola gun, Freed was not about to go quietly. With characteristic bravado, he reiterated that he had never taken a bribe, ominously adding, "If I go down the drain, a lot of others will go down the drain with me."

The first reporter to gain an advantage with the twice-fired Freed's eagerness to go public was *New York Post* columnist Earl Wilson, who maintained an office at the Broadway Theatre, in the heart of Tin Pan Alley. At the time, said the columnist, he had "a lot of [payola] information coming from various people in show business and the music business." Wilson, whose Fifty-seventh Street apartment was located not far from Freed's Manhattan dwelling, expressed uncertainty as to how his contact with the deejay came about. He speculated that "probably" it was he who "got to" Freed. Warren Troob insisted that it was Wilson, sensing a hot story, who initiated the contact by incessantly telephoning Freed in hopes of obtaining an exclusive interview. Troob, who recognized that Freed was in a situation difficult enough as it was without going public in the newspapers, warned his controversial client to keep his distance from Wilson.

Warren Troob, besides serving as Freed's legal counsel, was a close personal friend of the deejay's. He had spent enough time with

Freed in both business and social situations to realize that when the deejay began to drink, he became more unpredictable than usual, with his bravado often getting the better of him. Troob said he was so determined to keep Freed away from Earl Wilson that the attorney temporarily moved into Freed's apartment to "baby-sit" for his client and friend. But Troob's plan went awry when he was suddenly called away on business. On his return, the attorney said he discovered Freed and Jack Hooke, both of whom had obviously been drinking heavily, at Freed's apartment. At once, Troob realized the damage had been done—Earl Wilson had his Alan Freed "exclusive."

When the Monday-afternoon *New York Post* hit the newsstands, Troob's fears were confirmed. Earl Wilson had written that Freed told him the deejay "had information that some of the big brass of the broadcasting industry was on the take" and had accepted money to play records, although Freed refused to name them at that time. In the story, Freed insisted he was "no better or worse" than any of his fellow disc jockeys and that while he would "throw anybody down the steps" who attempted to bribe him and "most vigorously" denied ever requesting or accepting cash bribes, he did not deny following the "common practice of not sending back gifts."

Freed told Wilson somebody once asked the deejay, "If somebody sent you a Cadillac, would you send it back?" Freed brazenly replied that it would "depend on the color." He explained that while he would not take the car for playing a record, he would look like "an idiot" for rejecting the gift after having done somebody "a hell of a turn, inadvertently helping a company by playing a record for it." Echoing the philosophy of Tom Clay, Freed said that the taking of cash gifts "was the backbone of American business."

Wilson asked Freed about rumors that the deejay's Stamford house had been given to him. Freed replied that Grey Cliffe had been purchased with "nineteen years of sweat . . . and a few mortgages," claiming that as a result of trying to maintain "three houses" and "four children," he did not "have a dime" to his name.

In the *Post* story, Freed also said he felt Dick Clark "should be investigated" because "he's on 300 stations, I'm on one. . . . If I'm going to be a scapegoat, he's going to be one, too." The out-of-work deejay said that when he complained to WABC about Clark not having to sign the standard ABC payola affidavit, WABC told him that Clark was "out of our jurisdiction" because of his network status.

Freed boldly predicted that despite the loss of his radio and television programs, his upcoming Christmas show at the Brooklyn Fabian-Fox would produce the "biggest gross in my history in New York," because the deejay's fans still believed in him and he believed in them.

When Wilson told Freed he heard that the deejay planned to "blow the whistle" on various broadcasting practices, Freed laughed and said, "Leave me some ammunition for Washington and the District Attorney, will you?"

After reading Wilson's *New York Post* story, Morris Levy promptly called Freed and asked, "What the fuck did you do?"

On Tuesday, Freed came face-to-face with the press in an attempt at damage control over what Earl Wilson had written the previous day. Freed said he had received and rejected bribes in the past—not in New York, but in Cleveland, Akron, and other cities—and that he would be glad to tell Stone or the Harris subcommittee what he knew, but only if called to testify. Freed maintained that despite what Wilson had written, the deejay was not volunteering to blow the whistle on anybody.

In other developments that day, federal agents visited WABC and WNEW-TV, where, to satisfy tax liens against Freed's Stamford home, they seized approximately $6,000 that was due the deejay. "This shows how rich I must be!" exclaimed Freed.

A spokesman for Assistant District Attorney Stone's office confirmed that the subpoenaed books and records of various record companies were being studied and that "people in the companies and in the musical world" were being questioned. The spokesman also said that Stone's office was "still on the ground floor, but "sooner or later we'll get to those people who are sounding off in the papers."

Meanwhile, in Detroit another Storer employee lost his job. WJBK-TV deejay Jac LeGoff was fired after he said on the air that payola "in one form or another is a part of American business . . . let him who is without sin cast the first stone."

Teenagers queued up for Tuesday's "Big Beat" show hours before it began, and as they waited for the man many of them looked upon as a father figure, they reacted to the weekend's events. One girl thought the firing of Freed from WNEW-TV "was the station's way of getting rid of rock and roll," defiantly adding that she and her friends "don't want anybody else" as Freed's replacement. Another teenage girl said Freed's show gave the teens something to do after school and kept them "off the streets. What are we going to do with ourselves now?" she wondered.

When Freed finally arrived at the WNEW studio and headed for his dressing room, he waved a friendly greeting to his young following. "See how nice he is to us," remarked another girl. "He's a wonderful person, someone we can look up to."

But when a reporter suggested that the teens start a letter-writing campaign to WNEW-TV, it was reported that "interest lagged" among the group. Most of them were unaware of the details leading to Freed's firing, "nor were they capable of speaking rationally about the incident."

After the telecast, Freed attended what was described as a "final supper party" at a West Fifty-eighth Street restaurant. There, Freed told the press he had decided at about three that morning that he "was being played for a sucker," and the more he thought about it, "the more I realized I was being a real creep." Although Freed first intended to comply with WNEW-TV's wishes that he "be graceful" about his firing and say the decision was "amicable," he asked himself, "What's the difference? I'm being fired." Contrary to what the station had announced the day before, Freed said he would not do the rest of his "Big Beat" telecasts. The deejay said he decided "not to be an idiot any longer . . . I'm through! He concluded, "I'm not notifying them—let this be their notice."

Wednesday morning, November 25, WABC's Martin Block, the host of "Make-Believe Ballroom" and described as "dean of disc jockeys," met with Stone for over an hour. On emerging from Stone's office, Block only commented, "I answered all their questions." Stone said it was not certain yet if Block would be "invited back for additional questioning. Freed, too, had been "invited down" for questioning by the assistant district attorney that morning, but he failed to appear. Late Wednesday evening Freed was served with a subpoena by Stone, calling for the deejay's appearance "forewith" before a New York grand jury investigating broadcasting payola. By that time, Stone's investigation was gathering momentum. He said that he had made it a point to observe Freed "several times" on the deejay's "Big Beat" television show, noting that Freed "seemed to have a lot of personality."

When the Wednesday-afternoon *New York Post* hit the stands, Freed was at it again. ALAN FREED TELLING ALL TO PAYOLA PROBERS, said the full-page headline in type Morris Levy said "was the same size [as] when World War II ended." This time Wilson wrote that Freed, "the twice-fired disc jockey, has been busily but secretly telling all about payola practices to two Harris subcommittee investigators for the past 48 hours." According to Wilson's story, Freed said he had been quizzed primarily about "disc jockey practices in other cities." Freed also admitted being questioned about Dick Clark, but he refused to divulge exactly what was discussed, saying that he "merely answered some of their questions about him [Clark]. They seemed primarily interested in one individual," teasingly not revealing who that individual was. The Harris subcommittee probers also questioned Freed's radio producer, Johnny Brantley, and Jack Hooke, described in the press as a "former associate" of Freed.

Despite the mounting allegations against him, Freed continued to exude a cocky confidence, vowing publicly that "when the time comes I will clear my name" and "I'll wind up on the white horse before this thing is over." Hooke recalled that because "nothing would scare" Freed, the disc jockey "never dreamed" that the scandal would ruin his career. Ray Reneri said that Freed was convinced that after the deejay "laid out" everything in public and "got it over with [and] out of the papers," the payola scandal would subside in a matter of weeks. Alana Freed said that when her father was on top, "that's where he thought he was going to stay. He thought he'd come out a winner." She recalled hearing him say the payola scandal would make him "a bigger person"!

On Thursday, a representative of King Records of Cincinnati, responding to a subpoena by Joseph Stone, delivered the company's books to the assistant district attorney's office. King Records owner Syd Nathan, already on record as having had a monthly payola budget of $2,000, complained that the payola practice was "plain blackmail, and a dirty rotten mess that has gotten worse and worse." Nathan also delivered to Stone canceled checks which the label owner maintained was proof he had paid various disc jockeys.

The assistant district attorney's office also issued a subpoena to Freed ordering him to appear for a 10:00 A.M. Monday meeting with Stone. Also subpoenaed were the books and records of WNEW-TV, which program director Jack Lynn was ordered to deliver for the Freed meeting.

In Washington, while Oren Harris was hospitalized for a minor operation that temporarily kept the Arkansas congressman from his subcommittee duties, chief counsel Robert Lishman announced he would visit New York on Tuesday "to discuss the payola situation" with Stone. Lishman said the Harris subcommittee, rather than making a direct payola investigation of its own, "instead will cooperate with Mr. Hogan's office."

Also in Washington, it was announced that fifty-two witnesses, "including representatives of the major television networks, advertising, and education," were given a "blanket invitation" to testify between December 7 and 11 at FCC hearings on deceptive television practices, at which payola to disc jockeys was to be a topic. While no disc jockeys or record companies were slated to testify, the list of prospective witnesses did include members of ASCAP, which, said one news account, meant "there was no question that the subject of 'payola' would be brought up."

Thursday evening Freed was a guest on Barry Gray's late-night talk show, broadcast over WMCA radio, where he once again professed to having done nothing wrong in his broadcasting practices.

The next morning, Freed was served with a subpoena demanding he produce at his Monday meeting with Stone the financial records of any corporation in which he had an interest. The assistant district attorney's office was particularly interested in Freed's involvement with Figure Music.

Freed planned to squeeze the last drop of emotion from his final "Big Beat" telecast that Friday evening. Freed remained in his dressing room until seconds before the show began, at which time, clad in his familiar gold-buttoned plaid sport jacket, he made a dramatic entrance. Head bowed, Freed walked on camera to chants of "We want Alan! We want Alan!" Many of his teenage fans in the studio audience wept openly as Freed moved among them, consoling them saying, "Now, don't cry."

A group of what was described as "the most important record distributing companies in New York City" presented the deposed deejay with a scroll in appreciation of his services and his "sincere warmth, kindness, and devotion as a distinguished leader in the field of music." As Freed accepted the tribute, he shrugged and said, "Payola, payola, that's all we've been hearing. These guys are the nicest guys in the business."

At one point Freed "danced dolefully" with two teenaged girls and momentarily quelled the sobs of his young fans when he interrupted Little Anthony and the Imperials' recording of "Shimmy Shimmy Ko Ko Bop" to announce his "resignation." One boy angrily told a newsman, "I hope you're satisfied now—you and your damned headlines!"

Now visibly sobbing himself, Freed told his studio audience he was confident he had done nothing wrong, and urged them to keep calm and to shed no tears. "We know we are more adult than adults," he told them. "By no means is this goodbye," Freed reassured them. "I'm not going anywhere. I'll be back on the air soon." Freed then fired his parting shot: "Payola may stink, but it's here and I didn't start it. . . . I know a lot of ASCAP publishers who will be glad I'm off the air."

One teen was overheard saying to no one in particular, "Now they're trying to take our father away!"

At 6:00 P.M., November 27, 1959, Alan Freed vanished from New York's airwaves. Pop singer Richard Hayes, who already had his own television show, was set to take over Freed's "Big Beat" telecasts. At WABC, disc jockey Freddie Robbins was already presiding over Freed's old radio program.

After his final "Big Beat" telecast Freed called another press conference, where he reiterated he had never taken cash to play records, although he did concede he had received noncash gifts, which he characterized as "the backbone of American business." And for the first time, Freed publicly admitted that he had accepted checks from various record companies and distributors as compensation for "consultation work" he did for them. Freed went on to explain that those companies paid him for his "professional advice" in telling them whether or not he thought "they should release a new record," as well as "advising record manufacturers as to whether one of their new releases had a good chance of being successful."

On Saturday, disc jockey Mickey Shorr of WXYZ in Detroit became the next payola casualty. Shorr, a friend of Alan Freed's was fired after he denied any payola involvement and refused to resign from the radio station. After his firing, Shorr said he planned to get out of the broadcasting business because "I think it's lost all opportunities to create personalities."

Alan Freed was the first disc jockey to be subpoenaed for a meeting with Stone. At 10:45 Monday morning Freed, his wife Inga, and Warren Troob arrived at the New York Criminal Courts Building, where a grand jury was hearing testimony relevant to the payola scandal.

According to New York State law at the time, any witness appearing before a grand jury to give testimony was automatically granted immunity from having any part of that testimony later used for criminal prosecution of that witness. Stone wanted Freed to testify before the grand jury, but first insisted that Freed sign a waiver of immunity for his testimony, in effect legally enabling Freed to incriminate himself. Stone's insistence on the waiver of immunity stemmed from Freed's public protestations of innocence when the deejay was "making statements and blowing his mouth off" when "he would have been better off keeping his mouth shut." Had Freed been as innocent as he proclaimed, said Stone, then the deejay would have no reason to balk at signing away immunity for his testimony. Stone said his office was giving Freed "the opportunity to say [to the grand jury] he had nothing to hide."

As Freed entered the Criminal Courts Building he was "smiling frequently and chatting affably with reporters." One member of the press asked him if he would sign a waiver of immunity. "I will not," replied Freed.

"Any ideas you want to discuss with the grand jury?" Freed was asked.

"That depends on whether they give me immunity," replied the deejay, who once again denied he had ever taken payola, but admitted that he had accepted consultation fees. When another reporter asked what the distinction was, Freed replied, "They'll have to explain to me what 'payola' means."

When a reporter asked Freed if he felt "they are picking on you unnecessarily," his reply was a curt "Yes." With that, Freed stepped into the elevator that would take him upstairs to the waiting courtroom and grand jury.

Shedding the lighthearted demeanor of an hour earlier, Freed emerged from his meeting with Stone looking "disturbed," telling waiting reporters, "I'd love to answer all your questions, fellas. You know I like to be nice, but my attorney doesn't want me to say a thing." When pressed further, Freed replied, "I just can't say. I'm under subpoena." Not surprisingly, however, Freed was unable to hold his silence, and despite "the advice of my attorney and my grandmother, who told me never to volunteer for anything," he disclosed to the press that he refused to sign a waiver of immunity for

Stone. "I didn't go before the grand jury and I don't know what the future holds for me."

Ray Reneri said that in the beginning, Freed "thought he would fight the payola charge and beat it." But after the deejay was informed that "they can fine you heavily, they can put you away," for violating New York's commercial bribery statute, and after Stone refused to let Freed testify before the payola grand jury without first waiving his immunity, the deejay was no longer so confident.

A spokesman for Stone's office confirmed Freed's refusal to sign a waiver of immunity and explained that the assistant district attorney declined to let the deejay testify because "we are not prepared to grant him immunity on the questions we want to ask him."

Stone explained that since Freed "knew damned well he wasn't innocent," he did not testify before the grand jury because "it would have been worse" for him if he had done so. "What the hell would his answer be?" said Stone. "He knew we had the evidence."

It was also confirmed that Monday that Jack Hooke had also been subpoenaed, but not questioned. Like Freed, Hooke refused to sign a waiver of immunity before testifying. Stone's office also said it believed Freed had an interest in Figure Music. When Freed and Hooke emerged from the Criminal Courts Building elevator after their meeting with Stone, Hooke refused to comment when the reporters asked him if Freed had any affiliation with Figure.

Stone's office also said an "arrangement" had been worked out whereby it would be allowed to examine Freed's personal records at WNEW-TV. Station manager Jack Lynn had already been instructed "to keep everything locked up" in preparation for a visit by a representative of the district attorney's office later that afternoon. Shortly after 3:30 P.M. Lynn, Warren Troob, and Sam Lacter entered Freed's WNEW-TV office, only to emerge "empty-handed and without comment" about an hour later. A spokesman for Hogan's office explained that because of Freed's refusal to sign a waiver of immunity, the district attorney was not entitled to take anything of a personal nature from among the deejay's papers, although "anything of a corporate nature we can take." But Troob contended that all of Freed's papers were of a personal nature and the attorney refused to let Lacter take anything.

In Washington it was disclosed that the FCC had placed under review the broadcasting license of WGMA in Hollywood, Florida, one of the radio stations owned by Jack Barry and Dan Enright. The

FCC had already sent a letter to WGMA stating that Barry and Enright's quiz show testimony "raises serious questions concerning the character qualifications of Mr. Enright" and whether his and Barry's corporation "is qualified to own and operate a broadcast facility."

On Tuesday, December 1, Robert Lishman, chief counsel for the House Subcommittee on Legislative Oversight, arrived in New York to rendezvous with Stone. Afterward, Lishman was quizzed by reporters about his two-hour meeting with the assistant district attorney, but other than to say that problems "of mutual interest" were discussed, the subcommittee lawyer refused to elaborate. When one reporter asked if Freed would be called to testify before the subcommittee at its next session, scheduled to begin on December 9, Lishman cryptically replied, "That's the subcommittee's business to decide."

On December 2, the Federal Bureau of Investigation, which had been keeping a file on Freed since the deejay's 1958 Boston riot episode, reacted to Freed's prominence in the growing scandal. An FBI memorandum referring to Freed as a "New York rock and roll promoter" was sent to Cartha ("Deke") DeLoach, the "genial Georgian" Assistant to the Director, head of the Bureau's Crime Records Division, and one of Director J. Edgar Hoover's "chief 'axe-men.' " The subject of the memorandum: "Disc jockey payola scandal." The "confidential" two-page memo mentioned the "wide public attention [that] has been focused" on the payola practices of some disc jockeys as a result of the House subcommittee investigations. It was noted that one of the disc jockeys prominently mentioned in the payola scandal was Freed, whom the FBI referred to as "the New York radio and television personality who has been credited with originating the term 'rock and roll.' " The memorandum also stated the FBI's version of Freed's 1958 riot incident, when "the wrath of responsible citizens of Boston descended upon Freed" after one of his rock & roll "road shows" in that city "was followed by a teen-age riot." The memorandum also made mention of Freed's refusal to sign a waiver of immunity for his grand jury testimony, adding that the deejay "reportedly has admitted accepting 'consultant fees' but not 'payola.' " It was recommended that the FBI "continue to follow Freed's involvement in the current 'payola' scandal."

* * *

Since Freed had not reported as income the alleged payola he received, WABC and WNEW-TV received Internal Revenue Service tax liens against unpaid money the two broadcasting outlets owed the twice-fired Freed. WABC and WNEW-TV were ordered to hold the money until they were served with a tax levy by the IRS, at which time they were to turn the money over to the government tax collectors.

When the newspapers hit the streets on Thursday, December 3, they contained Jerry Blaine's disclosure that in 1956 the head of Cosnat Distributing Corporation gave Freed an $11,000 loan secured by a mortgage—subsequently transferred to Morris Levy's Roulette Records—on the deejay's Connecticut home. While neither Roulette nor Freed would comment on the transaction, a Roulette attorney stated that any transfer of real estate was "a matter of public record," and he did not see why there should be so much commotion over the arrangement.

Also made public was the incident in which Art Freeman of Cleveland's Benart Distributors alleged that Freed had demanded cash before he would play Freeman's records on the air. Freeman was reluctant to discuss the incident, which allegedly occurred in 1954, and insisted that he no longer had a copy of Freed's letter. Lou Platt, Freed's ex-manager, said he recalled the letter, adding that "there were too many things like that going on around Alan" and it was "because of things like that that Alan and I broke up."

Following Blaine's disclosure of Freed's mortgage transfer to Roulette, Stone subpoenaed the books and financial records of Roulette Records and Cosnat Distributors.

On December 11, the FBI initiated the next phase of its own investigation of Freed, linking the deejay to Morris Levy and alleged "fraud by wire." Robert J. Rosthal, FBI deputy chief of the General Crimes Section, sent to the Justice Department a memo stating that as requested by the assistant U.S. attorney general's office, the FBI would investigate the "Alan Freed-[censored] situation. In view of the racketeer influence" in the case, the deputy chief wished Freed to be "fully interrogated" to determine his payola involvement.

The FBI alleged that during a meeting between Roulette Records representatives and the Securities and Exchange Commission about an attempt by the label to gain additional financing by going public, those representatives had stated that Freed was "indebted" to Roulette for $18,000, which was secured by using Freed's Stamford home as collateral; that "[name censored by the FBI] has a racketeer or gangster background"; that Freed at one time had an interest in Roulette; that an individual (again the name was censored by the FBI) was permitted to purchase Roulette stock "to secure Freed's help in 'pushing' Roulette records"; that Freed "would 'push' Roulette records"; and that Freed received, expense-free, a 25 percent interest in an unnamed record company from a party whose name was censored by the FBI.

The FBI wanted Freed's association with Roulette and with the unnamed record company "fully explored" in regard to any payola made by them to Freed.

Meanwhile, New York State Attorney General Louis Lefkowitz initiated an investigation of his own into the business activities of Freed and Levy. On December 12, Freed was subpoenaed by Lefkowitz to give testimony.

Secluded in his Manhattan apartment, Freed gained a brief respite from his mounting problems by immersing himself in the preparation of his upcoming Brooklyn Fabian-Fox Christmas show, the first time the unemployed deejay had no radio program on which to promote such a production. Freed extended his thanks to theater owner Ed Fabian, who spent additional money to promote the show after Freed lost his radio and television programs.

To what extent the talent lineup for Freed's "Christmas Jubilee of Stars" was affected by the deejay's loss of airtime is uncertain, but overall, this was one of the deejay's weaker shows. Jackie Wilson returned after heading Freed's Labor Day show, this time to sing his latest hit, "Talk That Talk." Young Johnny Restivo, who also appeared at Freed's Labor Day show, sang his latest release, "I Dig Girls," which was to sell poorly, if at all. Artists with hot hits to plug were the Brooklyn-based Passions quartet with "Just to Be with You"; a quartet from New Jersey, the Knockouts, with "Darling Lorraine"; Billy ("Crash") Craddock and "Don't Destroy Me"; Brooklyn guitar duo Santo and Johnny with "Tear Drop"; seventeen-year-old Bobby Rydell, one of the newest teen idols, with "We Got Love"; and a singer with perhaps the oddest record of the year, twenty-year-old Tommy Facenda from Norfolk, Virginia, with "High School U.S.A." The song was little more than two minutes of stringing together the names of local high schools, but Facenda's record company came up with a novel promotional gimmick and released twenty-eight versions of the song, covering twenty-seven cities or states and one "national" version. The novelty of hearing one's high school mentioned in a song caught on, and "High School U.S.A." became a freak national hit. The Isley Brothers, who cut their first records for George Goldner in 1957–1958, reprised their huge RCA Victor hit "Shout" and performed their latest release, "Respectable." Other acts returning from Freed's Labor Day show looking for another hit record included Bo Diddley, who performed "Say Man, Back Again," a sequel to "Say Man" that would not match the latter's success. Likewise, the Pittsburgh-based Skyliners and their latest record, "How Much," would fail to match their previous hit, "It Happened Today." The Wheels, a vocal group that began recording in 1956 and had just signed with Roulette Records, sang their first Roulette release, "No One But You." Also on Freed's stage was Brooklyn singer Linda Laurie, who earlier in the year had had a novelty hit with "Ambrose—Part 5" but never again matched that success. Rounding out the bill was Teddy Randazzo, who was then recording for ABC-Paramount. Randazzo sang his fourth ABC-Paramount release (and fourth flop), "You Don't Care Anymore."

As the decade of the 1950s drew to a close, U.S. Attorney General William P. Rogers issued his deceptive broadcasting practices report to President Eisenhower. Rogers concluded that while the FCC and the FTC do have the power to consider programming content and should exercise that power "more vigorously," legislation to endow the FCC and the FTC with additional authority might be required. Rogers also raised the possibility of criminally prosecuting those individuals responsible for the rigged TV quiz shows. It was reported that some broadcasters were "stunned" by Rogers's prosecution suggestion, and while "few would comment publicly, privately they seethed."

The attorney general's report drew a mixed reaction from other sources in Washington. FCC chairman John C. Doerfer (who would be forced to resign his post under a cloud of suspicion of being bribed) said Rogers' report would be considered "among other viewpoints," while FCC commissioner Frederick Ford hailed the report for "resolving the legal issue" of the powers of the FCC. Oren Harris said the attorney general's recommendations "did not go far enough" in "ripping the veil from the quiz show chicanery."

* * *

Despite his public posturing, the pressures on Alan Freed began to take their toll. Now under the scrutiny of the New York district attorney's office, the House Subcommittee on Legislative Oversight, the FBI, the Internal Revenue Service, and the New York State attorney general, the bankrupt and out-of-work disc jockey watched his legal expenses (which had begun with his Boston defense) continue to mount, with no end in sight.

Betty Lou Greene said her ex-husband became so strung out that "he couldn't sit down." Freed's daughter Alana said the pressure and the emotional strain on her father "showed in his face. It showed in his habits—sleeping, eating, and drinking." She also said that unlike the time when the payola scandal first broke and Freed thought everything would be forgotten in a matter of weeks, "for the first time in his life he felt total panic. He didn't know what he was going to do. He didn't know which way to turn."

CHAPTER 13

As Clean as the Newly Driven Snow

"Nobody ever brought me a record in my twenty years in the business and said, 'Here is some money, play the record.' I've never been bribed to play any record. If anyone tried it, I'd throw them down the stairs myself."

THE decade of the 1950s had ended. *Billboard* wrote that 1959 would go down in the music business as "the year in which payola leaped out of the back rooms and into the newspaper headlines from coast to coast." But while the sensational initial disc jockey firings and resignations ceased, the payola scandal was far from being over. As January 1960 began, WINS program director Mel Leeds received a telephone call from a Boston reporter who warned Leeds that his telephone was tapped. The reporter also told Leeds that it was "stupid" of Alan Freed to have conducted his business by telephone. "Reels and reels" of Freed's conversations allegedly existed. The reporter also alleged that there was a spy at WINS who was "funneling out information" and that most of Freed's associates "have stabbed him in the back." With that, Leeds mysteriously disappeared for a week because of what he later said was a "heart problem." Leeds then announced he was going on vacation, but on January 26, WINS received a letter from Leeds stating he had resigned to become program director at radio station KDAY in Los Angeles.

* * *

As the New York district attorney's office, under the Assistant District Attorney Stone, stepped up its high-profile criminal investigation into broadcasting payola, criminal indictments became imminent and pop music executives grew tight-lipped. This industrywide reticence exacerbated the consternation concerning the actions of Freed, who more than ever was perceived as a loose cannon in the broadcasting business. One Tin Pan Alley executive warned, "If Freed ever starts talking, a lot of people may land in jail."

Ray Reneri said that those few individuals who had not abandoned Freed began telling the deejay, "You have to get out of New York. Don't you understand? They're going to get you. They're not going to be satisfied until you're out!"

Betty Lou Greene was then living with her husband, Tom, and Alana and Lance Freed in New Canaan, Connecticut. She remembered that when her ex-husband discovered "no one would be connected with him [or] would hire anyone associated with him," Freed "advised all the people who'd been close to him" to leave New York. The Greenes left for Tom Greene's native North Carolina. Freed's younger children, Sieglinde and Alan, Jr., remained in Connecticut with their mother, Jackie.

With or without Freed's testimony, Stone's office tightened the scope of its payola investigation. Under New York State's commercial bribery statute, while the giver and the taker of a bribe were equally guilty, a confession by one of the accused parties would not in itself be sufficient evidence for conviction. Such an admission had to be corroborated by other evidence. In layman's terms, explained Stone, "the law says we're not going to trust either party to testify against each other without some sort of additional evidence to connect the defendant with the commission of a crime." Stone said such corroborating evidence might be a "third-party witness, a check passed or endorsed, or any other bribes that were offered and accepted. . . . It could be anything."

Unlike Stone's frustrating quiz show investigation, in which no laws had been broken, this time he not only had the law but also both alleged guilty parties. Confronted with that situation, Stone said he began "testing the waters" to determine which of the two reluctant parties—the givers or the takers of alleged payola—would supply the corroborating evidence needed to prosecute the other.

Stone explained that in commercial bribery cases, "very rarely is the giver of the bribe prosecuted," because "philosophically" the taker is viewed as a "dishonest employee" violating the trust placed in him to be "faithful and dedicated." Stone also said that when an employee accepts a bribe, "it is inherent . . . that he is not going to do the best possible job for his employer."

As for the parties who offered the illegal bribes, "in our society, [where] businessmen rule the roost," explained Stone, "I think the authorities are inclined to believe in most instances that the receiver, a dishonest employee, is in effect also an extortionist and generally initiates the bribe."

In addition, Stone said it would have been "psychologically damaging" to grant immunity to the disc jockeys, because the public would perceive such an act as "back-room dealing" and would become skeptical of the entire case. Besides, the disc jockeys, who were protected by the Fifth Amendment, did not have to admit to any payola involvement, whereas the record company and distributor executives did not enjoy such constitutional protection. And, not to be forgotten, the prosecution of some well-known broadcasting celebrities would result in more press coverage than would the prosecution of some faceless record company executives. With District Attorney Frank Hogan considering a possible run for the governorship of New York in the fall, a successfully prosecuted sensational case such as the payola scandal would enhance Hogan's image as a tough, crime-fighting prosecutor.

Thus, it was decided that the record company executives, the alleged givers of commercial bribes, would not be asked to sign waivers of immunity before testifying before the payola grand jury. That testimony, along with corroborating evidence in the form of canceled checks, would then be used to prosecute the alleged takers of the commercial bribes—the disc jockeys and other broadcasting personnel.

Joseph Stone said that Samuel Lacter, head of the Accounting Units Division, "took a shot in the dark" and began what they called a "John Doe" investigation (one in which no particular individual is targeted). Using the Manhattan Yellow Pages as a guide, the head of the Accounting Units Division subpoenaed the books and financial records of every local record manufacturer and distributor listed. Stone said that with two-thirds of the companies subpoenaed, "we hit paydirt!" But, added Stone, despite the decision to prosecute the takers of the alleged commercial bribery, the record company and distributor executives remained wary of his investigation and "all gave me a hard time." Stone said that since "no one was exactly volunteering any information," in many instances his office had to resort to "legal compulsion" to force them to talk.

Despite the removal of the threat of criminal prosecution in New York, the record companies faced potential danger on another front. The TV quiz show rigging revelations of October 1959 caused President Eisenhower to have Attorney General William P. Rogers meet that November with the broadcasting networks, the FCC, and the FTC to look into the matter of deceptive broadcasting practices. Near the end of the year, FTC chairman Earl Kintner announced that the regulatory agency planned to bring charges against several record companies, based on its belief that payola given to disc jockeys to plug records was an "unfair trade practice" violating Section 5 of the FTC act prohibiting "unfair methods of competition [and] . . . unfair or deceptive acts or practices in commerce."

Kintner also disclosed that FTC investigators were already "active in several sections of the country," including the key areas of Philadelphia and New York, preparing charges against the companies alleged to have given payola to broadcasting personnel.

On December 3 the FTC charged the Radio Corporation of America and eight other concerns with giving illegal payola to radio and television disc jockeys to "expose" their recordings. The FTC defined exposure as the playing of a particular record repeatedly, "as much as six to ten times daily," thus creating a deception of the record's popularity. Such deception, said the agency, "tends to mislead purchasers into buying the 'exposed' records, which they might not otherwise have purchased," and, because it has the capacity to "divert trade unfairly from respondents' competitors," is in violation of the FTC act.

On January 3, 1960, the FTC lodged similar payola charges against fifteen additional concerns, including several owned by the boys. Among those companies charged were the Atlantic Recording Corporation, Jerry Blaine's Cosnat Distributing Corporation and Jay-Gee Records and Morris Levy's Roulette Records, Inc. Officials at the New York concerns either declined comment or could not be reached, but an executive with Cosnat's Detroit branch stated that they operated "just like everyone else" and refused further comment.

On January 31 the FTC issued nine more payola complaints, bringing to thirty-seven (four companies had been charged January

15) the number issued by that agency since the previous December. The boys continued to feel the government's squeeze. This time Sam Weiss, president of Superior Record Sales Corporation, Inc., and George Goldner, president of Gone Recording Corporation and End Music Company, Inc., were among those charged with payola practices.

The FTC attempted to have Levy sign a consent decree admitting he had done wrong in giving payola, but Levy refused to do so (RCA had done so and had complimented the FTC "for its crackdown of the practice"). The Roulette Records president said that because of his refusal to sign the consent decree, the Harris subcommittee investigators seized Roulette's books and "harassed the shit out of me." Levy recalled that, at the time, people said he was "an idiot" for not signing the decree, and that he received "plenty of grief" for refusing to do so, but he liked himself "better for not signing it."

Counting on heightened public interest from the still-developing payola revelations, ASCAP again attacked its chief competitor, BMI, and the nation's broadcasters. At a public hearing on January 12, ASCAP president Stanley Adams charged that payola was "becoming rampant as a big business operation" because of the actions of the broadcasters and their "wholly owned music publishing and licensing organization—Broadcast Music, Inc." Adams asked the FCC to deny operating licenses to 557 radio stations on the grounds that they "own conflicting interests" in the music field. But when Adams, who said he was not prepared "to be more specific" in his allegations, was ordered by the FCC to compile and submit evidence to support his claims, what evidence the guild president did submit was deemed "not sufficiently persuasive," and the FCC ultimately rejected ASCAP's complaint. BMI, in turn, asked the FCC for time to prepare a reply to what it described as the "unjustified attacks by ASCAP."

On February 2, 1960, after Stone had subpoenaed the books and financial records of more than fifty record companies and distributors, a grand jury began its investigation into the payola allegations. His office announced that although various record company executives would testify before the grand jury, no disc jockeys would be subpoenaed, because some of them loomed "as the potential defendants in any crimes that might be charged by the jury."

Five executives representing four record companies appeared at

A publicity shot for Freed's third WABC-TV "Big Beat" telecast, July 26, 1957. The show starred, clockwise from top, Jimmy Bowen and the Rhythm Orchids, Patsy Cline, Marvin Rainwater, Jimmy C. Newman, Dale Hawkins, Clyde McPhatter, Fats Domino, and an unidentified female singer. On Freed's TV show the week before, Frankie Lymon danced in front of the camera with a white girl. Two weeks later, Freed's show was canceled by ABC. *Courtesy of John Cavello, National Television Archives.*

Freed and Little Richard backstage at the Brooklyn Paramount, Labor Day 1957, shortly before the release of *Mister Rock and Roll,* in which Richard performed "Keep-a Knockin'." Note Richard's Bible; when the singer became an ordained minister that year, his record company tried to keep it a secret from Richard's record-buying fans.

Courtesy of John Cavello, National Television Archives.

Freed's "Third Anniversary Rock 'n' Roll Stage Show" at the Brooklyn Paramount, Labor Day 1957. Mark Stevens, who went on to become an actor in films, including *Gunsight Ridge*, was the radio host of WAKR's "Request Review" before Freed replaced him in 1946. *Courtesy of John Cavello, National Television Archives.*

Freed on stage in 1957. *Courtesy of John Cavello, National Television Archives.*

An uncommon publicity still from Freed's fourth movie, *Mister Rock and Roll,* which premiered in October 1957.
Courtesy of John Cavello, National Television Archives.

Monte Bruce, Freed, and Warren Troob in New Haven on May 8, 1958, after that city banned Freed's rock & roll show. *Courtesy of John Cavello, National Television Archives.*

WABC publicity photo, June 1958, when Freed began broadcasting on the station. *Courtesy of John Cavello, National Television Archives.*

A rare 1959 publicity still from Freed's fifth movie *Go, Johnny, Go!* The police officer on the right is played by Jack Hooke. Less than a year later Freed would find himself in serious trouble with the real police.

Freed, with some of that day's guests on the deejay's WNEW-TV "Big Beat" show, August 16, 1959. *Courtesy of John Cavello, National Television Archives.*

Teenagers dancing on Freed's WNEW-TV "Big Beat" show, August 16, 1959. *Courtesy of John Cavello, National Television Archives.*

| **FINAL** | # DAILY NEWS
NEW YORK'S PICTURE NEWSPAPER® | 5¢ |

Vol. 41. No. 130 New York 17, N.Y., Tuesday, November 24, 1959   WEATHER: Cloudy, some rain.

TV SHOW CLEAN, FREED SWEARS —AND HE'S OUT

Freed for New Role. Disk jockey Alan Freed, who helped make rock 'n' roll what it is today, and his wife, Inga, leave WNEW building. He and station parted company "by mutual consent" after payola scandal. Station said Freed's r 'n' r show is no longer "right" for WNEW. Alan said there were no hard feelings. —*Story on page 3*

"The type was the same size when World War II ended," said Morris Levy. *New York Post* front page of November 25, 1959.
© *1959 New York Post. Reprinted with permission.*

Freed's loss of two broadcasting jobs within a week was front-page news in New York. © *1959 New York News, Inc. Reprinted with permission.*

Freed on the defensive, with WMCA talk show host Barry Gray on November 26, 1959. Freed had been fired by WNEW-TV three days earlier. *Courtesy of John Cavello, National Television Archives.*

Freed, surrounded by his fans after the final telecast of his WNEW-TV "Big Beat" show, November 27, 1959. *Courtesy of John Cavello, National Television Archives.*

Freed and his wife Inga arrive at the New York City criminal courthouse on December 1, 1959, before he refused to sign a waiver of immunity before the New York grand jury hearing payola-related testimony. He was not permitted to testify before the grand jury. The effects of emotional stress and alcohol are evident on Freed's face. *Courtesy of John Cavello, National Television Archives.*

Freed's "Christmas Jubilee of Stars" at the Brooklyn Fox, held shortly after the deejay's firings from WABC Radio and WNEW-TV. Freed was to present one additional stage show in New York (at the Apollo Theatre in February 1960). *Courtesy of John Cavello, National Television Archives.*

The big payola "bust," Elizabeth Street police station, May 19, 1960. Standing left to right at desk, Hal Jackson (looking at the others), WLIB disc jockey; Jack Walker, WLIB disc jockey; Tommy ("Dr. Jive") Smalls, WWRL disc jockey; Joseph Saccone, WMGM record librarian; Peter Tripp, WMGM disc jockey; Mel Leeds, WINS program director; and Alan Freed. *Courtesy of John Cavello, National Television Archives.*

Freed emceeing a "Twist Revue" at Morris Levy's Camelot Club on November 17, 1962, shortly after Freed was fired by WQAM Radio in Miami. *Courtesy of John Cavello, National Television Archives.*

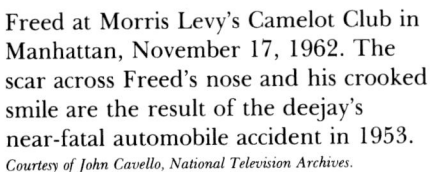

Freed at Morris Levy's Camelot Club in Manhattan, November 17, 1962. The scar across Freed's nose and his crooked smile are the result of the deejay's near-fatal automobile accident in 1953. *Courtesy of John Cavello, National Television Archives.*

Freed's simple memorial plaque at Ferncliff Mausoleum, Hartsdale, New York.

the first grand jury session, which lasted two-and-a-half hours. Stone refused to identify the officials or the companies, some of whom were scheduled to give additional testimony when the grand jury met again on Friday, February 5. A spokesman for the assistant district attorney's office announced to the press that no record company executives were asked to sign wavers of immunity before they appeared before the grand jury.

On behalf of Roulette Records, Morris Levy appeared before the New York payola grand jury, which he said was "hot" because of a $20,000 loan to Alan Freed that appeared on Roulette's books. Levy said that Joseph Stone "tried to break my balls [in an attempt] . . . to show [the loan] was for payola." Stone's ball breaking and Levy's immunity from prosecution evidently proved effective. The Roulette president allegedly told the grand jury that he had given Freed a loan with the "tacit understanding and agreement" that the disc jockey "would continue to favor and expose" Levy's records. Levy also allegedly told the grand jury he indicated to Freed that the disc jockey "could forget about repayment" of the "loan."

On February 3, it was announced that Mel Leeds had resigned as WINS program director because of an in-house payola investigation conducted by station owner J. Elroy McCaw. While confirming the rumors of his own payola investigation, McCaw said that Leeds "denied that he had done anything improper and we have no proof to the contrary."

NBC board chairman Robert W. Sarnoff had recently testified before the FCC that the broadcasting industry was fully capable of self-regulation and did not need any assistance from the government. When FCC commissioner John Cross asked Sarnoff if the practice of payola had been halted, the NBC network chief replied that he doubted if payola could be found anywhere in the nation. At that time, following the disc jockey purges, FCC threats to revoke broadcasting licenses, and the looming possibility of legislative action and criminal prosecution for participation in payola, Sarnoff was correct in his assessment of the industry.

The decision of the New York district attorney's office to prosecute the takers of payola, using the testimony of some of the givers of the bribes to help convict the recipients, sealed the fate of Alan Freed and other disc jockeys. The record spinners became payola's scapegoats, while other parties whose complicity in the illicit bribery was being scrutinized took part in a conspicuous bailout designed to show—recent history aside—that they did not condone the bribery practices.

Record companies and distributors, accomplices in the alleged commercial bribery, gave testimony—albeit with reluctance in some cases—to the New York district attorney in return for a promise that they themselves would not be prosecuted. The broadcasting networks, typified by NBC's David Sarnoff, preached renewed vigilance and self-regulation to prevent payola. Individual station owners, including George B. Storer and J. Elroy McCaw, conducted in-house investigations to root out payola.

In the late-January report that wrapped up the television quiz show rigging phase of its deceptive broadcasting practice investigation, the House Subcommittee on Legislative Oversight noted that the most conclusive evidence of the inadequacy of self-regulation was found in the testimony of witnesses who said they were "wholly ignorant of the facts constituting one of the most gigantic hoaxes ever perpetuated on the American people." The subcommittee further concluded that "it is not reasonable to expect persons who have profited in the past from deceptive use of the airwaves in blissful ignorance of the fraud to become rigorous guardians of the public interest." The subcommittee also criticized the "passive view" adopted by the FCC and FTC, which allowed a "public evil" to grow "unchecked in silence." The Harris subcommittee further concluded that Congress "must exercise its duty of legislative oversight to restore lost public confidence."

At the urging of the Attorney General William P. Rogers, the FCC—in the midst of weathering its own scandal—and the FTC adopted get-tough policies toward the alleged payola practitioners. On February 11 the FCC stated that under existing federal law it had jurisdiction over any payola practice "as it applied to a station license, but not to station employees" (although that jurisdiction was seldom utilized because of the severity of the penalty—the loss of a station's broadcasting license). The FCC further stated that it did not appear "such jurisdiction [over station employees] is warranted." "Greatly concerned" over broadcasting payola, the FCC instead proposed federal legislation making "deceit on the airwaves" a crime punishable by fines up to $5,000 and up to one year imprisonment.

Similar proposals for federal criminal sanctions on payola had recently been introduced by Rep. John B. Bennett of the House Special Subcommittee on Legislative Oversight and by Attorney General Rogers.

Meanwhile, the FTC continued to apply pressure to the boys, lodging two additional payola complaints. Charged with unfair practices were the Am-Par Record Corporation and its officers, including president Samuel H. Clark; and Herald Music Corporation and Ember Distributors, Inc., and their officers, including president Al Silver.

The nation's radio and television disc jockeys were about to take the fall for industrywide payola practices, but because most of them were employed in states with no commercial bribery laws, they would receive society's condemnation not in a courtroom but in a public flogging before the highly visible Washington hearings on deceptive broadcasting practices.

Of all the witnesses scheduled to testify before the subcommittee, Freed faced the most-dire consequences. Not only did he have many enemies eager to see him fall, but Freed was also the keystone figure in the commercial bribery investigation being conducted by Assistant District Attorney Stone, who was in the process of gathering evidence to support an indictment of the disc jockey.

With the television quiz show rigging phase of its investigation completed, Oren Harris' subcommittee turned its full attention to the nation's disc jockeys and other broadcasting personnel. From the start, the subcommittee's agenda was designed with drama in mind. To guarantee sustained public interest in the proceedings, the subcommittee decided to hear testimony from lesser-known broadcasting figures first, before culminating the hearings with the appearances of Alan Freed and Dick Clark. (Clark's request to appear first was denied by the subcommittee.)

The first session of the Washington payola hearings began in January 1960. While too much evidence in the form of canceled checks existed for the witnesses to deny that money had passed hands, when asked why such exchanges had taken place, most of the witnesses said they never asked for the money in question, that it was simply offered to them. Consequently, they maintained that since no agreement had been made in advance of receiving the money, it could not be considered payola.

The first subcommittee witness was Anthony Mammarella, who

had been the producer of Dick Clark's "American Bandstand" until the payola revelations revealed Mammarella's considerable music-related holdings. Like Clark, Mammarella was given the choice by ABC of divesting himself of his music business holdings or relinquishing his "Bandstand" producer's role. Unlike Clark, Mammarella opted to stay in the music business and so resigned as the "Bandstand" producer. After hearing of Mammarella's extensive music business interests, subcommittee member John J. Bennett of Michigan remarked that either Mammarella was "very naive" or Mammarella thought the subcommittee members were very naive. The Michigan congressman also said he had the feeling that Mammarella had been "less than frank" in telling his story to the subcommittee.

A parade of recently deposed disc jockeys followed Mammarella to the subcommittee's witness stand. Joe Finan, recently fired by Cleveland's KYW radio, admitted he had received $50 a week from Mercury Records for his "special attention or listening" to that company's records. In his own defense, Finan also pointed out numerous instances when he refused to play a Mercury record he thought was bad. Another ex-KYW deejay, Wesley Hopkins, estimated that in two years he received over $12,000 as a "listening fee" from various record companies, prompting Walter Rogers of Texas to remark that Hopkins "must have done a lot of listening." Disc jockey Arnie ("Woo-Woo") Ginsberg, recently of WMEX in Boston, said he received $4,400 "to establish feelings of good will" from various record distributors over the preceding two-and-a-half years.

A Boston record distributor revealed that WMEX's "Golden Platter of the Week" was once arranged thirteen weeks in advance. Disc jockey Stan Richards of station WILD in Boston admitted accepting more than $6,000 from various record companies while he worked at that station. Richards also told the subcommittee that payola was like "one pupil [giving] the teacher a better gift than the other pupil, hoping to get a favor in return." He thought payola typified "the American way of life, . . . a wonderful way of life," built on romance. "I'll do for you. What will you do for me?"

Harry Weiss, a promo man for Music Suppliers of Boston, a record distributor, said he obtained signed but otherwise blank radio station letter forms in his territory and filled in whatever "hits" he chose, including his own records, before mailing the letters to the music trade newspaper *Cashbox*, which then published the results as coming from radio stations themselves.

The subcommittee heard essentially the same story from each witness. Nobody who testified believed he had done anything wrong by accepting gifts he believed were earned. California congressman John E. Moss, Jr., said he noticed a unique characteristic of the record industry and described it as "brotherly love." He said that some kind of "telepathic communication" must have been evident, noting that by "intellectual osmosis" between disc jockeys and record manufacturers, money was passed and records were played.

The first series of House subcommittee payola hearings concluded on February 19, 1960. The biggest names in broadcasting—including Alan Freed and Dick Clark—were yet to be heard from.

Freed attempted as best he could to stay visible to his fans and to raise some much-needed cash. Despite the fact that Freed was off the air, Jack Hooke said that they "didn't want to spoil our system of doing three shows a year." A deal was worked out for Freed to host a rock & roll show at Harlem's Apollo Theatre, to begin February 5, 1960. That particular show reflected the sad state of affairs the once-proud disc jockey was now in. Show headliner Bo Diddley, a consistent crowd-pleaser ever since the years when he could not crack the white-dominated pop charts, was in the midst of a series of national charted hits (of which "Road Runner" was his latest). Freed's other perennial showstopper, Jo Ann Campbell, once again did not disappoint the Apollo audience, although as a recording artist Campbell was lacking not only a hit record (she had never made the national "Top 100" at this stage of her career) but a record label as well. "Beachcomber," the seventh (and last) of Campbell's singles for George Goldner, had flopped the previous summer, and Goldner had finally given up all hope of the "blonde bombshell" ever making a hit record.

The Skyliners, whose latest record, "How Much," was a dismal commercial failure, had not had a hit since the fall of 1959, before the payola scandal broke. Another great stage act, the Cadillacs, had just seen Jerry Blaine issue what would be the last of their Josie Records nineteen releases dating back to 1954. The Cadillacs, without a "Top 100" hit since 1958, would next record for Mercury Records, but time had passed the group by, at least as regards recording. The same could be said for another singer on Freed's Apollo bill, Bobby Day who had last had a hit record in the summer of 1959.

Despite the meager talent lineup, Hooke insisted Freed "did well" at the Apollo. But the disc jockey never played that theater again. Hooke said Apollo owner Frank Schiffman "drove a very hard bargain."

On February 25, 1960, three days after rock & roll disappeared entirely from WNEW-TV when Richard Hayes abandoned Freed's old "Big Beat" format, New York District Attorney Frank Hogan received New York Criminal Court Judge Gerald Gulkin's order to file an information from the New York grand jury charging Alan Freed with "requesting and accepting" $10,000 from Roulette Records on February 28, 1958. Stone had his first criminal indictment resulting from the payola scandal. The information was filed the following day, charging Freed with his first count of commercial bribery.

Early in March, FCC chairman John C. Doerfer resigned in the face of the charges that he had been influenced by broadcasting magnate George B. Storer by accepting a free cruise to Bimini on Storer's yacht at a time when Storer had a broadcasting decision pending before the FCC.

Later that month, Alan Freed racked up what was said to be a "solid gross" of $18,500 for two rock & roll show dates at Hartford's State Theatre, despite a howling northeast blizzard that raged for those two days. Meanwhile, rumors began to surface that Freed would soon return to New York's airwaves on an unspecified radio station.

Freed was scheduled to testify before the House subcommittee in Washington when the panel reconvened in Room 1334 of the New House Office Building on Monday, April 25, 1960. Freed, by far the biggest personality yet to appear before the subcommittee, and his attorney, Warren Troob, were as prepared as they could have been. The disc jockey was granted an executive, or closed, hearing, the transcript of which would not be released to the public. With one criminal indictment already lodged against him in New York and other indictments forthcoming, Freed, Troob, and the subcommittee members disappeared behind closed doors. While Freed remained without immunity from Assistant District Attorney Stone, if the House members expected more of the evasiveness that characterized the witnesses who testified during the winter session, they were in for a surprise.

The subcommittee's chief counsel, Robert Lishman, questioned

Freed about the disc jockey's dealings with WABC Radio before the panel got down to the real business at hand—payola. Noting Freed's sensitivity to the way ABC handled him as opposed to the manner in which the network dealt with Dick Clark, Oren Harris turned the questioning of Freed in that direction.

As Jack Hooke maintained years later, Clark was a "shrewd little businessman" and legally he was "clean as a whistle." If Clark's many music-related businesses had in many cases been deceptive, they had also been perfectly legal.

One bone that Freed had to pick was that when ABC's company payola affidavit was sent out to the network's employees the past November, Freed was told that he was expected to sign the company-authored document while Clark was permitted to respond with his own specially written statement declaring his innocence.

Freed was handed a copy of Clark's statement, in which the "Bandstand" host denied any payola involvement. In it, Clark's attorneys had adopted the narrow definition of *payola*, which called for an agreement to play a particular record in return for payment of some sort. When Lishman asked Freed if Clark's definition was Freed's idea of a commonly accepted definition, Freed turned to the subcommittee attorney and said, "No, it isn't." The deejay said he thought Clark's sounded more like a bribery explanation.

Lishman asked Freed if he agreed with Clark that an agreement had to be made between the two parties to constitute payola. Freed replied that such an agreement was not necessary. Lishman informed Freed that Clark said, "There had to be an agreement made."

"Then he was wrong," Freed responded, telling Lishman that if the attorney was going to refer to payola at all, he would have to use the word to define the practice of receiving money and gifts before plugging a record as well as for the practice of receiving gifts for being a "nice guy" after playing a record. "There can't be two types of payola," said Freed, contending that Clark's definition of the practice was not correct as it applied to the music business.

Lishman then asked Freed if he could have signed Clark's specially written payola denial without perjuring himself.

"Yes," said Freed, "I could have signed it."

"But you still would have been guilty of payola in the common sense we're talking about?" asked Lishman.

Freed replied that he would have been guilty just the same.

Seeking to drive home the point, Lishman asked Freed, "With

Clark's elaborate payola definition, could you swear to your innocence without any hesitation?"

Freed replied that under Clark's payola definition, he would be "as clean as the driven snow."

Freed said that because Dick Clark grossed about $12 million a year for the ABC network, compared to Freed's $250,000 yearly figure for the local WABC radio, there was no doubt in his mind that ABC had a double standard for him and for Clark. Freed maintained that while he let ABC know all along that he would sign "anything that Clark signed, . . . when a fellow can be sacrificed, he can be sacrificed."

Congressman John J. Bennett took over the questioning and asked Freed if he would be willing to tell the panel of his own payola activities. Freed explained that since he had been refused immunity to testify before the New York grand jury investigating payola, anything he told the subcommittee could be used against him for prosecution in New York. "Mr. Hogan would like to get an indictment to make somebody look like they are real criminals under the 439th Statute of New York State law of commercial bribery," Freed told Bennett.

Freed said that without touching on his own specific dealings, he would enlighten the panel on some of the general practices of the music business. Reminding the Michigan congressman that music business payola went back to the "Victor Herbert days," Freed pointed out that payoffs were actually more common in other areas of the music business than among disc jockeys and that deals made by music publishers to get an artist to record a particular song made the disc jockey payoffs look like "peanuts." The deejay said that song publishers were notorious for giving a record company A&R man cash in order to get a particular song recorded. Freed also described his weekly receipt of up to five hundred new record releases as a "completely ridiculous situation. There was no way I could have listened to each of them, and the manufacturers knew it." But even with such a large selection of records to choose from, Freed insisted that he always tried to "protect" his listening audience by not playing what he termed "junk," explaining that his listeners were not about to have anything "forced down their throats."

Freed also explained to the subcommittee the common practice whereby a record distributor received two or three percent of the pressings of a particular record "free of charge, to be used for promotion purposes." Such promo records were then divided up among the most important disc jockeys, a practice that "we call payola in the disc jockey end" of the business.

When Bennett questioned Freed about fellow ABC employees Dick Clark and Martin Block, Freed could no longer contain his anger at being made what he called ABC's "sacrificial lamb." Claiming that his own operation "was a piker's" compared to Clark's and Block's, Freed fumed that he "never made a dime" from Figure Music, the one publishing company he had an interest in. "Why should I be the scapegoat?" he angrily implored the subcommittee. "Why me!"

Bennett grasped the emotionally charged moment and asked the distressed Freed if he really felt he would incriminate himself before the New York grand jury if he discussed in detail his own payola activities. Freed hesitated, but then agreed to discuss certain of his dealings, explaining that he did not want to make himself "cannon fodder" before the grand jury. Bennett assured Freed that he did not want to ask him any questions that might be incriminating. Freed replied that he appreciated the congressman's avoiding such areas.

The congressman then questioned the subcommittee's celebrated witness about the circumstances whereby Figure Music obtained the publishing rights to the Royal Teens' "Short Shorts" (including a comical respite when the congressman from Michigan referred to the song as "Short Pants"), before relinquishing the microphone to Chairman Harris.

Harris, a Democrat, chastised his colleague, the senior Republican on the subcommittee, for his "unscheduled disclosures" concerning Dick Clark. Bennett then expressed his dismay at the subcommittee's delay in calling Clark to testify and offered his opinion that Clark was "obviously very seriously involved in payola." Bennett was upset that so far the subcommittee had exposed only "peanut deejays." He reminded the chairman that the panel now had more evidence to question Clark about than they had had on many of the small-time individuals they had questioned. "I hope he will be called as soon as possible," declared Bennett, who maintained that Clark's music business dealings "epitomized the evils of payola."

Harris continued to question Freed and expressed astonishment at the deejay's WABC contract requirement that he kick back $30,000 of his approximately $40,000 salary as payment for airplugs for Freed's stage shows. Freed responded that because WABC threatened to pull his show off the air if he failed to sign the contract, he had no choice in the matter. Freed also told the panel of the stage show on which he "made less than ABC made " from the contractual kickback deal.

When Robert Lishman again took up the questioning of Freed, he asked how many free records were supplied to disc jockeys by record distributors and manufacturers. "Too many," replied Freed. Referring to testimony in which Freed had alleged he was told at his WABC contract signing "to lay very heavily on ABC-Paramount records," Lishman asked Freed if Am-Par president Sam Clark had ever told the deejay he was not playing enough Am-Par records. "Many times," responded Freed, recalling that on occasion Clark would sent Freed a packet of Am-Par releases and remind the deejay that it was Clark who had had much to do with Freed being signed by WABC in the first place. Freed said he told Sam Clark that "he [Freed] didn't owe any part of his career to him." Freed further explained that sometimes when he did refuse to spin a particular Am-Par record, "Clark would call and ask why I wouldn't air the tune." Freed said he told the Am-Par President that he did not play the particular song because he did not like it "and that was that!"

Chairman Oren Harris paused for a moment. As far as he was concerned his subcommittee was finished questioning Freed. Nevertheless, Harris said that while he respected Freed's right not to discuss his personal payola dealings without a guarantee of immunity by the New York grand jury, the chairman would be "derelict" if he did not ask some additional questions that had been asked of everyone else who had previously appeared before the panel. Harris reminded Freed that the disc jockey did not have to answer the questions. "You testified a moment ago that you were on the payroll of record distributing companies," the chairman matter-of-factly began. "Will you name them?" Without hesitation, Freed answered that he was on the payroll of Alpha Distributing Corporation, Superior Record Sales, and Lou Klayman, all of New York City.

The subcommittee was astonished by Freed's unexpected candidness. Harris, trying not to appear surprised, asked if the deejay was also on Jerry Blaine's Cosnat Distributing payroll. Freed said he was not, claiming that those distributors he named were the only ones paying him. "Let me name manufacturers," continued Freed. He admitted receiving payment from "United Artists Records, Roulette Records, Atlantic Records. Those three . . . for my services as disc jockey" while at WABC and WNEW-TV. Freed explained that someone in his position could help a record distributor select future releases because "a lot of these guys are pretty dumb when it comes to making a record." Freed was speaking freely now, and Harris let him go on uninterrupted. The deejay explained how his extensive broadcasting experience made him "some kind of an expert" in knowing what kind of records the public would like. This expertise, he maintained, often saved distributors a few thousand dollars by not having them issue "junk that is going to get lost somewhere along the way." Freed said that in his "consultation" he tried to help the record manufacturers "make a little better records, classier records, a good-sounding record." He claimed to have sometimes sat in on record company sessions, "many nights until three or four in the morning, helping to get the right sound." Freed said he had done nothing wrong in accepting payments from record companies for such services because he earned the money.

When Harris asked if Freed would be more specific about the payments he had just referred to, the deejay said that he received most of them on a monthly basis, and recalled one specific $10,000 payment from Roulette made in 1958 (the payment that Morris Levy allegedly told the New York grand jury he gave to Freed to ensure that the deejay would keep playing Roulette records, the payment that Freed would be criminally indicted for receiving). Harris then asked if Freed had any way of knowing "how many or what" Roulette records he "played or promoted" that year. Freed replied that "it would be very hard to remember" such details. He then told the subcommittee that he received "maybe $5,000" from Atlantic Records in 1958 and "$400 a month" from United Artists, and "I think it was $500 month" in 1959 from each of the three distributors mentioned previously. Freed swore that WABC "did know [of] these outside dealings."

Harris stared at Freed. "They were fully aware you were on the monthly payroll of some of these companies and you received annual payments from other companies?" he asked.

"That is right," replied Freed. When the deejay explained that Ben Hoberman was Freed's immediate employer at WABC, Harris asked if Hoberman was aware of the payments. Freed said the WABC station manager was aware of them, but that "he did not complain about them then. He just asked me to sign the affidavit."

Congressman Bennett resumed his interrogation of Freed by saying he would have asked the questions Harris had just asked, but that he thought Freed "would take the Fifth Amendment or refuse to answer the questions because they would incriminate you." The Michigan congressman then stated, "You were receiving this money from the record companies to plug their records on the air. Is that not true?"

"Yes," replied Freed.

Warren Troob, who would say years later that Freed had been under a "great deal of tension" and that he (Troob) "didn't know" what Freed would tell the subcommittee, had agreed to permit Freed to admit that he had been paid by various record manufacturers and distributors. Too much evidence in the form of canceled checks existed for Freed to deny such payments had been made. In openly admitting the receipt of payments, Freed intended to establish the fact that they were perfectly legal "consultation fees" (at one point in his testimony Freed told the subcommittee that he "coined that phrase 'record consultant' ") and not illegal payola. But, by accident or design, Bennett had been able to get Freed to agree that he had taken money to plug records on the air. Troob could not let his client's answer stand.

"Wait a minute!" exclaimed Freed's attorney as he sprang to his feet. "What was the question?"

Bennett, more than satisfied with the answer he had elicited from Freed, said the deejay had already answered the question. He then admonished Troob that the attorney was not there to instruct his client how to answer the questions. Troob said he was not telling Freed how to answer any questions; he had simply asked his client if he had listened to the question, because "I know Mr. Freed does not listen to the question before he answers."

"Did you understand the question?" Harris asked Freed. The deejay replied that he had not understood it. The question was read back to Freed, after which the deejay explained, "My answer cannot be yes to that. I was not being paid to play any specific records by any of those people."

But a skeptical Bennett remained unconvinced, reminding Freed that he had already testified that Am-Par Distributors had "called you up and insisted that you play their records." Freed agreed with Bennett's contention that Am-Par had done so "because they had given you a good contract with WABC . . . and they expected you to reciprocate by playing or plugging Am-Par records." But Freed insisted there was a difference between the Am-Par arrangement and the deals he had with the other record distributors, "where it was always my prerogative to say yes or no as to the quality of the record."

Bennett, growing short of patience with Freed's distinctions, asked him if it was not true "that you were getting money to plug records?"

"Let us say they gave me a job, and one of the stipulations was to play records, Am-Par records," Freed coolly replied, reminding the congressman that in his deals with other companies, "if I didn't feel the record justified being played, it was not played."

Bennett said that if such was the case, then those companies could refuse to pay him each month, to which Freed agreed. "And they would have [refused to continue payment] if you had not plugged their records, would they not?" asked the subcommittee member.

"Not necessarily," replied Freed.

Bennett was incredulous. With his voice rising, he said to Freed, "You think this record company is giving you $10,000 a year if you had not plugged this record?"

Freed calmly replied that if he had not played any of their records, "I am sure that would have been it."

The questioning of Freed was concluded by Robert Lishman, who asked the deejay how he could be so certain that Ben Hoberman was aware of Freed's outside music business deals. Freed explained that the "only conversation" he could remember relevant to that point occurred at a time when the deejay was fighting to avoid paying a second $10,000 to WABC for stage-show plugs. Freed said that Hoberman "looked across the desk and winked at me," before saying, "Just a moment, Alan, you know you have a million outside deals; give up the $10,000."

At 7:25 P.M. the subcommittee hearing was recessed. Alan Freed's bout with the House Subcommittee on Legislative Oversight was over.

Hearing Freed's testimony, the subcommittee members felt they had at last obtained some honest answers. Still, Freed swore he had never taken a bribe, and while he would accept a gift if he had helped somebody, he "wouldn't take a dime to plug a record. I'd be a fool to. I'd be giving up control of my own program."

By openly admitting to the subcommittee that he was on the payroll of various record companies and distributors, Freed had potentially incriminated himself for the New York grand jury. Freed knew that the record companies and distributors, permitted by Stone to retain their immunity before the grand jury, were protecting themselves as best they could by cooperating with the district attorney's office. Morris Levy had become a sort of Judas, with his alleged testimony of the "loan" he had given to Freed. What is more, Freed knew that Stone not only had the testimony of the record companies but also the corroborating evidence in the form of canceled checks. In laying out his "consultant fee" defense, Freed had not admitted anything that Stone could not already prove in court. Clearly, Freed's back was to the wall. While his "record consultant" alibi was weak (why would a record distributor need to consult anybody about making or releasing a record?), it was the only one Freed had.

On Tuesday, April 26, the United Press International wire story out of Washington bore the title "A Closed Hearing Is Held on Clark; Payola Inquiry Goes into Disk Jockey's Business Ties—Alan Freed Testifies." Paul Porter, Clark's attorney, asked the subcommittee that his client be the first witness on Tuesday so he could "tell his story and get it over with." Although it was not disclosed what Freed had told the subcommittee, when Chairman Oren Harris asked if he thought Freed had been a cooperative witness, he replied, "I would say yes."

Freed's undisclosed testimony only heightened the anticipation of Dick Clark's scheduled April 29 appearance before the Harris subcommittee, especially after word was leaked to the press by Robert Lishman that during his testimony, Freed had "impugned Clark's purity."

Before hearing from Clark, the subcommittee heard testimony from George Goldner, at one time one of the most influential of "the boys" in New York. Goldner testified that he had assigned song copyrights to disc jockeys—Freed's and Clark's publishing companies included—in "hopes of having those songs played on the air." Congressman Moss asked Goldner if the New York record manufacturer regarded the four song copyrights he assigned to Dick Clark as payola. Goldner said he "did not think so."

When Moss pressed Goldner, asking, "How would you describe them?" the record executive said, "It is pretty hard." Goldner also listed some of the disc jockeys he allegedly had on his payroll. Goldner also swore he never paid disc jockeys to give him "advice" on the prospects of any records, but rather to get those deejays to play records in which his company "had a financial interest." He also told the subcommittee that it was a common practice for record manufacturers and distributors to reimburse television shows and stage shows for performing fees paid to their artists. Then, with his tongue planted firmly in his cheek, Goldner told the Harris subcommittee that as long as there were people like themselves in the country, "I still feel safe as an American citizen." The record manufacturer went on to thank the subcommittee members "very much for your interest in the music industry and what you are doing for the industry." Goldner closed by saying he was "sure that a lot of good will come out of what you are doing."

On Thursday morning, April 27, Bernie Lowe—songwriter, musician, arranger, and the principal owner of Cameo-Parkway Records—testified before the House subcommittee. Lowe told of his song-publishing "gifts," including 25 percent of "Butterfly" and 50 percent of "Back to School Again," two of Cameo's big hits, to Dick Clark. As for payola, Lowe estimated he paid almost $5,000 between 1956 and 1959 to various disc jockeys. Lowe cited a specific instance where he allegedly paid WMGM's Peter Trip "good will" of $1,000, because the record manufacturer "just wasn't getting my records played over there."

A brief appearance by Harry Chipetz, Dick Clark's ex-partner in Chips Distributing Company, followed Lowe's. Chipetz said he paid disc jockeys more than $5,000 in 1958 and almost $15,000 in 1959.

On Friday, April 28, 1960, Dick Clark appeared, sporting a conservative dark blue suit, a white, button-down shirt, dark blue tie, and black loafers, before the Washington subcommittee. It was reported by the press that Clark's "every hair strand was neatly lacquered in place" and that the "American Bandstand" host radiated "the same air of proper respectability he does on TV." Schoolchildren were interspersed among the packed gallery of 240 that eagerly awaited the star of Oren Harris's payola investigation.

Clark, intent on "selling his highly select adult audience the same moralistic image of himself that he had continually sold to the nation's teens," immediately jumped on the offensive, telling the subcommittee members he felt he had been "convicted, condemned and denounced" even before he had his chance to give his side of the story.

Clark said he wanted to "make it clear, immediately, that I have never taken payola . . . I followed normal business practices under the ground rules that then existed."

But when Clark maintained he had no agreement with Bernie Lowe about receiving anything for the publishing rights to "Butterfly," Robert Lishman produced a letter Clark had written to one of Lowe's publishing companies in which the "American Bandstand" host spoke of an "oral agreement" the two had whereby Lowe was to give Clark 25 percent of the song's publishing rights. Stating that he had never "in his life . . . used devious means of negotiating" any of his business deals, Clark thought perhaps he had forgotten about the "oral agreement" letter regarding "Butterfly." He still insisted that the $7,000 he received after the song's success was Lowe's "idea of gratitude" and that Clark had repeatedly reminded Lowe that such payment was "unnecessary." When Lishman suggested to Clark that it may have been convenient for him not to get to know too much about his business dealings so that when questioned, "you wouldn't have the answers," Clark replied that while that has not "been my practice, I have been pretty busy." With his blonde wife, Barbara, sitting three rows in back of him, Clark also told the subcommittee, while he knew that Chips Distributing had given out $20,000 in payola, "it never occurred to me to look into it in detail." Besides, said Clark, making such payments "was not a particularly unusual practice in the business."

As part of the subcommittee's scrutiny of Clark's recently divested music business ventures in thirty-three companies, it was pointed out that he owned copyrights to 160 songs, 143 of them received as outright gifts. Congressman Moss remarked to Clark that "once you acquired an interest [in a song] you really laid it on." The Californian accused Clark of exploiting "his position as a network personality" and asserted that "by almost any reasonable test," he played records he held an interest in "more than the ones you didn't."

Clark replied that while he did not consciously favor records he had an interest in, "maybe I did so without realizing it."

When the subcommittee questioned Clark about a $1,000 fur stole and $3,400 in jewelry he and his wife received from Lou Bedell, the owner of Era and Dore records, Clark said that while he was "embarrassed" over the fact that Bedell had written off the items in question as promotional expenses, they were nevertheless "given to us as gifts," and that he "did not receive them because of any agreement or understanding that I was to give Mr. Bedell's records any special treatment."

The pop music historian Arnold Shaw, who at the time of the payola scandal worked for E. B. Marks Music Publishing Company, remarked in 1959 that "someone like Clark is a one-man trust." But, as usual, the "suave, unruffled" Clark, who, according to the news media, "wiggled off each baited hook" of the members of the subcommittee, was correct: he had taken no payola. He had followed normal business practices under the ground rules that existed at the time.

Realizing they were not going to uncover any illegalities in Clark's business practices, the Harris subcommittee members instead focused on the preferential treatment afforded Clark by the ABC network, as opposed to the treatment Freed received. Congressman Bennett wasted no time in asking Clark if he knew Freed. Clark replied that the two had never met face-to-face, but that they had spoken on the telephone. The "American Bandstand" host also said he was not familiar with the practices Freed used to get himself on the payrolls of various record companies.

Bennett, already upset because the subcommittee had waited so long to call Clark as a witness, exhibited little patience with the star witness. He angrily pointed out that Clark ran practically the same kind of operation Freed did. Clark took exception, saying there was a big difference between a disc jockey such as himself on the payroll of a record company in which he held an interest and someone like Freed, who was on the payroll of a company in which no interest was held. Bennett impatiently responded that "it seems like the only difference was that ABC kept you and fired Freed."

Clark, refusing to be drawn in by Bennett's badgering, said that if he was on the payroll of record companies in which he held no interest, "I would say it would be difficult to explain."

"Frankly," replied Bennett, obviously not an "American Bandstand" fan, "I cannot see very much difference from the type of activities you were carrying on, except that yours involved a tremendous amount of money."

When Bennett made a reference to the contractual kickbacks Freed was required to pay WABC, Chairman Harris interrupted the Michigan congressman to remind him that Freed had been an "important witness" whose testimony had not been made public and to caution the subcommittee member to "stay away" from Freed's testimony. Bennett contended that Freed's testimony was an important reference in cross-examining Clark, but Harris said that the subcommittee quorum necessary to vote on releasing Freed's testimony was not present.

In his opening remarks, Clark had said he did not think he received preferential treatment from ABC, but the subcommittee had proof to the contrary. Robert Lishman produced a copy of the payola affidavit given to all ABC employees, except Clark, to sign. He asked Clark if the "American Bandstand" host could honestly answer no to each of the questions. Clark replied he could not—and then quickly added that he did not know why Freed could not do so. Clark "presumed" out loud that the reason Freed would not sign the affidavit was "mainly because he could not swear he had not taken payola."

Clark's concession that he could not honestly have signed ABC's payola affidavit while condemning Freed for not having done so was too much for the subcommittee. When Peter F. Mack (of Illinois) asked if "in effect" Clark drew up his affidavit on his own terms, Clark said he had done so, but added that his personal statement was a "forerunner" of ABC's payola affidavit. Robert Lishman reminded Clark that ABC's affidavits were distributed on November 13, three days before Clark's alleged "forerunner" was submitted. Steven B. Derounian of New York, who kept a low profile during the hearings, rose to the occasion, saying he would describe Clark's payola affidavit as a " 'Christian Dior affidavit,' because it was tailored to your need." An outburst of laughter rose from the gallery as Derounian pointed out to Clark that other disc jockeys who admitted taking payola could have honestly signed Clark's denial and still have accepted the money they received.

Unnerved, Clark said he was not aware of that fact. He then described the choice given him by ABC to either divest himself of his music-related businesses or resign as the "American Bandstand" host as "no choice" at all, because he "preferred TV" and wanted to be a star.

Chairman Harris summed up Clark's appearance before the House subcommittee on a sympathetic note, saying he did not think that Clark was the "inventor" of the payola system, but rather "the product that has taken advantage of a unique opportunity in exposing to the public, to the teenagers, the young people, the television productions of this country—and I say that in all sincerity."

Once again repeating that he had "followed the normal business practices under the ground rules that existed" in the music business, Clark added that he would not have been "completely frank" in saying he had been pleased to appear before the subcommittee and that he did not feel he had done anything "illegal or immoral."

While ABC may have defended Dick Clark in the payola scandal, the network apparently was not prepared to take any chances with his appearance before the subcommittee or with the public's reaction to it. It was reported that the network was "cautious, waiting to see which way the wind blows" after Clark's testimony. In the meantime, ABC had lined up a replacement for the "American Bandstand" host "just in case."

"American Bandstand" teen idols rose to Clark's defense. Frankie Avalon thought there was nothing wrong with having one business "and an interest in another." As for receiving gifts, Avalon saw nothing wrong with the practice, saying he had once given Clark "a shirt and a pair of shoes." Fabian thought the payola accusations were "a big shame," adding that the kids "really love Dick" because "you can always kid around with him." Bobby Darin said he "couldn't have more respect" for Clark if he was the singer's own brother. Darin thought Clark was "as innocent of doing any harm as any clergyman I know." Paul Anka said he was "a hundred percent Dick Clark man" and "they'd better get after some other cats."

In 1980, Warren Troob called Clark's appearance before the subcommittee a "whitewash" and said they "practically had a parade" in Washington for the host of "American Bandstand." Jack Hooke, who later worked for Dick Clark for eighteen years, was more philosophical. While Freed's former business associate recently conceded that Clark "got the best" legal defense and emerged from the Washington payola hearings "smelling like a rose," he maintained that Clark merely "did what he had to do." Hooke said ABC, in effect, "came along with a lifesaver [and pulled Clark] . . . out of the ocean when he was drowning," and anybody in Clark's predicament "would have grabbed that lifesaver too."

A decade after the Washington payola hearings, Clark dismissed them as "just politics," saying the congressmen "were just looking for headlines" in an election year. The "American Bandstand" host insisted that he was innocent and the Harris subcommittee had ignored the improprieties of others and instead focused their attention on him. Nevertheless, said Clark, he cooperated fully by turning over his business records to the subcommittee when he could just as easily "burned those motherfuckers in two minutes." Referring to the taking of payola, the "Bandstand" host said it was "offensive" to him that the Harris subcommittee "thought I was ignorant." In *Rolling Stone* in 1990, Clark told Henry Schipper that the members of the 1960 House subcommittee, who "knew little or nothing and cared less" about rock & roll, had attacked him for the "headlines" and that some members would leave the hearings early "to go make a statement to the press for the afternoon and evening newspapers and television." Clark maintained that since the payola scandal his motto has been Protect Your Ass at All Times.

In 1973, speaking of Alan Freed's fate, Clark said he thought Freed "made a lot of mistakes." While crediting the pioneering rock & roll disc jockey with feeling the "raw emotion" of the music and of having the "gut reaction" to it, Clark said he "knew the game" better than Freed had known it. Clark thought Freed "wasn't bright enough" to get himself safely through his own business dealings. More recently, Clark conceded that Freed "was the man who made it [rock & roll] happen" and that "we owe a great deal to him."

On Tuesday, May 3, the final day of the Washington payola hearings, ABC President Leonard Goldenson and WABC radio general manager testified. When asked what he knew about payola, Goldenson replied that he "probably" was not as aware of the practice as he should have been. He thought payola was more widespread among the independent stations, explaining that such stations "went in for rock and roll, which our owned-and-operated stations had not done." It was an eyebrow-raising statement, considering it came from the head of the ABC network. What, if not rock & roll, did Goldenson think Freed had been playing on WABC, the network's flagship radio station?

When informed of the alleged double standard ABC applied to Freed and Clark, Goldenson expressed surprise, saying there was "no basis to the charge of a double standard with respect to Mr. Freed." Goldenson explained that ABC had been "very patient" with Freed before firing him, trying for more than a week to get him to sign the network's payola affidavit. Goldenson also denied Freed's allegation that someone at ABC told the disc jockey to "lay it on" ABC-Paramount records. The network president said that Mortimer Weinbach, the attorney Freed had alleged made the "lay it on" statement, had never seen Freed or talked to him.

"I might point out to you, sir," Congressman Moss said to Goldenson, "that in my judgement Mr. Freed was one of the very completely truthful men we had before us."

When asked why Clark had been allowed to submit his own affidavit denying any payola involvement, Goldenson brazenly replied that there was no significant difference in the wording of Clark's affidavit and ABC's. The network president also said he was "not aware" that Freed had been contractually required to kick back three-fourths of his salary to WABC in return for the deejay's stage-show plugs.

"Quite candidly," Moss said to Goldenson, "I do not believe you."

Goldenson explained that in the final analysis, ABC fired Freed not for any disclosures made, but because "he refused to provide us any information at all under oath." He also maintained that about 110 ABC employees responded to the network's payola affidavit, with Freed "the single exception in this respect." Goldenson recalled that when he learned of Freed's refusal to sign the affidavit, he said, "If that is the case, I think we should terminate his contract."

Ben Hoberman was the final witness to appear before the payola subcommittee for the April session. If anybody at WABC had known of Freed's outside business dealings, it should have been Hoberman, the station manager. But Hoberman testified that Freed's charge that the station manager had been aware of the disc jockey's outside deals was "absolutely not true." Hoberman insisted all he knew Freed to be involved with were the deejay's WNEW-TV show, his stage shows, and the rock & roll movies he had made. The WABC station manager swore that until that very day, he was still uncertain of the association Freed had with various record companies.

Hoberman was also questioned about his apparent relentless quest to gain additional WABC revenue via Freed's advertising plugs. Hoberman conceded that his contract did stipulate that the station manager was to receive, above his base salary, a percentage of WABC's net profits and that such an arrangement did give Hoberman an incentive to increase airtime sales at the station.

On completion of hearing testimony concerning payola and other deceptive broadcasting practices, the House Subcommittee on Legislative Oversight began to prepare recommendations for federal legislation designed to safeguard against similar future abuses. Also, as a result of the Washington hearings, the networks lost their broadcasting autonomy and became (as individual stations had been) subject to FCC licensing. As for payola itself, the subcommittee hearings displayed the ethical ambiguity that existed in the music and broadcasting industries, wherein what were viewed as unethical practices by some were considered practical business strategy by others.

The anti–rock & roll forces used the payola revelations to support their specious claim that rock & roll had been foisted upon an unsuspecting and gullible public. The *New York Herald Tribune*, long a belittler of both Alan Freed and rock & roll, editorialized that while solace could be taken that the payola scandal revealed most of the music played by disc jockeys to be "so bad that it's almost a relief to learn they had to be paid to play it" and that punishing the "fakers and the takers" would be relatively easy to do; there were difficult as well as important tasks ahead, including the restoration of "lost standards" and the elevation of, instead of the pandering to, "low tastes" in music.

For all of the publicity, the payola subcommittee adopted a dilatory attitude toward exposing deeper levels of broadcasting corruption. Professor Bernard Schwartz, who was originally employed by the Harris subcommittee to investigate alleged FCC improprieties, continued to follow the proceedings closely after being fired by the subcommittee. Schwartz noted that while the word *payola* had recently become one of the familiar words in the American vocabulary, "what the country does not realize . . . is that improprieties other than those committed by Charles Van Doren, Alan Freed, et al.— what may aptly be determined the 'real payola'—have thus far remained buried in the Harris Committee's files."

It was Schwartz's contention—and he was not alone in the belief— that the public "sadly deceived" itself if it believed, as the newspaper headlines made it appear, that the congressmen had conducted "anything like the really thorough investigation of the federal regulatory agencies that is so urgently needed."

While Congress chose to take a safe yet sensational approach to the problem of broadcasting payola by exposing a handful of disc jockeys, the greatest irony of the scandal turned out to be that BMI, whose formation, wrote *Variety* editor Herm Schoenfeld, was at the root of rival ASCAP's "long-standing vendetta against the major networks," remained unscathed by the payola hearings.

* * *

By the time the Washington payola hearings concluded in the spring of 1960, rock & roll's first generation of fans had reached adulthood. Those who had been high school seniors in 1955 or before and had gone on to college had received their degrees. Others had received a different kind of education, one that included wives, children, nine-to-five jobs, and mortgage payments. Many of them looked wistfully to the past and wondered where the carefree days of the 1950s had gone. Naturally, the nostalgic feeling encompassed the music of that bygone era.

"The boys," who ran the independent record companies, also longed for those halcyon days when they gave the major record companies fits. Now, large record distributors that handled numerous independent labels called the shots in the rock & roll business. And in 1959, for the first time since rock & roll's inception, the major labels outgrossed the indies in sales and surpassed them in number of records that appeared on the national hit charts. Faced with their declining industrywide influence and a corresponding loss of sales revenue, many independent record companies were forced to adapt a new marketing strategy, one that involved the recycling of past hit songs.

About the time that the payola scandal broke in November 1959 Al Silver (one of the boys and the owner of Herald-Ember Records) rereleased the Five Satins' quintessential 1950s ballad "In the Still of the Nite." On the West Coast, Dootsie Williams, who owned the Los Angeles–based Dootone Records, rereleased the Penguin's 1954 do-wop classic "Earth Angel," and the song sold well enough the second time around to reach *Billboard*'s "Bubbling Under the Top 100" chart in January 1960, one week after the three-year-old "In the Still of the Nite" reappeared on *Billboard*'s national "Hot 100" chart. As the 1960s began, other indie record companies, including Chicago's Vee Jay label, which rereleased the Dells' 1956 recording of "Oh What a Nite" began to rerelease many of their tried-and-true 1950s ballads, heralding a mass recycling of previously issued hits. The first "do-wop revival" was under way, and dusty, forgotten hits began to take on new importance to the independent label owners who had originally produced them and, in most cases, now owned the publishing rights to them as well. There was additional gold to be mined from those classic songs lying dormant in the record company vaults.

During the summer of 1960, the do-wop revival continued to gather momentum. The Jacks' "Why Don't You Write Me" (originally a hit in 1955) and Johnnie and Joe's "Over the Mountain, Across the Sea" (from 1957) were reissued, with the latter reappearing on *Billboard*'s "Hot 100" chart. By the fall, with the boys of the New York record business in its vanguard, the do-wop revival reached its zenith. Morris Levy rereleased the Heartbeats' "A Thousand Miles Away" (from 1956); Al Silver, who, ten months earlier, began the practice of recycling gold, hit again, this time with the rerelease of the Mello-Kings' "Tonight, Tonight" (from 1957); and the New York–based Scepter label rereleased the Shirelles' "Dedicated to the One I Love" (1959). All three ballads sold well enough the second time around to reappear on *Billboard*'s "Hot 100" chart.

Shortly after the Washington payola hearings ended, Mel Leeds, then the program director at KDAY Radio in Los Angeles, called Freed in New York and told the unemployed disc jockey that there was a job waiting for him at KDAY if he wanted it. Freed, desperate for any broadcasting position, jumped at the offer.

Warren Troob insisted that at that point Freed had not given up hope of resuming his career. The attorney said that while Freed was "disappointed in a lot of people around him, his so-called 'real friends,' " the deejay was not "bitter." Troob recalled that Freed told him that he had built up a following once and "I can do it again." But the familiar Freed bravado was now tempered with trepidation. Alana Freed said her father left New York feeling he had "nothing" and that when he joined KDAY, he was unsure of his future and "didn't know what to expect."

KDAY, originally owned by Art Tobin and the "singing cowboy" Gene Autry, went on the air in 1948 in Santa Monica, California, with just five kilowatts of broadcasting power. In 1953, Tobin and Autry sold the station, which by that time had moved to Vine Street in Los Angeles and had increased its power to fifty kilowatts, to the owners of the *Santa Monica Times*. Bob Dye, KDAY's chief engineer, who joined the station in 1952, said at the time of the sale KDAY was "the leading Negro and foreign-language station this side of Chicago."

Keenly aware of the growing do-wop revival, the KDAY brass believed that Alan Freed and his vast experience with 1950s rhythm and blues would fit in comfortably with their new programming format. (As a result of the payola scandal KDAY, which had given its disc jockeys televised lie-detector tests to determine if any were guilty, had decided to deemphasize rock & roll and to specialize instead in rhythm and blues. The decision to offer Freed, now an East Coast pariah, a job was greatly abetted by the fact that Mel Leeds, who was under his own cloud of suspicion regarding payola, had been Freed's program director at WINS in New York.

Station manager Irving Phillips said KDAY had chosen Freed because "he's a dynamic personality and any problems he may have had are a thing of the past." The station manager added that Freed "has full knowledge of the way we operate and will abide by our restrictions." Phillips also disclosed that Freed's $25,000-a-year contract contained a clause that called for the disc jockey's adherence to the FCC "clarification" on selecting records to be played on the air. Phillips said that inclusion of such a clause in disc jockey contracts had become a "standard practice" since the FCC payola crackdown. In the wake of KDAY's rock & roll ban, Freed would "concentrate his talents on exposing rhythm and blues discs."

Bob Dye recalled Freed's hiring under different circumstances, saying it occurred at a time when KDAY was "trying anybody and everybody to make the station go." Whatever the case, Freed made his KDAY debut on May 16, 1960, filling the one-to-four afternoon time slot six days a week.

Alana Freed said her father received a lot of help in California, particularly from Randy Wood of Dot Records, who was very good friends with her father. Wood encouraged Freed to make the move to California and told the deejay he would "take care" of him until Freed was back on his feet again. Freed moved into the Mikado Apartments ("It was nice," said the deejay's daughter, "but it was nothing like what he was used to") in Los Angeles, where he began a low-key professional routine. Freed's daughter, who visited her father in Los Angeles, said that after her father's afternoon shift at KDAY, "he returned to the apartment, and that was it." But Freed was back on the radio and, said Alana, "was much more up" than he had been when he left New York.

Less than a month after his appearance before the House Subcommittee on Legislative Oversight and just four days after going on the air at KDAY, the besieged Freed again became front-page news in New York when he and seven others, including Mel Leeds, were arrested there on commercial bribery charges. The arrest came as no surprise to Freed, who was aware of the earlier New

York grand jury information charging him with accepting $10,000 in payola from Roulette Records in 1958. On May 5, Freed and Jack Hooke had met in New York with attorney Michael Di Renzo, who would defend the two against Assistant District Attorney Joseph Stone's payola charges. The following day the New York grand jury directed District Attorney Frank Hogan to file an information charging Freed and WMGM disc jockey Peter Tripp with commercial bribery charges.

On May 10, Hogan's office filed an information charging Tripp with thirty-nine violations of the state's commercial bribery statute, charging that the disc jockey, "as an agent and employee" of WMGM, "and without the knowledge and consent of his employer, requested and accepted gifts and gratuities from various phonograph record manufacturers and distributors, pursuant to agreements and understandings that the defendant would act in a particular manner in relation to his employer's business." On the same day, bench warrants for the arrests of Freed and Tripp were issued. After that, said Irving Phillips, Freed and Leeds "at their own expense" flew back to New York to surrender to the authorities.

Arrested and booked with Freed, Leeds, and Tripp at the Fifth Precinct Elizabeth Street station house in Manhattan were WWRL's Tommy ("Dr. Jive") Smalls; WLIB's Hal Jackson and Jack Walker; and record librarians Joe Saccone of WMGM and Ron Granger of WINS. With twenty-six counts of commercial bribery charged against him, Freed was the "big fish" in Hogan's payola catch. He was accused of accepting $30,650 in commercial bribery in 1958 and 1959, with the largest payoff being the $10,000 Freed received from Roulette Records in 1958. Freed's old radio rival Peter Tripp, "the curly-headed kid in the third row," was charged with twenty-nine counts of commercial bribery totaling over $36,000 received from eight companies. The largest payment was $10,400 from Alpha Distributors. Mel Leeds was charged with forty counts alleging he received almost $10,000 from five companies, the largest payment being $3,600 from London Records.

The other charges were as follows: Smalls, forty-eight counts totaling over $13,000 from eighteen companies, the largest contributor being Cosnat Distributing: Jackson, thirty-nine counts totaling almost $10,000, the largest payment being $3,800 from Alpha Distributors; Walker, thirty-three counts totaling over $7,000 from ten companies, the largest payment being $2,250 from Alpha; Saccone, seven counts totaling $2,000 in regular monthly payments from Alpha; and Granger, twenty-six counts totaling $7,550 from nine companies, the largest payment being $2,300 from Superior Record Sales.

In all, the grand jury informations handed up to the district attorney named twenty-three record companies and distributors with making illegal commercial bribery payments to the eight defendants. Hogan described the alleged commercial bribery as "graft payments," adding that two record companies, Coed and Laurie, had agreed to give Peter Tripp a 2.5-cent royalty on every copy sold of the Crests' "Sixteen Candles" and Dion and the Belmonts' "I Wonder Why." Hogan also charged that in return for payola, Freed often played a record "eight or nine times" in one night.

Tripp, whom WMGM had placed on "probation, pending developments" in the payola scandal after he had "voluntarily" given the station a sworn affidavit stating he had never taken payola, was immediately suspended by WMGM. Smalls was fired "at once" from his WWRL afternoon radio program. WWRL said that in the previous November, Smalls had submitted to them an affidavit stating he had not taken money from record companies. Jackson did his usual morning shift on WLIB that may 19, and Walker was scheduled to do his four o'clock program on WLIB that afternoon, when the two were arrested. The radio station had no immediate comment.

The arrests marked the culmination of Hogan and Stone's extensive payola investigation. The district attorney's office charged that the alleged illegalities had been going on for at least ten years, lending credence to the FCC charge that both WINS and WMGM had known of such practices as early as 1954. Hogan said it had "evidently been the judgement of some manufacturers and producers that the economic life of their companies depends on the amount of air time given to their records, and sales are based on popularity—however synthetic—which is created by disc jockeys repeatedly exposing their records." The initiative in those "corrupt arrangements," said Hogan, came "indiscriminately from either side."

When Freed arrived for his May 19 arraignment before Justice Joseph A. Martinez, he made a valiant effort to mask the internal anguish he felt. Barely recognizable as the national celebrity who not long ago arrogantly strutted onstage in his garish plaid sport jacket, Freed, now clad in a conservative suit and tie, idly laughed and joked with bystanders.

Stone told Justice Martinez of the Court of Special Sessions that the defendants "had exploited their responsibility to their employers and to the listening public, in order to line their pockets."

After being informed of their rights, Freed and Leeds pleaded not guilty to the charges and a trial date of September 19, 1960, was set for the Court of Special Sessions. Freed and Leeds then returned to California to resume their careers at KDAY. Irving Phillips called his new employees "fall guys" in Hogan's investigation. "We are 100 percent behind both men," said the station manager. "If Freed is free to do so, he'll definitely start his two-year contract with us this week."

On June 14, Peter Tripp pleaded not guilty to Hogan's payola charges. As in Freed's case, a trial date of September 19 was set in the Court of Special Sessions.

Although Morris Levy, along with other record manufacturers and distributors, escaped criminal prosecution in New York by allegedly giving testimony regarding payments made to various disc jockeys and other radio station personnel to the grand jury investigating payola, as president of Roulette he and his record company still faced potential punitive action from the Federal Trade Commission. Reacting to the threat of FTC action, several days after Freed's arrest Levy, who described Stone's indictment of Freed as "bullshit charges" brought against the deejay because he "stuck himself out front," wrote an "open letter" to radio disc jockeys and program directors regarding what Levy euphemistically described as "some historical and traditional concepts" of the music business. Levy wrote that during the payola investigations some "unjust accusations" had been made and he "wanted the air cleared" in relation to the charges. The Roulette president requested that disc jockeys do so by signing affidavits saying they never accepted any "consideration" for playing Roulette records.

Concomitant with his moderate West Coast radio success, Freed kept a watchful eye on the San Francisco area where Peter Tripp was living until the start of his payola trial back east. Since Freed and Tripp had both been charged with breaking New York's commercial bribery statute, Tripp's case would demonstrate what Freed could expect from his own prosecution. On September 13, 1960, Tripp's attorneys moved to have the charges against him dismissed in the New York Court of Special Sessions on the grounds that Tripp was not an employee of WMGM, but rather an independent contractor who did work for others, as well as for the radio station. Tripp's attorneys contended that as an independent contractor, the disc jockey should not be subject to commercial bribery charges, as WMGM "had consented to his conduct," and that the agreement "did not effect the 'business' of the station as required by the statute." Tripp's trial was adjourned until November 16, 1960. But on November 4 the motion to have the charges against Tripp dismissed was denied by Judge Thomas Dickens and a new trial date was set for January 23, 1961. Meanwhile, Freed's attorneys, wishing to see the outcome of Tripp's case, successfully employed delaying tactics in the trial of their own client. Freed's new trial date was March 13, 1961.

Also on September 13, as a result of the House Subcommittee on Legislative Oversight hearings and the subsequent recommendation of the FCC, Congress amended the Communications Act of 1934, making payola a federal offense punishable by a $10,000 fine and/or a year in jail.

In October 1960 twenty contestants, including Charles Van Doren and Vivienne Nearing, who had appeared on "Twenty-One" or "Tic Tac Dough," were indicted by a New York grand jury for second-degree perjury for lying to the 1958 grand jury investigating television quiz show rigging.

On January 16, 1961, Peter Tripp served District Attorney Hogan's office with an order to show cause why his case should not be transferred from the Court of Special Sessions (where it would be heard by three Special Sessions justices) to General Session, where it would be tried in front of a jury. Since New York State law specified that those defendants charged with misdemeanors (which includes commercial bribery) were entitled only to a trial heard and decided by three judges in the Court of Special Sessions, Judge Joseph A. Sarafite of the Court of General Sessions denied Tripp's motion on March 3, 1961, after finding "no evidence that the defendant can't receive a fair trial in Special Sessions."

Tripp's commercial bribery trial finally got under way on April 26, 1961. Tripp, then residing in San Anselmo, just north of San Francisco in Marin County, flew east to take the witness stand in his own defense. Tripp's attorney, Benjamin Shedler, with his back pushed to the wall by the overwhelming amount of evidence gathered by prosecutor Joseph Stone, pulled out all the stops for his client. Despite the fact that the courts had refused to dismiss Tripp's payola charges because of his contention that the deejay was an independent contractor entitled to make outside deals as he saw fit, Shedler introduced that argument at the trial. Tripp swore on the stand that he had never taken a dime in payola. Using the defense Freed had established shortly after he was fired during the payola scandal, Tripp said the money he received from various record companies was earned solely for "advice" he had given to them. While Tripp asserted that he advised various record companies as to what types of records to make and what tempos and instrumentation to use, as well as advising them to look for "new sounds," prosecution witnesses testified that they paid money to Tripp to play their records, which Tripp did repeatedly.

The trial was a stormy affair, marred by numerous outbursts. At one point Assistant District Attorney Jerome Kidder (who temporarily stepped in for the ailing Stone) asked Tripp why in August 1958 the disc jockey had asked George Goldner for $4,000. With a straight face, Tripp replied that he had some "extra expenses" and because he had found Goldner to be "nice," he thought the record manufacturer could afford to "help" the deejay with a loan.

Kidder called Tripp an "outright liar" and was admonished by Judge Edward F. Breslin to "refrain from making these observations" about the defendant.

As a last resort Tripp's attorney told the court that "everybody and his uncle knew that gifts were being sent to disc jockeys," but "nobody ever said a thing to stop it" while the practice was going on.

Tripp's trial concluded on May 3, and on May 15 the three Special Sessions justices rendered their decision. Judge Breslin said the three had "given the law and the evidence considerable thought" and were unanimous in holding that Tripp was guilty of thirty-five counts of commercial bribery. The convicted deejay was released in the custody of Shedler and returned to California to await sentencing (subsequently postponed from June until September). Tripp's attorney said his client was "penniless," and so the lawyer did not know if an appeal would be made.

Tripp's trial had been the first in the culmination of Stone's mass payola arrest the previous May. Freed and his attorneys, who had stalled for time until the outcome of Tripp's trial was known, could not have been pleased with the result. Grudgingly aware that he was next in line to visit Hogan's hallowed halls of justice, Freed now knew exactly what lay in store for him if he chose not to plea-bargain away some of the twenty-six commercial bribery charges against him.

The latest series of postponements in Freed's own trial had pushed his court date back to May 24, but when Stone collapsed in the courtroom, the event was postponed once more. After recovering from his brief illness, Stone warned that if Freed's trial did not begin by June, it would have to be held over until September 1961, because Special Sessions justices did not hear cases in July and August. A new trial date of June 15 was set, but when Peter Tripp's sentencing was delayed until September, Freed's trial was put off again, this time until the fall. Meanwhile, Stone insisted that Freed's trial "would definitely be on, sooner or later."

When Freed joined KDAY in 1960, the do-wop revival was gathering momentum. That summer, two enterprising New York record promoters urged Hiram Johnson owner of Johnson Records (inactive at the time), to rerelease a ballad called "Baby, Oh Baby," which had been recorded and released by the Shells, a Brooklyn-based R&B quartet, in 1957, but had then flopped in the commercial marketplace. As a favor to Johnson and to his bandleader-composer brother, Buddy Johnson, a friend of Freed's since the deejay's Ohio days, "Baby Oh Baby" was "broken" (introduced on the radio) by Freed in Los Angeles. Although the song had been recorded three years earlier in New York, *Cashbox* unwittingly referred to "Baby, Oh Baby" as a California sound. Freed got behind the song with heavy airplay, and "Baby, Oh Baby" spread across the country. By Christmas 1960, it was a national hit.

"Sure enough," said Jack Hooke, Freed, utilizing his old standbys, telephone book and cowbell, "started to make noise" on KDAY. Freed "was really plugging along," said his daughter Alana. "He had a great show!"

The revitalized Freed was also instrumental in breaking Kathy Young and the Innocents' "A Thousand Stars" in the fall of 1960, Rosie Hamlin's "Lonely Blue Nights" early in 1961, and the New Yorkers' (led by the Five Satins' former lead singer, Fred Paris) "Miss Fine" in the spring of 1961. Sparked by hefty doses of airplay by Freed, all three songs became national hits. *Billboard* noted a "coincidental upsurge of disk breakout activity" on the West Coast and credited Freed and Peter Tripp (who was then broadcasting on KYA Radio in San Francisco) with "injecting the kind of fast-talking excitement [that sells records] into the disk scene." The music trade newspaper noted that "today, many eyes look west to find out the initial score on a new record," adding that Cleveland, Philadelphia, and Detroit were "no longer the prime centers" of record breakout activity.

Early in 1961, things were going well enough for Freed to leave the Mikado Apartments and purchase a modest house at 309 Holly Circle in fashionable Palm Springs, about a hundred miles east of Los Angeles. Freed was also anxious to resume the most lucrative facet of the deejay's career—his stage show productions. Amid rumors that there was a "chance" Freed would take a rock & roll show starring Jerry Lee Lewis to England and Europe later that summer, Freed called Jack Hooke in New York and said to his former associate, "Everything's going great!" He also told Hooke to "start putting a [stage] show together."

Hooke knew from Mel Leed's tenure at WINS that the station manager was "a sharp operator" and that Freed would have to pay KDAY in order to plug his stage shows on the air. Hooke said that he intended to sit down with Leeds "and see what he wanted" in the way of advertising money. After lining up some talent for the projected show, Hooke caught a plane for California. But when Hooke met with Leeds and brought up the subject of Freed's intended show, Leeds professed to know nothing about it. The station manager explained to Hooke that Freed could not promote any shows on his own because KDAY worked with a local promoter who, for $30,000 a year, was "the only one who can promote rock & roll shows on this station. You can't promote the show."

Hooke said that he and Freed, obligated to the acts already signed, "were determined" to do the stage show. They booked the Hollywood Bowl for June 25 and bought advertising time for the show on other radio stations.

Freed's Hollywood Bowl show headlined the Shirelles, at the time one of the hottest rock & roll acts in the business. In addition to introducing "A Thing of the Past," which would turn out to be the group's fourth consecutive chart smash, the Shirelles also performed their previous three hits—"Will You Still Love Me Tomorrow," "Dedicated to the One I Love," and "Mama Said." Other hot artists with hit records included sixteen-year-old Brenda Lee, with her two-sided smash "Dum Dum" and "Eventually"; the Fleetwoods, from Olympia, Washington with "Tragedy"; Gene McDaniels, with "A Tear," his follow-up to "A Hundred Pounds of Clay"; the Ventures, with "(Theme from) Silver City"; and Clarence Henry, with "You Always Hurt the One You Love." Also a part of Freed's star-studded lineup was eighteen-year-old Bobby Vee, whose latest release, "Take Good Care of My Baby," would soon be the number-one song in

America; fifteen-year-old Kathy Young from nearby Long Beach, California, and the Innocents, who, after a national hit with "Happy Birthday Blues," produced a local favorite in "Our Parents Talked It Over"; and Etta James with her new release, "Don't Cry, Baby." Jerry Lee Lewis, attempting to pump new life into his sagging rock & roll career, drove cross-country to appear with Freed and promote his latest release, "It Wouldn't Happen with Me," on which "the killer" compared his own fidelity to the shortcomings of Elvis, Jackie Wilson, Ricky Nelson, and Fabian.

Not only was the hit-laden show a sellout, but it also kicked off a cross-country rock & roll tour joined by most of the artists on Freed's bill. Flushed with success, Freed naturally began to think of promoting additional stage shows, but when he again approached Leeds, the station manager "came down hard" and protested that KDAY's exclusive promoter had made a "big stink" over Freed's Hollywood Bowl production. Leeds told Freed that even though the deejay had promoted that one show, he was forbidden to promote any others.

"I'm on the air and I can't promote my own shows?" Freed protested. He again threatened to buy advertising time elsewhere and put on another show, but Leeds remained adamant. "I can't let you do it," he told Freed.

Freed fussed, fumed, and threatened to quit the station. At that point KDAY—like WAKR, WINS, WABC, and WNEW-TV—had heard enough from Freed. Several days after his Hollywood Bowl concert, Freed was fired by KDAY.

There may have been other factors involved in KDAY's decision to fire Freed. Bob Dye said that for all Freed's newfound success, the deejay was never accepted in California as he was in New York. It was Dye's contention that the black population in the Los Angeles area was "an entirely different story than back east and down south." KDAY's chief engineer said that while Freed played music that "fit some of the market back there" in New York, it "didn't fit" in California. Art Laboe, a KDAY disc jockey during Freed's tenure at the station, agreed with Dye that while Freed "loved being on the air again," the disc jockey was "frustrated at not being able to make the impact he had made in New York. The teenagers in California liked Freed, said Laboe, "but not the way they'd loved him in New York."

Many of Freed's first listeners in New York remembered life before rock & roll. To them, Freed symbolized the exhilaration and the pleasure experienced by the discovery of the music. This peculiar identification had helped Freed become as much—if not more—of a star as many of the artists he championed. During those glory days Freed bristled when he heard himself referred to as merely a disc jockey. He insisted he was a personality, a celebrity. But when Freed sought refuge on the West Coast in 1960 from the payola scandal, only a small portion of his new audience had even a hazy awareness of the deejay's glorious past. To the majority of Freed's new listeners, he was just another rock & roll disc jockey. They identified with the music he played to the extent that only days after Freed was fired, *Billboard*, in a story about the resurgent popularity of rhythm and blues disc jockeys, said that Freed, who "helped break many hits of new labels [and] . . . just left" his KDAY spot, "had a very high rating after only a few months there." But Freed's new audience evidently did not identify with the transplanted forty-year-old New Yorker, and his reduction from a celebrity to an ordinary disc jockey proved unrewarding to the man who, as rock & roll's prime mover, had once basked in the adulation of his New York audience. Despite his newfound radio success, Freed yearned in vain for the lionization of his New York heyday. This frustration unleashed Freed's longtime nemesis, alcohol, which had been held in check from the time he took the KDAY job. By the time Freed was fired, Bob Dye said the deejay's drinking was "quite noticeably" affecting his on-the-air manner.

Freed's ostensibly interminable payola case and his still-mounting legal fees, coupled with the loss of his KDAY program, caused him additional anguish. Drinking more heavily than he had in the past and haunted by the realization that not even a successful radio program could bring back his glory days, Freed and his wife Inga retreated to the sanctuary of 309 Holly Circle in Palm Springs.

CHAPTER 14

Payola's First Fatality

"He was a bigger man than those who turned their backs on him."

NOT long after Alan Freed lost his KDAY Radio program, word began to circulate in the broadcasting business that he was about to return to New York with a nightly seven-to-ten program on WADO Radio. "Persistent rumors" to that effect became such an embarrassment to WADO that station manager Sydney Kavaleer "officially scotched" them in August 1961 by stating in writing that WADO contemplated "no changes in our programming or personnel, which would include Alan Freed."

Off the air and drinking harder than ever, Freed was offered a job as an A&R man at Time Records by a sympathetic Bobby Shad, a blues and jazz producer who had been in the recording business since the 1940s and who had known Freed since the early 1950s in Cleveland. Freed's degradation by "pushing records" was what radio disc jockey Norm N. Nite described as "a difficult pill to swallow for a man who was on top of the record business."

In New York, WINS owner J. Elroy McCaw's worst fears were being realized. The FCC charged that WINS management had been aware of payola dealings at the station (Freed, Mel Leeds, and Ron Granger were specifically named) as early as 1954, yet had done nothing to stop the practices. The FCC claimed that besides tolerating payola practices, WINS management indulged in other dubious activities, including having a record distributor pay directly to the station portions of line charges and engineers' salaries for Freed's "Rock 'n' Roll Party" and billing Freed for the deejay's remote broadcasts, with the bills sometimes exceeding his station salary.

The FCC charged the Gotham Broadcasting Corporation (owner of WINS) with trying to "induce" Freed to get certain record manufacturers and distributors to pay the station directly, in return for Freed playing their records on his radio program. The FCC also criticized the arrangement whereby Freed paid WINS 10 percent of the profits from his stage shows in return for Freed being permitted to plug the shows on the air "without sponsorship identification."

On July 7, 1961, McCaw received notice from the FCC that, in light of the payola allegations, a hearing would be necessary to determine if renewing the broadcasting license of Gotham Broadcasting "would serve a public purpose." At the time, McCaw was negotiating the sale of WINS to the Storer Broadcasting Company, but with the FCC's refusal to grant a license renewal pending a hearing, the deal fell through. The owner of WINS was in danger of losing not only everything he had put into the station in the past seven years, but also the sizable profit guaranteed by WINS's sale.

On June 20, 1961, the Federal Trade Commission dismissed payola charges against the distributors of Columbia, Capitol, and Dot records, contending that the recent amendment to the Communications Act of 1934—which made it a federal offense to "bestow gifts on radio and television disc jockeys for broadcasting records"—assured the "protection of the public interest."

While most of the 106 payola complaints originally filed by the FTC had resulted in the issuance of cease-and-desist orders to the alleged offenders, a spokesman for the FTC said that five other payola cases still awaiting action "would presumably be dismissed."

Indeed, on August 31 the FTC dismissed payola charges against Bigtop Records, Bigtop Record Distributors, Decca Distributing, Mutual Distributors, and Morris Levy's Roulette Records, thereby avoiding "unnecessary and costly litigation."

Ultimately it was a handful of celebrity disc jockeys, pop music's link to the fickle public, that bore the brunt of payola's "justice"—firings, resignations, blackballings, and criminal prosecutions. Once the sensational headlines subsided, the public quickly lost interest in the payola proceedings. The House of Representatives acted in similar fashion, reaping publicity from the high-profile Washington hearings (the entire Harris subcommittee was reelected to Congress in November 1960) while being careful not to focus attention on individuals who wielded significant influence or political clout.

At Peter Tripp's payola conviction sentencing on October 16, 1961, Assistant District Attorney Joseph Stone recommended a jail sentence for the disc jockey, who had "boldly and flagrantly violated the law." Stone reasoned that if Tripp was given a "slap on the wrist," the court would give a "license to others to engage in this creeping corruption." The three Special Sessions justices showed compassion, however, and sentenced Tripp to a $500 fine and thirty-five concurrent workhouse terms of six months, which was suspended on condition of good behavior. Meanwhile, Freed's September trial date was postponed until October 23.

On October 18, 1961, the FCC decided that J. Elroy McCaw had been punished sufficiently for WINS's payola transgressions and voted 4–2 to renew the license of Gotham Broadcasting. Commission chairman Newton Minnow (who, in his "vast wasteland" speech five months earlier, had criticized television for its display of violence and mediocrity), casting one of the dissenting votes, said, "there remain substantial questions whether, for purposes of its own, it [WINS] willfully or recklessly tolerated the taking of 'payola' by several of its key employees." The first move made by the station owner was to have WINS herald a return to "pretty music." The new format was kicked off with sixty-six continuous hours of Frank Sinatra songs ("Murray the K" Kaufman, WINS's star rock & roll deejay, faithfully began each evening's show with a Sinatra number). Next, McCaw commenced negotiations with the Westinghouse Broadcasting Company for the sale of WINS. In April 1962 the deal was completed. The station, purchased by McCaw in 1953 for $450,000, was sold to Westinghouse for $10 million, the second largest sum paid for a single radio station to that point. As part of the deal, McCaw exercised his option to purchase the property at 7 Central Park West, where WINS was located. After paying about $450,000 for the property, McCaw turned around and sold it to a skyscraper developer for nearly as much money as he received for WINS.

While J. Elroy McCaw negotiated the sale of the New York radio station that was most responsible for the early promotion of rock & roll, one of the music's long-standing opponents continued his rock & roll diatribe. Stanley Adams, who spearheaded the prolonged Songwriters of America antitrust suit against BMI, was in January 1962 elected to his fifth term as ASCAP president. On reelection, Adams said he saw hopeful signs in the "sad and noisy regression that had beset music for over ten years." Although Adams conceded that some of the guild's writers now wrote and published rock & roll (which Adams derogatorily referred to as "a vast sprouting of weeds [that] had choked out the roses"), most ASCAP members were "relieved" at the decline of rock & roll "and its idiot derivations like twist music." As Adams spoke, Joey Dee and the Starliters' "Peppermint Twist," courtesy of Morris Levy's Roulette Records, was the hottest record in America, rapidly approaching number one on the sales charts.

Once Freed was forced off the air in New York by the payola scandal, Jack Hooke also fell upon hard times. While Hooke still had his interest in Figure Music, "without Alan's power I was struggling." Sorely in need of cash, Freed had already sold his share of Figure Music to Morris Levy. Although Levy proved to be "very helpful" to Hooke in administering the music publishing company and despite Figure's publishing of "three or four pretty good songs," Hooke said he "was starving."

Times were changing in the music business. Most record companies ran their own publishing companies, and many artists were beginning to retain publishing rights to their own songs. "The days of the independent music publisher were over," said Hooke. In need of cash, he eventually "grabbed whatever few thousand dollars" he could by selling his share of Figure Music to Morris Levy.

Late in 1961, Jack Hooke crossed paths with Dick Clark at New York's Peppermint Lounge, then the most hip nightspot in Manhattan, if not the entire country. Remembering the negative remarks Freed allegedly made in the newspapers about Clark during the payola scandal (Freed later claimed he had been misquoted), Clark "turned his head and he walked away" when he saw Hooke. Considering the circumstances, Hooke said he "couldn't blame" Clark for shunning the person who had been closest to Freed businesswise. But, Hooke said, sometime in 1962 he received a telephone call from Rosalyn Ross, a former talent booking agent acquaintance who was then working for Clark. Clark, in the process of organizing his "Caravan of Stars" rock & roll show tours, had hired Ross to coordinate the proceedings. Recalling her previous dealings with Hooke, as well as his experience in organizing and supervising Freed's live shows, Ross sought Hooke's assistance. Thus, despite the lingering antagonism between Clark and Hooke, Freed's former right-hand man came full circle and went to work for the Dick Clark organization.

As was to be expected, there were hard feelings in what was left of the Freed camp when Hooke joined Clark. Betty Lou Greene lumped Hooke with those whom she called her ex-husband's "fair-weather friends," who disappeared as soon as Freed's career fell apart. Alana Freed described Hooke as the type of person who "was going to go where the action was," adding that while Hooke was always near her father "in the good old days," as the payola allegations mounted, "he was not around nearly as much."

Morris Levy's acquisition of Jack Hooke's share of Figure Music was the music entrepreneur's latest move in the relentless consolidation of power in his entertainment empire. The previous September, Planetary Music (owned by Levy, Phil Kahl, and Morris Gurlek) purchased Joe Kolsky's 429,000 shares in Roulette Records, giving the music publishing company control of 80 percent of Roulette's stock. In January 1962, Kahl sold his interest in Roulette and three music publishing firms to Levy, giving the Roulette president complete control of Planetary Music and Roulette Records.

On January 17, 1962 Charles Van Doren and the nine remaining quiz show defendants pleaded guilty to charges of lying to the New York grand jury investigating the quiz show–rigging allegations. Justice Edward Breslin then suspended their sentences because the "humiliation was evident in their faces." Also that month, Dr. Jive Smalls, arrested with Freed in 1960, pleaded guilty to the payola charges against him. Assistant District Attorney Joseph Stone's commercial bribery conviction record from the mass arrests remained unblemished.

Freed's own payola case continued to drag on when his trial, scheduled for January 9, was postponed until March 5, 1962, at which time, announced the assistant district attorney, he planned to bring in "several out-of-town witnesses" to testify for the prosecution.

On February 8, Stone announced that all the commercial bribery charges against ex-WLIB disc jockey Hal Jackson would be dropped because there was a question as to whether his office would be able to prove "beyond a reasonable doubt" that Jackson was actually an employee of that station at the time of the alleged bribery incidents. In utilizing Peter Tripp's ill-fated "independent contractor" defense,

Jackson came up a winner, dropping Stone's payola conviction record in the arrests to two out of three.

Also in February, while Alan Freed remained off the air in California, back east George Goldner released a series of "oldies" albums with the deejay's name on them, consisting of rock & roll hits from the 1950s. The first album, "Alan Freed's Memory Lane" (End LP 314), on which Freed spoke on the record between the songs, much like he did on the radio, edged onto *Billboard*'s album chart. The second, "Alan Freed's Top 15" (End LP 315), according to *Billboard* was "also showing action."

It is uncertain how much of Goldner's intent in issuing these albums was his effort to capitalize on the do-wop revival (and on Freed's obviously still-commercial name) and how much, if any, was done for Freed's benefit (the Moonglow's "Sincerely," for which Freed received one-half of the writing credit, appeared on the first album). What is certain is that Goldner's oldies project was a musical paean to the glory days of "the boys." Of the twenty-nine songs included on the two records, six had originally been released on Al Silver's labels. Also represented were Jerry Blaine (three), Bobby Robinson (two), Leonard and Phil Chess (two), Hy Weiss, Sol Rabinowitz, and Goldner himself.

On April 7, 1962, ex-WLIB disc jockey Jack Walker pleaded guilty to three of the original thirty-three commercial bribery counts lodged against him, as Stone's payola conviction record rose to three out of four. Tommy Smalls, who had pleaded guilty to commercial bribery charges in January, was sentenced to six months in jail or a $250 fine, and was given one week to pay it.

On April 21, Westinghouse, which, it was reported, "hoped for a return to rock and roll," consummated its purchase of WINS radio from J. Elroy McCaw's Gotham Broadcasting.

As Freed's payola trial continued to be postponed (to May 1 and then to September 10, 1962), the deejay, largely through the efforts of Morris Levy, was given another crack at a radio program.

In the summer of 1962, Miami, Florida's two major top-forty rock & roll radio stations, WQAM and WFUN, were in the midst of a "battle royal" for ratings in the city then proudly billed as "the Sun and Fun Capital of the World." After being locked in this running battle for the Miami area's listeners all summer, WQAM announced it had signed Alan Freed to be one of the station's disc jockeys. Jack Hooke said it was Levy who "sold" WQAM on Freed.

Freed's WQAM contract, which began on September 1, 1962, called for twenty-six hours of airtime a week for the deejay. He was heard in the station's seven-to-ten slot six nights a week, Saturday mornings from nine until noon, and Sunday evenings from seven until midnight. After one week on the air it was reported that WQAM's new personality was in a "nip and tuck" ratings battle with WFUN.

In October, Freed called Hooke, who was in New York, and asked his old partner to come to Florida to help the deejay put on a rock & roll stage show. Miami's Dinner Key Auditorium was booked for a Saturday evening show on November 24. WQAM, cool to the idea of Freed's promotion, which was independent from the radio station, could do nothing to prevent it. But the Dinner Key show "didn't do well at all," remembered Hooke. Even Freed admitted that the Miami production "was a bomb."

Freed faced other problems at WQAM. As was the case with many radio stations in the wake of the payola scandal, WQAM was "against the development of a so-called personality cult on the rock level." Freed—who, Jack Hooke said, could be "a very rough guy to deal with"—arrived at WQAM with a reputation for managerial confrontation and wasted little time in antagonizing the station brass by promoting a rock & roll stage show against WQAM's wishes. By this time, Freed's drinking problem was apparently out of hand. Hooke, who described Freed as then a "big drinker," said that after traveling to Miami to assist Freed with the live show and hearing the deejay on the air, he recognized immediately that Freed "didn't sound the same" as he once had. Also, it became obvious to WQAM management that Freed was not making inroads into rival WFUN's audience. Hooke said that while Freed's sizable ego was as forceful as ever, WQAM "had their ratings," which indicated Freed's program "wasn't making it" against WFUN. Apparently, Freed's Dinner Key Auditorium show was the "last straw" to WQAM. On Monday, November 26, Freed was fired by the station.

Despite Morris Levy's bid to revitalize Freed's radio career, the deejay was once again off the air, this time in less than three months. Alana Freed said there was a time when she questioned whether Levy was "a true friend or not" to her father, but as both Freed's career and his personal life continued to spiral downward, it became obvious to her that unlike most of Freed's former friends and associates, who wanted nothing to do with her father, "Morris was there."

Chubby Checker had recently stood the entertainment world on its ear with his worldwide smash hit of a year-old Hank Ballard song called "The Twist." Soon, New York's society crowd twisted to a Neanderthal-like lounge combo called the Starliters, led by a young New Jersey singer named Joey Dee. That rudimentary rock & roll group almost single-handedly transformed a dingy West Forty-fifth Street storefront nightspot called the Peppermint Lounge into the twist mecca of the world. Joey Dee and the Starliters were signed by Roulette Records and subsequently had a number-one national hit record early in 1962 with "The Peppermint Twist—Part 1."

In November 1962, just after Freed lost his WQAM program, Morris Levy brought the floundering deejay from Miami, back to the city of his greatest triumphs, as emcee of a "Twist Revue" featured at Levy's Camelot Club on Manhattan's East Side. Since everyone else in the music business was twisting, why not Alan Freed? But, except for Freed's oft-postponed courtroom appearance to answer Stone's commercial bribery charges, Freed was still persona non grata in the Big Apple. Just days after Freed opened there, the Camelot Club was raided and closed down by the New York Police Department for allegedly serving alcohol to minors.

Then, after two years of legal maneuvering and postponments, Freed's commercial bribery trial seemed at hand. On December 1, before Freed could leave New York for his Palm Springs hideaway, Joseph Stone announced that the unemployed deejay's trial would begin on December 10.

While Freed's legal defense team was headed by attorney Michael Di Renzo, Warren Troob's recommendation to his friend Freed was "no deals, no bargaining." Troob said he wanted the case to go to trial, but by then Freed was "weary of the whole thing" and wanted to put the payola case behind him once and for all, no matter what the outcome. Despite Troob's recommendation that Freed not pleabargain, the deejay agreed to do just that.

At a pretrial meeting with the assistant district attorney, at which time Freed acted in what the prosecutor described as a "subdued manner" while giving a "gentlemanly impression," it was agreed that the deejay would plead guilty to just two of the twenty-nine commercial bribery counts lodged against him. Many years later Stone explained that Freed was prosecuted on only those two counts because by then Stone felt that Freed "had had enough."

On Monday, December 10, Freed pleaded guilty in the Special Sessions part of the New York Criminal Court of accepting on September 29, 1958, "without the knowledge or consent" of his employers, $2,000 from Cosnat Distributing Corporation and of having "sought and accepted" on February 16, 1959, a "gift" of $700 from Superior Record Sales. On receiving Freed's guilty plea, Justice John Murtagh sentenced him to a $500 fine, plus a six-month suspended jail term. Freed's fine, which he was given thirty days to pay, was reduced to $300 after his attorneys pleaded "lack of funds" for him. In the wake of his conviction, Freed noted that payola was then "just as prevalent in the music business" as it had been before the scandal.

Twenty years after the payola scandal, Stone called Freed's payola complicity "a waste." Stone, who had in the interim become a Criminal Court judge, said that while his 1959–1960 payola investigation uncovered some "very hungry" disc jockeys who were "putting the bite" on various record companies for money to play records, he did not place Freed in that category. It was the ex-prosecutor's opinion that Freed "drifted" into trouble, not only because he was "disorganized" and unaware of many things going on around him, but because the deejay was not very interested in discovering those things. Stone said that while Freed "did as he damned well pleased and played the music that he liked" during his glory years, he was also influenced by the alleged commercial bribery money, which was needed "to support three households and some bad [drinking] habits."

Stone said he "always suspected that the record companies, recognizing that he [Freed] was really coming across [by playing their records], made payments to him for insurance." He saw Freed as a "free and easy guy . . . [who] didn't ask too many questions when he was given money," but, rather simply, "fell in line with the practices within the record business at the time."

On March 8, 1963, awash in a sea of alcohol and staggering legal fees and facing potential federal tax-evasion charges, Freed paid his $300 fine, officially concluding the deejay's commercial bribery prosecution. Freed was the fourth and last of the eight defendants arrested on commercial bribery charges in May 1960 to be convicted. All of the charges against Mel Leeds, Joseph Saccone, and Ron Granger were eventually dropped.

After paying the fine, Freed remarked that while no one ever paid him to play a specific record, he regretted the way he had conducted some of his business activities. "I would never to it again," explained the deejay. "I've made too much money the other way. There's no need to get involved [with payola]."

Off the radio since his WQAM firing and without any type of job since his short-lived Camelot Club "Twist Revue" appearance, Freed's will to hold a job seemed to vanish altogether. Alana said that her father, whose life had consisted of "music, the kids, and being somebody," at that point gave up. Freed publicly lamented that he no longer heard from the fans who had remained loyal to him during the payola investigation, because "they're grown up, for the most part." When he returned to Palm Springs, Freed's daughter said, he "acted almost like someone who'd retired" and began the life of a near recluse.

Bob Rolontz, who knew Freed since the deejay's early days in New York, observed that Freed, "often a moody and injudicious man off radio, . . . became more so as his fortunes plunged downward."

In 1962, Freed's four children lived with their respective mothers—Alana and Lance with Betty Lou and Tom Greene in North Carolina and Siegelinde and Alan, Jr., with Jackie in Connecticut. Lance was about to enter his junior year of high school at the end of the summer of 1962 when he decided he had had enough of life with Tom Greene, with whom, Lance said, he did not see eye-to-eye on anything. Freed's older son packed his bags and headed for Palm Springs to live with his father. Alana, who shared a close sibling relationship with Lance, joined him and her father in California, where in 1963 she took a job as a cashier in a movie theater.

Alana said that while her father was not working he became involved doing things "he would have loved to have been doing for years, but just didn't have the time" to do. Freed taught himself to cook and, boasted his daughter, "he cooked every meal we ate. You name it, he could fix it!"

Alana said Freed established a routine whereby she and Lance would watch the nightly seven o'clock news on television, after which Freed would quiz them on the broadcast "to see if we'd been paying attention." She said much of the time spent with her father involved "the two of us getting to know each other," because of the fact that when she and Lance were little children, Freed had been "too busy to get to know them."

It was Freed's wish that Alana became an actress, and he did his best to push her in that direction. While Alana had no idea how her father planned to pay for it, she said Freed wanted her to attend the nearby Pasadena Playhouse school of acting. And just as Freed twenty years earlier had insisted on honing his own broadcasting manner by reading newspapers out loud to Betty Lou Greene, he now insisted that his daughter read out loud to him. Freed's house contained a fireplace with a raised hearth. He would give Alana books, magazines, and scripts and, said Alana, "I had to get up there and read the parts," while Freed corrected her and offered suggestions to improve her speaking. Freed's daughter said she loved acting "and really thought about going into it."

Alana conceded that other than cooking, quizzing her about the news, and coaching her in acting, her father "didn't do much of anything" but drink, and that Inga "probably kept up with him" in his drinking. She said that her father would fix himself a drink when he got up in the morning, he would drink all day, and "he would go to bed with one."

Warren Troob, his close personal friend as well as his lawyer, explained that Freed would periodically swear off alcohol. He recalled a time that Freed capped off a particularly heavy drinking binge by downing a tumbler of straight Scotch for breakfast and then vowed that he would no longer take a drink before sundown. Not long after that, when Freed and Troob were offered a drink at some function, Freed looked out the window and, observing the sunlight, refused the drink. But, by 1963, Freed's periods of alcoholic abstinence grew fewer in number and shorter in duration. If he had not already lost his battle with alcohol, Freed was close to doing so.

Apparently, Inga gave Freed solace as a drinking partner. Alana said that rather than work, Inga "sat on her tail most of the time and drank." Freed's daughter estimated that her father's drinking doubled during his last year in Palm Springs, in part because support from Inga "was not there" and Freed "didn't have a whole lot to fall back on."

Randy Wood visited the Freeds almost every weekend, but Alana recalled that other than Wood and his family, "we didn't see very many people." One person they did seen was Troob, who came to Palm Springs shortly after Alana joined Lance there in 1963. Troob said that while he knew Freed's situation was "unbearably bad," when the attorney arrived in Palm Springs he saw Freed "acting in front of them [Alana and Lance] as though all were right with Alan Freed and with the world."

In November 1963 yet another rumor swirled around the unemployed and alcohol-drenched Freed. According to the story, the deejay's return to New York via WWRL, a black-oriented radio station located on Long Island, was imminent. Despite the fact that WWRL was a small radio station, Alana Freed said, the idea of working for WWRL affected her father as if he had been "offered a job at WABC [then the top-rated rock & roll station in New York]. It just brought him back!"

Freed confided to his daughter that the WWRL offer was "what I've been waiting for" and that he was going to go back to New York and "be on top again!"

Freed became obsessed with the idea of returning to New York radio, and while Alana had no doubts that her father would have "given it his best shot," she did not believe he would have been happy, because "he would never have been where he was before. Too much had happened, too much time had passed."

On February 4, 1964, four long-haired English youths who went by the name of the Beatles made their American debut with an appearance on Ed Sullivan's long-running and highly rated television variety show. That night, the Beatles appeared on more than 70 percent of all the television sets in use in New York City (the highest Nielsen rating up to that time), as well as on television screens of twenty-three million households nationally. Beatlemania had begun. The group's Sullivan show appearance (the first of three consecutive Sunday-night spots) precipitated a sudden and unequivocal change in pop music. And, ironically, what the Beatles—and, to a greater extent, other groups such as the Rolling Stones—did was what Alan Freed had done a decade earlier: they introduced a generation of young white Americans to black rhythm and blues music.

Alana Freed recalled that the Beatles' televised introduction to America occurred shortly before her father "got sick." Her voice trailed off without completing the thought.

On March 15, 1964, Freed was indicted by a federal grand jury on charges of evading income tax from 1957 to 1959. Assistant U.S. Attorney Robert J. McGuire said the tax charges against Freed stemmed "in large part, from the failure to report the payola as income that he received for pushing records." The federal government contended that from 1957 through 1959, Freed "willfully failed to report" taxable income totaling $56,652. McGuire noted that a significant portion of the government's tax-evasion figures came from alleged "fraudulent deductions or business expenses" claimed by Freed, amounts paid to Betty Lou Greene for support of Alana and Lance.

Freed knew there would be no stopping the Internal Revenue Service. He had to look no further than his friend Al Silver for proof. Silver said that in 1962 the IRS "disallowed [as business expenses] all the payola—all cash payments that they found in my checkbooks—if I couldn't account for those payments." Silver said that the IRS subsequently "persuaded" the label owner to sign a waiver of the statute of limitations, enabling them to search Silver's books back to 1953. Silver said that so many of his cash-payment expenses were disallowed that he received a tax bill from the federal government for about $150,000 and they wanted the money, "no ifs, ands, or buts" about it.

The federal government was certain that Freed had some assets that it could lay its hands on. Government agents appeared at Betty Lou Greene's home in North Carolina and searched it for an entire day, because they believed "there was money somewhere." But they were wrong.

While Freed had earned enormous sums of money during his heyday, Jack Hooke said it had meant nothing to the deejay. Freed's former right-hand man recalled a time when he was short on cash and told Freed so. Freed opened up a closet in his Grey Cliffe home to reveal what Hooke said were shoulder-high "piles of hundreds."

"Grab a handful," Freed told him. "Take as much as you want!"

Hooke described Freed as a "chemist"—someone who could "take money and make shit out of it!" Freed "sold this, lost that . . . and wouldn't say no to anybody," all the while taking care of every part of the deejay's own family, "as remote as they were." When the tax-evasion charges were levied against Freed, he did not have a dime to his name.

Alana Freed recalled that during her father's income tax troubles she was questioned and briefed by some attorneys who came to Palm Springs to prepare Freed's case, in the event that the government questioned her concerning her father's activities. As Freed's daughter sat in on some of the legal sessions and listened to tape recordings, she became "very scared because there was talk of him going to jail." "What's going to happen now?" she wondered.

Jack Hooke said Freed spent his last days in Palm Springs "drinking and picking up the phone and calling people" to ask them to send him some money to live on. Hooke said the situation reached the point where Leonard Chess called him to say he did not mind Freed's requests for a few hundred dollars, but that his requests for "four, five thousand dollars" was too much. "I've got to stop somewhere," Chess said to Hooke. "He's been off the air for years and he keeps calling."

By that time, Freed had been almost totally abandoned by all but Randy Wood and Morris Levy (who, according to Hooke, gave Freed money "to the very end"). Alana Freed remembered her father calling Wood to ask for grocery money, and Wood was always there, "100 percent" of the time. But other than Wood and Levy, Freed's daughter could not recall anyone helping her father near the end of his life.

Despite his having no assets, Freed thought he did have something else to lose. Shortly after he was indicted for income tax evasion in March 1964, Freed experienced the added personal agony of seeing Alana pack her bags and leave for Alaska to marry someone who, he believed, did not have his daughter's best interests at heart.

Dick Libertore had been Alana's high school boyfriend in New Canaan, Connecticut, in 1958 and 1959. Freed's daughter maintained that her father "distrusted" Libertore when the two were dating and thought the high school senior was only out to capitalize on Freed's name.

Early in 1960, at the height of the payola scandal, Alana left Connecticut with her mother and moved to North Carolina. After graduating from New Canaan High School in 1960, Libertore joined the military service and was stationed in Alaska, where he became involved with Armed Forces Radio. The Freed-Libertore high school romance appeared to have suffered the fate of many similar relationships: it was dampened by distance. It was not unusual, then, that when Alana received a telephone call from Libertore early in 1964, she was quite surprised. Freed's daughter was even more taken aback when Libertore told her he was coming to Palm Springs to visit.

Libertore said that when he arrived Palm Springs, he found Freed "pretty bitter" that the deejay's friends in the music business had abandoned him and "despondent over his inability to find work."

Freed soon learned he had more to be despondent over. Dick Libertore came to California determined to take Alana Freed back to Alaska and marry her. Libertore stayed in California for two weeks, during which he, Alana, and Freed "did a lot of talking." Ultimately, Freed's daughter decided to accompany Libertore to Alaska, where she would marry him.

At first, Freed was shocked at his daughter's decision because, said Alana, he still believed Libertore was "using her." Freed tried his best to dissuade his daughter from marrying Libertore, keeping her up one night for twelve hours straight. "Don't do it," Freed pleaded. "You're going to be sorry. You're going to ruin your life!"

Alana said that while her father swore he "would do anything" to keep her with him, "I went anyway, and I got married." The couple left for Alaska in March 1964 ("It wasn't a very happy parting," recalled Alana) and were married in the base chapel in May. Alana saw her father just once more after she moved to Alaska, "and that was when he got sick."

Late in 1964, when Warren Troob's son paid a visit to Freed in Palm Springs, he called his father in New York and told him, "Alan's very sick. He's in bad shape." By then, Freed was indeed an extremely sick man. Physically weakened from the serious internal injuries sustained in his near-fatal automobile accident in 1953 to the extent that even a common cold meant a possible bout with pneumonia, Freed's body was further ravaged from years of chainsmoking cigarettes and drinking heavily. To that was added the emotional stress of Freed's payola ordeal and tax-evasion charges, which pushed the deejay to a point where, Alana said, "he was drinking a lot heavier than I had ever seen him drink." When Alana then left for Alaska with Dick Libertore, Freed hit bottom.

On receiving the distressing telephone call from his son, Warren Troob flew to California. When he arrived in Palm Springs, he saw immediately why his son had been so concerned about Freed's health. Freed "looked bad," so bad that Troob sensed Freed knew he was dying. "He had to know," said Troob. But Freed uttered not a word about his failing health. Troob, out of desperation, told his friend to "quit drinking," but "it did no good."

In December 1964, the twenty-five year old verbal battle between ASCAP and BMI entered a showdown phase when the U.S.

Department of Justice filed an antitrust suit against BMI in New York Federal Court. It was said that, in filing the lawsuit, the Justice Department "reiterated the basic allegations" made several years ago in the Songwriters of America antitrust suit against BMI, which eventually petered out in inconclusive pretrial rulings.

The Justice Department originally asked the courts to order the nation's broadcasters to divest themselves of any BMI ownership, but after months of negotiation, the federal government accepted from BMI a watered-down consent decree by which no divestiture of BMI holdings was required. BMI was also permitted to continue its practices of extending advances and guarantees (an ASCAP target for nearly twenty-five years) against a song's future royalties. Once again, ASCAP was thwarted by BMI.

While BMI continued to thrive, the individual who did more than any other to make that song-licensing organization a viable concern neared the end of his life. Alan Freed entered Desert Hospital in Palm Springs in December 1964, shortly after the Justice Department filed its antitrust suit against BMI. He suffered from uremic poisoning, a toxic blood condition resulting from kidney failure. Alana Freed said her father did not realize how serious his physical condition was "until the night they put him in the hospital" and he was informed by doctors that he had only a 20 percent chance of surviving.

Living in Ohio at the time, David Freed and his wife received a telephone call from Inga, in which she said her husband "was quite ill and was in the hospital." Inga told David Freed that because of complications stemming from Freed's automobile accident, his doctor cautioned him against drinking, "but that he would not quit drinking."

Lance Freed called Alaska and told Alana the grim news of their father. She caught the first available flight to Palm Springs, only to be stopped outside her father's hospital room by a doctor who, not wanting Freed to become upset by anything, asked her what kind of a relationship she had with her father. Alana replied that she had "a good relationship" with him and indignantly added that she had not come all the way from Alaska to upset him. "I'm going in there!" she declared.

On entering her father's room, Alana was met by Lance, who told her that their father was periodically "in and out" of a coma and, in his lucid moments, would carry on a conversation. Lance urged his sister to talk to Freed to let him know she was there. Alana took hold of her father's arm and squeezed it as she began to talk to him. When Freed squeezed his daughter's arm with his other hand, she took it as a sign that "he knew I was there." When Freed eventually came out of his coma, Alana discovered he "was not scared" of dying, but he was greatly disturbed by "the thought of leaving his children with nothing—no money, no insurance, nothing! That's what scared him."

Alana spent a week—"day and night"—at the Palm Springs hospital with her father until her money ran out and she could no longer stay away from her job in Alaska. When she left on January 17, 1965, she recalled her father "sitting up in bed, reading a newspaper, and drinking a Hires root beer." Freed joked with his daughter, "just like his old self," telling her "not to stay away so long this time, and not to come back just because he was sick."

Dick Clark said he was called on January 18 for a "contribution" to help keep Freed in Desert Hospital. Curiously Clark maintained that while the stricken Freed was "grovelling around" during the last few months of his life, Clark had been "the last friend Alan had" and that he had tried to land Freed a job shortly before Freed succumbed to uremic poisoning.

Lance Freed recalled his father languishing in the hospital as visitors, some bringing food with them, stopped by. But he recalled no such visit from Clark. "No way," agreed Alana. A visit at Desert Hospital by Clark "did not happen." Lance was unable to recall so much as a telephone call from Clark.

When challenged, Clark conceded he and Freed did not have a close relationship. And, thought Clark, perhaps he was not "the last friend that Alan had," but only one of several people who tried to get Freed back on his feet again.

On January 19, two days after Alana left her father, Jack Hooke, in California on business for Dick Clark, called Freed's Palm Springs residence. Inga answered the telephone, and Hooke asked her how Freed was. She replied that her husband was in the hospital with yellow jaundice "and they don't expect him to live more than another day or two."

"I'll be right there!" said a stunned Hooke. He and his daughter, who was traveling with him, began the drive from Los Angeles to Palm Springs.

If Freed was on the verge of death, not given more than a few days to live, it would appear unfathomable why Freed's wife was not at the hospital, by his side. Lance said that at one point Inga appeared at the hospital "after she had been drinking" and that when Freed smelled the alcohol on her breath, "he didn't want her anywhere close to him" and became so agitated that she was allegedly told by the hospital staff that if she could not come to the hospital sober, she was "not to come at all."

Jack Hooke said it was only after he and his daughter entered Freed's hospital room and saw the stricken deejay that the shock of what was happening overwhelmed him. Freed's former business associate said Freed "looked up at me, but he was fucked up." He said Freed appeared "semiconscious" and was "shot full of morphine" to alleviate his pain. Freed mistook Hooke's daughter for his former partner's wife, and then asked if Hooke had brought him "any hot dogs from Nathan's." When Hooke replied that he had not done so, Freed lamented, "Oh man, how could you come here without bringing me some Nathan's hot dogs?"

Hooke sat down and lit a cigarette. While Freed "looked awful," Hooke was not dismayed, "because the guy was in good spirits."

"Inga's got to be wrong," thought Hooke. "This man isn't dying!"

But Hooke had caught Freed at the beginning of one of the deejay's lucid periods. Freed, speaking in an abnormally loud manner, asked Hooke how he was doing and how his job was going. Again, Hooke thought, "This man isn't dying. He looks terrible, but he's not dying!" Hooke thought Freed, who "was asking for hot dogs," would soon be out of the hospital. Neither he nor Freed made reference to the deejay's illness. When there was nothing more to be said, Hooke told Freed he would be in town for a few days. "I'll see you tomorrow, Alan," he matter-of-factly said. But, recalled the man who most likely knew Freed best, "he died twelve hours after I saw him."

The date was January 20, 1965, the day Lyndon B. Johnson was inaugurated in Washington as the thirty-sixth president of the United States. David Freed, en route home to Ohio after attending the inauguration, stopped on the Pennsylvania Turnpike to telephone his wife. There, in Somerset County, some twenty miles south of Windber, where he and Alan had been born, and "overlooking the courthouse where the birth records are kept," David Freed's wife told him that his brother was dead. One of the thoughts that flashed through the youngest Freed brother's mind was a favorite saying of Alan's:

"Live fast, die young, and make a good-looking corpse." Alan Freed had managed to accomplish the first two.

By that time, perhaps the only newsworthy event of Freed's remaining life was his death, and the New York press reacted in a manner consistent with their irresolute attitude toward the once-famous personality in the reaction to his demise. The *New York Daily News*, a longtime foe of rock & roll and of Freed, credited him as "one of the nation's best-known deejays," but then went on to emphasize the fines that Freed had paid during his career. The *Herald Tribune*, another acerbic critic of Freed, credited him as "the discoverer of rock and roll," who had defended the music "at every opportunity and also defended his fans as decent youngsters." The United Press International wire story in the *World Telegram* simply referred to Freed as a "former deejay."

True to its noted journalistic tradition, the *New York Times* described the "slim, youthful-looking announcer" as "the nation's leading rock and roll disc jockey." In the concise, informative obituary, it was noted that at his stage shows Freed "was accorded the same shrieking welcome the Beatles got nearly a decade later." Freed's ultimate downfall" was said to have occurred when the television quiz show scandals "brought the subject of payola into the public view." The story concluded by noting that Freed had moved to the West Coast "after admitting that he took bribes in New York to publicize certain records on his radio programs."

It was the *New York Post*, however, that best captured the emotional feeling evoked by Freed's death. In a romanticized editorial, two schools of thought on Freed's demise were given. The "up-tempo" version held that the fallen deejay died of a broken heart, while the "slow blues" version attributed Freed's death to an excess of alcohol. Paul Sherman agreed with the latter, saying that many people believed Freed deliberately drank himself to death in a long-term suicide. It was also the opinion of Hermie Dressel, another of Freed's close friends, that Freed, bitter over the fact that many of those he helped over the years "never called him, never even corresponded with him, . . . drank himself to death," completely forsaken. "He died of a broken heart."

Music reporter June Bundy attributed Freed's inability to overcome the payola setbacks (most other deejays implicated had) on his being "far more sensitive and vulnerable" than most of the other disc jockeys involved in the scandal. Of the others arrested on payola charges with Freed, said Bundy, only he "failed to bounce back," becoming instead "payola's first fatality, a tragic lesson for the entire industry."

In the instances when Freed's death was discussed by the music industry, it was grudgingly conceded that he had, indeed, "taken the rap" for the entire industry. *Cashbox* editorialized that of all the disc jockeys involved in the payola scandal, Freed "had suffered the most and was perhaps singled out for alleged wrongs that had become a business way-of-life for many others."

June Bundy, writing in *Music Business* magazine, "condemned" the industry, in which one individual who was "stupid, weak, naive, call him what you will," bore the brunt of payola retribution, "while hundreds of others . . . escaped because they were shrewd enough to 'legalize' their take." Bundy said that Freed was "much used" by people who "profited far more from his power than Freed himself did."

George ("Hound Dog") Lorenz, another white disc jockey who championed early 1950s rhythm and blues, also attributed Freed's death to a broken heart, "which of course, no hospital could mend." Lorenz wondered "how expensive" would be the floral pieces sent to Freed's funeral by those many individuals made "mighty rich" by Freed's "tremendous assistance and advice" throughout his career.

Honoring a request Freed had made before he died, his body was cremated at Woodlawn Memorial Park in Los Angeles. His ashes were returned to New York, where a public memorial service arranged by his widow was held at the Campbell Funeral Home on Manhattan's Park Avenue on February 6, 1965. While David Freed described Campbell's as a "nondenominational chapel used by show people," he said "nobody was a star that day" at his brother's service.

Freed's father, Charles, Sr., attended the service without his wife, Maude, who was in ill health herself at the time. Also absent from the service was Freed's older brother, the enigmatic Charles, Jr. Lance Freed attended the service, but his sister Alana, who had exhausted her savings on her recent two-week trip to Palm Springs, "just couldn't afford to go back to New York" and was forced to rectify her failure to do so with her own conscience, which, she said, "was not easy."

Morris Levy and Warren Troob also attended Freed's memorial

service. At the brief ceremony, Troob cited Freed's passion for classical music, and pieces by Bach were played at its beginning and at its conclusion. Troob also composed and delivered a eulogy for his old friend. As recordings of the Moonglows' "Sincerely" and "Most of All" played in the background, Troob spoke of how Freed "raised the standard of the disc jockey from that of the performer, who repeats what others have created, to that of the originator and creator."

Troob urged the small gathering to remember Freed for "the happiness he brought to the millions of people by the brilliance of his talents," for his "fire, zeal, and energy," for his being a "soft touch, who could never turn away from a request for help," and for his "warmth as a friend."

Troob closed by saying that none who heard Freed throughout the deejay's career would be able to pay a final tribute to him because Freed's voice and personality were such that "the inner ear will again and again hear the sound of Alan Freed, so that he will be with us forever."

On February 26, 1965, Freed's ashes were interred at Ferncliff Memorial Mausoleum amid the suburban greenery of Hartsdale, New York, a short drive from Manhattan. As one turns left from Hartsdale Avenue onto Secor Road and heads west, Ferncliff's two imposing gray stone buildings, surrounded by a meticulously landscaped, rolling grassy terrain, soon appear to the right. On entering the building to the right, a cordial receptionist unsolicitedly points out the locations of the interred remains of Joan Crawford, Judy Garland, and Ed Sullivan among other celebrities.

Alan Freed?

"One flight down," visitors are told.

There, on the "first floor" (the basement, just the same), out of sight around a corner and inconspicuously surrounded by a wall full of similar plaques, is Freed's memorial plaque, simply inscribed "Freed—Alan 1921–1965."

Across Secor Road, not more than a few hundred yards from Ferncliff's stone steps, is located WDAS Radio. On Saturday evenings the station broadcasts a program of 1950s rock & roll transmitted by satellite from Los Angeles. That music, beamed to surrounding Westchester County from WDAS's tower standing vigil over Freed's final resting place, is a far more appropriate memorial to Alan Freed than any basement wall plaque ever could be.

POSTSCRIPT

WHEN Alan Freed died, he owned nothing but the residences in Stamford, Palm Springs, and Miami, which, said Betty Lou Greene, the federal government "slapped liens on" and auctioned off for a "minimal amount." The IRS attached Freed's BMI songwriting royalties, which they took "for twelve years," recalled Alana Freed. Only after the government "finally got theirs, said Freed's daughter, did her father's estate begin receiving a portion of the BMI royalties. It did not amount to much, but "it was more than we'd had," said Alana.

After Alana and Dick Libertore divorced late in 1965, she moved back to North Carolina to be closer to her mother, who by then was divorced from Tom Greene.

Lance Freed, who said he was not keen on entering the music business, lest he be accused of attempting to gain a free ride on his father's coattails, in 1966 began undergraduate studies in psychology at UCLA. To finance his education, Lance took a part-time job as a gofer in the shipping department of Herb Alpert and Jerry Moss's A&M Records in Los Angeles. By 1970, Lance's interests had changed, so he shifted his area of study to English literature. After graduating from UCLA and teaching in Ireland for a short time, Lance decided that the music business was his calling after all. He took a full-time position at A&M, where he eventually worked his way up to the presidency of Almo/Irving Music and its international music-publishing affiliate, Rondor Music.

After her 1958 divorce from Alan, Jackie Freed remained in Connecticut, where she eventually remarried. Sieglinde, her daughter by Freed, for a time lived with her uncle David Freed and his family at their home near Cleveland. David Freed, who became an attorney after leaving the music business, still practices law in Ohio. Alana said she has not seen her stepsister "Siggy" since 1966 and "wouldn't recognize her today if she was sitting in front of me." Alana also said she would not recognize Alan, Jr., "a vagabond [who] just roams [so that] nobody ever knows where he is."

Charles, Jr., the oldest of the three Freed brothers, became music director of the Columbia Broadcasting System after World War II. He later worked as a free-lance composer and performer and is now retired in Utah.

After Alan's death Inga Freed returned to New York, where she took a job at Scepter Records as secretary to Florence Greenberg. Inga remained in New York until the early 1980s, when she remarried and moved west again. Like Freed's second wife, Jackie, Inga declined to be interviewed for this book.

After a life of chronic illness, Freed's mother, Maude, passed away late in 1969. Freed's father, Charles Sr., who, Alana said, was "never sick a day in his life," died suddenly four months after his wife died.

J. Elroy McCaw, who "had had big dreams about building a media empire and . . . had taken big risks," died in 1969. Despite McCaw's purchase of WINS radio for $450,000 and the sale of it for $10 million less than a decade later, it took his widow eight years to pay off his debts. All that remained in the family was one cable television system, which McCaw's son Craig took over in 1973. The younger McCaw, who subsequently built that system into McCaw Cellular Communications, the nation's largest cellular telephone company, called his father "a visionary who did not hire great people." Apparently the young executive had never heard of Alan Freed, by far J. Elroy McCaw's most famous employee.

Morris Levy, who, as Freed's manager, helped orchestra the influential deejay's career in the 1950s, also had the foresight, when others did not, to recognize the sustained value of rock & roll from that era. In 1978, Levy predicted that the 1950s would because "the most important era in U.S. music in terms of resurgence and in the use of copyrights." Noting that the major music publishers of the 1950s had said the rock & roll songs of that era "would never become standards" and their copyrights wouldn't mean anything," Levy said it was ironic to see how wrong they had been. By the 1980s, Levy had acquired the ownership of so many songs from the 1950s and 1960s that he was known in the industry as the Godfather of Rock and Roll. By 1988 his assets—which included a controlling interest in Roulette Records, Big Seven Music Publishing, and Strawberries, a chain of eighty retail music stores, as well as his two-thousand-acre horse farm in upstate Ghent, New York, worth approximately $15 million—were estimated to total some $75 million.

But Levy has had his share of trouble with the U.S. government. A 1986 FBI affidavit described him as an "associate and victim" of the Genovese crime family, reputedly controlled by Vincent ("the Chin") Gigante. The FBI contends that Gigante developed a "stronghold" on Levy's music enterprises, making him a "lucrative source of cash and property for leaders" of the Genovese family. Of his alleged mob connections, which go back as far as Thomas ("Three Fingers Brown") Luchese, Levy said, "A lot of them I like. But I'm not in business with them."

In a 1986 conversation recorded by the FBI, one Genovese soldier, speaking of Levy, told another, "When I'm around him, I need dancing shoes because, ah, he puts ya, he spins you around, you need the toe dancing shoes so you could spin easier . . . he's a pretty cute guy, ya know."

Following an investigation by the U.S. attorney's office, Levy was arrested by federal authorities in September 1986 and charged with three counts of extortion in a plot allegedly engineered by the Genovese crime family. (The scheme involved taking over the wholesale record business of John La Monte and using threats to force La Monte to pay a debt to Levy.) In May 1988, after deliberating less than five hours in a federal courtroom in Camden, New Jersey, a jury found Levy guilty on two of the three counts of "conspiring" to extort La Monte. In November, Levy was sentenced to ten years in prison and fined $200,000, but he remained free, pending appeal of his conviction. Around the time of his conviction, the usually reticent Levy agreed to a lengthy profile by Fredric Dannen, in which it was revealed that the music entrepreneur had recently sold his combined interests in Roulette Records and his publishing companies for a total of $16.5 million, before the federal government had the chance to "finish burying me off." Early in 1989, Levy sold the Strawberries music chain for a reported $40.5 million, but that October his extortion conviction was upheld by the U.S. Court of Appeals for the Third Circuit in Philadelphia. Scheduled to report to federal prison by July 16, 1990, Levy died in May of liver cancer at age sixty-two at his farm in Ghent.

One obituary credited Levy, described as a "longtime power behind the scenes in the music industry" who remained "relatively unknown to the public," with having produced Frankie Lymon and the Teenagers' "Why Do Fools Fall in Love"—a contention George Goldner, the creative force behind Gee Records, for which the song was recorded, would dispute, were he still alive.

Goldner, the founder of Tico, Rama, and Gee records, sold his interest in them to Levy in 1957. Late in 1962, Goldner sold his Gone/End recording and publishing resources to Levy and returned to Roulette to do production work. Several of the label's 1963 releases bore the familiar notation "Produced under the personal supervision of George Goldner." In 1965, Goldner, in partnership with the songwriting team of Jerry Leiber and Mike Stoller, formed Red Bird Records. But despite commercial success (Red Bird's first release, the Dixie Cups' "Chapel of Love," went to number one on the charts), the label came to an untimely demise because of personal differences among the owners. About to start the Firebird label in association with his cousin Sam, Goldner died in April 1970, at age fifty-two.

The 1950s payola scandal and the subsequent subcommittee hearings in Washington had a significant effect on broadcasting and, to a lesser extent, on the development of rock & roll itself. Carl Belz wrote in *The Story of Rock* that the 1960 congressional payola hearings, in frequently straying from issues of legality to the area of aesthetics, "demonstrated that the music had made a profound and revolutionary impact on the American public." But that impact was not necessarily born of fact. While payola had been inbred in the pop music business since its inception, the Washington hearings further tarnished rock & roll's already battered image by giving the public the impression that the music—and Alan Freed—had originated the illicit practice. (Belz incorrectly concluded that the hearings would not have occurred if rock & roll had been aesthetically pleasing to the pop music audience. It was ASCAP's relentless, financially motivated campaign, not aesthetic considerations, that ultimately turned the Washington hearings toward rock & roll.) Many adversaries of rock & roll, including some members of the Washington subcommittee, erroneously maintained that payola was the reason for the development and the sustained popularity of the controversial music, when in fact rock & roll had simply intensified the music industry's traditional practices by stimulating a tremendous increase in competition for record sales.

While the payola hearings did not directly inhibit the development of rock & roll, they ultimately altered the sound of the music that the public heard on radio and television. Since Freed, along with other influential 1950s disc jockeys, had wielded unqualified power in selecting records that would or would not be played on their respective programs, the flow of payola was directed toward them. But the payola scandal removed that programming power from the deejays' hands and placed it into the hands of station directors. Station playlists stripped from disc jockeys like Freed—who, in some ways, were as vital to their listeners as was the music they offered—the power to create shows to correspond to their individual personalities, which, wrote music critic Robert Christgau, caused rock & roll to become "almost as bland as the average legislator no doubt believes it should be." Or, as one rock writer noted, "the rock revolution had fallen into the hands of Connie Francis."

The loss of programming individuality also reinforced the top-forty format, which had gained prominence during the 1950s, and stations across the country assembled their staffs of "good guys"—disc jockeys who, while conforming to a frantic on-the-air manner, were "rarely singled out as the creators of a distinctive show." In response to the restrictiveness inherent in the popular top-forty format on AM radio, in 1966 stations in major cities across America began to offer "alternative" FM rock & roll programming, which reflected what Carl Belz called a "growing seriousness and sophistication of the music" (which had gained a measure of respectability with its renaming as "rock").

Anyone who believes that the 1950s payola scandal rid the music industry of such practices is naive, not only about the machinations of the business but also about the difficulty of teaching an old dog new tricks. Not long after the 1960 payola hearings, Jerry Blaine, head of Cosnat Distributing (from which Freed was convicted of taking commercial bribes), lamented that he wished the payola system had been left as it was, when "at least we knew what records were being played." Blaine liked the old system because it was "economical." He said that after making a payoff, "at least we knew we got the record played . . . and if the record didn't have it, we got off the record." The record executive said the 1950s payola system was "a lot cheaper to have" than the situation immediately following the scandal, when "we don't know how long the record's going to take or who's playing it." Blaine died in May 1973.

Shortly before George Goldner, one of the most prolific of the boys of New York's 1950's rock & roll scene, passed away, he mourned the loss of the 1950s payola system. He echoed Jerry Blaine's contention that after a payoff was made to a particular disc jockey, that jock would "play a record for two or three days," and if it did not become a hit, it "would come off the air." Goldner thought that process "more just" than the "more subtle system of parties and whores" that replaced it, and he felt radio airplay in 1970 was determined "artificially by people who don't know anything about music."

In 1972, syndicated columnist Jack Anderson claimed, without naming names, that "big-time disc jockeys" were offered what music critic Robert Christgau described as "cash, drugs, prostitutes, cars and vacations to push records." Christgau also said that certain rhythm and blues disc jockeys were "paid off in records that they sold in bulk to retailers and then plugged." The following year, the federal government undertook an investigation of the music business, but no charges were ever leveled.

In May 1989 independent record promoter Ralph Tashjian pleaded guilty in a Los Angeles courtroom to a misdemeanor—making undisclosed payments of drugs to a radio station employee in exchange for getting records added to the station's playlist. Tashjian's payola conviction was the first one under the federal payola statute adopted in 1960 as a result of the congressional hearings earlier that year.

In 1972 music critic Al Aronowitz wrote that if rock & roll became "the greatest story ever told," Freed "would have to be worshipped as the man who told it first." In telling the rock & roll story, not only did Freed introduce white America to black rhythm and blues, but he also had a profound effect on society itself.

Before the advent of rock & roll, rhythm and blues was unknown to most whites, and those black artists (including Nat Cole and Billy Eckstine) who did manage to gain pop success did so by altering their style to conform to that of the popular white crooners of the day. Freed's introduction of rock & roll to whites afforded rhythm and blues artists the opportunity to gain acceptance by that audience while performing in their own genre. Bob Rolontz, a 1950s rhythm and blues producer and a music writer for *Billboard*, knew Freed well. Shortly after the deejay's death, Rolontz wrote that Freed "would have liked to have been remembered for introducing Negro artists to a wider audience, and for popularizing them and their music." Indeed, Freed was most proud of that accomplishment, not because rhythm and blues was black but because he believed it to be an "honest" form of music.

It is arguable to what extent this new role of the black artist affected a generalized social change in white America's assimilation of black culture, but early rock & roll afforded many white teens of the 1950s their first (and often their only) exposure to blacks and their culture. Concomitant with white teenage acceptance of black music and idolization of black artists came a certain level of awareness that the two races were able to form some common bond. This familiarization of the black and white races was marked by pronounced resistance from a large segment of white society: Freed, for example, claimed to have received "batches of poison-pen letters" calling him a "nigger-lover."

Rock & roll in the 1950s was vilified as lowbrow trash by a large segment of adult society. Jeff Greenfield has said that those with intellectual pretensions considered the music "like masturbation: exciting, but shameful." But, as critic Albert Goldman put it, by the 1960s, aided by the Beatles and the English "invasion," the "rock age [had] . . . assimilated everything in sight, commencing with the whole of American music."

Almost four decades after rock & roll's inception, many teens who cut their teeth on the exhilaration of that newly discovered music are now among the Madison Avenue corporate executives who decide the most effective ways to catch the buying public's attention. Thus, rock artists and musicians from the 1950s to the present day are now being employed in commercials, making it difficult, if not impossible, to distinguish the commercials from the music itself.

There is no way of proving whether or not rock & roll would have happened without Freed. Dick Clark said in 1981 that without Freed's "insight that white people would listen to black music, this whole industry might have never gotten off the ground," but taking into account those cultural and musical forces at work in the late 1940s and early 1950s, the music most likely would have evolved much as it did, albeit under a different name. Freed, after all, had nothing to do with the creation of rhythm and blues. He simply brought its attention to white America and called it rock & roll; white America did the rest.

Tragically, as rock & roll's first spokesman, Freed fell victim to all the perils of the pop music business and became inexorably linked to payola. Robert Christgau wrote in 1973 that he did not believe payola "has ever done anyone much harm," a thought that Freed would have undoubtedly disputed. Describing Freed as "the most creative deejay of his age," Christgau credited him with having "had the good sense to take [payola] . . . for good records." While romantically appealing, that perception is historically false. The rock & roll writer Wayne Stierle got closer to what Freed was about when he wrote that to Freed's "everlasting credit [he] . . . played many bombs, but at least we were exposed to them." Freed and the wide variety of sounds he (for whatever reason) offered proved how essential the disc jockey was to the growth of rock & roll.

In 1984, Freed was inducted into the Akron (Ohio) Radio Hall of Fame for his contributions to broadcasting on WAKR in the 1940s. An editor from the *Salem News*, Freed's hometown newspaper, attending the ceremonies was shocked when Freed's plaque went unclaimed. On November 24, 1984, the plaque was presented to the city of Salem, where it is permanently displayed at the Salem Music Centre. Shortly thereafter, it was decided to honor Freed, Salem's belated favorite son, at the city's "Jubilee 179," a four-day celebration held in July 1976, to commemorate the city's founding in 1806. Ohio State Representative John D. Shivers of Salem presented a letter of commendation to each of Freed's relatives present, calling Freed the "father of rock and roll [whose] . . . truly laudable accomplishments" in radio were honored. It was further noted in the commendation that Freed, through his "admirable perseverance in promoting rhythm and blues music of black artists . . . fought tirelessly for . . . free expression through new music."

Early in 1986 the Rock and Roll Hall of Fame Foundation, a nonprofit group led by prominent industry executives, inducted its first ten members. In addition to those performer-inductees, five individuals were inducted in a special "non-performer and early influences" category. Among them were Jimmie Rodgers, country music's "Singing Brakeman"; Mississippi Delta blues singer Robert Johnson; Chicago boogie-woogie pianist Jimmy Yancey; Sam Phillips, owner of the Memphis-based Sun studio and record company; and Freed, described by *Rolling Stone* as "one of rock & roll's first heroes—and villains," who, as a result of the payola scandal, was "blackballed" in the music business and "died a broken man."

Cleveland was subsequently chosen as the city in which to erect the Rock and Roll Hall of Fame because that was where Freed began to popularize the term rock & roll."

Freed's impact on society may have been summed up most succinctly by Bob Rolontz, who twenty-five years ago wrote that while the deejay's "temper and hotheadedness lost him many friends over the years, . . . it could be that Alan Freed fulfilled his mission in the world of pop music in those glowing years when he made rock and roll a household word."

MAGAZINE AND NEWSPAPER ABBREVIATIONS

BTR	*Big Town Review*
BB	*Billboard*
BBB	*Bim Bam Boom*
CB	*Cashbox*
CPD	*Cleveland Plain Dealer*
DB	*Downbeat*
GM	*Goldmine*
NYDM	*New York Daily Mirror*
NYDN	*New York Daily News*
NYHT	*New York Herald Tribune*
NYJA	*New York Journal-American*
NYP	*New York Post*
NYT	*New York Times*
NYWT	*New York World Telegram*
RCM	*Record Collector's Monthly*
REX	*Record Exchanger*
RS	*Rolling Stone*
SN	*Salem* (Ohio) *News*
VV	*Village Voice* (New York)

NOTES

Chapter 1 • Moondog's Coronation

1 "If rock had any particular beginning": Scott, "Thirty Years Ago, 'Moon Dog' Howled," *CPD*, March 14, 1982.
1 Temperatures dipped into the low forties: *CPD*, March 22, 1952.
1 Calling himself "Moondog,": Freed's radio name has appeared in print both as "Moondog" and "Moon Dog." Printed advertisements by WJW radio, photographs of banners displayed at Freed's Ohio dances, as well as Freed's own WJW "Moondog House" letterhead, indicate that "Moondog" was the form originally employed. That form has been used throughout this book for consistency.
1 Of what were then called "hepcats": The word *hepcat* originated in 1925 and stems from the adjective *hep* or *hip,* a term of unknown origin that originated in 1904. To be "hep" means to be "characterized by a keen informed awareness of or interest in the newest developments." In 1952 the *CPD* used the term *hepcats* to describe Freed's Cleveland Arena audience.
2 He was nontheless astounded by its size: Scott, "Thirty Years Ago, . . . ," *CPD*, March 14, 1982. The black newspaper the *Cleveland Call and Post* estimated the crowd at the Cleveland Arena to be 99 percent black.
2 "I was worried whether there would be enough people . . . the lid blew off": Helen Bolstad, reprinted in Buzzell, *Mister 'Rock 'n' Roll' Alan Freed* p. 24. (Hereafter cited simply as Buzzell.)
2 Assaulted the arena in a human wave: *CPD*, March 22, 1952.
2 "I can still see the crowd below us": Scott, "Thirty Years Ago, . . . ," *CPD*, March 14, 1982.
2 "Slowly and reluctantly filed out": *CPD*, March 22, 1952.
2 MOONDOG BALL IS HALTED: *CPD*, March 22, 1952.
3 "Crushing mob of 25,000": Scott, "Thirty Years Ago, . . . ," *CPD*, March 14, 1982.
3 "The Moondog Coronation Ball was almost all black": Interview with David Freed, September 28, 1982.
3 "We were having a real great time": "Moondog House" audiotape, March 22, 1952.
3 "It was strictly a breakdown": Interview with David Freed.
3 About 9,000 tickets were sold in advance: Scott, "Thirty Years Ago, . . . ," *CPD*, March 14, 1982.
3 "Everybody had such a grand time": Buzzell, p. 64.
3 "It was those who didn't have tickets that caused the problem": Scott, "Thirty Years Ago, . . . ," *CPD*, March 14, 1982.
3 "The shame of the situation": Valena Minor Williams, quoted by Scott, "Thirty Years Ago, . . . ," *CPD*, March 14, 1982.
3 "Low-brow, cheap entertainment . . . frequently obscene": *Call and Post* reporter Marty Richardson, quoted by Scott, "Thirty Years Ago, . . . ," *CPD*, March 14, 1982.
4 "Did not make a fetish of integration": Kusmer, *A Ghetto Takes Shape*, p. 270.
4 "More isolated from the general life": Kusmer, p. 274.
4 "Lowbrowed" rhythm: Valena Minor Williams, quoted by Scott, "Thirty Years Ago, . . . ," *CPD*, March 14, 1982.

4 "Gutbucket" rhythm and blues: Marty Richardson, quoted by Scott, "Thirty Years Ago, . . . ," *CPD*, March 14, 1982. The term *gutbucket*, which came into widespread use after the Civil War, denoted a small bucket used to catch the drippings from whiskey kegs. The black honky-tonk music commonly heard in barrelhouse establishments that utilized gutbuckets was soon associated with the gutbucket itself.
5 "Cleveland's well-known R&B jock": Bob Rolontz, "R&B Notes," *BB*, June 7, 1952.
5 "Blues and rhythm" records: "Moondog House" audiotape, March 31, 1954.
5 "If anybody . . . had told us . . . the 'Moondog' program will leave the radio!": "Moondog House" audiotape, March 22, 1952.
6 Company of Connecticut settlers in 1796: Vexler, *Cleveland*, p. 1.
6 Seventh-largest city in the United States: Ploski, *The Negro Almanac*, p. 380. Cleveland's total population in 1952 was just under one million.
6 "Exceptional" race relations . . . "crystallization" of discriminatory practices: Kusmer, *A Ghetto Takes Shape*, pp. 64, 174.
6 Rechristened it "rhythm and blues": Whitburn, *Top R&B Singles*, p. 11.
6 "Garbage trash . . . gutbucket blues and lowdown rhythms": Valena Minor Williams, quoted by Scott, "Thirty Years Ago, . . . ," *CPD*, March 14, 1982.
7 "Sixty-Minute Man," in the summer of 1951: Whitburn, *Pop Memories*, p. 128.
7 "Saw it as big business": Scott, "Thirty Years Ago, . . . ," *CPD*, March 14, 1982.
8 "He generated the same kind of electricity as Mickey Mantle or Judy Garland": Bob Rolontz, quoted by Arnold Shaw, *Honkers and Shouters*, p. 512.
8 Came to America as a five-year-old: Interview with David Freed.
8 On December 21, 1921: There remains some question as to Freed's birth date. While some biographical articles from the 1950s give 1922 as the date (most likely Freed made himself a year younger for his youthful audience), more reliable sources, including Freed's Ferncliff Mausoleum memorial, list 1921 as his birth date.
8 The Freed family moved three times: Interview with David Freed.
8 Charles Sr. was hired as a clerk: Interview with Lozier Caplan, August 26, 1982.
9 "Very aggressive, very protective": Interview with Robert Dixon, August 26, 1982.
9 "Quiet and gentle man": Interview with David Freed.
9 "Mild and meek-mannered": Interview with Dixon.
9 "There was never a time": Interview with David Freed.
9 Minstrel-performing brothers Al and Don: One promotional advertisement for Al Palmer ("Actor, Musician, Singer, and Composer") claims that he composed "many songs, several of which were hits all over the country." Palmer, of whom it was said had "vast experience in all parts of the amusement world," worked for the Al G. Field and Neil O'Brien Minstrels as well as for other companies.
9 "Some of their style": Buzzell, p. 24.
9 "Believe it or not . . . I got the dance band bug": Buzzell, p. 75.
9 "We always had records": Interview with David Freed.
10 "Always picked 'em right": Fanselow, "Alan Freed," *SN*, July 16, 1985.
10 "The musician of the family . . . some heavy differences": Interview with David Freed.
10 "Charlie was brilliant in high school": Interview with Dixon.
10 Chester Brautigam . . . did not have to teach: Fanselow.
10 "Entertaining all by himself": Interview with Daniel E. Smith, August 26, 1982.
11 "We got fifty cents a man": Buzzell, p. 63.
11 "Someday I'll have a dance band": Sklar, reprinted in Buzzell, p. 68.
11 Warm, favorable memories of him: Fanselow.
11 "A good guy . . . Pretty much a loner": Interview with Don I. Rich, August 26, 1982.
11 "Go-getter . . . Long and mushy": Interview with Betty Bischel Lowery, August 26, 1982.
11 "Opportunist . . . Get four, Bob . . . One of those individuals . . . I have to make good": Interview with Dixon.
12 "If he couldn't find it": Raymond, quoted in Fanselow.
12 "Factual basis . . . A tremendous amount of faults": Interview with David Freed.
12 "He wasn't too interested": Brautigam, quoted in Fanselow.
12 Freed and a classmate performed: "Seniors Receive Diplomas," *SN*, June 7, 1940.
12 "Somewhat a person of destiny": Interview with David Freed.
12 Met with disapproval by his father: Buzzell, p. 27.
12 "He had his heart set": Buzzell, p. 63.
13 "My father was not ever opposed": Interview with David Freed.
13 "That was it. I was gone!": Buzzell, p. 63.
13 Hooked on broadcasting: Fanselow, "Alan Freed," *SN*, July 16, 1985.
13 "I hung around": Buzzell, p. 63.
13 "For a brief period": Interview with David Freed.
13 Tomah in west-central Wisconsin: Fields "Only Human," *NYDM*, March 18, 1957.
13 "Believe it or not": Interview with David Freed.

NOTES

13 Attack on Pearl Harbor: Buzzell, p. 27. This so called "fact" has been printed several times in various publications. This particular source is most likely the first.
13 Medical discharge because of flatfeet: Interviews with David Freed and with Betty Lou Greene, November 21, 1982.
14 "Obvious . . . After graduation . . . I realized I'd seen him before" : Interview with Greene.
14 Earned a degree in mechanical engineering: Alicia Evans, reprinted in Buzzell, p. 38.
14 "It's been told over and over": Interview with Greene.
15 Off to State in the fall of 1940: Interview with David Freed.
15 "That was his life . . . We spent a great many evenings" . . . She would return to Lisbon: Interview with Greene.
15 "Doing more to enthuse me": "Freed's Preaching Style Attracts $75,000 Contracts," *Youngstown Vindicator*, August 1954.
15 Announcing on a nightly classical music program: Theodore Irwin, reprinted in Buzzell, p. 18.
15 Did "mainly announcing": Interview with Greene.
16 Freed began work for seventeen dollars a week: Irwin, reprinted in Buzzell, p. 18.
16 "Moved into a little three-room upstairs apartment": Interview with Greene.
16 Beethoven's "Pastorale" . . . "Pathetique": Irwin, reprinted in Buzzell, p. 18.
16 Bach and Brahms . . . *Der Ring des Nibelungen*: "Rock 'n' Roll Pied Piper," *NYT*, May 20, 1960.
16 "He liked the big bands, too": Interview with Greene.
16 "Good-looking, tall and slender . . . a way about him": Interview with Ruth Cruikshank, August 25, 1982.
17 Called himself Albert James Freed: WKBN Employment Application Card, 1943.
17 Freed's given name as Aldon James: Interview with David Freed.
17 Styled himself Albert J, Albert James: Interviews with David Freed and Greene.
17 "I think he manufactured that one in high school" . . . Al J, as well as Alan: Interview with David Freed.
17 "Summer theatre work and directing" . . . as well as with civic symphonies: WKBN Employment Application Card.
17 "It took a lot of guts": Interview with Dixon
17 Just across the Ohio state line; WKBN Employment Application Card.
17 Was afraid to stay there . . . forty-two dollars a week at WKBN: Interview with Greene.
18 "Dean of Ohio Sportscasters": Interview with Smith.
18 "A little bit of everything . . . Rub elbows with the big shots . . . he'd step on your face": Interview with Don Gardner, August 25, 1982.
18 "We went over to WKBN . . . a person to look up to": Interview with Smith.

CHAPTER 2 • BIRTH OF A DISC JOCKEY

20 "Alan and I got in some trouble": Interview with Herman ("Hermie") Dressel, July 3, 1979.
20 America's disc jockey phenomenon: *Disc jockey* is defined as "an announcer of a radio show of popular recorded music who often intersperses comments not related to the music" (Mish). The term *record jockey* first appeared in print in the show business tabloid *Variety* in April 1940. The term *disc jockey* first appeared in print in *Variety* in July 1941.
20 Unobtrusively and with dignity: Barnouw, *A Tower in Babel*, p. 26.
20 Any sort of listener identity develop: Sterling and Kittross, *Stay Tuned*, p. 71. At first, radio announcers were identified on the air by code initials, not names. For example, Thomas A. Cowan, who began announcing for WJZ in Newark in 1922, was known on the air simply as "ACN," which stood for "Announcer Cowan Newark."
20 Reginald A. Fessenden, an electrical engineer: Barnouw, *The Golden Web*, p. 216.
20 The first "disc jockey": Barnouw, *A Tower in Babel*, p. 287.
21 Strong opposition to broadcasting them on the nation's airwaves: Sterling and Kittross, *Stay Tuned*, p. 72.
21 "Attempted everything this side of public hangings": Passman, *The Deejays*, p. 36.
21 "In effect a fraud upon the listening public": Passman, *The Deejays*, p. 38.
21 "Identified as such before they were played on the air: Barnouw, *The Golden Web*, p. 217.
21 To create the illusion of a live radio broadcast: Shaw, *The Rockin' '50s*, p. 61.
22 "It was this style . . . Staple of American radio": Passman, *The Deejays*, p. 60.
22 As much as 80 percent of their programming: Sterling and Kittross, *Stay Tuned*, p. 164.
22 Identifying all prerecorded music: Barnouw, *The Golden Web*, p. 217.
23 With 55 percent of that music being prerecorded: Dachs, *Anything Goes*, p. 151.
23 "Musical clock" format . . . plenty of commercial announcements: Sterling and Kittross, *Stay Tuned*, p. 275.
23 "Such programming seemed to require a minimum": Barnouw, *The Golden Web*, p. 218.
23 WKBN in Youngstown on November 4, 1944: WKBN Employment Application Card.
23 To WIBE radio in Philadelphia: Perhaps the earliest mention of the phantom WIBE occurred in the fall of 1956, in a story about Freed by Alicia Evans, reprinted in Buzzell, p. 39.

23 No recollection of WIBE: Interview with Greene.
23 "In some sort of retail establishment" Interview with Phyllis Simms, September 15, 1980.
23 "Some development" . . . the announcer would be right for WAKR: Interview with Simms, August 24, 1982.
23 Berk offered the announcer $62.50 a week: *BB*, March 4, 1950.
24 "Publicity-conscious" Berk: Interview with Simms, August 24, 1982.
24 "Jesus, I have to take a piss" . . . at Westgate Manor: Interview with Greene.
24 Disc jockey for the 11:15 program had not yet shown up: Interview with Greene.
24 Silverman told him which ones to play: Interview with Simms, September 15, 1980. Simms said Freed "just sat behind a desk with a microphone" and was cued by Silverman from the control room.
24 "He fired the other guy and gave me the job": Buzzell, p. 63.
25 "Extensive" training . . . "thousands" of dollars: Interview with Simms, August 24, 1982.
25 "Became a well-known figure in the area . . . the wildest things he could get ahold of": Interview with Simms, September 15, 1980.
25 WAKR had a "music committee" . . . "more up-tempo": Interview with Simms, September 15, 1980.
25 "From time to time" . . . playing unsanctioned records: Interview with Simms, August 24, 1982.
25 On an "adult level" . . . "precious little patter between records": Interview with Simms, September 15, 1980.
25 Freed served as its first program director: Fanselow.
25 "Deejays were just really beginning": Interview with David Freed.
26 "From pop . . . to Spike Jones": Buzzell, p. 63.
26 "A big fish in a little pool . . . would not leave him alone": Interview with Greene.
26 A drummer . . . "playing some real music?": Interview with Dressel.
26 He would stay with the Freeds: Interview with Greene.
26 "Lifting a few glasses" . . . "wigged out": Interview with Dressel.
27 "At that time my career": Buzzell, p. 63.
27 "Really attractive" blonde divorcée: Interview with Dressel.
27 "But everybody called her Jackie": Interview with David Freed.
27 "Completely shocked" . . . "he knew the judge": Interview with Greene.
28 "Very definitely . . . a lot of evidence I didn't enjoy gathering": Interview with Greene.
28 Freed . . . agreed to the divorce: Buzzell, p. 64. Freed's and Greene's accounts of their marital breakup differ. He said the couple "agreed on a mutual divorce" and that after they split up "the whole world seemed to collapse, but what we did turned out to be the right thing" (Buzzell, p. 64). Greene said she and Freed "split up" shortly before son Lance was born. The couple were not legally divorced until December 1949. Freed and Jackie were married in Toledo, Ohio, in 1950.
28 Cut it out and sent it to her: Interview with Greene.
28 As he would an impudent child's: Interview with David Freed.
28 Should he leave WAKR . . . pay Freed to do a disc jockey program: *BB*, march 4, 1950.
29 Prohibiting the wayward deejay from continuing: Interview with David Freed.
29 To whichever radio station was interested . . . "for its appeal to advertisers": *BB*, March 4, 1950.
30 His "right to be heard" . . . "offered me anything it hadn't before": *BB*, March 4, 1950. Since Freed's WAKR contract was the only one at issue, reference to other contracts was ruled irrelevant by the court.
30 "Bit of a troublemaker" . . . "all his life": Interview with David Freed.
30 "About six months" . . . "died a natural death": Interview with David Freed.
30 Six commercial television stations . . . entire country: Jackson, *Big Beat legends*, p. 5.
31 "Never before equalled in the city's history": Yust, *1952 Britannica Book of the Year*, p. 188.
31 Television viewing in 1950 matched radio listening: Jackson, *Big Beat Legends*, p. 6.
31 "Practically all . . . operating profitably": Yust, *1952 Britannica Book of the Year*, p. 670.
31 WEWS-TV, opened in 1947: Kane, *The World Book*, Vol. 4, "Cleveland," p. 516.
31 Would not be linked . . . until September 1951: Jackson, *Big Beat Legends*, p. 6.
31 One that dwarfed even Akron's: Yust, *1952 Britannica Book of the Year*, p. 668.
31 "Did some records": Interview with David Freed.
31 "One of the worst things I've ever seen": Interview with Dixon
31 "Television records . . . didn't last long": Interview with David Freed.
31 Upheld Judge Roetzel's earlier ruling: *BB*, December 16, 1950.

Chapter 3 • The Dog Howls

33 "I had a program on WJW": Freed, "Alan Freed Says, 'I Told You So . . . ' " *DB*, September 19, 1956, p. 44.
33 "A very heavy drinker": Interview with David Freed.
33 Land a job playing classical music on WJW: WAKR's restrictive clause prohibiting Freed from radio broadcasts within a seventy-five-mile radius of Akron expired in February 1951.

NOTES

34 Taken aback by the "unusual" sight . . . "alien to their culture": Gillett, *The Sound of the City*, p. 36.
34 "Accepted" Mintz's invitation": Freed, "Alan Freed Says . . . ," *DB* p. 44.
34 "Played on black radio stations": Interview with Jack Hooke.
34 "At first attracted an audience": Buzzell, p. 64.
34 "First inkling . . . that white people enjoyed": Irwin, reprinted in Buzzell, p. 18.
35 Mintz noticed: Interview with Hooke.
35 "I'll buy you a radio show": Bolstad, reprinted in Buzzell, p. 24.
35 "Not anymore": Buzzell, p. 62. Mintz's remark implies that white teenagers were buying race records at his Record Rendezvous shop in 1951. Most likely Mintz's alleged quote was manufactured by Freed at a later date to reinforce the deejay's tale of discovering white teenagers in Mintz's record store.
35 "Two girls with real contralto voices": Freed, "Alan Freed Says ," *DB*, September 19, 1956, p. 44.
35 "The hoarse, husky tenor sax": Shaw, *The Rockin' '50s*, p. 88.
35 "Radio is dead": "High Lama of Rock 'n' Roll."
36 "I wondered for about a week": Freed, "Alan Freed Says . . . ," *DB*, September 19, 1956, p. 44.
36 "Was interested in selling": Interview with Hooke.
36 "Confirmed rhythm and blues fan": Buzzell, p. 62.
37 Listening with "fascination" . . . "some jazz research": Buzzell, p. 62.
37 "Knowledge of spirituals": Interview with David Freed.
37 "Blues record": Interview with David Freed.
37 "Prowling" . . . "knew what rhythm and blues was all about": Interview with Dressel.
37 "Blaring mixture of stepped-up folk songs": Sklar, reprinted in Buzzell, p. 68.
37 "It was the beat": Freed, "Alan Freed Says . . . ," *DB*, September 19, 1956, p. 44.
37 "Hot, freewheeling platters . . . ": Buzzell, p. 13.
37 "Complimented, rather than sublimated": Hopkins, *The Rock Story*, p. 17.
37 "Naive piece of 'pure corn' ": Yust, *1952 Britannica Book of the Year*, p. 483. "Goodnight, Irene" reportedly sold over two million copies and was the number-one song in the United States for thirteen weeks (Whitburn, *Pop Memories*, p. 441).
37 "Commercially successful": Yust, *1952 Britannica Book of the Year*, p. 484.
38 "Starved for entertainment" . . . "soupy and languid": Irwin, reprinted in Buzzell, p. 18.
38 "Ballads" . . . "great for dancing": Buzzell, p. 75.
38 "Powerful, affirmative jazz beat" . . . "an exciting discovery": Irwin, reprinted in Buzzell, p. 18.
38 "It found me": Buzzell, p. 64.
38 "Was as much his idea as mine": Buzzell, p. 76.
39 "This left his evenings open": Buzzell, p. 52.
39 "As soon as I got command": Sklar, reprinted in Buzzell, p. 68.
39 "Had the foresight": Buzzell, p. 64.
39 "Two of a kind": Interview with David Freed.
40 "Serious appraisal" . . . "to black listeners": MacDonald, *Don't Touch That Dial!*, p. 356. In 1943 there were only four radio stations in the U.S. that programmed specifically for blacks.
40 "Intense" pressure within American broadcasting: Sterling and Kittross, *Stay Tuned*, p. 253. From 1945 to 1952 the number of AM radio stations in the United States increased from 930 to 2,350.
40 In 1948 full-time radio broadcasting aimed at blacks came into being: Redd, *Rock Is Rhythm and Blues*, p. 25.
40 "Jump band jazz" . . . "as far north as Canada": Courtney, "Blues in the Night," *GM*, February 1984, p. 183.
41 Almost overnight: Redd, *Rock Is Rhythm and Blues*, p. 26.
41 "Many jocks were doing it in the South": Passman, *The Deejays*, p. 175.
41 "The first announcer" . . . "the West Coast Alan Freed": Shaw, *Honkers and Shouters*, pp. 518, 508.
41 "Forgotten 15 million black consumers in America": MacDonald, *Don't Touch That Dial!*, p. 365.
42 "The potential rhythm and blues explosion": Redd, *Rock Is Rhythm and Blues*, p. 26.
42 "But still represented": MacDonald, *Don't Touch That Dial!*, p. 368.
42 "Although other white disc jockeys": Shaw, *Honkers and Shouters*, p. 513.
42 "A weird number" . . . "wanted to know the score": Slifka, "Freed's Preaching Style Attracts $75,000 Contract," *Youngstown Vindicator*, August 1954.
42 Adopted the name himself: "Moondog Symphony," recorded on the obscure Temple label by a sightless street musician-beggar named Thomas Hardin, the "Viking poet," who went by the name Moondog on his recordings, was never copyrighted.
42 Would change the song title to his liking: Freed's original theme, Todd Rhodes's "Blues for the Red Boy," was later renamed "Blue Night". Freed also used that theme on his original one-hour WINS program in New York.
43 Bones shaking and rattling in the background: Interview with Jim Russell, May 13, 1986.
43 "All right, Moondog": "Moondog House" audiotape, March 31, 1954.
43 "Used to carry on . . . "Tore" the town apart: Interview with Dressel.
43 "All right": "Moondog House" audiotape, March 31, 1954.

43 "Period of adjustment": *CPD*, February 2, 1952.
44 "Got called down for that": Passman, *The Deejays*, p 176.
44 "Never directed": Interview with David Freed.
45 Reportedly selling more than two million copies: Whitburn, *Pop Memories*, p. 362; *Top R&B Singles*, p. 343.
45 Her version of "Wheel of Fortune": Whitburn, *Pop Memories*, p. 167; *Top R&B Singles*, p. 442.
45 "More willing to submit": Cotten, *Shake, Rattle, and Roll*, Vol. 1, p. 17.
45 Performers were "virtually nonexistent": Cotten, *Shake, Rattle, and Roll*, pp. xxii, 17.
46 "Only an employee": Scott, "Thirty Years Ago, 'Moon Dog Howled," *CPD*, March 14, 1982.
47 Royal Roost . . . "a bottle of beer!": Interview with Hooke.
47 "So, folks, you take a tip": "Moondog House" audiotape, March 31, 1954.
47 "Ol' king and give it a try": "Moondog House" audiotape, March 31, 1954.
47 "Revelation to watch": Interview with Hooke.
48 "We knew guys were taking money" . . . "accompanied by Jackie": Interview with Hooke.
48 "I stayed four days": Interview with Hooke. Betty Lou Greene said that "no one was closer" to Freed's situation than Hooke, who "was by Alan's side a good bit of the time" (interview with Greene).
48 "Cleveland's chief station": Full-page WJW Radio advertisement in *Cashbox*, 1953.
49 Noting the "strong upsurge": *Variety*, February 25, 1953, quoted by Redd, *Rock Is Rhythm and Blues*, p. 39.
49 "Key positions" . . . "one of the most potent": *Variety*, February 25, 1953, quoted by Redd, *Rock Is Rhythm and Blues*, p. 39.
49 Damage to both his spleen and liver: Interview with David Freed.
49 Some 260 stitches: The operation left a visible scar across Freed's nose, and after the incident the deejay sported his famous crooked smile, a visual reminder of his close brush with death.
49 "He was not expected to live": Interview with Alana Freed.
49 "Small and meaningless": Buzzell, p. 64.
49 Did not expect him to live more than ten years: Passman, *The Deejays*, p. 222.
50 "He was told . . . take another drink": Interview with Alana Freed. The grim prediction of ten more years of life for Freed would prove prophetic. David Freed said he, and "a lot of people, attributed [his brother's] early demise, in part, to that accident."
50 "He didn't drink anything": Interview with Greene.
50 Don Gardner . . . while working there: Interview with Gardner.
50 "Might have had a glass of wine": Interview with Greene.
50 "Almost a teetotaler" . . . "in Akron": Interview with David Freed.
50 "Never came home" . . . "a social drink now and then": Interview with Greene.
50 "Lifted a few glasses" . . . "goof up on a show": Interview with Dressel.
50 "Was not a teetotaler" . . . "drinking problem": Interview with Simms, September 15, 1980.
50 "A ten-cent beer drinker" . . . "that goddamned saloon": Interview with Hooke.
51 Took turns sitting in . . . did not broadcast from the hospital: Interview with David Freed.
51 "Moon Dog, aka Alan Freed": *BB*, June 6, 1953.
51 "Well, here's a letter from Korea": "Moondog House" audiotape, March 31, 1954.
51 "Now, Faye Adams": "Moondog House" audiotape, March 31, 1954.
52 A "daring project": *BB*, January 29, 1955.
52 ALL SEATS RESERVED!: *CPD*, advertisement, June 28 and July 5, 1953.
52 "Now it's Joe Louis": "Fighter Capers in Revue," *CPD*, July 19, 1953.
52 "Almost 20,000" turned out at the Arena: Cotten, *Shake, Rattle, and Roll*, p. 109.
52 "Joe Louis Packs in": "Joe Louis Packs in 10,000 Trained Squeals for Show," *CPD*, July 21, 1953.
53 Was "very, very small": Interview with Hooke.

CHAPTER 4 • THE MOONDOG MESMERIZES MANHATTAN

55 "[Freed] was a character": WJW station manager Bill Lemmon, quoted by Scott.
55 "Over 10,000 admissions were racked up": Freed, quoted by *BB*, August 29, 1953.
55 "I'm gonna take you guys": Interview by Bobby Lester, June 23, 1979.
56 They were now the Moonglows: Lyle Kenyon Engel, "The Moonglows Sincerely," *Rock 'n' Roll Stars*, p. 53.
56 "Moon puppies" . . . "we glow in the dark": Interview with Bobby Lester, June 23, 1979.
56 "Scores of suggestions": Engel, "The Moonglows Sincerely," *Rock 'n' Roll Stars*, p. 53.
56 "Was a pretty funny thing to see": Interview with Bobby Lester.
56 He signed them . . . in October 1953: "Chance Records Signs Moonglows, Managed by Al (Moondog) Freed," *BB*, October 24, 1953.
57 As a result . . . took what the record distributor gave: Tosches, *Country*, pp. 242, 245.
57 David Freed quit Ohio Sales: *BB*, September 19, 1953.
57 "Sittin' around waitin' " . . . "a quick minute": Interview with Sam Griggs, September 10, 1980.

NOTES

57 Their first release for Chess: "Nadine" and "I'm All Alone" (Chess 1549) was released on September 19, 1953.
58 The group's first two: "Whistle My Love" and "Baby Please" (Chance 1147) was released in October 1953. "Just a Lonely Christmas" and "Hey, Santa Claus" (Chance 1150) was released in December 1953.
58 "Our little hit": Interview with Griggs.
58 The same package had done well in Steubenville and Youngstown: "Moondog Ball Pulls 2,480," *BB*, November 28, 1953.
59 The song reportedly sold: Millar, *The Drifters*, p. 49.
59 "It was the worst thing you ever heard" . . . "Very aggressive": Interview with Hooke.
60 A "dilly" of a ball: *BB*, January 9, 1954.
60 Until then . . . sales of perhaps 250,000 copies: Cotten, *Shake, Rattle, and Roll*, p. 75.
60 But that year . . . over a million copies each: Whitburn, *Top Pop Singles*, pp. 128, 425.
60 As 15 million rhythm and blues singles were sold in 1953: Cotten, *Shake, Rattle, and Roll*, p. 76.
60 Day's top-selling pop hit "Secret Love": "Secret Love," backed by "Real Gone Mama" (Chance 1152), was released in February 1954.
60 "Got all the acts he wanted": Interview with Bobby Lester.
61 Their second Chess release: "It Would Be Heavenly" and "Baby's Coming Home" (Chess 1553).
61 Freed expected "great sacrifices" . . . "Ruthless" . . . "hustling records": Interview with Griggs.
61 Becoming a network radio disk jockey: *BB* reported in its January 30, 1954, issue that Freed, "Cleveland's top r&b jock," was negotiating for a network rhythm and blues program.
61 "Making a strong bid for pop market acceptance": Redd, *Rock Is Rhythm and Blues*, p. 58.
61 First "reverse crossover" rhythm and blues hit: Whitburn, *Top R&B Singles*, p. 105.
62 "What happened there soon happened elsewhere": Redd, *Rock Is Rhythm and Blues*, p. 32.
62 "Regretfully deemed advisable": "Station WINS Sold, If FCC Approves," *NYT*, August 10, 1953.
62 To slash operating costs: Sklar, *Rocking America*, pp. 10, 11.
63 Wagner refused to cross: "Mayor Passes up Yankee Opener, Bowing to Musicians' Picket Line," *NYT*, April 16, 1954.
63 "All other union members at WINS:" "Pitcher Wagner Stays Away," *NYT*, April 17, 1954.
64 "Being heard on New York radio": Interview with Hooke.
64 Harptones, a tremendously popular group: The Harptones had recently enjoyed two huge New York–area hits, "A Sunday Kind of Love" (Bruce 101), released in December 1953, and "My Memories of You" (Bruce 102), released early in 1954.
64 "A sight to see": Interview with Hooke.
64 "11,000 screaming teens": Buzzell, p. 12.
64 Trade paper accounts noted: Expenses for talent and for the armory rental amounted to $5,000, which left a $15,000 profit for the two nights.
65 "The kids want that music with a beat" . . . 20 percent of the rhythm and blues audience was white: *BB*, May 15, 1954.
65 "Put this guy [Freed] on": Interview with Hooke.
65 On May 23 . . . Freed flew to New York to meet with WINS: *BB*, May 29, 1954.
65 Capacity crowd . . . "about $75,000": "Moondog to WINS; Freed Freed of WJW to Start in New York," *BB*, July 10, 1954.
65 MOONDOG TO WINS: "Moondog to WINS," *BB*, July 10, 1954.
66 "Second Annual Biggest Rhythm and Blues Show": Cotten, *Shake, Rattle, and Roll*, p. 183.
66 Art Freeman . . . "kicked up a fuss" . . . "Exposed some of Freed's activities": "WINS Places Freed Show in 5 Markets," *BB*, August 28, 1954.
66 Freeman displayed a letter: *Variety*, August 25, 1954.
66 "Until further action, if any": "WINS Places Freed . . . ," *BB*, August 28, 1954.
66 "Whenever he [Freed] was fighting with Leo Mintz": Interview with David Freed.
67 They "wanted [the R&B market]" . . . "engineered": Interview with David Freed.
67 "New York got up and took notice": Tancredi, "The Flamingos," *BBB*, February-March 1972, p. 6. The quote was attributed to cousins Jake and Zeke Carey of the Flamingos.
67 Their summer release of "219 Train": "219 Train" and "My Gal" (Chance 1161).
67 "Kind of messin' up": Interview with Bobby Lester.
67 Alan "wanted me to go with him" . . . attended law school: Interview with David Freed.
67 "Special incentive plan": "WINS Places Freed . . . ," *BB*, August 28, 1954.
67 "Applicable discounts and agency commissions": Eliot, *Rockonomics*, p. 257. The wording is taken from Freed's original WINS contract, dated August 10, 1954.
68 Thus precluding a Moondog-Milkman confrontation . . . "Long live the new king": *BB*, September 9, 1954.
68 WINS also paid for the deejay's move: Interview with M. Warren Troob, April 30, 1980.
68 "Definitely not a R&B town": Shaw, *Honkers and Shouters*, p. 514.
68 "Billion dollar plus" potential: MacDonald, *Don't Touch That Dial!*, p. 365.
68 "One of the largest concentrations . . . in the country": Redd, *Rock Is Rhythm and Blues*, p. 46.

68 "Accepted white voice": Passman, *The Deejays*, p. 67.
68 "Hippest guy in the business": Shaw, *Honkers and Shouters*, p. 362, which attributes the quote to 1940s record executive Lee Magid.
68 "Gravelly voice . . . with a southern accent": Gourse, *Louis' Children*, p. 208.
68 "After-dark Negro market": Passman, *The Deejays*, p. 67.
69 "Did not command the respect": Interview with Screamin' Jay Hawkins, July 9, 1979.
69 "WWRL" . . . "was where you got your plays": Interview with William Miller, September 26, 1979.
69 "Few whites [who] went all the way up the dial": Interview with James McGowan, July 17, 1979.
69 "Hi, everybody": "Rock 'n' Roll Party" audiotape, February 12, 1955. The introduction of Ruth Brown's "What A Dream" has been substituted for a song actually introduced on the tape.
69 "Freed had ten people in there": Interview with Ray Reneri, July 9, 1979.
70 "Now we're gonna send": "Rock 'n' Roll Party" audiotape, February 12, 1955.
70 Freed had the volume up to "double ten": Gillett, "Alan Freed," *Stormy Weather*, January 1970, p. 4.
70 Hearing loss as "very slight" . . . "Always greatly exaggerated": Interview with Alana Freed.
70 Often a caller: Gillett, "Alan Freed," *Stormy Weather*, January 1970, p. 4.
70 "crap" . . . "I give him one week": Whelton, "He Was the King of Rock and Roll," *NYT*, September 24, 1972.
71 McGowan said . . . "banging and shouting" . . . "Automatically assumed": Interview with McGowan.
71 "Took this town over before you could turn around": Interview with Hooke.
71 "The same station [WINS] everywhere you went": Interview with Reneri.
71 "Had to rig up a roof antenna": Hoffman, *Woodstock Nation*, p. 24.

CHAPTER 5 • ROCK & ROLL PARTY

72 "Teenagers Demand . . . Rhythm & Blues": *Billboard* headline from an April 1954 issued, quoted by Cotten, *Shake, Rattle, and Roll*, p. 162.
72 Rhythm and blues began to evoke open derision and outright hatred: Fox, *Showtime at the Apollo*, p. 170.
72 Music's allegedly "smutty" lyrics: Passman, *The Deejays*, p. 189.
72 "It Ain't the Meat (It's the Motion)" . . . "Roll with My Baby": "It Ain't the Meat ("It's the Motion)" (King 4501), recorded by the Swallows, released in December 1951; "Sixty-Minute Man" (Federal 12022), recorded by the Dominoes, released in 1951; "I Got Loaded" (Aladdin 3097), recorded by Peppermint Harris, released in July 1951; "Rock Me All Night Long" (Mercury 8291), recorded by the Ravens, released in October 1952; "Roll with My Baby" (Atlantic 976), recorded by Ray Charles, released in January 1954.
73 Advocated sex or drinking or that ridiculed blacks: Cotten, *Shake, Rattle, and Roll*, p. 151.
73 "Such a Night" . . . across the country: Cotten, *Shake, Rattle, and Roll*, p. 155. The first station to do so, on March 13, 1954, was Detroit's WXYZ.
73 Released a song called "Work with Me Annie": "Work with Me Annie" and "Until I Die" (Federal 12169), released in March 1954. The group's name was originally the Royals, then changed to the Midnighters.
73 An old jazz expression that could mean "anything": Lydon, *Boogie Lightning*, p. 84.
73 Called "Annie Had a Baby (She Can't Work No More)": "Annie Had a Baby" and "She's the One" (Federal 12195), released in September 1954.
73 What type of work Annie was fond of: Hank Ballard, lead singer of the Midnighters, as well as the writer of the group's "Annie" records, said that the Midnighters' white audiences knew exactly what he was singing about and that "they loved those dirty records" (Pollack, *When Rock Was Young*, p. 109).
73 Robins' "Riot in Cell Block #9" was banned: "Riot in Cell Block #9" and "Wrap It Up" (Spark 103), released in the summer of 1954 (Cotten, *Shake, Rattle, and Roll*, p. 178).
73 Needing his "honey love": "Honey Love" and "Warm Your Heart" (Atlantic 1029), released in May 1954.
73 Banned all records with "suggestive" lyrics: Cotten, *Shake, Rattle, and Roll*, p. 194.
73 "Work with Me Annie" appeared on the best-selling pop charts: Whitburn, *Pop Memories*, p. 308. "Annie" first appeared on the chart on June 5, 1954, and remained there for twenty-three consecutive weeks, while peaking at #22.
73 Referred to . . . as a "nigger lover": Irwin, reprinted in Buzzell, p. 17.
73 The *Pittsburgh Courier* . . . "showcasing Negro talent": "Bryant Story—R&B Hassle Envelops Alan Freed," *BB*, October 9, 1954.
74 "A voluntary association to protect their property rights": Dachs, *Anything Goes*, p. 216.
74 In 1923 it was decided: A "blanket" licensing fee was instituted, whereby a radio station paid a designated portion of its gross time-sales revenue to ASCAP as a performance royalty.
74 But in 1937 ASCAP: Barnouw, *The Golden Web*, p. 110.

NOTES

75 ASCAP members were "panic-stricken": Passman, *The Deejays*, p. 180.
75 "Was probably the most vital factor": Interview by David Freed.
75 "Impending breakdown" . . . "on a level with dirty comic magazines": Shaw, *The Rockin' '50s*, p. 115.
75 "The most astonishing thing" . . . "marketing filth": *Variety*, March 9, 1955.
75 "All rhythm and blues records": *BB*, March 26, 1955.
76 To eliminate "flagrantly pornographic songs": Passman, *The Deejays*, p. 189.
76 "Any performance whatsoever" . . . "any sort of deal": "Split Copyrights: ASCAP Rule Confuses Publishing Fraternity," *BB*, April 23, 1955.
76 The antitrust suit brought against BMI: "Suit Vs. BMI Moves Ahead," *BB*, December 12, 1955.
76 At an uptown rally . . . outsider who imitated blacks: Shaw, *Honkers and Shouters*, p. 515.
76 "We just wanted the best talent": Passman, *The Deejays*, p. 202.
76 "'Tis said he [Freed] apes Negroes": Shaw, *The Rockin' '50s*, p. 108.
76 "Things got very heated" . . . "than Alan Freed could": Passman, *The Deejays*, p. 202.
76 The first black deejay to host a network radio music program: "Night Life," a CBS network summer series, featured a racially mixed cast, but the series was quickly dropped by CBS after the network's southern affiliates objected to its racial composition (MacDonald, *Don't Touch That Dial!*, p. 357).
76 "After-Hours Session" . . . on New York's WHOM: Shaw, *Honkers and Shouters*, p. 362.
77 Carroll "couldn't get arrested": Interview with Hooke.
77 "I have nothing against Freed": "Bryant Story—R&B Hassle Envelops Alan Freed," *BB*, October 9, 1954.
77 Syndicating Freed in up to sixty radio markets: "WINS Places Freed . . . ," *BB*, August 28, 1954.
77 Would "shove aside" black disc jockeys: "Bryant Story—R&B Hassle . . . ," *BB*, October 9, 1954.
77 "Alan just got bigger and bigger": Interview with Hooke.
77 "Alan had already touted us to them": Engel, "The Moonglows Sincerely," *Rock 'n' Roll Stars*, p. 54.
77 Freed and Harvey Fuqua were listed as cowriters: "Sincerely" (Chess 1581) was released the first week in November 1954. Later that month the Moonglows signed a personal-appearance contract with the New York–based Shaw Agency. "Sincerely" appeared on the R&B best-selling charts on December 12, 1954. It eventually reached the #2 position (Whitburn, *Top R&B Singles*, p. 297).
77 The McGuire Sisters . . . copied the song: The McGuire Sisters' version of "Sincerely" (Coral 61323) appeared on the pop charts on January 8, 1955, where it remained for twenty-one consecutive weeks, becoming a #1 best-seller (Whitburn, *Top Pop Singles*, p. 334).
77 Freed maintained the practice . . . was "anti-Negro": Irwin, reprinted in Buzzell, p. 66.
77 The practice of covering . . . not limited to pop covers of R&B material: Cotten, p. xxiv.
78 The cover stimulated sales of the original . . . "Only the artists suffered": Shaw, *The Rockin' '50s*, p. 129.
79 Freed played only the original R&B . . . music was "honest": Irwin, reprinted in Buzzell, p. 66.
79 "Note-for-note" copies of "Tweedle Dee" . . . "modern-day pirates" . . . "Thefting my music note for note": "There Ought to Be a Law: LaVern Baker Seeks Bill . . . ," *BB*, March 5, 1955.
79 "Oh, they can always excuse it" . . . "any of those others is poor": Millar, *The Drifters*, p. 51.
79 By the close of 1954 the practice had turned into an industry of its own: Cotten, *Shake, Rattle, and Roll*, p. xxv.
80 "Interest of fairness" . . . "completely ethical": "WINS Issues Ban on Copy Records," *BB*, August 27, 1955.
80 "Antiseptic, sterile-sounding" . . . "cover their records": Roeser "I'm Tired of Being Called a Rip-Off Artist!", *Sh-Boom*, March 1990, p. 25.
80 Wanting to do his "own thing": Alan Kozinn, "Moondog Returns from the Hippie Years," *NYT*, November 16, 1989.
81 "For a fast few days" . . . "like Jesus Christ": Interview with Hooke.
81 Played one of Hardin's records on the air: "Sightless Musician Sounds Off in Court," *NYT*, November 24, 1954.
81 Nearly incapacitated "sick old man": Interview with Warren Troob.
81 "Jungle sounds" . . . "buried his face in a handkerchief": "Sightless Musician . . . ," *NYT*, November 24, 1954.
81 "Very bright guy, a musicologist" . . . "You boys go out and settle it": Interview with Troob.
81 The judge also said . . . the two were in some way connected: "Freed Enjoined from Use of 'Moondog' Label," *BB*, December 4, 1954.
81 "Not only did he [Hardin] win": Interview with Hooke.
82 A "bad one" . . . "on with the show": Interview with Troob.
82 "I think I'm . . . "call the show!": Interview with Hooke. This scenario is certainly plausible, given that Freed had for some time referred to his show on the air as a "Moondog Rock 'n' Roll Party" ("Moon Dog House" audiotape, March 31, 1954).
82 While still in Cleveland . . . "with blues and rhythm records": "Moon Dog Rock 'n' Roll Party" audiotape, March 31, 1954.
82 "In order to cultivate a broader audience": Irwin, reprinted in Buzzell, p. 18.
82 "I agreed": Fields, "Only Human," *NYDM*, March 18, 1957. Until the day he died, Leo Mintz

- 82 maintained—as does his son, Stuart—that it was Mintz who came up with the "rock & roll" phrase.
- 82 Claimed he gave rock & roll its name: Buzzell, p. 76.
- 82 By 1960 the deejay incorrectly maintained: Album liner notes from "Alan Freed's Top 15" (End LP 315). Freed wrote, "It is impossible for me to present this album without thinking back to 1951 in Cleveland, where I named our music 'rock 'n' roll.' "
- 83 Trixie Smith . . . "Rock Me, Mama": Tosches, *Unsung Heroes of Rock 'n' Roll*, p. 5. "My Daddy Rocks Me" was subsequently recorded no less than five times during the 1920s.
- 83 "Connoted a new sensuality of rhythm": Tosches, *Unsung Heroes*, p. 5.
- 83 In 1945 Luther Johnson . . . "rock and roll the house down": Marshak, "The Birth of Rock 'n' Roll," *Rock*, July 6, 1970, p. 32.
- 83 By 1944 Capitol Records . . . "It Rocks, It Rolls": Tosches, *Unsung Heroes*, p. 6.
- 83 Wynonie Harris . . . in 1948: Whitburn, *Top R&B Singles*, p. 182. Also in 1948, Wild Bill Moore recorded "We're Gonna Rock, We're Gonna Roll" for Savoy Records.
- 83 "If it rocked, it sold": Tosches, *Unsung Heroes*, p. 6.
- 83 Little Son Jackson's "Rockin' and Rollin' ": Released in 1952 on Imperial Records.
- 84 Came to him . . . "colorful and dynamic": Buzzell, p. 76.
- 84 Appropriated the phrase from the rhythm and blues music he listened to: It hardly seems mere coincidence that in the Dominoes' recording of "Sixty-Minute Man," released early in 1951 (and a #1 R&B hit by the time Freed began his WJW "Moondog" program that year), the line "Gonna rock and roll you all night long" was repeated throughout the song.
- 84 "P.J. Moriarty's, a local saloon": Goldblatt, "Boys of Rock 'n' Roll: The Teenagers After 25 Years," *VV*, April 15–21, 1981, p. 69.
- 84 "Took her wig off" . . . Ubangi Club: Fredric Dannen, "The Godfather of Rock & Roll," *RS*, November 17, 1988, p. 92.
- 84 "Morris was a very aggressive young kid": Interview with Hooke.
- 85 "Everybody in the world's gotta pay?": Dannen, "The Godfather . . . ," *RS*, November 17, 1988, p. 92.
- 85 "Had a lot of talent": Dannen, "The Godfather . . . ," *RS*, November 17, 1988, p. 92.
- 85 A copyright on the phrase "rock & roll": Dannen, "The Godfather . . . ," *RS*, November 17, 1988, p. 92. Seig was a shortening of Sieglinde, the name of Freed's recently born second daughter. Seig Music was originally formed to promote Freed's "Rock 'n' Roll Jubilee Ball" at the St. Nicholas Arena in January 1955 (*BB*, February 19, 1955).
- 85 "Freed is now calling his program the 'Rock and Roll Show' ": "Freed Enjoined . . . ," *BB*, December 4, 1954.
- 85 "I'll take the risk": Interview with Hooke.
- 85 "Birdland executive" Morris Levy: "Freed Enjoined . . . ," *BB*, December 4, 1954.
- 85 There were other parties involved: The Gotham Freed Corporation consisted of Freed, Levy, Lew Platt, and WINS.
- 86 "Dear Fellow 'Rock 'n' Roller' ": This promotional letter was most likely printed early in December 1954; it could be the first printed mention of rock & roll as a specific type of music.
- 86 *Variety* . . . "rhythm and blues bash": "Alan Freed to Promote 'Rock & Roll Ball' in N.Y.," December 22, 1954.
- 86 *Billboard* . . . describe Freed as a "key r&b deejay": "Freed to Sponsor 'Rock & Roll' Ball," December 25, 1954.
- 86 "Pandemonium from 8 P.M. to 2 A.M.": Passman, *The Deejays*, p. 202.
- 86 Racial composition: Marion, "In the Beginning: A New Excitement," *Record Exchanger* no. 14, 1973, p. 16.
- 86 "Oh my God, this is crazy": Dannen, "The Godfather . . . ," *RS*, November 17, 1988, p. 92.
- 86 "America's #1 'Rock 'n' Roll' Disc Jockey": The full-page WINS radio advertisement was identified as a "thank you tribute . . . for the greatest advance sale in the history of American dance promotions . . . thousands turned away" (*BB*, January 29, 1955).
- 87 "The big beat in the pop music business . . . rock and roll disc jockey": Schoenfeld, "Teenagers Like 'Hot Rod' Tempo," *Variety*, January 19, 1955.
- 87 *Billboard* continued to classify Freed as a rhythm and blues deejay: "Talent Topics" column, *BB*, February 5, 1955.
- 87 Featured "only rhythm and blues talent": "Rock 'n' Roll: Freed Ball Takes 24G at St. Nick," *BB*, January 22, 1955.
- 87 Hello, everybody . . . 'Rock 'n' Roll Party Number One'!": "Rock 'n' Roll Party" audiotape, February 12, 1955.

Chapter 6 • The Big Beat

- 88 "The Big Beat has arrived": Alicia Evans, reprinted in Buzzell, p. 38.
- 88 WINS showed . . . profit for the first time: Bundy, "Alan Freed's 'Rock 'n' Roll' Show Opens," *BB*, April 16, 1955.

NOTES

88 *Billboard* and *Variety* . . . refer to Freed as a "rock and roll" disc jockey: "Freed Mum About Coral Negotiations," *BB*, March 12, 1955.
88 "Rock & roll" in their trade advertising: *BB*, March 12, 1955.
88 "Rocks 'n' Rolls with 2 Smash Hits": *BB*, March 12, 1955. Taken from a Mercury Recording Company trade advertisement, p. 47.
89 Red Prysock's . . . "Rock 'n' Roll" . . . Dinah Washington's "That's All I Want from You": Mercury 70540 and Mercury 70537, respectively.
89 Played by Freed: "Rock 'n' Roll Party" audiotape, February 12, 1955.
89 "It would have meant filing a thousand lawsuits": Levy, "The World of Soul," *BB*, Special Summer Issue, 1967. Levy claimed that royalties were actually collected from certain record companies (Capitol, for one) that used the "rock & roll" phrase on their album covers (Dannen, p. 92).
89 Morris Levy, with strong connections . . . "sell job" by Levy: Interview with Hooke.
90 Instead of leaving: Interview with Ray Reneri.
90 Saw both the movie and the stage show for 90 cents: The price of admission was raised to $1.75 at noon and to $2.00 for the prime evening shows.
90 "A superior tenor": Feather, *The New Edition of the Encyclopedia of Jazz*, p. 438.
90 "Much about . . . rhythm and blues and rock and roll": Dance, *The World of Swing*, p. 375.
91 "Lay out" . . . "I can't hear you!": Interview with Dressel.
91 "One of the best visual acts on the bill": Bundy, "Alan Freed's . . . ," *BB*, April 16, 1955.
91 Fontaine . . . just covered the rhythm and blues song "Rock Love": The original recording by Sonny Thompson and Lulu Reed appeared on King Records.
91 Freed hyped Fontaine's "Rock Love": "Rock 'n' Roll Party" audiotape, February 12, 1955.
92 "Coon-style, really raucous": Peter Smart, "Eddie Fontaine: The Shakin' Story," p. 18.
92 Levy . . . did production work for RCA: Dannen, "The Godfather of Rock & Roll," *RS*, November 17, 1988, p. 93.
92 "Unique deal" . . . "nurture new talent": "RCA Near on M. Levy Deal," *BB*, August 27, 1955.
92 "Pleased the kids . . . [but] seemed out of place": Bundy, "Alan Freed's . . . ," *BB*, April 16, 1955.
92 "In the predominantly r&b line-up": Bundy, "Alan Freed's . . . " *BB*, April 16, 1955. It was not easy to book a white rock & roll act in April 1955. Aside from R&B cover specialist Bill Haley, virtually no other white rock & rollers appeared on the best-selling record charts, and few, if any, white singers classified themselves as rock & rollers.
92 "Break up the steady stream of record talent": Bundy, "Alan Freed's . . . ," *BB*, April 16, 1955.
92 Box-office gross of $107,000: "Freed Breaks Record," *BB*, April 28, 1955.
92 "Dancing in the aisles": Buzzell, p. 65.
92 Freed described the Brooklyn crowds: Buzzell, p. 13.
92 Benny Goodman's . . . audiences: Bolstad, reprinted in Buzzell, p. 24.
93 "Well-behaved and appreciative" . . . "frequently exciting": Bundy, "Alan Freed's . . . ," *BB*, April 16, 1955.
93 "Began shoving a fireman": Theater manager Gene Pleshette, quoted by Buzzell, p. 13.
93 "Money rules": Interview with Hooke.
94 "A safe form of rebellion against authority": Freed, "Alan Freed Says, 'I Told You So . . . ,' " *DB*, September 19, 1956.
94 "One, two, three o'clock": Rock Around the Clock (Decca 29124) by Bill Haley and His Comets.
94 An energy never before experienced in movie theaters: Milt Gabler, Haley's record producer, explained that while early 1950s film musicals had their soundtracks "pinched" at the top and bottom of the sound spectrum so that the giant theater speakers would not irritate the ears of the customers, *The Blackboard Jungle*'s producers let the movie's soundtrack "go wide open" (Fox *In the Groove*, p. 92).
95 "Hollywood is to blame": Irwin, reprinted in Buzzell, p. 19.
95 "A potent force in breaking down racial barriers": A June 1955 edition of *Variety*, quoted by MacDonald, *Don't Touch That Dial!*, p. 369.
95 Blacks and whites would dance together: Szatmary, *Rockin' in Time*, p. 122.
95 As much to break down America's racial barriers: Ralph Bass, quoted by Lydon, *Boogie Lightning*, p. 92.
96 *Pittsburgh Courier* . . . "Command Performance": Buzzell, p. 13. Performers at the benefit included the Charms, the Penguins, Dinah Washington, and the Count Basie Combo.
96 Bristled . . . that he was a racial do-gooder: Buzzell, p. 66.
96 "This so-called 'madman'": Interview with Reneri.
96 "Obviously Negro music": *Heroes of Rock 'n' Roll* film documentary, 1979. The first quote is taken from a filmed speech by the executive secretary of the Alabama White Citizens Council in 1955 or 1956. The second quote is by the chairman of one of the chapters of the Alabama White Citizens Council.
97 "Like jungle tom-toms": Passman, *The Deejays*, p. 224.
97 Freed met "strong opposition" . . . "immoral": Interview with Hooke.
97 Freed was told not to put his show on: Interview with Dressel.
97 "Joint was jumping": "Hub Faithful Rock 'n' Roll," *BB*, June 4, 1955.

97	A disappointing $27,000: Expenses for the rental of the theater and talent totaled $15,000.
98	A disturbance . . . for which Fats Domino had been booked: "Fear of Rock-Roll Nixes Connecticut Date," *BB*, June 4, 1955.
98	In Washington, D.C., . . . at the National Guard Armory: *Time*, June 18, 1955.
98	"Was gettin' bricks throwed at his house": Bo Diddley, "Live at Five," WNBC-TV, April 1980.
98	"If a stage show is well-policed": *BB*, April 7, 1956.
99	"Everything from . . . a race singer to doing Mario Lanza": Shaw, *The Rockin' '50s*, p. 37.
99	"An outstanding rhythm and blues rendition": "It's Too Soon to Know" (Columbia 40427) was released in the spring of 1955. At the time, Columbia's advertising said of Bennett, "He Swings!! He Rocks!! He Goes!!"
99	"On a whim . . . after three or four beers": Interview with Hooke.
99	"Box-office insurance": Bundy, "Rock & Roll Supports 2 Big-Budget Shows," *BB*, January, 1956.
100	"Other associations [had] convinced Freed": Lew Platt letter to Jim Russell, February 26, 1956.
100	A "very nice man . . . not the New York type": Interview with Hooke.
100	"Deemed it advisable" . . . "and white people love him": Lew Platt letter, February 26, 1956.
101	"Who wants him!" . . . "something the people liked": Leroy Kirkland interview, "Music, Maestro, Please," *Big Town Review*, no. 2, p. 44.
101	"Wiped the doubt clear" . . . "in the big business": Chuck Berry, *The Autobiography*, p. 115.
101	"The cut looked worse than it was" . . . "about $200 for the week": Interview with Reneri.
102	Freed's week-long Labor Day stand . . . shattered his own box-office record: There is disagreement as to how much the show actually grossed. *Billboard* originally reported a take of "more than $154,000," with Freed's net reportedly $125,000 before he made the split with Levy and WINS ("Deejay Freed Has Himself a Busy Week," September 17, 1955). By the end of the year the box-office gross was being reported as $156,000 (Bundy, "Rock & Roll Supports . . . ," *BB*, January 7, 1956).
102	"With some artists working . . . for $200": Bundy, "Rock & Roll Supports . . . ," *BB*, January 7, 1956.
102	"Free ten-day home trial": "Rock 'n' Roll Party" audiotape, February 12, 1955.
102	"More than you ever dreamed it was worth": "Rock 'n' Roll Party" audiotape, February 12, 1955.
103	WINS bowed to the opposition: "Deejay Freed . . . ," *BB*, September 17, 1955.
103	"Year R&B took over the pop field": *BB*, November 12, 1955.
103	*Billboard* instituted . . . the "Top 100": The new chart first appeared in the November 12, 1955, edition.
103	Ed Sullivan's "Toast of the Town" variety show: Ackerman, "All Are Getting Hip," *BB*, February 4, 1956.
104	Freed's local popularity was validated: *BB*, December 17, 1955. Survey conducted by Teen Age Survey, Inc.
104	"Fast gaining stature": " 'Teen' Tune Is Freed's 15th," *BB*, January 14, 1956.
104	"Helped us independent record companies get established": "Chess, Marshall," on "The Old Rock and Roll Show," WPIX-FM, New York, November 24, 1979.
104	An alternative to outright cash: De Witt, *Chuck Berry*, p. 25.
105	His "proudest memories": "Alan Freed's Memory Lane" (End LP 314). On this record narrated by Freed, he states that he wrote "Sincerely" in 1951.
105	"Alan used to sit around": Interview with Hooke.
105	"A long time before we met Alan" . . . "A beautiful man": Interview with Lester.
105	"Businessman out for a buck" . . . "nothing else would happen": Interview with Griggs.
105	Berry had high hopes for . . . "Wee Wee Hours": Christgau, "Chuck Berry's Back from the Blues," *Creem*, February 1973, p. 45.
105	"Ida Red," a song Berry called "a joke": De Witt, *Chuck Berry*, p. 37.
105	One unlikely account of the incident: Gillett, *The Sound of the City*, p. 40.
106	Almost as unlikely . . . "discussed Chuck's talents": De Witt, *Chuck Berry*, p. 25.
106	Chess said he gave Freed a dub . . . "his biggest record ever": Lydon, *Rock Folk*, p. 10.
106	Berry maintained that because of his "rookiness": Fries, "Chuck Berry Interview," *GM*, November 1979, p. 7.
106	"Totally ignorant" of the intricacies: Berry, *The Autobiography*, p. 104.
106	"Had written the song with me": Fries, "Chuck Berry Interview," *GM*, November 1979, p. 7.
106	"Would get more attention": Lydon, *Rock Folk*, p. 10.
106	Two-hour airing one night on Freed's "Rock 'n' Roll Party": De Witt, *Chuck Berry*, p. 39.
106	"Maybellene" was also the first: Both the singing disc jockey Jim Lowe (on Dot) and country singer Marty Robbins (on Columbia) recorded versions of "Maybellene."
107	"The beat, man" . . . "he emphasized the beat": Interview with Miller.
107	The theater would not give Freed the deal he wanted: Interview with Hooke.
108	Freed's "Holiday Jubilee" . . . "at the Academy": Bundy, "Rock & Roll Supports . . . ," *BB*, January 7, 1956. It is unlikely that the movie *Dig That Uranium*, starring the Bowery Boys, increased Freed's box-office take.
108	"Has its share of jockeys who indulge": "Jocks Make Hay," *BB*, December 31, 1955.
108	BMI's December awards dinner: *BB*, December 10, 1955.

NOTES

CHAPTER 7 • THE BOYS

109 "The first time": Interview with Miller.
110 Tenth Avenue . . . came to be called . . . "and few Cadillacs": Rolontz, "Many Indie Disk Houses Struggle for Survival in Vital 14-Block Area," *BB*, September 5, 1953.
110 "There's a guy making noise": Interview with Hooke.
110 Ahmet Ertegun, the "playboy" son . . . "had an ear for the black sound": Grendysa, "Jubilee," *GM*, June 2, 1989, p. 18.
111 "Innovating and forcing": Grendysa, "Spotlight on LaVern Baker," *RCM*, November-December 1985, p. 1.
111 "Hard-headed, hard-working, and highly opinionated": Shaw, *The Rockin' '50s*. Nathan died in 1967, and King Records was sold to Fort Knox Music.
111 "Sell records to colored people" . . . "plunged into recording with a vengeance": Porter, *The Roots of Rock 'n' Roll* (Savoy SJL 2221) liner notes.
112 "I knew I had to sign her" . . . "induced": Bailin, "Herald-Ember (The Al Silver Story)," *BBB*, July 1972, p. 24.
112 Robinson . . . "worked closely" with Freed: Turco, "Bobby Robinson Interview," *REX*, May 1972, p. 6.
113 "I was up there" . . . "who can you bring to the Paramount?": Interview with Miller.
113 In 1948 Goldner . . . formed a record company: Newman, "The George Goldner Story," *BBB*, September 1972, p. 30.
114 "You really hurt my label" . . . "get my record on the air": Dannen, "The Godfather of Rock & Roll," *RS*, November 17, 1988, p. 93.
115 "One-man operation": Interview with Herbert Cox, July 3, 1979.
115 "Signed the groups": Galgano, "Cleftones Interview," *BBB*, August-September 1971, p. 4.
115 "Okay, fellas" . . . "what was happening there": Interview with Cox.
116 Shot to number six on *Billboard's* "Top 100": Whitburn, *Top Pop Singles*, p. 312.
116 "White stations wouldn't play our records" . . . "Guerilla tactics" . . . "all over the country": "Chess, Marshall," on "The Old Rock and Roll Show," November 24, 1979.
116 "You made me a millionaire": Interview with Hooke.
117 "Myopic, anemic, . . . high school dropout" . . . "wily old Syd": Grendysa, "King Records . . . ," *RCM*, November-December 1985, p. 5.
117 "Hey, man, . . . you just made me 400,000 bucks": Interview with Hooke.
117 "It sold ten thousand copies": Interview with Reneri.
117 "Beautiful person" . . . "Also made 'Life Is But a Dream' a hit for us": Jones, "The Harptones," *GM*, March 1983, p. 14.
118 "You couldn't find the [Bruce] label": Interview with Reneri.
118 Exemplified by a sequestered gathering: Cotten, *Shake, Rattle, and Roll*, p. 231.
118 "Would be restricted": "Alan Freed Deal with Coral Label Definitely Tabled," *BB*, May 7, 1955.
118 "Alan promised to make it up": Bailin, "Herald-Ember . . . ," *BBB*, July 1972, p. 25.
119 "Getting him to play our records" . . . "professional respect and courtesy you deserved": Interview with McGowan.
119 "Very bad sonofabitch to a lot of people" . . . "I'm giving the rights to you": Interview with Hooke.
120 "His [Freed's] thumbs-up": Rolontz, "Alan Freed—An Appreciation," *Music Business*, February 6, 1965, p. 22.
120 "Top Negro entertainers": *BB*, September 4, 1954.
120 Repackage . . . into twelve thirty-six minute shorts: Cotten, *Shake, Rattle, and Roll*, p. 218.
121 *Harlem Variety Revue* . . . released nationally in May: Cotten, *Shake, Rattle, and Roll*, p. 243.
121 "A small part" in Katzman's film . . . "up-front" cash guarantee: Whelton, "He Was the King of Rock and Roll," *NYT*, September 24, 1972.
121 "Would have done the picture for 2 cents": Interview with Hooke.
122 "Dummy, take a piece!": Whelton, "He was the King . . . ," *NYT*, September 24, 1972.
122 "Yessed the deal in a second": Interview with Hooke. Shooting of *Rock Around the Clock* began on January 7, 1956.
122 *Rock Around the Clock* achieved instant notoriety: *Time*, June 18, 1956, reprinted in Redd, *Rock Is Rhythm and Blues*, p. 54.
122 "Eisenhower-led plot": *NYT*, January 23, 1957, p. 24.
123 Somewhere in Liverpool . . . John Lennon had attended: Norman, *Shout!*, p. 33.
123 "Hooligans were hooligans": "37 Held After Riots in London," *NYT*, September 17, 1956.
123 "Fake folk music" . . . "nothing obscene": *NYT*, April 1, 1957.
123 "Could have bought Freed for $15,000": Whelton, "He was the King . . . ," *NYT*, September 24, 1972.
123 "Rather pleased" . . . "the way he did on screen": Interview with Troob.
124 "Ripe for rock and roll": *BB*, April 7, 1956.
124 "Riotously introduced rock and roll to England": Buzzell, p. 65.
124 "Became a propaganda weapon": Bolstad, reprinted in Buzzell, p. 23.

124 "First full-scale invasion": "What Would Victoria Say," *BB*, April 14, 1956.
124 "Most popular of the men in rock and roll": CBS Radio supervisor of network programs Harlan Dunning, quoted in "How Rock and Roll Started," 1956, unidentified source.
124 At the time, the networks were rebuked: Bundy, "Indie Station Balking at 'Farm Club' Role Re Deejays," *BB*, May 28, 1955.
125 "In the advantageous position": "CBS Plots Sun. Evening Rock, Roll Net Show," *BB*, January 28, 1956.
125 "Of particular interest" . . . "contrary to general belief": "CBS Plots . . . ," *BB*, January 28, 1956.
125 "Acknowledge . . . pop conventions": Giddens, *Riding on a Blue Note*, p. 91.
125 Put two hit records onto the pop charts: "Softly with Feeling" (Clef 89112) reached #29 in May 1954; "16 Men Swinging" (Clef 89147) reached #29 in October 1954 (Whitburn, *Pop Memories*, p. 47).
125 "One of our biggest fans": Murray, *Good Morning Blues*, p. 327.
126 "Birdland Stars of 1955" tour: "Talent Topics" column, *BB*, February 5, 1955.
126 Basie, who knew rock & roll "wasn't our thing" . . . "an almost empty house": Murray, *Good Morning Blues*, pp. 316, 318.
126 "Fit in any kind of way": Murray, *Good Morning Blues*, p. 317.
126 "Basie is a good friend": Giddens, *Riding on a Blue Note*, p. 92.
126 "First full-scale venture": "1st Full-Scale Straight R&B Pact by Coral," *BB*, February 25, 1956.
126 Thiele said . . . "only as an artist": "Freed's Post at Coral Clarified," *BB*, March 3, 1956.
127 "Dance sets for teenagers": "1st Full-Scale . . . ," *BB*, February 25, 1956.
127 "Additional r&b flavor": "Freed's Post . . . ," *BB*, March 3, 1956.
127 "Why don't we go into the studio": Interview with Hooke.
127 "Very difficult" . . . "how not to write so good" . . . "hired all the musicians and everything": "Music, Maestro, Please," *Big Town Review*, April-May 1972, p. 43.
128 "No big deal" financially: Interview with Hooke.
128 Coral termed a live "party" effect: "1st Full-Scale . . . ," *BB*, February 25, 1956.
128 "Hard-driving uninhibited performance" . . . "a stronger kick than six Moscow mules": Bundy, *Rock 'n' Roll Party—Vol. 1* (Coral CRL 57063) liner notes.
128 Indicative of the deejay's subsequent recordings: Refer to the Discography.
128 Propaganda of pressure groups": Ackerman, "Square Circles Peg Rock and Roll Idiom as a Beat to Stick," *BB*, February 4, 1956.
129 Prompted its city fathers . . . was nearly mobbed: *BB*, March 17, 1956.
129 In Birmingham: *Time*, June 18, 1956, reprinted in Redd, *Rock Is Rhythm and Blues*, p. 54.
129 "Roughhouse riots": *BB*, March 24, 1956.
129 "Attending the rites of some obscure tribe" . . . "what a motorcycle club at full throttle does": Quoted by Szatmary, *Rockin' in Time*, p. 23.
129 "Musical junk" . . . "a mere perversion of rhythm and blues, . . . too many" . . . "Were failing to live up to the importance of their jobs": Bolstad, reprinted in Buzzell, p. 23.
129 "While the r.&b. craze is still at its peak": "R&B Disk Jockeys to Form Own Org.," *BB*, February 4, 1956.
129 "Corrupting influences of rock and roll": *BB*, March 24, 1956.
130 "Public safety was endangered" . . . "outlandish things": Psychiatrist Dr. Francis J. Braceland of Hartford's Institute of Living, quoted by *BB*, April 7, 1956.
130 Who saw integration . . . as being fostered by . . . rock and roll: Szatmary, *Rockin' in Time*, p. 22.
130 "Appeals to the base in man": *Newsweek*, April 23, 1956, quoted by London, *Closing the Circle*, p. 24.
130 "Basic, heavy beat . . . of the Negroes": Quoted by Szatmary, *Rockin' in Time*, p. 22.
130 "A plot to mongrolize America": *Newsweek*, April 23, 1956, quoted by London, *Closing the Circle*, p. 24.
130 "Where the KKK didn't want us performing": Bo Diddley to interviewer Lou Cohen, quoted by Szatmary, *Rockin' in Time*, p. 23.
130 "Jam sessions . . . along the primrose path to hell": Szatmary, *Rockin' in Time*, p. 23.
130 "Smells of discrimination of the worst kind": *Look*, June 26, 1956, quoted by Redd, *Rock Is Rhythm and Blues*, p. 48.
131 "Appeals to morons of all ages": Bolstad, reprinted in Buzzell, p. 23.
131 Labeled it "completely biased . . . conspiracy": *BB*, April 7, 1956.
131 "Fumed, fretted, legislated, and pontificated": London, *Closing the Circle*, p. 50.
131 Paul Whiteman . . . "crazier" . . . "Run an engine or bust a boiler" . . . "the 'Rock and Roll Waltz' ": Bolstad, reprinted in Buzzell, pp. 23–24.
131 Restless "natives" . . . "heavy on groups": "Freed's R&R Run pus Stops Traffic at Brooklyn Par," *BB*, April 16, 1956.
132 "The show would just stretch out": Interview with Dressel.
132 "Couldn't put them on the show unless": Little Walter and Vance, "Richard Barrett Remembers," February-March 1972, *BBB*, p. 31.
132 "On our way" . . . "really on cloud nine": "Unbelievable . . . we owed them money": Ifill, "The Royaltones," *Yesterday's Memories*, 1975, p. 26.
132 "You want royalty?": Eliot, *Rockanomics*, p. 48.

NOTES

132 "A strong connection": Interview with Hooke.
133 "Whether we were on third or eighth": Interview with Cox.
133 "He had no concept of time": Interview with Reneri.
133 The Platters . . . with three successive chart smashes: "Only You [and You Alone]" (Mercury 70633) reached #5 on *Billboard's* "Top 100"; "The Great Pretender (Mercury 70753) reached #1; "[You've Got] The Magic Touch (Mercury 70819) reached #4 (Whitburn, *Top Pop Singles*, p. 392).
133 The Teenagers . . . first two releases: "Why Do Fools Fall in Love" (Gee 1002) reached #7 on *Billboard's* "Top 100"; "I Want You to Be My Girl" (Gee 1012) reached #17 (Whitburn, *Top Pop Singles*, p. 312).
133 "As long as the rock and roll beat was there": "Freed's R&R . . . ," *BB*, April 16, 1956.
133 Jackie . . . took a bow: Evans, reprinted in Buzzell, p. 40.
133 Playing the record "regularly" . . . "Man, what does this mean?": Interview with Cox.
134 "Wasn't too friendly" . . . "a thrill to do his [Freed's] show": Interview with Cox.
134 "Frantic rock 'n' roll rumpus": "Freed's R&R . . . ," *BB*, April 16, 1956.
134 First grossed $125,000, then $155,000: Bundy, "Deejay Emerges as a Powerhouse Promoter of R&B Personals," *BB*, February 4, 1956.
134 And now $240,000: "Freed's R&R . . . ," *BB*, April 16, 1956. The $240,000 figure was "estimated" by the Paramount management.
134 "That's all you can get into the place with a shoe horn": Buzzell, p. 65.
135 "Pretty much" . . . "and it wasn't always friendly": Interview with Cox.
135 Freed felt he would be promoting his competition: Interview with McGowan.
135 "We [the Cleftones] were personally" . . . "They felt we owed them something": Interview with Cox.
135 More than two thousand fan clubs: Evans, reprinted in Buzzell, p. 40.
135 "Primary target" . . . he was "allowed" to state his case: Bundy, "Freed Replies to R&R Press Slurs," *BB*, April 28, 1956.
136 "Symptomatic of something wrong" . . . "makes a virtue out of monotony": Bundy, "Freed Replies . . . ," *BB*, April 28, 1956.
136 "As long as there are radio stations": Bundy, "Freed Replies . . . ," *BB*, April 28, 1956.
136 In May . . . Bob Smith left to join his ex-boss: "Smith Leaves for WOR," *BB*, May 26, 1956.
137 A half-century old, sixteen-room stucco mansion: Buzzell, p. 65.
137 "Falling apart" . . . "had to rebuild the house": Interview with Hooke.
137 Freed planned to install remote broadcasting facilities: "Freed Eyes London for Fall R&B Show," *BB*, July 14, 1956.
137 "Looked like a stately mansion" . . . "Bullshit! Wait'll you see this": Interview with Dressel.
137 "That's what we got to show . . . two mortgages": Buzzell, p. 65.
137 Mortgages . . . held by Jerry Blaine and . . . Morris Levy: Wilson and Carr, "Record Man Says He Gave Freed $11,000 Interest-Free Loan in '56," *NYP*, December 3, 1959.

CHAPTER 8 • DON'T KNOCK THE ROCK

138 "I think Elvis Presley is": Irwin, reprinted in Buzzell, p. 19.
138 "Striking parallel" . . . "tremendous headway" . . . "Rock and roll country-style artists" . . . "back shack" sound: "Diskeries Race for R&R Country Talent," *BB*, May 12, 1956.
138 "Hillbilly boogie, when it was called anything at all": Tosches, *Unsung Heroes of Rock 'n' Roll*, p. 5.
139 Presley's "Heartbreak Hotel" and Carl Perkins's "Blue Suede Shoes": "Heartbreak Hotel" reached #1 pop, #1 country, and #6 R&B on *BB*'s charts; "Blue Suede Shoes" reached #3, #2, and #3, respectively, on the same charts ("Pop and R&B Charts Spot Same 8 Disks," *BB*, May 12, 1956).
139 "Felt it necessary to go with listeners' preferences" . . . "Everywhere the search is on for another Elvis Presley": "Pop and R&B . . . ," *BB*, May 12, 1956.
139 "Young hillbilly singer": Castleman and Podrazik, *Watching TV*, p. 106.
140 "Too much unfavorable mail": Bream, "Elvis on TV," *GM*, January 29, 1988, p. 14.
140 "Finally beginning to have programming 'eyes' for rock and roll and rhythm and blues": "Nets Find R&R No Butt for Jokes," *BB*, April 28, 1956.
140 If Freed's one-shot appearance "clicked": "Nets Find . . . ," *BB*, April 28, 1956.
140 "America's new singing sensation": Bream "Elvis on TV," *GM*, January 29, 1988, p. 16.
140 "Phenom from Mississippi": "2D Jackpot for Presley," *BB*, May 26, 1956.
140 On Berle's June 5 television show: "2BB Crowns for Presley on Berle's TV," *BB*, June 2, 1956.
140 "Rock and roll sensation": "Elvis Presley Pacted for Day by Tupelo Fair," *BB*, June 2, 1956.
141 "Rock and roll variation" . . . "abdominal gyrations" . . . "Present-day craze" . . . "grunt and groin": "Presley on Pan But Cash Keeps Rolling," *BB*, June 14, 1956.
141 "Where do you go": Gillett, *The Sound of the City*, p. 17.
141 Berle to top: "Presley on Pan . . . ," *BB*, June 14, 1956.
141 Presley sold 75,000 records a day: Eliot, *Rockonomics*, p. 63.
141 1,350,000 in sales: "E.P. Is V.I.P. for Victor," *BB*, May 12, 1956.

141 "Emerged a winner" . . . "next" Presley: "Pop and R&B Charts . . . ," *BB*, May 12, 1956.
142 "Rockabilly" . . . first appeared in *Billboard* in August 1956: "Bruce Debs New Label," *BB*, August 25, 1956.
142 "Painfully subdued" . . . Presley "rolled not—nor did he rock": "You Can't Do That to Elvis," *BB*, July 14, 1956.
142 Presley's first Sullivan appearance took place on September 9: Erroneous reports to the contrary, it was during Presley's third and final "Toast of the Town" appearance, January 6, 1957, that Sullivan ordered the TV cameras to show the controversial singer from the waist up only. That "waist-up" TV appearance has become Presley's most remembered.
142 "The big fight [over rock & roll]": Alan Freed, from a letter to his fans, published as "The Story of Rock 'n' Roll" in his "Easter Jubilee of Stars" program book, 1956.
142 "A real live sex idol": Redd, *Rock Is Rhythm and Blues*, p. 70.
143 Claiming rock and roll as its own: Redd, *Rock Is Rhythm and Blues*, p. 70.
143 "Really sings hill-billy, or country-and-western style": Irwin, reprinted in Buzzell, p. 19.
143 "Greeted with distaste" . . . "by no means on the skids as yet": "No Skids for R&B or R&R," *BB*, July 14, 1956.
143 Jimmy Cavello . . . instrumental in signing: "Freed Recommends Two for Coral Pacts," *BB*, August 25, 1956.
144 "A most important release" . . . "roundly scolded the unruly youngsters": Buzzell, pp. 32, 34.
144 "Bunnies" ("my word for delinquents"): Fields, "Only Human," *NYDM*, March 18, 1957.
144 "Just outrageous": Buzzell, p. 32.
144 "Know in order to get" . . . drew over 140,000 patrons: Buzzell, pp. 30, 32.
144 Box-office gross of nearly $221,000: Buzzell, p. 65.
144 Freed would be in competition with himself: *BB*, July 14, 1956.
145 "The station didn't want it" . . . "don't do this, don't do that": Interview with Reneri.
145 A thousand letters and telegrams requesting certain records: Sklar, reprinted in Buzzell, p. 69.
145 "To dominate and control" . . . "Massive and expensive propaganda campaign" . . . "cretinous goons": Sanjek, "The War on Rock," *DB*, pp. 18, 58.
146 " 'Payola' and the Product 'Plug' ": Memo from Carl Watson to Stockton Helfrich, July 14, 1955, quoted in " 'Payola'—An Inside Story Told Four Years Ago," *U.S. News & World Report*, December 21, 1959, pp. 81, 82.
146 "A danger that an exposé": "House Unit Spurs Payola Inquiry," *NYT*, November 19, 1959.
146 "Has its place" . . . "in good taste" . . . "Quite convinced" . . . "name-calling and rock-knocking": Sanjek, "The War on Rock," *DB*, p. 19. Sanjek says that the Songwriters of America proceeded to book Celler "on every talk program available, like the writer of the newest best-selling novel.
146 "The greatest song in the world": Dachs, *Anything Goes*, p. 124.
147 "All phases of the music field": Sanjek, "The War on Rock," *DB*, p. 19.
147 "Strong mail response" . . . "Blue-printed" an extensive . . . tour:"Freed Eyes London for Fall R&B Show," *BB*, July 14, 1956.
147 A leading role in its rock & roll sequel: "Joyce Pacts Haley to 2d Columbia Pic," *BB*, September 16, 1956.
147 Hi-Fi . . . to *Rhythm and Blues*: "Title Change for Haley Pic," *BB*, September 22, 1956.
148 "Is for morons" . . . "a quote from the Middle Ages!": Dialogue from *Don't Knock the Rock*, produced by Sam Katzman, directed by Fred F. Sears, Columbia Pictures, 1956.
149 "Just a couple of cameras and you": Jones, "Nate Nelson Interview," *GM*, March 1978, p. 12.
149 "Amidst considerable hoopla": Kramer, "Rhythm and Blues Notes," *BB*, December 15, 1956.
149 "Should be rolling in the long-green": Bundy, "Freed's New Movie Adds Up to Triple-Threat $s," *BB*, November 17, 1956.
149 "Rhythm and Blues Week," beginning on December 7: *BB*, December 15, 1956.
150 "Somehow, some way" . . . "fifteen cigarettes a minute": "Moondog Coronation Ball—30th Anniversary" audiotape, March 21, 1982.
151 "Gave us a balling out": "Moondog . . . 30th Anniversary" audiotape, March 21, 1982.
151 The $180,000 taken in during Freed's "Christmas Jubilee": Asbury, "Rock 'n' Roll Teen-Agers Tie Up Times Square Area," *NYT*, February 23, 1957.
151 Doubled the $100,000 "neighborhood" figure: Buzzell, p. 65.
152 "Didn't know nothing": Dannen, "The Godfather of Rock and Roll," *RS*, November 17, 1988, p. 92.
152 Freed allegedly expected to receive up to a 50 percent share of Roulette: "Freed, Levy Come to Parting of the Ways," *BB*, March 30, 1957.

Chapter 9 • The King Is Crowned

153 "As soon as the name": Buzzell, p. 61.
153 Levy had made public his desire to gain control of Roost: In 1955 Levy was "reported buying into Roost Records" ("RCA Near on M. Levy Deal," *BB*, August 27, 1955; "Levy Again Wants in on Roost Label," *BB*, March 3, 1956).

NOTES

153 "That was my thing": Interview with Hooke.
154 Hooke released both songs on one record: Royal Roost 624.
154 Follow-up to "Priscilla": "Driftwood" and "A Spark Met a Flame" (Royal Roost 626).
154 Winley then released the song on his own Winley label: "You" and "Must Be Falling in Love" (Winley 212).
154 Lacked the "power". . . "your record was played": Turco, "Little Anthony Interview," *REX*, 1973, p. 5.
154 "It probably sold about twelve copies": Pollack, *When Rock Was Young*, p. 175.
154 "Great" . . . "at the Paramount": Interview with Hooke.
156 "The vigor with which": Crowther, *The Girl Can't Help It* review, *NYT*, February 9, 1957.
156 "He should keep his ass inside the theater" . . . "We almost got killed": Interview with Dressel.
157 "Fell back from the barriers" . . . "that's their problem": Asbury "Rock 'n' Roll Teen-Agers Tie Up Times Square Area," *NYT*, February 23, 1957.
157 "Used to belong to Elvis": Asbury, "Rock 'n' Roll . . . ," *NYT*, February 23, 1957.
157 "I love being mobbed by kids": Irwin, reprinted in Buzzell, p. 17.
157 "The ol' king of rock 'n' roll": Greenfield, "But Papa, It's My Music, I Like It," *NYT*, March 7, 1971.
157 "Seven-shows-a-day bit" . . . "All you had to do was go up on stage": Gart "Ruth Brown Interview," *BBB*, 1973, p. 15.
158 "Quite often worked you to death" . . . "loan" their bassman: Interview with Cox.
158 "The ceiling, the walls, the floors": "Moondog . . . 30th Anniversary" audiotape, March 21, 1982.
158 "Precautionary measure" . . . "but not such a large one": Asbury, "Rock 'n' Roll . . . ," *NYT*, February 23, 1957.
158 "I'm pinning my hopes": Asbury, "Times Sq. 'Rocks' for Second Day," *NYT*, February 24, 1957.
158 "Swing with a modern name" . . . "somewhat of a gamble": Asbury, "Rock 'n' Roll . . . ," *NYT*, February 23, 1957.
159 ROCK 'N' ROLL TEEN-AGERS TIE UP THE TIMES SQUARE AREA: Asbury, *NYT*, February 23, 1957.
159 "Terrible little film" . . . "if it is still standing": Thompson, "Frenzy 'n' Furor Featured at Paramount," *NYT*, February 23, 1957.
159 "Increasing sales for many segments of American business": Hammer, "Fad Also Rocks Cash Registers," *NYT*, February 23, 1957.
159 "Medieval type of spontaneous lunacy" . . . "decline and passivity": Bracker, "Experts Propose Study of 'Craze,' " *NYT*, February 23, 1957.
160 "Nonsense" . . . "keeps them from delinquency": Fields, Only Human," March 18, 1957.
160 "Sway precariously" . . . "just about every continent": "Rock 'n' Roll Exported to 4 Corners of Globe," *NYT*, February 23, 1957.
160 "Freed, Levy Come to Parting of the Ways": "Freed, Levy . . . ," *BB*, March 30, 1957.
160 "The contract actually called for a much smaller percentage": "Freed, Levy . . . ," *BB*, March 30, 1957.
160 "I can no longer limit myself": Buzzell, p. 65.
161 "Never trusted anyone": Eliot, *Rockonomics*, p. 50.
161 "A condition he was increasingly in": Chuck Berry, *Autobiography*, p. 188.
161 "Presumably to make him easier to manipulate": Eliot, p. 50.
161 "Inability to carry out his [business] obligations": Chuck Berry, *Autobiography*, p. 188.
161 "You know how junior partners are": Goldblatt, "Lewis Lymon Interview," *GM*, January 1983, p. 24.
161 Goldner sold his share . . . for a reported $250,000: *BB*, April 6, 1957.
161 Formation . . . of Figure Music Publishing: *BB*, April 13, 1957.
161 "Wasn't doing well" . . . "we'll split it, fifty-fifty": Interview with Hooke.
161 With Hooke owning a 55 percent controlling interest: House of Representatives, Special Subcommittee on Legislative Oversight of the Committee on Interstate Commerce, Alan Freed testimony, April 25, 1960, p. 40. (Hereafter cited simply as House subcommittee hearings.)
162 Blacks and whites reportedly clashed: Richard, "Banned in Boston," *GM*, October 1979, p. 125.
162 "Tame caper of gangsters and counterfeit money, set in Havana": Maltin, *TV Movies 1985–86*, p. 69.
162 "Into the living room . . . healthy, normal music": Carlyle and Wood, *TV Personalities Biographical Sketchbook*, Vol. 4. p. 83.
163 "Paid so well" . . . "temptation": *BB*, May 20, 1957.
163 *Billboard* reported . . . that the two had reassociated: "Freed-Levy Back Together Again," *BB*, May 27, 1957.
163 "So short you got to get it from all angles": Buzzell, p. 65.
163 "Stopped talking to Freed" . . . "argument for a few months": Dannen, "The Godfather of Rock & Roll," *RS*, November 17, 1988, p. 92.
163 An extended Alan Freed television series: "Freed-Levy . . . ," *BB*, May 27, 1957.
163 "Assigned" the original mortgage: Wilson and Carr, "Record Man Says He Gave Freed $11,000 Interest-Free Loan in '56," *NYP*, December 3, 1959.
164 "Actively engage" in Levy's other interests: "Freed-Levy . . . ," *BB*, May 27, 1957.
164 A thirteen-week series . . . "Alan Freed's Big Beat": "Rock & Roll Summer on TV," *BB*, June 27, 1957.
164 George Goldner . . . "shocked": "Freed-Levy . . . ,"

164 "Improving production techniques": Gillett, *The Sound of the City*, p. 90.
165 "In hopes" that the songs would receive airplay . . . Joe Niagara . . . Tom Clay "approximately" $100 a month: House subcommittee hearings, Goldner testimony, April 27, 1960, p1096 1099, 1101.
165 Treated "beautifully" . . . "this is super!": Interview with Alana Freed.
165 "I want to bring the kids here": Interview with Hooke.
165 Her husband "wanted out" . . . She and Jackie "became very good friends": Interview with Greene.
165 "There was such an age difference": Interview with Alana Freed.
166 Freed's "true love" . . . "Tommy Greene had a job": Interview with Hooke.
166 "Black Vincent Price": Newman, "Screamin' Jay Hawkins," *BBB*, September 1972, p. 35.
166 "Don't tell me what to do!": Interview with William Miller.
166 "I have just the thing for you": Newman, "Screamin' Jay Hawkins," *BBB*, September 1972, p. 35.
166 "Go on and do it": Interview with Miller.
166 "Are you sure?" . . . "Yes" . . . "Was in the coffin and loving it": Newman, "Screamin' Jay Hawkins," *BBB*, September 1972, p. 35.
167 ROCK 'N' ROLLERS COLLECT CALMLY: *NYT*, July 4, 1957.
167 "Rock and roll may be dead": *BB*, July 22, 1957.
167 "Stronger than ever" . . . "ballads and sweet music": *BB*, July 15, 1957.
167 "Host and conductor for a new series": *TV Guide*, July 12, 1957, p. A79.
168 "More ambitious plans" . . . "healthy sign for the music with a beat": "On the Beat," *BB*, July 29, 1957.
168 "Alan's show closed" . . . "the flak was unbelievable": Interview with Hooke.
168 "But only if they had all ofay [white] acts": "Music, Maestro, Please," *Big Town Review*, April-May 1972, p. 43.
168 "Continues rating kudos": *BB*, August 5, 1957.
168 "Rough, unpolished manner" . . . "somewhat threatening": Castleman and Podrazik, *Watching TV*, p. 121.
170 "Bandstand" soon drew as much as 60 percent: Fong-Torres, "Dick Clark," *RS*, August 16, 1973, p. 18.
170 "There were no skeletons in his split-level closet": Richard Goldstein, quoted in Hopkins, *The Rock Story*, p. 39.
170 "Necessary stabilizing control and guidance": Castleman and Podrazik, *Watching TV*, p. 121.
170 "Gruff, a street man": Eliot, *Rockonomics*, p. 87.
170 "Technical shambles" . . . "mild success": *BB*, August 12, 1957.
170 Clark . . . nothing more than an "imitator": Interview with Hooke.
171 "A couple of U.S. acts": "Busy Jockey," *BB*, August 19, 1957.
171 "He did entertain a lot": Interview with Alana Freed.
171 "Sort of a home for the down-and-out" . . . "Drinking Scotch": Interview with David Freed.
171 "Many top r&b tradesters" . . . "radio, TV and film personalities": *BB*, September 2, 1957.
172 "Well, pay them thirty-two": "Music, Maestro, Please," *Big Town Review*, April-May 1972, p. 43.
172 "Involuntary dunking": *BB*, September 2, 1957.
172 "Wasn't playing enough Atlantic records": Eliot, *Rockonomics*, p. 81. This story was related to Eliot by Lance Freed, who said that he heard it from Morris Levy.
172 "Who had never been on a boat" . . . "take me back to the dock!" . . . "Hooke, the boat is yours!": Interview with Hooke.
173 "A wife and a mother": Interview with Greene.
173 "Did a beautiful job": Interview with Alana Freed.
173 "Alan, Jackie and all the little Freeds": "Rock 'n' Roll Party" audiotape, February 12, 1955.
173 "The Three Musketeers" . . . "One of them has to go!": Interview with Hawkins.
173 "Wanted to be a mother" . . . "was not for her": Interview with Alana Freed.
174 "Main reason" . . . "Alan Freed beckoned!" . . . "Always hated" . . . "I loved him very much": Pollack, *When Rock Was Young*, pp. 94–95.
174 "Hottest acts on the bill" . . . "breaking it up": "Alan Freed 'Breaking It Up' at Brooklyn Paramount," *BB*, September 9, 1957.
175 "90 percent sure" . . . "new, important international phase" . . . "Underscores the highest interest": *BB*, September 16, 1957.
175 "Diminutive and wiry" Mel Leeds . . . "show-biz flair": Sklar, *Rocking America*, p. 26.
176 "For music, news, time, and the weather" . . . By October WINS was . . . share leader: Sklar, *Rocking America*, pp. 27, 28.
176 "Will find this a wonderful picture": Buzzell, p. 59.
176 "Latest quickie film" . . . "where do we go from here?": Nason, *Mister Rock and Roll* movie review, *NYT*, October 17, 1957.
177 "Had a knack for bringing together": Blair, "Early Rock Cinema," *GM*, September 1979, p. 12A.
177 "Atomic Alan Freed": *BB*, November 11, 1957.
178 "Very, very well" . . . "working for money" . . . "The music was picked for me": Whelton, "He Was the King of Rock and Roll," *NYT*, September 24, 1972.
178 Freed's "90 percent sure" English tour: *BB*, November 11, 1957.

NOTES

178 "Tension in the air" . . . Domino's contract stated that he close the show: De Witt, pp. 59, 60.
179 "Shrieking, pushing, stamping teens" . . . "20,000 Rock 'n' Rollers Queue for Block in Midtown to Crowd Into Holiday Show": "20,000 Rock 'n' Rollers . . . ," *NYT*, December 28, 1957.
179 "Traditional occurrence" . . . "Everybody got drenched!": Interview with Hooke.
180 His 1957 take-home earnings: Goldberg, "Alan Freed Story," *Rock*, July 20, 1970.

CHAPTER 10 • BANNED IN BOSTON

181 "When kids stand on seats": Irwin, reprinted in Buzzell, p. 19.
181 "All any musical trend needs" . . . "there was no stopping": From the program booklet for Freed's 1958 Christmas show.
181 "Youth revolution" . . . "interesting popular music": Buzzell, p. 62.
182 While no white rock & roll vocal groups appeared on *Billboard*'s national "Top 100" in 1956: A distinction has been made here between rock & roll groups and pop-oriented groups such as the Rover Boys, the Four Coins, and the Four Lads and between cover groups such as the Diamonds and the Crew Cuts. All of these groups did appear on the "Top 100" chart in 1956, but not as rock & roll acts.
182 "For a long time to come": Grevatt, "On the Beat," *BB*, February 24, 1958.
182 "Felt sorry" . . . "didn't like him at all": "Music, Maestro, Please," *Big Town Review*, April-May 1972, p. 44.
183 "Knew the times were changing" . . . "teenage thing": Interview with Reneri.
183 Was not capable of relating on more than a limited basis to those black artists: "Got Live If You Want It," *Rock*, January 5, 1970, p. 22.
183 " 'Sweet Little Sixteen' rocking on 'Bandstand' ": "Sweet Little Sixteen" (Chess 1683), reached #2 on *BB*'s "Top 100" (Whitburn, *Top Pop Singles*, p. 47).
183 "First and foremost as a special business enterprise" . . . "safer, more accessible surroundings": Castleman and Podrazik, *Watching TV*, p. 121.
184 "Good singers and good songs": Hopkins, *The Rock Story*, p. 44.
184 "I don't want to limit myself": Grevatt, "On the Beat," *BB*, February 24, 1958.
184 "Very strong rivalry" . . . "get together in some way": Interview with Hooke.
184 "Saw nothing from Power" . . . "at a very early age": Eliot, *Rockonomics*, p. 122.
184 "Why the people gave him half" . . . "for Mr. Clark to play": House subcommittee hearings, Alan Freed testimony, p. 40.
184 "Short Shorts" reached number three: Whitburn, *Top Pop Singles*, p. 435.
185 "Represented the future" . . . "remained tethered to its inglorious past": Eliot, *Rockonomics*, p. 88.
185 Lowe said Clark agreed . . . a "friend" . . . "Because things worked out pretty good": House subcommittee hearings, Bernard Lowe testimony, p. 1117.
185 No "arrangement" concerning "Butterfly" . . . "said it was unnecessary": "Royola," *Time*, May 9, 1960, p. 30.
185 Made payable to Margaret Mallory: House subcommittee hearings, Lowe testimony p. 1117.
185 Clark had formed the Click Corporation in March: House subcommittee hearings, Harry Chipetz testimony, p. 1153.
186 Lowe assigned 50 percent of the song's performance rights to Clark: House subcommittee hearings, Lowe testimony, p. 1126.
186 Number thirty-six on *Billboard*'s "Top 100" by the fall: Cameo 116, Whitburn, *Top Pop Singles*, p. 429.
186 "At the Hop" assigned to Clark . . . "wouldn't be a hit" without him: House subcommittee hearings, Clark testimony, p. 1178.
186 Formed Swan Records: House subcommittee hearings, Clark testimony, p. 1173.
186 "To try to get as many artists" . . . "made out checks to Click Corporation": House subcommittee hearings, Chipetz testimony, p. 1154.
187 Fifteen hundred disappointed ride-seekers had to be turned away: *BB*, January 20, 1958.
187 "Higher and higher" . . . "and how are you?" Passman, *The Deejays*, p. 224.
188 "Closely resembled Freed's 'The Big Beat' ": Castleman and Podrazik, *Watching TV*, p. 121.
188 "Sizzling for months": *BB*, February 3, 1958.
188 Competition among "key jocks": "Competition Hits All-Time High in DJ Field," *BB*, February 10, 1958.
188 Publishing rights to several "hot tunes": *BB*, February 3, 1958.
188 "Started taking songs [to record] George Goldner": Interview with Hooke.
188 Assigned the publishing rights to "three or four" of his songs: House subcommittee hearings, Goldner testimony, p. 1101.
188 "Or any phase of the record business" . . . "great job for the business": Grevatt, "On the Beat," *BB*, February 24, 1958.
189 "Financial difficulties" . . . "could forget about repayment": FBI Memorandum, May 20, 1960.
189 Demise of "creative programming" . . . "eight-to-fourteen-year-olds": Eliot, *Rockonomics*, p. 67.
189 "It sounded like sour grapes": *BB*, March 8, 1958.

189 "Let's face it, rock and roll is bigger than all of us": Shaw, *The Rockin' '50s*, p. 222.
189 "Just because they reach eighteen" . . . "saturated with rock and roll": Grevatt, "On the Beat," *BB*, February 24, 1958.
190 "Pickin' on the Wrong Chicken" by the Five Stars: (Hunt 318), released in April 1958. The Five Stars were a white group from Philadelphia.
190 "Down the Aisle of Love" by the Quin-Tones: (Hunt 321). The song appeared on *BB*'s "Hot 100" on August 18, 1958, and eventually reached #20 (Whitburn, *Top Pop Singles*, p. 407).
191 Planned to spend $35,000 a week for talent: *BB*, February 24, 1958.
191 "Put our acts on the bus": Interview with Hooke.
191 "Smashing $17,000": *BB*, April 14, 1958.
192 Touring "Big Beat" had taken in $150,000: *BB*, April 14, 1958.
192 "Pulled from the road": *BB*, April 28, 1958.
192 "Open and vulnerable target": Pollack, *When Rock Was Young*, p. 96.
192 Freed "hated" Boston: Interview with Reneri.
192 "Began pushing the kids back" . . . "rednecked old men": Interview with Reneri.
192 Brawlers were quickly "hustled" out: *BB*, April 21, 1958.
193 "5,000 hip kids": *Time*, "Rock 'n' Riot," May 19, 1958, p. 50.
193 "The worst section in Boston": Interview with Hooke.
193 "Perhaps 60 percent white" . . . "As Jo Ann rocked off stage" . . . "tension began to mount": Moonoogian, "Wax Fax," *RCM*, February-March 1985, p. 10.
194 "Several times" . . . "to quiet everybody down": Pollack, *When Rock Was Young*, p. 96.
194 Boston police "were all around us" . . . "Happened in every other place" . . . "in this town!": Interview with Hooke.
195 "This show is not going on" . . . "Alright, kids," . . . "a show with bright lights on!" Interview with Hooke.
195 "We don't like your kind" . . . "serious-faced" Freed: *Time*, "Rock 'n' Riot," April 19, 1958, p. 50.
195 "The big statement": Interview with Hooke.
196 "It looks like the Boston police don't want": Richard, "Banned in Boston," *GM*, October 1979.
196 "We'd like to get the lights out . . . they're not letting us": FBI Report, December 2, 1959, p. 2.
196 "They won't put out the lights": Moonoogian, "Wax Fax," *RCM*, February-March 1985, p. 10.
196 "Off the cuff . . . unfortunate chance remark": *BB*, May 19, 1958.
196 "Certainly wasn't made to incite anyone" . . . "Had on different colored bandanas": Moonoogian, "Wax Fax," *RCM*, February-March 1985, p. 10.
197 "There's no other word for it" . . . "great deal of activity" . . . "Just a few yards" . . . "Sal came puffing in": Moonoogian, "Wax Fax," *RCM*, February-March 1985, p. 10.
197 "Finished the show in bright lights": Interview with Hooke.
197 Never actually "ended": Moonoogian, "Wax Fax," *RCM*, February-March 1985, p. 10.
197 "Got dressed and . . . left" . . . "A couple of kids were milling around": Interview with Hooke.
198 "Stood on a street corner [outside the arena] signing": *BB*, May 19, 1958.
198 "Hard to believe": Moonoogian, "Wax Fax," *RCM*, February-March 1985, p. 10.
198 "Unsettled crowd milling by the stage door": Pollack, *When Rock Was Young*, p. 96.
198 "Took a good hour back in those days": Moonoogian, "Wax Fax," *RCM*, February-March 1985, p. 10.
198 "At no time did we" . . . "what happened in Boston" . . . "Minor interruption" . . . "knew of any trouble": *BB*, May 19, 1958.
199 "How girls were raped" . . . "Is this America?" Interview with Hooke.
199 ROCK AND ROLL STABBING: "Rock 'n' Roll Stabbing," *NYT*, May 5, 1958.
199 "Beat, robbed, and molested" . . . "robbed three men of $50": Richard, "Banned in Boston," *GM*, October 1979.
199 "We were witness to it" . . . "good news copy": Moonoogian, "Wax Fax," *RCM*, February-March 1985, p. 10.
199 "That's how far" . . . " 'hot nut' they had for Alan": Interview with Hooke.
199 "Conflicting reports" . . . "Not only will this show not be": Richard, "Banned in Boston," *GM*, October 1979.
200 "The next thing we knew": Interview with Hooke.
200 "Would do everything possible": "Boston, New Haven Ban 'Rock' Shows," *NYT*, May 6, 1958.
200 "We tried to fight it": Interview with Hooke.
200 "Contributed by a substantial amount": "Freed Show Fights Ban in New Haven," *NYT*, May 7, 1958.
200 "Never seemed to be racial": Moonoogian, "Wax Fax," *RCM*, February-March 1985, p. 10.
200 "Fled before they could be seized": Richard, "Banned in Boston," *GM*, October 1979.
201 "Not against rock": "Boston, New Haven Ban . . . ," *NYT*, May 6, 1958.
201 "Juvenile delinquency and unrest" . . . "narcotics—were sold": Richard, "Banned in Boston," *GM*, October 1979.
201 "Inciting the unlawful destruction" . . . "arrested and extradited": "Freed Is Indicted over Rock 'n' Roll," *NYT*, May 9, 1958.

NOTES

201 "He was convicted": Interview with Hooke.
201 "Warren, I've just been indicted" . . . "work of the [Catholic] church": Interview with Troob.
201 "Alan stood a chance of going": Interview with Hooke.
202 "Just so much hogwash": "Alan Freed Says . . . ," reprinted in Buzzell, p. 62.
202 "Threw the book" . . . "I'm the scapegoat": FBI Report, December 2, 1959, p. 2.
202 "The greatest—swell": "Rock 'n' Riot," *Time*, May 19, 1958, p. 50.
202 "There's no question" . . . "get him there": Eliot, *Rockonomics*, p. 67.
202 "If certain forces": Pollack, *When Rock Was Young*, p. 97.
202 "What Alan Freed . . . sock it to": Passman, *The Deejays*, p. 190.
203 "At least as early as": Dannen, "The Godfather of Rock & Roll," *RS*, November 17, 1988, p. 99.
203 "Corrupting influence": FBI Memorandum, December 2, 1959, p. 2.
203 "Alan wanted to defend himself": Interview with Hooke.
204 "An impossible person to work with": Passman, *The Deejays*, p. 202.
204 "The music industry's worst-kept secret" . . . "very few times in his life": Eliot, *Rockonomics*, pp. 69, 261.
204 Freed had "resigned" . . . "wishy-washy": "Freed Is Indicted . . . ," *NYT*, May 9, 1958.
205 "Stand behind my policies" . . . "publicity from Boston": "Freed Is Indicted . . . ," *NYT*, May 9, 1958.
205 "As a complete surprise" . . . "within a reasonable time": *BB*, May 12, 1958.
205 "The public's safety": "Jersey Guard Bars Rock 'n' Roll Show in Newark Armory," *NYT*, May 8, 1958.
205 Hooke allegedly received a cash payment of $750 from Kenneth Luttman: FBI Memorandum, May 20, 1960, "Payments by record companies introduced into evidence and included in the Information." See also New York Grand Jury Information, May 9, 1960, Twenty-third Count, p. 14. Freed testified that he was on the payroll of United Artists Records for his "services as disc jockey": House subcommittee hearings, Alan Freed testimony, p. 51.
206 "Not the kind that soothes" . . . "There was a time": *NYHT*, May 13, 1958.

Chapter 11 • "We Start 'Em; the Others Chart 'Em"

207 "There were times that money passed hands": Interview with Hooke.
207 "Unlawfully, wickedly, and maliciously": "Freed Indicted Again," *NYT*, May 15, 1958.
207 "Inciting unlawful destruction": "Freed Denies Charges," *NYT*, May 17, 1958.
207 "Job hunting": Interview with Hooke.
208 "And who better to have" . . . "he arrived there!" . . . "The big bucks": Interview with Hooke.
208 "Never got a dime": House subcommittee hearings, Freed testimony, p. 38.
208 "Other money, gratuities, from other people" . . . "Was acceptable to Mr. Freed": Interview with Hooke.
209 "Taken back" . . . "play nothing but Paramount theatres": House subcommittee hearings, Freed testimony, p. 8.
209 "Quieter" . . . "better" rock & roll: *BB*, June 9, 1958.
209 "Music for older people" . . . "whole ASCAP" situation: Buzzell, p. 60.
209 "Without incident": *BB*, June 9, 1958.
209 "Was unconstitutional as it was applied to Mr. Freed": "Freed Denies Riot Role," *NYT*, June 5, 1958.
210 "Power to line up top artists": *BB*, July 21, 1958.
210 "Dancing Youngsters": *BB*, June 16, 1958.
210 "Reacting to Boston": Shaw, *The Rockin' '50s*, p. 236.
210 "Didn't like television": Interview with Reneri.
210 "Positively subdued": *BB*, July 7, 1958.
211 "The music with the big beat": *BB*, August 11, 1958.
211 "Well-known host": Eliot, *Rockonomics*, p. 69.
211 "Unparalleled success": Hopkins, *The Rock Story*, p. 40. By mid-1958 there were forty-six million TV sets in use in the United States.
212 "Dick got behind it": Hopkins, *The Rock Story*, p. 46. "Venus" was recorded in December 1958.
212 "Over 100,000 from distributors": Berry, Foose, and Jones, *Up from the Cradle of Jazz*, p. 111.
212 "People know that Clark will lay it on": "Facing the Music," *Time*, December 7, 1959.
212 "Just good business": Fong-Torres, "Dick Clark," *RS*, August 16, 1973, p. 18.
212 Lozier Caplan . . . handled . . . Greene's divorce: Freed's first wife said that she and Freed "ended up with a lot of respect for each other, even with the things that happened" (Interview with Greene).
212 "Was supporting two families": Interview with Caplan.
212 "Get the jump on Clark": *BB*, June 9, 1958.
213 Assets as "nil": *BB*, July 28, 1958.
213 "Certain image to keep up": Interview with Alana Freed.
213 "Stopped doing some of the things": Interview with Greene.
214 "Had already met Inga" . . . "past, present, and future": Interview with Hooke.

214 "Too young": Interview with Alana Freed.
214 Ramistella . . . meet Freed out in front of WINS: Glenn A. Baker, "Johnny Rivers, the Singer Not the Song," *GM*, June 19, 1987.
215 Rivers recorded for various record labels: Rivers wrote and recorded for various labels from 1958 to 1963, including Era, Riveraire, Chancellor, Cub, Guyden, and Dee Dee.
215 The soaring ballad "The Fires Burn No More": "The Fires Burn No More" and "Lift Up Your Head" (Apollo 521), released in 1957.
215 "Really big locally": Turco, "Little Anthony Interview," *REX*, 1973, p. 6.
215 "In his tracks": Pollack, *When Rock Was Young*, p. 176.
215 He maintains . . . "stinks": Turco, "Little Anthony Interview," *REX*, 1973, p. 6.
215 "Didn't have any 'zing' . . . outraged": Pollack, *When Rock Was Young*, p. 177.
215 "And now . . . making a lot of noise": Apugliesi, et al., "Little Anthony & the," *BBB*, 1973, p. 8.
216 "Did not know it was me": Turco, "Little Anthony Interview," *REX*, 1973, p. 6.
216 "Remembered me from the Duponts": Pollack, *When Rock Was Young*, p. 177.
216 "Had a little voice": Jones, "Talks with Little Anthony," *GM*, April 1981, p. 11.
216 "They thought I was . . . thirteen years old": Pollack, *When Rock Was Young*, p. 177.
216 "Just spread like": Jones, "Talks With Little Anthony," *GM*, April 1981, p. 11.
216 "Jumped up and sold about 800,000": Turco, "Little Anthony Interview," *REX*, 1973, p. 6.
216 Freed allegedly received a $400 payment from Superior: FBI Memorandum, May 20, 1960, "Payments by record companies introduced into evidence and included in the Information." See also New York Grand Jury Information, May 9, 1960, Seventh Count, pp. 4, 5.
216 "Was in the middle": Interview with Hooke. See also FBI Memorandum, May 20, 1960.
217 "Alone and unique": Rosen, *Americana Annual, 1956*, p. 623.
218 "Other than a true test of skill": "Rogers Proposes Strict Controls on TV & Radio," *NYT*, January 1, 1960.
218 Questioned in several leading national magazines: "Rogers Proposes . . . ," *NYT*, January 1, 1960. Two magazines mentioned were *Time*, April 22, 1957, and *Look*, August 20, 1957.
219 "Take a dive" against Charles Van Doren: Castleman and Podrazik, *Watching TV*, p. 125.
219 "The smoldering rumors": Barnouw, *The Image Empire*, p. 122.
219 "Saddened and shocked": Castleman and Podrazik, *Watching TV*, p. 125.
220 "Down the road" . . . "oppose Alan Freed at all": *BB*, August 11, 1958.
220 "Pretty slick dude": Interview with Hooke.
220 "Came in . . . strong!": Interview with Hooke.
220 "Under no circumstances would he": House subcommittee hearings, Ben Hoberman testimony May 3, 1960, p. 1449.
220 "They got 10 percent . . . profit": Interview with Hooke.
221 "Forbidden" . . . "That's all that matters": Interview with Hooke.
221 "Keep things cool": . . . "Every intention of returning": *BB*, September 8, 1958.
221 The Elegants, whose Am-Par-distributed recording: "Little Star" was released on the Apt label, a subsidiary of ABC-Paramount Records.
222 "Sighs of admiration" . . . "sent furthest": *BB*, September 8, 1958.
222 Proclaimed it "a winner!": Interview with Hooke.
222 "Alan Freed Rocks Brooklyn with 'Big Beat' Show": *BB*, September 8, 1958.
223 "Rocky" basis: Interview with Hooke.
223 "A better deal": House subcommittee hearings, Alan Freed testimony, p. 11.
223 Hooke and Bernie Friedlander allegedly agreed: FBI Memorandum, May 20, 1960.
223 "Did request and accept": New York Grand Jury Information, May 9, 1960, First Count, p. 1.
223 Accepted another $700 check from Superior: New York Grand Jury Information, Eighth Count, p. 5.
223 On November 21 . . . $500 payment from Sam Weiss: New York Grand Jury Information, May 9, 1960, Ninth Count, pp. 5, 6.
223 Dees allegedly continued United Artists payments: FBI Memorandum, May 20, 1960.
223 On December 18, Sam Weiss: New York Grand Jury Information, May 9, 1960, Tenth Count, p. 6.
224 "The truth will win out": Castleman and Podrazik, *Watching TV*, p. 125.
224 "An element of unreality" . . . "Crystal clear that": Bergreen, *Look Now, Pay Later*, p. 193.
225 "Nothing could be played" . . . "Alan had to have the list" . . . "Somewhere down the line" . . . "with the list": Interview with Hooke.
225 "Mr. Freed's bailiwick" . . . "limits of good taste": House subcommittee hearings, Hoberman testimony, p. 1447.
225 "Never really equalled": Rolontz, "Alan Freed—An Appreciation," *Music Business*, February 6, 1965, p. 23.
226 "Tried very hard" . . . "out of his element": *BB*, December 29, 1958.
226 "Highly dramatic style": *BB*, December 29, 1958.
226 Nat ("the Rat") Tarnapol, also worked: "Disc Jockeys: Now Don't Cry," *Time*, December 7, 1959, p. 47.
226 Inga had recently cut her first record, "Silly Willy": Interview with Hooke.

NOTES

227 "I want to put my wife in there . . . "I had my Christmas gift": "Moondog Coronation Ball—30th Anniversary," Joey Villa interview, "Do Wop Shop," WPIX-FM, New York, March 21, 1982.
227 "Broke it up most of all" . . . "nearly packed the house": *BB*, December 29, 1958.
228 "Lots of people walking" . . . "surely on the payroll": Chuck Berry, *Autobiography*, p. 187.
228 "I'm not much good": Mendheim, *Ritchie Valens*, p. 102.
229 "Seemed more important": House subcommittee hearings, Alan Freed testimony, p. 11.
229 "Several incidents": House subcommittee hearings, Hoberman testimony, p. 1450.
229 "Wasn't doing any [advertising] business": House subcommittee hearings, Leonard Goldenson testimony, May 3, 1960, p. 1399.
229 "Unfortunate thing[s]": "Alan Freed's Big Beat" audiotape, March 12, 1959.
230 "Tell Sam Clark": "Alan Freed's Big Beat" audiotape, March 12, 1959.
230 WABC was trying to ax him: House subcommittee hearings, Alan Freed testimony, p. 12.
231 "Not be one of the sponsors" . . . "effective as of such time": House subcommittee hearings, Freed testimony, p. 12.
231 Hoberman allegedly conducted interviews: House subcommittee hearings, Hoberman testimony, p. 1453.
231 "Usual type of arrangement": House subcommittee hearings, Hoberman testimony, p. 1453.
231 "Silenced rumors of several weeks": *BB*, April 13, 1959.
231 "Wasn't doing any business": House subcommittee hearings, Goldenson testimony, p. 1399.
232 The payments he regularly received: In each of the first three months of 1959 Lester Dees allegedly delivered a cash payment of $400 to Freed on behalf of United Artists Records (FBI Memorandum, May 20, 1960). In February and March 1959, Sam Weiss of Superior Record Sales allegedly paid Freed $700 (New York Grand Jury Information, May 9, 1960, Eleventh and Twelfth Counts, pp. 7, 8).
232 Already conferred with the Securities and Exchange Commission: FBI Report, December 11, 1959.
232 "No useful purpose": "Alan Freed Wins Point," *NYT*, March 7, 1959.
232 "Well ahead of the previous ratings": *BB*, April 13, 1959.
233 Freed's "highlight performers": *BB*, April 13, 1959.
233 "Couldn't sing a note" . . . Hooke said when Darin: Interview with Hooke.
234 Grossed a disappointing $167,000: *BB*, April 13, 1959.
234 "Paragraph Twenty" . . . "blackjacked": House subcommittee hearings, Freed testimony, pp. 15–17.
234 "No one knew what Alan's": Interview with Reneri.
234 *Go, Johnny, Go* . . . was about to be released: The film had been released to theaters in other areas of the country in April and, in the words of talent booker Jolly Joyce, "was doing very well" (*BB*, July 11, 1959). The film opened in Brooklyn and the vicinity in Loews' Theaters on July 29, 1959.
234 "We're going to play it again": Interview with Reneri.
235 "Presentment," which called attention: Castleman and Podrazik, *Watching TV*, p. 125.
236 "With an understanding" . . . "played them on his program": FBI Memorandum, May 20, 1960.
236 Formed two corporations . . . in Maryland and Delaware: Salutem Corporation (Maryland), formed in August 1959, and Wallingford Corporation (Delaware), formed in September, 1959.

Chapter 12 • Payola

238 "What they call payola": Wilson, "Alan Freed's Story," *NYP*, November 23, 1959.
238 "To probe the morals of radio and television": *CPD*, May 22, 1952.
239 "Shook the industry": Sterling and Kittross, *Stay Tuned*, p. 359.
239 "Almost from the start . . . a prime target" . . . "Little patience for diplomatic conventions": Sterling and Kittross, *Stay Tuned*, p. 360.
240 "Neglect of duty": Sterling and Kittross, *Stay Tuned*, p. 361.
240 Four days after Alan Freed allegedly received the second of two $500 payments: This arrangement between Klayman and Hooke allegedly began in July 1959. Freed was to "favor the exposure of records distributed" by Action on his WABC radio program (FBI Memorandum, May 20, 1960). The first payment was allegedly made to Hooke on September 2, 1959. The second payment was allegedly delivered on October 2, 1959 (New York Grand Jury Information, May 9, 1960, Twenty-first Count, pp. 12, 13). Also in September 1959, Mayfair Distributing Company allegedly gave Hooke $500 in cash, intended for Freed. In October 1959, Freed also received the third (and final) $2,000 check from Jerry Blaine's Cosnat Distributors (FBI Memorandum, May 20, 1959).
241 "Controls": Castleman and Podrazik, *Watching TV*, p. 133.
241 "Unable to pinpoint any legal violations": *1960 Britannica Book of the Year*, p. 251.
241 "Deception": Castleman and Podrazik, *Watching TV*, p. 133.
241 "Terrible thing" . . . "no power in the Executive Department": "Payola," *Broadcasting*, February 15, 1960, p. 98.
241 "Symbol of ingenuity": Barnouw, *The Image Empire*, p. 222.
241 "Give almost anything to reverse the course": Barnouw *Tube of Plenty*, p. 244.
242 Stempel . . . "virtually unbeatable": Barnouw, *The Image Empire*, p. 222.

242 "The good looks and engaging manner": Eliot, *Rockonomics*, p. 75.
242 Aid the cause of the "intellectual": Castleman and Podrazik, *Watching TV*, p. 134.
242 "Foolish, naive, prideful, and avaricious": Van Doren, transcript of speech, *NYT*, November 3, 1959.
242 "Ought to be commended for telling the truth": Barnouw, *The Image Empire*, p. 134.
242 Eliminate other broadcasting "deceits" . . . "policed, not cancelled": Dodge, 1960 Britannica Book of the Year, p. 578.
243 "Shocking state of rottenness" . . . "common cheats and liars": Mayer, *About Television*, p. 119.
243 "Favor the exposure" . . . "Spotlight Song of the Week" . . . Pick of the Week: FBI Memorandum, May 20, 1960.
243 Enough checks had been passed to establish: Because of the New York State statute of limitations governing prosecution of certain crimes, the NYPD constructed its case against Freed only as far back as 1958.
244 "Chosen" four distributors . . . Sleeper: FBI Memorandum, May 20, 1960. Neither "One Hundred Years from Today" nor "Wear This Ring" appeared on *BB*'s "Hot 100" or "Top 30 Hot R&B Sides."
244 November 4, Weiss allegedly delivered $1,000: New York Grand Jury Information, May 9, 1960, Nineteenth Count, pp. 11, 12.
244 "Surreptitiously induced to buy": "Wider TV Inquiry to Study Bribery & Paid Plugs," *NYT*, November 7, 1959.
244 "To suppress genuine talent": Sanjek, "The War on Rock," *DB*, p. 63.
245 *Variety* called . . . PAYOLA—WORSE THAN EVER: Eliot, *Rockonomics*, pp. 70, 72.
245 "Flagrant and rampant": Passman, *The Deejays*, p. 184.
245 WKMH and WJBK . . . "Album of the Week": Purchasing the Album of the Week guaranteed that one cut from the album, or a single record, would be played 114 times a week, with commercials aired on both sides of the spin.
245 "Cash accounting formula": "Block That Schlock," *Time*, November 23, 1959, pp. 65–66.
245 "Normal fringe benefits": Barnouw, *The Image Empire*, p. 69.
246 "Advisable" to draft a company affidavit: House subcommittee hearings, Goldenson testimony, p. 1371.
246 "New arrangement" . . . Pick of the Week: FBI Memorandum, May 20, 1960. See also New York Grand Jury Information, May 9, 1960, Twenty-second Count, p. 13. "Humorock" did not appear on *BB*'s "Hot 100" chart.
246 "As a result" . . . "substantial doubts": Wise, "52 Witnesses Due at F.C.C. Quiz on TV," *NYHT*, November 28, 1959.
247 Placed Freed's 1958 riot charge "on file" . . . "Were scattered over the country": "Disc Jockey Freed; Boston Won't Press Riot Case Against Alan Freed," *NYT*, November 13, 1959.
247 "Good relations" with Ben Hoberman: House subcommittee hearings, Freed testimony, p. 18.
247 "Acceptance of gratuities": . . . "In any music publishing, recording, or merchandising concern . . . explained in detail": ABC payola affidavit. November 13, 1959.
248 "Where is your affidavit" . . . "in the music business": . . . p. 19. "Cases of Scotch" . . . "I will sign it": House subcommittee hearings, Freed testimony, pp. 19, 20.
248 "Shotgun to your head" . . . "which would you like to be": Fong-Torres, "Dick Clark," *RS*, August 16, 1973, pp. 18–19
248 "Preferred" television: House subcommittee hearings, Clark testimony, p. 1204.
248 "Renewed faith and confidence": Adams, "House Unit to Query D. Clark," *NYT*, November 18, 1959.
249 More than 70 percent: House subcommittee hearings, Freed testimony, p. 20.
249 "You must be kidding!": Interview with Troob.
249 "Are you going to sign?": House subcommittee hearings, Freed testimony, p. 21.
249 "Lied under oath": Interview with David Freed.
249 "Evidence[d] a lack of faith": Alan Freed, letter to WABC, November 21, 1959.
250 "We will expect all three answers to be no" . . . "Too much American Broadcasting Company" . . . "That was that": House subcommittee hearings, Freed testimony, pp. 21, 22.
250 "Abruptly dismissed" . . . "contractual right": Shephard, "Alan Freed Is Out in Payola Study," *NYT*, November 22, 1959.
250 "Jeopardizing" . . . Virtually to a man" . . . "complete overhaul": Marino and Smee, "TV Will Ask Freed Today: Any Payola?" *NYDN*, November 23, 1959.
251 "Shenanigans . . . "we ought to take a look": Interview with Joseph Stone, 1980.
251 "After payola itself": Interview with Hooke.
252 "Corrupt influencing of agents": New York State Penal Law of 1909, Section 439.
252 "Little boy who takes an apple to his teacher" . . . "was not unusual": "Jockey Fired, Defends Payola," *NYDN*, November 23, 1959.
252 "Were they wrong": "Detroit Radio Star Confesses 'Payola,' " *NYT*, November 23, 1959.

NOTES 365

253 "Desirable music": "Disc Jockeys Curbed," *NYT*, December 1, 1959.
253 FREED FACES TV PAYOLA PROBE; WNEW ASKS DETAILS OF SHOW: Marino and Smee, "TV Will Ask Freed . . . ," *NYDN*, November 23, 1959.
253 "What are you doing" . . . "reporters are waiting": Wilson, "Alan Freed Telling All About Payola to House Probers," *NYP*, November 25, 1959.
253 "By mutual consent" . . . "suspect he did anything wrong": Marino, "Freed Swears 'No TV Payola' & Loses Job," *NYDN*, November 24, 1959.
253 "Long in coming" . . . "to control our own show": "Alan Freed Loses 2D Broadcasting Job," *NYT*, November 24, 1959.
253 No longer felt Freed was "right" . . . "At no time during my" . . . "We discussed this several weeks ago": Marino, "Freed Swears . . . ," *NYDN*, November 24, 1959.
254 "Go home and don't talk": Dannen, "The Godfather of Rock & Roll," *RS*, November 17, 1988, p. 92.
254 "Alan was very publicity-conscious": Interview with Hooke.
254 "If I go down the drain": Williams, "Freed Replaced on Today's Ch. 5 Show—Union Sets Payola Talk with DA," *NYP*, November 23, 1959.
254 "A lot of . . . information": Interview with Earl Wilson, September 12, 1980.
255 Troob insisted that it was Wilson . . . "baby-sit": Interview with Troob.
255 "Had information that some of the big brass" . . . "Should be investigated": Wilson, "Alan Freed's Story," *NYP*, November 23, 1959,
256 "What the fuck did you do?": Dannen, "The Godfather of Rock & Roll," *RS*, November 17, 1988, p. 92.
256 "This shows how rich": Wilson, "Alan Freed Telling . . . ," *NYP*, November 25, 1959.
256 "People in the companies" . . . "sounding off in the papers": Crist, "Alan Freed Now Out at WNEW-TV," *NYHT*, November 24, 1959.
256 "In one form or another" . . . "the station's way": Torre, "Alan Freed Still Idol to His Teen-Age Fans," *NYHT*, November 25, 1959.
257 "Final supper party" . . . "I'm being fired" . . . "Not to be an idiot" . . . "their notice": Wilson, "Alan Freed Telling All . . . ," *NYP*, November 25, 1959.
257 "Dean of disc jockeys" . . . "forewith": Abrams and Quirk, "Subpoena Invites Freed to DA's Payola Show," *NYDN*, November 26, 1959.
257 "Several times": Interview with Stone.
257 ALAN FREED TELLING ALL TO PAYOLA PROBERS: Wilson, "Alan Freed Telling All . . . ," *NYP*, November 25, 1959.
258 "Was the same size [as] when World War II ended": Dannen, "The Godfather . . . ," *RS*, November 17, 1988, p. 92.
258 "Twice-fired disc jockey" . . . "About payola practices": Wilson, "Alan Freed Telling All . . . ," *NYP*, November 25, 1959.
258 "I'll wind up on the white horse": Wilson, "Alan Freed's Story," *NYP*, November 23, 1959.
258 "Nothing would scare": Interview with Hooke.
258 "Laid out" . . . "out of the papers": Interview with Reneri.
258 "That's where he thought": Interview with Alana Freed.
258 "Plain blackmail": Shaw, *The Rockin' '50s*, p. 274.
259 "To discuss the payola situation"; Shepard, "Hogan Subpoenas Freed's Papers," *NYT*, November 28, 1959.
259 "Including representatives of the major television networks": Wise, "52 Witnesses . . . ," *NYHT*, November 28, 1959.
259 "We want Alan!" . . . "don't cry": "Disc Jockeys: Now Don't Cry," *Time*, December 7, 1959, p. 47.
259 "The most important record distributing companies" . . . "nicest guys in the business": "Payola Axes King Freed," *Life*, December 7, 1959, pp. 30–31.
259 "Danced dolefully": "Disc Jockeys . . . ," *Time*, December 7, 1959, p. 47.
260 "I hope you're satisfied": "Payola Axes . . . ," *Life*, December 7, 1959, pp. 30, 31.
260 "We know we are": "DA Calls for Alan Freed's Accounts; 'I'll Be Back,' Disc Jockey Tells Fans," *NYP*, November 29, 1959.
260 "Payola may stink": "Disc Jockeys . . . ," *Time*, December 7, 1959, p. 47.
260 "I know a lot of ASCAP publishers": *BB*, November 30, 1959.
260 "Now they're trying to take" . . . "The backbone of American business": "Payola Axes . . . ," *Life*, December 7, 1959, p. 30.
260 "Consultation work": "NBC Explains Its TV Position," *NYT*, November 29, 1959.
260 "Professional advice" . . . "release a new record": Kosner, "DA Calls . . . ," *NYP*, November 29, 1959.
260 "Advising record manufacturers": "NBC Explains . . . ," *NYT*, November 29, 1959.
260 "I think it's lost all opportunities": Kosner, "DA Calls . . . ," *NYP*, November 29, 1959.
261 "Making statements": Interview with Stone.
261 "Smiling frequently": Scaduto and O'Grady, "Freed Faces DA, Balks at Waiver," *NYP*, November 30, 1959.

261 "Any ideas"... "disturbed": Sheard, "Freed Balks at Testifying Before Payola Jury," *NYJA*, November 30, 1959.
261 "I'd love to answer": "Big Beat Legends," documentary film.
261 "The advice of my attorney": Scaduto and O'Grady, "Freed Faces DA...," *NYP*, November 30, 1959.
262 "Thought he would fight"... "put you away": Interview with Reneri.
262 "We are not prepared to grant": Scaduto and O'Grady, "Freed Faces DA...," *NYP*, November 30, 1959.
262 "Knew damned well": Interview with Stone.
262 "Arrangement"... "everything locked up": Scaduto and O'Grady, "Freed Faces DA...," *NYP*, November 30, 1959.
262 "Empty-handed"... "we can take": Crist, "Freed Won't Sign Waiver for Inquiry," *NYHT*, December 1, 1959.
263 "Raises serious questions": Scaduto and O'Grady, "Freed Faces DA...," *NYP*, November 30, 1959.
263 "Of mutual interest"... "business to decide": "CBS Chief Issues a Bribe Warning," *NYT*, December 2, 1959.
263 "New York rock and roll promoter": FBI Memorandum, December 2, 1959. It was this particular memorandum that made reference to Freed's "intense dislike for the Director [J. Edgar Hoover]." At that point, the FBI dossier on Freed consisted of a handful of newspaper articles clipped from New York newspapers, pertaining to Freed's WNEW-TV firing and subsequent payola allegations lodged against him. The file also contained a copy of a scathing *NYHT* editorial attack on Freed following the Boston riot incident.
263 DeLoach, the "genial Georgian": Theoharis and Cox, *The Boss: J. Edgar Hoover and the Great American Inquisition*, p. 221.
263 Hoover's "chief 'axe-men' ": Nash, *Citizen Hoover: A Critical Study of the Life and Times of J. Edgar Hoover and His FBI*, p. 239.
264 "A matter of public record"... "broke up": Wilson and Carr, "Record Man Says He Gave Freed $11,000 Interest-Free Loan in '56," *NYP*, December 3, 1959.
264 "Fraud by wire": FBI Memorandum, December 11, 1959.
266 "More vigorously"... "few would"... "Among other viewpoints"... "chicanery": "Payola," *Broadcasting*, February 15, 1960, p. 98.
267 "Couldn't sit down": Interview with Greene.
267 "Showed in his face"... "For the first time": Interview with Alana Freed.

Chapter 13 • As Clean as the Newly Driven snow

268 "Nobody ever brought me a record": House subcommittee hearings, Freed testimony, p. 51.
268 "Year in which payola leaped": "A Rock Chronology," *Rock*, January 5, 1970, p. 9.
268 "Stupid"... "heart problem": Sklar, *Rocking America*, p. 58.
268 January 26, WINS received a letter: *BB*, February 1, 1960.
269 "If Freed ever starts": Wilson, "Alan Freed Telling All About Payola to House Probers," *NYP*, November 25, 1959.
269 "You have to get out": Interview with Reneri.
269 "No one would be connected": Interview with Greene.
269 "The law says": Interview with Stone.
270 "Took a shot": Interview with Stone.
271 "We hit paydirt!"... "legal compulsion": Interview with Stone.
271 An "unfair trade practice... unfair methods of competition... active in several sections": "Payola Givers Facing FTC 'Unfair' Charges," *NYP*, December 1, 1959.
271 To "expose... as much as six to ten times... Tends to mislead purchasers... Divert trade unfairly... Just like everyone else": "15 More Accused of Disk Payolas," *NYT*, January 3, 1960.
272 The FTC issued nine more payola complaints: "9 Payola Charges Added by FTC," *NYT*, February 1, 1960.
272 "For its crackdown of the practice": "15 More Accused of Disk Payolas," *NYT*, January 3, 1960.
272 "Harassed the shit"... "better for not signing it": Dannen, "The Godfather...," *RS*, November 17, 1988, p. 92.
272 "Becoming rampant"... "To be more specific"... "sufficiently persuasive": Sanjek, "The War on Rock," *DB*, p. 64.
272 "Unjustified attacks by ASCAP": *NYHT*, January 13, 1960.
272 "As the potential defendants": "Jury Here Opens Payola Inquiry," *NYT*, February 3, 1960.
273 "Hot"... "for payola": Dannen, "The Godfather of Rock & Roll," *RS*, November 17, 1988, p. 92.
273 "Tacit understanding"... "forget about repayment": FBI Memorandum, May 20, 1960.
273 "Denied that he had done": Sklar, *Rocking America*, p. 65.
274 "Wholly ignorant"... "public confidence": "Payola," *Broadcasting*, February 15, 1960, p. 98.

NOTES

274 "As it applied to a station license . . . Greatly concerned . . . Deceit on the airwaves": Blair, "FCC Urges Law on Deceit on air," *NYT*, February 12, 1960.
276 "Very naive" . . . "less than frank": House subcommittee hearings, Anthony Mammarella testimony, January 20 and 28, 1960, p. 776.
276 "Special attention or listening": House subcommittee hearings, Joseph Finan testimony, February 9, 1960, p. 132.
276 "Listening fee" . . . "a lot of listening": House subcommittee hearings, Wesley Hopkins testimony, February 10, 1960, p. 182.
276 "Establish feelings of good will": House subcommittee hearings, Arnie Ginsberg testimony, February 15, 1960, p. 325.
276 "One pupil": "Goodbye, Ookie Dookie," *Newsweek*, February 22, 1960, p. 60.
276 Whatever "hits" he chose: House subcommittee hearings, Harry Weiss testimony, p. 498.
277 "Brotherly love" . . . "intellectual osmoses": Subcommittee member John E. Moss, quoted in "Music Business Goes Round and Round: It Comes Out Clarkola," *Life*, May 16, 1960, pp. 118–120.
277 "Didn't want to spoil our system": Interview with Hooke.
278 "Did well" . . . "drove a very hard bargain": Interview with Hooke.
278 "Requesting and accepting" $10,000: New York Criminal Court Order, Judge Gulkin, February 25, 1960; see also New York Grand Jury Information, February 26, 1960.
278 FCC Chairman John C. Doerfer resigned: *BB*, March 14, 1960.
278 "Solid gross" of $18,500: *BB*, March 28, 1960.
279 "Shrewd little businessman" . . . "clean as a whistle": Interview with Hooke.
279 "No, it isn't" . . . "two types of payola": House subcommittee hearings, Freed testimony, pp. 29–30.
279-281 "Yes, . . . I could have signed it": House subcommittee hearings, Freed testimony, pp. 31, 33–36, 38–39.
281 "Unscheduled disclosures" . . . "evils of payola": Passman, *The Deejays*, p. 244.
282-284 "Made less than ABC": House subcommittee hearings, Freed testimony, pp. 45, 47, 50–55, 57.
284 "Great deal of tension" . . . "didn't know": Interview with Troob.
284-285 "Coined that phrase 'record consultant' ": House subcommittee hearings, Freed testimony, pp. 31–32, 58–60.
285 "Wouldn't take a dime": Passman, *The Deejays*, p. 221.
286 "A Closed Hearing is Held": "A Closed Hearing Is Held on Clark; Payola Inquiry Goes Into Disk Jockey's Business Ties—Alan Freed Testifies," *NYT*, April 26, 1960.
286 "Hopes of having those songs played on the air": House subcommittee hearings, Goldner testimony, p. 1099.
286 "Did not think so": House subcommittee hearings, Goldner testimony, pp. 1110–1111.
287 His song publishing "gifts": Fong-Torres, "Dick Clark," *RS*, August 16, 1973, p. 18.
287 "Good will" . . . "just wasn't getting my records played": House subcommittee hearings, Lowe testimony, p. 1130.
287 "Every hair strand" . . . "highly select adult audience": "Music Business Goes Round . . . ," *Life*, May 16, 1960, p. 118.
288 "Convicted, condemned and denounced" . . . "make it clear": House subcommittee hearings, Dick Clark, testimony, May 2, 1960, pp. 1168, 1187.
288 "I followed normal business": House subcommittee hearings, Clark testimony, pp. 1170, 1177, 1184, 1187.
288 Was "unnecessary": "Royola," *Time*, May 9, 1960, p. 30.
288 "You wouldn't have": House subcommittee hearings, Clark testimony, pp. 1189, 1190.
288 "Once you acquired an interest": "Music Business Goes Round . . . ," *Life*, May 16, 1960, p. 120.
289 "Maybe I did so without realizing it" . . . "special treatment": "Nobody Blew the Whistle," *Newsweek*, May 9, 1960, p. 30.
289 "Someone like Clark is a one-man trust": "Facing the Music," *Time*, November 30, 1959, p. 70.
289 "Suave, unruffled" . . . "wiggled off each baited hook": "Nobody Blew the Whistle," *Newsweek*, May 9, 1960, p. 30.
289-291 "It seems like the only difference": House subcommittee hearings, Clark testimony, pp. 1170, 1185, 1200, 1204, 1211–1212, 1219, 1221, 1305–1306, 1351.
291 "Illegal or immoral": Fong-Torres, "Dick Clark," *RS*, August 16, 1973, p. 18.
291 "Cautious, waiting to see" . . . "you can always": "Music Business Goes Round . . . ," *Life*, May 16, 1960, p. 122.
291 "Couldn't have more respect" . . . "some other cats": "Music Business Goes Round . . . ," *Life*, May 16, 1960, p. 122.
291 "Whitewash" . . . "had a parade": Interview with Troob.
291 "Got the best . . . "grabbed that lifesaver too": Interview with Hooke.
291 "Just politics" . . . "looking for headlines": Fong-Torres, "Dick Clark," *RS*, August 16, 1973, p. 19.
292 "Burned those motherfuckers" . . . "I was ignorant": Fong-Torres, "Dick Clark," *RS*, August 16, 1973, p. 19.

292 "Knew little or nothing" . . . Protect Your Ass at All Times: Schippers, "Dick Clark," *RS*, April 19, 1990, pp. 68, 70.
292 "Made a lot of mistakes" . . . "wasn't bright enough": Fong-Torres, "Dick Clark," *RS*, August 16, 1973, p. 19.
292 "The man who made it [rock & roll] happen": Schippers, "Dick Clark," *RS*, April 19, 1990, p. 68.
292 "Probably" . . . "went in for rock and roll": House subcommittee hearings, Goldenson testimony, May 3, 1960, pp. 1372–1373, 1399.
293 "Truthful men we had before us" . . . "not aware": House subcommittee hearings, Goldenson testimony, pp. 1372, 1432.
293 "Quite candidly": "House Unit Plans Payola Remedies," *NYT*, May 4, 1960.
293 "He refused to provide us": House subcommittee hearings, Goldenson testimony, pp. 1372, 1399.
293 "Absolutely not true": House subcommittee hearings, Hoberman testimony, May 3, 1960, p. 1445.
294 "So bad that" . . . "low tastes": Dachs, *Anything Goes*, p. 125.
294 "What the country does not realize": Sanjek, "The War on Rock," *DB*, p. 64.
294 "Sadly deceived" . . . "long-standing vendetta against the major networks": Quoted by Sanjek, "The War on Rock," *DB*, pp. 63, 64.
296 "Disappointed in a lot of people": Interview with Troob.
296 "Nothing" . . . "didn't know what to expect": Interview with Alana Freed.
296 "Leading Negro and foreign-language station": Interview with Bob Dye, September 15, 1980.
297 "He's a dynamic personality" . . . "on exposing rhythm and blues discs": *BB*, May 16, 1960.
297 "Trying anybody and": Interview with Dye.
297 "Take care" . . . "much more up": Interview with Alana Freed.
298 "As an agent and employee" . . . "in relation to his employer's business": Peoples Trial Memorandum Against Peter G. Tripp, p. 1.
298 "At their own expense": *BB*, May 23, 1960.
299 "Graft payments" . . . "Eight or nine times" . . . "at once": Cotter and Carr, "DJ Alan Freed and 6 Others Arrested in Payola Probe," *NYP*, May 19, 1960.
299 "Evidently been the judgement" . . . "given to their": Abrams and Patterson, "Hogan Slaps Payola Rap on Freed and 7," *NYDN*, May 20, 1960.
300 "Had exploited their responsibility": Cotter and Carr, "DJ Alan Freed . . . ," *NYP*, May 19, 1960.
300 "Fall guys" . . . "with us this week": *BB*, May 23, 1960.
300 "Bullshit charges" . . . "stuck himself out": Dannen, "The Godfather . . . ," *RS*, November 17, 1988, p. 92.
300 "Open letter" . . . "consideration": *BB*, May 30, 1960.
301 "Had consented to his conduct": Peter G. Tripp, Trial Transcript, March 1961, p. ii.
301 "No evidence that the defendant can't receive a fair trial": *BB*, May 31, 1961.
302 Solely for "advice" . . . "new sounds": "Decision Due May 15 in Trial on Payola," *NYT*, May 4, 1961.
302 "Extra expenses" . . . "help": "Testimony Ended in Disc Jockey Suit," *NYT*, May 3, 1961. Kidder, who, like Joseph Stone, went on to become a New York City criminal court judge from 1968 to 1979, died in 1988 at age seventy-nine.
302 "Outright liar": "Decision Due . . . ," *NYT*, May 4, 1961.
302 "Refrain from making these observations": "Testimony Ended . . . ," *NYT*, May 3, 1961.
302 "Everybody and his uncle": "Decision Due . . . ," *NYT*, May 4, 1961.
302 Special Sessions justices rendered their decision: The justices were Edward F. Breslin, Vincent R. Impellitteri, and Aaron Goldstein.
302 "Given the law" . . . "penniless": "Tripp Guilty of Taking Payola While Radio Disc Jockey Here," *NYT*, May 16, 1961.
303 "Would definitely be on, sooner or later": *BB*, May 22, 1961.
303 By Christmas 1960, it was a national hit: "Baby, Oh Baby" was the first [but not the last] rerelease from the 1950s to become a hit after flopping the first time around. The song reached #21 on *BB*'s national "Hot 100" chart.
303 "Sure enough" . . . "started to make noise": Interview with Hooke.
303 "Was really plugging along": Interview with Alana Freed.
303 "Coincidental upsurge" . . . "the prime centers": *BB*, February 13, 1961.
304 "Chance" Freed would take a rock & roll show: *BB*, June 19, 1961.
304 "Everything's going great!" . . . "Were determined": Interview with Hooke.
305 "Came down hard" . . . "can't let you do it": Interview with Hooke.
305 "Entirely different story" . . . "didn't fit": Interview with Dye.
305 "Loved being on the air again": Eliot, *Rockonomics*, p. 88.
306 "Helped break many hits": *BB*, July 3, 1961.
306 "Quite noticeably": Interview with Dye.

NOTES   369

CHAPTER 14 • PAYOLA'S FIRST FATALITY

307 "He was a bigger man than those": Rolontz, "Alan Freed—An Appreciation," *Music Business*, February 6, 1965, p. 23.
307 "Persistent rumors" . . . "no changes in our": *BB*, August 21, 1961. It was about this time that Bruce ["Cousin Brucie"] Morrow left WINZ Radio in Miami to join Dan Ingram on WABC. Morrow would soon surpass WINS's Murray the K as New York's top nighttime rock & roll deejay of the early 1960s.
307 "Pushing records" . . . "a difficult pill to swallow": "Moondog Coronation Ball—30th Anniversary" audiotape, March 21, 1982.
307 Aware of payola dealings: *BB*, July 10, 1961.
308 FCC charged the Gotham Broadcasting . . . to "induce" . . . "Without sponsorship identification": *BB*, July 10, 1961.
308 "Would serve a public purpose": Shephard, "FCC Action Near on WINS, WMGM; Reports Requested," *NYT*, July 8, 1961.
308 To "bestow gifts" . . . "Protection of the public interest" . . . "Would presumably be dismissed": "FTC Dismisses Charges of Payola," *NYT*, June 21, 1961.
308 "Unnecessary and costly litigation": "Payola Cases Dropped, FTC Dismisses Charges Against Five Companies," *NYT*, September 1, 1961.
309 "Boldly and flagrantly violated the law . . . Slap on the wrist . . . License to others": Roth, "Tripp Fined $500 in Payola Case," *NYT*, October 17, 1961.
309 Freed's September trial date was postponed: The commercial bribery trials of Leeds, Joe Saccone, Ron Granger, and Jack Walker were also postponed [*BB*, September 25, 1961].
309 "There remain substantial questions": Lewis, "Miami TV Station Loses Its License," *NYT*, October 19, 1961.
309 "Pretty music": *BB*, January 27, 1962.
309 The second largest sum paid for a single radio station: In December, 1961 Storer Radio, Inc. purchased WMGM in New York from Loew's Theatres for $10,950,000, after which Storer changed the station's call letters to its original WHN.
310 "Sad and noisy regression" . . . "idiot derivations like twist music": Sanjek, "The War on Rock," *DB*, p. 65. Adams's quotes were taken from a Sidney Fields column in the *NYDM*, January 1, 1962.
310 Joey Dee and the Starliters' "Peppermint Twist": "Peppermint Twist—Part 1" [Roulette 4401] appeared on *BB*'s "Hot 100" chart in November 1961. It became the #1 song in the United States in January 1962.
310 "Without Alan's power I was struggling": Interview with Hooke.
310 "Turned his head" . . . "couldn't blame" Clark: Interview with Hooke.
311 "Fair-weather friends": Interview with Greene.
311 "Was going to go" . . . "nearly as much": Interview with Alana Freed.
311 The previous September, Planetary Music: *BB*, January 20, 1962.
311 "Humiliation was evident in their faces": Castleman and Podrazik, *Watching TV*, p. 134.
311 Dr. Jive Smalls . . . "several out-of-town witnesses": *BB*, February 3, 1962.
311 "Beyond a reasonable doubt": *BB*, February 9, 1962.
312 Stone's . . . conviction record: Tripp had been found guilty in May 1961; Smalls pleaded guilty in January 1962.
312 "Also showing action": *BB*, February 17, 1962. "Alan Freed's Memory Lane" album entered *BB*'s chart at #146.
312 Smalls . . . sentenced to six months in jail: *BB*, April 4, 1962.
312 "Hoped for a return to rock and roll": *BB*, April 21, 1962.
312 "Battle royal": *BB*, August 4, 1962.
313 Levy, who "sold" WQAM: Interview with Hooke.
313 "Nip and tuck" ratings: *BB*, September 8, 1962.
313 "Didn't do well at all": Interview with Hooke.
313 "Was a bomb": *BB*, December 8, 1962.
313 "Against the development of a . . . personality cult": *BB*, December 8, 1962.
313 "Very rough guy to deal with" . . . "Big drinker" . . . "wasn't making it": Interview with Hooke.
313 "Last straw" to WQAM: *BB*, December 8, 1962.
314 "True friend" . . . "Morris was there": Interview with Alana Freed.
314 Trial would begin on December 10: *BB*, December 8, 1962.
314 "No deals, no bargaining" . . . "weary of the whole thing": Interview with Troob.
315 "Subdued manner" . . . "had had enough": Interview with Stone.
315 "Without the knowledge" . . . "gift": *BB*, December 29, 1962. These were the first and second counts of commercial bribery Freed had been charged with.
315 "Lack of funds" . . . "just as prevalent in the music business": *BB*, December 29, 1962.
315 "A waste" . . . "very hungry" . . . "Free and easy guy" . . . "the record business at the time": Interview with Stone.

316 "I would never do it again": Sullivan, "Alan Freed, Rose and Fell to Music of Rock 'n' Roll," *NYHT*, January 21, 1965.
316 "Music, the kids, and being somebody": Interview with Alana Freed.
316 "They're grown up, for the most part": Sullivan, "Alan Freed, Rose . . . ," *NYHT*, January 21, 1965.
316 "Acted almost like someone": Interview with Alana Freed.
316 "Often a moody and injudicious": Rolontz, "Alan Freed—An Appreciation," *Music Business*, February 6, 1965, p. 23.
316 "He would have loved": Interview with Alana Freed.
317 "Probably kept up with" . . . "we didn't see": Interview with Alana Freed.
317 "Unbearably bad": Warren Troob, Alan Freed Eulogy, February 6, 1965.
318 "Offered a job at WABC" . . . "time had passed" . . . Her father "got sick": Interview with Alana Freed.
319 "In large part": "Freed, Ex-Disc Jockey, Indicted in $37,920 U.S. Tax Evasion," *NYT*, March 17, 1964.
319 "Willfully failed": "Freed, Ex-Disc Jockey . . . ," *NYT*. Freed's claimed taxable income for 1957 was $123,818; for 1958, $33,850; and for 1959, $35,529. The IRS taxable income for those years was $137,977; $55,981; and $55,891, respectively.
319 "Disallowed [as business expenses]" . . . "no ifs, ands or buts": Shaw, *Honkers and Shouters*, p. 459.
319 "There was money somewhere": Interview with Greene.
319 "Piles of hundreds": Interview with Hooke.
320 "Very scared" . . . "What's going to happen now?": Interview with Alana Freed.
320 "Drinking and picking up the phone" . . . "Four, five thousand dollars": Interview with Hooke.
320 "100 percent" . . . "distrusted": Interview with Alana Freed.
321 "Pretty bitter" . . . "a lot of talking": Chernin, "Alan Freed's Heyday to Be Filmed," *CPD*, June 10, 1977.
321 "Using her" . . . "Don't do it" . . . "You're going to be sorry" . . . "he got sick": Interview with Alana Freed.
321 "Alan's very sick": Interview with Troob.
321 "Drinking a lot heavier" . . . "Looked bad": Interview with Troob.
322 "Reiterated the basic allegations": Herm Schoenfeld, *Variety*, December 1964, quoted by Sanjek, "The War on Rock," *DB*, p. 66.
322 "Until the night": Interview with Alana Freed.
322 "Was quite ill" . . . "would not quit drinking": Interview with David Freed.
322 "A good relationship" . . . "in and out": Interview with Alana Freed.
323 "He knew I was there": Interview with Alana Freed.
323 "Contribution" . . . "last friend Alan had": Fong-Torres, "Dick Clark," *RS*, August 16, 1973, p. 19.
323 "No way" . . . "did not happen": Interview with Alana Freed.
323 Lance was unable to recall . . . "the last friend": Fong-Torres, "Dick Clark," *RS*, August 16, 1973, p. 19.
323 "And they don't expect him to live": Interview with Hooke.
324 "After she had been drinking" . . . "want her anywhere" . . . "Not to come at all": Interview with Alana Freed.
324 "Looked up" . . . "Was asking for hot dogs": Interview with Hooke.
324 "Overlooking the courthouse": Interview with David Freed.
325 "One of the nation's best-known deejays": *NYDN*, January 20, 1965.
325 "The discoverer of rock": Sullivan, "Alan Freed, Rose . . . ," *NYHT*, January 20, 1965.
325 "Former deejay": "King of Rock 'n' Roll Dies," *Daily Oklahoman*, January 20, 1965.
325 "Slim, youthful-looking": "Alan Freed, Disk Jockey, Dead; Popularized Rock 'n' Roll Music," *NYT*, January 21, 1965.
325 "Up-tempo" . . . "slow blues": Editorial, *NYP*, January 21, 1965.
325 "Never called him": Interview with Dressel.
326 "Far more sensitive": Bundy, "Payola's First Fatality," *Music Business*, February 6, 1965, p. 23.
326 "Taken the rap": "Alan Freed, 'King of Rock & Roll,' Dies," *Cashbox*, January 30, 1965.
326 Bundy . . . "condemned": Bundy, "Payola's First Fatality," *Music Business*, February 6, 1965, p. 23.
326 "Nondenominational chapel": Interview with David Freed.
326 "Couldn't afford to go back" . . . "Was not easy": Interview with Alana Freed.
327 "Raised the standard": Interview with Troob.

POSTSCRIPT •

329 "Slapped liens on" . . . "minimal amount": Interview with Greene.
329 "Twelve years" . . . "more than we'd had": Interview with Alana Freed.
330 "Wouldn't recognize her" . . . "never sick a day in his life": Interview with Alana Freed.
330 "Had had big dreams" . . . "Visionary who did not hire": Fabrikant, "Craig McCaw's High-Risk Phone Bet," *NYT*, May 6, 1990.

NOTES

331 "Most important era" . . . "wouldn't mean anything": "Roulette to Reissue Alan Freed LP's for 'Hot Wax' Spinoff Try," *Variety*, May 4, 1978. .
331 "Godfather of Rock and Roll": Dannen, "The Godfather of Rock and Roll," *RS*, November 17, 1988, p. 89.
331 "Associate and victim" . . . "cash and property for leaders": Bastone, "Runnin' Scared" column, *VV*, May 29, 1990.
331 "A lot of them I like": Dannen, "The Godfather . . . ," *RS*, p. 92.
331 "I need dancing shoes": Bastone, *VV*, May 29, 1990.
331 "Conspiring" to extort La Monte . . . "finish burying me off": Dannen, "The Godfather . . . ," *RS*, November 17, 1988, pp. 96, 164.
332 "Longtime power": "Morris Levy Is Dead; Power in Recording and Club Owner, 62," *NYT*, May 23, 1990.
332 "Demonstrated that the music": Belz, *The Story of Rock*, p. 109.
333 "Almost as bland": Christgau, "So Payola Isn't Good, But It Isn't Such a Bad Thing Either," *Newsday*, June 17, 1973.
333 "Rock revolution had fallen": Marshak, "A Decade of Rock," *Rock*, January 5, 1970, p. 8.
333 "Rarely singled out" . . . "sophistication of the music": Belz, *The Story of Rock*, p. 117.
334 "At least we knew" . . . "who's playing it": Dachs, *Anything Goes*, p. 122.
334 "Play a record for two or three days": "George Goldner: Production Through Two Decades," *Rock*, April 27, 1970, p. 6.
334 "Big-time disc jockeys": Christgau, "So Payola . . . ," *Newsday*, June 17, 1973.
334 "The greatest story ever told": Aronowitz, "Murray the K's Entitled," *Fusion*, July 1972, p. 26.
335 "Would have liked to have been remembered": Rolontz, "Alan Freed—An Appreciation," *Music Business*, February 6, 1965, p. 22.
335 "Nigger-lover": Irwin, reprinted in Buzzell, p. 18.
335 "Like masturbation: exciting, but shameful": Greenfield, "They Changed Rock, Which Changed the Culture, Which Changed Us," *NYT Magazine*, February 16, 1975, p. 12.
335 "Rock age . . . assimilated everything in sight": Podell, *Rock Music in America*, p. 41.
335 "Insight that white people would listen": Eliot, *Rockonomics*, p. 85.
336 "Has ever done anyone": Christgau, "So Payola . . . ," *Newsday*, June 17, 1973.
336 "Everlasting credit": Stierle, "Considering the Source," *Rock*, May 24, 1971, p. 28.
336 "Father of rock": Ohio House of Representatives Proclamation, July 1985.
337 "One of rock and roll's first heroes": Fricke, "The Rock & Roll Hall of Fame Forefathers," *RS*, February 13, 1986, p. 48.
337 "Temper and hotheadedness": Rolontz, "Alan Freed—An Appreciation," *Music Business*, February 6, 1965, p. 22.

BIBLIOGRAPHY

Government Documents

CRIMDEL-CRS, "New York City District Attorney Charges Disk Jockies With Commercial Bribery," To: Director, FBI (63-4296)-34-, serial 602, From: SAC, New York (94-1138). Attached to the memo were two two-page reports, "Payments Put into Evidence and Included in the Information" and "Payments by Record Companies Introduced into Evidence but Not Included in the Information," May 20, 1960. Federal Bureau of Investigation.

"Disc Jockey 'Payola' Scandal; Alan Freed, New York 'Rock & Roll' Promoter," To: Carla D. ("Deke") De Loach, Assistant to the Director, From: [censored] 67c, Freed file #63-5721-1. Included in the file were the following newspaper clippings: Carr, "Disc Maker Says He Cut Clark In," *NYP*; Crist, "Alan Freed Now Out . . . ," *NYHT*; "Disk Jockey Won't . . . ," *Washington Post*; Marino, "Freed Swears . . . ," *NYDN*; "Rock 'n' Riot" editorial *NYHT*; and Scaduto and O'Grady, "Freed Faces DA . . . ," *NYP*. "Freed Pleads Guilty . . . ," *Broadcasting*, was added to the file on January 8, 1963. Memorandum originally dated December 2, 1959. Federal Bureau of Investigation.

"Request for Investigation in 'Payola'; Alan Freed [censored; probably Morris Levy] Fraud by Wire," To: Malcolm R. Wilkey, Assistant Attorney General, Criminal Division, From: Robert J. Rosthal, Deputy Chief, General Crimes Section, December 11, 1959. Federal Bureau of Investigation. Eliot, *Rockonomics*, pp. 263, 264.

The People of the State of New York v. Alan Freed, Court of Special Sessions, City of New York, Bench Warrant After Conviction (December 17, 1962), dated March 29, 1963.

The People of the State of New York v. Alan Freed, Court of Special Sessions, City of New York, Bench Warrant Charging to Arrest, dated May 10, 1960.

The People of the State of New York v. Alan Freed, Court of Special Sessions, City of New York, Notice of Appearance by Moses L. Kove, attorney for Alan Freed, May 19, 1960.

The People of the State of New York v. Alan Freed, Court of General Sessions, City of New York, Court Order by Judge Gerald P. Gulkin to NYDA to file the New York Grand Jury Information in Special Sessions, February 25, 1960.

The People of the State of New York v. Alan Freed, Court of General Sessions, City of New

York, Court Order by Judge Gerald P. Gulkin to NYDA to file New York Grand Jury twenty-five-count commercial bribery Information, fifteen-page Information attached, May 9, 1960.

The People of the State of New York v. Alan Freed, Court of General Sessions, City of New York, New York Grand Jury twenty-five-count commercial bribery Information, February, 1960.

The People of the State of New York v. Alan Freed, Recommendation by ADA Stone for DA Hogan that the Court of Special Sessions Order filing an information, May 6, 1960.

The People of the State of New York v. Peter G. Tripp, Court of Special Sessions, City of New York, Peoples Trial Memorandum, Joseph Stone and Michael Juvilier, ADAs, March 1961.

New York State Penal Law of 1909, Section 439: Corrupt influencing of agents, employees, or servants, pp. 367–368.

Ohio House of Representatives (116th General Assembly of Ohio), Rep. John D. Shivers, House District no. 3, July 1985.

U.S. House of Representatives, *Responsibilities of Broadcasting Licensees and Station Personnel: Hearings Before a Subcommittee of the Committee on Interstate and Foreign Commerce.* 86th Congress, 2d Session on Payola and Other Deceptive Practices in the Broadcasting Field. Part I: February 8, 9, 10, 15, 17, 18, 19, March 4, 1960. Part II: January 27, 28, 29, May 2, 3, August 30, 31, 1960, Washington D.C.: U.S. Government Printing Office, 1960.

U.S. House of Representatives, Special Subcommittee on Legislative Oversight of the Committee on Interstate and Foreign Commerce, Washington, D.C., *"Payola" and Related Deceptive Methods in the Broadcast Field,* Executive Session—Confidential Testimony of Alan Freed, Accompanied by Counsel Warren Troob, April 25, 1960, unpublished.

Books

Barnouw, Erik. *A Tower in Babel,* Vol. 1, *A History of Broadcasting in the U.S. to 1933.* New York: Oxford, 1966.

———. *The Golden Web,* Vol. 2, *A History of Broadcasting in the U.S., 1933–1953.* New York: Oxford, 1968.

———. *The Image Empire,* Vol. 3, *A History of Broadcasting in the U.S. from 1953.* New York: Oxford, 1970.

———. *Tube of Plenty: The Evolution of American Television.* New York: Oxford, 1975.

Belz, Carl. *The Story of Rock,* 2nd ed. New York: Oxford, 1972.

Bergreen, Lawrence. *Look Now, Pay Later: The Rise of Network Broadcasting.* Garden City, N.Y.: Doubleday, 1980.

Berry, Chuck, *The Autobiography.* New York: Harmony, 1987.

Berry, Jason; Foose, Jonathan; and Jones, Tad. *Up from the Cradle of Jazz: New Orleans Music Since World War II.* Athens: University of Georgia, 1986.

Buzzell, John, ed. *Mister 'Rock 'n' Roll' Alan Freed.* Los Angeles: National Rock 'n' Roll Archives, 1986. Includes the following reprinted magazine articles:

"Alan Freed . . . 'Mr. Dee-Jay' " (written late 1956)

"Alan Freed, Mr. Rock and Roll Himself" (December 1956), From *Who's Who in Rock 'n' Roll, 1958*

"Alan Freed," *Rock 'n' Roll Songs* (October 1957)

"Alan Freed Says: The Beat is Here to Stay" (summer 1958)

"Alan Freed . . . the Man Who Invented . . . Rock 'n' Roll" (fall 1959).

"Alan Freed's Teenage Crusade" (April 1956), from *Hit Parader,* June 1956

"Allan's King of the Rock 'n' Rollers" (August 1955), from *Star Date,* September 1955

"A Salute to Alan Freed," from Labor Day Stage Show Program Book, 1956

"A Story You Helped Write" (March 1956)

BIBLIOGRAPHY

    Helen Bolstad, "Rock 'n' Roll" (June 1956)
    George Christy, "Backstage at the Big Beat with Alan Freed" (late 1958)
    Alicia Evans, "The Rock 'n' Roll Story Featuring Alan Freed" (April 1956), from *Rock 'n' Roll Jamboree* (fall 1956)
    Theodore Irwin, "Rock 'n' Roll 'n' Alan Freed," from *Pageant*, July 1957
    Richard Sklar, "Why You Flip Over Freed" (written 1956).
Castleman, Harry, and Podrazik, Walter J. *Watching TV: Four Decades of American Television*. New York: McGraw-Hill, 1982.
Chapple, Steve, and Garofalo, Reebee. *Rock 'n' Roll Is Here to Pay*. Chicago: Nelson-Hall, 1977.
Clark, Dick. *Rock, Roll, and Remember*. New York: Popular Library, 1978.
Cotten, Lee. *Shake, Rattle, and Roll: The Golden Age of American Rock 'n' Roll*, Vol. 1, *1952–1955*. Ann Arbor, Mich.: Pierian Press, 1989.
Curtis, Jim. *Rock Eras: Interpretations of Music and Society, 1954–1984*. Bowling Green, Ohio: Bowling Green University Popular Press, 1987.
Dachs, David. *Anything Goes: The World of Popular Music*. New York: Bobbs-Merrill, 1964.
Dance, Stanley. *The World of Swing*, Vol. 1. New York: Scribners, 1974.
De Witt, Howard A. *Chuck Berry: Rock 'n' Roll Music*. Ann Arbor, Mich.: Pierian Press, 1985.
Dodge, John V., ed. *1960 Britannica Book of the Year*. Chicago: Encyclopaedia Britannica, 1960.
Eliot, Marc. *Rockonomics: The Money Behind the Music*. New York: Franklin Watts, 1989.
Ewen, David *The Life And Death of Tin Pan Alley (The Golden Age of Popular Music)*. New York: Funk and Wagnall's, 1964.
———. *Great Men of American Popular Song*. Englewood Cliffs, N.J.: Prentice-Hall, 1970.
Feather, Leonard. *The New Edition of the Encyclopedia of Jazz*. New York: Bonanza/Crown, 1960.
Fox, Ted. *Showtime at the Appollo*. New York: Holt, Rinehart and Winston, 1983.
———. *In the Groove: The People Behind the Music*. New York: St. Martin's, 1986.
Frederics, Vic, ed. *Who's Who in Rock 'n' Roll*. New York: Frederick Fell, 1958.
Gelatt, Roland. *The Fabulous Phonograph*. New York: Appleton-Century, 1965.
Giddins, Gary. *Riding on a Blue Note: Jazz and American Pop*. New York: Oxford, 1981.
Gillett, Charlie. *The Sound of the City: The Rise of American Rock and Roll*. New York: Outerbridge and Dienstfrey, 1970.
Gonzales, Fernando L., ed. *Disco-File: The Discographical Catalog of American Rock and Roll and Rhythm and Blues, 1902 to 1976*, 2nd ed. Flushing, N.Y.: Fernando L. Gonzales, 1977.
Gourse, Leslie. *Louis' Children: American Jazz Singers*. New York: William Morrow, 1984.
Groia, Phil. *They All Sang on the Corner*. Setauket, N.Y.: Edmond, 1973.
Hoffman, Abbie. *Woodstock Nation*. New York: Vintage, 1969.
Hopkins, Jerry. *The Rock Story*. New York: Signet, 1970.
Jackson, John A. *Big Beat Legends: Television's Golden Age*. Point Pleasant, N.J.: Renaissance Home Theatre, 1987.
Kane, Russel W., ed. *The World Book*, Vol. 4. Chicago: World Book, 1986.
Karshner, Roger. *The Music Machine*. Los Angeles: Nash, 1971.
Kusmer, Kenneth. *A Ghetto Takes Shape: Black Cleveland, 1870–1930*. Urbana: University of Illinois Press, 1976.
Lewis, Myra, and Silver, Murray. *Great Balls of Fire: The Uncensored Story of Jerry Lee Lewis*. New York: Quill, 1982.
London, Herbert I. *Closing the Circle: A Cultural History of the Rock Revolution*. Chicago: Nelson-Hall, 1984.
Lydon, Michael. *Rock Folk*. New York: Dial, 1971.
———. *Boogie Lightning*. New York: Dial, 1974.
McCutcheon, Lynn Ellis. *Rhythm and Blues*. Arlington, Va.: Beatty, 1971.
MacDonald, J. Fred. *Don't Touch That Dial! Radio Programming in American Life from 1920 to 1960*. Chicago: Nelson-Hall, 1979.
Maltin, Leonard. *TV Movies 1985–86*. New York: Signet, 1984.
Mattfield, Julius. *Variety Musical Cavalcade: Musical History Review*. Englewood Cliffs, N.J.: Prentice-Hall, 1962.

Mayer, Martin. *About Television.* New York: Harper and Row, 1972.
Mendheim, Beverly. *Ritchie Valens: The First Latino Rocker.* Tempe, Ariz.: Bilingual, 1987.
Millar, Bill. *The Drifters: The Rise and Fall of the Black Vocal Group.* New York: Macmillan, 1971.
Mish, Frederick C., ed. *Webster's Ninth New Collegiate Dictionary.* Springfield, Mass.: Merriam-Webster, 1987.
Murray, Albert. *Good Morning Blues: The Autobiography of Count Basie.* New York: Random House, 1985.
Nash, Jay Robert. *Citizen Hoover: A Critical Study of the Life and Times of J. Edgar Hoover and His FBI.* Chicago: Nelson-Hall, 1972.
Norman, Philip. *Shout!: The Beatles in Their Generation.* New York: Warner, 1981.
Passman, Arnold. *The Deejays.* New York: Macmillan, 1971.
Ploski, Harry A., *The Negro Almanac.* New York: Bellwether, 1976.
Podell, Janet, ed. *Rock Music in America.* New York: Wilson, 1987.
Polk's Directory: Salem, Ohio City Directory. Volumes from 1937, 1940, 1957–1958, and 1960.
Pollack, Bruce. *When Rock Was Young.* New York: Holt, Rinehart and Winston, 1981.
Quaker Annual: Salem High School Yearbook. Volumes from 1935, 1937, 1938, 1939, 1940, 1941.
Redd, Lawrence N. *Rock Is Rhythm and Blues (The Impact of Mass Media).* Ann Arbor: Michigan State, 1974.
Rosen, George, *Americana Annual, 1956.* New York: Americana, 1956.
Salem (Ohio) Story: Sesquicentennial Souvenir Book, 1806–1956.
Shaw, Arnold. *The Rockin' '50s: The Decade That Transformed the Pop Music Scene.* New York: Hawthorn, 1974.
———. *Honkers and Shouters: The Golden Years of Rhythm and Blues.* New York: Macmillan, 1978.
Sklar, Rick. *Rocking America.* New York: St. Martin's, 1984.
Sterling, Christopher H., and Kittross, John M. *Stay Tuned: A Concise History of American Broadcasting.* Belmont, Calif.: Wadsworth, 1978.
Szatmary, David P. *Rockin' in Time: A Social History of Rock and Roll.* Englewood Cliffs, N.J.: Prentice-Hall, 1987.
Theoharis, Athan G., and Cox, John Stuart. *The Boss: J. Edgar Hoover and the Great American Inquisition.* Philadelphia: Temple University Press, 1988.
Tosches, Nick. *Country: The Biggest Music in America.* New York: Stein and Day, 1977.
———. *Unsung Heroes of Rock 'n' Roll: The Birth of Rock 'n' Roll in the Dark and Wild Years Before Elvis.* New York: Scribners, 1984.
Vexler, Robert I., ed. *Cleveland; A Chronological and Documentary History, 1760–1976.* Dobbs Ferry, N.Y.: Oceana, 1977.
Whitburn, Joel. *Pop Memories, 1890–1954: The History of American Popular Music.* Menomonee Falls, Wis.: Record Research Inc., 1986.
———. *Top Pop Singles, 1955–1986.* Menomonee Falls, Wis.: Record Research Inc., 1987.
———. *Top R&B Singles, 1942–1988.* Menomonee Falls, Wis.: Record Research Inc., 1988.
———. *Top Country Singles, 1944–1988.* Menomonee Falls, Wis.: Record Research Inc., 1989.
Wood, Carlyle, ed. *TV Personalities Biographical Sketchbook,* Vol. 3. St. Louis: 1957.
———. *TV Personalities Biographical Sketchbook,* Vol. 4. St. Louis: 1958.
Yust, Walter, ed. *1946 Britannica Book of the Year.* Chicago: Encyclopaedia Britannica, 1946.
———. *1952 Britannica Book of the Year.* Chicago: Encyclopaedia Britannica, 1952.
———. *1959 Britannica Book of the Year.* Chicago: Encyclopaedia Britannica, 1959.

Articles and Documents

Abrams, Norma, and Patterson, Neal. "Hogan Slaps Payola Rap on Freed and 7," *New York Daily News,* May 20, 1960.
Abrams, Norma, and Quirk, David. "Subpoena Invites Freed to DA's Payola Show," *New York Daily News,* November 26, 1959.

BIBLIOGRAPHY

Ackerman, Paul. "All Are Getting Hip," *Billboard*, January 4, 1956.
———. "Square Circles Peg Rock and Roll Idiom as a Beat to Stick," *Billboard*, February 4, 1956.
"A Closed Hearing Is Held on Clark; Payola Inquiry Goes Into Disk Jockey's Business Ties—Alan Freed Testifies," *New York Times*, April 26, 1960.
Adams, Val. "House Unit to Query D. Clark," *New York Times*, November 18, 1959.
"Age of Payola," *Look*, March 29, 1960.
"Alan Freed And 7 Arrested Here," *New York Times*, May 20, 1960.
"Alan Freed Bankrupt," *New York Times*, July 19, 1958.
"Alan Freed Bars Immunity Waiver," *New York Times*, December 1, 1959.
"Alan Freed 'Breaking It Up' at Brooklyn Paramount," *Billboard*, September 9, 1957.
"Alan Freed: Daddy of the Big Beat," *Hit Parader*, December 1958.
"Alan Freed Deal with Coral Label Definitely Tabled," *Billboard*, May 7, 1955.
"Alan Freed, Disc Jockey, Dead; Popularized Rock 'n' Roll Music," *New York Times*, January 21, 1965.
"Alan Freed Is Out in Payola Study," *New York Times*, November 22, 1959.
"Alan Freed, 'King of Rock & Roll,' Dies," *Cashbox*, January 30, 1965.
"Alan Freed Loses 2D Broadcasting Job," *New York Times*, November 24, 1959.
"Alan Freed—Obituary," *Variety*, January 27, 1965.
"Alan Freed—Obituary," *Time*, January 29, 1965.
"Alan Freed—Obituary," *Newsweek*, February 1, 1965.
"Alan Freed Pays $300 Fine," *New York Times*, March 13, 1963.
"Alan Freed Receives Subpoena from Hogan on Payola Inquiry," *New York Times*, November 26, 1959.
"Alan Freed Rocks Brooklyn with 'Big Beat' Show," *Billboard*, September 9, 1958.
"Alan Freed to Play Discs on Miami Station WQAM," *New York Times*, August 29, 1962.
"Alan Freed to Promote 'Rock & Roll Ball' in N.Y.," *Variety*, December 22, 1954.
"Alan Freed Top 25—November 24, 1956," *Bim Bam Boom* No. 1, August-September 1971.
"Alan Freed Wins Point; Boston Won't Press Anarchy Case," *New York Times*, March 7, 1959.
Apugliesi, John, Sr.; Flam, Steve; and Newman, Ralph M. "Little Anthony & the," *Bim Bam Boom* no. 9, 1973.
Aronowitz, Al. "Murray the K's Entitled," *Fusion* no. 76, July 1972.
Asbury, Edith Adams. "Rock 'n' Roll Teen-Agers Tie Up Times Square Area," *New York Times*, February 23, 1957.
———. "Times Sq. 'Rocks' for Second Day," *New York Times*, February 24, 1957.
Bailin, Fred. "Herald-Ember (The Al Silver Story)," *Bim Bam Boom* no. 6, July 1972.
Baker, Cary. "Johnny Rivers Weathers the Storm," *Goldmine* no. 80, January 1983.
Baker, Glenn A. "Johnny Rivers, the Singer Not the Song," *Goldmine* no. 180, June 19, 1987.
Bastone, William. "Runnin' Scared" column, *Village Voice* (New York), May 29, 1990.
Belaire, Felix, Jr. "Rogers Proposes Strict Controls for TV & Radio," *New York Times*, January 1, 1960.
Blair, John. "Early Rock Cinema," *Goldmine* no. 40, September 1979.
Blair, William M. "FCC Urges Law on Deceit on Air," *New York Times*, February 12, 1960.
"Block That Schlock," *Time*, November 23, 1959.
"Boston Indictment Sought," *New York Times*, May 8, 1958.
"Boston, New Haven Ban 'Rock' Shows," *New York Times*, May 6, 1958.
Bracker, Milton. "Experts Propose Study of 'Craze'; Liken It to Medieval Lunacy," *New York Times*, February 23, 1957.
Bream, Terry. "Elvis on TV," *Goldmine* no. 196, January 29, 1988.
"Bruce Debs New Label," *Billboard*, August 25, 1956.
"Bryant Story—R&B Hassle Envelops Alan Freed," *Billboard*, October 9, 1954.

Bundy, June. "Alan Freed's 'Rock 'n' Roll' Show Opens," *Billboard*, April 16, 1955.
———. "Indie Station Balking at 'Farm Club' Role Re Deejays," *Billboard*, May 28, 1955.
———. "Rock & Roll Supports 2 Big-Budget Shows," *Billboard*, January 7, 1956.
———. "Deejay Emerges as Powerhouse Promoter of R&B Personals," *Billboard*, February 4, 1956.
———. "Freed Replies to R&R Press Slurs," *Billboard*, April 28, 1956.
———. "Freed's New Movie Adds Up to Triple-Threat $s," *Billboard*, November 17, 1956.
———. "Payola's First Fatality," *Music Business*, February 6, 1965.
"Busy Jockey," *Billboard*, August 19, 1957.
Carr, H. A. "Disc Maker Says He Cut Clark In," *New York Post*, November 30, 1959.
"CBS Chief Issues Bribe Warning," *New York Times*, December 2, 1959.
"CBS Plots Sun. Evening Rock, Roll Net Show," *Billboard*, January 28, 1956.
"Chance Records Signs Moonglows, Managed by Al (Moondog) Freed," *Billboard*, October 24, 1953.
"Charges Dropped Against Hal Jackson," *New York Times*, February 9, 1962.
Chernin, Donna. "Alan Freed's Heyday to Be Filmed," *Cleveland Plain Dealer*, June 10, 1977.
Christgau, Robert. "Chuck Berry's Back from the Blues," *Creem*, February 1973.
———. "So Payola Isn't Good, But It Isn't Such a Bad Thing Either," *Newsday* (Long Island), June 17, 1973.
"Clark Is Accused of Giving Payola," *New York Times*, April 27, 1960.
"Competition Hits All-Time High in DJ Field," *Billboard*, February 10, 1958.
Cotter, Joseph, and Carr, William H. A. "DJ Alan Freed and 6 Others Arrested in Payola Probe," *New York Post*, May 19, 1960.
Courtney, Ron. "Blues in the Night: The Story of WLAC Radio," *Goldmine* no. 93, February 1984.
Crist, Judith. "Alan Freed Now Out at WNEW-TV," *New York Herald Tribune*, November 24, 1959.
———. "Hogan Hears Singer Tell of Payola," *New York Herald Tribune*, November 28, 1959.
———. "Freed Won't Sign Waiver for Inquiry," *New York Herald Tribune*, December 1, 1959.
Crowther, Bosley. *The Girl Can't Help It* review, *New York Times*, February 9, 1957.
Dannen, Fredric. "The Godfather of Rock and Roll," *Rolling Stone*, November 17, 1988.
Davis, Steve. "Payola '70," *Rock*, no. 17, April 27, 1970.
"Decision Due May 15 in Trial on Payola," *New York Times*, May 4, 1961.
"Deejay Freed Has Himself a Busy Week," *Billboard*, September 17, 1955.
"Detroit Radio Star Confesses Payola," *New York Times*, November 23, 1959.
"Disc Jockey Freed; Boston Won't Press Riot Case Against Alan Freed," *New York Times*, November 13, 1959.
"Disc Jockeys Curbed," *New York Times*, December 1, 1959.
"Disc Jockeys: Now Don't Cry—Wages of Spin," *Time*, December 7, 1959.
"Disc Jockey Won't Waive Immunity," *Washington Post*, December 1, 1959.
"Diskeries Race for R&R Country Talent," *Billboard*, May 12, 1956.
"Elvis Presley Pacted for Day by Tupelo Fair," *Billboard*, June 2, 1956.
"End of Payola Charge Urged," *New York Times*, July 1, 1961.
Engel, Lyle Kenyon, ed. "The Moonglows Sincerely," *Rock 'n' Roll Stars* no. 2, 1957.
"E.P. Is V.I.P. for Victor," *Billboard*, May 12, 1956.
Escott, Colin, and Booth, David. "Ronnie Hawkins: A Legend in His Spare Time," *Goldmine* no. 258, June 15, 1990.
Fabrikant, Geraldine. "Craig McCaw's High-Risk Phone Bet," *New York Times*, May 6, 1990.
"Facing the Music," *Time*, November 30, 1959.
Fanselow, Julie. "Alan Freed: 'Al J,' Just Your Average Salem Teen, Went on to Become 'Mister Rock and Roll,'" *Salem* (Ohio) *News*, July 16, 1985.

Farlekus, Mike. "Memory Lane," *Bim Bam Boom* no. 7, September 1972.
"Fear Of Rock-Roll Nixes Connecticut Date," *Billboard*, June 4, 1955.
Fields, Sidney. "Only Human" column *New York Daily Mirror*, March 18, 1957.
"15 More Accused of Disk Payolas," *New York Times*, January 3, 1960.
"Fighter Capers in Revue," *Cleveland Plain Dealer*, July 19, 1953.
"1st Full-Scale Straight R&B Pact by Coral," *Billboard*, February 25, 1956.
Fong-Torres, Ben. "Dick Clark: Twenty Years of Clearasil Rock," *Rolling Stone*, no. 141, August 16, 1973.
Freed, Alan. "Alan Freed Says, 'I Told You So . . . ,' " *Downbeat*, September 19, 1956.
"Freed Breaks Record; Jive Big in Harlem," *Billboard*, April 28, 1955.
"Freed Denies Charges," *New York Times*, May 17, 1958.
"Freed Denies Pay to 'Plug,' " *New York Times*, November 29, 1959.
"Freed Denies Riot Role; DJ Asks Dismissal at Boston Fracas Indictment," *New York Times*, June 5, 1958.
"Freed Enjoined from Use of 'Moondog' Label," *Billboard*, December 4, 1954.
"Freed, Ex-Disc Jockey, Indicted in $37,920 U.S. Tax Evasion," *New York Times*, March 17, 1964.
"Freed Eyes London for Fall R&B Show," *Billboard*, July 14, 1956.
"Freed Falls in New Haven," *New York Times*, May 8, 1958.
"Freed Family: He Died for This Music," *Rock*, February 15, 1971.
"Freed Indicted Again," *New York Times*, May 15, 1958.
"Freed Is Indicted over Rock 'n' Roll," *New York Times*, May 9, 1958.
"Freed-Levy Back Together Again," *Billboard*, May 27, 1957.
"Freed, Levy Come to Parting of the Ways," *Billboard*, March 30, 1957.
"Freed Mum About Coral Negotiations," *Billboard*, March 12, 1955.
"Feed Pleads Guilty, Is Fined For Payola," *Broadcasting*, December 31, 1962.
"Freed Recommends Two for Coral Pacts," *Billboard*, August 25, 1956.
"Freed Show Fights Ban in New Haven," *New York Times*, May 7, 1958.
"Freed's Post at Coral Clarified," *Billboard*, March 3, 1956.
"Freed's R&R Run pus Stops Traffic at Brooklyn Par," *Billboard*, April 16, 1956.
"Freed to Sponsor 'Rock & Roll' Ball," *Billboard*, December 25, 1954.
Fricke, David. "The Rock and Roll Hall of Fame Forefathers," *Rolling Stone*, no. 467, February 13, 1986.
Fries, Dan. "Chuck Berry Interview," *Goldmine* no. 42, November 1979.
"From One Scandal to Another," *U.S. News & World Report*, December 7, 1959.
"FTC Dismisses a Case; End of Payola Urged," *New York Times*, July 1, 1961.
"FTC Dismisses Charges of Payola," *New York Times*, June 21, 1961.
"FTC Names 9 Companies in Payola Deals," *New York Times*, December 5, 1959.
Galgano, Bob. "Cleftones Interview," *Bim Bam Boom* no. 1, August-September 1971.
Gart, Galen. "Ruth Brown Interview," *Bim Bam Boom* no. 11, 1973.
"George Goldner: Production Through the Decades," *Rock* no. 17, April 27, 1970.
Gillett, Charlie. "Alan Freed," *Stormy Weather* no. 3, January 1970.
"Gimmee, Gimmee, Gimmee on the Old Payola," *Life*, November 23, 1959.
Goldberg, Lenny. "Alan Freed Story," *Rock*, July 20, 1970.
Goldblatt, David. "Boys of Rock 'n' Roll: The Teenagers After 25 Years," *Village Voice* (New York), April 15–21, 1981.
———. "Lewis Lymon Interview," *Goldmine* no. 80, January 1983.
"Goodbye, Ookie Dookie: Payola," *Newsweek*, February 22, 1960.
"Got Live If You Want It," *Rock*, January 5, 1970.
Grasso, Bob. "TV DJ's," *Goldmine* no. 23, February 1978.
Greenfield, Jeff. "But Papa, It's My Music, I Like It," *New York Times*, March 7, 1971.

———. "They Changed Rock, Which Changed the Culture, Which Changed Us," *New York Times Magazine*, February 16, 1975.
Grendysa, Peter. "Spotlight on LaVern Baker," *Record Collectors' Monthly* no. 19, April 1984.
———. "King Records, Born of War & Shortages, Thrived by Serving Peripheral Markets," *Record Collectors' Monthly* no. 33, November-December 1985.
———. "Jubilee," *Goldmine* no. 231, June 2, 1989.
Grevatt, Ren, "On the Beat," *Billboard*, February 24, 1958.
Hall, Doug. "NY Exploded Via Clevelander Freed," *Billboard*, December 2, 1978.
Hammer, Alexander R. "Fad Also Rocks Cash Registers," *New York Times*, February 23, 1957.
Healy, Paul, "DJ Kicked Back 30G to ABC for Airing His Plugs," *New York Daily News*, May 4, 1960.
"Hit Parade Omits Words of Song Banned by WWJ," *New York Times*, November 26, 1951.
"Hogan Questions Stars," *New York Times*, December 5, 1959.
"Hogan Studies Fraud in TV; Payola Denied by Deejays," *New York Times*, November 8, 1959.
"House Unit Plans Payola Remedies," *New York Times*, May 20, 1960.
"House Unit Spurs Payola Inquiry," *New York Times*, November 19, 1959.
"House Unit to Query Clark," *New York Times*, November 18, 1959.
"How Rock and Roll Started," Unidentified source, 1956.
"Hub Faithful Rock 'n' Roll," *Billboard*, June 4, 1955.
Ifill, James. "The Royaltones," *Yesterday's Memories* no. 3, 1975.
"Jersey Guard Bars Rock 'n' Roll Show in Newark Armory," *New York Times*, May 8, 1958.
"Jockies on a Rough Ride," *Newsweek*, December 7, 1959.
"Jocks Make Hay," *Billboard*, December 31, 1955.
"Joe Louis Packs in 10,000 Trained Squeals for Show," *Cleveland Plain Dealer*, July 21, 1953.
Jones, Wayne. "Nate Nelson Interview," *Goldmine* no. 24, March 1978.
———. "Talks With Little Anthony," *Goldmine* No. 59, April 1981.
———. "The Harptones—Willie Winfield Interview," *Goldmine* no. 82, March 1983.
"Joyce Pacts Haley to 2d Columbia Pic," *Billboard*, September 16, 1956.
"Jury Here Opens Payola Inquiry," *New York Times*, February 3, 1960.
"King of Rock 'n' Roll Dies," *Daily Oklahoman*, January 20, 1965.
Kosner, Edward. "DA Calls for Alan Freed's Accounts; 'I'll Be Back,' Disc Jockey Tells Fans," *New York Post*, November 29, 1959.
Kozinn, Alan. "Moondog Returns from the Hippie Years," *New York Times*, November 16, 1989.
Kramer, Gary. "Rhythm & Blues Notes," *Billboard*, December 15, 1956.
Levy, Morris. "The World of Soul," *Billboard*, Special Summer Issue, 1967.
"Levy Again Wants In on Roost Label," *Billboard*, March 3, 1956.
Lewis, Anthony. "Miami TV Station Loses Its License," *New York Times*, October 19, 1961.
Lewis, Milton. "Payola Probe Hears 5 in Disk Firms," *New York Herald Tribune*, February 3, 1960.
Little Walter, and Vance, Marcia. "Richard Barrett Remembers," *Bim Bam Boom* no. 4, February-March 1972.
Marino, Anthony, "Freed Swears 'No TV Payola' & Loses Job," *New York Daily News*, November 24, 1959.
Marino, Anthony, and Smee, Jack. "TV Will Ask Freed Today: Any Payola?" *New York Daily News*, November 23, 1959.
Marion, Jean-Charles, "In the Beginning: A New Excitement," *Record Exchanger* no. 14, 1973.
Marshak, Larry. "A Decade of Rock," *Rock*, January 5, 1970.
———. "The Birth of Rock 'n' Roll," *Rock*, July 6, 1970.
"Mayor Passes up Yankee Opener, Bowing to Musicians' Picket Line," *New York Times*, April 16, 1954.

BIBLIOGRAPHY

"Moondog Ball Is Halted As 6,000 Crash Gate Area," *Cleveland Plain Dealer*, March 22, 1952.
"Moondog Ball Pulls 2,480," *Billboard*, November 28, 1953.
"Moondog to WINS; Freed Freed of WJW to Start in N.Y. in Fall," *Billboard*, July 10, 1954.
" 'Moondog' Wins a Point," *New York Times*, November 25, 1954.
Moonoogian, George. "Wax Fax" column, *Record Collectors' Monthly* no. 28, February-March 1985.
"Morris Levy Is Dead; Power in Recording and Club Owner, 62," *New York Times*, May 23, 1990.
"Music Business Goes Round and Round: It Comes Out Clarkola," *Life*, May 16, 1960.
"Music, Maestro, Please—Leroy Kirkland Interview," *Big Town Review* no. 2, April-May 1972.
Nason, Richard W. *Mister Rock and Roll* review, *New York Times*, October 17, 1957.
"NBC Explains Its TV Position," *New York Times*, November 29, 1959.
"NBC Scores Time on Quiz Scandals," *New York Times*, November 23, 1959.
"Nets Find R&R No Butt for Jokes," *Billboard*, April 28, 1956.
Newman, Ralph M. "The George Goldner Story (As Told by Sam Goldner)," *Bim Bam Boom* no. 7, September 1972.
———. "Screamin' Jay Hawkins," *Bim Bam Boom* no. 7, September 1972.
"9 Payola Charges Added by FTC," *New York Times*, February 1, 1960.
"Nobody Blew the Whistle," *Newsweek*, May 9, 1960.
Nolan, Tom. "America Waxes Hot," *Village Voice* (New York), March 20, 1978.
"No Skids for R&B or R&R," *Billboard*, July 14, 1956.
"On the Beat," *Billboard*, July 29, 1957.
"Pay-Offs Disclosed," *New York Times*, November 22, 1959.
"Payola," *Broadcasting*, February 15, 1960.
"Payola Axes King Freed," *Life*, December 7, 1959.
"Payola Blues," *Newsweek*, November 30, 1959.
"Payola Cases Dropped, FTC Dismisses Charges Against Five Companies," *New York Times*, September 1, 1961.
"Payola Givers Facing FTC 'Unfair' Charges," *New York Post*, December 1, 1959.
"Payola—An Inside Story Told Four Years Ago," *U.S. News & World Report*, December 21, 1959.
"Peter Tripp Trial: Testimony Ended in Disk Jockey Suit," *New York Times*, May 3, 1961.
"Pitcher Wagner Stays Away," *New York Times*, April 17, 1954.
"Pop and R&B Charts Spot Same 8 Disks," *Billboard*, May 12, 1956.
"Presley on Pan But Cash Keeps Rolling," *Billboard*, June 14, 1956.
"R&B Disk Jockeys to Form Own Org.," *Billboard*, February 4, 1956.
"RCA Near on M. Levy Deal," *Billboard*, August 27, 1955.
"Record Concern Has Freed's Mortgage," *New York Times*, December 4, 1959.
Richard, Mike. "Banned in Boston," *Goldmine* no. 41, October 1979.
"Robert Montgomery Says TV Long Had Hints of Rigging," *New York Times*, January 16, 1960.
"Rock & Roll Summer on TV.," *Billboard*, June 27, 1957.
"Rock 'n' Fight with Alan Freed," *Rock & Roll Songs*, July 1956.
"Rock 'n' Riot" (editorial), *New York Herald Tribune*, May 13, 1958.
"Rock 'n' Riot," *Time*, May 19, 1958.
"Rock 'n' Roll Exported to 4 Corners of Globe," *New York Times*, February 23, 1957.
"Rock 'n' Roll: Freed Ball Takes 24G at St. Nick," *Billboard*, January 22, 1955.
"Rock 'n' Roll Pied Piper—Alan Freed," *New York Times*, May 20, 1960.
"Rock 'n' Roll Plays; Young Moviegoers Jam Times Square, But Are Orderly," *New York Times*, February 25, 1957.
"Rock 'n' Roll Stabbing," *New York Times*, May 5, 1958.
"Rock 'n' Rollers Collect Calmly," *New York Times*, July 4, 1957.

"A Rock Chronology," *Rock*, January 5, 1970.
"Rock from the Beginning," *100 of the Greatest Rock & Roll Hits*, 1972.
"Rockin' And Rollin' Again," *Newsday* (Long Island), March 12, 1978.
Roeser, Steve. "I'm Tired of Being Called a Rip-Off Artist!" *Sh-Boom*, March 1990.
Rolontz, Bob. "R&B Notes" column, *Billboard*, June 7, 1952.
———. "Many Indie Disk Houses Struggle for Survival in Vital 14-Block Area," *Billboard*, September 5, 1953.
———. "Alan Freed—An Appreciation," *Music Business*, February 6, 1965.
Roth, Jack. "Tripp Fined $500 in Payola Case," *New York Times*, October 17, 1961.
"Roulette to Reissue Alan Freed LP's for 'Hot Wax' Spinoff Try," *Variety*, May 4, 1978.
"Royola," *Time*, May 9, 1960.
Salvo, Patrick William. "A Conversation with Chuck Berry," *Rolling Stone*, no. 122, November 23, 1972.
Sanjek, Russell. "The War on Rock" (lecture delivered during second session of Atomic Youth and the Rock Mushroom, New School for Social Research, New York City), *Downbeat 17th Annual Yearbook/Music '72*, 1972.
Scaduto, Anthony, and O'Grady, Jack. "Freed Faces DA, Balks at Waiver," *New York Post*, November 30, 1959.
Schippers, Henry. "Dick Clark," *Rolling Stone*, no. 576, April 19, 1990.
Schoenfeld, Herm. "Teenagers Like 'Hot Rod' Tempo," *Variety*, January 19, 1955.
Scott, Jane. "Thirty Years Ago, 'Moon Dog' Howled," *Cleveland Plain Dealer*, March 14, 1982.
"2D Jackpot for Presley," *Billboard*, May 26, 1956.
"Seniors Receive Diplomas; Go to Alumni Rally Tonight," *Salem News*, June 7, 1940.
Sheard, Don. "Freed Balks at Testifying Before Payola Jury," *New York Journal-American*, November 30, 1959.
Shephard, Richard F. "Alan Freed Is Out in Payola Study," *New York Times*, November 22, 1959.
———. "Hogan Subpoenaes Freed's Papers," *New York Times*, November 28, 1959.
———. "FCC Action Near on WINS, WMGM; Reports Requested," *New York Times*, July 8, 1961.
"Sightless Musician Sounds Off in Court," *New York Times*, November 24, 1954.
Slifka, Adrian, "Freed's 'Preaching' Style Attracts $75,000 Contract," *Youngstown Vindicator*, August 1954.
Smart, Peter. "Eddie Fontaine: The Shakin' Story," *Goldmine* no. 58, March 1981.
"Smith Leaves for WOR," *Billboard*, May 26, 1956.
"Station WINS Sold, If FCC Approves," *New York Times*, August 10, 1953.
Stierle, Wayne. "Considering the Source," *Rock*, May 24, 1971.
———. "The Shells," *Bim Bam Boom* no. 7, September 1972.
"Suit Vs. BMI Moves Ahead," *Billboard*, December 12, 1955.
Sullivan, James W. "Alan Freed, Rose and Fell to Music of Rock 'n' Roll," *New York Herald Tribune*, January 21, 1965.
Tancredi, Carl. "The Flamingos," *Bim Bam Boom* no. 4, February-March 1972.
"Teen Tune Is Freed's 15th," *Billboard*, January 14, 1956.
"Testimony Ended in Disc Jockey Suit," *New York Times*, May 3, 1961.
"There Ought to Be a Law; Lavern Baker Seeks Bill to Halt Arrangement 'Thefts,'" *Billboard*, March 5, 1955.
"37 Held After Riots in London," *New York Times*, September 17, 1956.
Thompson, Howard H. "Frenzy 'n' Furor Featured at Paramount," *New York Times*, February 23, 1957.
"Title Change for Haley Pic," *Billboard*, September 22, 1956.

Torre, Marie. "Alan Freed Still Idol to His Teen-Age Fans," *New York Herald Tribune*, November 25, 1959.
"Tripp Guilty of Taking Payola While Radio Disc Jockey Here," *New York Times*, May 16, 1961.
Turco, Art. "Bobby Robinson Interview: Part 1," *Record Exchanger* no. 10, May 1972.
———. "Little Anthony Interview," *Record Exchanger* no. 14, 1973.
"TV Abuses Ended, Sarnoff Testifies," *New York Times*, January 29, 1960.
TV Guide, May 4–11, July 7–13, 14–20, 21–27, July 28–August 3, 1957.
"20,000 Rock 'n' Rollers Queue for Block in Midtown to Crowd Holiday Show," *New York Times*, December 28, 1957.
"2BB Crowns for Presley on Berle's TV," *Billboard*, June 2, 1956.
"U.S. Ban on Payola Accepted by RCA," *New York Times*, December 16, 1959.
Vance, Marcia, and Groia, Phil. "The Willows," *Bim Bam Boom* no. 6, July 1972.
Van Doren, Charles. Transcript of his "confession," *New York Times*, November 3, 1959.
"The Voice & Payola," *Time*, September 9, 1957.
"WABC Debut of Freed Radio Show," *New York Times*, May 20, 1958.
Watson, Carl. Memo to Stockton Helfrich, dated July 14, 1955, "Payola—An Inside Story Told Four Years Ago," *U.S. News & World Report*, December 21, 1959.
"What Would Victoria Say," *Billboard*, April 14, 1956.
Whelton, Clark. "He Was the King of Rock and Roll," *New York Times*, September 24, 1972.
"Wider TV Inquiry to Study Bribery & Paid Plugs," *New York Times*, November 7, 1959.
Williams, Bob. "Freed Replaced on Today's Ch. 5 Show—Union Sets Payola Talk with DA," *New York Post*, November 23, 1959.
Wilson, Earl. "Alan Freed's Story," *New York Post*, November 23, 1959.
———. "Alan Freed Telling All About Payola to House Probers; Drops TV Shows," *New York Post*, November 25, 1959.
Wilson, Earl, and Carr, H. A. "Record Man Says He Gave Freed $11,000 Interest-Free Loan in '56," *New York Post*, December 3, 1959.
"WINS Issues Ban on Copy Records," *Billboard*, August 27, 1955.
"WINS Places Freed Show in 5 Markets," *Billboard*, August 28, 1954.
Wise, David. "52 Witnesses Due at F.C.C. Quiz on TV," *New York Herald Tribune*, November 28, 1959.
"WNJR Sold by Paper," *New York Times*, September 9, 1953.
"WWJ, WWJ-TV (Detroit) Bans Lyrics of 2 Songs," *New York Times*, October 27, 1951.
"You Can't Do That to Elvis," *Billboard*, July 14, 1956.

Television and Radio Programs; Documentary Films

"Alan Freed's Big Beat" (audiotape), WABC-AM Radio, New York, March 12, 1959.
"Alan Freed's Big Beat" (audiotape), WABC-AM Radio, New York, April, 1959.
Big Beat Legends: The Evolution of Rock on Television (videocassette), Produced by Renaissance Home Theatre, 1987.
"Chess, Marshall," Installment of "The Old Rock And Roll Show" (audiotape) with Ralph M. Newman, WPIX-FM, New York, November 24, 1979.
"Diddley, Bo," Installment of "Live at Five," with Jack Cafferty and Connie Collins, WNBC-TV, New York, April, 1980.
Don't Knock the Rock, Columbia Pictures, produced by Sam Katzman, 1956.
Heroes of Rock 'n' Roll (film documentary), produced by Jack Haley, Jr., 1979.
"Moondog Coronation Ball—30th Anniversary" (audiotape), "Don K. Reed's Do-Wop Shop," WPIX-FM, New York, March 21, 1982.
"Moondog House" (audiotape), WJW-AM, WJW-FM, Cleveland, March 22, 1952, March 31, 1954.

"Rock 'n' Roll Party" (audiotape) with Alan Freed, WINS-AM Radio, New York, February 12, 1955.

Interviews (All conducted by John A. Jackson except where otherwise noted.)

Burlison, Paul. Interviewed by Rick Whitesell. July 26, 1980.
Caplan, Lozier. August 26, 1982.
Cox, Herbert. July 3, 1979.
Cruikshank, Ruth. August 25, 1982.
Dixon, Robert. August 26, 1982.
Dressel, Herman. Interviewed by John A. Jackson and Marcia Vance. July 3, 1979.
Dye, Robert. Interviewed by Rick Whitesell. September 15, 1980.
Freed, Alana. November 21, 1982.
Freed, David P. September 28, 1982.
Gardner, Donald. August 25, 1982.
Greene, Betty Lou. November 21, 1982.
Griggs, Sam. Interviewed by Rick Whitesell. September 10, 1980.
Hawkins, Screamin' Jay. Interviewed by John A. Jackson and Marcia Vance. July 9, 1979.
Hooke, Jack. Interviewed by John A. Jackson and Marcia Vance.
Lester, Bobby. June 23, 1979.
Lowry, Betty Bishel. August 26, 1982.
McGowan, James. Interviewed by John A. Jackson and Marcia Vance. July 17, 1979.
Miller, William. September 26, 1979.
Quick, Clarence. June 23, 1979.
Reneri, Ray. Interviewed by John A. Jackson and Marcia Vance. July 9, 1979.
Rich, Don I. August 26, 1982.
Russell, Jim. Interview by Rick Coleman. May 13, 1986.
Shoe, Robert. August 26, 1982.
Simms, Phyllis. August 24, 1982. Also interviewed by Rick Whitesell. September 15, 1980.
Smith, Daniel E. August 26, 1982.
Stone, Joseph. September 25 and 29, 1979; March 8, 1980.
Troob, M. Warren. April 30, 1980.
Walken, Nat. August 26, 1982.
Wilson, Earl. September 12, 1980.

Miscellaneous Items

Bundy, June. Album liner notes, *Rock 'n' Roll Party—Vol. 1* (Coral LP CRL 57063), March 1956.
Everett, Todd. Compact disc liner notes, *The Best of Jimmie Rodgers* (Rhino R2 70942), 1990.
Freed, Alan. Album narration, *Alan Freed's Memory Lane* (End LP 314), 1960.
———. Album liner notes, *Alan Freed's Top 15* (End LP 315), 1960.
———. Album liner notes, *Music with the Big Beat* (MGM 10" LP E293) by Sam ("the Man") Taylor, 1955.
———. "Christmas Jubilee of Stars" program booklet, December, 1958.
———. Fan club promotional letter, "Rock and Roll Jubilee Ball," January 1955.
"High Lama of Rock 'n' Roll," from "Third Anniversary Show" program book, Labor Day 1957.
Hyde, Bob. "Frankie Lymon and the Teenagers: A Recording History" booklet, accompanying Murray Hill Records 5-album boxed set (Murray Hill #000148), 1986.

Platt, Lew. Letter written to Jim Russell, at the time a disc jockey at WAND Radio, Canton, Ohio, February 26, 1956. Letter courtesy of Rick Coleman.

Porter, Bob. Album liner notes for *The Roots of Rock 'n' Roll* (Savoy SJL 2221), 1977.

Troob, M. Warren. Alan Freed Eulogy, Campbell Funeral Home Service, New York City, February 6, 1965.

WKBN Radio Employment Application—Alan Freed, Youngstown, Ohio, 1943.

DISCOGRAPHY

45 RPM

Coral 9-61363: "I Wanna Hug You, Kiss You, Squeeze You" and "Smoke from Your Cigarette," by the Billy Williams Quartet. Released April 1955. Freed can be heard introducing the record. Alan Freed and His Rock 'n' Roll Band are acknowledged on the label. Freed not on B-side.

Coral 9-61626: "Right Now, Right Now" and "Tina's Canteen," by Alan Freed and His Rock 'n' Roll Band, with Alan Freed's Rock 'n' Rollers. Released April 1956.

Coral 9-61660: "I Don't Need Lotsa Money" and "The Camel Rock," by Alan Freed and His Rock 'n' Roll Band, with Alan Freed's Rock 'n' Rollers. Released June 1956. B-side was used as a theme for Freed's CBS Radio program, sponsored by Camel Cigarettes.

Coral 9-61693: "The Space Man" and "Jazzbo's Theory," A-side by Alan Freed, Steve Allen, Al ("Jazzbo") Collins, and the Modernaires, with George Cates and the Out of Spacers. This was a copy of Buchanan and Goodman's "The Flying Saucer." B-side by Collins, recorded at Max's Pawn Shop, New York City. Released September 1956.

Coral 9-61749: "Rock 'n' Roll Boogie" and "The Grey Bear," by Alan Freed and His Rock 'n' Roll Band. Released December 1956.

Coral 9-61818: "Stop, Look, and Run!" and "Sentimental Journey," by Alan Freed and His Rock 'n' Roll Band, with the Rock 'n' Rollers. Released April 1957.

33-1/3 RPM ALBUMS

Coral 57063: *Rock 'n' Roll Dance Party—Vol. 1*, by Alan Freed and His Rock 'n' Roll Band, featuring the Modernaires. Album is narrated by Freed. Released March 1956.

Coral 57115: *Rock 'n' Roll Dance Party—Vol. 2*, by Alan Freed and His Rock 'n' Roll Band, with Jimmy Cavello and His House Rockers. Released April 1957.

Coral 57177: *Go Go Go—Alan Freed's T.V. Record Hop.* Released August 1957. An all-instrumental album designed to capitalize on Freed's WABC-TV show.

Coral 57213: *Rock Around the Block*, by Alan Freed and His Rock 'n' Roll Band, and featuring

Buddy Holly, Billy Williams, and the Modernaires. Narrated by Freed. Released November 1957.

Brunswick 54043: *Alan Freed Rock 'n' Roll Show*, featuring Jackie Wilson, Buddy Holly and the Crickets, and Terry Noland. Narrated by Freed. Released March 1958.

Coral 57216: *Alan Freed Presents the King's Henchmen*, featuring King Curtis, Sam ("the Man") Taylor, Count Hastings, Kenny Burrell, Everett Barksdale, and Ernie Hayes. Released 1958.

Radiola LP 1087: *Rock 'n' Roll Radio*, Released 1978. U.S. Armed Forces transcriptions of Freed's 1956 CBS Radio studio broadcasts.

WINS LPs 1010–1014: *Rock 'n' Roll Dance Party Recorded Live on Stage*, Vols. 1–5. Released 1978. Live recordings taken from Freed's CBS Radio shows, among other sources.

Silhouette Music 10006–10008: *Dedication*, Vols. 1–3. Released 1982. Compilation of live acts from Freed's CBS Radio show and dialogue from "Moondog House," WJW Radio, Cleveland.

Silhouette Music 10016: *Alan Freed . . . and This Is Rock 'n' Roll*. Compilation of Freed's "Moondog House" on WJW, Cleveland; Freed's "Spaceman" recording; and segments from his WINS Radio program and WNEW-TV "Big Beat Dance Party," including his farewell to his fans in 1959. Released 1985.

FILMOGRAPHY

Rock Around the Clock. Produced by Sam Katzman for Clover Productions. Directed by Fred F. Sears. Released by Columbia Pictures, April 1956. Running time: 77 minutes. Starring Alan Freed, Johnny Johnston, John Archer, and Alix Talton. With Bill Haley and His Comets, the Platters, Freddie Bell and His Bellboys, and Tony Martinez and His Band.

Rock, Rock, Rock. Produced by Max J. Rosenberg and Milton Subotsky. Directed by Will Price. Released by Distributor Corp. of America, December 1956. Running time: 85 minutes. Starring Alan Freed, Tuesday Weld (in her screen debut), Teddy Randazzo, Jacqueline Kerr, Fran Manford. With the Chuckles, Ivy Schulman, the Coney Island Kids, Cirino and the Bow Ties, the Moonglows, Jimmy Cavello and His Houserockers, the Flamingos, LaVern Baker, the Johnny Burnette Trio, Chuck Berry, Frankie Lymon and the Teenagers, and the Freed Band, featuring Freddie Mitchell.

Don't Knock the Rock. Produced by Sam Katzman for Clover Productions. Directed by Fred F. Sears. Released by Columbia Pictures, December 1956. Running time: 85 minutes. Starring Alan Freed, Alan Dale, and Patricia Hardy. With Bill Haley and His Comets, Little Richard, the Treniers, and Dave Appell and the Applejacks.

Mr. Rock And Roll. Produced by Ralph Serpe and Howard B. Kreitsek. Directed by Charles Dubin. Released by Paramount Pictures, September 1957. Running time: 86 minutes. Starring Alan Freed, Rocky Graziano, and Lois O'Brien. With Teddy Randazzo, Lionel Hampton, Frankie Lymon and the Teenagers, Chuck Berry, LaVern Baker, Clyde McPhatter, Little Richard, Ferlin Husky, Brook Benton, the Moonglows, Shaye Cogan, and Lionel Hampton and His Band.

Go, Johnny, Go! Produced by Alan Freed for Valiant. Directed by Paul Landres. Released by Hal Roach Studios, April 1958. Running time: 75 minutes. Starring Alan Freed, Sandy Stewart, Jimmy Clanton, and Chuck Berry. With Eddie Cochran, the Cadillacs, the Flamingos, Jackie Wilson, Ritchie Valens, Jo Ann Campbell, and Harvey Fuqua.

INDEX

A

Action Distributors, 237, 240, 246
Adams (Scruggs), Faye, 51, 58, 65, 66, 112, 118, 120
Adams, Stanley, 272, 309, 310
A.D.T. Enterprises, 150
Akron, Ohio, 18, 23–32, 37, 46, 50, 71, 174, 256; Armory, 53, 58, 60, 64, 65; Radio Hall of Fame, 336; University of Akron, 24. *See also* WAKR
Aladdin Records, 117, 150
Al and Dick's, 118
Alan Freed and Associates, 29
Alan Freed band, 90, 91, 127, 128, 131, 132, 157, 171
Alan Freed Enterprises, 213
Alan Freed School of Radio and Television, 30
Alan Freed's Memory Lane (record album), 312
Alan Freed's Top 15 (record album), 312
Alpha Distributing Corporation, 110, 171, 235, 236, 237, 282, 298, 299
"American Bandstand," 169, 170, 182–188, 190, 210–212, 224, 248, 276, 287–291. *See also* Clark, Dick
American Broadcasting Company (ABC), 23, 89, 132, 163, 168–170, 183, 188, 208–210, 224, 229, 231, 242, 246, 253, 254, 276, 280–282, 289–293; ABC Paramount Records, 132, 150, 171, 184, 209, 226, 229, 266, 282, 292, 300; ABC-TV, 162, 164; Am-Par Distributors, 221, 226, 229, 230, 275, 282, 284, 285; payola affidavit, 247–250, 254, 279, 280, 290; WABC (radio), 130, 131, 207–210, 220, 221, 223, 225–227, 229–232, 234, 237, 243, 249, 250, 252, 253, 255–257, 260, 264, 279–285, 289, 292, 293, 305, 318
American Federation of Musicians, 63
American Federation of Television and Radio Artists (AFTRA), 253
Angel, Jack, 111, 112, 118, 134
Anka, Paul, 166, 178, 182, 187, 191, 192, 291
Apollo Records, 110, 112, 215
Apollo Theatre, 45, 68, 118, 120, 134, 135, 144, 149, 155, 277, 278
Aposteleris, Harry, 110, 171, 235
Applejacks, Dave Appell and the, 147, 148
ASCAP (American Society of Composers, Authors, and Publishers), 74, 75, 99, 136, 145, 147, 181, 202, 209, 225, 236, 243, 251, 259, 260, 272, 294, 310, 321, 322; opposition to rhythm and blues, rock and roll, 73, 75, 76, 162, 163, 243, 244, 246, 332. *See also* Song war (ASCAP/BMI)
Ash, Bob, 16
Atlantic Records, 69, 110, 111, 117, 143, 149, 151, 171, 172, 180, 199, 271, 282, 283; Atco Records, 168, 180
Avalon, Frankie, 182, 212, 222, 226, 236, 291

B

Baby Grand (Harlem nightclub), 68, 149
Baker, LaVern, x, 35, 66, 79, 88, 91, 103, 107, 149, 162, 166, 176, 191
Baker, Michouston ("Mickey Guitar"), 86, 91, 107, 127. *See also* Mickey & Sylvia
"Bandstand" (WFIL-TV), 169, 170
Barlowe, Dean, 134; and Crickets, 112
Barrett, Richard, 132, 215
Barry, Jack, 217–219, 224, 241–243, 262, 263
Basie, William ("Count"), 25, 26, 40, 52, 91, 107, 119, 120, 125, 126, 130
Bass, Ralph, 73, 95, 111
Baton Records, 110, 112
Beatles, 318, 325, 335
Bell, Freddy, and the Bellboys, 122
Belvin, Jessie, 150
Benart Distributors, 66, 264
Bennett, John J. (U.S. Representative, House Subcommittee on Legislative Oversight), 275, 276, 280, 281, 283–285, 289, 290
Bennett (Debenedetto), Tony, 99–102
Berk, S. Bernard, 23–25, 28–30
Berman, Bess, 112
Berry, Chuck, x, 100, 101, 105–107, 116, 149, 161, 166, 168, 176, 183, 190, 191, 194–197, 210, 222, 226, 228
"Big Beat, The" (song), 178
"Biggest Show of '53" (rhythm and blues tour), 52
"Biggest Show of Stars for 1958" (rock and roll tour), 190–192
Big Maybelle (Smith), 127, 149
Big Seven Music publishing, 331
Bihari Brothers (Joe, Jules, Lester, Saul), 117; Saul, 117, 118
Billboard, 66, 89, 108, 138–140, 168, 170, 188, 244, 245, 251, 268, 335; comments on Alan Freed, 5, 51, 55, 60, 64, 65, 85–88, 92, 99, 125, 131, 140, 149, 160, 163, 171, 174, 175, 177, 190, 191, 222, 227, 231, 303, 306;

390

INDEX 391

names rhythm and blues music, 6, 110; record charts, 85, 157, 162, 177, 205, 214, 219, 234, 239, 257, 285, 286, 291, 293; uses phrase "rock and roll," 85
Binnick, Bernard, 186
Birdland (Manhattan nightclub), 84, 85, 100, 114, 125, 164, 203; "Stars of 1955" (tour), 126
Blackboard Jungle, The (movie), 94, 95, 103, 120, 121
Blackwell, Otis, 112, 154
Blaine, Jerry, 67, 110, 111, 137, 151, 157, 163, 223, 264, 271, 277, 282, 312; comments on payola, 333, 334
Block, Martin, 21, 207, 248, 257, 281. *See also* "Make Believe Ballroom"
"Blues for the Moondog" (song). *See* "Blues for the Red Boy"
"Blues for the Red Boy" (song), 42
"Blue Suede Shoes" (song), 139, 140
BMI (Broadcast Music International), 74–76, 85, 104, 108, 145–147, 163, 186, 202, 225, 236, 243, 272, 294, 310, 321, 322, 329. *See also* Song war (ASCAP/BMI)
Bob (Elliott) and Ray (Goulding), 62, 136
Bonnie Sisters, 127, 151
Boone, Pat, 80, 107
Boston, 71, 97, 98, 129, 161, 162, 177, 180, 192–210, 212, 213, 219, 221, 225, 227, 232, 247, 263, 267, 276; Archdiocese of, 97, 202; Arena, 193, 194, 196, 198–200, 207, 225; Band of Angels (street gang), 194; blue laws (curfew), 198; Police Department, 194, 200, 202
Bowen, Jimmy, 152, 157, 162, 168, 181
Boys, the, 110–120, 132, 134, 136, 150, 151, 180, 286, 312, 334; and Freed, Alan, 115–120, 132, 143, 149, 150, 157, 171; and payola, 271, 272, 275, 295
Brantley, Johnny, 82, 145, 243, 244, 258
Brautigam, Chester, 10
Briggs, Lillian, 100, 150, 174
Brooklyn Fabian Fox Theatre, 219, 221–223, 232, 233, 236, 256, 265, 266
Brown, Charles, 33, 46, 64, 86
Brown, Nappy, 97, 100, 157
Brown, Paul, 195, 196
Brown, Ruth, 33, 52, 58, 69, 86, 106, 107, 110, 120, 157
Bruce, Monte, 112, 113, 117, 120
Bruce Records, 110, 113, 118
Bryant, Willie, 68, 69, 76, 77, 90, 120, 131
Bundy, June, 99, 325, 326
Burnette, Johnny, Trio (Rock and Roll Trio), 141, 149
Burns, Stan Z., 175
"Butterfly" (song), 162, 185, 187, 287, 288
Byrne, Garrett H. (Boston District Attorney), 201, 205

C

Cadillacs, 107, 151, 157, 226, 228, 233, 277
Cameo Records, 185, 287

Campbell Funeral Home, 326
Campbell, Jo Ann, 155, 174, 175, 178, 183, 191, 193, 194, 222, 228, 233, 236, 277
Capitol Records, 83, 141, 170, 308
Caplan, Lozier, 212
Carnegie Hall, 80, 103
Cashbox, 5, 126, 244, 276, 303, 326
Catholic church (Roman Catholic church), 319–321; Legion of Decency, 97. *See also* Boston, Archdiocese of
Cavello, Jimmy, and the House Rockers, 143, 149, 150
Celler, Emanuel (U.S. Representative). *See* House of Representatives Judiciary Committee Hearings (1956)
Champagne Records, 56
Chance Records, 55, 57, 58, 60, 67
Chantels, 164, 187, 188, 191, 215
Checker, Chubby (Ernest Evans), 314
Cheers, 107
Chess brothers, 77, 106; Leonard, 66, 104–106, 116, 134, 149, 157, 312, 320; Phil, 66, 105, 116, 149, 157, 312
Chess, Marshall (son of Leonard), 104, 116
Chess Records, 57, 60, 61, 77, 104–106, 150
Chesters, 215
Chicago, 56, 57, 88, 105, 106, 118, 150, 245, 295, 296, 337
Chipetz, Harry, 186, 287
Chips Distribution, 186, 287, 288
Christgau, Robert, 333, 334, 336
Chuckles (Three Chuckles), 92, 107, 149
Chudd, Lew, 117
Cirino (Del), and the Bow Ties, 143, 149, 154
Clanton, Jimmy, 182, 212, 224, 226, 228, 233, 236
Clark, Dick, 170, 171, 182–184, 190, 210, 224, 230, 233, 258, 311; and ABC payola affidavit, 248, 255, 279, 280, 293; "Caravan of Stars" 1962 (rock and roll tour), 310; comments on Freed, Alan, 323, 335; and House Subcommittee on Legislative Oversight, 249, 275, 277, 279, 281, 287–292; music-related businesses, 185–187, 190, 211, 212, 236, 248, 276, 286, 288; "Saturday Night" (ABC-TV), 188, 211
Clark, Samuel H., 171, 230, 275, 282
Clay, Tom, 164, 252, 255
Cleftones, 115, 125, 131–135, 143, 157, 158, 162, 173, 222; Corbin, Warren, 158; Cox, Herbert, 115, 132–135, 157
Cleveland, 1–8, 16, 18, 24, 25, 30, 31, 33, 36–55, 57, 59, 66–68, 71, 73, 79, 82, 99, 102, 110–112, 125, 128, 139, 176, 191, 303, 330, 337; Arena, 1–5, 7, 8, 34, 46, 52–55, 66; black community, 4, 6; as "break-out" city, 44; broadcasting history, 24, 31, 41, 43, 44; Circle Theatre, 45, 58, 60; Mullins' bar, 33, 36, 48, 50; and payola, 256, 264, 276; Shaker Heights, 44, 49, 51. *See also* Freed, Alan: dances; radio; television
Clovers, 46, 52, 64, 86, 91, 110, 149, 155, 162
Cochran, Eddie, 141, 155, 226, 228
Cogan, Shaye, 173, 176
Cole, Nat "King," 83, 130, 334

Colombo, Joseph, crime family, 203
Columbia Broadcasting System (CBS), 21, 73, 124–126, 130, 140, 144, 217, 224, 242, 330; CBS-TV, 103, 135, 139, 141, 142, 209, 216, 218; Columbia Records, 75, 78, 99, 109, 127, 136, 141, 145, 189, 211, 308
Columbia Pictures, 121, 123, 147, 148, 156
Commercial bribery. *See* New York City, (Manhattan) Grand Jury, and commercial bribery; New York City, Police Department, commercial bribery investigation; New York State Penal Law of 1909 (Section 439)
Communications Act of 1934, 301, 308
"Contact" (radio program), 136, 213
Cooley, Eddie, 127, 161; and Dimples, 150, 151, 153, 154
Cooper, Joe, 36, 65
"Copy" records, ix, x, 77, 79, 151, 180
Coral Records, 118, 126–128, 141, 143, 147–149, 171
Coronets, 57, 58, 60, 61, 105
Cosnat Distributing Corp., 110, 111, 118, 223, 237, 264, 271, 282, 298, 315, 333
Cover records, ix, 58, 60, 77–80, 88, 91, 94, 106, 116, 151, 168
Craft, Morty, 113, 132
Crests, 226, 236, 299
Crosley Broadcasting Company, 62
Crossover records (rhythm and blues charts to pop), 6, 7, 34, 58
Crows, 61, 114
Cruikshank, Ruth, 16
"Crying in the Chapel" (song), 58–60
Curtis, Mac, 141, 150

D

Dale, Alan, 147, 148
Danny and the Juniors, 178, 182, 186, 187, 191
Darin, Bobby, 168, 232, 233, 291
Davis, Joe, 112, 134
Decca Records, 109, 141, 168
Dee, Joey, and the Starliters, 310, 314
Dees, Lester, 223
Dells, 150, 295
Dell Vikings, 162, 174
DeLoach, Cartha ("Deke"), 263
DeMilo Sisters, 143
Derby Records, 109, 110, 113, 119
Derounian, Steven B. (U.S. Representative, House Subcommittee on Legislative Oversight), 242, 290
Desert Hospital (Palm Springs), 322–324
Detroit, 115, 164, 220, 245, 252, 256, 260, 271, 303
Diamonds (white vocal group), 151, 155, 174, 187, 191
Diddley, Bo (Ellas McDaniel), 97, 98, 103, 107, 116, 130, 132, 134, 162, 227, 236, 266, 277
Dillard, Varetta, 1, 70, 86, 111
Dion and the Belmonts, 226, 236, 299
Di Renzo, Michael, 298, 314
Disc jockeys, 65, 75–77, 86–88, 100, 108, 117, 119, 124, 125, 128, 129, 167, 183, 186–188, 219, 225, 229, 246, 280, 306, 326, 333, 336; country and western, 138, 139; rhythm and blues:
   black, 49, 59, 68–71, 98, 114; white, 7, 39–42, 48, 68, 69, 100
   and payola firings, 252, 260, 268
Dixon, Robert, 9–12, 16, 17, 31
"Dr. Jive." *See* Smalls, Tommy ("Dr. Jive")
Doerfer, John C., 241, 246, 266, 278
Domino, Antoine ("Fats"), x, 33, 55, 58, 60, 80, 86, 98, 106, 143, 155, 168, 178, 179, 190, 232
Dominoes, 1, 34, 53, 60, 117; Billy Ward and, 51, 234; with Clyde McPhatter, 6, 7, 53; with Jackie Wilson, 51, 53
Donahue, Tom ("Big Daddy"), 41
"Don't Knock the Rock" (song), 148
Doo, Dickey, and the Don'ts, 186, 187
DooTone Records, 117, 295
Dorsey brothers, 139, 140; Jimmy, 127, 139; Tommy, 11, 127, 139, 179
Dot Records, 80, 297, 308'
Downbeat (Manhattan nightclub), 85
Do-wop revival (1960), 295, 296, 303, 312
Dressel, Herman ("Hermie"), 26, 37, 43, 50, 91, 97, 132, 137, 156, 158, 325
Drifters, 60, 66, 155; with McPhatter, Clyde, 58, 72, 73, 86
Dubs, 164, 166, 178, 187, 214
Duke/Peacock Records, 117
Dumont Broadcasting Company, 210, 211
Duponts, 127, 154, 157, 215, 216
Dupree, Champion Jack, 117
Dye, Robert, 296, 297, 305, 306

E

Eddy, Duane, 185, 186, 211, 212, 232
Eisenhower, Dwight D., 122, 240, 241, 266, 271
El Dorados, 80, 119
Ellington, Edward Kennedy ("Duke"), 35, 83, 90, 112
Ember Distributors, Inc., 275
Ember Records, 110, 112, 151, 295
End Music Company, Inc., 272
End Records, 188, 214, 215, 312, 332; and payola, 164, 165
England, 124, 132, 137, 147, 184, 199, 244; London, 122–124, 147, 160; prospective tours by Alan Freed, 147, 171, 175, 177, 178, 304
Enright, Dan, 217, 219, 224, 240–243, 262, 263
Ertegun, Ahmet, 110, 111, 118, 149, 151, 157, 168, 171, 172, 180
Everly Brothers, 166, 167, 178, 181, 190, 191, 221, 226

F

Fabian (Forte), 182, 232, 233, 236, 291, 305
FBI, 202, 203, 263–265, 267, 331
Fearnhead, H. G. ("Jock"), 136, 137, 205

INDEX

Federal Communications Commission (FCC), 22, 40, 62, 224, 225, 294, 297, 299, 307–309; and House Subcommittee on Legislative Oversight, 238–240; internal corruption on, 239, 240, 259, 278, 294; and payola, 251, 259, 271–274, 301, 307–309; and television quiz show rigging, 241, 246, 259, 262, 263, 266
Federal Radio Commission (FRC), 21
Federal Trade Commission (FTC): and payola, 271, 272, 274, 275, 300, 308; and television quiz show rigging, 218, 241, 266
Ferncliff Memorial Mausoleum, 327
Figure Music publishing, 161, 184, 188, 208, 220, 222, 247, 248, 259, 262, 281, 310, 311
Fisher, Lew, 62, 70
Fi-Tones, 134
Five Keys, 65, 80, 88, 97, 103, 107, 174
Five Satins, 151, 295, 303
Flamingos, 56, 87, 100, 107, 131, 155, 164, 228; Nelson, Nate, 149
Foglia, Marty, 229, 230
Fontaine, Eddie, 91, 92, 99
Ford, Art, 68, 163, 209
Four Fellows, 107, 108, 125, 135; McGowan, James, 69–71, 119
Francis, Connie, 148, 149, 167, 333
Francis, David Albert ("Panama"), 90, 91, 171
Fratto, Russ, 106
Freed, Aldon James ("Alan"):
 and alcohol, x, 31–33, 48, 50, 51, 69, 101, 125, 161, 171, 255, 267, 306, 307, 313, 315, 317, 318, 320–322, 324, 325; audience: age of, 64, 65, 102, 125, 229; his popularity, rapport with, 8, 18, 19, 25, 26, 38, 53, 55, 71, 86, 99–101, 104, 133, 135, 136, 143, 144, 156–158, 165, 167, 173, 177, 179, 180, 183, 202, 211, 213, 221, 222, 226, 229, 256, 257, 259, 260, 280, 296, 305, 306, 316, 325; racial composition of, 1, 3, 4, 34, 42, 44, 46, 53, 65, 86, 102, 135, 144
 automobile accident, 49–51, 130, 321, 322; and "big beat," 87, 91, 122, 128, 153, 168, 179, 211, 222; broadcasting, first interest, 13–15; commercial bribery conviction, 256–260, 262, 264, 267, 269, 273, 275, 278, 280–283, 285, 286, 297–303, 306, 309, 311, 312, 314, 315; and consultation fees, 260, 261, 263, 282–284, 286, 302; dances, 169, 170;
  Avon Oaks Ballroom (Youngstown), 46; "Biggest Rhythm and Blues Show" (Cleveland), 52, 53, 56; "Big Rhythm and Blues Show" (Cleveland), 53–55; Crystal Beach Ballroom (Lorraine, Ohio), 46; "Harvest Moon Ball" (Akron), 58; Holiday Ball (Akron), 60; "Moondog Birthday Ball" (Akron), 65; "Moondog Coronation Ball" (Cleveland), 1–8, 34, 46, 52, 111; "Moondog Holiday Ball" (Akron), 116; "Moondog Maytime Ball" (Cleveland), 46; "Moondog Memory Ball" (Akron), 60; Myers Lake Park (Cleveland), 1; Olympia Arena (Detroit), 96; "Rock 'n' Roll Jubilee Ball (New York), 85–87, 100, 155; "Second Annual Biggest Rhythm and Blues Show" (Cleveland), 66; "Second Annual Moondog Birthday Parties," 53; Stambaugh Auditorium (Youngstown), 53; Summitt Beach Ballroom (Akron), 46; Sussex Avenue National Guard Armory (Newark), 64, 65; "Twist Revue" (Camelot Club, New York), 314, 316
 disturbances at dances, movies, show, 1–5, 92, 93, 122, 123, 129, 130, 136, 143, 144, 156, 157, 161, 162, 192–204, 207, 209, 221, 363; fan clubs, 80, 86, 135; House Subcommittee on Legislative Oversight testimony, 225, 237, 243, 256–258, 263, 267, 277–286, 289, 290, 292, 293, 297; illnesses, 13, 14, 70, 321–324; managerial conflict, 25, 28–30, 137, 144, 145, 147, 177, 203–205, 219–221, 223, 225–227, 229–231, 234, 235, 237, 247–250, 253, 254, 257, 281, 282, 304, 305, 313; as Moondog, 1–8, 42–44, 46–48, 51–56, 58–60, 64–73, 76, 77, 79–82, 84, 85, 110–112; movies, 163, 176, 177, 179, 184, 293;
  Don't Knock the Rock, 147–159; *Go, Johnny, Go*, 226–229, 233, 234, 236; *Mr. Rock and Roll*, 171, 176; *Rock Around the Clock*, 121–124, 128–130, 135, 147, 148, 160; *Rock, Rock, Rock*, 148, 149, 152, 154, 156, 228
 musical interests, personal, 9–11, 16, 327; musical talent, 9–12, 104; music publishing, 92, 120, 149, 150, 152, 160, 161, 188, 208, 211, 248–250, 260, 281; at Ohio Sate, 12–14, 17; payments received from record distributors, manufacturers, x, 116, 189, 205, 207, 216, 218, 223, 232, 235–237, 240, 243, 244, 246, 247, 260, 261, 263, 264, 273, 278, 282–286, 289, 293, 298, 299, 315, 325, 336; and payola, x, 66, 104–106, 116, 118–120, 132, 189, 204, 235, 236, 247–250, 253–265, 268, 269, 273, 278–286, 289, 290, 292, 293, 325, 326, 332, 333, 336, 337; personality characteristics, x, 5, 11, 12, 96, 119, 133, 134, 150, 151, 204, 210, 254, 255, 258, 267, 284, 296, 299, 306, 313, 315, 316, 319, 325, 326, 337; radio, 1, 5, 25, 34, 42, 44, 46–48, 60, 65, 66, 79, 110, 112, 125;
  KDAY (Los Angeles), 296, 297, 300, 303–307; WABC (New York) "Alan Freed's Big Beat," 225–227, 229–231; WADC (Akron), 29, 30; WAKR (Akron) "Request Revue," 25, 28, 29, 32, 46, 174; WCBS (New York) "Camel Rock and Roll Party," 124–126, 130, 135, 140, 144; WINS (New York) "Rock 'n' Roll Party," x, 82, 84, 85, 87, 89, 91, 98, 102, 103, 106, 107, 115–118, 124, 133, 135, 137, 144, 175, 177, 188, 204, 205, 308; WJW (Cleveland) "Moondog House," 2, 5, 43, 44, 48, 51, 53–55, 59; WKBN (Youngstown), 15–18, 20, 23, 25, 50; WKST (New Castle, Pennsylvania), 15, 16, 22, 24; WNJR (Newark, New Jersey) "Moondog House," 59, 60, 64, 117; WQAM (Miami, Florida), 312–314, 316

Freed, Aldon James ("Alan") (*continued*)
recordings by, 118, 126–128, 149, 312; rhythm and blues, introduction to, 33–39; songwriting, 56–58, 61, 77, 79, 104–106, 117, 132, 250, 283, 312, 329; as sportscaster, 18, 20, 24; stage shows: Apollo Theatre (1960), 277, 278; "Big Beat" tour (1958), 190–202, 205, 263; "Christmas Jubilee" (1956, Brooklyn Paramount), 150, 151; "Christmas Jubilee of Stars" (1958, Loews' State, Manhattan), 223, 226, 227; "Christmas Jubilee of Stars" (1959, Brooklyn, Fox), 265, 266; "Christmas Jubilee of Stars" (1957, New York Paramount), 178, 179; "Diddley Daddy" road show (1955), 97, 98; Dinner Key Auditorium (1962, Miami), 313; "Easter Jubilee of Stars" (1957, Boston), 161, 162; "Easter Jubilee of Stars" (1957, Brooklyn Paramount), 162; "Easter Jubilee of Stars" (1956, Brooklyn Paramount), 131–134; Easter road show, Boston, 192; Easter show (1959, Brooklyn Fox), 232–234; Hollywood Bowl (1961, Los Angeles), 304, 305; Labor Day "First Anniversary" show (1955, Brooklyn Paramount), 98–102, 119; Labor Day "Second Anniversary" show (1956, Brooklyn Paramount), 143, 144; Labor Day 1958 stage show (Brooklyn Fox), 219–233; Labor Day 1959 stage show (Brooklyn Fox), 236, 237; Labor Day "Third Anniversary" show, (1957, Brooklyn Paramount), 173, 174; "Rock 'n' Roll Easter Jubilee" (1955, Brooklyn Paramount), 89–93; "Rock 'n' Roll Halloween Party" (1955, Brooklyn Paramount), 103; "Rock 'n' Roll Holiday Jubilee" (1955, Academy of Music, New York), 107, 108, 126; "Summer Festival" (1957, New York Paramount), 166, 167; Washington's Birthday show (1957, New York Paramount), 155–159, 179, 215
studio manner, 26, 42, 43, 47, 51, 59, 69, 70, 107, 141, 229, 230, 259, 260, 303; television, 135, 136, 140, 162–164, 189, 209, 262, 264; WABC-TV (New York) "Alan Freed's Big Beat," 164, 167–169, 188; WNEW-TV (New York) "Alan Freed's Big Beat," 170, 210, 211, 231, 232, 253, 254, 256, 257, 259, 260, 278; WXEL-TV (Cleveland), 31, 33, 38
in U.S. Army, 13, 17; as worldwide personality, ix, 122–124, 135, 147, 160, 175, 179, 199
Freed, Alan Junior (son), 165, 269, 316, 330
Freed, Alana (daughter), 24, 28, 49, 50, 165, 171, 173, 188, 213, 214, 258, 267, 269, 296, 297, 303, 311, 313, 314, 320–323, 326, 329, 330
Freed, Charles Junior ("Dugie") (brother), 8–10, 12, 326, 330
Freed, Charles (father), 8, 9, 12, 143, 326, 330
Freed, David Palmer (brother), 3, 8–10, 12, 13, 15–17, 25–27, 30–31, 36, 37, 39, 44, 50, 51, 57, 66, 67, 75, 171, 249, 322, 324, 326, 330
Freed, Inga (nee Boling) (third wife), 136, 213, 214, 216, 226, 230, 236, 260, 306, 317, 322–324, 330; recordings by: "Get Off the Phone," 226, 227, 233; "Silly Willy," 226
stage show appearances, 226, 227, 233
Freed, Marjorie ("Jackie") (nee McCoy) (second wife), 27, 48, 53, 57, 119, 120, 133, 137, 165, 172, 173, 197, 212–214, 269, 316, 330
Freed, Lance (son), 28, 57, 143, 165, 202, 269, 316–319, 322–324, 326, 329
Freed, Maude Palmer (mother), 8, 9, 143, 326, 330
Freed, Mitzi (sister), 9
Freed, Sieglinde ("Siggy") (daughter), 16, 165, 269, 316, 330
Freedman, Albert, 224, 235, 242
Freeman, Art, 66, 264
Friedlander, Bernard, 205, 223
Furness, George, 65

G

Galley, Lou, 215
Gardner, Don, 18, 50
Gayles, Juggy, 47, 48
"Gee" (song), 61, 62, 114
Gee Records, 114, 115, 134, 143, 151, 152, 157, 161, 162, 164, 173, 332
Genovese crime family, 331
Gibbs, Georgia, 79
Gigante, Vincent ("The Chin"), 331
Ginsberg, Arnie ("Woo Woo"), 276
Girl Can't Help It, The (movie), 155
Godfrey, Arthur ("Red"), 21, 22, 139
Goldenson, Leonard, 229, 246, 292, 293
Goldner, George, 113–116, 132, 133, 143, 149, 151, 152, 157, 161, 164, 214–216, 266, 272, 277, 286, 287, 302, 312, 332; and payola, 164, 165, 186, 272, 286, 287, 302, 334
Goldner, Sam, 113, 332
Gone Recording Corp., 272
Gone Records, 164, 165, 174, 214, 332
Goodman, Benny, 11, 92, 135, 137
Goodman, Gene, 11, 92
Gotham Broadcasting Corporation, 62, 308, 309, 312
Gourdine, "Little Anthony," 154, 215, 216. *See also* Chesters; Duponts; Imperials, Little Anthony and
Gracie, Charlie, 162, 185, 187
Granger, Ron, 298, 299, 307, 315
Greene, Betty Lou (nee Bean) (first wife of Alan Freed), 13–17, 23, 24, 26–28, 50, 165, 172, 173, 212–214, 267, 269, 311, 316, 317, 319, 320, 329
Greene, Tom, 28, 165, 166, 269, 316, 329
Grey Cliffe, 137, 163, 165, 171–173, 213, 255, 256, 264, 265, 319, 329
Griggs, Sam. *See* Coronets
Gurlek, Morris, 311

INDEX

H

Haley, Bill, and the Comets, ix, 51, 94, 95, 121–123, 147, 148, 181, 222
Halonka, Johnny, 110, 171, 235, 236
Hampton, Lionel, 25, 35, 90, 120, 176
Hancock, Hunter, 41, 59
Hanover Signature Records, 216, 247
Hardin, Thomas Louis ("Moondog"), 80, 81, 85
Harlem, 10, 68, 69, 76, 112–115, 117, 120, 134, 155, 187, 277
Harlem Variety Revue (movie), 120
Harptones, 64, 86, 100, 113, 117
Harris, Oren (U.S. Representative, House Subcommittee on Legislative Oversight), 235, 237–239, 246, 258, 266, 275, 284, 286, 287, 290
Harris, Wynonie, 52, 83, 117
Hartford, Connecticut, 129, 130, 177, 278; State Theatre, 98, 129, 191, 278
Hawkins, Jalacy ("Screamin' Jay"), 69, 150, 162, 166, 173, 191, 193
Hayes, Richard, 260, 278
Heartbeats, 107, 113, 134, 150, 151, 155, 296
"Heartbreak Hotel" (song), 139–141
Heinz (Sales), Soupy, 44
Heller, Eddie, 113, 151
Henry, Haywood, 91
Herald Music Corporation, 275
Herald Records, 51, 110–113, 118, 295
Hibbler, Al, 97, 101
Hillbilly boogie, 138, 141
Hoberman, Ben, 220, 221, 223, 225, 229–231, 234, 235, 247, 248, 250, 283, 285, 293
Hogan, Frank, 219, 235, 241, 251, 259, 262, 270, 278, 280, 298–302
Holly, Buddy, 141, 181, 231
and Crickets, 174, 178, 190, 191
Hooke (Horowitz), Jack, 36, 53, 59, 63, 64, 71, 77, 80–82, 97, 99–101, 105, 107, 111, 116, 117, 121, 128, 137, 151, 153, 165, 166, 168, 179, 191, 193–195, 197–201, 203–205, 208, 214, 220–222, 225, 233, 258, 277, 278, 303, 304; and Alan Freed, 46–48, 50, 119, 172, 173, 205, 207, 213, 216, 223, 240, 255, 313, 319, 320, 323, 324; and Dick Clark, 170, 184, 279, 291, 310, 311; and Figure Music, 161, 184, 188, 262, 310, 311; and Morris Levy, 84, 85, 89, 93; and New York commercial bribery, 251, 254, 262, 298
Hoover, J. Edgar, 203, 263
Hopkins, Jerry, 184, 211
Horn, Bob, 169, 170
House of Representatives Judiciary Committee Hearings (Celler Congressional hearings, 1956), 145, 146, 163, 249
House of Representatives Subcommittee on Legislative Oversight, 146, 147, 246, 248, 249, 256, 272, 275, 285–287, 289–296, 301, 308, 309, 332–334; and commercial bribery, 244, 249, 251, 259, 263; FCC, investigation of, 238–240; history of, 238–239; and television quiz show hearings, 235, 240–242, 246, 274, 275. *See also* payola, and House Subcommittee on Legislative Oversight
Hugg, Dick ("Huggie Boy"), 41
Hull Records, 107, 113
Hunter, "Ivory" Joe, 35, 151, 162

I

"I Just Can't Tell No Lie" (song), 56
Imperials, Little Anthony and, 164, 215, 216, 260
Internal Revenue Service (IRS), 264, 267, 319, 329

J

Jackie Music publishing, 160
Jackson, Hal, 59, 71, 98, 298, 299, 311, 312
"Jamboree" (movie), 186, 212
Jamie Records, 185, 187
Jarvis, Al, 21
Jay-Dee Records, 110, 112
Jay-Gee Records, 271
"Jocko" (Douglas Henderson), 155, 156, 174, 187
Johnnie and Joe, 166, 167, 296
Johnson, Buddy, Orchestra, 52, 64, 86, 97, 155, 232, 303
with Johnson, Ella, 64, 86, 97, 155
Johnson Records, 164, 303
Josie (JOZ) Records, 110, 111, 151, 277
Joyce, Jolly, 121, 168
Jubilee Records, 110, 111
Justice Department, United States, 146, 264, 322

K

Kahl, Phil, 85, 152, 160, 161, 163, 173
Kahl Music publishing, 164
Kaslin, Blanche ("Bea"), 113
Katzman, Sam, 121, 122, 147
Kaufman, Murray ("The K"), xi, 246, 309
Kavaleer, Syndey, 307
KDAY (Los Angeles), 268. *See also* Freed, Alan; radio
King Curtis (Curtis Ousley), 91, 155
King Records, 116, 141, 150, 258
Kirkland, Leroy, 101, 127, 168, 171, 172, 182
Klayman, Lou, 240, 246, 282
Knox, Buddy, 152, 157, 162, 181
Kolsky, Joe L., 171, 311
Korn, Bennett, 253

L

Laboe, Art, 305
Lacey, Jack, 62, 103, 124, 175
Lacter, Samuel, 251, 262, 270
Lance Distribution, Inc., 56, 57, 61, 67, 112, 118

Lance Records, 143
Lanphear, Al, 59
Leder, Bob, 63, 65, 67, 136, 171
Leeds, Mel, 175, 176, 204, 268, 273, 296–298, 300, 304, 305, 307, 315
Lefkowitz, Louis, 265
Lemmon, Bill, 2, 3, 68
Lennon, John, 123
Levy, Morris, 115, 125, 149, 151, 153, 180, 188, 215, 216, 226, 232, 296; and Alan Freed, 84–86, 89, 92, 93, 99, 100, 102, 116, 126, 132, 137, 143, 149, 152, 155, 157, 160–165, 171–173, 189, 254, 256, 257, 264, 272, 273, 283, 286, 310, 312–314, 320, 326, 330; and copyright of "rock and roll" phrase, 84, 89; extortion arrest, conviction, 331, 332; and FBI, 203, 264, 331; music publishing, 85, 114, 149, 152, 160, 164, 173, 310, 311, 330–332; organized crime, alleged ties to, 203, 331; and payola, 265, 271, 272, 308
Lewis, Jerry Lee, 169, 178, 179, 181, 191, 194, 195, 304, 305
Libertore, Dick, 320, 321, 329
Lido Records, 113, 150
Lip-syncing, 170, 188, 210
Lisbon, Ohio, 14, 15
Lishman, Robert, 244, 259, 263, 278, 279, 282, 285, 286, 288, 290
Listening fee, 276. *See also* Freed, Alan, and consultation fees
Little Richard (Richard Penniman), x, 80, 147, 148, 155, 174–176
Little Sylvia (Sylvia Vanderpool Robinson), 127
Little Theatre (New York City), 188
Little Walter (Jacobs), 97, 116; and his Jukes, 60
Lorenz, George ("Hound Dog"), 41, 100, 326
Louis, Joe, 51–53
Lowe, Bernard, 185, 186, 211, 287, 288
Lowe, Don, 229, 230
Lowry, Betty (nee Bischel), 11
Lubinsky, Herman, 59, 111, 127, 157
Lucas, Buddy, 46, 111, 214
Luttman, Kenneth, 205
Lymon, Frankie, 161, 168, 216; and Teenagers, 91, 115, 116, 122, 131–134, 143, 149, 151, 157, 158, 166, 176, 178, 246, 332
Lymon, Lewis, and the Teen Chords, 155, 161, 166
Lynn, Jack, 253, 258, 262
Lyons, Bob, 11

M

McCarthy, John, 70
McCaw, J. Elroy, 62, 63, 65, 88, 124, 136, 137, 175, 176, 203, 204, 273, 274, 307–309, 312, 330
McFadden, Ruth, 132
McGowan, James. *See* Four Fellows
McGuire Sisters, 77, 79
Mack, Peter F. (U.S. Representative, House Subcommittee on Legislative Oversight), 290

McPhatter, Clyde, 107, 149–151, 166, 168, 176, 191. *See also* Dominoes; Drifters
"Make Believe Ballroom;" Al Jarvis, 21; Jerry Marshall, 141; Martin Block, 21, 207, 257
Mallard Pressing Company, 211
Mammarella, Anthony, 184, 186, 275, 276
"Maybelline" (song), x, 101, 104–107
Mayflower Hotel (Akron), 26
Mello Kings, 182, 232, 296
Mendelsohn, Fred, 59, 111
Mercury Records, 80, 87, 88, 89, 105, 109, 127, 169, 276, 277
Merrian, Leon, 91, 171
Messner brothers (Leo and Edward), 117
Metromedia Corporation, 211, 253
Miami, Florida, 312–314, 329
Mickey (Baker) and Sylvia (Vanderpool Robinson), 127, 155, 169. *See also* Baker, Michouston
Midnighters (Royals), 73
Miller, Glenn, 128, 135
Miller, Mitch, 78, 99, 136, 189, 211
Miller, William, 69, 107, 113
Millinder, Lucius ("Lucky"), 69, 76, 90, 91
Mintz, Leo, 1, 8, 32–39, 42, 46, 52, 57, 64, 66, 82–84
Mitchell, Freddie, 91, 128
Modernaires, 128
Modern Records, 117, 150
"Moondog". *See* Freed, Alan; Hardin, Thomas Louis
"Moondog Symphony" (song), 42, 81
Moonglows, 55–58, 67, 77, 79, 105, 116, 134, 174, 175, 312, 327; Barnes, Prentiss, 55, 56; Crazy Sounds, 56; and Alan Freed, appearances with, 56, 60, 86, 91, 97, 100, 143, 149, 150, 166, 176, 226; Fuqua, Harvey, 55, 56, 226, 228;
 songwriting credit with Alan Freed, 58, 77, 104, 105
Lester, Bobby, 55, 56, 60, 67, 77, 105;
Moonlighters (Fuqua and Lester), 86, 91, 97
Moonoogian, George, 193, 194, 196–200, 202
Morris, Joe, Orchestra, 65, 112
Moss, John E. (U.S. Representative, House Subcommittee on Legislative Oversight), 277, 286, 288, 292, 293
Music Publishers' Protective Association, 244, 245
Music publishing, 45, 78–80, 85, 106, 108, 247, 280, 289, 295; ASCAP monopoly on, 73–75. *See also* Song war (ASCAP/BMI)
Mutual Radio network, 188

N

"Nadine" (song), 57, 58, 61, 105
Nathan, Sydney, 116, 117, 150, 258
National Broadcasting Company (NBC), 21, 124, 146, 242; NBC-TV, 142, 169, 218, 219, 242; and payola, 146, 273, 274; and television quiz show rigging, 217–219, 224, 242

INDEX

National Records, 83, 110, 111
New Castle, Pennsylvania, 15–17
New Haven, Connecticut, 200; Arena, 98, 192
Newton, Larry, 109, 113, 119
New York City: Court of Special Sessions, 299–303, 309, 315; Manhattan district attorney, 256, 267, 269, 273, 274, 299; Accounting Investigation Unit, 251, 270
Manhattan grand jury, 301;
  and commercial bribery, 257, 261, 262, 270, 272, 273, 278, 280–283, 285, 286, 297–300; and television quiz show rigging, 224, 235, 238, 240, 241, 311
  Police Department, 203, 251, 314; commercial bribery investigation, 251, 252, 256–264, 269–275, 278, 280–283, 285, 286, 297–303, 308, 309, 311, 312, 314, 315
New York State Attorney General, 265, 267
New York State Penal Law of 1909, Section 439 (commercial bribery), 252, 262, 269, 280
Nite, Norm N., 307
Nobles, Gene ("Daddy"), 40, 49
Nutmegs, 100, 118, 119

O

Ohio Record Sales, 57
Ohio State University, 10, 15; See also Freed, Alan, at Ohio State
Okeh Records, 127, 150
Old Town Records, 110, 112, 132
Oliver, Sy, 127
Orioles, 58, 60, 99

P

Palm Cafe (Harlem), 155
Palmer, Al and Don (uncles of Alan Freed), 8, 9, 37
Palm Springs, 304, 306, 314, 316, 317, 319–323, 326, 329
Paramount Theatres, 89, 113, 132, 209, 212, 219, 223, 226, 228, 230, 233; Brooklyn Paramount, 89–93, 97–103, 107, 108, 119, 129, 131–134, 140, 143, 144, 147, 150, 151, 156, 160, 162, 173, 174, 191, 212, 219, 220; New York Paramount, 89, 92, 154–159, 166, 167, 171, 178, 179, 206, 215, 226, 228; Paramount Studios, 176
Passman, Arnold, x, 22, 202
Patricia Music, 85, 114, 164
Payola, 47, 104–106, 108, 116, 118, 129, 154, 163, 186, 204, 211, 215, 243–265, 268–277, 279–303, 332–334; federal legislation against, 238, 241, 251, 252, 266, 273–275, 293, 301, 308, 334; first use of term, 245; history of in music business, 244, 245; and House Subcommittee on Legislative Oversight, 257–259, 263, 278–296. See also American Broadcasting Company, Payola affidavit; Boys, the; Commercial bribery; Record distributors; WINS
Penguins, 88, 91, 143, 295
Peppermint Lounge (New York), 310, 314
Perkins, Carl, 139
Petrillo, James C., 22; Petrillo ban on recording, 22, 111
Pfund, Jane (cousin of Alan Freed), 11
Philadelphia, 23, 164, 169, 170, 183–185, 187, 188, 212, 245, 249, 252, 303, 332. See also WFIL
Phillips, Brad, 63
Phillips, Dewey, 41
Phillips, Irving, 297, 298, 300
Phonograph records: history of radio use, 20–23, 245
Planetary Music, 164, 311
Platt, Lew, 1, 28–30, 46, 52, 56, 57, 64, 65, 85, 99, 100, 264
Platters, 122, 125, 131, 133, 157
Pleshette, Gene, 92, 93, 108
Portem Distributors, 110
Power Records, 113, 184
Presley, Elvis, ix, 103, 104, 139–143, 145, 146, 148, 150, 151, 157, 181, 183, 189, 190, 305
"Priscilla" (song), 150, 151, 154, 161
Prysock, Wilbert ("Red"), 35, 86, 87, 89, 91

Q, R

Quiz shows, television: history of, 216–218; rigging, 218, 219, 237, 246, 251, 266, 269, 271, 275, 301, 325. See also House Subcommittee on Legislative Oversight; New York City, Manhattan grand jury; Van Doren, Charles
Rabinowitz, Sol, 112, 119, 312
"Race" music, 6, 33, 35–37, 68, 83, 110, 176
Radio Act of 1927, 21
Radio Corporation of America (RCA), 271, 272; RCA Victor Records, 75, 91, 92, 103, 109, 114, 118, 139–142, 145, 151, 171, 189, 266
Radio Luxembourg, 124, 135, 147
Rainbow Records, 110, 113, 127, 151
Rama Records, 110, 114, 143, 150, 152, 161, 162, 164, 332
Randazzo, Teddy, 148, 149, 166, 171, 175, 176, 222. See also Chuckles
Randle, Bill, 7, 44, 45, 51, 52, 139
Ray, Johnnie, 45, 226
Record distributors, 56, 57, 66, 108–110, 120, 221, 222, 225, 226, 259, 295; and payola, 104, 108, 245, 252, 270–272, 274–276, 280–282, 286, 287, 298, 299, 308
Record Rendezvous, 33–38, 57, 84
Reed, Don K., 158
Regent Music publishing. See Goodman, Gene
Reig, Teddy, 46, 111, 149, 151, 153, 216
Reneri, Ray, 69, 71, 89, 96, 101, 117, 118, 133, 144, 183, 192, 210, 234, 258, 262, 269
Rhodes, Todd, 42

Rhythm and blues: naming of, 6, 110; objections to lyrics, 72, 73, 75, 76, 129; racial opposition to, 72–76, 82, 89, 130, 142; radio broadcasts of, history, 39–42, 44, 48, 49, 68, 69, 76, 77; "rock" and "roll," lyrical references to, 123–125; and television, 103, 120; touring circuit, 45, 52, 53, 66;
  chitlin' circuit, 45, 53
  transition to rock and roll, 85–89, 98–100, 109, 115, 120, 121, 142, 143, 183, 336
"Rhythm and Blues Review" (movie), 149
Richbourg, John ("John R"), 40
Rivers (Ramistella), Johnny, 214, 215
Robbins, Fred, 129, 260
Robey, Don, 117
Robinson, Bobby, 69, 112, 312
Rockabilly, 142, 150, 152, 169
Rock and roll: and Alan Freed:
  copyrights phrase, 84, 85, 89; defends music, 135, 136, 160, 176, 182, 189, 202, 209, 325; names music, 82, 83, 86, 87
  bans on, 98, 122, 123, 128, 129, 150, 192, 200, 201, 205, 212; country and western music, influence of, 59, 138, 139, 141, 142, 181; effects of payola scandal on, 332, 333; as a fad, 99, 102–104, 129, 143, 159, 167, 176, 189, 221; first reference to, music trade newspapers, 86; first use as musical description, 82, 83, 85–87, 89, 90; opposition to, 93–98, 108, 122, 123, 128–131, 135, 136, 142, 145, 146, 159, 160, 176, 189, 192, 193, 200–203, 205, 206, 209, 243, 294, 309, 310, 332; overseas reaction to, 122–124, 147, 160; and teenage violence, 92–95, 98, 122, 123, 128–130, 135, 136, 160–162, 196–199; and television, 139–142, 162–164, 167–170, 188, 189, 209–211, 232, 256, 257, 259, 260, 318
"Rock and Roll" (Boswell Sisters song), 83
"Rock and Roll" (Bill Moore song), 43
"Rock 'n' Roll" (song), 87, 89
Rock 'n' Roll Dance Party—Vol. 1 (phonograph record), 128
Rock and Roll Hall of Fame Foundation, 336; Rock and Roll Hall of Fame, 337
Rock and Roll Revue (movie), 120, 121
"Rock Around the Clock" (song), 94, 95, 121, 128, 145
Rodgers, Jimmie, 173, 181
Roetzel, Bernard (Ohio judge), 29–31
Rogers, Leo, 113, 150, 184
Rogers, William P., 241, 266, 271, 274, 275
Rollings Broadcasting Corp., 59
Rolontz, Bob, 64, 110, 118, 120, 171, 225, 316, 335, 337
Rose, Billy, 75, 145, 146
Rose, Phil, 119
Roulette Records, 157, 161, 165, 171, 173, 188, 215, 216, 226, 232, 234, 264, 265, 271–273, 300, 310, 311, 314, 331, 332; and Alan Freed, 152, 157, 160, 162, 163, 165, 173, 188, 189, 236, 264, 265, 266, 273, 282, 283, 298; formation of, 152, 153, 160; and payola, 264, 265, 271, 308

Royal Roost (nightclub), 84
Royal Roost Records, 34, 46, 47, 110, 111, 127, 143, 149, 150, 153, 154, 157, 161, 216
Royal Teens, 184, 188, 191, 221, 226, 227, 281
Royaltones, 131, 132; Ifill, James, 132
Rupe, Art, 66, 117
Rydell, Bobby, 182, 265

S

Saccone, Joseph, 298, 315
Salem, Ohio, 8–11, 14–18, 36, 143, 212, 236; High School, 10, 12–14, 16, 25; "Jubilee 179," 336; Music Centre, 336
Santly-Joy publishing, 173
Sarnoff, David, 274
Sarnoff, Robert W., 273
Savoy Records, 43, 59, 70, 83, 111, 117, 127
Schoenfeld, Herm, 87, 294
Schwartz, Bernard, 239, 240, 294
Sea-Lark Enterprises, 186, 187
Sears, Alfred Omega ("Big Al"), 35, 90, 112, 128, 131, 171
Sears, Zena ("Daddy"), 41, 59
Securities and Exchange Commission (SEC), 232, 264
Seig Music, 85
Society of European Stage Authors and Composers (SESAC), 76, 225
Shad, Bob, 127, 307
Shapiro, Robert, 158, 179
Shaw, Arnold, 35, 42, 68, 75, 78, 210, 289
Shepherd Sisters, 143, 178
Sheridan, Art, 56–58, 60, 67; Sheridan Distributors, 57
Sherman, Paul, 70, 121, 123, 177, 178, 204, 221, 229, 325
"Short Shorts" (song), 184, 188, 191, 281
Silver, Al, 111, 112, 118, 134, 151, 275, 295, 296, 312, 319
Silverman, Danny, 24
Simms, Phyllis, 23, 25, 50
Sinatra, Frank, 92, 145, 155, 179, 309
"Sincerely" (song), 77, 79, 80, 104, 105, 312, 327
"$64,000 Question, The" (television quiz show), 216–219, 224
"Sixty Minute Man" (song), 6, 7, 34, 72
Sklar, Rick, 176
Smalls, Tommy ("Dr. Jive"), 69, 71, 103, 154, 165; and Alan Freed rivalry, 98, 107, 119, 134, 135, 144, 155, 156, 165; commercial bribery conviction, 298, 299, 311, 312; stage shows, 107, 118, 134, 155
Smith, Bob, 63, 65, 76, 79, 80, 124, 125, 136, 171, 204
Smith, Daniel, 10, 18, 19
Smith, Irv, 175
Smith, Paul, 202, 209
Snapper Music Inc., 152
Solitaires, 134, 162
Song plugging, 244, 245

INDEX

Song war (ASCAP/BMI), 74–76, 145, 162, 163, 202, 244, 260, 272, 309, 310
Songwriters of America, 75, 145, 147, 309, 310, 322
"South Philly" sound, 183, 188
Sproat, Bill (cousin of Alan Freed), 9–11
"Stage Show" (television program), 139, 140
Stanton, Frank, 224
Stempel, Herbert, 217–219, 240, 242
Stamford, Connecticut, 137, 144, 145, 163, 165, 213, 256, 265, 329
Stern, Bill. *See* "Contact"
Stewart, Lee, 169, 170
St. Nicholas Arena (New York), 85–87, 89, 100, 155
Stone, Joseph, 251, 256, 258, 261, 262, 264, 269–273, 275, 278, 286, 298–303, 309, 311, 312, 314, 315; and House Subcommittee on Legislative Oversight, 259, 263; and television quiz show rigging, 219, 223, 224
Storer, George B., 252, 274, 278; Storer Broadcasting Company, 256, 308
Storz, Todd, 175
"Street of Hope," 109, 112–114, 132
Studio Films, 120, 121, 149
Sullivan, Ed, 103, 142, 318, 327
Sultans of Swing, 10, 12
Sun Records, 103, 141, 337
Superior Record Sales Corporation, Inc., 216, 218, 233, 235, 237, 243, 244, 272, 282, 299, 315
Supreme Court, United States of America, 22, 96
Swallows, 46, 111
Swan Records, 186, 187, 236

T

Tarnapol, Nat, 226
Tate, Buddy, 119
Taylor, Samuel L. ("Sam the man"), 90, 126–128, 131
Teenagers. *See* Lymon, Frankie, and Teenagers
Teen Age Survey, Inc., 167, 229
Teen idols, 166, 182, 183, 187, 189, 226, 236, 265, 291
Thiele, Bob, 126, 127, 171
Thomas, Al ("Fats"), 55
"Thousand Miles Away, A" (song), 150, 151, 155, 296
Three Friends, 150, 151, 227
Tico Distributing Company, 161, 164
Tico Records, 113–115, 152, 161, 162, 164, 332
Time Records, 307
Tin Pan Alley, 64, 181, 182, 244, 254, 269
"Today" (television program), 218, 219
"Tongue-Tied Blues" (song), 117
Top forty radio format, 175, 176, 189, 207, 243, 312, 333
Torin, "Symphony Sid," 68, 69
Trace, Gene, 15, 16, 50

Tripp, Peter, 104, 229, 287; commercial bribery arrest, conviction, 298–303, 309, 311
Troob, M. Warren, 81, 82, 123, 147, 150, 171, 201, 202, 249, 250, 254, 255, 260, 262, 278, 284, 291, 296, 314, 317, 321
Turner, "Big" Joe, 55, 58, 65, 83, 86, 106, 110, 143, 166
"Tweedle-Dee" (song), x, 79, 88
"Twenty-One" (television quiz show), 217–219, 224, 235, 240–242, 301

U, V

United Artists Records, 205, 207, 223, 235, 282, 283
Valens, Ritchie, 228, 231
Valentines, 107, 115, 131, 132
Van Doren, Charles, 217–219, 235, 241–243, 294, 301, 311
Variety, 49, 66, 68, 75, 86, 87, 92, 93, 217, 294; calls Alan Freed "rock and roll disc jockey," 87, 88; "payola," first use of term, 245
Vee Jay Records, 105, 150, 244, 295
Villa (Francavilla), Joey, 150, 151, 227

W

WABD-TV (New York), 163, 210
WADC (Akron), 28. *See also* Freed, Alan, radio
WADO (New York), 307
WAKR (Akron), 23–31, 46, 50, 174, 305, 336. *See also* Freed, Alan, radio
Walker, Jack, 298, 299, 312
Wallace, Mike, 163, 189
Walter, Carroll G. (New York City Judge), 81, 82, 84
Washington, Dinah (Ruth Jones), 44, 89, 97, 127
Washington, D.C., 41, 45, 64, 98, 110, 190, 241, 259, 262, 266, 275, 278, 286, 291, 293, 294, 332; Howard Theatre, 45
Waters, Muddy (McKinley Morganfield), 64, 100, 105
WDIA (Memphis), 40, 41, 73
Weinbach, Mortimer, 208, 209, 292
Weiss, Hy, 112, 132, 134, 312
Weiss, Sam, 112, 216, 223, 243, 244, 246, 272
Weld, Tuesday, 148
Westinghouse Broadcasting Company, 309, 312
Wexler, Jerry, 110, 171, 199
WFIL (Philadelphia), 169, 170
WFUN (Miami), 312, 313
WHB (Kansas City, Missouri), 104, 175
"Wheel of Fortune" (song), 45, 109
White Citizens Councils, 96, 130
Whiteman, Paul, 22, 131, 212
"Why Do Fools Fall in Love" (song), 116, 122, 151, 332
WIBE, 23
Wilkins, Ernie, 91

Williams, Dootsie, 117, 295
Williams, Larry, 174, 191, 193, 222, 232
Williams, Paul, 1, 111, 120
Wilson, Earl, 254–256, 258
Wilson, Grant, 31
Wilson, Jackie, 226, 228, 232, 234, 236, 265, 305. *See also* Dominoes
Windber, Pennsylvania, 8, 324
Winley, Paul, 154
WINS (New York), 62, 63, 65–69, 71, 73, 76, 77, 82, 84–88, 97–100, 102–104, 107, 117, 120–122, 124, 125, 135–137, 144, 145, 147, 152, 167, 171, 175–177, 188, 203–205, 208, 209, 213, 214, 219, 220, 225, 227, 229, 246, 268, 297, 298, 304, 305, 330; bans copy records, 79, 80; and payola allegations, 66, 251, 273, 299, 307, 308; sold by McCaw, 308, 309, 312
WJW (Cleveland), 1–3, 5, 33, 35–39, 42–44, 46–48, 51, 53–57, 61, 66, 68, 82, 112, 125. *See also* Freed, Alan, radio
WKBN (Youngstown). *See* Freed, Alan, radio
WKST (New Castle, Pennsylvania). *See* Freed, Alan, radio
WKSU (Kent State), 25
WLAC (Nashville), 40
WLIB (New York), 298, 299, 311, 312
WMGM (New York), 104, 229, 287, 298–300
WNEW (New York), 21, 67–69, 80, 141, 163, 175, 207
WNEW-TV (New York), 211, 232, 243, 244, 253, 254, 256–258, 262, 264, 278, 282, 293, 305. *See also* Freed, Alan, television
WNJR (Newark, New Jersey). *See* Freed, Alan, radio
Wood, Randy, 297, 317, 320
Woodlawn Memorial Park, 326
"Work With Me, Annie" (song), 73
WOSU (Ohio State), 13
WOV (New York), 69, 155, 187
WQAM (Miami, Florida). *See* Freed, Alan, radio
Wright, Jimmy, 91, 116
WWRL (New York), 69, 154, 298, 299, 318
WXEL-TV (Cleveland). *See* Freed, Alan, television

X, Y, Z

X Records, 91, 92
Youngstown, 15–18, 20, 23, 46, 50, 53, 58
"Your Hits of the Week" (radio program), 104
Zacherle, John, 230

Visit us online!
Oldies.com

Over 10,000 rare & hard-to-find audio CDs
Boxed sets & special collections
Over 10,000 45RPM Records
Classic Movies & TV Shows
Over 1,000 Music & Movie Books

SEND FOR A FREE CATALOG
Collectables Records, PO Box 35, Narberth, PA 19072
Or call **1-800-336-4627**